Get a camera

Get some stock

Go shoot a MOVIE...

The Guerilla Film Makers Handbook

Dedicated to the memory and inspiration of
John Holland, and to mum and dad.

To Chris and Jo.

For Terry.

Continuum
The Tower Building,
11 York Road, London SE1 7NX

15 East 26th Street
New York, NY 10010

First Published in 2000, Reprinted 2000, 2001, 2002 (twice), 2003

British Library Cataloguing-in-Publication Data
A catalogue record for this book is available from the British Library.

ISBN 0 8264 4713 9

Layout and design by Chris Jones.
Printed and bound in Great Britain by CPI Bath

The Guerilla Film Makers Handbook

By
Chris Jones and
Genevieve Jolliffe

continuum
LONDON • NEW YORK

The Guerilla Film Makers Handbook

Introduction

It's true that the road to becoming a successful film maker is a rocky, often bizarre and certainly unpredictable one. Neither of us expected to be writing the introduction to a book about film making on this hot July night, more likely our acceptance speech for the Oscar we would surely have been nominated for by now. That's the first lesson. Film making can take a very long time. There are exceptions the press love to quote, but on the whole, carving out a career in film making is not dissimilar to mounting an expedition to tackle the North face of the Eiger.

During our first expedition into film making, we made many mistakes. After regrouping we discovered a small group of persistent wannabe first time film makers pounding at our door, asking questions, the answer to which we had learned the hard way only weeks before. To keep these potential movie makers from consuming our every waking hour, we compiled some notes about how we made our first film and what pit falls could have been avoided. Soon after, due to great demand and overwork, our photocopier broke down. We realised then that there was a genuine need for a book about low-budget film making in the UK. Not some crusty manual written by a frustrated accountant, or an American guide that is so localised to Hollywood that it's all but useless, but a book that tells how it really is in the UK, how it's really done, what the penalties are, and what the rewards can be. And so, back in 1991, *The Guerilla Film Makers Handbook* was born.

If you have enough energy, half a brain and can convince enough people that you could be the next Orson Welles, you will become a film maker. Don't be put off by ridicule, poverty (although that can be very tough) or fear. You can do it. You will do it. Good luck.

Chris Jones & Genevieve Jolliffe
July 30th '96 (03.52 hours)

The Guerilla Film Makers Handbook

Introduction to the 2nd Edition

Since the GFMH hit the streets four years ago the film business has changed dramatically. Lottery money, the New Producers Alliance and perhaps in a small way, this book, have all paved the way for new film makers in the UK to make their voices heard.

Since the last edition we have made another feature film, *Urban Ghost Story* and like all movies it has been a labour of love. Again a Living Spirit production that was against all odds with a new set of problems, pitfalls and rewards. This time however the heavy doors of Hollywood have creaked open just enough for us to get our foot in.

In this edition you will see that there are a number of anonymous interviews. This is because we wanted the interviewees to be free to answer honestly, not politically as often that would put a person in a difficult position. So we have protected their identity.

Digital technology is also moving very quickly. It's impossible to predict how things will change but a few guesses would include DVD style distribution, international sales across the Internet, digital cinema projection (meaning you don't need a print) and most of all, origination on digital formats, of which DV is the cheapest and is accessible to all people. Undoubtedly, this liberation will spawn a plethora of dull and slow movies, but from this sea of mediocrity, a few unique film makers will rise. It's up to you to be that person, that original film maker. Be vocal. Be heard. Make your movie.

Chris Jones & Genevieve Jolliffe
April 10th 2000 (23.13 hours)

structure
plot
character
dialogue

Acknowledgements

We would like to thank all the contributors in this book for sharing with them their experience and expertise, helping to shed light on the way parts of the British film industry works. We would also like to thank everyone who has helped Living Spirit produce it's first three feature films; *The Runner, White Angel* and *Urban Ghost Story,* especially those who have supported us, both financially and emotionally, whilst navigating the shark infested, ship wrecked waters that is low-budget film making. You were our life jackets - *literally.*

To all those people who said it can't be done, eat humble pie. To all those people who said it could be done, our sincere thanks for your encouragement.

Special thanks in particular for words of advice received on a running track all those years ago.

Thanks also for the phrase 'the surest way to succeed is to be determined not to fail'.

We would also like to express our gratitude to the following for their help in producing this book - Helen Tulley, Cpt. CCR Jolliffe, Claire Trevor-Roper (neé Moore), Jon Walker, Amanda Roberts, Julie McKay Simon Cox and Kevin Foxe.

Thanks also to Mums, Dads and families.

And for their support we thank the following companies.

Special thanks on behalf of the authors must be extended to two other people without who's hard work, grit and determination, this book would not have been possible.

Jon Walker
For tirelessly programming the software that accompanies this book, navigating the murky waters of multiple platforms and versions ensuring that you can use the *Screenplay* formatter on both Mac's and PC's.

Claire Trevor-Roper - Researcher
For relentlessly keeping us on schedule, sourcing that hard to find information and typing up what must feel like a million words.

Contents

Section 1 - Anatomy of a Movie

Pre Production

Production

Post Production

Sales

What Next?

Section 2 - Case Studies

Hot Tips

Section 3 - The Toolkit

Section 4 - The Software

Section 5 - The Directory

What's on the CD Rom?

Accompanying this book is a CD Rom packed with software, documents, demos and sound files. You'll need a PC or Mac with CD drive to access it.

Screenplay Software

A powerful screenplay formatter to take the headache out of writing your movie. It works with MS Word and the full manual for it is included later in this book. This software has been specially written for TGFMH. Some features are disabled in this demo version although there is no restrictions on how much you want to write.

Production Forms

Included and saved in MSWord form are a multitude of production forms - from Continuity to Call Sheets - which are easy to use, adapt and print out, saving you time and money.

Contracts

All the contracts contained in this book are also included on the CD Rom in MS Word format. Use of these contracts is restricted by the disclaimer. Please read the disclaimer carefully as we don't accept any responsibility for their use or misuse whatsoever.

Sound Odyssey

Recorded and produced by Mark Bygrave and Paul Hamblin. Copyright File Effects Limited. Not to be reproduced or copied without permission.

Pop this CD into a great quality HiFi, crank up the volume. Included as an example of the quality you should aspire to in your soundtrack.

Extreme Music

Interactive multimedia demo of some of the music available from The Extreme Music Library. Included as an example of the type of high quality music available from libraries. Mac and PC friendly. Copyright restrictions apply.

Shareware

Contained on the disk are a number of Shareware programs developed by other companies. The use of these programs are governed by their individual licenses, but generally you can try them out and if you like them, pay the author.

Cool Edit 2000 (win)

Extremely sophisticated audio editing software, ideal for digital recording and cleaning up of sound effects. Can be used to track lay, or export sounds for track laying, in other program such as Adobe Premiere. www.syntrillium.com

TransMac (win)

Essential for anyone who works with a PC and Mac. TransMac allows your PC to read and write to Mac formatted disks. You may only use it once or twice, but when you do, it will save your life. www.asy.com

VAT Calc (win)

Calculating your VAT is a pain in the neck. Use this tiny but indispensable utility to do the hard work for you.

Time Code Calculator (win)

Anyone who has tried to calculate time in minutes and seconds will understand just how complex it is working in base six opposed the base ten that we use every day. This baby takes the strain out of it. Will handle PAL and NTSC as well as 24, 25 and 30fps. www.sssm.com/frcc/frcc.html

Poster (win)

This nifty program will print a poster for you, on multiple sheets that come out of your printer, then you paste them all together. Prepare a slick poster image in Photoshop, import and print out from your colour printer to create a full size high impact poster. www.cadkas.com

Check out our website every so often for software updates and new programs that make film production more creative, easier, cheaper and more professional.

www.livingspirit.com

The Guerilla Film Makers Handbook
Legal Disclaimer

Read This First!

The copyright in and to the sample contracts and documents in this book is owned and retained by the originator of the work ("the Owner"). These sample contracts and documents have been created for your general information only. The Owner, the authors of this book and the publishers cannot therefore be held responsible for any losses or claims howsoever arising from any use or reproduction. Nothing in this book should be construed as legal advice. The information provided and the sample contracts and documents are not a substitute for consulting with an experienced entertainment lawyer and receiving counsel based on the facts and circumstances of a particular transaction. Furthermore case law and statutes and European and International law and industry practise are subject to change, and differ from country to country.

Quick Guide To Low Budget Movie Making

Get a Great Idea

write a script + get a bit of cash + Determination

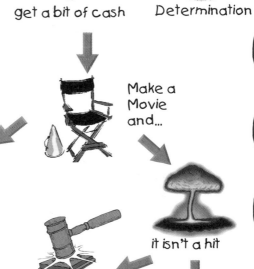

Make a Movie and...

it's a hit

it isn't a hit

Bankruptcy

HOLLYWOOD MOVIES
the rest is history

Short holiday

Make enough to survive before back to square one

Section 1
Anatomy Of
A Movie

Simon Moore
Screenplay &
The Spec Script
Market

Q - How did you get started in the film business?

Simon - I knew no-one in the business so I started from scratch. I studied drama at University and put on plays there, then went to film school. I was determined that after film school I was going to be working in the business so I worked hard while I was there, not just on the course, but writing scripts in my spare time. I am a great believer in the theory that you need to write a million words of crap before your work is good - so I wrote unfilmable feature films as well as making a couple of short films.

Q - From a writers point of view, what first steps should you take?

Simon - I think that the priority of the writer is to get things made, even if film people don't really see value in the end product, it's important to experience an audience reaction. Writers work in a vacuum and it's hard to get genuine feedback about a film that might cost $100m. You can sit down and write it but how on earth are you to gauge whether you are going in the right direction or not. The real route to success for me has been to write scripts speculatively and then take my chances selling them. The disadvantage of that is that you have to be prepared to go for a year or two without making any money. The advantage is that if and when you sell the script, you have tremendous power to negotiate yourself into a better position, role, credit and of course, money. The interesting thing is that you start off and no one will pay you to write in advance, then when you have completed, everyone gets excited and they pay much more than if they had paid you to write it in the first place.

Q - How did 'The Quick and the Dead' happen?

Simon - I wrote the movie for myself to direct as a spaghetti western on a budget of $4m. I had sent the script to my agent who had circulated it in LA. It was a Friday night and I was out for dinner with friends. I was broke and was lamenting the fact. When I returned home there was a message on the answerphone that said *somebody has read your script and they really want to do it, and they want to offer you some serious money and there is a major star attached.* The truth is that I had no idea which script they were talking about as I had several scripts circulating. So I phoned him and it was all very hush, hush and they would not tell me who was interested in doing it. The tactical advantage that I had was that this was a film that I was trying to set up for myself to direct, and they thought that I was in the process of getting it made. I had spoken to a producer a few weeks earlier and said *look, I am sorry but I have already decided to make it with someone in Britain and we are going to do it this way.* And this message had filtered through the Hollywood system (laughs). So I had this crazy night where I had no money and was feeling very lost, when suddenly there was this huge pressure. Over the course of the weekend they kept offering more - they started with $370k and my agent said *if they are opening with that, they will go really high - and they want to conclude the deal before Monday* ...and this is Friday night. Obviously they thought that on Monday morning all the other studios would be out-bidding them, which was nonsense of course. It went on for 48 hours and I felt like I had been in a minor car crash. I was just sitting there, there was nothing I could do and he kept saying *no, they are really going to offer you a lot of money, just sit tight.* Then he phoned me on Sunday and said *we've agreed on $1m* and I found out that it was Sharon Stone and Columbia TriStar. There was a narrow window to make the film because Sharon Stone was committed to making another movie afterward, so not only did the deal happen, but I thought it is actually going to happen as a film. So in less than two weeks I was flying back and forth to LA having meetings and the movie was happening.

Sharon Stone had decided that she wanted Sam Raimi to direct, which was a good and interesting choice. There were a group of people around Sam who were not unlike European independent film makers which was creatively good, but unfortunately, that was also part of their downfall because they had no experience of how to face the corporate might of the studio.

I did ten re-writes over three months and anybody who came on board gave me notes and I just said *yeah, yeah I'll do that.* Script meetings were with 12-14 people, and of course the person who is in charge as far as anyone is, is not at the meeting. And so it goes on. As a scriptwriter it is hard to protect and re-emphasise the story telling, people forget the storytelling when they get involved with all the other elements that come together when making a film.

Q - How did you feel at this point?

Simon - I've had largely good experiences working on all kinds of projects, but it quickly became clear that *The Quick And The Dead* was not going to be one. I sat in a room in LA with Gene Hackman, who is just about my most favourite fucking actor in the world (laughs), Sharon Stone who turned up ten minutes late, and Leonardo DeCaprio. Sharon Stone being ten minutes late was the first test, you could see the sweat pouring off the executives, *do we begin this read through or not, if we don't begin the read through, she has won, she is now in charge,* and if you do begin the read through, your star walks through the door ten minutes late because she has got 'flu. I sat there thinking this is a great moment in my life, but the actual read through was terrible. It largely consisted of Gene Hackman saying out loud *that was a terrible line, oh that's awful, you are going to have to change that.* There were people leaning across me to Sam Raimi talking about script notes and just ignoring my presence. I was never acknowledged by any of the 'A' list cast, no-one said *this is a good script and I am pleased to be doing it.* I was routinely asked to leave the room for meetings and you wonder just what it is that they are talking about that you cannot hear? Actually it has nothing to do with you, it is just hierarchy. But as you know the reasons that films get made are nothing to do with the quality of the script.

When shooting started and I thought *I can't fucking do a hundred*

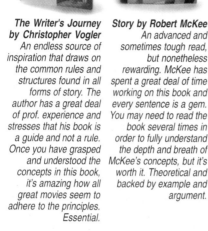

The Writer's Journey by Christopher Vogler
An endless source of inspiration that draws on the common rules and structures found in all forms of story. The author has a great deal of prof. experience and stresses that his book is a guide and not a rule. Once you have grasped and understood the concepts in this book, it's amazing how all great movies seem to adhere to the principles. Essential.

Story by Robert McKee
An advanced and sometimes tough read, but nonetheless rewarding. McKee has spent a great deal of time working on this book and every sentence is a gem. You may need to read the book several times in order to fully understand the depth and breath of McKee's concepts, but it's worth it. Theoretical and backed by example and argument.

The Screenwriter's Workbook by Syd Field
Along with several other books written by Syd Field, TSWW has proved invaluable to authors at all levels, although those starting out will probably benefit from his clear, concise and structured concepts. 'Four Screenplays', another book by Syd Field is particular fun for the dissection of four Hollywood movies. Very practical.

Writing Screenplays That Sell by Michael Hague
A great starter book that really gets the juices flowing. Light-weight in comparison to Vogler and McKee but probably the best place to start if you are working on your first screenplay. Also includes details on getting agents and selling your screenplay. Practical and pragmatic.

days of this humiliation, I am going home, it really can't get any worse, so I went up to Sharon Stone and said I am flying back to England now, and I just wanted to wish you luck with production and she said You can't go, you haven't fixed my scenes yet!

Q - How long was it between sending Quick and the Dead out, and interest coming back?

Simon - About four months, something like that. My agent always sends things to several people at once, I think that is a very good strategy. If there is no reaction, you have to re-think and re-group. I believe in consensus, if you can find one person who thinks that your script is fantastic then that is fine, but when you get four out of five people saying we like this but the ending isn't very good, or it is not a star vehicle then I think you have to listen. Unfortunately, I don't think many people appreciate how much work you have got to do in order to write a great screenplay.

Q - So should you go to LA if you want to write a Hollywood movie?

Simon - Lots of people said to me you can't sit in London and write a studio film on spec and expect to get it made - and I want to say that they are wrong because I did it and other people have done it - maybe half a dozen people do it every year. I am very much against the notion that you can calculate this business, I think that people who get on are on the whole people who have the confidence to express their individual voices. There is a danger in thinking that if you get the formula right you can sell a script. I think people still write a film and say oh, this won't sell in

Hollywood, I must put it through some sort of machine, put in guns, car chases and sex. I would also say that it is just as hard to get a small movie made as it is a big movie, the studios have got to churn out loads of movies every year and someone has to make them.

Q - How does a writer get a script circulating in LA?

Simon - You need to have an agent, perhaps one in LA too, but that isn't essential. It is hard to get a script read by someone who has the power to make it, but if you have written a great script, it will be recognised by an agent.

I made a film called *Under Suspicion* with Liam Neeson and then went out to Hollywood which was good timing for me. If you go out as a nobody with nothing you are going to get nowhere. I saw all the agents and in the end I went for a small agent who had good clients. I think that a good agent will send a spec script out with some kind of heat attached. My agent usually sends out a script to six people on a Friday night, and then on Monday morning phones them, and if nobody is interested you know it's not as hot as you hoped. You want an agent who will work with you too, one who will tell you when your script needs more work, one who is willing to put their reputation on the line when the script is ready. Remember, Hollywood is a paranoid place and as William Goldman says, *no-one knows anything.*

The agent should be able to do the deal, ideally in an atmosphere of hysteria - it does happen, you give studio execs three hours to read the script (laughs) - I mean to helicopter scripts out to people because they think that if they don't get it, they will come in on Monday and somebody will say *The Crighton went to somebody else.* It's down to hype, but also down to the fact that the script really is shit hot.

Q - With the Quick and the Dead did they change it a lot when you left?

Simon - The big battle was that the studio people all had favourite Westerns, so somebody said *show Sam Red River, I want it to be like Red River* another would be saying *High Noon...* and I wrote a spaghetti western. The studio people had cottoned on to the fact that I was from London, so no matter what they thought about the script initially, they now thought *we can't have this English guy telling us about the wild west..!*

I feel very passionate about people re-writing other writers work and had said to Sam that the only thing I ask is that no-one re-writes, I would re-write as much as they liked, but no-one can come in to rewrite. He agreed and understood why and how I felt that way.

So the studio insisted that John Sayles was brought in to give it the authentic smell of the Old West and he wrote another 40 pages, some of which was very good I thought. I then said *you got another writer on board so you can forget my involvement, you have betrayed my trust.* And I flew back to the UK. I got this phone call about a month later saying *Well, here's the thing. You see they have read this new script and they don't like it, as it has become a bit woolly and they would like to get you back to de-wool.* So I cut out everything that John Sayles had put in, except for a couple of key things that were an improvement. And then they said *OK, that is fine, we will do it now.*

It was an anti-violence film when I wrote it (laughs), but by the time the Americans had finished

with it they were testing it to see whether Gene Hackman should flip over backwards twice when he was shot!

Q - What was Sam Raimi like?

Simon - Sam was a good guy, but he just wasn't prepared to face the might of the studio. You just have no idea quite how much they are going to force you at every stage to do things in a certain way. I think that it would have been interesting if Sam had made the movie in the same kind of way that he made his other movies, it would have been a lot better.

Q - What observations did you make about the way stars and directors work in Hollywood?

Simon - Directors are fighting a constant battle with the studio, so unless you turn yourself into someone like James Cameron, directors don't really have the power that they are perceived to have and I know toward the end of post production, Sam was feeling very battered. So if Gene Hackman says *no, I am not doing it,* there is no debate, the studio doesn't say, *no, you do what Sam says.* Stars run pictures, it gets to 3 o'clock and they say *I don't want to shoot anything any more, I am going home.* Stars have got their money, they know why they have been hired, they are not hired to make a film successful, they are hired to open the film.

Q - What about screenwriting courses and books?

Simon - There is a proliferation of quick courses and although you should read books and take some courses, I think that they encourage people to think that it is something you can learn overnight, it's just a matter of doing AB and C. As I said before, I believe you need to write a million words of crap before you get it right. In the long run it is the people who go the distance and have original voices who succeed.

Remember, films get made because of an alignment of planets, just the right two stars there, just the right producer, just the right director but that only lasts for a while, it all moves around again and then you have to start from scratch. Once you can see how genuinely complex it is, then you begin to understand how the business works.

Q - What advice would you offer new writers?

Simon - Films, and therefore screenplays, should be shorter. Rarely do people come out of the cinema and say *gee, I loved that film, but it was too short,* and almost every film you see apart from your own is too long. Writers shoot themselves in the foot by writing their screenplays 30 pages too long.

Drew's Script-o-rama, a place where writers can freely download movie screenplays, mainly from major Hollywood features. Sometimes there are just transcripts, but often they are shooting scripts complete with deleted scenes and often different dialogue. Especially interesting to compare with the completed movie.

Go to www.script-o-rama.com

Film Script Title	Script Type	Size	Available From
Kids	First Draft	Zipped	Script Marta's Formatted Scripts
The Killer (Walter Hill's remake)	Unproduced	400K	Donated by Cotton Weary
Killing Zoe	Script	432K	ES Inc
King Kong (The Peter Jackson One)	Script	155K	Moon's Script World
Kramer Vs. Kramer	Revised Third Draft	400K	Anonymous Donation
Kundun	Script	206K	Film Manuskripten Arkiv
L.A. Confidential	Shooting Script	300K	Ann Omms
La Jetee (The Short Film 12 Monkeys Was Based On)	Script	12K	Gods Among Directors
Labyrinth	Early Script	110K	Think Labyrinth!
Last Of The Mohicans Script	Revised Script	16.386() Bytes	On The Trail Of The Last Of The Mohicans
Legend	2nd Draft	13 Forces	The Legend Glen
Lethal Weapon	Script	222K	Gods Among Directors
Little Monsters	First Draft	200K	Wordplay

I test my ideas out on people at every stage and the way to do it is to present more than one idea. Writers often say *I have got this great idea for a script* tell you it and then say *do you think that was good?* - then you tend to say *I liked it* because you don't want to upset them. The technique I have found is to present someone with two ideas and they will tell you which one they prefer. So when you say *don't you think the one about my dad in Zimbabwe in the 1920s is really good?* you can say *no, dull as ditchwater*.

The other trick is to forget the first draft. Some writers send me scripts with notes saying *I know it is 30 pages too long, the end doesn't work and I have not quite got the relationship between these two people, but see what you think.* That is disastrous as it encourages people to think that they can't write without your help. I put thousands of hours of work into a script and end up with something that is shootable. I believe that the first script you send to anyone should be a shooting script. You will still have to do ten redrafts but you will be building on something that is structurally sound. If you show people something that is structurally sound and you get fifty different voices and comments on it, you are not pulling down the house, you are re-decorating it. Someone could say *I just love this house, I really love this house, I only want to make one change to it, I want to move it six inches to the left* and that actually means dismantling the house, or you could have someone who says *I really hate this house, it is really awful* and you say *what do you hate about it?* and they say *it's green* and it will take a morning to paint it white. The structure is the key. You need to present a script that is as fully formed as you can make it, has been read, has been talked about, then you can enter this difficult and competitive world with a degree of confidence.

Don't demonise institutions, don't talk about *them*, be specific about the forces that you feel are stopping you from articulating what you want to say or what you want to do. The truth is that there are a tiny number of people who share your values, but they do exist, they are the people to seek out, they are the people that you should form alliances with and that is the way to make what you want to make.

PRE-PRODUCTION

Script Reader
Identity Witheld

Q - What is your job?

Anon - I'm a script reader which involves reading scripts, writing reports and assessing their strengths, weaknesses and potential for commercial success.

Q - How many scripts do you read and do the good ones really stick out?

Anon - I read and write reports on two scripts a day, depending on length, quality and potential. Other readers can read more, it depends on the individual and their employer's requirements. And yes, "good" scripts do stick out for two reasons. Firstly if they have an engaging and/or original premise in terms of subject matter and/or structure, or secondly if they are well written in terms of structure, plot, character and dialogue.

Q - How much is personal taste?

Anon - It depends on the individual and their employer's requirements. Script readers will definitely respond to scripts that they find personally engaging. However, when the script reader writes a report their personal responses should be tempered by two objective considerations - first, does the script reflect the "type" of film that their employer is seeking in terms of subject matter, genre, budget and so forth, and second, does the script fulfil generally accepted conventions of what makes a good script in terms of structure, plotting, characterisation and dialogue.

Q - How much do you charge and what do you get for the fee?

Anon - Readers are paid per script, the basic starting rate is being around £25.00 each. What you get from the reader is a report, often referred to as "coverage". This contains a brief "logline" which sums up what the script is about in two or three sentences, a "synopsis" of what happens in the script (which can vary from one half to two sides of A4), a "comment" outlining what the script reader feels the script is trying to do, how well it does it, whether the premise is original and engaging, what could be done to improve it and the sort of audience that it is likely to appeal to. The comment's would probably be a side of A4 in length. Finally, a "verdict" or "recommendation" on the script which will indicate whether it should be accepted, rejected, or developed.

Q - What makes a script stand out as not professional?

Anon - Unbound or badly bound scripts, spelling mistakes, bad grammar or typo errors. Also the script layout is important and the generally accepted format conventions should be adhered to.

Q - What makes a script stand out as being hot?

Anon - There is no definitive answer to this question. If there were, every script could be made "hot". However, beyond the basic qualities of an original premise and being well written, there are certain factors that are potentially "hot". Firstly, if the script addresses a contemporary subject or issue that is likely to be relevant and of interest to a broad cross section of the public. Secondly, if the script manages to find a new "angle" on a type or genre of film that has already been successful. And, thirdly, external factors, such as whether it has been adapted from a successful book, who the production team are, what actors are attached.

Q - What are the common mistakes that you encounter?

Anon - They divide into three categories: conceptual, dramatic and technical. The most common conceptual mistake with a script is that it is better suited to television than film. This distinction between the two is notoriously hard to define but involves questions of premise, genre and dramatic intensity. The most common dramatic mistake with a script involves failing to fully exploit the main story line. This occurs when a script fails to focus on the establishment, development and resolution of the central character/s' story, and is instead padded out with too many secondary characters and story lines. The most common technical problem is excessive description of the characters' actions and feelings. This usually indicates that the dialogue and action are not strong enough in themselves and also means the writer has encroached upon territory belonging to the producer, director, casting agents, actors and so on.

Q - What advice would you offer a new screenwriter wanting to break in?

Anon - Firstly, screenwriting requires talent and skill: talent is innate but skill is acquired. Study screenwriting manuals, take relevant courses and look at the differences between a range of television programs and feature films. This won't necessarily make you a great screenwriter, but it will make you a better screenwriter. Secondly, think laterally about getting your work read as production companies are inundated with scripts from established writers. Nurture contacts with people who work in the film industry. Enter screenwriting competitions because even if you don't win your script may be good enough to be brought to the attention of someone who can help you. Find the companies and organisations that accept unsolicited material and are willing to offer their professional opinion on them. And remember that most successful writers have had to experience a great deal of rejection, so don't take it personally. Success consists of going from failure to failure without loss of enthusiasm.

Solicitor
Helen Tulley
Of Hammond Suddards

Q - Do you need a company to make a film?

Helen - As a producer you need a limited company which you can currently buy off the shelf for about £125 (inclusive of VAT). A limited company means limited liability so that, provided you have not acted unlawfully or wrongfully, if everything goes wrong, you can walk away without losing your personal property. Without a limited company, your liabilities would then be *personal* and you could be made bankrupt - everything you own, home and belongings (except for the tools of your trade), will go to the Trustees in bankruptcy. If you don't have a company no-one will do business with you anyway. Some people will try and get round your limited liability status by asking you to give personal guarantees. If you were borrowing money from the bank, they may say *yes your company can borrow money but we want the directors to personally guarantee the loan.* You should try and avoid this where possible and just say that it's unreasonable. If you give a personal guarantee, that makes you personally liable and you can be made bankrupt which defeats the whole purpose of having a limited company. You can go two ways with a limited company - either set up a company and have an agreement as to how you want to treat individual projects brought in by the directors of the company. Alternatively, you can set up a separate company for each project, which is more usual.

Q - We were advised initially to set up a limited company for each film, but never got around to it, now it's very complicated?

Helen - I think the reason why people are put off by getting another limited company is really because of the administration, it's another company you have to file accounts for, it's more money, just another thing to think about. People do make more than one film through a single company, but it does mean you have to be a little more careful when giving any security to a financier. If the company is borrowing from a bank, you must make sure that the loan for one production doesn't jeopardise other projects by the fact that they also become security for the loan.

Q - How important is a good solicitor to a film project?

Helen - I appreciate that legal costs can be high, but I think what people sometimes forget is that they could be entering into an agreement where the money involved may not be substantial but the liabilities are huge. That's why it's important to have proper protection, to have somebody to say *this is what you've got to watch out for.* When it comes to the agreements, if you don't have very much money then you should concentrate on obtaining agreements to secure your rights in the underlying material or screenplay. Make sure that you own or have a licence to what it is that you are going to exploit. I have seen, for example, options from quite established agents which give you absolutely nothing, yet the paper says that it is an option. A proper option agreement will have the terms of the licence or assignment annexed. If you tried to get development money based on an imperfect option, a broadcaster or financier would not be interested. If you wrote a screenplay based on the underlying material you could be at risk and waste time and money if the owner then refused to grant a licence or assignment. Obviously you can go back to the person who owns the rights and say we didn't have a proper deal, but then you're in a difficult negotiating position and they can be awkward. They could refuse to give you the rights or they could turn round and say *Ok, we now want £10k for it.* That's why it's important to have a solicitor look at those agreements and say *it's ok, you can go ahead.* I appreciate that most new film makers will be making a film from their own screenplay or from something a friend wrote, but it's still essential to have those rights sewn up before you shoot.

Q - How important are sales agents agreements?

Helen - Most operate on standard terms and you don't have much leeway. However, if you're not happy with the agreement for certain reasons, then you should negotiate with them, particularly in relation to the level of commission.

Q - Can a conversation over lunch be interpreted as a binding contract?

Helen - It depends on the circumstances. For a contract to be legally binding (apart from there being an offer, acceptance and consideration), what you have to look at is the intention of the parties. Did they intend, when having this conversation or even in letters or quite detailed memos, to create a legal relationship? If the parties did not intend that, at the time, there is no legally binding contract. It very much depends on what the practice is in the industry - a casual conversation over lunch with an actor saying *I'd like you to be in the film* is not going to be considered in the film industry as an offer which if accepted and consideration being agreed, is legally binding. If you're worried about your correspondence being misconstrued, you should always write at the head of any letter, *SUBJECT TO CONTRACT,* so it's clear.

Q - So to be safe, you should get it all in writing - don't go with verbal agreements?

Helen - It's better to do so, but it's not always possible to get everything in writing. A contract can be made orally, but it is then difficult to prove the terms of any verbal agreement. Even if you are dealing with friends on a business level, confirm the arrangement in writing as this will help avoid bad feeling over any dispute at a later stage.

Q - If a solicitor felt that a project was good, would they introduce one client to other clients with a view to investment?

Helen - If I thought I knew somebody who would be interested in a project, I would introduce them. You can say informally to someone that you've *read something and think it's quite good, have a look and see what you think'* That's the level it works on, we're not acting as agents for people. It's in our interest to help clients, but we do not take commission. Conversely, if you know that somebody has had a bad experience with a certain company or they're not reliable, a sales agent or distributor for instance, I would pass that information on too.

Q - How is your time charged?

Helen - I think nearly all firms work on the same basis - you have an hourly rate. With smaller productions, where there is a fixed amount for legal fees, we can do an all in deal - you say, *OK we'll do a flat deal for £20k and that's it'-* which is quite often the case. If things get more complicated then you might have to negotiate for a little more.

Q - Would you read the script?

Helen - Yes, I read the script because there could be areas that clients might not have thought about which could cause problems. I think it's quite good to pass it by a friendly insurance company as references to names and places should be checked to ensure there is no living person who may be innocently defamed. For example: if your screenplay contains a bent copper working for the Met - make sure there is or has been no PC of that name working for the Met. Generally if you're doing anything about living people it is an area of difficulty.

Q - How much should be budgeted for a solicitor's time on a low-budget picture?

Helen - On a very rough estimation, depending on how much work you're doing, anywhere between £10k and £15k really. It does depend on what the project is and if you're going to be doing artists contracts, directors, producers etc. If you're doing all the finance agreements and negotiating deals then I think between £5k and £10k is realistic. It depends a lot on how much you have to negotiate on behalf of the producer, because it's the negotiating process that can take up a lot of your time, particularly if you're dealing with agents.

Q - Could producers draw up their own contracts & bring them to you to be checked?

Helen - Yes, and that would normally reduce the costs, depending on the quality of the drafting.

Q - Most film makers would be put off from approaching a professional like yourself due to the fear of expensive charges?

Helen - There is a certain amount of leeway that we can give, for example, if a project is likely to get off the ground, what we sometimes do is run the clock whilst it is in development, and when it goes into production and there is money available, we'll then recoup our fees.

Q - In what areas do film makers have the most legal questions?

Helen - I would say, copyright and the payment or receipt of money, the financial side is of most interest to producers.

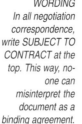

LTD. Co.	THE DEAL	WORDING	JUST IN CASE	ON PAPER
Always set up a limited company to make a film. This will afford limited protection for you as the directors	Always have a contract between your company & the author, especially if a friend has written the screenplay as friendships do end. Also an assignment of rights must be in writing.	In all negotiation correspondence, write SUBJECT TO CONTRACT at the top. This way, no-one can misinterpret the document as a binding agreement.	Always send a copy of your screenplay to yourself (or your solicitor) in a sealed and postmarked envelope, don't open it, store it away for use should someone contest your original authorship.	Wherever possible, get it in writing, signed and dated.

Q - Have you ever had any cases where producers have come along to you after they've signed a deal, and found themselves in a sticky situation?

Helen - It doesn't happen often, but there are disputes and claims when people are owed money, or are in dispute over the interpretation of the contract.

Q - What should a film maker do to protect the copyright of a project?

Helen - If you're basing it on a work that's already in existence, like a book, then obviously you have to get the rights of the author of the book, or whoever owns the rights. They may have already assigned them to a publisher, or they might belong to the estate if the author has died. You have to get the *right* to make the film. Most of the time, you'll either get an assignment just to make the film (i.e. the owner retains certain rights, like novelisation, theatrical, radio rights) or a licence which is restricted in time, and that'll be subject to negotiation. If you're getting somebody to write the screenplay, then you should commission them to write it and you will want them to assign all their rights in that screenplay to you. The most important thing is to have the necessary rights. If you don't have them and you go ahead and then you try and sell a screenplay or film, for instance, a small distributor who doesn't check the rights, who then shows the film - the person who owns the underlying work can go to court and get an injunction which will stop the film being shown. As a basic form of protection, it's a good idea to post a copy of your work to yourself in a sealed envelope and not open it (then the postmark - make sure it is clear - is evidence that you wrote it before a particular date). If somebody comes along saying you stole the idea from them, and they say that your idea was created a year after theirs, then you have evidence that it was created earlier - it's just added security.

Q - What happens when somebody puts an injunction on a film?

Helen - They go to the court and prove that they've got reasonable grounds and evidence to warrant an injunction. The court may order the film to be withdrawn from distribution until the issues in dispute are resolved. The party seeking the injunction, if successful will issue and serve a writ on the Defendant and the matter will be decided by the courts or otherwise settled.

PRE-PRODUCTION

Q - Does it cost to get an injunction?

Helen - Yes - in two ways. Firstly, if you engaged a solicitor you will be asked for money on account and it could cost £10-15k to obtain an injunction. Secondly, the person who applies for the injunction often has to make a payment in court so that if the injunction has been wrongly granted, due to evidence that later comes to light, there is money secured in court to pay the defendant, who might have suffered damages because of the injunction.

Q - If you've written the script yourself, what's the procedure for copyright?

Helen - Generally speaking, if you create it, you own it (unless you are an employee and create work as part of your employment). In the UK there is no formality with which you must comply.

Q - What about copyright in America - if you know your film is going to be released in the States, is it worth registering it?

Helen - You don't have to register your work in the USA, but a lot of people still do because if you want to produce your copyright as evidence in a court in America, your copyright has to be registered.

Q - What is your job after the film is completed?

Helen - Ensuring all the documentation is complete and signed off correctly. More and more producers are entering into sale and leaseback deals.

Q - What happens if a production company can't pay off a debt?

Helen - You can do a deal with your creditor. Ultimately, if you can't do a deal or pay, your company could be wound up by the creditor, and the creditor could end up owning your film. Unless, as a director you were found guilty of wrongful trading or unlawful trading, you won't have any personal liability - the company owes the money, not you - all the assets belonging to the company will go to pay off certain parties (Inland Revenue, Customs & Excise, secured creditors) including finally, the creditors.

For extra protection, you may wish to register the copyright for your film in the USA. It will cost you $20. To get the forms, write to The Register Of Copyrights, Library Of Congress, Washington D.C. 20559 USA

CHARGES	COLD TRAIL	PSYCHOS	GOOD ADVICE	DON'T FORGET
Keep in contact with your solicitor with regard to their fees. You don't want to build up a big bill without knowing it, and you should be able to ask for conversations off the record for which you aren't charged.	If you get on the wrong side of someone else's solicitor, don't allow negotiations to go silent or stale or you may well end up in court.	Just because you have a solid contract don't assume that you won't be ripped off. Some people are just plain bonkers and will try anything on, regardless of the contract.	Remember, your solicitor is an advisor. YOU make the decision and you can choose to disregard what they say.	In all this legal quagmire you may forget that you are here to make your film and launch your career. Resist the urge to spend time making your contract watertight and spend time developing your script.

Q - How does a low-budget film maker go about independently raising investment from private sources?

Helen - There are a lot of problems with this area and I know that people do it, but they usually don't comply with the Financial Services Act 1986. This Act was brought in to protect people from unscrupulous investment companies who went to unsuspecting people and said, *look at this wonderful proposal, you give me all your life savings and in ten years time I'm going to give you this huge return.* Since the Act, you can only seek private investment if you're an authorised person as set out in the Act. You also have to have the approval of an authorised person to give out an advertisement or prospectus that says *invest in this.* You must also give warnings, you have to say that this investment is not guaranteed, there are risks in doing it, and you're not necessarily going to get your money back. The people who are authorised to do that include accountants or solicitors. I've had people who've said to me, I want to send out letters to investors, saying invest in my film, this film is going to be a great success and you're going to make a lot of money - they're infringing the Financial Services Act and it's a criminal offence. If you do not comply with the Act a further problem is that if someone says to you, we'll give you £100k and then when it comes to the crunch they don't, you wouldn't be able to legally enforce that promise because what you're doing is not itself authorised or legal.

Q - What are the most common problems to resolve?

Helen - Ensuring that the producer has sufficient rights in the work to go ahead and exploit a project with the maximum opportunity to make the film (and ancillary rights) a commercial success. This also means ensuring the stream of income from the film is properly and fairly distributed. If you think about the time you are going to invest in making your film, then it does make sense to have the correct basic structure.

Accountant
Christine Corner
Of Baker Tilly

Q – Why do I need an accountant?

Christine – You need accountants to ensure that your finances are properly managed and that you are receiving proper advice on financing your company and film productions.

Q – What is the job of the production accountant?

Christine – The job of the production accountant is to prepare and monitor the film production budget. They need to go through every single item and analyse what is required and then produce a detailed budget, not only looking at the costs, but the timing of each line item so that the correct amount of drawdown can be obtained from the film financiers. The actual monitoring of costs against the budget is important so that you can see how the budget is going throughout the production. Once the film is up and running, the production accountant's day to day job will be checking that all the information is coming in, processing and paying invoices and ensuring they are genuine costs that are allocated properly to the right cost code, then comparing costs with the budget.

Q – What kind of complications peculiar to film making should a film maker be aware of?

Christine – There are many sources of finance and many ways to finance a film. A film-maker should be aware of all sources and the costs of each type of finance. Often a film is financed using more than one source of finance which makes the deal more complex and thus more costly from a legal point of view.

The producer needs to be aware that it is often difficult to get all sources of finance lined up at the same time and therefore some may end up not coming up with the money. The producer should never start spending money until the full budget is financed.

Q – Are you involved in negotiating deals with the actors or crew members?

Christine – We don't normally get involved with this. This is really the job of the producer and the lawyers because the legal terms, particularly if an actor takes a share of the profits, are often complicated and important to get right in a legal agreement.

Q – Do you help put proposals together, for the Lottery fund for example?

Christine – Yes, we do. We help clients in raising money through all sources, whether it be a business plan for a bank, an information memorandum for private EIS investors (see below) sale and leaseback transactions (see below) or applications for lottery or other public funds.

Q – Are there any tax incentives to invest in the UK?

Christine – Currently, tax incentives are available for investors in two ways. The first is via the Enterprise Investment Scheme (EIS). Baker Tilly have been involved in several successful fund raising ventures under which the investors qualified for EIS reliefs. The reliefs available are 20% income tax relief on investments up to £150k, per individual per tax year. 40% Capital Gains Tax deferral, no maximum investment. Disposal of the EIS shares is outside the scope of Capital Gains Tax if they have been held for at least five years (three years for investment after 5th April 2000).

The second method, which has proved popular in the last couple of years is investing via the various film partnerships that are currently being marketed, under which the 100% film write off can be taken by the individual as a tax deferral.

Q – What about Sale and Leaseback?

Christine – The sale and leaseback of films has always been popular with the US studios on big budget movies. Recently, however, sale and leaseback arrangements have become popular for films with production budgets generally from £1m upwards. Smaller budget movies can sometimes obtain a deal if they have a completion bond, but the costs often mean it is not worthwhile. Film production and acquisition expenditure on qualifying "British Films" of £15m or less can be written off on the date the film is ready for distribution or acquired. It is possible for deferrals to be included as part of the production expenditure for the sale and leaseback. The film production company ("Producer") sells certain rights in the film to the Purchaser (an individual or company with UK tax capacity). The film and all rights are then leased back to the Producer by the Purchaser for a series of increasing annual lease payments over a period of up to 15 years. This length of lease is normally acceptable to the Inland Revenue, provided the Film can reasonably be expected to generate income for at least that term. The Purchaser normally requires the lease payments to be secured by the Producer, by obtaining a bank guarantee payable to the Purchaser. This is typically achieved by a substantial amount of the proceeds of the sale being placed on deposit at the guarantor bank which, when combined with deposit interest over the period, is sufficient to cover the rental payments. The difference between the purchase price and the proceeds placed on deposit is the Net Benefit to the Producer and typically ranges between 5 and 10%. Every sale and leaseback transaction is different, because all the constituent parts are open to negotiation and obviously the transaction will not occur unless both parties are satisfied with their side of the agreement.

CHRISTINE CORNER
Partner
Arts Entertainment and
Media Group

BAKER TILLY

Chartered Accountants
2 Bloomsbury Street
London WC1B 3ST
Tel: +44 (0)20 7413 5100
Fax: +44 (0)20 7413 5101
E-mail: christine.corner@bakertilly.co.uk
DX: 1040 London/Chancery Lane

www.bakertilly.co.uk

An independent member of Summit International Associates, Inc.

Q – How do I make sure my film qualifies as a British Qualifying Film?

IRELAND'S SECTION 481 TAX INCENTIVE

The Irish Government is committed to the development of an Irish film industry and supports the industry through tax incentives and the Irish Film Board. As a result, Ireland is an attractive location and continues to be used by overseas producers.

Section 481	**Amount**	**Shares**	**Break**	**Producer Benefit**	**Tax**
Film Finance Incentive is a tax break for both corporate and private investors. Generally, 75% of the production work must be carried out in Ireland.	Individual investors can invest up to £25k per film per year. Companies can invest up to £3m per film per year.	The investor buys shares in a company that must be incorporated and based in Ireland. Up to 66% of the budget for a low-budget film can be raised under Section 481.	Both private and corporate investors receive an 80% tax break on their investment.	On top of any other deals, producers get to keep up to 17% of any returns under Section 481.	Film makers and other artists who relocate in Ireland may enjoy tax free earnings whilst companies can enjoy a range of low taxes. Irish corporation tax is being gradually reduced to reach a rate of 12.5% from Jan 2003.

Christine – The definition of a British Qualifying Film was changed on 27 August 1999. Films delivered before 27 August 2000 can qualify under the old or new rules. A British Qualifying Film certificate is issued by the Department for Culture, Media and Sport (DCMS). Under the new rules, the film must conform to the following - the producer (production company) must be either a person ordinarily resident or a company incorporated and managed from an EU or EEA member state. 70% (excluding payment to one person) or 75% (excluding payment to two persons, one of whom must be engaged only as an actor) of total labour costs must be payable to citizens or ordinary residents of an EU or Commonwealth country. Note – that deferrals are included as part of the calculation. At least 70% of the total expenditure incurred in the production of the film must be spent on film production activity carried out in the UK. (Note not the cost of goods and services supplied from the UK). Stock footage from a previously certified film or a film not made by the same film maker cannot make up more than 10% of the total playing time. (This does not apply to a documentary film).

It's also possible to qualify under one of the seven co-production treaties with Canada, Australia, New Zealand, France, Germany, Italy or Norway and under the European Convention on Cinematographic co-productions.

Q – How can an accountant help me obtain a British Qualifying Certificate?

Christine – A media accountant can advise on ensuring that all the elements planned for the film allow you to qualify in advance and will then carry out the audit and report to DCMS once the production is completed.

MONEY MATTERS

If you make a film, you will almost certainly have to register for VAT. From that point on you will be able to reclaim the VAT on purchases, but must charge VAT on invoices to UK companies and individuals. Each quarter you balance books and either reclaim VAT or pay VAT to Customs & Excise. Books MUST be done quarterly and VAT returns sent in on time or hefty penalties may be charged. NEVER cook the books for the VAT man or you could go to prison.

Pay As You Earn. As a director of a Limited company, you are technically an "employee" and must therefore calculate your wages on a PAYE system. This will calculate the amount of income tax and national insurance to be deducted each month and to be forwarded to the Inland Revenue (Tax and NI tables are provided by your tax office). You MUST pay the PAYE/NI due each month, or fill in a declaration if you have received no salary. If you earn less than £66 per week per individual then you will not have to operate this system. At the end of each tax year (5th April) you will have to fill in a return (P60) for each employee and an annual return (P35) for the company as a whole. Most crew on a film will be self employed and there are certain categories where PAYE need not be applied (see Schedule D). However, it is important to check their positions with the Inland Revenue otherwise the IR might declare them as 'employees' and therefore you may be liable to pay their PAYE plus severe penalties.

Contact the Film Industry Unit of the IR for more information: **Film Industry Unit, Inland Revenue, Tyne Bridge Tower, Gateshead, Tyne & Wear, NE8 2DT:** *Tel: 091 490 3500. Fax: 0191 390 3501.*

Income Tax: *Any and all income is liable to tax. If you operate PAYE then the tax for your employees will be calculated under that system. If you are self employed, your tax bill will be payable under the self assessment regime. If you pay taxes at 40%, then you may be required to complete a self assessment tax return. Failure to submit this return on time may result in penalties.*

Corporation Tax: *Tax on profits. Where a company makes a taxable profit, corporation tax generally must be paid within nine months of the year end, unless taxable profits exceed £1.5m, when quarterly payments on account will be required. Where a company makes a loss, these losses can be set off against future profits of the same company in the same trade or may be carried back and set off against profits which have been taxed in the previous year. A corporation tax return must be filed within 12 months of the year end, otherwise penalties will be charged.*

Capital Gains Tax: *A company will pay corporation tax on chargeable gains accruing during an accounting period. An individual will be chargeable to capital gains tax in respect of chargeable gains accruing to him in a year of assessment after an annual exempt amount for individuals of £7,100 in the year to 5 April 2000.*

Accounting Year: *This is generally set when you set up a company, but can be changed on application to the Registrar of Companies. For tax purposes, an accounting period generally ends 12 months after the inning of the accounting period. Individuals are taxed in the year to 5 April.*

There are five categories of National Insurance Contributions:

Class 1 – Primary: paid by employees
        Secondary: paid for employees by employers (12.2%)
Class 1A - Paid by employers who provide employees with cars/fuel for private use and other benefits in kind
Class 2 - Paid by people who are self employed (£6.55 per week)
Class 3 - Voluntary contributions
Class 4 - Paid by those whose profits and gains are chargeable to income tax under
Schedule D. These are normally paid by self employed people in addition to Class 2.

If you operate PAYE then the national insurance contributions for your employees will be calculated under that system. As an "employee" you will also have to deduct Class 1 national insurance contributions from your income. However, if you are self- employed (run a partnership not a limited company, or provide your services as freelance), then you will be liable to pay Class 2 National Insurance and Class 4 if your profits and gains are over a certain limit. You may be entitled to 'small earnings exemption' if your net earnings from self employment are under a certain limit.

Freephone Social Security Telephone No: 0845 741 3355

AUDITED ACCOUNTS – As a Limited Company, it is a requirement to submit audited accounts to Companies House and to fill in an annual return, giving details about the company's directors, secretary, registered office address, shareholders and share capital. There is a filing fee payable of £15.

If your company has an annual turnover less that £350,000 your company is exempt from any requirements to have its annual accounts audited. However, your investors or shareholders may request and insist on audited accounts.

There are few specific tax incentives in the UK for investors in films and those which currently exist favour investment by individuals rather than companies. A new scheme, called Corporate Venturing, is being introduced with effect from 5 April 2000. The intention is for this to be similar to EIS relief but for corporate investors. Relief is anticipated to be upfront tax relief of 20% on investments held for at least three years. At the time of going to press, the final legislation in respect of Corporate Venturing relief has not been published.

Individuals: The "Enterprise Investment Scheme" (EIS) replaced the BES with similar rules. The capital cost of shares in certain circumstances may be treated as a reduction against an individual's taxable income and/ or as a deferral of capital gains tax (see before). Where such shares are held for at least three years, any capital gain arising is exempt but where a loss arises, this can be set against chargeable gains or other taxable income.

Q – What about incentives for filming in Ireland?

Christine – The main tax incentive under Section 481 is a tax break for investors which gives them an additional deduction against their other income. However, producers can also obtain benefits as set out before.

Q – What happens about TAX, PAYE, NI on a film and will the producer deal with all of that?

Christine – Yes, or the production accountant can deal with it. They must notify the Revenue office that the film is being produced. The responsibility for the company to make sure that the books and records are kept up to date and that payments are made on time is quite significant. The question is whether the people working on the production are going to be employees or self- employed. The Revenue have published guidelines which should help and it's best to follow them rather than accept somebody's word that they are self-employed. At the end of the day, if you cannot prove that a worker is self-employed, you may be held responsible for their tax and national insurance, plus possible penalties and interest.

Q – What happens with deferred fee films with regard to paying PAYE, TAX and NI contributions to the cast and crew members?

Christine - The deferred fees which you pay to cast and crew, will be tax deductible as and when you pay them.

Q – Do you deal with sales agents?

Christine – Generally the producer will be dealing directly with the sales agent although, initially, we might advise the producer on the terms of the contract with the sales agent.

Q – What's the easiest type of investment structure to manage?

Christine – Often it isn't up to the producer to decide on the structure, because the investor will pick the route that they think will protect them the most, and also be the most attractive in terms of tax. They may wish to invest under EIS (see above) which means they will have to invest in the company or they may wish to invest via an off shore company or merely to take a share of the film. The best scenario for you as the film producer is for somebody to put the money directly into the business without taking shares in the company, but taking a share of the profits from just one film if possible.

Q – How can a film maker keep costs down?

Christine – It is all dependent on day to day control and knowing what is going on and ensuring that costs are kept down. If you know that there is a specific amount of money and no more, it's in your interest to

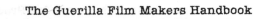

keep the costs down, but if you think that the backers will put in more money, then there is no incentive to keep costs down and stick to the film budget.

Q – What does a filmmaker need to do with regard to keeping books?

Christine – It is important to keep proper accounting records. On the simplest level, this can be done on a spreadsheet, recording each cost as it is paid out. The main requirement is to keep proper records for Customs & Excise. It is in the producer's interest to do this, as initially you will be able to reclaim VAT paid on expenses as the film is being made. Usually, you will have a separate company for each film and you should also set up a separate bank account for that company and film. This bank account needs to be reconciled with the accounting records.

Q – Is it true you don't need an audit if your turnover is under £350,000

Christine – Yes, it is true, however, your backers and bankers may want an audit.

Q – What is an audit?

Christine – An audit is a review by an external, independent, Chartered Accountant of the accounting records, to check that the figures have not been misstated.

Q – Would a high street accountant do as a good a job as a media accountant?

Christine – Probably not. A media accountant will understand how production works and what items can be allowed for tax, etc. The main benefit of a media accountant is the advice they can give in helping to raise and structure finance for films. It would be perfectly acceptable for a high street accountant to prepare the accounting records, look after the payroll and the VAT returns of the company as long as a production accountant was employed during the filming of each production.

Q – So once the film is made and you have a distribution or sales agent, then it's worth going to your accountant to check over the royalty agreements before you sign?

Low Budget films that cannot afford a Production Accountant can rely on dedicated accounts software to keep track of the budget, expenditure and cashflow. It's probably a good idea to still hire a book keeper to enter all the details as there will undoubtedly be more pressing problems for the production team to deal with.

Christine – Having an accountant and lawyer go through all the agreements and documentation can make the difference between getting money and getting no money. For instance, a distributor may try to get you as the producer to pay for all marketing costs. A good accountant or solicitor would make sure that the marketing costs are capped.

Q – How is your time charged?

Christine – By the hour. It is important to use accountants and lawyers who understand the film industry. One thing film producers should always get before any work is carried out is an estimate of fees to be charged.

Q – For a film that was budgeted at around £500k, how much should be set aside for accounting?

Christine – For advisors in general, including legal, I would suggest 15%. It may seem like a huge amount, but it should ensure that everything is above board and that you, as the producer, have negotiated the best terms and are protected.

Q – What are the most common mistakes that you have encountered?

Christine – Not properly estimating the budget. You should use a production accountant to prepare the budget and include a 10% contingency for unexpected costs. A good production accountant is also worth their weight in gold during the shoot, as they will control costs and prepare all the figures for the film which may be needed for investors reports or for sale and leaseback deals. Tax, PAYE and VAT are all relatively easy to deal with, and if not dealt with properly, could cause very serious problems. If a producer doesn't wish to deal with these things, get someone in who can.

Q – What basic advice can you offer to new film makers?

Christine – Surround yourself with people who know what they are doing, whether it be cast, crew or professional advisors, they will provide you with a professional approach and advice which should prevent you from appearing too naive as an up and coming producer. Otherwise, there are people out there who will try to rip you off. Although costs will be a problem, make sure you can get every agreement checked before you sign. Lastly, film-making is a business which should be run professionally. There is much more to running a company than you may think. It's important to learn and understand just how a small business runs – there are plenty of good books you can get to answer most questions, plus your bank manager should be able to provide help, as can your solicitor and accountant.

Bank Manager Stephen Shelley
Of Barclays, Soho Square.

Barclays in Soho Square have for many years been a source of specialised film banking offering a service backed up by expertise in both the film making and financial areas.

Q - How does a normal business account differ from a film business account?

Steve - Your normal personal account is something that you use for paying bills and paying in your salary- it's just a means of making payments and receiving payments. For a business account the same principles apply - it's a way of collecting money and paying money out, but with a business account, you tend to get a bank manager along with it.

The bank manager will also have expertise in the running of small businesses and will be able to advise on many basic issues, as well as suggesting contacts for things like solicitors and accountants. In many ways, they are a kind of free consultant. For a film company, two types of account are normally set up. One for the running of the film production company, and a second for the running of an individual production.

Q - So I am a new filmmaker with a great idea, and I only need £100k - are you going to give it to me?

Steve - The quick answer is no. However, what we often do is advance a film maker the money, prior to production, as long as there is evidence that sales exist. This might be a contract with a broadcaster like Sky, or an overseas distributor in France. They will have given you a contract that will say something like *when you deliver this film to me I will pay you £X* and then we can advance you the money. This is very common in the film business. A fee of around 1% of the sum borrowed would be charged, plus an interest rate of probably two and a half percent over base rate. In terms of running a simple bank account for your production company, like all the major banks, we would apply a small business tariff, although the first year would be free.

Q - So it is better than your credit card?

Steve - Absolutely. Borrowing on a corporate level is somewhat cheaper than borrowing personally. There is another type of finance too, it's called gap finance. You say you are making a film for £2m of which £1m comes from the Arts Council, £0.5m comes from Channel Four, leaving a gap of £0.5m - even though there is no determined buyer we and other banks do sell gap finance to plug that hole. This will be based on things like sales agents and distributors estimates, and the gap finance will be insured too. We don't get involved in gap finance for micro budget films though.

Q - Clearly a media based bank manager is better for a film company than a high street manager who is used to a greengrocers buying and selling potatoes?

Steve - One of the biggest things that clients need is that the bank manager understands their language - we understand the industry so when they say that they have a project greenlighted or a script in development they are all terms that we are familiar with. Plus we know all the big players in the industry, so a film maker does not have to waste time educating the bank about the industry in which they work.

Q - What common problems for new or young film makers do you see?

Steve - Making sure that they can deliver the film on budget and on time. If we are financing a contract for somebody who is relatively new to the industry we will need to ensure they have the ability to deliver what they say they are going to deliver, on time and on budget.

Another issue, and I think one of my predecessors, Peter Hitchen, mentioned this in the last edition of your book, is that it takes a lot of ideas to get to a completed film, and there is generally a high attrition factor. Determination is vital.

Also, we don't, and other banks won't, give money to fund the development of an idea. So if someone wants £20k to get the first script written, then that kind of finance is not available.

Q - You clearly deal with multi-million dollar projects regularly. Is it really worth a small production setting up with you?

Steve - Absolutely. It is in their interest to work with somebody who understands their industry. Even if they already have their money raised there can be timing differences and that can force a position where a service from the bank may be needed. At the end of the day, you want to be building relationships for the future and everyone has to start somewhere.

Q - What basic advice would you offer a new film maker?

Steve - Firstly, although it sounds quite corny, don't give up. I have seen some people who have come to us with good

Stephen Shelley
Corporate Director

Media Banking Centre
27 Soho Square
London
W1A 4WA

Tel 020 7445 5716 (Direct)
Fax 020 7445 5784

Regulated by IMRO and the
Personal Investment Authority.

GFMH
OFFICIAL
SPONSOR

BARCLAYS

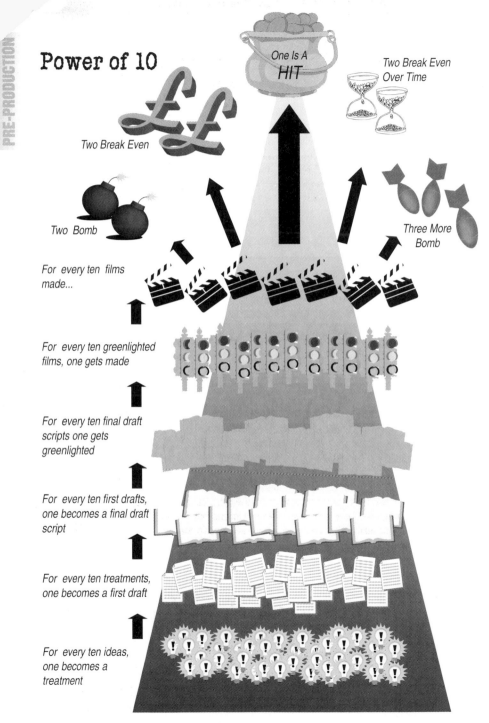

Power of 10

One Is A **HIT**

Two Break Even Over Time

Two Break Even

Two Bomb

Three More Bomb

For every ten films made...

For every ten greenlighted films, one gets made

For every ten final draft scripts one gets greenlighted

For every ten first drafts, one becomes a final draft script

For every ten treatments, one becomes a first draft

For every ten ideas, one becomes a treatment

SEPARATION	CONTACT	CHEQUE BOOKS	MEDIA BANK
Keep your business account separate from your production account. Don't underestimate how messy things can get during production, and this simple separation will make it 50% easier.	Keep your bank manager informed, especially if you have problems. They want you to succeed and they can't help if they don't know.	Before shooting, make sure you have heaps of cheque books as you can rip through them quickly. If you run out of cheques you could have problems for a week or two.	Get a bank manager who understands the business, can put you in contact with others, and can grow with you over the years. Relationships are everything.

ideas and we've never seen them again. Other people have come into us with good ideas and then made it happen.

The other thing that I would say is ensure that the calibre of people they get involved with is high. I am not saying that you should spend lots of money hiring expensive accountants or solicitors, but get involved with and take advice from good people in the industry.

Another simple problem is when new producers don't separate funds, keeping everything in one place. They should have at least two accounts, one for their production company, the other for each individual production and the monies are then separate.

Q - What can a new producer do to make your life easier?

Steve - Dialogue with the bank. Whatever they are doing, whether they are having difficulties or successes, they should speak to the bank. Just treating the bank as somewhere to deposit money and withdraw money means that you will never have a good relationship, and the better the relationship, the better the bank will be able to deliver.

PRE-PRODUCTION

First Film Foundation
Jonathan Rawlinson

Q - What is the First Film Foundation?

Jonathan - The First Film Foundation is a charity that exists to help new British writers, producers and directors make their first feature film. We provide a range of educational and promotional programmes that give filmmakers the contacts, knowledge and the experience they need to achieve this goal.

Q - Who can you help?

Jonathan - Usually screenwriters, producers and directors who have achieved some level of experience in the industry, either by making short films or having written their first scripts. We do have a guidebook, 'First Facts', which gives introductory advice for new filmmakers, however as most of our schemes are tailored towards feature film production, the people who participate are usually a little further along in their careers.

Q - What do you offer?

Jonathan - Our work is structured through various schemes that run throughout the year. 'New Directions' is an annual scheme that takes short films and their filmmakers to meet the industry in London, New York and Los Angeles. Filmmakers are selected on the basis of their short films and on their feature length projects in development. 'North By Northwest' is a screenwriter-training programme that develops projects during workshops spread over a six-month period. In the final workshop, the writers pitch their work to agents and producers with the aim of moving their projects towards production. Throughout the year, people can submit scripts to the Script Feedback Service where, for a small fee, they can receive a script report giving advice on their work. We also launched a competition in Spring 2000 to write or direct a short film on a Sci-Fi theme. The winning films are going to be shown in UCI cinemas, and the winning writer and director will also be taken on Universal Studios' 'Cinemaster' masterclass programme in Los Angeles. In addition, we are always developing new initiatives, including a short film completion fund that we hope to launch later in 2000, and 'First Feedback', a series of script development workshops for writers from throughout the UK, which culminate in the writers being presented to the industry.

Q - What have been your biggest successes?

Jonathan - We have been running schemes since '87 so many of the filmmakers who have been helped by us over the years have achieved great success such as Lynne Ramsey, Peter Mullan, Andrea Calderwood, Andrzej Sekula, Paul Anderson and Richard Holmes. However, the schemes we operate are all about helping filmmakers find the long-term contacts that they will need throughout a whole career in the film industry.

Q - How do people submit to you?

Jonathan - People should visit our website or send us a 39p SAE stating whether they are interested in the writers, directors or producers schemes and we can send them the relevant information. The New Directions and North By Northwest schemes invite applications in December, with the Script Feedback Service operating throughout the year. The competitions are developed on a more individual basis, such as the Sci-Fi competition that ran in Spring 2000. Any current news is included in the material we post out, or can be accessed on our website.

Q - Do you see a lot of common mistakes and what are they?

Jonathan - We still get people writing standard letters to us who clearly haven't tried to find out what we do, and that we aren't a production company. With scripts, there are common weaknesses, some of which are easily rectified. It is always frustrating to receive scripts that aren't properly formatted, particularly given the number of screenwriting books that are now available. This isn't just for convention's sake, it is actually a lot harder to assess how a script is structured and paced if the layout is wrong. More generally, with new writers there is often a lack of distinct characterisation and characters tend to speak with one voice. With the short films, there has been an increase in recent years of technically proficient films, even ones with very high production values, but they are often lacking the *thing* that makes them stand out. Not many of the films we see really take risks with material, or with their visual language, which is something that you can afford to play around with in short films, you can push a device over ten minutes that wouldn't work in a feature format. Too many shorts feel like slices taken out of a longer piece, there's no sense of it being a miniature, complete in itself.

Q - Do good projects stand out and why?

Jonathan - There is always fluency and a drive to good projects, whether script or film, that draws you in and keeps you interested. The pacing is really important, and knowing that people have really thought about what each scene is doing, what we the audience are gaining from each scene. However behind every good project is just a really strong idea. Whether it is a plot line, or even something as simple as a visual image or an emotional situation, there needs to be something that interests an audience enough for them to stay with your story and become involved.

Q - What advice would you offer a new film-maker?

Jonathan - The film industry is very competitive so you need to make yourself stand out and be better prepared than everybody else. Research the field before writing your script or making your film. Find out where short films are shown and see what type of material works, what other people are making. Research which organisations are out there, what mailing lists you can get on, and who might be able to help you. Make

FIRST FILM FOUNDATION

9 Bourlet Close
London W1P 7PJ
Tel. 020 7580 2111
Fax. 020 7580 2116
Registered Charity No. 297614

Jonathan Rawlinson
Director

sure that you have a clear idea about how you feel they can help before approaching them, and that you have developed your ideas about what you are trying to do. Organisations will be less likely to help you if you haven't found out even the most basic information about what they do.

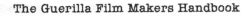

John Woodward
of the Film
Council

Q - What is the Film Council?

John - The Film Council is the new strategic lead body for the UK film industry. Our job is to advise government about all matters relating to the film industry and channel all public funding for film production previously allocated to other bodies by the Department for Culture, Media and Sport. The only exception to this is the grant to the National Film and Television School.

The formal integration of the British Film Commission which focuses on attracting inward investment to the UK, the British Film Institute's (*bfi*) Production Department and the Arts Council of England's Lottery Fund Department into the Film Council started in April and a new structure will be in place by the end of September.

By October, film production and development agency, British Screen, will be incorporated into the Film Council to form the basis of a united production entity with a number of entry points responsive to the needs of the industry and offering a diversity of decision making. The British Film Institute will continue as an independent body delivering cultural and educational objectives for film but funded by the Film Council and responsible to it.

Q - What is the remit of the Film Council?

John - The Film Council can't create a new British film industry, it can only aim to encourage an environment in which we can have a successful industry. It has been set up with two specific and equal aims. First, it is looking to create a more sustainable domestic industry within the UK and part of its strategy to achieve this will be the development of a long-term coherent approach to film production funding.

Secondly, it aims to develop film culture by improving access to and education about the moving image. In order to achieve these aims, the Film Council will build a coherent strategy for film culture, the development of the film industry and the encouragement of inward investment. In providing this direction for the film industry, the Film Council will be looking to eliminate gaps and overlaps in services to encourage greater efficiency and effectiveness.

Q - What are the key priorities of the Film Council in addressing its remit?

John - Overall we are looking at how the educational, industrial and cultural imperatives can be harnessed together more effectively to benefit the development of the industry and the audience for the moving image.

In terms of the Film Council's cultural objectives, our strategies and policies have been developed with the objective of nurturing an environment in which new talent can be supported and creative endeavour encouraged. Taking film development and production specifically, the Film Council recognises that it will be essential to ensure that sufficient resources are available to support film-makers with a distinctive cinematic style and a strong personal vision. This helps to enhance the diversity of UK cinema and can also help to broaden the audience.

Assisting the development of the film industry infrastructure across the UK takes into account both cultural and commercial objectives. Culturally, an increased degree of diversity in moving image presentation of life and society in the UK can be encouraged whilst at the same time the strengths of the different types of organisations which comprise the regional industry infrastructure, particularly outside of London, including media development agencies, screen commissions, local cinemas, etc, can be maximised.

All cinema audiences should have access to film and the opportunities offered by developing the moving image industry. The needs of those people most disadvantaged in society have been and will continue to be, considered by the Film Council from a number of angles. The opportunities need to be widened both for people and communities to see films as well as participating in film-making activities.

And then there is the audience of the future, young people.

Clearly investing in both formal education and lifelong learning has cultural and industrial value. Creating an environment on which people can develop their knowledge and awareness will help foster a deeper understanding of film and the richness of different types of cinematic experience. It may also encourage people to become professionally involved in the industry.

Other business considerations include looking at how to encourage more private finance into the industry to create better-capitalised companies which may invest and reinvest in the industry, sustaining and increasing the level of inward investment from overseas into the industry, boosting film exports and developing the foundations to maximise the commercial and educational opportunities offered by digital technologies.

The full development of the Film Council's strategies and polices will unfold in the coming months.

FILM | COUNCIL

John Woodward

10 Little Portland Street, London W1N 5DF
Tel: 0207 436 1357   Fax: 0207 436 1391

Finance
Jenny Borgars
of British Screen

Q - What is British Screen?

Jenny - It's a private company, funded in part by an annual grant from the British Government through the DCMS (Department of Culture, Media and Sport). We are a mechanism for state intervention in the film industry with an agenda which is a mix of business and culture. We're involved in the development and production funding of films that wouldn't get made without our support, that promote new talent, that are in some sense definably British and which also answer a marketplace demand. Technically, projects for production need to qualify as British films under the Films Act of 1985 (which is changed and amended from time to time).

Q - What kind of funding is available?

Jenny - We do two main sorts of funding. Development Funding and Production Funding. You don't have to have Development Funding from British Screen before you apply for Production Funding, but the projects developed here often graduate to the production fund. For development there are two main streams of finance. Screenplay Loans are a low level loan of £5k to a writer in order to get to first draft. This is intended for writers new to cinema and payment is fairly straight-forward - 50% on signature, 50% on delivery. The writer retains the copyright in the script that they have written. The loan is repayable, plus 50%, if the film goes into production, so it's a soft loan. The Development Loan is a loan to production companies, designed to enable the script to get written and cover all the other costs of getting a film through development. We lend to the production company, and the producer uses the money for example, to pay the writer, prepare the budget, recce locations etc. Everything that is needed to get the film into 'official' pre production. Again, there is a premium of 50% on those loans and all of it is payable on the first day of principle photography. We also take 5% of a film's net profit. If the film doesn't go into production we do not get our money back.

Q - How does the production side work?

Jenny - We have two main funds from which we loan money for production. They are The British Screen Fund and the European Co-production Fund. In essence, the British Screen Fund is there to support films made by British directors, British writers etc. The European Co-production Fund is there to support films which are, as the name suggests, European co-productions. So in order to qualify for a British Screen Fund loan for production, the film must be British under the Film's Act, in most cases have a British director and in many cases a British writer. In order to qualify for the European Co-production Fund a film must be a genuine European co-production with a co-producing partner in another EC country. If it all works out then our money is loaned to a British production company. Also, for the European Co-production Fund, there must be some interest in the UK from a distributor. You don't necessarily have to have a signed distribution deal but when you come here you must be able to show evidence that there is someone else apart from the European Co-production Fund that is interested in this movie in the UK. We would not be disposed to get involved in a film which is entirely supported by subsidy money from around Europe for example, because we want evidence that there is demand for the film in the market place. If that evidence is strong then that's another reason for us not to invest. If the film can get financed without us, because the casting is so attractive for example, then we can't get involved. Our money is there to target films that wouldn't get made without our support. And there have been successful British films which we have declined because we knew that they would be financed without our help.

Q - How does somebody approach British Screen?

Jenny - Applicants submit whatever they have, be it a script, a treatment, writer's notes on a book or play they want to adapt. Once we've assessed the project we decide whether or not we want to take it further for development finance. If we do, then we prepare the project in conjunction with the producer and writer and present it on their behalf to a panel of industry consultants who meet every ten weeks or so to review the development projects here at British Screen. Any paperwork that goes into an application is usually decided between ourselves and the applicants. Anything that helps the application look stronger is acceptable. That includes things like statements of intent from directors, writers and producers. Supporting material which has helped give a flavour of some of the previous projects we have been involved with have included books of poetry, writing samples, art work and even in one case, a prosthetic latex head. Screenplay loans are much the same except simpler, because there is only a writer involved. If a Development Loan project is passed by the panel then the producer comes to a meeting here at British Screen where we determine the exact amount of money that we are going to invest. We then start the legal process of contracting the loan.

Q - If someone has limited experience, is that a problem?

Jenny - We are driven by enthusiasm for a project. If a project comes in and there are things that we might be worried about, for instance, the lack of experience of various people, then we would do our best to alleviate those problems. Not by taking people off the project but by introducing them to more experienced people - that more experienced person may take on the role of the executive producer or simply act as an advisor.

Q - Is a producer more likely to get production investment if they have already received the development loan?

Jenny - 20-30% of projects that we put money into come out of the development department here. It helps if you can get a project through development here, because you have an inside track, if you like, but as you can see from the statistics, it's not a decisive inside track.

British Screen
Finance Limited

14-17 Wells Mews
London W1P 3FL
Tel 020 7323 9080
Fax 020 7323 0092

Jenny Borgars

BRITISH Screen

BRITISH SCREEN FINANCE SCHEMES

All productions must be *'intrinsically'* British and demonstrate that the project has a place in the commercial marketplace.

Screenplay Loan

For Who - Writers
To - Get to first draft
Amount Available - £5k
Turnaround - Up to 8 weeks
Terms - Paid 50% upfront and 50% on delivery. Repay in full plus 50% if screenplay is made into film

Development Loan

For Who - Producers
To - Support producers through development
Amount Available -Typically up to £15k (first stage), £35-50k in total.
Turnaround - Up to 10 weeks
Terms - Paid in instalments throughout development. Repay in full plus 50% on first day of principal photography. Plus British Screen receives 5% of profits.

Preparation Loan

For Who - Producers
To - Finance final development of a project where British Screen intend to provide Production Finance
Amount Available -Typically up to £50k (very negotiable)
Turnaround - Up to 8 weeks
Terms - Repay in full plus 50% on first day of principal photography. Plus British Screen receives 2.5% of net profits additional to 5% if Development Loan was secured.

Production Loan From The British Screen Main Fund

For Who - Production Companies
To - Be used as part of the production budget.
Amount Available - Up to £500k
Turnaround - Up to 10 weeks
Terms - Repay in full plus 50% from receipts of film. Plus British Screen receives a share of net profits.

Production Loan From European Co-production Fund

For Who - Production Companies with European partners
To - Be used as part of the production budget
Amount Available - Up to £500k
Turnaround - Up to 10 weeks
Terms -Repay in full plus 50% from receipts of film. Plus British Screen receives a share of net profits.

Greenlight Fund - currently suspended

For Who - Established director driven productions
To - Be used as part of the production budget
Amount Available - Up to £1.5m

BSkyB Output Deal

For Who - British Screen productions
To - Provide production finance secured against a Pay TV deal with BSkyB.
Amount Available - Typically 8% of total budget.

Q - What is the deal British Screen has with BskyB?

Jenny - It's a straightforward output deal - every film that British Screen and The European Co-production Fund (excluding films not in the English language or budgeted at under £1m) is automatically acquired by BSkyB for pay television broadcast in the UK and Ireland. It is worth 8% of the budget for films budgeted at £2.5m or less and the money is paid out for production.

Q - What should a Producer supply to make an application for the full production loan?

Jenny - You're required to have a script and a fairly rigorous idea of the personnel involved. You don't have to have all your cast or a director. But if you don't then it becomes a lower priority for us - projects that have a director attached are dealt with more quickly. Simply send to 'admissions for production' a copy of the script and a letter detailing whatever you think we ought to know about the project, that is, the history of it up to date, the ideas you have for the financing, the interest with third parties, the cast, the crew, and various other interested financiers to give an idea of how the producer thinks the finance will be brought in. Once you have the script and the letter, we then read the script, and if the script interests us, there will then be a meeting.

Q - What kind of films are British Screen looking to become involved in?

Jenny - We're not looking for specific genres, however, there is a bias towards contemporary projects. We get involved in projects that would not get made without our help, but at the same time we also have to try to make a sound commercial investment. Films, that once they're made, the commercial marketplace thinks, God, we should have funded that film, we should have seen that it would work. So it's not completely off the wall films, but it is not completely mainstream films either. Exactly what those are, and how you identify them is a very interesting question because it changes all the time and it's very difficult to actually make the correct choice.

Q - How many applications do you get, and what is the turnaround?

Jenny - For production investment, we get something in the region of 400-500 a year. Of those probably 250 are serious, in the sense that they are a complete package that could go if the production money came together. In the development department we get triple that. But in development, conversely, we have at any one time, around 90 active projects as opposed to the 20 or so in production. The turnaround for production should be around 6 to 7 weeks before you get a detailed response. For development, I'm afraid, it's slightly longer. In fact sometimes, it can take up to 10 weeks or more. We try and keep it down to 6-8 weeks. It really depends on what time of year you apply.

Q - What can a producer do to make your life easier?

Jenny - Make sure you send in the right material. In order to make a decision about something, we need to see a serious amount of work put into an application. We expect a treatment of 10-15 pages. If you have the script, send the script. Also write a clear and concise letter detailing everything we need to know.

Finance
Jane Wittekind
of The Film
Consortium

Q - What is your relationship to the Arts Council?

Jane - The Film Consortium (TFC) is one of the three companies awarded a franchise by the Arts Council in 1997 to finance British feature films using funds from the National Lottery. £30.25m was made available to The Film Consortium for production funding over the six year term of the franchise, and the award enables us to operate as an independent "mini-studio".

Q - What kind of films do you make?

Jane - The films we've made so far have been very diverse, ranging from romantic comedies to thrillers. We're about to start shooting a teenage comedy set in Birmingham. Primarily, we're looking for commercial projects.

Q - How should a new film-maker submit to you?

Jane - Projects should be submitted by producers rather than writers or directors because TFC is a film finance company and not a production company. That said, we do provide a nurturing environment and often take an executive producer role. In the case of new or relatively inexperienced producers, we can attach a more experienced producer, possibly one of our shareholders, to act as a godparent or we can suggest line producers.

We make an initial assessment of each script submitted and decide if we want to put it forward to the Arts Council for funding. It's helpful if producers approach us with a package already in place (e.g. writer / director / partial finance and business plan), but the script is ultimately the most important thing in our decision making process. If we really like a piece of material, we will use our financing leverage to try and make it happen.

Q - How important is the quality of presentation?

Jane - Obviously, the more professional the presentation the better. It helps if the script is properly formatted with accurate page and scene numbers.

Q - What kind of budgets do you work with?

Jane - The Film Consortium will invest up to 50% or £2m of the production budget, whichever is the higher, using funding available from the Arts Council. The budget range is generally between £1.2 - £9m. However, we can become involved in bigger budget films and invest more by way of gap funding or a licence fee from Film Four with whom we have an output deal.

Q - What happens about distribution?

Jane - The Film Consortium has an "output" deal with UIP (UK) Distribution so we can guarantee distribution for all our films. The Film Consortium is also a shareholder of the Sales Co which ensures that our films secure the widest international distribution possible on the best possible terms.

Q - How do you put an application forward to the Arts Council?

Jane - Should TFC wish to take a project forward for funding, it will consult with the producer to establish the basis of the deal. Then we'll make a formal application to the Arts Council, submitting the script and supporting documentation, including CVs of key personnel (producer, director, key cast and crew), the budget, schedule, a full finance plan identifying rights to be granted and other sources of funding, and the full chain of title.

Q- So if you recommend a film it's likely to get backing through the Arts Council?

Jane - Yes. It's not automatic, but none of our applications have been turned down so far. The franchises offer a fast track for applications which are considered by the Film Panel and Council at their monthly meetings.

Q - What in your opinion do you think a new film maker should be making?

Jane - The films we've backed so far have, I hope, demonstrated originality and a distinctive voice which single them out. I wouldn't say we're looking for any specific genre or subject, but we like good stories that are handled in a cinematic rather than a televisual way.

The Film Consortium Limited
6 Flitcroft Street
London WC2H 8DJ
Tel +44 (0) 20 7691 4440
Fax +44 (0) 20 7691 4445

Q - What advice would you offer new film makers?

Jane - To persevere and try to get as much experience as they can, working on shorts if possible as they're always a good calling card.

TheFilmConsortium

Finance
Robin Gutch
FilmFour Lab

Q - What is the FilmFour Lab?

Robin - The FilmFour Lab was specifically created in 1999 to find new filmmakers with original creative voices who need support in the world of independent cinema. We co-finance only four films a year, and this year we have one digital film, two Super 16mm and one 35mm. We are linked into FilmFour Production, Distributors and International.

Q - What kind of projects are you looking for?

Robin - We want debut features that can find a cinema and television audience. I am looking for poets, pioneers, renegades and hackers. Lynne Ramsey is a cinematic poet, and her audience exists as *Ratcatcher* has shown. I want pioneers to explore the new digital technology which in America and Europe is acknowledged as the way of the future for new film makers. I want people who not only make their films using new technologies, but want to market and distribute them in new ways such as the FilmFour portal. I want renegades who have vision and experiences that make good stories. I am interested in the hackers that take the solid generic core of a thriller, gangster, sci-fi etc., and subvert it with the language that they use, both in dialogue and the way that the film is made and shot. So there's this promotable and marketable core, recognisable to the audience, but interpreted from an entirely different and new perspective. A film that we are co-financing now has these qualities. It is called *Large*, directed by first timer Justin Edgar. It's a generic teenage bad taste comedy but it is set in a part of Birmingham with its own rules, language and characters which are unusual and not part of that genre.

Q- What kind of budgets are you working with?

Robin - We usually budget at £1m, sometimes lower, rarely higher.

Q - How should projects be submitted?

Robin - The best way is to write in with an outline which indicates what sort of film it is and what you are trying to achieve with it. Bare plot synopsis are very dull so I would prefer getting the idea or premise and why you think audiences would want to see the film. I like receiving treatments rather than scripts because I do not have the time or the resources to get through them all. If we like it we will option the script and put in seed development money, leaving a window for us to pursue it or pass on it if we feel that it is not for our distinctive remit.

Q - How long does it take for a script that you take on to reach the cinema?

Robin - From script to cinema is about two years, although all our films are intended to go onto FilmFour Channel and Channel 4. This seems a long time to new filmmakers but it has advantages. There is enough development, production and post production time. So many low budget British movies race through development to get into production so that producers earn money and can survive, especially if there has been very little development money. They also tend to rush the post production in an attempt to get the movie sold to recoup as fast as possible. The other advantage is that we try to choose films that we believe will have a lasting value. If it takes two years to reach the screen we don't want something that is merely following the fashion and will look out-dated in two years time. It is a good test for the film if it survives the wait.

Q - What mistakes do you see new film makers making?

Robin - The biggest mistake is chasing the phenomenon of the day rather than thinking ahead. I know that this is very hard to do but in 1999 I had so many *Lock Stock* pitches. Some had merit but you could hear '*that was a success, they will want more of these*'. New film makers often seem to have unrealistic expectations. They say that the movie will be cheap and we will go into production in two weeks. Institutionalised finance is grindingly slow and that kind of attitude of *let's go* when the script is only in its second draft does not indicate that you take us or your film seriously. Do I really want to give this money to this person who really does not have a clue how to make a film? Lastly telling us your film will be really cheap to make as the winning pitch is not going to work. All it does is indicate to us that you undervalue the film. Maybe it will be cheap to make, but we would rather be pitched with the dramatic intrigue or the tense claustrophobic build-up or the fascinating relationship. There seems to be this conviction that financiers of low budget films will want to do your film simply because it is cheap.

I feel that British Filmmakers are curiously reluctant to take advantage of digital technology. Directors and DoPs in particular seem to be reluctant to embrace it. Both Dogma and some of the films at Sundance this year use digital camerawork to great effect. We partner with the BFI in the New Directors Scheme and we specifically encouraged digital submissions and out of the 800 or so films that we received only 10% were digital. The digital film that we have this year is using this technology really well, it is really fresh and unusual rather than just a 35mm film shot on DV.

Q - What advice would you offer a new film maker?

Robin - Work out what it is that will make people go and see your film in reasonable numbers. In two, possibly three, years what will make it shine among 500 other films at Cannes or another market? It has to have something, otherwise it gets lost and collects dust.

ROBIN GUTCH
HEAD OF FILMFOUR LAB

FILMFOUR 4

FilmFour Ltd
76-78 Charlotte Street
London W1P 1LX
Telephone: +44 (0) 20 7868 7700
Direct Line: +44 (0) 20 7868 7744
Direct Fax: +44 (0) 20 7868 7772
rgutch@channel4.co.uk
www.filmfour.com

Finance & Support
James Wilson
Deputy Head of Production, FilmFour

Q - What is FilmFour looking for?

Jim - We look for distinctive material that will turn into low-budget British films in the £2-3m bracket; through to £4-6m films where you get a level of cast and production value that can help you out of the 'little British movie' niche. We also now make a couple of big budget movies a year, say £8-10m and over, where we are looking for significant directors and cast.

Q - Are you making more commercial films?

Jim - We're not scared of the 'c' word anymore. People often confuse conventional with commercial. We're looking for films that make an impact whether it's a feel good crowd pleaser or in your face, edgy and provocative. There are different ways to crack the nut, but either way a film has to cut through the crowd. We market aggressively but we don't have the marketing dollars of the US studios, so we choose films that in content and style will draw attention to themsleves, especially important when dozens of films are opening every week.

Q - How should a film maker submit a project to you?

Jim - We don't accept unsolicited scripts but that doesn't mean that we'll only deal with agents. We request that you get to know us before you send it. Send me a fax describing the project and I'll respond to that. We try to be prompt and get back to people within 3 or 4 weeks, but we do have an enormous volume to deal with. Remember if you're a new writer/film maker you're not going to get an overnight response.

Q - If a new film maker had a fantastic idea and wanted money to turn it into a screenplay would you put money into developing it?

Jim - Yes, if the idea was really strong. Development is a key part of our business. We're cautious, careful developers and unlike the Hollywood studios we don't have hundreds of projects on our development slate. Don't develop a gangster movie right now like everyone else, we're looking for stories that are distinctive. A producer with just an idea has to find a writer and a director which takes a long time. If you bring in a book with a writer who wants to do it and an exciting director it's easier to see the light at the end of the tunnel.

Q - If you were presented with a screenplay how long would it take to get going?

Jim - It's variable. About a year is pretty good which includes getting the right draft, arranging the financing, casting etc. Other developments may be longer or shorter. There was a movie we made with Alison Anders last year called *Sugar Town*, which was made for under a $1m. We got a script, they needed a relatively modest amount of money. They shot the movie in 19 days and cut for 29 days. We had moved from script to movie and out the door in a matter of months. If you've got a script that's finished, ready to cast, we can be shooting within a few months. We try and make twelve films per year incorporating some acquisitions, where at script stage we will buy UK rights, like David Lynch's *Straight Story*.

Q - What are the common mistakes made by film makers submitting projects?

Jim - Number one is sending scripts in cold. I dislike naive overselling when people send budgets with marketing plans, lots of pictures and cast lists that say *we're thinking of Sean Connery...* This is meaningless unless Sean Connery has actually agreed to do it. So keep it simple. Send me your script with a covering letter, explaining anything I need to know, this director is interested, that cast is interested. Simple and strong. The other mistake people make is obsessive badgering.

Q - What advice would you give to a scriptwriter submitting a project?

Jim - Learn from the industry, find out from the trades whether the companies are doing your sort of project. Find out about the company you're submitting to, what they're doing, how they're working in the business, be smart. Don't send me proposals for a TV series.

Q - Did you think East is East was going to take off like it did at the beginninq?

Jim - It was an engrossing, funny, involving script that also had pathos and it fitted into the British working class comedy niche. We only undertake a project if it's going to have an impact on an audience but no, we didn't know that this would be such a mainstream hit. It's test screening went through the roof, they did an aggressive advertising campaign and it paid off.

Q - Has FilmFour got it's own sales company?

Jim - Yes, it is called FilmFour International and it sells to distributors around the world. There is also FilmFour Distribution which distributes theatrically in the UK, and we are also a TV end user, the Ch4 network and now the FilmFour Channel. We have strong relationships with American distributors and producers, Fine Line, Miramax, Artisan and Fox Searchlight.

Q - What advice would you offer a new filmmaker?

Jim - The challenge for everyone in the UK is to make distinctive films in an environment where the small, disappearing, British movie has become common-place. We need new voices, like the ones you hear in the best of American or European cinema, like Todd Solondz or Thomas Vinterberg. I see it in the work of Lynne Ramsay, Shane Meadowes and Chris Cunningham from music videos. So think cinemati-cally. I despair of a film culture that can't think beyond the stylistic language of *Eastenders*. Film is it's own language, not an extension of the language of TV drama or theatre. It's about having a strong voice, whether it's *Happiness*, *The Idiots*, or *Being John Malkovich*. Who's got voices like those in the UK? Who's got the balls?

JAMES WILSON
DEPUTY HEAD OF PRODUCTION

FILMFOUR 4
PRODUCTIONS

FilmFour Ltd
76-78 Charlotte Street
London W1P 1LX
Direct Line: +44 (0) 20 7868 7700
Direct Fax: +44 (0) 20 7868 7771
www.filmfour.com

Finance
Luke Alkin of
BBC Films

Q - What is this organisation and what are its affiliations?

Luke - This is BBC Films. We have a broad output, ranging from large feature films to small-scale low budget films for TV. Because we are affiliated to the BBC, everything we make is destined for a TV slot so even if it is years down the line you know it will get screened. In terms of what we commission, because we are the BBC, our remit is on the whole to make films that reflect British life.

Q - What kind of movies are you looking for and how should I submit it to you?

Luke - Screenplays are dealt with by the in-house development team and our freelance readers who decide what to reject and what is worth a second look. This could be the case if it is something we might want to commission or if we think that the author has a strong original voice, even if the screenplay itself has problems. We prefer being approached by a company or agent that we have worked with before and new writers should submit their work to Lucy Hannah who co-ordinates the New Writer's Initiative.

Q – What is the procedure if you like what you read?

Luke - We would option the screenplay and put it into development. At the right time we would get a producer involved, then director. It can happen incredibly quickly or it can take years depending on how the script develops.

Q – What sort of budgets do you work with?

Luke - Anything from under £1million to £10million. The BBC has not fully funded its own projects for years so we have to look for co-production funding and we have an in-house department whose job it is to raise those funds.

Q – How long does it take to get a rejection or an acceptance?

Luke - Our target is eight weeks although often we are quicker than that.

Q – Do the people that supply the screenplays get access to the readers notes?

Luke - No. The letter of rejection is designed to be helpful and give some indication why the screenplay could not be taken on.

Q – What do you think film makers should be making and what should they be avoiding?

Luke - There is always a market for formulaic material if it is good, but we are looking for people with a new voice, with a new eye. I would like to see less low key stories where nothing much happens, where all you get is lots of characters and shifting relationships, people should be more ambitious in their storytelling in this country.

Q – How realistic is it making a living out of being a writer?

Luke - Depends on where you set your sights. Writing for a series on TV is obviously an easier way to make money than trying to write a high-budget experimental feature film. Either way, you will need to get yourself an agent to promote your work and negotiate contracts. And when you do get your script commissioned, be prepared for plenty of work re-drafting it!

Q – There is this naïve belief that the BBC is a charity but it is in fact a business, producing commercial theatrical films - is this right?

Luke - To a certain extent, yes. If we raise funding with a company like Miramax we have to be commercial, and of course we want to make films people want to see. But we have a broad enough output to be able to make smaller, more challenging films for under-served sections of the community.

Q – What else do you offer?

Luke - Our main strength is our ability to give scripts the development time they need until they are absolutely ready to be made. Because we are a large organisation we don't have the financial pressures of smaller companies and therefore we have the luxury to incubate the projects so that they do not go before they are ready. Script is key.

Q – What are the common mistakes with screenplays and submissions?

Luke - Something we see over and over are the dialogue-driven scripts with no real story and little character development. This is because the writer has started at page one, rather than spending the necessary time on the narrative and the characters. It is crucial to have a well-worked out, detailed treatment before even thinking about the dialogue.

Q – What advice would you offer?

Luke - Think about the story as much as you can, try and get some distance from the script. Do everything to your script before sending it out. It might take a long time, but keep at it, until it as genuinely as good as you can make it.

B B C Films

Luke Alkin
Script Editor

Centre House
56 Wood Lane
London W12 7SB
Tel: 0208 743 8000
Fax: 0208 576 7054
e-mail: luke.alkin@bbc.co.uk

PRE-PRODUCTION

Next Wave Films
Peter Broderick

Q – What is Next Wave?

Peter – As a company of the Independent Film Channel, we're much more than a finishing fund for low budget films. We get involved at some stage of post-production when film makers have run out of money and need to finish the movie. Often they also need help solving certain technical problems in post-production, figuring out where to do the blow-up or the video-to-film transfer, how to get better post deals, sort out music rights, all those things that people making their first or second feature get confronted with. We also help develop a film festival strategy, application and positioning as we have relationships with all the major festivals. We can't guarantee that any movie gets into a festival but we can ensure that it's seriously considered. We also act as a sales agent, for both the US and overseas. We help frame the movie in the press with as much free media as possible, and we support the movie when it comes out theatrically, and on the Independent Film Channel in the US. We now have a production arm too, it's called Agenda 2000 which provides production financing for digital features. Our focus is on low budget films, either shot on film or video. They must be in English, but they can be from any country. Video tape to Imax, if we love the movie we'll figure out a way to get it out to the world.

Q - What kind of budgets are you looking at?

Peter – Budgets have ranged from $5k-$1m. The money we provide is up to $100k. Because we are good at getting deals from labs and other places, our $100k goes a long way. Unless someone has an unaffordable music rights situation, usually we can figure out a way to make it work.

Q - I understand that you can submit on the Internet?

Peter – A lot of the films are coming in over the Internet, because new film makers use it as a tool and they can easily find us. *Envy,* our feature from Australia, came to us that way. Then it turned up in the mail, I watched it, liked it, called them up that night and said we were interested and it went from there.

Q - How good is the digital video to film transfer?

Peter - Hocus-Bogus and Swiss Effects, two of the best places to do transfers from digital to film, literally do magic. There used to be a video look and a film look but nowadays you can look at digital features and not know if they originated on film or video. There's a spectrum of looks for the style you're after and we have confidence that the stuff can look great, even when it started on mini-DV. It's something people shouldn't worry about; they should just work backwards from the resources they have. Currently (circa 2000) the cost of the transfer for a feature is roughly the same as the blow up from S16mm, about $40k for a 90 minute feature.

Q – What kind of technical problems should filmmakers be aware of when shooting on miniDV?

Peter – Make sure that your sound is good all the way through. I know that it is hard to find sound people who are experienced and affordable, but you could say the same thing about actors. You can see a movie that visually has some problems, maybe there can be some fixes or some re-shoots or you can cut around it, but if the sound is bad, nobody including critics, festival people, distributors, audiences will have the patience to deal with the movie. The sound recording quality on miniDV is very good, as long as the sound going in is good. Don't rely on the microphone on the front of the camera, get a good quality external microphone.

Q - What advantages are there shooting on DV?

Peter - You can have a much higher shooting ratio which will help to get the right performance, coverage or shot. Lighting requirements are much more forgiving, crews can be smaller, set-ups can be faster, you have so much more freedom. You can take as long as you like. If you make your movie for $3k and it doesn't quite work out then you don't have to show it to anyone. Nowadays you can take your movie to a festival digitally so you don't have to pay for the cost of the transfer. If there's enthusiasm for a theatrical release then you can do the transfer. If not, you don't need a film print, you can still show it on TV, video, DVD, Internet etc. Video pushes the cost curve back, and with digital projection at festivals you can push it far enough back that completing your film should not be an insurmountable obstacle. Because the medium is so accessible, film makers will be prepared to take more risks practising their craft and style, so we'll be in for more interesting films. Make your movie stand out. There are more and more no-budget independent films being made with the same amount of theatres. Your film can't be the same as the other 5000 romantic comedies that are being made, you must have something distinctive to break through. Many film makers think that their chances of distribution will be better if they shoot on 35mm but it isn't so, it's the creativity in the movie, the uniqueness of the script. They should always focus on, no matter what they're shooting on, the script, direction and acting.

Q – When you have these pictures, do you push for theatrical release?

Peter – Yes, the movies that we get involved with are all expected to be theatrical and we will do whatever we need to do to get them into theatres in as many countries as we can. After having a theatrical and video release, the film will also be seen on TV. In the US, all of our films are shown onthe Independent Film Channel, during the basic cable window, which follows pay cable. The Independent Film Channel is available in more than 30 million homes in the US.

next wave films ⟨N⟩›

Liz Rosenthal

U.K. Representative

tel / fax: +44 (0) 207 449 9779
mobile: 07957 34 28 96
email: LizRosen@aol.com

US Office:
2510 7th St., Suite E, Santa Monica
CA 90405
tel: 310 392 1720
fax: 310 399 3455
email: launch@nextwavefilms.com
www.nextwavefilms.com

Q - What is Agenda 2000?

Peter - It's our new digital production arm. It provides production financing for digital features from more experienced film makers who have already made at least one feature.

We will also work with some new film makers but I will have to see some short that really knocks my socks off. It has to be a good project, a good script, not just a director that I believe in. You submit a sample (hopefully a previous feature and a couple of paragraphs about what you want to do). If I'm really excited by the filmmaker and it seems to fit into what we're doing, then we'll ask to see the script. We are not set up to read a million scripts; we are very filmmaker driven.

Q – What kind of films do you think new filmmakers should make?

Peter – Make movies that are original! Make movies that have to do with parts of the world you've experienced, stories you're passionate about, something that matters to you. If you try to make a genre film on $10k it isn't going to work! There was a time that every US Indie was under the shadow of Tarantino but now that's over. Chris Nolan's *Following* is 70 minutes and black and white: they didn't spend a lot of time worrying whether it was in colour or linear or long enough, they just made a great movie.

Q - Are there too many digital movies out there?

Peter - There are a lot of gatekeepers who are terrified of being drowned in a sea of digital mediocrity. We haven't drowned in a sea of Hollywood mediocrity so they will probably survive. Beyond that, nobody would say that too many poems are being written, that too many paintings are being painted. The talented people will rise and we are all better off if more talented filmmakers come along.

Q - What mistakes do you encounter with new film makers?

Peter - The common mistake is the use of unaffordable music. Get original music. There are plenty of composers out there who will record an entire score for $5k. If you want to get that Bruce Springsteen song in your movie, good luck, but it is going to be painfully long, and if you can even manage to get an answer, expensive. What filmmakers often do is just get something called festival rights, which I think is a trap - so a distributor comes along and says *did you clear your music?* and they say *we cleared festival rights*, and they say *whats the cost of ultimate rights?* The filmmakers say *I don't know*, so already the distributor knows that there is going to be a problem and they may not want to pay for those ultimate rights. You get into a situation where you cannot afford the music rights, but you have already shown it in the festival and it has got reviews, and it has been identified with certain music.

Few film makers budget post production correctly. If you're editing on your own computer then you have affordable time, but if you're renting an Avid or

'Blood, Guts, Bullets & Octane', 'Following' and 'Envy', three features that Next Wave Films has helped get to the big screen and find an audience.

working every other Tuesday from 5pm to 7am on a friend's Avid, you have to be realistic. We are only able to give finishing funds to one out of 200 movies that we see, so there are 199 other movies who are desperately trying to find the money to finish.

Another mistake is that people show their film to distributors and festivals too early. Don't show it to anybody until it is as good as it is going to get, with the exception of people who can give you money to complete. Distributors are not in the finishing funds part of the business, and don't know how to evaluate movies that are unmixed low res outputs. You only have one shot, first impressions are last impressions, if even the janitor doesn't like a film, it is then in a company's computer, *we passed on this movie.* When considering distributors, do your homework, talk to other film makers who've dealt with them. If you have a festival movie, figure out which festivals are right for your movie. Every film maker has to do research, it takes as much time and effort to get a movie into the world as it is to make it.

Q - What's going to happen in the not too distant future?

Peter - I think we're approaching an exciting frontier. We'll have an alternative universe of independent production, mini studios where four or five film makers get together, buy the camera, buy the computer and software, make as many movies as they want. I think people are going to figure out ways to use a combination of new and old technologies to market their movies and you will be able to aggregate audiences across national boundaries, if 5 people in the UK want to see a movie, 20 in the US, 3 in Australia etc., you can achieve critical mass.

Q - What advice would you offer a new filmmaker?

Peter - No more excuses. Ask yourself *how much do I have now to make a film?* rather than spending years trying to raise $5 million. People need to have a good idea, a great script and solid acting. Make it on film or make it on video but make it. At Next Wave, we watch everything, hoping that each cassette we put in the VCR is our great new movie. We see a lot of movies that are flawed, but where the filmmakers are really talented. Because of a bad performance, these movies may never get to festivals, or get any critical attention, despite the film makers talent.

There is only one reason to be an independent filmmaker and it's because you have to be. If there are other things that appeal to you, like being a solicitor or a journalist, I seriously recommend you pursue those more rational fairer routes. You need to make a movie, that is going to give you the opportunity to keep making movies - it is about building a career, and I think that the opportunities have never been greater. Many people get locked into the old way of doing things, make their first short and then work their way up the ladder to the third short. Why not make a feature now, if there is a feature in you? Take it into your own hands and just make the movie. If in the end the movie doesn't work, at least you had a shot, you tried it, you took the risk. But if the movie is great, I believe that in most cases the film maker will have many opportunities to keep making movies.

Completion Bonds
Identity Witheld

Q - What is a completion guarantee?

Anon - A completion guarantee or bond is an instrument whereby a completion guarantor promises to the providers of the finance for a film that the film will be completed in accordance with the budget, the timescale and the script which they have approved. It is not a guarantee to the producers of the film that those things will happen, it's a guarantee to the providers of the finance, and it's quite an important feature of the completion guarantee that the producers are not able to invoke it or call upon it.

Q - What does a Producer need to furnish you with?

Anon - The producer will approach us with the script, budget and production schedule. We don't look at material before they have the finance for their film because reviewing the script, budget and schedule is time consuming. Once we've reviewed the material we ask the producers to come in for a meeting where we will ask them to explain particular things in the script that have struck us as being difficult or unusual such as crowd scenes, special effects, action sequences which might be logistically difficult. We'll ask them about locations, who their heads of department would be etc., so we can see whether they are people we know and feel comfortable with. It's at that meeting the producers would be able to give an account of themselves. At some stage we will also need to see the director to satisfy ourselves that he or she is a responsible individual who knows what they are going to do and they are indeed going to do what they say they are going to do. The script should be written clearly so it's apparent how everything that is described is going to be realised. Flowery language and vague generalities of what the producers hope to see on screen should be avoided.

Q - What is the lowest budget you would expect to issue a guarantee for?

Anon - About a £1m. We have done a film for £750k but that is unusual. On the basis of a £1m budget, the guarantee would work out at about 5%. We also require a contingency of 10% of the direct and above and below the line costs in the budget.

Q - When is a guarantee called in, when an actor dies or the director is imprisoned etc.?

Anon - Producers will take out insurance on the cast, negative and other things, so if the lead actor dies, that would be covered by that insurance. If the director is imprisoned it would be our problem and we would take the view that either we would wait for him to come out of prison and reschedule the whole thing or we would get another director in. If a director was very slow we might have to apply some pressure and tell him to get on with it, otherwise you're going to replace him. Sometimes this works, but some directors are incapable of working more quickly than the speed at which they are working. Remember, the director has assured us beforehand that he can do it within the allocated schedule so he's going to be aware that he's not keeping to what he originally said he was going to do.

Q - At what point do you decide to step in?

Anon - We wouldn't usually take action right away because it wouldn't be apparent that there was a terrible problem. If projections showed the film was going to go over schedule by 50% then that would be a serious thing which would have major cost implications. It would almost certainly follow that the director was shooting too much material and we might consider cutting certain things out of the script for which you would probably need the consent of the financiers. If there were a 50% over-run we would probably decide that we wanted to exert more control over expenditure. We would probably have decided that we become counter signatories on cheques so payments are directly controlled by us. At this point we probably wouldn't replace anybody on the production team, although we might send a full time representative to keep an eye on them. We get daily progress reports while they're shooting which tells us things like how much they've shot, how many people were there for lunch etc. On a weekly basis we get reports to show how much money has been spent and how much they are projecting to spend. If the reports are accurate, which we hope they are, then we know where the production is at and can take the view as to whether we need to do anything or not.

Q - How do film makers regard you?

Anon - I don't think we should be regarded as ogres because that's not really how we go about our job. We're usually quite humane about anything that has to be done, even if it's fairly draconian. The producers who work best with us really regard us as some sort of consultancy, able to provide advice whenever it's required. Ultimately, we can be relied upon to be there and see that the production gets completed.

Q - What basic advice would you offer?

Anon - The main thing is that they should be absolutely open with us. If they are making a film and perceive anything to be a potential problem they should let us know straight away because we can give our advice to avoid them getting into difficulties. It's important to realise that when we give a completion guarantee to financiers we also take direct contractual control over the production company and we do have very sweeping powers to step in to dismiss people, replace producers, or even move in and complete the film ourselves. It's unusual for us to take that step because the producers are often the best people to get the film finished - so even if they need to be put under a great deal of pressure in one way or another, it is usually better to leave them in charge.

THE

BOND COMPANY

TEL 0207
FAX 0207

Insurance
Paul Cable of
Media & Entertainment
Insurance Services

Q - How much should a low budget producer put in the budget for insurance?

Paul - Every film is different so the producer should call me when they are doing their budget so I can advise them what to allow for. I will ask for certain things, the script, draft shooting schedule, top sheet of the budget, and ask questions like when do you start filming? what is it about? what format are you shooting on? where are you getting your equipment from? any aspects of hazardous filming? I then approach insurance companies for a quote. Hopefully the producer is satisfied with the quote. I then issue an insurance summary, and certificates of insurance so that they can show them to hire companies.

As a bare minimum there are two types of insurance that you legally must have in this country. *Employers Liability* and *Motor Insurance*. *Employers Liability* should provide cover up to £10m *Public Liability* which is not compulsory but very much recommended should be at least £1m, motor insurance, unlimited.

For all policies, the insurers will expect the premium to be paid by first day of principal photography.

If the budget is £100k the producer should take what is called a 'production package'. This includes cover for key people going sick causing delay, the physical material - like the negative - because if you are shooting on neg, the labs won't accept any responsibility for any damage to it. The equipment should be insured on a new for old basis, so you should get an idea of the costings - if you are shooting on 35mm you may be looking at a £1m worth of equipment. You should know that irrespective of whether you are insuring the equipment or not the hire company will charge for 'loss of use' which is their loss of hiring charges during the period that their equipment is being repaired or being replaced. You need replacement values for props, sets and wardrobe. You need to know where you keep the equipment overnight. A major exclusion for all insurance companies is 'mysterious disappearance', so if you do have a claim call the broker straight away. Most of these covers run through the entire production right up to completion. An area we must discuss is hazardous filming, which includes filming from boats, aerial photography, pyrotechnics, use of animals, anything that could be construed as hazardous.

Q - A new film maker may just assume that "shot of man punching another man" is just part of the story, but it might be a red flag for you?

Section 1 - Anatomy Of A Movie, Pre-Production

Paul - Yes, that is why it's useful to have a copy of the script, to spot the potential hazards and ask the producer things like *are you using a stunt co-ordinator for this fight scene?*

Q - Who would you normally liase with on a film?

Paul - I would initially deal with the producer, then the production manager.

Q - Low budget film producers are used to blagging to get everything cheaply, but insurance should not be one of those areas?

Paul - Once someone lied about their budget, they said it was £300k and it was actually £2.5m. There was a claim and the insurer declined. The relationship with your broker is one of trust, as your broker can only support you if you tell him the truth.

Q - So a claim on insurance is based on the cost of production per day?

Paul - If your processing and running costs are as little as £500 a day and you are having to pay the first £500 under a negative insurance policy then maybe there is little need in insuring the negative. Obviously you still have the post production process where the negative could be damaged. Public Liability which you have to have, is about £250. Most equipment suppliers will insist that the producer has an insurance policy for their kit. There is also Errors and Omissions insurance which covers you for libel, slander, defamation, breach of contract, plagiarism. On major films this insurance would be in place from the first camera day, this is to give injunctive relief against somebody saying this film was my idea and bringing an action against the film producer. Clearly on micro budget films this won't be possible, but you may have to take out a policy in order to give the film to a sales agent at the end. You should always get legal advice about Errors and Omissions because it is dependent on the subject matter. The problem is that it is expensive, and the premiums range between $2.5k to as much as $15k.

Q - If you lose the free camera from Arri Media into the deep blue sea, how long would it take for an insurance claim to go through?

Paul - You should call me straight away, which is very important, and tell me how long it will take to get a replacement camera and how long this would affect the filming. If people are going abroad and they have little money and cannot afford back-up cameras I always ask them to find out how long it would take to get a replacement camera out to wherever they are. This becomes part of the insurance policy. If I have to engage the services of a loss adjuster this

MEDIA and ENTERTAINMENT
Insurance Services Ltd

Paul Cable
Director

Tel: 020-8460 4498 ·
Fax: 020-8460 6064 · Mobile: 079-7740 9520
Email: pdc-media@netway.co.uk

Media & Entertainment
Insurance Services Ltd
49 Glanville Road
Bromley
Kent BR2 9LN

Tel No.(+44) 0181 460 4498
Fax No.(+44) 0181 460 6064
Mobile. (+44) 07977 409520
email: pdc-media@netway.co.uk

CLAIM FORM

1 Name and address of insured
PETER SWANN
37 OLD OAK LANE
LONDON   Policy No AL/4703 LTDE0002
Postcode E7 2DE   Home Telephone No. 0181 789 1234
                                Office Telephone No. 0171 143 1222
Business/Occupation FEATURE FILM PRODUCER

2 Are there any other insurances (eg Motor, Travel, All Risks) on the lost or damaged property?
                                Yes/No
If so, give particulars

X

CIRCUMSTANCES OF LOSS

3 Date property was last seen
      /   /
                     time   am/pm
4 Where was property last seen
      /   /
                     time   am/pm
5 Date loss or damage was discovered
      03/07/98
                     time 10.00   am/pm
6 Address where loss or damage was discovered
   EDWARDS FILM STUDIOS
   ST. ALBANS. HERTS
                     Postcode AL3 2RS

may take as little as two weeks but it is subject to how much invoice documentation the company gives you. If hire companies can receive confirmation from you that the claim is covered they will re-hire you new equipment.

Q - What is the difference between an insurance policy and a completion guarantee?

Paul - A completion bond is there at the requirement of the financier to make sure that the film is completed. The completion bond will cover what is not covered by the production insurance.

All completion bond companies are concerned with any exclusions. We could have an elderly cast member who has a cardiovascular problem which the insurance company won't cover. The completion bond company will want to know that because if that actor does suffer a heart attack, they pick up any losses. They are there to pick up where the insurance company doesn't.

Q - What happens if mid-shoot the writer decides to change the ending of the main actor driving off into the sunset, to a helicopter chase, and the Producer neglected to inform the insurers?

Paul - If this resulted in a claim, my reaction would be that the insurance company would decline to pay.

Q - What about dangerous things like explosions and weapons? Does a stuntman come with his own insurance?

Paul - They sometimes have their own insurance. I will ask who the stunt person is, whether they are on the registry of stunt personnel, what their qualifications are etc. If a stunt person does not have insurance and the stunt goes wrong and people are injured, it is the production company's responsibility. It is also a legal requirement in this country to have a Health and Safety person. PACT has Health and Safety guidelines, and there are many Health and Safety advisors in the field.

| Employers Liability - required by law, protects employees from accident or damage. | Public Liability - required by law, protects the public from accident or damage. | Negative Insurance - insures your master negative during production and post. May be cheaper not to bother and take the risk. | Equipment Insurance - insures equipment hired from loss or damage, and lost hire charges. You won't get kit from a sales agent. | Other Insurance - insures against other potential losses, from stunts and action, to lost props or damaged locations. |

Q - What are the common mistakes that you have experienced?

Paul - People often ring around other insurance companies for quotes to save £10 and these companies may not be aware of the film business. Then they phone me in distress because they have needed to make a claim and the company won't pay up, because the insurance was not suited to their needs, just so that they could save £10. I get calls about props or equipment damage when the production stopped filming three months ago, I need to know as soon as it is discovered.

Q - What could a new film maker do to make your life easier?

Paul - Have the conversation with me at the budgetary stage. Then contact me at least three days before filming. Tell me everything, the more that I know the easier it is to insure. So they may find the first conversation a rather painful process, but like other brokers I have things like insurance guides which explain all the types of cover that are available. Give me enough time to sort it out.

Public Relations
Ginger Corbett of
Corbett & Keene

Q - What is your job?

Ginger - Our job is to bring the film to the attention to distributors, other film makers and to the public via the press. The earlier we can be involved in the film-making process the better. To alert everyone that the film is being made, we send out start of picture releases as well as listings of cast and crew to the trade press worldwide. We also place pictures in the trade press and general media, plan interesting feature articles and ideas for location stories etc. The earlier we are involved, the better.

Q - Photographs are vital for international sales agents, but they only want shots of the actors in scenes - do you need shots of directors etc?

Ginger - Yes we do, but not too many of them. What we REALLY need is the story in photographs. There is on every film, a still that every publication will use, so we have to decide, with the photographer, what those key scenes are and make sure they are photographed. For feature articles, covers etc. a far greater selection is required. We also keep an eye on the quantity and quality of the stills during the production, making sure that the photographer is taking the stills that reflect the mood of the film.

Q - There are different areas of publicity - trade press, national press, magazines, television, radio and the international variations, do you take care of the whole lot?

Ginger - Yes, everything.

Q - So why should a low-budget film maker who's confident of getting on the phone themselves not do it, and you do it instead?

Ginger - A low-budget film maker has enough on his plate just making the film, without concerning himself with the press. First timers in general also try to get articles published at every opportunity. If they do manage to get something published in a major magazine during production they should try to limit this to one or maybe two articles. Too much and you destroy your chances of coverage when the film is being released - as the press rarely give you a second spread. By all means try to get a journalist or two on set, but get an agreement that they will hold the pieces until distribution. Another thing that happens with low-budget films is that friends/or relations are invited to be the publicist or stills photographer. A recent case where we worked on the distribution campaign for a film, the actor's wife was the only person allowed on set as a journalist/stills photographer. Everyone was thrilled that she had a commission from a leading publication, but the ensuing piece made the production look tacky and very amateurish - not at all good for the film.

Q - So when people hire you, they're hiring you for experience and contacts?

Ginger - Yes.

Q - What materials do you need from the production?

Ginger - When we start at the beginning of the production process, we have scripts, cast and crew lists, schedules, locations, the biographies from the actors agents, we also research the projects to find out anything exciting about the locations etc. Then we put a writer on the job, to compile production notes - they will interview all the artists and principals and put together a press kit.

Q - If money is tight, what are the barest minimum requirements from a publicity point of view that you would need?

Ginger - Stills are very important. I can't ever place too much emphasis on good quality stills, even if you only have a photographer on for a few key days.

Q - Would you suggest it's a good idea, if the budget can afford it, to set up the lead actors in a studio with a professional photographer to take shots which are ideal for, say the cover of Premiere?

Ginger - It is more important for the production to spend money on good unit photography, if time and budget allow, then either the unit (if they are experienced) or a 'specials' photographer should take some special set ups and portraits of the principals in costume against a plain background.

The production will need to supply to the distributor a quantity of good quality materials which will normally include approximately 200 pieces of colour and 100 black and white photographs.

Q - If the budget could stretch to it can a production take high quality images to offer to the glossy magazines with a story. Not a photograph on set but in a studio?

Ginger - This need not be a budgetary item. There are plenty of photographic agencies who will, if the actors are interesting enough and the film has potential, take them into a studio for a session with a top photographer and stylist. And they'll pay for it. They will retain the rights to exploit these pictures, normally in conjunction with the publicist at the time of release. The costs of the photographer, studio etc. will be recouped from picture sales.

Ginger Corbett

Corbett & Keene
122 Wardour Street, London, W1V 3TD
England

tel: 020 7494 3478   fax:020 7734 2024

PUBLIC RELATIONS HOTLIST

PRE-PRODUCTION

The Phone - get on it and make contacts, stir up controversy, pitch ideas to magazines.

Stills - The absolute cornerstone of good publicity is the image. Make sure you have plenty of good shots, and try to isolate a single image that will become synonymous with the project.

The Press Kit - Typed interviews with key cast and crew members, biographies, interesting facts, synopsis and treatment of the film. Also include stills.

The EPK - Electronic Press Kit is a Beta SP tape that has interviews with key cast and crew members, plus clips from the film and a trailer. All loosely edited. Never give away your master!

Radio Interviews - Supply notes to radio progs., plus taped interviews with key cast and crew on either 1/4" or DAT tape.

Q - Are Electronic Press Kits and video taped interviews with cast and crew important?

Ginger - Yes, because there are now many outlets on satellite TV stations around the world. Often, you believe that your cast will be available for the distribution campaign, but the young actress gets snapped up to star with Robert Redford, an elderly lead has died etc. Despite promises and good intentions you could be left with nothing, so it's a good idea to shoot interviews during or just after production ceases.

Q - What should the tape contain?

Ginger - It should be a Betacam SP tape with 20 minutes of edited interviews with the principal cast and director (plus costume/art director and cinematographer - but only if their work is particularly unusual or interesting). There should also be some B-roll (behind the scenes footage of the crew at work) and some clips. As MiniDV is so cheap now, there is no reason why every film should not have some good behind the scenes footage and interviews.

Q - Is there a low-budget film you've done where you've got a bit more mileage than you perhaps thought possible?

Press Armoury - Press Pack (paper), BetaSP EPK, Stills on transparency and now CD. You can even do your own interactive CD ROM.

Orlando - A film where the photographic images were so strong, they're still in use today with reference to British films.

Ginger - *Orlando* is a movie that went very well - a lot of its success was down to the brilliant stills which were simply fantastic. Publications are using the stills well after writing about that movie and they're constantly used when talking about British Films. The stills were so beautiful and so rich.

Q - So the Orlando team was smart enough to make sure they got good pictures, which gave you the correct tools to do the job?

Ginger - Yes. We were sending out pictures during production and publications were calling saying *'these are wonderful pictures', 'have you got any more', 'we'll do a spread'*. So it's worth while having good pictures.

Q - Assuming somebody's making a low-budget picture and they have no money for PR and they have to do their own, what tips would you give them to maximise the impact and minimise the damage during production, to set it up for somebody like yourself when it comes to the distributor coming on board?

Ginger - To try and get as much information together - anything that's written about the film or the subject of the film, all your research material, notes on anything, such as shooting in an interesting location - keep a copy of every useful brochure and telephone number.

Q - Do you have any basic advice?

Ginger - Let the publicist know as much as possible, even things that you don't want the rest of the world to know. Tell us so that we know not to mention or do it. Get a publicity plan worked out. Even if sometimes you can't afford a publicist, it doesn't hurt to have a chat, and get some advice.

Casting Director Identity Witheld

Q - What is the job of a casting director?

Anon - To cast the movie, all lead and support players right down to the *couple of liners.* The buck, in my book, usually stops with extras/walk-ons although it can happen that your director wants you to extend the continuity in the look and feel of the film to extras. Beyond that it depends on the relationship you have with that particular director, some want a sort of elaborate creative nannying, others are more militant and self-possessed, some haven't got a clue. My favourite variety are egocentrically balanced enough to be reasonable human beings who welcome your collaborative interpretation of their ideas and pursue them as literally or left-field as the producer/financier can tolerate.

Q - What do you need?

Anon - It helps to have a director who knows what and whom they like, this gives me a good reference to work on. I also need a screenplay so that I can work through it and start to form ideas. Often, on low budget films, the screenplay is the best tool you have - it could be unique writing with unique characters that under other circumstances might not get made, and therefore that interesting part would not have been offered to an actor. Also, a good casting director could advise on cutting down on characters or merging characters to save money on the cast.

Q - How much does it cost?

Anon - It depends on the project and how much 'we' all want to work together. You'll find that a lot of producers have not that much pro rata figured out for little old us. We're important mythically but not financially.

Q - How does it work?

Anon - Normally, I would make up a short list and work with the director, looking at those people. Depending on their stature we would then ask to meet, perhaps have a reading and go from there. Sometimes it is hard to find the right person, but often the right person just jumps right out at you. Then you speak to the agent, check availability and cut the deal etc.

Q - Can you access big names?

Anon - We do not have a direct conduit to the mega-stars but we do know who to contact and how to make a professional approach, then it will be up to the script, director and the deal. Sometimes a

PRE-PRODUCTION

casting director might get approached early in a project prior to any kind of funding in order that they help attach a cast to the film so that the 'package' is more attractive for financiers.

Q - Could a producer cast a film themselves?

Anon - Yes of course, but what a casting agent brings to the table is experience and knowledge. We will have had dealings with agents so there will be a degree of trust and understanding. More importantly, we often make suggestions that the film makers would never think of such as casting against type or bringing a hot new actor to the attention of the film maker. Some Casting Directors keep their eye on fringe theatre, or TV drama, spotting people who shine and then putting them up for jobs when the right part comes along.

To find actors you could place ads in *PCR, SBS* and *The Stage,* but you will have to sort through a lot of CVs and photos to find the actors that you might want for your shoot. You should also buy *The Spotlight,* either the books or on CD, as all professional actors are listed there.

Q - Do you cut the deals, or does the producer cut the deals?

Anon - It is up to the producer. The best way to approach it however is to use the registered low budget scheme negotiated between PACT and Equity as it takes most of the negotiation out of the loop. There is still some minor negotiation with the agent, but that is usually over things like billing and per diems.

Q - What about minor roles?

Anon - These are cast when you have the leads in place, usually in the run up to the shoot. It is important to make sure that everyone in front of the camera is as good as the time and budget can accommodate. Often you can draw minor parts from the people you may have seen for the lead but passed on.

Q - What common mistakes do you encounter?

Anon - Ego, Ego, Ego. It does not mean that you have talent. Low budget films are often blighted with a poor cast because the film makers think that the actors are like the cameras, just a resource to hire. It's important to get the right person for the character and please don't cast your mates, even in small parts. Every so often you get the privilege to work with someone truly gifted and creatively exceptional and you in yourself will pull the stops to get them the best they could get.

CASTING

Q - What advice would you offer?

Anon - Strive to get the best possible cast for your film. When you and your producer truly want advi you'll truly listen.

PRE-PRODUCTION

Actors Agent
Jeremy Conway
Of Conway Van Gelder

Q - What is an agent's job?

Jeremy - An agent's job is to get actors work, to create a career, to try and get the actors to work with the best directors and do the best projects.

Q - Does an agent act as a buffer between the production company and the performer?

Jeremy - To some degree, but if an actor behaves badly on set, you're the one who has to sort it out. If an actor has a serious problem, they can tell us and we can do our best to sort it out. We also take care of all the negotiating and contracts which could be both embarrassing and problematic if an actor were to do that themselves.

Q - With what would you supply an interested producer?

Jeremy - Initially a CV and photo, and if they have one, a showreel.

Q - How soon before principal photography would you expect to be approached?

Jeremy - To do a deal on the actor? I think one gets less time these days but one can get everything done and sorted out with a months notice - more than that I think is a mistake.

Q - What's your usual response if you find out the film is low-budget?

Jeremy - If it's a good script it doesn't matter. There's an awful lot of low-budget films with poor scripts in which I'm not interested, but if there is a wonderful script with absolutely no money, I would much rather an actor did that, than a major movie that's not very good for a lot of money. Certainly, I think English actors appreciate that, and would rather do a quality film than rubbish for bucks. A lot of new film makers believe their scripts are wonderful, but often I don't share their enthusiasm, so it is important for them to remember that if I say I don't think it's suitable, it's not because I don't want an actor to do a low-budget film, it's because I believe the script is below par. Everything stems from the screenplay - if it is good, everyone believes in it and most of your problems are over.

Q - There is a myth in film making that the agent is simply an obstacle to get around. How would you feel about film makers who contact an actor directly, either by phoning them or sending a screenplay?

Jeremy - If an actor meets film makers socially and they chat and it all works out then fine, but I know actors do not appreciate getting phone calls from desperate film makers. Nor do they like getting their post box filled with wannabe scripts.

Q - If the budget is very low, what can a producer do to make you more interested in a project?

Jeremy - All sorts of things, they can offer percentages of the gross afterwards, although they are not often in a position to do that. They can give really good billing or they can defer payments.

Q - What are the main problems dealing with a low-budget production?

Jeremy - There are basic things like transport, expecting an actor to get up at four o'clock in the morning and catch a tube to Neasden to start filming. I just say that is not on, it is the producer's job to provide transport. An awful lot of low-budget films are being made by first time film makers who have no real background you can check up on so I just have to go with my gut feeling. They've just got to be honest to make you trust them.

Q - If producers do not come to you directly, where should they advertise the jobs that are available?

Jeremy - We keep an eye on most industry journals and will always investigate a new production. I look at both *Screen International* and *Variety*. You could also put information in newsletters like PCR or SBS and whilst I do not usually look at them, many other agents do.

Q - Would it be a good idea for them to come and meet you?

Jeremy - Absolutely. I'd be very wary of sending an actor off to a very low-budget film with people I've never heard of and never met.

Q - What are the main concerns of an actor, especially if the budget is low?

Jeremy - They're not being paid a lot of money so what they do want is comfort. I think pushing them all into the same car to take them to the location is not what you want to do because they need that time to be quiet, to think about what they are doing. Nor do you want to put them up in crummy hotels. I know it's difficult because the money should be on the screen, but I think the actors comfort is something that is often forgotten. Basic things like no chairs to sit on, no umbrellas if its pouring with rain, no tents - the sort of things which often don't cost very much. Everyone else on the set is busy most of the time, rushing around doing things, but often, the actor isn't doing much and is waiting for the next scene to happen. A green room is ideal, a place where they can sit and

CONWAY · VAN GELDER LTD

JEREMY CONWAY, NICOLA VAN GELDER, JOHN GRANT
18-21 JERMYN STREET, LONDON SW1Y 6HP
TEL 020 7287 0077   FAX 020 7287 1940

concentrate on what they are doing without being distracted by the crew. Somewhere warm, dry and quiet, even a kettle with tea and coffee can be so easily forgotten.

Q - What is your worst experience of a low-budget film?

Jeremy - A client of mine made a film in Scotland that has never seen the light of day - it was an absolute nightmare. They hadn't scheduled anything, so he never knew if they wanted him the next day or not, that is until 10 o'clock at night - even then, they might not use him the next day as arranged. I think the most important thing is the pre planning, making sure everything is worked out well in advance and they know what they are shooting each day. Obviously things can go wrong and no-one expects any less, but one has to know what one is doing, when and where. Actors get cross if they don't know what's happening and they feel they've been mucked around, especially if they turn up and then they're not used.

Q - How is payment usually made on a film?

Jeremy - Usually it's weekly cheques, one week in arrears. Sometimes, especially on the continent, they like to do a sum up front, then one in the middle and one after the shooting is over. I would prefer to get a regular weekly cheque. Of course other agents may well prefer a whole chunk up front, it's up to the individual deal. Also, there is the per diem - it's a sum of money that is agreed between the agent and producer for living expenses. Normally, on location the hotel is paid and some sort of per diem for the actors to buy food, lunch and dinner. Obviously it varies between £10 per day, to stars who get hundreds and thousands of dollars per diem. It's above and beyond the salary, and is agreed at the time of the contract.

Q - What are the main areas in the contract that you would be looking to nail down?

Jeremy - Definitive dates. On a low-budget production, if an actor is doing just a couple of days, I would really like the days to be nominated rather than on or about. Billing is very difficult to negotiate and terribly important for the actor. On low-budget films, when actors aren't being paid very much, I try and make sure that everyone's on favoured nations (which is when the actors get the same, nobody is going to get more). If an actor is taking a big cut in salary and suddenly discovers that one of his contemporaries is getting a lot more, it can become very difficult, but if it's favoured nations there is no argument.

NEVER WORK WITH CHILDREN OR ANIMALS

Anyone under 16 (who has not completed the school term following their 16th birthday) requires a licence to act. Licences are NOT required for children who work less than 3 days within a 6 month period.

Licences are obtained from the child's local education authority. These licences list numerous requirements with regard to child employment, including hours of work, education, rest periods, meals, accommodation & matrons.

The use of animals on a production is governed by the Protection of Animals Act 1911, the Cinematograph Films (Animals) Act 1937, The Dangerous Wild Animals Act 1976, The Wildlife & Countryside Act 1981, relevant quarantine laws & The Royal Society for the Prevention of Cruelty to Animals (RSPCA).

Q - What is The Spotlight?

Jeremy - It's a directory of professional actors and actresses, stuntmen, young actors and the like. It is the main point of reference for agents and producers as I could say, turn to page one thousand and twenty to see a photo. I believe It Is being released on CD Rom for computers too.

Q - What can a producer do to make your life easier?

Jeremy - I think being honest and absolutely straightforward. You know when people aren't telling the truth - when I ask, *is so and so's client getting more than our client?* and the reply is, *well no, not exactly* - well, *what do you mean?* - the answer - *well, I can't say.* You just want them to be straightforward and honest and say, *well yes they are getting more money, because they're doing 6 weeks more work on it.* I just think that good honesty in this business pays off in the long run. Agents all talk to one another and confer on deals. An awful lot of producers, especially young producers who are starting out, have very little respect for rather senior, well known actors, and expect to meet them without even giving them a script. The actor thinks *why should I, I've never heard of this person.* Producers should be careful not to sound too arrogant - if they are trying to get a star to work for them, they should be extremely respectful.

THE SPOTLIGHT

Spotlight produce directories including actors, actresses, stuntmen, North American actors (in the UK), ethnic background actors, actors with disabilities, children, new actors and traditionally, these publications were only available as a set of books that when stacked measure more than two feet! However, most of their information is now available on a couple of CDROMS and also over the internet. Sometimes Spotlight have a backlog of older directories that they sell at reduced rates.

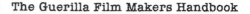

The British Film Commission
Steve Norris

Q - What is the British Film Commission?

Steve - We are a government funded body and our role is to facilitate film-making in the UK for international film-makers, particularly from Hollywood, a role which we will retain and enhance as part of the new Film Council. Even though we don't help with funding films, we aim to build bridges with all areas of the film sector including financing bodies, fully-equipped studios, and state-of-the-art special effects houses. We can also help advise the government on how best to legislate to make filming in Britain more attractive and competitive, and that's not possible unless we ensure the industry's infrastructure is sufficiently resourced to match the new challenges and new technology of the marketplace.

Q - What are the problems the BFC faces from producers?

Steve - Having been a producer myself, I know what problems can arise when you're making a film, so I would like to think I'm sympathetic to other producers' needs. We're here to make sure that a film can be made successfully no matter what problems need resolving in terms of granting licences or legal procedures that need to be followed. However, it means that we have been able to open doors because of the trust we have fostered between ourselves and a whole range of organisations, institutions, government offices, and local authorities. If a film company abuses that trust, it can hamper our continuing efforts to develop these vital relationships. We give additional help by publishing Check Book 4, our annual guide to film production in the UK along with other guides and information, and by putting the information on our website.

Q - How can the BFC help a British production, especially one that is on a lower budget?

Steve - As I mentioned earlier, our main role is to enable more film-makers from abroad to come and make their films in Britain. So we help to promote all areas of British talent and expertise which can be employed by visiting producers. However, our resources are limited and channelled towards broader inward investment opportunities for bigger budget films. The continued strength of the British film industry is important though and depending on the nature of the enquiries, we want to guarantee that they are given access to the right information and the right people. The UK film commission network is better suited to dealing with lower budget film production since they are trying to create a support structure for personnel and organisations based in their region or city as well as assisting all producers who are looking to make films in their specific area.

Q - What are the problems BFC faces in finding locations?

Steve - Strictly speaking, we are not a national location agency. Whilst we hold information about many location sources, we prefer to guide producers to our network of local film commissions, who have a more direct role in matching the requirements of a particular production to suitable locations in their area. However, we do make every effort to liaise with location managers at a higher level in order to understand what support they might need.

Q - Could you offer alternatives to locations that are out of the question?

Steve - The fun part of the film industry is making you believe what you see on the screen is real. If a production has a specific setting, then the local commissions will get clearance to use specific buildings, town spaces or natural locations. However, it is possible with imagination and solid local knowledge that any foreign, exotic, or alien location can be found. For example, Liverpool has stood in for Moscow and Jedi knights have trod deepest Hertfordshire.

Q - What can a producer do to make your life easier?

Steve - We are not miracle workers and we need time to arrange for the demands of a production to be met. Problem shooting is part of the course, but not if left to the last minute. Having devised a shooting schedule, you should know what locations you will be using and when. That means also knowing if any specific regulations need to be approved. Of course, there are always unforeseen circumstances that force a swift change of plan and we have learnt to adapt too.

Q - How do the local commissions link up with the BFC?

Steve - We are like the central office which establishes direct contact with producers, and then filters their requirements through to a network of regional commissions, which now number twenty five across England, Scotland, Wales, and Northern Ireland. They in turn will use their own staff and resources to deal with specific enquiries. If they feel they can offer the facilities, location and personnel that a production company is looking for, then they will liaise directly with the producers.

Q - What's the best job the BFC has done?

Steve - We have great satisfaction in knowing that we have been instrumental in ensuring British talent has played major roles in some of the biggest box-office hits in recent years such as Bond movies, *Saving Private Ryan*, *Shakespeare In Love*, *The Phantom Menace* for example. As part of the new Film Council, we will have even stronger support for what we are striving to do: to create and support a British film industry that is the envy of the world.

THE BRITISH FILM COMMISSION

70 BAKER STREET · LONDON W1M 1DJ
TEL: 020 7224 5000   FAX: 020 7224 1013
e mail: steve@bfc.co.uk
http://www.britfilmcom.co.u

STEPHEN A NORRIS
Commissioner

GFMH
OFFICIAL
SPONSOR

PRE-PRODUCTION

PACT
Bertrand Moullier
Head of Film

Q - What is PACT?

Bertrand - PACT stands for the Producers Alliance for Cinema and Television. It's the film and TV producers trade association that represents limited companies, not individuals. It's about assisting the growth of UK based independent production companies which supply content to a whole range of audio visual media.

Q - What kind of services does PACT offer?

Bertrand - The core service is the industrial relations service, it's in the business of maintaining an ongoing negotiating platform with the technical, talent and other unions that form the industry. As a result of this service we have standard agreements that our members can use, with the Writers Guild, Bectu, Equity, Musicians Union etc. It is a significant advantage to use these agreements as they are widely recognised and trusted. We also provide an information service, members phone here for diverse information such as contacts, a list of top line producers, or for TV finance companies in Europe etc. Specifically for TV producers we have a business advisory service run every Wednesday, giving people advice on how to negotiate with the BBC, Ch4 or anybody else in the broadcasting world. There is a whole other range of services which has to do with events - we try and sense the emerging trends in the industry and hold specific events to help people stay on top of developing technologies, developing financing opportunities, become familiarised with new players, new financiers, new broadcasters etc. These include serminars, workshops and courses.

Q - If somebody has a legal problem can they call PACT?

Bertrand - We do offer legal advice informally and can help producers put things in context and form a realisic expectation of what they can achieve in negotiation. We never try to substitute ourselves for a professional lawyer. Often, people can find out if there are any precedents for deals so that they can gauge if they can get any more or are paying too much. Although we cannot reveal confidential information about other deals, we can put things in context.

Q - How much does membership cost?

Bertrand - Producer membership is turnover related, if your turnover is under £0.5m per annum then you'll pay £560, between £.5-2m it would be £705 and over £2m it would be £845. If you're a start up film maker with under £100k turnover and a limited company, you can join for £210. If you get a movie off the ground, there is a fee called the PACT levy that is 0.5% of the budget, capped at £4500.

Q - What is the PACT / Equity Registered Low Budget Scheme?

Bertrand - It is an agreement between PACT and EQUITY for the employment of actors. It's designed to reduce the upfront cost of making low budget films and is welcomed by producers and agents. It's useful for low budget films, but micro budget films working with deferred payments would not be eligible.

Q - Do you have to be a member of PACT to access the PACT EQUITY low budget registered scheme?

Bertrand - No, but if you do use the scheme we will charge you the 0.5% levy once the film is in production.

Q - Do PACT lobby?

Bertrand - Yes. We have tried to convince successive governments to have some kind of film policy and with Labour there has been some success - they've decided to establish a stable structure, a centralised body that will look after a whole range of film activities. The good news is that the Film Council as it is now known will largely be staffed by people from the industry rather than government bureaucrats.

Q - What advice would you offer a new film maker?

Bertrand - Be young, don't have children and be unattached! (laugh) I see many people with enormous enthusiasm but unrealistic expectations - they go from the highest expectation to the lowest of disappointment. Many new producers simply believe that somebody out there is going to give them £5m to make their first movie with their best mate attached to direct. It just isn't going to happen. Also, don't do this alone. There are a number of companies and individual producers out there who are very credible potential mentors for you who don't want to rip you off. It might mean that you may have to share your fees to begin with but if you're still at the stage of trying to prepare the calling card film then try to set it up with someone strong as exec. producer who can help move obstacles out of your path. There are people who's generosity in imparting their knowledge and experience has helped many get started.

This business is tough and many good films fail. There can't be an expectation that this industry is going to be self sustaining overnight. There are only two self sustaining film industries in the world, India and the US, and even then one is dependent on export for its survival. Never rush a film into principal photography because you have to earn your fee. It's easy for me to say because I'm not out there waiting for the next meal, but if you can, go for that additional script polish, change the writer if you feel it's not right and lastly don't be derivative. Believe in your creative vision.

pact

producers
alliance for
cinema and
television

Bertrand Moullier
Head of Film and
European Affairs

45 Mortimer Street
London W1N 7TD
T 020 7331 6000
F 020 7331 6700
E moullier@pact.co.uk

Raindance
Elliot Grove

Q - What is Raindance?

Elliot - The organisation started in '92. Briefly, we do several things - training courses, a monthly magazine, the Raindance Film Festival, the British Independent Film Awards (BIFA), and this year we intend to branch out into our own distribution company.

Q - What happens on your courses?

Elliot - The courses are all run by instructors who are working industry professionals. We provide fresh, cutting edge information, the kind of information new film makers need, and tech craftsmanship too. The thing we notice on our courses is that many people are uninformed about all aspects of film making, be it production, editing, but especially screen writing. I think that the traditional film school route is woefully inadequate. They should be imprisoned for some of the things they teach in film school about writing and directing, because they get it so totally wrong.

Q – What questions, or reasons, do people have for taking your courses?

Elliot – There are three reasons - they want to write, they are finishing their screenplay or they want to make a movie, and it is the same three reasons regardless of age or level they are at. First reason is they lack confidence to actually go and do it, and you know yourself having done it, it is pretty scary - you go, *Oh my God I should have taken that job at Sainsbury's to stack shelves.* The second reason is they self-destruct, everyone has their own pet method of self destructing. The third reason, my personal favourite, is procrastination. *I will take this course then finish it, I will see that movie then finish it, Christmas is coming and then I will finish it.* And they never do.

Q – And the British Independent Film Awards?

Elliot –We started the BIFA's last year because other film awards in the UK basically gave awards in Britain for American Films. We wanted awards for British films in Britain. British, British, British. We managed to get a very strong advisory committee and jury together which meant that it was taken very seriously, and the new films being judged were seen by top level British film people. We were amazed how seriously the juries took the remit, they watched many, many movies, which takes hours and hours. The first BIFA's were a tremendous success and we anticipate the following ones to grow in strength. It's also a place where micro budget feature films can take on multi-million pound features, and win!

Q – What about the Raindance newsletter?

Elliot – The newsletter is to promote networking and information exchange and is published and sent to our members every month. It contains a billboard, information on festivals, articles of interest etc., and costs £15 per year.

Raindance isn't funded as such, so everything we do is blatant self-promotion on one hand, but on the other hand it is a way that people can meet - Matthew Vaughn and Guy Ritchie (*Lock Stock*) Simon Hunter (*The Lighthouse*), and Jake West (*Razorblade Smile*) met many of the people they work with through Raindance. We also have a website at www.raindance.co.uk.

Q – Tell me about the Raindance Festival?

Elliot – The Raindance Film Festival is the only Festival in Britain devoted to independent film. All the acquisition executives come because it is held in central London during the pre-MIFED week, and this year we had over 350 acquisitions executives attending. The Festival is a great place to meet other filmmakers, and we host panels and workshops on topics of interest to filmmakers and the general public.

Q – One of the things that I think is interesting is that once you put your film on a screen and an audience puts their butt on a seat it is a level playing field because they are just responding to a story, and Raindance is probably the only event in the UK where you can get your movie shown.

Elliot – Not all films submitted get into Raindance, but yes, once you get inside the cinema, even if your movie is gritty and cost 3p, as long as it is a great story well told, you will get the audience. Raindance screens features, shorts and documentaries that are sourced from all over the world, but a high proportion of those shown are by first time British directors.

Q – As you see hundreds of new film makers movies, what general criticism would you give?

Elliot – They don't tell a story. It all comes down to a shitty script. If you want to make your first movie and break in and you want to achieve notoriety and celebrity status, then you need a great screenplay. If you have that great screenplay, you probably won't make it with your own money, so it won't be low budget, and you will get a higher budget to make it. The minute your budget goes up you bring in all these people who interfere with the creative process, and you may even get fired. So do you make the film you want to make for less, or do you take the money and go through the hell of compromise and possibly even get fired? It's a huge paradox. And don't copy anybody – I can't tell you how many Tarantino movies I have looked at over the years, you just throw them out.

81 Berwick Street, London, W1V 3PF
TEL: 020 7287 3833 FAX: 020 7439 2243

PRE-PRODUCTION

Q - And from a technical view point?

Elliot - Don't put credits on the front end, put the title but little else, it's boring. Most people put far too many credits at the front, making it far too long, just put them all at the end. Shoot in colour, you will devalue your film by 90% if you shoot in b&w. There are several first time movies in b&w, I love them, but they can't be sold because when people buy the film they want to see colour. I hear it from acquisitions executives or sales agents all the time, *Oh, my God, it is b&w, I can't put this on TV.* Seriously, people phone up the BBC and say that they have paid their licence fee for colour. They won't screen letterbox films because people *disgustedly yours from Tunbridge Wells* will write in and say *I have paid my licence fee for the whole screen, not half of it.*

If you send a film into us, give us a press kit. Get great stills, fantastic ones, because I am sending them out to all the newspapers. Get Beta clips of the trailer not the whole movie, make sure that the Beta clips are at the most two minutes long, 45-60 seconds is best, and make sure that everything in those clips are cleared for TV broadcast because I might put it out on TV.

On your VHS submission tape put the trailer at the head of the tape, because tapes will go out for review and sometimes journalists will read the press kit, take a look at the trailer, fast forward half way through and see if they are still interested, and base what they write on that. It's brutal but unfortunately journalists may have 30 tapes to watch in a day.

Q – Interestingly, few people ever want to sell a movie, everyone wants to write, produce or direct?

Elliot – I am Canadian and I can sit on both sides of the pond. The difference between European and American film industries is that in Europe they divide the film making process into three, financing and script development, the actual production of the movie, and then the marketing and sale of the movie. In America you make the movie and then sell the movie, and not necessarily in that order. Often you sell the movie and then make it, so at all times during the process they are aware of the sale, and film makers educate themselves as to what distributors and sales agents want, and then supply that demand.

The biggest mistake I have experienced is that most film makers want millions of people to see their film which is totally wrong. The only people that you want to see your film are the acquisitions executives and there are only about 50-100 in the world that would be right for your film. You need to work out how to tantalise them, tease them so that they go absolutely mental. Once you learn how that game is played then you are going to be much better off. This is the basic reason that *Blair Witch* succeeded, they drove everybody nuts. By the time the acquisitions people saw the movie even though, let's face it, it was not a great movie, a great first movie maybe, but not great movie, they still wanted it. When they were making their movie they were thinking of the 50-100

Scene stealing - the essential point upward whenever a stills camera is on you. Elliot Grove on a 35mm shoot in the streets of Soho.

people who could buy it, and then marketed the movie to them.

Film making is so often about savvy. How do you teach savvy? You can't, it just sort of filters through you, which is why we push the networking thing, you sort of figure it out and get better with practice.

Q - What advice would you offer a new film maker?

Elliot – Find a great script. If you don't have a great script you are fucked. You can turn a great script into a bad movie, but you cannot turn a bad script into a great movie. So you find a great script, get a little bit of money, you don't need a lot especially with DV, you shoot a feature, edit on a computer, you can make it for £5k, possibly less.

You need to develop excellent interpersonal relationship skills, for pitching, building rapport with investors and talent. You need to develop the ability to be very firm, learn to say no. You also need boundless energy, which keeps you going through your lack of confidence, and you have to just bash thorough this concrete wall.

The formula that seems to work in launching American film makers is that they get a stage play, and shoot it as if it is a movie in a single location. Take this kind of material and shoot it like cinema - that's what they call talent in the industry, then you can step up and start making movies with serious money and your career is launched. I mean look at *Blair Witch*, it was three actors, some trees and the amount of money you would need to buy a London Cab. That was all they needed.

New Producers Alliance
Phillida Lansley

Q - How did the NPA come about?

Phillida - The NPA started in 1993 with 12 producers who, frustrated with the existing sources of funding and lack of interest or recognition in first and second time film-makers, teamed up to pool information, resources and contacts. Each year it has grown in numbers and strength.

Q - What is the primary function of the NPA, and what do you get for your money?

Phillida - The NPA's remit as a charitable membership organisation is to foster and sustain new generations of filmmakers. These days with around 1300 members this is achieved by providing a range of benefits.

You can take advantage of 4 events each month covering educational seminars, each discussing a specific production skill with a panel of experts, screenings of independent British features with discussions from the filmmakers, workshops and master classes with opportunities to meet key industry decision makers.

We also hold regular networking sessions to enable members to form alliances and friendships. Part of being an NPA member is meeting other people with a passion for film making as often, new film makers are unaware of others who share their dreams.

We also have a range of free hotlines from legal advice to music advice. There are services and discounts available to members, and a monthly magazine outlining the events and profiling members and other organisations.

In 1998 we launched our website which has a wealth of information, articles and vital links to other film related sites. Each year we produce a directory in which members are listed with their most recent credits.

Last September we launched our Foundation Workshops, a series of nine seminars and lectures over nine months, each month covering the next stage of a production. It is intended that this course will run every year, September to May, and that it will become a recognised qualification.

A lobby group exists to negotiate on behalf of all first and second time filmmakers better access to funding in the UK.

Each year, we have a presence in Cannes for the festival and market, and for film makers who have never been to Cannes, we are often a first stop off in order to get pointers on where to go and what to do.

Unfortunately, we do not have any money to invest in films or their development, it simply isn't our remit to do so.

Q - How much does it cost?

Phillida - We offer a range of memberships and application forms are available at the office on 0207 580 2480 or can be downloaded from our website www.newproducer.co.uk.

The fees depend on your status - unemployed is £50, a Producer, Writer or Director is £65, Affiliates are £90, Overseas is £80 and Corporate members are £250.

Q - What mistakes do new filmmakers most often make?

Phillida - A common situation, as it is not always purely a mistake, more an unavoidable occurrence, is script development or lack of it. Very little development money and cost of living pushes many low-budget films into production when frequently the script needs more work. Another area often overlooked is the audience. Even low-budget films will end up on the video shelves next to the likes of *Titanic* and *The Beach* As a filmmaker you have to be aware of the audience you are trying to attract, and why they might choose your film above a Hollywood blockbuster or high profile British feature.

Q - What advice would you offer a new filmmaker?

Phillida - If it's your first film, keep the budget realistic, put together a good package of Director, cast etc. If it's a first time Director try to get an experienced Director of Photography and as experienced an Editor as possible.

Join the NPA and learn as much about the whole filmmaking process, including sales, marketing and distribution.

Finally get networking and enjoy!

new producers alliance

phillida lansley

9 bourlet close london w1p 7pj e: info@npa.org.uk
t: +44 (0) 20 7580 2480 f: +44 (0) 20 7580 2484

Equity
Judy Franks

Q - What is Equity?

Equity - We are the union that represents performers in the UK with around 36,000 members. Our main role is to make agreements with producers which will form the basis of a contract between the producers and the performers. We don't represent children or extras in feature films, but we do represent stunt people and all other featured performers. If you hire an Equity member, you know you are getting a professional.

Q - What is the procedure for making a film with Equity agreements?

Equity - Equity has a Cinema Films agreement with PACT which has special provisions for registered low budget films. This is ideal for film makers with budgets under £2.4m - it's good for the producer and it's good for the performer. In essence, this is what happens as the agreement currently stands; the producer supplies to both PACT and Equity, a copy of the budget for the film which has been audited and verified by a film chartered accountant. The producer then pays 0.25% of this budget to PACT as a levy, even though they do not need to be a member of PACT. The budget must also reflect that in excess of 5% of the budget is spent on the performers.

The producer would then lodge the performer's fees in an Escrow bank account where it would attract interest, or they could supply an acceptable letter of financial guarantee. Equity would then release contracts to the producer who would then be able to hire the chosen performers. The contract is a simple form that is filled out very quickly, it's not a thirty page contract at all. The fees are also very reasonable, and they are paid on either the daily or weekly rate (for a breakdown of current rates contact Equity but specify it is a registered low budget film). The producer does not pay the performer out of the money in Escrow. The money held in Escrow is a guarantee until after the shoot wraps and the performers have been paid, then the money is released back to the producer.

Usually, for low budget productions, no-one is paid more than anyone else and other than the 70% for cinema and UK free TV use fees, other uses are not pre-purchased until after the film has recouped between 1.75% and 2.75% dependent on it's registered budget. Agents may also negotiate extra things like credit billing on the film and poster, per diems for the cast etc.

Q - One major advantage is the simple form contract?

Equity - Yes, it's a standard Equity contract that everyone recognises and is practical for everybody.

Q - *I found that being a registered Equity film made agents happy.*

Equity - More often than not if you go to an agent with a low budget production that is registered and regulated then they are happy to help, hoping they will be the film makers of the future. There are well known performers with successful careers who often take part in things because they want to encourage a particular director, they like the project or even the production company. If the film is successful it helps everyone and the industry. Everyone wants to be involved in a production tohelp nurture a success.

Q - *How many have actually reached recoupment level?*

Equity - *Trainspotting* and *Wish You Were Here* are the only ones so far. A film may well continue for decades and it represents a revenue stream for the film makers and the performers.

Q - *What power does Equity have?*

Equity - We try to persuade our members not to work without Equity contracts. Contrary to some myths, we do not and should not, have the power to go on set and shut a production down. Under European Law, no trade union can force or coerce an employer to use union members so a film maker is free to hire people who are not Equity members. However, both producer's and Equity's preference is always to use professional performers.

Q - *What about students making films?*

Equity - We now also have an agreement for film schools which means that film students can access professional actors and the actors are assured that their residual rights are protected. This is only for productions produced while students are in attendence at their school.

Q - *What are the common problems you encounter from new film makers?*

Equity - They offer Equity rates but not Equity contracts. If you can afford to pay Equity rates, it doesn't make sense not to use Equity contracts. Equity contracts are about more than rates of pay, they also protect performers and their rights. Before producers make the film they should call me because there is no point putting a budget together with inaccurate figures based on the myths that they have heard from other producers. And keep in touch at all times.

Q - *What advice would you offer?*

Equity - Do it, make your film. We are very keen for new film makers to make their films. Do it with a professional attitude.

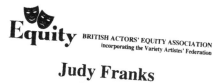

Equity BRITISH ACTORS' EQUITY ASSOCIATION
incorporating the Variety Artistes' Federation

Judy Franks
Organiser
Films, TV & Radio

Guild House, Upper St Martin's Lane, London WC2H 9EG
TEL: 020 7379 6000   FAX: 020 7379 7001

BECTU
Martin Spence

Q - What is BECTU?

Martin - BECTU is the Broadcast Entertainment Cinematograph & Theatre Union, with about 30,000 members in the entertainment industries. On the film/TV side, we represent permanently employed members – at the BBC, ITV companies, film studios, post-production and facilities houses, etc. - and freelancers, who make up much of the production workforce. The "Freelance Production Agreement" with PACT sets out minimum rates of pay and a framework of other working conditions (hours, travel etc.), and acts as a benchmark across a wide range of film/TV production.

Q - What can you offer your members?

Martin - We can give advice and assistance to freelance members, although we are not an employment agency. We also advise members on career development, training needs, and qualifications. We work with training bodies such as Skillset, FT2, and the regional training consortia. We can advise on rates of pay, contract queries, insurance cover, the do's and don'ts of working abroad and on whether the prospective employer is known to us as a dodgy customer. We give private advice and support, or take up disputes directly with the employer, depending on the circumstances. When the job's over, unfortunately some employers try to get away without paying so we run a "debt collection" service, and we take employers to court to recover what's due to our members. With a paid-up freelance membership you're covered by our Public Liability Insurance scheme which gives you £3m worth of cover. We have also negotiated special deals on insuring your tools or equipment, covering yourself against sickness or accident and motor insurance (which can be difficult to get on the High Street if they clock that you work in "the media"). We also run a Script Registration Service where you can register a treatment, script, or design with us, to protect yourself against copyright theft.

Q - What benefits can you offer producers?

Martin - We are a trade union, so our role is to represent the interests of our members as workers, in relation to their employers, who are usually the producers. It follows that we don't represent producers in their dealings with their workers, nor do we represent them in their commercial dealings with funders, commissioners, etc. However, some are line producers, engaged on freelance contracts like other members of the crew and we would represent a line producer member in any dispute with the company that employed them. Other producers are movers and shakers in their own production companies, developing and pitching ideas, raising the money, negotiating the rights, and generally making new things happen. These are the people we negotiate with every day, because they need our members' skills to make their films, and we need them to employ our members.

Q - What are the BECTU rates?

Martin - We have negotiated agreed pay rates with PACT and the AFVPA and we track "going rates" across the whole range of film and TV production. All of this information is available free to members, and the PACT and AFVPA ratecards are available for a small fee from our Head Office.

Q - What is your magazine?

Martin - The BECTU magazine Stage Screen & Radio comes out ten times a year. It contains the 'Ask First' list where we identify companies which have failed to honour their obligations to our members. Usually, though not always, this means they have refused to pay for work done. The 'Ask First' list is widely consulted in the industry, not only by our members but by facilities houses, post-production houses etc., who are keen to avoid getting stung by rogue production companies.

Q - What advice would you offer new film makers?

Martin - Our starting point is that the film/TV industry is just that: an industry, not a hobby. Within that industry, we do our best to ensure that the people whose skills underpin the whole business are properly treated and properly rewarded. Low/no-budget filmmaking is encouraged by colleges offering a glut of superficially attractive media courses, regardless of the fact that the number of graduates vastly exceeds employment prospects in the industry. The low/no budget production sector exists because a lot of young people coming off media courses see no other way to get started. And because a few grubby characters who like to call themselves "producers" want to make a few bob by ripping these same eager young people off. These are the ones who insist on going into production even though they can't, or won't, raise the budget to pay for it. We all know how they try to square the circle, by begging or borrowing money from family, friends, or ads in "Loot", by calling in favours, by offering "deferred pay" deals to prospective crew members. We have three problems with this. Firstly, low/no-budget production undermines pay rates, budgets, expectations and standards right across the industry. It plays right into the hands of the worst, most brutal, cost-cutting employers. Secondly, to get people to "defer" all of their pay is actually illegal as a result of the National Minimum Wage. Thirdly, there is increasingly little justification for it, because the industry is putting the pieces back together in terms of skills, training and career patterns. We have a whole suite of high-quality N/SVQ (National/Scottish Vocational Qualification) standards. We have a highly-regarded training co-ordination body in Skillset. And we have new money coming into the industry to fund training and tackle the looming skills crisis – most importantly, the new Skills Investment Fund in the feature film sector.

BECTU

Martin Spence

111 Wardour Street London W1V 4AY
tel 020 7437 8506 fax 020 7437 8268

BROADCASTING ENTERTAINMENT
CINEMATOGRAPH & THEATRE UNION

So my advice to would-be new filmmakers is that film and TV is not a hobby, but an industry. If you seriously want to make a career in this industry – to earn a living in it – you've got to put in the groundwork, get the careers advice, decide on your line of attack, research the training opportunities, do the training, build your network, work your way up. You may even get to make "your film" – but on real money, rather than a wing and a prayer.

Film Stock
Roger Sapsford
Of Fuji Film

Q - What different gauges are available for film makers to make a feature film?

Roger - 16mm, Super 16mm and 35mm. 16mm is not really used for features now, but that is not to say that it cannot be used, it is just that Super 16mm is much better at the job. However, 35mm is the international feature film standard format.

Q - What's the difference between 16mm and Super 16mm?

Roger - The only difference between 16mm and Super 16mm is that Super 16mm is perforated on one side only - Standard 16mm is perforated on both sides. The Super 16mm format allows for the picture area to be exposed to the absolute edge of the non perforated side which when blown up to 35mm (aspect ratio of 1:185) gives 40% more visual screening area than standard 16mm. So you could say the negative yields 40% more usable picture area whilst staying on a 16mm compatible gauge.

Q - What length is 16mm delivered in?

Roger - The standard lengths are 400 foot and 100 foot rolls. For special purposes, we can supply it in 1000 foot rolls, but this is very unusual. 400 foot lasts about 11 minutes at 25fps.

Q - What is film speed?

Roger - The film speed or ASA relates to the latitude against failing light. To put it simply, the higher the ASA, the less light is needed to properly expose the negative. Daylight photography with harsh sunshine would cope admirably with the slower speeds of stock, for instance the 64 or 125 ASA. Other speeds like 250 ASA can also be used for daylight exterior photography but can also be used for twilight or dusk. There are higher speeds such as 500 ASA stock which is mainly used for night photography where there are very low light levels.

Q - Am I correct in saying, the slower the speed of the film, i.e. the lower the ASA, the less grainy the film looks?

Roger - Yes, to some degree. As little as five years ago a cameraman would select lower speeds to keep the grain finer, as opposed to choosing higher speed with increased grain. However in the last five years, things have changed and high speed stocks have improved dramatically. Several factors have brought that about, one of which is demand from productions with restricted budgets and low light levels.

Q - What is the best average all round stock for shooting in Britain?

Roger - From a personal point of view, I would go for the mid range 200 to 250 ASA but other cameramen may select another speed like the 125 ASA. That is true for both 16mm formats and 35mm.

Q - What does the colour balance of film mean?

Roger - All light has a colour, interior light bulbs are 'orangey' whereas natural daylight is 'blueish'. Your brain can make adjustments for your eyes, but a camera can't adjust the film stock. There are two kinds of film stock, *Tungsten* which is generally used for shooting indoors with lights, and *Daylight* which is generally used outdoors for shooting in natural light. Different lights also have different colour temperatures or colour balance. *Tungsten* balanced stock is designed for use with tungsten lights - If you have selected HMI lights then it would generally be accepted that you use a *Daylight* base stock because of the colour temperature of these lights. With HMI lights the colour temperature is a lot higher than tungsten and they yield a very daylight looking light.

Q - If you find yourself having to shoot with tungsten stock whilst filming outside, or daylight stock whilst shooting inside (with tungsten lights), what can be done?

Roger - With tungsten stock outside one should always use a WRATTEN 85 filter on the camera (which should be supplied with every camera kit), otherwise known as a Daylight filter. This filter changes the 'colour' of the light entering the lens and exposing the negative. It isn't the end of the world if the filter is not used - indeed there are some leading photographers who do not use that filter and still get a lovely result. The negative is technically exposed incorrectly, but once it is graded at the labs, it falls within the realms of acceptability. You can also change the colour temperature of the lights by using specially coloured gels on the front of the lights, but this limits your latitude.

Q - What are the advantages of shooting 35mm over Super 16mm?

Roger - 35mm is a global standard gauge that's recognised instantly. Super 16mm isn't (unless it is subsequently blown up to 35mm). Plus the negative is two and a half times bigger, sharper and also has two and a half times less grain on screen.

Fuji Photo Film (U.K.) Ltd.,
Fuji Film House, 125 Finchley Road,
London NW3 6JH, U.K.
tel 020 7586 5900
fax 020 7722 4259

Roger Sapsford
Field Sales Manager
Features & Commercials
Motion Picture &
Professional Video Division

Q - What are the main problems shooting Super 16mm and blowing up to 35mm?

Roger - When blown up, Super 16mm is very good. It's

GFMH
OFFICIAL
SPONSOR

95

FILM STOCK FORMATS

(ACTUAL SIZE)

*Super
8mm*

*Standard
16mm*

*Super
16mm*

35mm

65mm

16MM & SUPER 16MM BLOW UP TO 35MM

(NOT ACTUAL SIZE)

*Standard 16mm -
Only the middle part
of the negative can
be blown up to
35mm losing some
20% at the top and
bottom of the frame.*

*Super 16mm occupies a wider
negative which can be
completely blown up to 35mm
without loss. The combination
of a larger negative and NO
part of the image being cropped
away yields 40% more negative
to blow up to 35mm.*

*35mm theatrical print with 1:185 aspect ration. The
Super 16mm aspect ratio fits comfortably whereas the
standard 16mm has to be cropped at the top and bottom
which limits further the amount of negative that can be
blown up to 35mm.*

economic to shoot Super 16mm, but as step printing is so expensive, it's possible you could have shot on 35mm for the same price, if not cheaper. It could be a false economy.

Q - In what length is 35mm delivered?

Roger - 35mm comes in 100 foot, 200 foot, 400 foot and 1000 foot lengths. 1000 foot lasts about 11 minutes at 25fps. The ASA speeds are also the same as 16mm and Super 16mm.

Q - What are the commonest problems with stocks?

Roger - Long term storage outside the manufacturers warehouse. The life of the base negative can be affected by long exposure to heat whilst still in its tin. In places of high temperature like the desert, faults with the negative could occur because of the extreme heat. Always store the negative in the way the manufacturer recommends on the tin i.e. in a fridge.

Q - Once film is exposed, must it be processed as quickly as possible?

Roger - No, it can stay as long as a year without any problem as long as its kept at room temperature and doesn't go over 60° Fahrenheit. However, it is advisable to process exposed footage as soon as possible.

Q - Is the X ray machine at airports a film makers myth?

Roger - In places like Heathrow and New York you are fine, you can go back and forth through the X ray machine eight or nine times without any problem, but the machines that are based in third world countries may not be so safe. It's most dangerous in places that are far flung outposts with equipment we used to have 30 years ago. The problem is that they can adjust the level of X-rays emitted - if they come across a can they may just whack it up to full power - if you were using 100 ASA stock, that still isn't too much of a problem, but with the faster stocks, like 500 ASA, the possibility of damage is much more significant. The higher the ASA, the more susceptible the stock is to X rays. Even if a customs official is still unconvinced and opens the can you should be alright because inside is a non reflective black bag wrapping the stock in such a fashion that daylight cannot penetrate it. But if he insists on opening the bag, then you've got a problem.

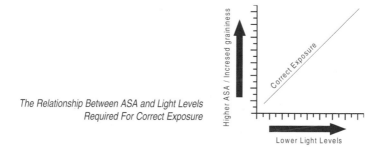

The Relationship Between ASA and Light Levels Required For Correct Exposure

FILM
GRAININESS

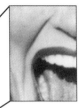

Lower ASA speed with decreased granular structure.

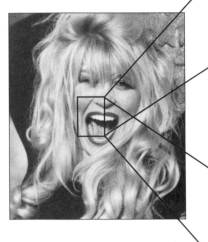

Graininess is in essence an aesthetic quality. There is no practical point where an image becomes too grainy, however, many people do find increased grain unacceptable. Grain structure also takes on different qualities depending upon lighting and incorrect exposure (which has been subsequently corrected).

Higher ASA speed with increased granular structure. Grain is surprisingly acceptable if the image is sharp and in focus.

UK CAMERA NEGATIVE FILM STOCK CHART

FUJI daylight	ASA	Gauge	Code
	F-64D	35MM	TYPE 8522
		16MM	TYPE 8622
	250D	35MM	TYPE 8562
		16MM	TYPE 8662

KODAK daylight	ASA	Gauge	Code
	50D	35MM	FILM 5245
	50D	16MM	FILM 7245
	250D	35MM	FILM 5246
	250D	16MM	FILM 7246

FUJI tungsten	ASA	Gauge	Code
	F-125	35MM	TYPE 8532
		16MM	TYPE 8632
	F250	35MM	TYPE 8552
		16MM	TYPE 8652
	F-500	35MM	TYPE 8572
		16MM	TYPE 8672

KODAK tungsten	ASA	Gauge	Code
	100T	35MM	FILM 5248
	100T	16MM	FILM 7248
	200T	35MM	FILM 5274
	200T	16MM	FILM 7274
	320T	35MM	FILM 5277
	320T	16MM	FILM 7277
	500T	35MM	FILM 5279
	500T	16MM	FILM 7279

PRODUCTION

Q - On a low-budget film people are tempted to use outdated stock - is there any way a producer can be confident that this stock is fine?

Roger - If you are in doubt about the stock, you could send it in for a clip test. The laboratory would cut off 15 feet from the end of a roll and produce a gamma test which would determine whether the stock was still within the realms of commercial acceptability.

Q - If one roll was all OK, would it be safe to assume that the whole batch would be OK, as long as they were all stored together?

Roger - If they were all stored together with the manufacturer, then yes. If not with the manufacturer, then not necessarily - it would be wrong to assume that all the cans were OK, but it would be a fair bet.

Q - At the beginning of rushes, I see a colour chart - what is that?

Roger - The colour chart is put on the front of each camera negative roll to assist in rushes grading at the labs - it ensures that the labs are printing the way the cameraman had intended. We can supply those charts to a production, as well as the labs.

Q - What are edge numbers?

Roger - The edge numbers are a series of numbers generated at the time of manufacturing the stock. These numbers are unique to any particular roll and are used when negative cutting. All stocks now carry digital bar codes which are an electronic edge number. These are used to speed up post production and are mainly used with non linear editing systems.

Q - Does Fuji do deals for bulk purchase?

Roger - Every single purchase is different - it depends whether you're a long standing customer, a new customer, a low-budget, medium budget or even God forbid a higher budget film. Everyone is different. The trend has been to help the low-budget film makers with cash deals, obviously that would affect the discount.

Q - What common mistakes have you experienced with regard to selection of stock?

Roger - The main problem I have encountered is that of pressure when a new cameraman is given his first bite of the cherry. He's under enormous pressure to make the right decisions and choose the right stock - half way through that decision may have been proven to be the wrong stock but it's too late then.

Camera Hire
Phil Cooper
of ARRI Media

Q - How do you hire?

Philip - Camera hire is normally based on a daily rental charge, however on a weekly hire a 16mm production would be charged at a four-day rental rate and a 35mm production at a three-day rental rate. Equipment orders will only be accepted from a member of the production team, never by the camera crew. If we were not strict on this policy we could get into the situation where we have shipped extra cameras out and no one wants to pay for them because they weren't authorised. Be aware!

Q - What is the difference between Super 16mm and 35mm?

Philip - 35mm film is larger than S16mm so the image is clearer and sharper. It's also the same format that is used in cinemas for projection, but it's more expensive to shoot on. We would like more things shot on 35mm but the success of S16 is apparent in films like *Lock Stock and Two Smoking Barrels* which are blown up to 35mm and then go theatrical. S16 is very attractive to low budget film makers. It's also more compact and lighter so you don't require so much crew.

Q - What is in a basic camera kit?

Philip - Between 16mm & 35mm it is a very similar package. The camera kit would comprise of 3 x 400ft magazines, follow focus, mattebox, batteries etc. It would then go on to include a set of prime lenses, possibly a zoom, a fluid head, tripods and even a video assist. Dependent on where you hire your camera kit from, it's a good idea to check exactly just what you get for your money. But don't forget consumables - you always need that gaffer tape, empty film can and clapperboard!

Q - If you have four lenses as suggested, could you hire an extra body and share the lenses in order to have a second camera?

Philip - Yes, you may even find it's a requirement from an insurance perspective, but if you do intend to use it as a second camera you will need all the extra equipment like head, tripods, filters and magazines too.

Q - Do you hire creative filters?

Philip - Yes. There are many choices of different filters such as promists, soft FX, diffusions etc, depending on the type of look you're after. For instance if you want to give the film an 'older look' you could use a sepia filter.

Q - Why have so many lenses?

Philip - Why not! It's great to cover every filming possibility, however cost will always outweigh the practical side. Generally primes are faster, ideal for handheld work and give great results but if you can't afford to have a certain focal length in your primes set, then use the zoom.

Q - If you're a new film maker shooting on S16mm, what camera should you hire?

Philip - From us it would be the Arri SR2. They're a robust and reliable camera that's easy to use. You could achieve a movie like *Lock Stock...* with an SR2. There are other S16mm cameras too, like Aaton. You should make sure everyone knows about the equipment before you use it, there are always things you pick up by coming to see us. We expect a camera team will come and test the cameras here, and familiarise themselves with the kit.

Q - As a producer, you do live in fear of lost or damaged cameras as they are so expensive.

Philip - If we were to add up every zoom bar that has been lost or damaged then I'm sure we could have purchased a brand new lens. Filters are easily scratched if not taken care of correctly. This can all be avoided if the crew look after the equipment in a professional manner in which case there should be no damages!

Q - What happens about insurance?

Philip - In the event of loss or damage we look for the cost of replacement plus 13-weeks loss of hire. We won't let any kit go out until we have received a copy of their insurance policy, which must include this. The majority of productions will always have their own insurance; however if not we can always recommend an insurance company for you.

Q - If a low budget film maker came to you and said 'I am going to pay you on day one of principal photography' would you give them a better deal?

Philip - Definitely. It's a great incentive for us and puts the production in a good position regarding price. No one likes to chase bills, it wastes everyone's time. If you haven't got much money be honest. Don't be afraid of getting us excited - we love movies. Show us your scripts, tell us about the project, who is already onboard. It could help us make the right decision in pushing your film forward.

PHILIP COOPER
RENTAL MANAGER

Media Film Service Ltd, 45 Airlinks, Spitfire Way, Heston, Middlesex, TW5 9NR, England
Tel: 020 8573 2255
Fax: 020 8756 0592
E-Mail: pcooper@arrimedia.com
Web: http://www.arri.com

CAMERA BODY
(Arri SRII pictured). The heart of the camera. All the other bits in the camera kit are attached to the body.

MAGAZINE
Film is loaded into the magazine, commonly called a 'mag', by the assistant camera person. Three 'mags' are normally supplied. One 400' mag will run for approximately 10 minutes.

FLIGHT CASE
All the kit is mounted in separate flight cases for protection. Can be bulkier than you expect and the small ones can be easily mislaid. Often used by the crew for cast or crew to stand on during a take where extra height is needed.

LENSES - ZOOM LENS
Common length is 10-100mm, giving a fairly wide shot to a good close up. Cheaper zoom lenses can be heavier, are physicaly longer, and need more light than prime lenses.

LENSES - PRIMES
Usually supplied in a kit of three or four - common prime lenses are 9.5mm (very wide), 12mm (wide), 15mm (mid), 25mm (mid/long) and 50mm (long). Much shorter and lighter than a zoom, crisper image and needs less light for exposure.

MATTE BOX WITH BARS
Affixes to the camera body and protects the camera from stray light entering the lens and creating lens 'flare'.

BATTERIES
A charger and several batteries should be supplied as standard. Ensure batteries are recharged as soon as possible as you just can't plug the camera into the wall.

INTERVALOMETER
Used to control the speed of the camera so that it can shoot at extreme interval such as 1 frame a second, or hour. Used for time lapse shots.

APERTURE CONTROL
Used to control the opening or closing of the aperture electronically and smoothly. Used in conjunction with a variable speed control, sequences where the speed changes mid shot are achievable.

SPEED CONTROL
This device allows the camera to be used at various speeds, usually from around 5fps to 70fps. Note, the camera speed can be set independently of this device, but not altered with ease or during a take.

FOLLOW FOCUS
Device used by the assistant camera person or focus puller to alter the focus of a lens during a take, so that when an actor moves they stay in focus.

ZOOM CONTROL
Device to control the zoom lens so that it can zoom in and out smoothly and at the right speed. If you intend to use zoom shots, you MUST use a zoom control as no operator will be able to perform a smooth zoom.

LIGHT METER
Device used by the DoP (Director of Photography) to measure the amount of light in a scene. They come in two basic varieties.

Spot meter (above)
Used much like a camera lens and gauges the amount of light reflected off a selected area of the subject.

Incident light meter (below)
Used to measure the amount of light falling on to all sides of the subject. This is the most common type of light meter used.

FILTERS

Colour correction filters to convert between tungsten and daylight are essential. Effects filters are only rented on the day needed and cheap semi pro photographic filters will usually do the same job for a fraction of the price.

PHASE ADJUSTER

Used to alter the frame rate of the camera so that it can be used to film television screens. Without this device it is possible a dark band or bar will appear on the TV.

EYEPIECE EXTENSION

Useful for when the camera is mounted high or low, or in an awkward position.

CHANGING BAG

Used to load and unload magazines with the film. Remember you will need empty cans when shooting so that you can unload film, perhaps with short ends being re-canned.

HIGH SPEED CAMERA

If you want to do slow motion shots of up to 150fps, you will need to hire a special high speed camera body. Note that this SRII is grey in colour. You can use your existing lenses and tripod/head with this body.

TAPE MEASURE

Used to measure the distance between focal point on the camera and the subject being filmed. Aids in focusing to ensure the image is sharp and crisp. Don't make the common error of mixing up feet and inches with centimetres and metres on the tape measure or the lenses.

CONSUMABLE STUFF

Compressed air for cleaning, torch for checking the gate, camera tape, gaffer tape, clapper board, camera report sheets, dulling spray (to reduce reflected highlights), empty cans, stickers for the cans etc.

VIDEO ASSIST

Device that connects to the camera so that the director can watch the shot on a small TV monitor. The quality is as good as the kit and can be recorded for instant 'playback'. Don't expect too much out of old kit.

HEAD

The camera sits on the head. The better the head, the smoother the action. Rent the best head you can afford. Ensure you have the right bracket to connect the camera to the head.

PRODUCTION

LEGS

The tripod - comes in two sets, tall and short.

SPREADER

Connects the base of the tripod for use in places where the tripod spikes will damage the floor, or just won't hold fast.

BARNEY

A blimp that covers the camera body and deadens some of the sound. Leather coats draped over the camera will also help.

CAR

You will need a large estate car or mini-van to drive all this kit around. Ensure one person is responsible for all the kit being packed away and checked so that no equipment is accidentally left. Think about where you are going to park overnight and if the gear will be loaded and unloaded at the end of each day.

Q - How quiet are cameras and what can you do with a noisy camera?

Philip - Cameras are quieter now than they have ever been. However in confined spaces, such as a bathroom scene, we would always recommend using a soft Barney.

Q - What happens about slow motion?

Philip - The SR2 or SR3 standard cameras will go to 75fps, the high speed SR2 and SR3 to 150fps. Faster than that and you are in to specialised cameras like the 16mm photosonics with a speed up to 500fps. For ramping high speed but keeping the aperture constant, the ARRI ICU can be used. For a TV drama, items like these would be hired on a daily basis to keep the costs down.

Q - What is anamorphic?

Philip - Anamorphic is a 35mm system where the taking lenses contain elements that squeeze the image by 50% horizontally, allowing an image twice the normal width to be photographed on regular width film. The reverse process is used to restore the wide screen image when it is projected. This system produces what many regard as a visually pleasing look with very little grain. The lenses tend to be physically larger than spherical ones and being slower, require more light. A typical working stop would be between 4.0 and 5.6.

Q - What is video assist and how does it work?

Philip - Video assist is a small video camera that sits on the side of the film camera feeding a picture to a TV monitor which the director can watch. It's great for the director because they can see exactly what movements the camera operator is making, what they are doing. The disadvantages are that it could slow the production down due to other members of the crew getting involved watching the monitor and giving their input. More DoPs and directors ask for the video assist in the early stages of their career for safety measures. On the more recent features we have serviced, video assist isn't being used at all. Not only does this save them time but also money.
All video assist really does is show you the frame and tells you if the operator has captured in frame what you had hoped but don't be fooled by the colour or lighting as it is only as good as the monitor you are watching on!

The camera team is encouraged to go to the hire facility to shoot tests and familiarise themselves with the kit before finding out the hard way in the field.

Q - What are the most common mistakes producers make?

Philip - Cutting the package down too much, then getting stung by the little things they hadn't considered. Choosing the right format is also a problem too, there are a lot of different formats, each with advantages and disadvantages.

Q - What advice would you give to a new film maker?

Philip - Honesty is the most important thing. Getting people to support you on a lie will get you into trouble. Visit the rental house and have a look of what equipment is available and understand how it works. Testing the equipment before the shoot will prepare you for the shoot ahead. Don't be afraid to ask any questions. Speak to us, we like to work with the crew so don't get scared off. Come down and see what we have, you can pick up some brilliant ideas and not only can we help make that shot work but give you enough confidence and support for a smooth shoot.

Grips Hire
Mark Furssedonn
Of Panavision UK

Q - What is grip equipment?

Mark - It's all about camera support and movement. We can supply anything from a top hat so that you can get low shots, up to camera cranes which give you aerial shots looking down on the action. Essentially, we supply the equipment that allows the camera to move in a controlled manner. We also hire camera equipment.

Q - What is the most versatile piece of grip equipment?

Mark - The camera dolly is the bread and butter of grips every day hire. It's a support which can run on track or rubber tyres, depending on the model. They are heavy and therefore stable, producing smooth moving shots. Some models have hydraulic arms enabling the camera to be moved up and down in shot. Most producers normally hire track and dolly.

Q - Are there any particular extras that would be very useful?

Mark - Track is the most common, but there are tongues which can offset the camera, a snake arm which drops the camera down lower, a small jib arm to give a crane effects etc. Most of the advanced dollies come with a full set of accessories. You will need a minimum of a Mercedes Sprinter van to move it all around in as well.

Q - What are your main considerations when hiring kit out from the grips point of view?

Mark - Who the grip is. We generally know how good the grips are and if you've got a good grip, you'll probably never hear from him during the shoot. Whereas the opposite applies to the less experienced grip - he'll be ringing every day asking questions. All our kit is in good condition when we send it out and it should return in that condition - unfortunately, it doesn't always return in good condition and sometimes we may have to make a charge if serious maintenance work is needed. The grip must maintain and service the kit to ensure that it stays in good working order.

Q - What's your policy for insurance on the equipment?

Mark - We ask the client to supply their own cover and we need to see documentary evidence as proof of cover. No equipment goes out without full cover.

Q - What are the most common problems you have to sort out?

Mark - It depends who you get on the phone. With the producer, the most common problem is that they don't have enough money in their budget. The crew come to us with technical problems - something is not working - maybe they are not doing something correctly. We try to help wherever we can.

Q - Does grip equipment differ between 16mm and 35mm?

Mark - No, that is the advantage of our equipment. We can put anything on it, any camera - 35mm, 16mm, video, all can be mounted. You would probably hire a slightly more lightweight dolly for 16mm than 35mm.

Q - What other types of equipment can you supply?

Mark - It's never ending really. We actually design equipment for specific shots so you could put a camera on the front of a roller coaster or on a camel's back for example. We have cranes, we put cameras on helicopters, we have put a crane on the back of a tracking car and driven down the motorway at high speed. The list is endless.

Q - What kind of cranes are there?

Mark - We have everything from a 9' to a 50' crane. Cost wise, the smaller the crane, the cheaper it is to hire. We also have electronic telescopic cranes which can telescope in and out during a shot. Nowadays, cranes tend to be used with a remote head instead of a camera man sitting on the end. The head is remote controlled and we can supply it as part of the package as well as the remote lens control. All our cranes have a dolly base which would run on track.

Q - Cranes can be dangerous if abused, what is your policy?

Mark - We would never send a crane out without one of our technicians. I would always advise that in addition to our technician the production company should supply two experienced grips but we can't stipulate that, only advise. At the end of the day, they are dangerous and we have people's lives in our hands. Because we have to pay the technician, it can make the hire of cranes more expensive than say dollies. All our cranes are regularly checked for fatigue by an independent company.

Q - Give me a short run down of the different bits of kit.

Mark - The Fisher 11 Camera Dolly is one of the most versatile and well manufactured dollies available. It covers all cameras, 35mm, 16mm and video. As with all dollies, track is extra and is hired in sections. The dolly comes as a package which includes comprehensive accessories.

Mark Furssedonn
OPERATIONS DIRECTOR

Direct Line: 020 8839 7318
Mobile: 0410 313102

PANAVISION LONDON,
METROPOLITAN CENTRE,
BRISTOL ROAD, GREENFORD,
MIDDLESEX UB6 8GD
TEL: 020 8839 7333
FAX: 020 8566 6123
E-MAIL:
mark.furssedonn@panavision.co.uk

GFMH
OFFICIAL SPONSOR

The Super PeeWee 4 is of American manufacture and is probably the most popular dolly at the moment. It is good for 35mm, 16mm and video shoots on both location and in the studio. It may be slightly lightweight for some 35mm cameras though. The Panther is a German made dolly which is operated electrically and has a centre column that moves up and down so you can actually get up and down movement in shot - you can also put a small crane on to get high shots at 12'-14'. An example of a small bit of grip equipment would be a turntable which can be used to put a camera in the centre of a table for 360° pans.

Q - What about vehicles?

Mark - We have car rigs and accessories and we can supply various types of rigs to mount the camera anywhere on a car, the bonnet, roof, looking at the wheel, looking at the bumper, the driver. Boats, trains, helicopters - we've done it all over the years. If we haven't got a rig to suit, then we'll build one for a specific shot. There is also a range of tracking vehicles that are fully equipped with various mounts and platforms for the camera, and wherever needed, the crew. These are used for high speed car shoots, chasing horses down a race track etc. Some vehicles can also be mounted with cranes, again using the remote head, others just for a camera crew to sit on with the camera mounted on the tripod to shoot off the back of the vehicle. We supply a trained driver as it's very dangerous at high speeds.

Q - What can a producer do to make your life easier?

Mark - Have greater knowledge of the equipment available. In general they do not know enough about the current equipment and this has an affect when they're budgeting. Most professional Grips are excellent but there are occasions when production companies employ grips who don't know enough about the equipment. We often get calls from guys on location actually asking us how to operate the equipment. Obviously we tell them, but this should not be the case.

Q - What are the most common mistakes made by a producer?

Mark - Budgeting. I understand that there is never enough money and I know that it is not always their fault but a problem they inherit. To the producer, a Grip often appears to be little more than manual labour therefore the level of professional hired for a production can be poor. Gripping is a highly skilled profession.

Elemack Cricket. One of the cheapest dollies available.

Snake Arm fitted to Elemack - be aware that the head and camera could add up to 8" from the base.

Super Pee Wee 4 dolly. Mid range price and all round performer.

Panther fitted with Panther Super Jib - low cost crane effects.

Low Price Wheelchair Dolly - cheap and cheerful!

Dolly Track, available in curves and straights in different lengths.

Tripod Legs - available both short and long. Tripod legs need a head to attach to the camera.

Giraffe crane - camera operator is positioned on the end of the crane.

Fluid Head - Dutch Head to attach to camera and then either to legs or dolly / crane.

Mamba Tracking Vehicle with mounted crane.

Bazooka - used instead of a tripod where space is tight.

Python Crane with dolly wheels and base.

PRODUCTION

111

Steadicam Operator
John Ward

Q - What is Steadicam?

John - Steadicam entails putting a rig on a person which holds the camera steady, enabling the operator to walk over rough ground, follow the action and still keep the camera movement smooth. It fills the gap between tripod and the encumbrance of a track dolly. Sometimes you can also get shots that you would not get on either.

Q - Is it feasible to strap a Steadicam onto any camera operator?

John - No. Steadicam is specialised kit requiring training and experience. It takes time to learn how to use Steadicam, especially to get the challenging shots directors demand.

Q - Are there any considerations with regard to the cameras used?

John - The most dynamic shots use wide lenses. On longer lenses you don't tend to see the Steadicam motion as much. It will handle both 35mm and 16mm comfortably and there is even a smaller Steadicam for DV cameras (SteadicamJR).

Q - Is it possible to shoot a whole film on Steadicam without a tripod or track and dolly?

John - I've shot a whole film on Steadicam so yes it can be done. But you still need to understand the nature of drama and using Steadicam exclusively isn't often the best way to tell your story.

Q - How much does it cost?

John - A full size Steadicam in feature film mode with operator will cost £800-£1000 per day. The lighter Steadicam with operator will cost you about £500 a day. It does cost money, but it can save a lot of time and can enable you to get more shots in a day. I am always willing to help out with new film makers as long as they are professional and honest. Often I have time between bigger jobs, and if I like the people and the script, I get involved. But don't try and con me into a deferred payment because the only way I work on deferred payment is that you pay me now and I work for you in a few years time. People say *'no, you don't understand'* and I say *'no it's not me that doesn't understand, I understand all too well'*. If you come to me saying that you have no money, you're being up front. If I can help you, I will. Steadicam operators are usually hired by the week or day.

Q - How do actors respond to the fluidity of Steadicam moving around them?

John - A common mistake is to think *'Oh, I don't have to rehearse the actors, all I have to do is set them off and leave the Steadicam operator to blunder his way through, catching the spontaneous drama'*. That's the worst of all worlds because the actors don't know where the camera is, the camera operator doesn't know where the actors are going to be, and nobody hits anything. You still need to rehearse your shots and work out what is going to happen just like you would in a normal tracking or tripod shot. Those rehearsals give the actors the confidence to say 'ah, I know where I am supposed to be now and I know where the cameras going to be at that moment'. And the operator also knows where the actors are going to be so he can keep them in frame.

Q - You don't look through the camera when using Steadicam - how do you see what is in shot?

John - I can see, however in low light situations it is often not as easy to see the actors as it would be through the viewfinder. It's important to remember that even though you can move the Camera around with speed and fluidity, lights, crew members and passers-by can often creep into shot. Again, rehearsals are vital.

Q - What mistakes do you encounter with new film makers?

John - They tend to be uninspired with the movement and think in terms of a dolly-like tracking shot and I end up walking in a straight line. The great thing about Steadicam is it can go around things and it really opens up a set. It makes much more of your locations. The other thing they expect is that you move in and finish on a pin head - absolutely rock steady. Steadicam moving in onto static objects is not as good as a dolly, and it never will be. There's always a place for a dolly and tripod as well as Steadicam because each fill the gaps the others leave. Strangely enough, it's using the Steadicam more dynamically is something that you usually to talk people into.

Q - What is the most common mistake that you come across?

John - Trying to construct the shot because you've got a Steadicam rather than make the shot work in dramatic terms and then realise you need the Steadicam to cover it. You should let the action and drama take you along and then decide what the best way to cover it would be legs, rig, dolly, hand held or Steadicam etc. If you really do want Steadicam, before you get on set it's a good idea to study movies that have used Steadicam very successfully.

Q - What single piece of advice would you offer a new film maker?

John - Make sure the project holds up dramatically - if it is a good story and you have good actors - the rest is relatively easy.

johnward@jwfilms.demon.co.uk

JW FILMS
STEADICAM

JOHN WARD 5 DULWICH WOOD PARK LONDON SE19 1XU
PHONE: 020 8761 5431 FAX: 020 8701 3545

Lighting Hire
Eddie Dias of
VFG Lighting

Q - What would be a good, basic lighting kit?

Eddie - The BBC used to have the best idea, they used to give a fixed package to the cameraman and send him off to shoot on location - *six weeks and there's your lights*. It really shouldn't be any different with feature films. The lighting cameraman had a 60Kw package including a large source, either a 12k or 6k, a couple of 4ks, four 1.2ks, a couple of 5.75ks, that's the HMI package - and the tungsten package may be two baby 5ks, four baby 2ks, four to six pups, some small lights, mizars, blondes, redheads - and that would cover them for all eventualities. They would also take a 60kw generator.

Q - With that lighting set up, what kind of personnel do you need to service it?

Eddie - You could have a two person camera crew, camera operator (lighting cameraman / DoP) and camera assistant, who would pull focus and clapperload. You're going to have the gaffer, chief electrician and the best boy. The gaffer usually sits on the cameraman's shoulder, the cameraman explains what he actually wants and the gaffer will relay that to his electricians and tell them what they need. The best boy's job is to liaise between the lighting office and the production office, making sure he's got adequate crew, cranes are going to be there in place etc. - making sure that they're covered for all eventualities. If extra equipment needs to be ordered, the gaffer doesn't need to be tied up ordering it, that's the best boy's job.

Q - So in terms of servicing the lighting you're going to have a gaffer, best boy, plus two or three sparks?

Eddie - Yes, one of those sparks will be driving the lighting vehicle and one driving and operating the generator.

Q - Would you normally have a generator with that kind of kit?

Eddie - Yes. You're not always going to be able to plug into the mains. Plus, many lights just can't be plugged into a socket on the wall. If you want to use all your lights at one time, you can do that with a generator without having to worry about a good solid electric source.

Q - And you supply the sparks as part of your package?

Eddie - Yes, we have to by law. Once you get to a vehicle that's over 3.5 tonnes, which is basically a transit van, you then have to have a licence to operate heavy goods vehicles - so every 7.5 or 16 tonne vehicle is on our operator's licence. The people driving the vehicles are paid by us, the onus has to be shown to be on us from a safety point of view.

Q - What's the situation if a producer hires out your people and they overrun?

Eddie - They carry on into overtime which would be paid at an agreed rate. The average daily rate is £150 - £200. If they're doing an extended day they have a set fee, if they're doing a night shoot, they have a set fee on top. It's always good to set up those parameters beforehand. We understand that films will sometimes overrun slightly, and if there's a bit of give and take, for instance if they finish early another time, we can be accommodating. As long as people are clear on that beforehand. People have lives outside the film industry. It may be very important to the producer and director, but an electrician, rigger, painter or a carpenter, isn't going to be taken on for their artistic abilities - to them it's just a job, at the end of the day they've got to bring the bacon home and put it on the table.

Q - If we scale it down a bit, if we think small, what kind of lighting kit would you suggest to keep the costs down?

Eddie - We have made feature films on very tight budgets, but it's like going into a rent-a-car company and asking for a JAG with only £30 a day to spend. They'll turn round and give a bargain basement car, you've got to expect the same in equipment hire. We had a production come to us and said *we know we haven't got a lot but this is what we need*. I welcomed them to my bargain basement and told them that they could have anything they wanted from there. So they took it and four weeks later, the equipment came back and the film was made. They didn't do any special effects or high speed shots so they didn't have to worry about flicker free lighting or strobing.

Q - What is flicker free lighting?

Eddie - If you're taking daylight lights - HMI's - you're susceptible, if you're changing camera speeds, to flicker. If you're shooting at 25fps there's no need to worry. Most productions now hire flicker free lighting which is obviously more expensive. For the lower budget films you can take non-flicker-free lights, they'll be cheaper to rent. If you do use more expensive flicker free lights, there is a ballast unit which gives you a high frequency hum. If your sound man says *we're getting a hum on the sound*, then we can supply special ballasts that don't hum.

Q - With non-flicker-free lighting, can you run slow motion at all?

Eddie - Yes you can - what you do is adjust the shutter angle in the camera. A lot of cameraman are scared of doing this but there's a simple calculation you can do, and all cameramen should know this - after all, you're paying the cameraman for his expertise. For example, if you're shooting at

MICHAEL SAMUELSON

Eddie Dias
Managing Director

PINEWOOD STUDIOS PINEWOOD ROAD
IVER HEATH BUCKINGHAMSHIRE SL0 0NH
TEL 01753 631130 FAX 01753 630485
HOME 01582 660747 MOBILE 0836 777800

Gels - Put over the front of lights to change their colour balance - orange to turn day-light into tungsten balance, blue to turn tungsten-light day-light balanced. Also trace and spun to diffuse light.

Spare Lamps - Keep lots of spare bulbs. Lights are susceptible to shock and water spray. Spare bulbs can range between £10 and £2k for an HMI bulb. You should not be responsible for bulbs that blow, unless your crew was negligent.

Torches - If you want a torch in shot, your normal domestic torch won't do, you will need to hire a special, extremely powerful one from an effects or lighting company.

Extension Cables - Can't get enough. Make sure that the cables you get can handle the power. Hire extra ones from the lighting company. Some lights don't use domestic square pin plugs, but round pin plugs designed for studio use or generators - you may need adapters.

Gloves, Clothes Pegs & Gaffer Tape - Lights are hot and heavy. Gloves are a necessity. Pegs are used to attach gels to the barn doors of the lights. Don't use plastic ones, they melt! Gaffer tape will stick pretty much anything to anything, if you use enough of it.

Stands - Used to mount lights. You will also need various poles and flag stands. Make sure you have enough for all your lights.

Bounce Boards - Used to reflect light. Some are small and hand held, used to fill actors faces in daylight. Large sheets of polyboard are ideal and cheap. Use netting to reduce the amount of light emitting from the lamp.

Van - Large! Transit or Luton van size. You won't need a special licence to drive it but it will guzzle petrol.

Practical Light - A light that actually lives within a scene and is usually tungsten balanced - table lamps, angle poise, ceiling lights - loaded with a standard light bulb from 100watt to 275 watt (beware of melting lights at 275 watt!). Beware of using strip lights as they do not have specific colour balance and may turn out green or pink on film.

Sun Gun - A hand held light, usually battery operated. Ideal for shooting with small crews where only a little fill light is needed. In a pinch, cheap battery operated camcorder lights will do a similar job.

Pepper Light - Very small 200 watt tungsten light. Used for highlighting small areas or creating small pools of light. Also used to place an attractive highlight dot in actors eyes.

Red Head - Blunt instrument and working horse of micro budget film. 750 watt tungsten balance usually coming in kits of three. Ideal for small shoots and close up shots. Don't expect too much out of them though! Can plug into the wall.

Blonde - More powerful version of the Red Head at 2k / tungsten. Ideal to use with a Red Head kit. Can plug into the wall.

Fresnel Light - Large tungsten light, from between 1k - 10k. Used for studio lighting. Fresnel means the light uses a lens which focuses the light in a given place. May need an adapter to plug into the wall. Larger lights will need specialised power sources such as a generator or studio power source.

HMI Lights - Comes in various guises. Daylight balanced and very powerful. All lights come with a ballast which sits at the base of the light or can be hidden away. Come in two varieties, flicker free and non flicker free - non flicker free means shooting at 25fps but is cheaper. Rating from 0.5k to 20k.

52.778 fps, then adjust the shutter angle to 190°, if you shoot at 40 fps, put your shutter angle at 144°.

Q - Would you advise an inexperienced producer who has an inexperienced, artistic cameraman to sit on him like a ton of bricks?

Eddie - Yes, or it will cost you. A lot of inexperienced cameramen want to be creative - but if you're on a low budget, you can't necessarily afford that. You need someone who is going to deliver the goods, to the technical standard needed, on time.

Q - How does the process of booking and paying for lights work?

Eddie - Anybody who's waving money around, instead of asking for credit or thirty days, is going to get a good deal. The scary thing for us is somebody saying w*e're doing a low budget film -* immediately you tense up! (laughs). As soon as someone says low budget, it scares people - don't say low budget, say *we haven't got a big budget.*

Q - What do you do about insurance?

Eddie - We ask the client to insure everything (plus 13 weeks loss of hire). Things do get broken and lost, we're usually quite lenient on the odd bolt and screw and there are some things we can equate to wear and tear. But if something is blown over in the wind, then the production company has got to accept that damage. We also ask to see a certificate of insurance. We can insure the equipment, but we're not insurance specialists and we have to charge a premium rate. You'd probably be better off taking out your own insurance.

Q - Does insurance cover bulbs?

HMI CHEAP	*DAYLIGHT*	*PRACTICALS*	*GELS*	*POWER*
Shooting at 25fps means you can use cheaper Non flicker free HMI Lighting. Remember, not all lighting can be plugged into the socket on your wall.	*It's bright, it's free and you can use a large white poly-board for fill light. Use bright summer days. But remember, winter days are very short though.*	*A 275w photoflood bulb plugs straight into a normal light socket. It's cheap and it's bright, and ideal for low key interior scenes.*	*The coloured gels that go on the front of lights (as well as trace and spun) are easily consumed and very expensive. Get your lighting crew to re-use rather than throw away.*	*HMI lighting is more efficient than tungsten lights. Don't underesti- mate the impact lighting your flat for three weeks will have on your electricity bill.*

Eddie - Yes, unless of course, the damage is through misuse. A 12k HMI bulb costs £2,000 and if they're misused or burnt incorrectly, it affects the bulb's life considerably.

Q - And what are the most common mistakes that could be avoided?

Eddie - There are weekly consumables that the crew will go through. If the cameraman wants to adjust the colour (and colour temperature) of the lighting, he'll do that with CTB, blue transfer gels, orange transfer gels, neutral density gels, frosts and diffusers. When you're given a quote, 90% of the time, it's plus consumables. Always bear in mind that there are consum-able costs on top of that - if you've got a generator and a truck and another truck, you've also got fuel to think of, which can be quite considerable. Even when crews are shooting in a studio, they often draw power from a generator as studio power is very expensive, sometimes five or six times more expensive than what comes out of the wall. We can give advice about how much should be budgeted for this kind of consumables. Don't be afraid to ask if you don't know something - if you ask a company for their advice they will give it to you open heartedly.

Production Sound
Richard Flynn

Q - What exactly is the sound recordist's job?

Richard - The production recordist's first concern is to record as much useable production dialogue as possible, dialogue that will end up in the finished film. Because of the on-set technology available today, there's no reason why dialogue has to be post synchronised in the studio, unless you are shooting action or effects for instance. Your second concern is to try and record any sound effect that is unique to a production or location, a sound that would be difficult to recreate later. Things like water and crowds have very specific sounds that are very hard to find in audio libraries or to recreate in a studio.

Q - Why not post sync the entire film?

Richard - The whole issue of post synching is down to the director. There are some directors like Robert Altman and Woody Allen who absolutely insist on using the original performance, and there are others, like John Boorman, who are very happy to post sync almost everything. Your job as a sound recordist really depends on what the director wants and what their attitude is. Having said that, I always try and make a scene work no matter what. If you need wild tracks to make a scene cut together and want to avoid expensive post synching sessions in the studio later, it's vital to get them on set.

Q - So when a director is looking for locations, it's not only important to consider it's appearance, but also to stand and listen to see if you're right next to something like the M4?

Richard - Exactly. However, if there is a location that has a unique look to it, a big building or stunning exterior for instance, then obviously compromises may have to be made in order to capture that visual element. But when it comes down to a living room interior, quite honestly there is no excuse for shooting in a location where noise is a problem. If you can't afford a set, at least try and find a quiet street, a cul-de-sac.

Q - What is the most basic kit?

Richard - The most basic requirement is that whatever audio recorder is used, the sound is going to stay in sync with the picture. For that reason you can't use an ordinary domestic tape recorder, you must either use an analogue recorder like a Nagra with a sync pulse on it, or a digital recorder which is very stable. Either recorder will suffice. I would say use the best microphone you can afford as you really do need directional microphones. The Sennheiser 416 mike type is probably the most commonly used, although a lot of people use the 816, which is much longer and more directional. The point of using very directional mics is that they cut down on unwanted background noise, but the down side is that you will need a very good boom operator because the 816 is precise and unforgiving if it's not pointing in the right direction. As I said earlier, the idea is to get the dialogue as clean as possible and that's the reason we use that sort of mic.

Q - What about radio mics?

Richard - I wouldn't attempt a drama production without radio mics, mainly because the way things are shot these days. The camera is a lot more portable than it used to be, the use of steadicam and long tracking shots are very common, and that complicates matters from a sound point of view. The major advantage of a small radio mic is that you can get it very close to the actors mouth without having to connect the actor via a long cable. You don't necessarily need radio mics in the studio, but anywhere else they are pretty much essential. I'd advise hiring the most expensive ones you can afford, because the cheap ones are prone to interference.

Q - When a producer hires the sound recordist, does he usually come with his own kit or does that have to be hired as well?

Richard - Most sound recordists who are freelance, own all their own equipment and will generally hire it out as a package, which for most film productions is actually pretty fixed. It doesn't make any difference if your film costs £100k or £50m, the basic sound kit would be the same for all films, it's not like lighting and special effects.

Q - So when a producer comes to you, they have to write out one cheque that covers the whole production sound department?

Richard - No, you would hire a recordist at a particular fee and then the kit for a particular fee. On top you would employ a boom operator and a sound maintenance person, but on low-budget productions the sound crew is usually two plus a trainee - if it's really low, there's no trainee.

Q - How much of a problem can camera noise present?

Richard - Not much of a problem with modern cameras, even with 16mm cameras. 35mm cameras are very quiet. If you're using older equipment, it's essential to have a blimp for the camera. It's mainly a problem in small hard surfaced areas as the sound bounces around.

Ultra low-budget feature productions can buy a cheap DAT recorder onto which they can record their sound in the knowledge that they should get excellent quality and rock solid sync.

Recording device - DAT, Digital Audio Tape, is now the defacto. For low budget productions, cheap semi-pro machines are affordable to buy, never mind rent. Beware of distortion and of non professional connectors that don't deal with the rigours of film making very well. Resist the urge to use ¼" tape.

Recording device - MiniDisc isn't ideal, especially when DAT is so affordable. However, it may be used at a push, especially for weekend re-shoots where only a few lines of dialogue may be used.

Headphones - essential to use high quality 'cans'. Enclosed earpeices mean you hear more of what is going down onto tape, although some recordists prefer the open type. Don't use walkman earphones.

Microphones - undeniably the most important part of the sound recordists kit.

Tie Clip Mic (powered) - can be concealed on an actor when a normal mic isn't appropriate. Radio mics are expensive and excellent, but beware of radio interference with cheaper ones.

Directional Mic (powered) - Several mics produce excellent results and a nominal hire charge will get you the best mic available. Rent. Sennheiser 416 is a good workhorse.

Large Diaphragm Mic - Ideal for recording foley sessions or close mic. singing. No use on a film set. Avoid.

Omni-directional Mic (un powered) - Cheap and cheerful and pretty much no use except in emergencies for guide tracks. Avoid.

Jammer / Baffle - Fits over the mic to protect it from wind. Usually comes with a 'furry' jacket that reduces wind noise even more. Essential.

Cables - Must be high quality and shielded. XLR cables are the professional norm and cheap semi-pro cables should be avoided and one short cable just isn't enough.

Batteries - Batteries must be replaced regularly. You can't wait for the battery to go down as quality might be compromised. Buy in bulk before shooting.

Stock - Whatever format you record sound, make sure you have enough stock for the shoot, plus a few extras. Work on recording a one hour tape a day and always label clearly.

Connectors - Most cheap semi pro equipment will use ¼" jack plugs which are unbalanced. Pro kit will use XLR connectors which are balanced and more suited to the job. If you have a both, you will need an adapter to convert between the two. Before you shoot, make sure you can connect everything up as needed.

Telescopic Mic Boom Pole - Used by the assistant sound recordist to place the mic over the actors, getting the mic as close as possible. Must use lightweight pro kit, fishing rods and clothes poles just don't cut it.

Leather Jacket - Use to put over the camera in order to help deaden noisy cameras.

Mixing Desk - On complicated jobs where multiple mics may be used, you may need a small portable mixing desk. This does add headaches though and isn't ideal for low budget productions.

PRODUCTION

SOUND ADVICE

KIT	LOCATION	BLIMP	CLEAN	WILDTRACK
Always hire or buy the best kit you can afford, both recorder and mics. If you can afford it, hire radio mics.	Always recce a location for sound as well as visual splendour	Always make sure you can blimp the camera, especially if it is old.	Always get dialogue as clean as possible. Always shoot guide tracks, even if the sound would be unusable.	Always shoot a wildtrack of any problematic dialogue or effect. Always run off 30 secs of Atmos after each scene.

Q - How much is the production sound recordist involved in post sound?

Richard - The best way to educate yourself about production sound is to actually start the other end. Sit through a final mix of a film as it's only at that point the problems show up. Post production sound is usually a separate part of the film making process in this country, although there are a few exceptions. Before I start a film, I always phone up the people who are going to mix it and the people who are going to be doing the sound editing and have a good chat with them. For example, with stereo recording, some sound editors prefer things to be recorded in MS Stereo, I won't get into the details but there are different ways of recording stereo and different post production sound people prefer different ways of recording it, so I always check with them what they prefer. Similarly if recording digitally. It's important to sort out any technical problems with sync and timecode with the post production people before you start.

Q - What are atmos and wild tracks?

Richard - Atmos tracks tend to be used to fix something in the sound editing, to smooth out any problems you have in a scene. For example, perhaps you've got a dialogue shot with tracking and there's tracking noise which doesn't actually cross the dialogue. If you have some atmos recorded from the same set up then you can use that atmos to fill in the gaps where the tracking noise was, which means that the sound editor can usually smooth out everything. There may also be other sounds like the directors cue's going along as the dialogue is being spoken. If you get through a whole scene and you're pretty sure that there aren't any major holes, then it's good to get a good thirty seconds of wildtrack 'ambience' and that's usually enough. It does depend on the scene that you're shooting as to what you need to get. For example, if you were shooting a dialogue scene in a real pub, then you'd shoot it without any actual background sounds and record the main actor's dialogue as cleanly as possible. The idea is to lay a crowd track, preferably with the real crowd from the real pub (who are actually there when you're shooting) over the whole scene later. If there are a few extraneous noises, they should be covered by the wild track. If there's an intimate scene between two people in a room, then any background noise is distracting and you have to really insist that there aren't any unnecessary compromises made.

It's very important if you're recording wildtracks of actors, that you do them immediately, straight

MICROPHONE DYNAMICS

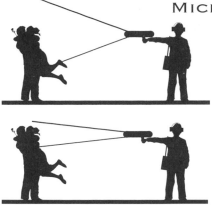

Whilst a directional microphone clearly gives better sound due to it's ability to 'focus' on a smaller area, it would be a mistake to draw the zoom lens analogy. Unlike a camera which has absolute crop off, a microphone, no matter how directional, is still subject to extraneous sound from all around. If you hear it, there's a good bet the microphone did too.

after a scene has been shot, as the actors still have it fresh in their minds - there's little point doing it an hour later because the actors won't remember how they performed in the shot. If you can't get good dialogue, still take sound because when it comes to post synching, the actors will need to hear the original performance in order for them replicate it in the studio.

Q - What are the most common mistakes you come across?

Richard - The most common problems are things like roads, flightpaths, building works in close proximity, the list is almost endless. If the lighting unit has a generator, try to pick a sensible location, it doesn't have to be a hundred miles away but insist that it's far enough not to cause a problem for dialogue. Most modern generators are quite good, you only have to get a hundred yards away and they're effectively quite dead. On an interior, if it's near a busy road, pick a building with double glazed windows which can be closed - what you need to do is to communicate with the gaffer and arrange for cables to come round the back of a building, not the front where you're shooting, so you don't have to have the windows open to run the cables through. That is all part of the sound recordist's job, to try and get the cleanest possible sound, because you want control when you come to final mix.

Q - What basic advice would you give to a film maker considering the sound?

Richard - Always consider the implications of poor on-set sound due to location noise etc. Think carefully about whether actors are going to be capable of reproducing their performance in the studio, and consider cost implications (studio and actors fees), plus you'll probably never get it as good as the original. Think carefully about any locations that aren't that specific to the visual look of the film and always pick the quietest possible. Never try to save money by getting someone who can't boom operate - the boom is the key to getting good sound. By far the most important thing is to have someone who knows where to put the microphone.

PRODUCTION

Director Of Photography
Jon Walker

Q - How do you approach the look of a film?

Jon - The *look* is more than just the photography, it's a joint effort between the set design, costume, make-up and other creative departments, they can all enhance the final look of the film. As well as being a 'science' combined with an 'art', lighting has an element of 'philosophy' in it, *what do I show? what do I hide? should the scene be bright and happy or dull and sad?* The Director of Photography (DOP) can literally change the tone of a scene by the quality and style of the lighting used.

When a person watches a film they should be oblivious of the technical processes involved in making the film. If they are distracted by the editing, the sound effects or the lighting then something has probably gone wrong. The job of the technician on a film is to re-create reality, or the illusion of reality. Both film and video are now very good at copying reality, however, they are not as accurate as the human eye and by understanding this, a good DOP can manipulate the medium to create a natural look. A DOP needs to understand four very important things. First, film stock is far less sensitive to light than the human eye. Second, film produces an image about 1.5 times more contrasty than the original scene. Third, our eyes and our brain adjust for different light temperatures and situations; the amount of light striking the eye can vary greatly and yet the eye and the brain can even it all out. You can read a book with a torch or on a blazing summer day where the quantity of light coming from the sun is hundreds of times greater than with the torch. Lastly, we don't just see with our eyes; we interpret what we see with our brains.

Q - How important is the lab?

Jon - The best place to start when your are just about to shoot a film is to go where the film is going to end up, the laboratory. An understanding of what the lab can and can not do is crucial - you need to know what grading can do for you and the technicians may be able to tell you something about the film stock you are using that isn't immediately obvious in any tests you might shoot. The most important principle when dealing with the labs is communication. They will only do what you want if you tell them what you want and you can't assume anything. The lab is a very powerful tool if you bother to find out how it operates.

For example, the grader can change the look of the film in a way that could completely destroy the effect you had intended. On the other hand, if you help them they can make your film look fantastic - it's vital that you sit down with the grader and watch the film, discussing exactly what you intended when you lit the film. The grader hasn't read the script and may never hear the sound track - how are they supposed to know what you intended if you don't tell them?

Q - What is the most important technical aspect of photography?

Jon - A properly exposed negative - it sounds obvious, but because modern negative emulsions are so flexible there can be a temptation to over rely on their latitude. I shot a film on Super 16mm which was subsequently blown up to 35mm. To get the best result I slightly over exposed the negative - this resulted in a dense negative, producing a final print where the low key and night scenes have good solid blacks. If I had not done this the blacks might well have looked milky (where the blacks look grey and the grain of the film becomes so obvious it can be distracting).

Q - What is the difference between 35mm and 16mm?

Jon - Simply put, the 35mm frame is much bigger so you're spreading your image over more grain to get a sharper, richer image which means you need a bigger lens to get more light in. The problem is that to get a decent depth of field you need a small aperture. For instance, on 16mm you could probably shoot at f2.8 but to get the equivalent depth of field on 35mm you'd need at least f4-5.6. This means that for 35mm you need up to four times as much light and a bigger, heavier camera, all of which will add to your budget.

Q - How noisy are cameras?

Jon - Properly blimped 35mm cameras are extremely quiet. 16mm can be noisier, but modern cameras are still very quiet. If there's a real problem, you can resort to covering the camera and blimp with coats, but that's an operator's nightmare. Film stock varies. Most noise comes from the misalignment of the sprocket holes and registration pin. 16mm is more prone to this as it is so much smaller. You should always take some of the stock you intend to use to your camera hire company and run tests so that if adjustments need to be made, they can be done then and not on set.

Q - How long does it take to change a roll of film?

Jon - A few minutes although you should always have pre-loaded magazines available so that you're never waiting on set. But if you've just got one cameraman who's doing the lighting, operating and loading, as you might on a low budget film, it's going to take much longer.

Q - What are gels and filters used for?

Jon - There are two basic areas. One is to correct light so it looks natural. For example, if you're filming inside and you've only got redheads and daylight is coming in through the windows, then you'll need to put a blue filter (gel) over the redheads to make the redhead's 'orange' light look blue to match the

daylight. Daylight is 'blue', and tungsten lights (anything that has a filament) is generally 'yellow'. Tungsten balanced stock (the most commonly used) produces accurate colours in tungsten light. Daylight balanced stock produces accurate colours in daylight. The other use of filters is to create an effect. You might want blue moonlight so you put blue gel on your redhead, or you want to have warm skin tones, filming with a candle for example, you'll put half an orange on the front of an already warm light.

Q - What about Day for Night?

Jon - Essentially you under expose. On a film I did recently we shot some sequences in a house during the day, but it needed to be night. I simply added a bit of extra back light and under exposed by about 4 stops. I also put lots of neutral density grey filters over the windows so they wouldn't be too bright - sky is always the problem. On screen, the normal background light was basically black, the bits I added were highlights and it looked as though it was shot at night. If you're filming outside, as long as you don't have sky in the shot you can do day for night but as soon as you get the sky in shot it's no good. The best time to film day for night is the magic hour - which is just before it goes dark. There's enough light to pick up details but it's definitely night.

Q - What is trace and spun?

Jon - The smaller the source of light, the harder the shadows produced. Most film lights have 'small' filaments and therefore produce hard shadows, which isn't very flattering on people's faces. If you put spun or trace, which is actually like tracing paper but fireproof, over the light, it 'widens' the source of light and produces 'softer' shadows.

Q - What are practical lights?

Jon - Practicals are lights that actually exist in the scene. For example an angle poise light is a practical. You can either use domestic bulbs, 60-100watt which might be enough, or you can buy 150-250watt bulbs (photofloods) that screw into the same socket. They give much more punch and are a good way to light moody interior scenes very quickly and cheaply - but be on the lookout for smoke rising because they do get hot and can cause a fire!

Q - Would it be feasible to film an entire low budget movie using practicals?

Jon - Yes, if you were really low budget, I would suggest shooting on slightly faster stock because this requires less light, something like 250ASA, and add a couple of red heads to the list.

Q - What is the basic lighting kit you can get

The American Cinematographers Manual is the bible for cameramen. It's crammed with every piece of technical information you could ever want.

GET IT RIGHT FIRST TIME

Make sure each shot has a board on it - either a sound clapper or a mute board.	*Shoot a colour test chart at the beginning of each roll or when the scene changes.*	*Keep accurate lab report sheets - which shot is on which roll, etc.*	*If you watch projected rushes make sure the projector is set up properly - some aren't bright enough or are the wrong colour temperature.*

away with to make a low budget movie?

Jon - If look isn't your primary concern and you just want to get something exposed then you could go for a kit that an average ENG crew would use - a battery powered light that's used in the field (a PAG light or SUNGUN) to fill up shadows. A couple of redheads for indoors and plenty of practical bulbs. This isn't going to look too pretty though. If you do want to create a 'look' then lighting is very important and a basic lighting kit should include at least one big light (2.5k HMI min.) as well as a range of smaller but controllable lights (fresnel lights 500w and 1k). I find I use eveything I have got. If a DoP is always struggling to get enough light on the scene because of the lack of lights, making the film look good as well may be asking too much.

Q - What about stock mixing?

Jon - Some stocks you can mix and some you can't but I would try to avoid it. Mixing speeds (ASA) is the same, it can be done, but it's best avoided.

Q - Shooting outside usually means you don't need lights, although you may need a little fill light - what are the basic elements of actually lighting a shot?

Jon - The three most important lights are the Key Light, the Fill Light and the High Light.

The Key Light is the most important - it's the 'modelling light' and it's usually the main source of light, and sets the mood and texture in the scene. The positioning of the key light is dictated by the requirements of the scene - for example, the sun is the key light in a room where the only source of light is the sunlight coming through the window. Outside, on a clear day, the sun is the key light producing bright highlights and strong dark shadows. On an overcast day with heavy cloud cover, the sun is still the key light, but it is completely diffused by the clouds producing a very flat look, soft shadows and not much contrast between highlights and shadows.

When you light a scene the first question to ask is *what is the most important source of light in this scene?* It may not be obvious; you might be in a tunnel or in a sitting room at night with various light sources (lamps, candles, etc.). Often the job of the DOP is to enhance an existing 'key light'.

The scene might be set in a room where the only light is coming from a candle set between two actors facing each other at a table. Without extra lighting the film will come back from the lab with a candle flame surrounded by complete darkness - remember film is not as sensitive as the human eye. So what do we do? We want to create the subtle look of a candle lit atmosphere without killing it by using too much extra light. By adding a slightly diffused key light that just adds to the candle light we can achieve a look on film that matches what the eye sees. The key light should be placed at the same height as the candle and on an axis. That means that when you look through the camera, the light from the key light looks as if it is coming from the candle. When you view the film you now see the flame and the actor.

Sun lit interiors can also be tricky. Overcast days can mean that without added light the windows are bright but the interiors are very dull (overcast light tending to come from above). The difference in contrast between the exposure needed inside the room and the exposure outside (through the window) is too great to be accommodated by the limited latitude of the film stock. The easiest solution, in order to simulate the look of a day lit room, is to place a very powerful and diffused key light outside the window. The further away from the window this light can go the more even the light in the room (the exposure drop is proportional to the distance from the light source - the further away the less difference it makes). The key light's colour temperature is the same as the daylight, but the key light only adds to the amount of light coming into the room; it does not add to the outside light so the contrast between inside and outside has been reduced and can now be captured on film, (important if the scene requires that both inside and outside the room be seen). The more diffused the key light can be the less harsh the shadows inside the room should be.

Q - What if there isn't a single main source of light?

Jon - Sometimes you may have to deal with multiple key lights - a simple case would be a tunnel with overhead lighting at regular intervals. The scene requires the camera to follow the actors as they walk down the tunnel. The overhead lights may only be domestic 100 watt bulbs and provide very little light for the scene. By replacing the 100w bulbs with 275w or 500w photoflood bulbs (which look the same), you don't change the look of the scene, but it is now bright enough to expose film.

Q - How does the fill light help?

Jon - If the key light 'creates' reality by enhancing the natural light sources, the fill light is the tool a DOP can use to give film the 'latitude' that the eye has.

Take the candle on the table again. Turn off the key light and look at what you've got. The candle light decreases rapidly the further from the flame you get. There's a ring of light around the candle on the table, the actor's faces are darker but still clearly visible and the walls, maybe 10 feet away, are just visible - not totally black. Now turn on the key light(s); you might have set a key light for each actor and put a light over the table shining down to simulate the ring of light produced on the table by the candle. Now film the scene. You should expose for the light on the table so that this is correctly or just under exposed and the actors (whose key light is slightly dimmer) look correctly and proportionally darker. However, the scene looks too contrasty and the background walls are completely black, this is not what we saw with our eyes. The solution to this problem is the fill light.

1. The candle is the only light in the scene. The actor's face and surroundings are too dark.

3. The Key Light is the primary source of light in the scene, sometimes called the modelling light. In this case, the light is placed to look as though the illumination is coming from the candle.

LIGHTING MASTERCLASS

2. The candle light is enhanced with a light directly above, creating a pool of light around the candle on the table, but still the actor's face is dark.

4. A Fill Light lifts the 'ambient' light of the scene (reducing contrast), adding detail to the dark areas of the frame.

PRODUCTION

5. A Back Light increases depth and enhances the visual impact of the final picture.

131

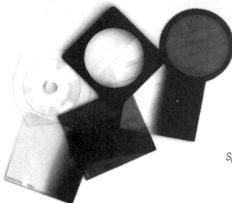

CREATIVE FILTERS

If you cannot afford to hire expensive special effects filters, gelatin filters can be used to great effect. Stills photographers use them with a special plastic holder which snaps onto the front of the lens.

Split diopters, graduated, star, close up, diffusion - all can add to the image if used in a subtle manner. Best of all, they're very cheap.

SPLIT DIOPTER

The narrow depth of field means that the extreme foreground is out of focus.

The split diopter, half of a close up lens for want of a better description, allows both extreme foreground and background to be simultaneously in focus.

GRADUATED

The sky is bright and bleached out.

The graduated filter darkens the sky slightly, creating a more broody look. Use graduated filters with extreme caution as it's easy to go over the top.

MASK

Mask - Binoculars and a keyhole are perhaps the most common type of mask. They work best on the longer end of the lens and can be done in the lab instead, although that will cost significantly more. Mask shots tend to look cheesy.

If you were sitting in a room with light coming through the windows, but the room was painted black, all the objects in the room would be side lit from the window, and the other side would be dark. The walls reflect none of the sunlight back onto the objects. If, however, the room is painted white the objects in the room would be lit by the light reflecting off the walls, as well as from the window. The objects would appear to be lit from all around. The white walls are acting as a fill light. The fill light must supply an equal amount of light to the whole scene without adding shadows to it. In the case of the candle scene, the easiest way to do this would be to bounce light from a powerful light off a white reflector placed just behind the camera. Reflected light is the softest light you can achieve and the position behind the camera means that any shadows created appear directly behind the subject and therefore are invisible to the camera. Experience is the best guide as to how much fill light to use. If there's too much the scene will lose all the texture provided by the key light and the scene will look over lit and flat. To the naked eye the addition of fill light will make the scene look slightly over lit and flat, however, remember that film is more contrasty and less sensitive than the eye. The use of the fill light reproduces the sensitivity of the eye on film. By using fill light the candle scene now looks on film as it did to the naked eye.

Outside on an overcast day the need for fill light may not be immediately obvious. However, overcast days, where the light is essentially overhead, can produce dark eye sockets on your actor. A simple piece of white polystyrene or a photographic reflector placed below the actor's face just lifts the details in their face, removes the harsh shadows and creates a softer more attractive look.

Sometimes providing a bounced fill light behind the camera is not possible. In a tunnel for example, the overhead lights provide the necessary quantity of key light, but also produce harsh and ugly shadows. There might also be pools of darkness between the lights. A light mounted on the camera might be the solution. The light is close to the camera so that shadows are kept to a minimum and by diffusing and dimming it the dark areas and shadows on the actor's faces are reduced without becoming obvious to the viewer. As long as the distance between the camera and the actors doesn't vary too much, the quantity of fill light will remain constant producing a natural look. If this distance is difficult to maintain then a hand held light (on the same axis as the camera) might overcome this problem. Discussing the positions of the actors should also ensure optimum lighting - if they stop and talk in a dark patch the scene might not work.

Q - What is the back light?

Jon - The back light makes actresses look beautiful, bad guys look mean and can get around the problem of providing a light source where, in reality, none would exist; a forest at night for example. Subtlety is the key in most cases. Like the fill light, overdoing the high light can destroy the 'real' look of the shot.

In the candle scene we've created a realistic look on film, however, the actor's close-ups look a little dull. A light placed behind and slightly above the actor produces a highlight on the head. As long as it's not too bright the 'real' look will not be spoilt, however, the depth and texture of the shot has be enhanced - the high light separates the subject from the dark background and a sense of 'space' has been created.

Key lights and high lights can sometimes be the same. In a room lit by various lights - angle poise on the table, standard light by the sofa - one actor's key light might be the other actors high light.

A real problem for a DOP is where in reality there would be no light at all. For example, a narrow unlit street at night or the woods at night have no natural sources of light for the DOP to enhance. Front lighting the subject with a key light would destroy the 'night time' look. A well placed back light is the solution to this problem. The intensity of this back lighting can help set the mood, harsh strong back light can create a powerful look suitable for action and a more gentle diffused back light might create the illusion of moonlight. Back lit smoke and shiny wet surfaces can be very effective in creating mood.

Q - Why do you put coloured gels on lights, or coloured filters on the front of the camera? What is colour temperature?

Jon - Light is essentially radiation produced as a result of heat (red hot and white hot). A domestic light bulb produces light when its filament is super heated, as the light source gets hotter the spectrum of light goes from red to blue. Candles burn at a 'low' temperature and are orange, the sun is very hot and produces white/blue light, (sunsets and dawn are coloured by aberrations in the atmosphere; a bit like putting a coloured gel over a light).

The human eye and brain balances these different colour 'temperatures'. Within a range 3200 Kelvin (about 3273°C) which is yellowish and 6000 Kelvin (6273°C) which is bluish to the eye, a piece of white paper is seen as white! However, film doesn't interpret what it sees. Given that you film within these two light temperatures the lab can probably grade the colours correctly. Most film stock is balanced to produce accurate colours in Tungsten light, which is 3200 Kelvin and is produced by heating a filament (Incandescent). If this film is used in daylight everything looks blue. Although the grader at the lab can correct this, a filter put on the lens to correct the colours at the time of filming provides a more evenly exposed negative and therefore a better looking picture.

Mixing light sources with different colour temperatures unintentionally could cause considerable problems. You might use Tungsten light inside, but the windows and outside are daylight. The result would be either correct colours inside but a blue exterior or a yellow interior and a correct exterior. You can deal with these differences by using coloured gels on the lights to produce a constant even light temperature for the scene. If in doubt, light your scene with one type of light source. Overhead striplights come in all sorts of different colour temperatures, the commonest are 'tungsten' sometimes called 'white' and 'daylight'. Because the spectrum of the light they produce is uneven - 'tungsten' is not true tungsten and 'daylight' not true daylight - when filming, make sure that all the striplights are the same type and you might rig up a 'light box' using the same type of lights for use as a fill light or key light. The lab can then make the small changes necessary to correct the colours.

Q - You mention grading, what can the lab do to correct problems?

Jon - Grading shouldn't really be to correct your mistakes, it is to even out the small difference in exposure and colour that occurs when scenes are shot in different places and at different times. For example, you might film in a field all day, but in the final edit a shot from the beginning of the day is cut next to a shot from the middle of the day. Nature cannot be controlled and the colour temperature of the light might change, clouds form and you might even have to shoot some close-

DEPTH OF FIELD

Stopped Down

There's plenty of light here, so the aperture is closed down. This creates a greater depth of field. Notice how sharp the foreground post to the left and background tree to the right are.

Wide Open

There's much less light now and the aperture is opened up. This reduces the depth of field. Notice how soft the foreground post to the left and background tree to the right is.

Depth of field can be controlled for effect using Neutral Density filters and extra lighting.

LENS & FOCAL LENGTH

Telephoto

The background is crushed and the figure appears more normal. There is less spillage of 'set and props' to the left and right.

Wide

The background is more distant and the figure appears more distorted - depth is enhanced with objects closer to the camera appearing much larger than those slightly further away.

135

THE 'LINE OF ACTION'

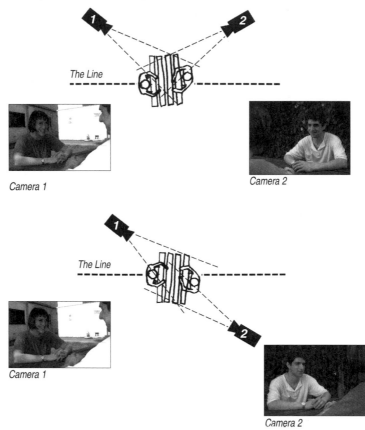

The Line Of Action, or 'line', is an imaginary line drawn through the action of a scene so that the audience understands the layout of the world in the scene they are watching. In these two examples you can see when the line is OK and when it is broken.

The top diagram shows two camera angles on a scene. Camera 1 is on the left of the scene and pointing right. Camera 2 is on the right of the scene and pointing left. When the two shots are cut together it is clear who is sitting where and the line remains unbroken. The people appear to be looking at each other.

The lower diagram shows the same scene with cameras on the left and right, but this time, camera 2 has moved across the line of action. Note how the two resulting shots show the characters sitting on the right of frame and looking left. Cutting these two shots together will jar. In this instance the line is 'broken'. The people don't appear to be looking at each other.

The 'line' is a very simple concept but desperately easy to break. If in doubt, make short video movies and practice by actively breaking the line and examining just how awkward the shots will look when cut.

ups in the studio later. The grader can even out the colour differences so that from shot to shot, the flesh tones and the colour of the grass stay the same - the scene has continuity. The grader has a 50 point scale for the three colours - red, green and blue - with which to grade the film. The closer to the middle of the scale the negative is, the more variations the grader can make; this is why properly exposed negative is so important. If you shoot tungsten film in daylight without a correction filter (Wratten 85), the negative will have too much in the blue layer and not enough in the red. The grader will have to compensate by putting in less blue and more red light at the printing stage; if the negative is under or over exposed the grader's chance of correcting the problem completely will be seriously reduced.

Q - What should you do in advance to ensure problems are ironed out?

Jon - Shoot tests. Film stock is a tool; it is the mechanism whereby the image is captured, copied and then transmitted. Film is made of several layers of light sensitive material - when light strikes it there is a chemical reaction, the more light the more reaction. Not enough light - no reaction and you get nothing on the negative (black), too much light and there's a complete chemical reaction and nothing on the negative (white). Most scenes you shoot will have varying degrees of light and dark; it is important to understand the sensitivity of the film. Your eye may be able to see into the shadowy areas, but will the film negative pick up that detail? Both stocks available in the UK - Kodak and Fuji - are different; their grain structure may not be exactly the same and their sensitivity to different colours may vary. Contact the manufacturers who are usually more than happy to supply a free roll of any stock for tests. Design a series of tests that help you to access the characteristics of the film. A test scene should have a selection of different light and dark areas; you should know what the reflective quality of each area is (a spot meter may help), and by shooting a range of exposures you can see what they look like and how they relate to each other. Talking to the lab is crucial and shooting tests are a great way to gain experience in a short period of time. I have always tried to shoot tests in advance of tackling tricky situations. For example, filming a TV screen and incorporating it into a scene so that it looks as it would in real life is very tricky. Shooting tests enables me to experiment and therefore get the best results.

Q - How much input should a director have with the look of the film?

Jon - It's vital to read and discuss the script with the director. It sounds obvious, but it's so often overlooked. A film should have a style and the photographic look should not radically change during the film unless the story requires it.

Q - What are the most common mistakes made by the production?

Jon - Expecting stunning images with very basic lighting and crew. Getting a good image takes time and resources and that means money. Outdoor locations at night take a long time to light, it's really hard work especially when you don't have enough lights. You're adding time, tiredness, and don't forget it's colder, long cable runs, all sorts of problems.

Possibly the quickest way to shoot a low budget film would be entirely outdoors during the day - with a few good poly boards and reflectors you can be shooting shot after shot after shot.

PRODUCTION

Costume Hire
Tim Angel
of Angels The
Costumiers

Q - What kind of costumes do you hire out?

Tim - We hire out any costume and any uniform from the beginning of time through to contemporary.

Q - What if you don't have a specific type of costume?

Tim - We have production facilities within the company so we can make up any outfits - whatever needs making, we can get made.

Q - Is that just the gowns themselves or do you take care of shoes, hats?

Tim - We don't actually make shoes in-house, but we can get those done. Hats we do make inside. We've got full millinery, dressmaking and tailoring facilities.

Q - How many different styles of gowns do you have in stock?

Tim - Millions.

Q - In terms of budgeting, is there a great price difference between a very basic costume and something that is extremely elaborate and extravagant?

Tim - No, with films you tend to have a set price per costume that's dependent on the number of weeks and number of costumes hired. We'll always start with a book price, and then we'll discuss it with the producer or the accountant. When we're making up a costume, the prices can vary - if it's a simple outfit it will be a lower price and if it's a complex outfit it will be a much higher price. It depends on how much handwork, what sort of fabric and how much time is involved.

Q - How do you usually hire out, is it a daily rate, a monthly rate, a weekly rate or by the production?

Tim - For a film, it basically works out by the number of weeks and the daily rate wouldn't apply. Unless of course, a costume is only needed for a day or two.

Q - Is it usual for a producer to come to you and say, we want all the costumes for our production from you and for you to do a deal based on that?

Tim - It's better I think for the producer to do that, some producers do that, others don't and split it up between lots of different places. The advantage for a producer doing an overall package is that we can offer a much better deal.

Q - Who usually comes to you first?

Tim - Initially, a designer will come with a production, sometimes the producer but at the end of the day we always deal with the producer when it comes down to the money as they are paying the designer.

Q - Do you have your own in-house designers?

Tim - No.

Q - If a producer comes to you with a low-budget period drama and assuming nothing needs making up, would you be able to offer a good deal?

Tim - Yes, we'll always do a deal. We view each project as it comes along. One does negotiate prices and there are times when one does low-budget films.

Q - How much should a basic costume budget be?

Tim - It depends on the production. Even if the costumes are from stock I couldn't give you an estimate - it's a bit different from cameras and sound equipment as everything is so variable.

Q - But it's not going to be £500?

Tim - No, but if a producer rang us up, we would discuss the particular project with them - there is no magic figure. What a producer should do is ring up when they are budgeting, ask us for an estimate and work backwards from there.

Q - What does the producer get for his money?

Tim - Angels is the only costume house in the world that is fully serviced. We have 150 staff and a costume designer would have backup from each of the departments, whether it be mens, ladies or military. Therefore, in preparation time, the producer doesn't need a great deal of backup staff for the costume designer. They are going to end up with one bill from one company and they are going to

Tim Angel OBE

Angels
The Costumiers

40 Camden Street London NW1 0EN
Tel: 020 7387 0999   Fax: 020 7383 5603

PRODUCTION

end up with a much more competitive package than they would if they went to three or four different houses. They get a fully serviced, one stop costume house.

Q - What are your terms for hire?

Tim - Normally we like to get 100% before the production shoots, in other cases, it might be staggered payments that tie in with deliveries we've got. It really depends, but there is always an upfront payment.

Q - What's your policy for insurance?

Tim - That's the responsibility of the production company and they have to insure the goods to the value that we specify.

Q - Do you require to see that certificate of insurance?

Tim - Most of the companies would show us that they have a policy.

Q - Do you ever get involved in science fiction films where you have a bizarre production design?

Tim - Sometimes, but when we do, most of the costumes tend to be made. We'll get involved in anything that requires costumes, but low-budget science fiction films tend to be very difficult.

Q - What are the greatest mistakes made by new film makers, first time film producers and first time costume designers?

Tim - I think the first thing they do is think that a place like this is too expensive for them to afford, so they try and find all different ways of doing it. The easiest way to deal with that is to ask the question at the beginning, come and see us. We might say no, but we might say yes. Even if you've got no money you should at least try and follow the path that the people with money have rather than try and cut the corners.

For a low-budget contemporary film, they'll probably employ somebody who'll think *Oh, I can't afford to hire anything* and they end up in Oxfam, charging around everywhere - and if they're first time people, that takes away a lot of their creativity. As a producer you're getting bills from Oxfam, Marks &

STORY DAYS
Work out how many specific days your story runs over. This will determine what costumes are worn on which days.

SIMPLICITY
Keep costumes simple and don't invent costume changes if they are not needed - this will save money and enable you to move scenes in editing with less chance of continuity problems.

TEMPERATURE
Remember, depending on a costume and location, an actor might freeze or boil. Make sure they have a private place to change on location.

Sparks, wherever, whereas if somebody actually asked the question the worst thing that could happen is we say *No, you can't have all that*, or *we'll cut some of the crowd number*. There's usually a way.

Q - So your advice would be, regardless of the budget, come in here with a wish list if only to have 'no' said to you?

Tim - Yes, if you can get the best, why go for second best. There are problems for us though as we don't have unlimited resources. If we are inundated with requests for Victorian gowns and a low-budget producer comes to us wanting Victorian gowns, we're less likely to do a competitive, low-budget deal. Also, there is a cost to simply organise and put clothes together and therefore there is a point when it just becomes uneconomical for us to do a production.

Q - Do you have any tips for low-budget producers?

Tim - Come and discuss things at the beginning as it makes everything much easier.

PRODUCTION

Props Hire
George Apter
of Studio & TV Hire

Q - What is a Prop House?

George - It is a hire company that rents props to television, film, theatre, dressing displays and photographic shoots. We have been here for forty years so we have a lot of experience.

Q - What do you have here?

George - We are specialists in *'smalls'* which means that we have props ranging from pens and pencils to TVs, radios, bicycles, stuffed animals, kitchen equipment, games, mannequins, Americana, neons, musical instruments, prams, even a yeti. We have over half a million varied items.

Other companies specialise in other things like furniture, modern or period, tanks, armoury, weapons, costumes, curtains, etc. If it needs to be in front of the camera there is a specialist out there for it. We also buy and make up new props all the time. When the World Cup was on we made the only existing World Cup replica.

Q - How does the rental system work?

George - Every item has a value, the first week's hire is 10% of the value, thereafter you go on a sliding scale, the longer you have the prop, the cheaper the weekly rate. The minimum charge is £15 + VAT. Selecting the props means walking around the warehouse and putting post-it labels on the large objects, and putting the smaller ones on a shopping trolley. Then we give you the quote and we go from there.

Q - So if a Production Designer comes to you with a list of say 300 things you would do a deal?

George - Yes, we try and work with people's budgets. We are here to work with the customer, and the bigger the hire the more we can do for them.

Q - What about transport?

George - They should have their own transport. I would rather they checked with us about the sort of vehicles they plan to use, so we can suggest an alternative if we feel the props will suffer. We can also recommend good companies for transport.

Q - What about insurance?

George - The customer organises their own insurance. Sometimes a customer will not insure and then if there is any loss or damage they will have to pay for it out of their own pocket. Some people just insure over a certain value, i.e. insure anything over £1k.

Q - What happens about damages?

George - We always suggest that their driver checks props when they are returned to avoid any misunderstanding. The problems tend to occur when the production has cut corners and not hired good vans and drivers who take their responsibility seriously, or they won't let the driver spend time at the various prop stores checking everything. Prop hire companies welcome anyone who takes the time to check everything and pack it sensibly for transport.

Q - What common mistakes do you encounter?

George - We need official orders on paper and often this doesn't happen, even with the biggest companies. Everyone needs to know what and when they are ordering and how much it will cost. Productions often rent for one week and then end up needing the prop for several weeks, therefore escalating the cost. Props get stolen or lost because they don't have an experienced props masters, props get damaged when they don't employ proper couriers.

Q - What advice would you offer?

George - Get professional and work in a professional manner. Don't lie, you will do far better if you tell us what you have rather than pretending that you have lots of money.

Either come to us with a list of what you want or an amount you want to spend and we can tell you how the deal will work. Be honest. I prefer film companies where the producer is frank and tells me when he can pay rather than fobbing me off with empty promises. We are all in the same industry, no one really wants to put someone else out of business, keep in touch, keep them updated.

Studio & TV Hire

Half a million props and antiques for hire for television, film, theatre, display and photography.

ESTABLISHED
40 YEARS

GEORGE APTER

3 Ariel Way, Wood Lane,
White City, London W12 7SL
TEL 0208 749 3445   FAX 0208 740 9662

Special Effects Mike Kelt
of Artem Visual Effects

Q - What is the job of the Special Effects man?

Mike - In very simple terms, to make the various things that are in a script that are difficult or impossible to achieve through normal channels, achievable. That could be anything from building a miniature of a medieval landscape to setting fire to a stately home which you can't actually damage.

Q - There's a vague line between make-up and special make-up. Where does it cease to become the job of the set make-up artist and become the job of the effects team?

Mike - The cross over is in the area of prosthetics. Make-up artists have facilities to make small prosthetic pieces but anything larger than say a false nose or a scar will usually be an effect and could entail making a full body prosthetic such as turning someone into a stone sculpture or an alien creature. Obviously we would work closely with the make-up department where such cross overs occur.

Q - How easy and safe are bullet hits?

Mike - They are perfectly safe providing you know what you are doing. On films they tend to want bullet hits that are theatrical. They are easy enough to do but can be costly because the pyrotechnics that you use tend to be expensive.

Q - Is there a special way to shoot models or miniatures?

Mike - Yes. We would liaise with the DoP as to how they are going to fit into the other shots and what lighting is going to be used or perhaps even duplicated to match other live footage, find out what lenses are to be used etc. It's easy to ignore all those things and just assume you can turn up with a model, plonk it down and hope that someone can light it and film it. It just doesn't work that way. We would be involved all the way through, in supervising the model, setting it up, helping to rig it and shoot it, and putting it in the skip afterwards.

Q - For ultra low-budget pictures, can you do it yourself with an Airfix kit for spaceships and Dick Smith's £9.99 make up kit from Woolies?

Mike - You can certainly try, yes. There are big areas in special effects where there's no reason why you can't do it yourself, providing you have the basic knowledge and know what you are

PRODUCTION

doing. The only areas where I'd say you couldn't do it yourself is where safety is involved, or where pyrotechnics are involved - that would be a legal minefield too. Anybody trying to do the special effects on their own films has got to draw the line at the point where safety starts to become an issue, but if you're doing a model, an Airfix spaceship say, then there's obviously no reason why somebody can't do it themselves, providing they've read enough books.

Q - What effects are more costly - a car explosion or blue screen model shot for instance?

Mike - Blowing up a car would be much cheaper than doing a blue screen model. Generally, the more things you can do for real the cheaper it is. Man hours are the expensive thing - if you can do something quickly with the minimum preparation then that is the route to go down.

Q - At what stage should a producer come to you and get you involved?

Mike - The earlier the better. Ideally when costing out a film, the producer should call us, then we can look at the script and actually make suggestions on how something could be achieved, rather than coping with problems which have been created after being brought in at the last minute. Often, there are things which can be done for a fraction of the price if we had only just been brought in at the start. It also means that the people involved have a more realistic idea of what the effects budget is going to be instead of just picking a figure out of the air. To keep costs to a minimum, there are always compromises of one sort or another that can be made and providing people are prepared to listen, substantial savings can be made with minimal loss of impact. I think the only area where that doesn't apply is safety where compromises can't be made.

Q - Are there any spectacular cheat effects where you can avoid expense but still achieve something special?

Mike - One of the things which tends to be forgotten about these days which works very well is a hanging miniature - you're filming a scene with people in it, but you want to show say, people coming out of a spaceship, or walking up to a castle. If you make a miniature and hang it infront of the camera between the live action and the lens, you can get a very realistic feel, because the lighting is correct, it's out in daylight, and providing you dress the edge between the model and whatever the background is that it's sitting against, it can be totally convincing. It's exactly the same effect as a matte painting but it has the advantage of being three dimensional so you don't have to worry about the light - as the light changes in the background so it changes on the model, but with a matte painting you're stuck with it. So if it's painted on a sunny day and on the day you shoot it, it's overcast, you have problems.

Q - Rain, wind, mist and snow - people write those things into scripts without thinking - does that fall under the production design department or is that special effects?

Mike - It comes under special effects and can be costly because, more than anything, man

SPECIAL EFFECTS - ROUGH GUIDE

Atmospheric
smoke, rain, snow etc..

Fire
ranging from making something look like it's on fire to a campfire that will always burn at exactly the same rate for continuity. Safety is always an issue with fire effects.

Pyrotechnics
blowing things up, ranging from huge fire balls to bullet hits on bodies.

Models & Miniatures
miniatures are a small version of a real object, a boat for instance. Models are things that are there to represent objects that are difficult to film or control, like an AIDS virus or an atom.

Mechanics
anything from a rig to control milk pouring out of a jug on cue and at just the right rate to a massive rig to knock down a wall (if it needs to be done mechanically rather than pyrotechnically).

Animatronics
making creatures up which have realistic movement, operated by radio control servos, cables, or computer operated these days.

Sculpture
covers a huge area; it could be a sculpture of an animal that's going to be used in animatronics, or an inanimate object that's going to be standing in the shot somewhere, a chocolate bar for instance.

Prosthetics
a latex piece that is attached to an actor that sometimes requires body and face casting enabling artists to sculpt 'onto' actors faces and bodies.

power is required. Plus, if you're not in a place where there's a ready water supply, it can be very costly because you have to tanker the water. 2000 gallons of effects rain doesn't go that far. If it's written willy nilly into the script for a low-budget film, the producer should weed it out very early on to avoid unnecessary expense. Smoke machines, on the other hand, are very cheap and don't have to be used by special effects people.

Q - What about computers and special effects?

Mike - I think as the years go by, the computer side of the business that actually generates images that go directly onto the screen, will play a bigger part. What is starting to happen is no

longer just a question of post production tinkering, it's the actual replacement of images with CGI. Replacing actors or animals with a computer generated image is now common, usually because it's cheaper to do that than try to get an animal to perform, or even because the actor died halfway through filming.

Q - What are the most common mistakes made by the producer and how can producers make your life easier?

Mike - By giving us more time, telling us about their requirements as soon as possible, then we can get our heads around what needs to be achieved and what the best and most cost effective way of doing that actually is. I've even come across people who've said, *we don't want to give you too much time because we don't want it to cost much -* I haven't quite got my head round that.

Q - What basic advice would you offer a new filmmaker when it comes to special effects?

Mike - Don't be afraid to talk to people who are in the business. If you are going to use special effects, make sure you use people who are recognised and who have a track record because this industry is littered with instances of people being used who are not competent and in the worst instances, it's been very dangerous. Using inexperienced people can also end up costing more money than it otherwise would have done because something didn't work and it has to be done again. It's certainly worth talking to people who have a track record and even if at the end of the day you can't afford them and you use somebody else, at least you might learn something.

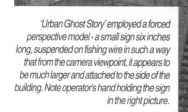

'Urban Ghost Story' employed a forced perspective model - a small sign six inches long, suspended on fishing wire in such a way that from the camera viewpoint, it appears to be much larger and attached to the side of the building. Note operator's hand holding the sign in the right picture.

Stunt Co-ordinator
Terry Forrestal

Q - What are the most common stunts for low budget films?

Terry - Fights. No matter the genre there's always some kind of fight, be it between lovers, friends or a bar room brawl. An experienced co-ordinator can choreograph that making sure it works for the drama and the camera; whereas young or inexperienced people have a tendency to overcomplicate things. This is especially problematic when you have actors trying to perform action sequences without professional guidance as this is not what they're trained to do.

Q - Are any stunts a real problem?

Terry - All stunts need proper organising and preparing, so from a low budget persepctive, all stunts are a potential problem. Many areas are specialist such as motorbikes, high falls, cars and horses. Most stunt people should be happy to fall out of a saddle, but pulling a horse down is a potential leg breaker.

Most injuries are caused by motorbike crashes and car knock downs. High falls don't hurt, unless you get them wrong; then you're very dead. It's knowing how to shoot the hard things that makes them easier and much less dangerous.

Q - What basic precautions does a film maker need to take?

Terry - Clearly preparation and discussion are essential. The first and foremost precaution that any young producer should take is not to listen to all those people around them who aren't in the film business who say *I know a fireman and my kid brother's mate can race motorbikes.* Use professional people, look at their CVs, don't listen to anyone who cuts short on safety, and if they do, get rid of them.

Whether you're low or big budget, you're responsible for health and safety, not just morally, but by law. If anyone gets hurt you could be dealing with a serious offence.

Q - The rule here is to find a way of achieving what your drama needs without doing a major stunt?

Terry - Yes, if necesary, cut away to a driver's face for the car impact and use a loud sound effect for instance. There are some co-ordinators and stunt performers who are happy to help out on low budget films because many people see new film makers as the future of the industry. Who knows, help them now and in the future they may give you a fully paid job.

Q - How involved is a stunt sequence?

Terry - It depends on the stunt. A serious stunt such as someone catching fire and falling out of window will need some dedicated support - the art department will need to build the window, a special effects team will need to handle the glass and the fire, official paramedics will be needed, one to drive and one to do the tending should something go wrong, the fire brigade etc. etc.

Even something that seems simple, such as two lovers on a lake having an argument and one falls in (and drowns), need full prep. You'd need the boat people, divers, the water needs to be tested beforehand in case there is a metal pole sticking up for instance. Also, film makers need to remember simple things like hot tea and coffee, towels and blankets if someone is going to fall in a lake. It's an easy oversight, but it can cause very bad feeling. Every film unit must have a unit nurse by law. Speak to the co-ordinator, they'll tell you what you need.

Q - What happens about weapons - a killing weapon in story can also be a killing weapon in real life?

Terry - More than likely you will need an armourer, like the guys from Perdix Firearms. Anything that's a practical weapon that actually fires out of the barrel must by law be taken away from set and put in the hands of a registered armourer who has a section 5 licence. When weapons are not in use, actors and extras and to a certain extent stunt people should not be allowed to handle them. Only at the last minute will the armourer load the weapon and shout *gun loaded* to let everyone know about the potential hazard. It may seem over-precautious but even blanks at close range have killed people before.

However, dummy weapons, made of plastic or blunt knives for instance, can be used and kept by the props master. If you're out and about, the location manager must inform local police and civilians that weapons will be on the streets. It has happened in the past that the police have swept in on what they thought was a robbery only to find a bunch of actors.

Q - What happens about stunt insurance, above and beyond other normal insurances?

Terry - All Equity stunt people have their own insurance covered by Equity. If a stuntman is injured and it is not the fault of a ridiculous demand

Get information about qualified stunt performers and co-ordinators from the Equity Stunt Register, available directly from Equity.

from the director or producer, the production company is not liable. If I decide on a stunt and how to do it, then it goes wrong, then it is not the fault of the production company but my responsibility and it would end up on my insurance. However, if for example, an inexperienced A.D. wasn't doing their job correctly and at the last minute a pedestrian, dog or pushbike comes from nowhere and the stunt performer is forced to swerve and has an accident then they'd have a right to claim.

Q - What are 'adjustments'?

Terry - Adjustments are a long standing tradition in the stunt business. The risk factor and potential for serious injury increases according to the severity of the stunt - accordingly a stunt person would want to be paid more. Also, each time you perform the stunt you will be repaid.

Q - What about camera tools like slow motion?

Terry - Many tricks with the camera are used to help the overall effect of a stunt. Slow motion is a great tool. Stunts can happen very quickly and a little slow motion can slow the action down so that you can see it more clearly. Many stunts are shot in slow motion and audiences don't even know that it is slow motion, they think that it happened at that speed. Similarly, under-cranking the camera slightly can make some stunts look much faster, such as a car knock down.

Q - What is your relationship to the first assistant director?

Terry - I work very closely with the first AD as the set must be completely controlled. I know that stunts are very exciting to watch but you should try to avoid letting people get over excited as it can be very distracting. Making sure everyone knows exactly what is happening and keeping everyone a safe distance is also essential. Clarity and co-ordination are essential.

Q - Can you advise on better ways of achieving the same ends in the drama of the script?

Terry Forrestal makes a huge leap from a building for a publicity stunt to launch the new Bond movie.

Real or fake? Even when examined close up, replica guns can be totally convincing and don't require a costly armourer or stunt co-ordinators presence. However, if blank firing weapons are to be used, an expert must be present.

Terry - Nothing should be impossible for a good stunt co-ordinator given enough time and money - but you often don't have either of those. I can advise about possible script changes to take advantage of a simpler, safer and therefore cheaper stunt that might have equal impact. Again, if money is tight, be creative about getting around the story without having to show the stunt - that's the cheapest and safest way by far!

The flipside is that often I can suggest ways of making something that seems fairly mundane in the script into something more spectacular.

Q - What common mistakes do you encounter?

Terry - In general, overall inexperience of young or new crew members. For example attitudes to saftey, and another classic is the person doing the budget. The latter often leads to conversations like *I didn't realise that was a stunt* or *What? This isn't a stunt picture.* Usually I then say *well if it isn't a stunt picture, why are you talking to me?* An old lady with a walking stick who trips and falls, that's a stunt.

Virtually everything has been done before, check out other movies and make what you are doing different somehow. Hire a professional - the people to go for are Equity stunt registered performers and co-ordinators, and remember you need Health and Safety on the set - by law, no matter what the budget. Lastly, remember, even though a stunt person is highly trained, they are putting their life on the line for a production and you must respect their experience and decisions.

Q - What basic advice would you offer a film maker?

Terry -This isn't a glib answer, I will quote my school motto - *'think well on it'.*

Addendum. As of going to press, we learnt that Terry had been killed in a base jumping accident. His untimely death serves to illustrate that even under controlled conditions with seasoned professionals, stunts can be mortally dangerous. He was a dear friend and inspiration to all at Living Spirit and will be missed.

PRODUCTION

Studios
Steve Jaggs of
Pinewood Studios

Q - Do low-budget films tend to shoot in studios or on location?

Steve - Generally, they tend to shoot on location due to budgetary restraints and the fact that it may be easier to pull favours in from locals. Plus, hiring of stages may appear to be expensive. But in the long run it may work out cheaper - you have total control in a studio - guaranteed weather coverage, sets can be built, you can get the right camera angles (which you can't necessarily do if you've rented a house for a couple of days). Also, if you have a situation where there is an effect, like somebody charging through a glass door, I don't think anybody would be too happy about you doing that in their home.

Q - From a production point of view, what other things can benefit a production?

Steve - There are lots of things in the studio that have to be arranged for on location - you don't have to get involved in catering, it exists, they can just break for lunch and go to the cafeteria or restaurant. There's all the other ancillaries like toilet blocks around the studio and dressing rooms in situ. We have a medical block with a nurse and a doctor, you're close to companies on the lot like accountants, special effects, preview theatres, and there's ample car parking, security, etc. There are so many extra costs whilst shooting on location that you don't have in a studio - transport, hotel bills, and the inconvenience of being far from the labs (if you're shooting in Yorkshire for instance).

Q - What does the film maker get for their money when they hire a studio?

Steve - They get a sound stage, plus all the facilities that are on site that you need. On top of that there is an extra cost for production offices if required. They may wish to have make up and dressing rooms for the period of the picture or they may want them just on Tuesdays and Thursdays depending on when their artists are in. Certainly with new film makers, we like to be involved as early on as possible so that we can advise them as to exactly what they will need and then there are no nasty shocks when the bill comes. Often, new film makers don't realise that they need production offices, make-up and hair, a wardrobe area, a props area, a work shop - if there's plaster work involved they need a plaster shop, do they require an area where they need special effects work? etc. Another thing that often gets forgotten is a build and strike period for sets - remember, sets and rubbish have to be cleared away by the production, and that takes time.

Q - So whilst the studio is a hire thing, it's more of a service?

Steve - Yes. We're effectively supplying them with property for a limited amount of time, and a specific property for a specific purpose. Things like make up or hair, they are fully fitted, you don't have to hire a chair or hot and cold running water, we have proper barbers chairs to sit in, the same with art departments, with drawing boards, rooms for model making, set building etc.

Q - Are studios as expensive as they sound?

Steve - No they're not - the perception is that they are. We always ask film makers to come to us and discuss the situation, let's see what your requirements are and let us give you a quote - maybe you'll be surprised. On the surface, it may look more expensive to shoot in a studio rather than on location, but there are so many inherent advantages to shooting in a studio, it will save you time and therefore money. Even your cast and crew don't need to be accommodated, you just say, we're in the studio, make your own way there.

Q - What other companies are available on the studio lot?

Steve - That's one of the other advantages of coming here, we have about sixty tenants - we have several special effects companies, lighting hire companies, even a travel company that handles the film industry, accountants, insurance etc. There are too many to list here, but we have almost everything you could need, right here. If a bulb blows in a light, you only have a five minute walk to replace it, not an overnight delivery.

Q - When productions are shooting at Pinewood, do they take production offices?

Steve - Normally they base themselves at the studio and they can come in and out as they wish.

Q - What is the procedure for booking?

Steve - This is difficult because films tend to change dramatically over time - we just ask for the film makers best guess, and ask them to keep us informed of any changes so we can alter any pencil bookings accordingly. However, there comes a point where we have to say pay up or shut up as we cannot indefinitely hold a stage on a pencil. If you've agreed the hire and the film is all set to go, then something halts it, we will still have to charge. We do our best to sell that time and space to another production and if we do, we'd give you the money back.

Q - Are there any rules or etiquette for working in a studio that cannot be broken?

Steve - Obviously there are certain restrictions, for instance if there's going to be a night shoot we like to be notified because out of courtesy we'd like to let the local residents know. There are certain things that you can't do - there are yellow lines on the stage where we request nothing is to be built over it because that's the fire escape. Also, we ask photographers not to wander around taking pictures as that can cause problems for other productions.

Pinewood Studios
STEVE JAGGS
Pinewood Studios Ltd
Pinewood Road, Iver, Bucks SL0 0NH
Tel: (01753) 651700 Fax: (01753) 656844

PRODUCTION

SPACE	POWER	FACILITIES	KUDOS
If you can't afford a studio but need to build a set, find an old warehouse or barn. But beware of noise or echo.	Most studios will sell you their power at a marked up price - check this before booking.	Check out if services like catering, toilets and production offices are available. These are all major headache savers.	Don't underestimate the kudos you will get from being based at a film studios - even if you do rent the boiler room at Ealing Film Studios, just like Living Spirit!

Q - What's the procedure if the production over runs - do you throw them out?

Steve - It could happen, but we've never thrown anyone off a stage. We juggle the elements so everyone's happy and don't book studios back to back as we know we need manoeuvrability.

Q - What basic advice would you offer to film makers?

Steve - Don't dismiss studios, always discuss with the studio management what's happening. Also, for financial restraints, don't spoil your script to suit your location. For instance, you're using your mother's house, it's a lovely house but actually I really need to knock that wall out because I can't get my camera back far enough so therefore your script changes. Talk to studios as early as you possibly can because they may be able to advise about budgeting so that you can make a decision as to whether to shoot on location or in a studio. The age old problem to avoid is when you have run out of money and still have two weeks to shoot. There are a lot of people in this industry, us included, who want to encourage young film makers because they're the film makers of the future, a lot of people are quite prepared to give up their time and talk - utilise it, don't think you know everything about this industry because, believe me you don't.

Right - the world famous 007 stage where many of the epic Bond movies were shot is yours for a mere £13,500 per week - and that's without a deal!

Left - a big space in a studio is an ideal place for a low budget set build. Ealing Film Studios Stage 4 is a non sound stage, designed for special effects, but is ideal for low budget work. Depending on the deal you cut, it's cheap and includes facilities such as loos, production offices, green rooms, wardrobe, catering etc.

Studio	Phone	Stages	Size	Sync	Lighting Rig	Tank
Bray Film Studios	01628 622111	1	113x91x34.5	Y	Gantry	34.5x21.6x7'6"
Down Place		2	120x85x35	Y	Gantry	33x17.8x8
Water Oakley		3	71x36x13.5	N	N	10x8x4.6
Windsor Road		4	47x40x18	N	Gantry	10x8x4.6
Windsor SL4 5UG						20x12x8 (free standing tank)
Ealing Film Studios	020 8 567 6655	1	54x52x18	N	Gantry	N
Ealing Green		2	125x75x34	Y	Gantry	25x20x7 & 40x17x6
London		3A	85x70x32	Y	Gantry	30x17x6
W5 5EP		3B	85x70x32	Y	Gantry	35x20x7'6"
		3A/3B	145x85x32			
		5	44x22x16	Y	Scaffold	
Elstree Film Studios	020 8 953 1600	1	130x118x50	Y	Gantry	N
Shenley Road		2	130x118x50	Y	Gantry	N
Borehamwood		7	77x64x32	Y	TV Grid	N
Herts		8	97x77x32	Y	TV Grid	30x30x9
WD6 1JG		9	97x77x32	Y	TV Grid	30x30x9
		10	160x60x20	N	N	N
		Exterior Lot	5 acres			Exterior & Inner Tank
Millennium Studios	020 8 236 1400	X	80x44x24$^{1/2}$	Y	Scaffold Rig	N
Elstree Way						
Borehamwood						
Herts WD6 1SF						
Pinewood Studios	01753 651700	A	165x110x35	Y	Gantries	40x30x8
Pinewood Road		B	110x81x34	Y	Gantries	N
Iver		C	100x81x34	Y	Gantries	10x8x6
Bucks		D	165x110x35	Y	Gantries	40x30x8
SL0 0NH		E	165x110x35	Y	Gantries	40x30x0
		F	75x100x35	Y	Gantries	20x20x8
		G	54x49x23	Y		N
		H	89x36'36"x28	Y	Gantries	N
		J	11x80x29'3"	Y	TV Grid	N
		K	11x80x29'3"	Y	TV Grid	N
* World's largest silent stage		L	105x90x30	Y	TV Grid	N
Largest Outdoor tank in Europe		M	105x90x30	Y	TV Grid	N
		N/P	80x104x19	Y		N
		South Dock	174x96x28	N		N
		007	334x136x40'6"	N	Gantries	297X73X8'10" *
		LG Process	175x28x28	Y	Gantries	
Shepperton Studios	01932 562611	A&C	150x120x40	Y	Gantry	36x20x7
Studios Road		B&D	100x120x35	Y	Gantry	16x8x7
Shepperton		E	72x44x24	Y	Gantry	N
Middx		F	72x44x24	Y	Gantry	N
TW17 0QD		G	94x72x24	Y	Gantry	N
		H	250x120x45	N	Gantry	230x120x5
		I	124x57x20	Y	Gantry	24x18x8
		J	150x100x40	Y	Gantry	N
		K	120x100x40	Y	Gantry	N
		L	100x65x24	Y	Gantry	N
		R	85x120x45	Y	Gantry	N
		S	100x100x45	Y	Gantry	N
		T	42x67x24	Y	Gantry	N
		W	80x100x34	N	N	N
Three Mills Island Studios	020 7 363 0033	1	31x28x18	Y	Y	N
Three Mill Lane		2	33x28x18	Y	Y	N
London		3	14x28x18	Y	Y	N
E3 3DU		4	87x77x23'7"	Y	Y	N
		5	143x74x22	Y	Y	N
		6	101x77x27	Y	Y	N
		7	212x77x33'5"	Y	Y	N
		8	84x49x31	Y	Y	N
		9	104x84x33	Y	Y	N
		9B	157x50x33	Y	Y	N
		10	121x46x23	N	Y	N
		11	106x89x33	N	Y	N
		12	51x32x20	N	Y	N
		14	84x43x27	N	Y	N
		The Foyer	106x34'10"x33	N	Y	N

UK MAJOR FILM STUDIOS CHART

see yellow pages at back of book
for full listing

PRODUCTION

Product Placement
Identity Withheld

Product placement and sponsorship is always a favourite prospective source of finance for low-budget film makers. Because this side of the industry is often frowned upon by advertising regulatory bodies, the interviewee requested anonymity.

Q - What is product placement with regard to feature films?

Anonymous - A producer will come to someone like myself, or approach a manufacturer direct, and offer to 'place' a specific brand product in a shot or sequence, in return for payment. Many Hollywood feature films do this and sometimes it's a little too obvious where a deal has been struck. We are concerned with getting our clients brand name promoted in a way that we feel is appropriate. So we may impose certain restrictions.

Q - What kind of restrictions?

Anonymous - For instance, we might insist that if an alcoholic beverage was featured in the film, it was only consumed by the 'good guys' and not the villains and that the bottle was never used as a weapon etc.

Q - How much money is available?

Anonymous - For a low-budget film, very little, as the film maker probably won't have the calibre of cast that we need, or a distributor who is going to really push the film out. It is a film myth that new film-makers will be able to finance their film from the product placement of huge brand names like Coca Cola or Panasonic. I am sure that both these companies will have large advertising budgets, but they are looking for the calibre of Mel Gibson or Julia Roberts, not some unknown actor in a film that might never see the light of day.

Q - What about simply supplying the products for use in a film?

Anonymous - Very often we can help there as the cost of simply supplying a product is minimal to the manufacturer. We often supply anything from beer and chocolate bars to cars. Obviously, we expect the crew to drink the beer and eat the chocolate after all the shots have been covered, but we will want the car back! Also, with regard to cars, the producer will almost certainly have to cover the insurance for the driver. We may also ask for some photos of the cast with the product.

Q - What do you need from the producer for you to make a decision?

Anonymous - In the first instance, if the producer was looking for some kind of payment, we would need to know about the film, the subject matter and theme, who is in it, who is making it etc. If we represent a client whom we think would be interested, we would ask to see the screenplay and if we decided to proceed, we would stipulate where and how we wished the products to be featured in a contract.

If you are simply looking for products to feature and no money, more than likely we would just send them to you, especially food and drinks. Often we will supply some hardware products, but then we do look for more assurances from the producer about the type of coverage in the film, plus an assurance that the various products are insured whilst being used by the film unit.

Q - How much coverage of a product are you looking for?

Anonymous - We don't want to bombard the audience with product names to the point where they feel they are watching a commercial, so we aren't looking for excessive or unnecessary coverage. It's just that if there is a camcorder in a scene for example, we want it to be one that comes from one of our clients.

Q - What advice would you offer a new film maker?

Anonymous - Don't waste your time trying to get large sums of money from huge corporations. Do deliver what you promise in terms of coverage of the products we promote, because you will be coming back to us for your next film and it's a small world.

Q - What are the most common mistakes you come across?

Anonymous - Many films are simply not suited to placement of products, a period drama and some science fiction for example. So in those instances, it's just not worth making the call. Producers often bend the truth too and I know that things can and do fall through. It's just frustrating for us when we are told that the lead is going to be a big Hollywood star, and that person simply doesn't materialise.

Often, we will only pay a deposit and hold on to the balance until the film is completed and we have viewed it to agree the level of product coverage.

The Laboratory
Brian Dale
of Technicolor

Q - What is the job of the laboratory?

Brian - To take the exposed raw camera stock, process it, probably make telecine rushes, or maybe print it, then deal with the post production of that material in terms of producing the necessary facilities up to and including bulk release prints. Television transmission tapes may be made by the lab or an associated company, but more usually by a specialist facilities house.

Q - How important is it for the production team to meet the laboratory contact person?

Brian - The contact technician becomes the 'technical eyes' of the production and it's vital the producer and director meet him, to understand who they are and what they will be doing. Also, the cameraman and editor should meet the lab contact - he is a named individual who will be completely responsible for looking after the production, right the way through to the answer print and maybe beyond. If you've got a problem, a good contact man will be able, subtly of course, to suggest the changes that may be necessary to improve the look of the picture. After meeting the cameraman and discussing the 'look' he is trying to achieve and after the first one or two days rushes, the contact man will be able to advise what changes, if any, should be made - indeed it's his job to report on technical problems like hairs in the gate or a boom in shot for example.

Q - What is the lab report sheet?

Brian - The report sheet is a list of scenes and takes which contains key numbers as well as the printing lights (a laboratory measure of the exposure of the red, green and blue emulsion layers). It's a listing of all the material that's shot, roll by roll, scene by scene, key number at the start of the scene, key number at the end of the scene, or in the case of telecine rushes, a timecode reference, colour grading and any comments from the contact man.

Q - What is the camera report sheet?

Brian - The camera report sheet comes from the production and is usually produced by the camera assistant on the job. It lists the material in use, by stock type, batch, roll, everything down to the strip number. If there is a problem and with the best will in the world, stock manufacturers, all have their problems from time to time, they need to be able to trace back. It's an advice document for us to tell whether there is any special effect, whether there's been any problems or if there's been a jam in camera, so that we can deal with it accordingly. It will also give us information on scenes and takes, preferred takes, those takes that are to be printed and those takes that aren't.

Q - How should they supply the exposed negative to you?

Brian - Tape the can lids down, have the rolls of film gaffer taped together, with the camera report sheets (or better still, box everything up), and drop it off at film reception at the lab. Some labs offer a collection service from designated sites.

Q - What happens about sound?

Brian - Sound is an entirely separate channel as far as we're concerned. The only time that we would see sound at this stage of the operation is if all the materials from the shoot were coming in to us and we'd simply been asked to pass the sound on to an audio facility where the sound tapes are transferred. In the case of film rushes, it is normal for the assistant editor to sync up the sound with the rushes and to project the picture - mute picture with the separate mag soundtrack. In the case of video rushes transfer, if sync sound is required, then the master audio tapes will need to be delivered along with the negative to the telecine facility, be it in the lab or another company.

Q - What are the differences in the way 16mm & 35mm is handled?

Brian - Fundamentally there's no difference in that both are received the same way, but separated into Super 16mm or 35mm channels. They are processed in the same way, different machines, but the design of the machines is identical. Generally, 16mm is graded roll by roll, so you come up with a grading light for a complete camera roll which is an average of all the scenes on that roll. With 35mm, selected takes will be circled on the camera report sheet which will be extracted from the negative roll and printed or transferred so you end up with 2 rolls of 35mm negative - one of which is selected takes and the other B Roll, (unused takes) which is stored away, to be called up if alternate takes are needed, but in general it will probably never see the light of day again. With regard to 16mm and Super 16mm - most labs have a mixture of Super 16 and Standard 16 equipment, and the Standard 16 equipment doesn't have the relieved edges that are necessary for Super 16 film. To ensure that your Super 16 film doesn't get tangled up in a Standard 16 winder or something like that, then it is vital to identify it as Super 16 on the can and on the camera report sheet.

Q - Can rushes be viewed at the labs?

Brian - Yes, rushes can be viewed at the labs. We would need prior advice to make sure we have enough theatre or viewing space available and that your contact man was here in the lab - subject to that, it's no problem at all.

Q - If a film is cut using traditional techniques, what happens after the fine cut is completed by the editor?

Brian - Obviously, the first stage would have been to process the negative as it comes from the production and supply a rush print which the editor cuts. Once the film is cut, we would then hold a cutting copy

Technicolor
Hollywood ■ London ■ Rome ■ New Yo

BRIAN DALE

Technicolor Ltd.

PHONE: 020 8759 5432
FAX: 020 8759 5016 PRODUCTION

BATH ROAD
WEST DRAYTON
MIDDX · UB7 0DB
ENGLAND

GFMH
OFFICIAL
SPONSOR

Technicolor NO. 70940
BATH ROAD, WEST DRAYTON, MIDDLESEX Tel: 081-759 5432 Telex: (851) 22344

PINK Production Room Copy BLUE Cutting Room Copy GOLD Accounts Room Copy GREEN Camera Room Copy
WHITE Technicolor Copy

PICTURE NEGATIVE REPORT

PROCESS NORMAL + SEE BELOW

Technicolor RUSH PRINT VIEWING REPORT E 420897

GRADING COPY

VIA W.CARGO

screening with the grader - the guy who's ultimately going to balance the colour and density of the image - plus the cameraman, director, producer and usually the editor, all of whom can have creative input. Comments will be made by all present and the grader will take notes from rather generic terms like *we need more density, we need this colour* - whatever the changes are that are requested from the existing cutting copy. The grader will convert this subjective guidance into an objective assessment of client requirements. The negative will then be neg-cut, either in house or usually with a neg-cutting company. The big consideration here is that it is in the production's interest to talk to the laboratory about what they believe the schedule to be. The laboratory will be perfectly honest about it, they won't try and grab themselves more time than they actually need, but this particular stage is very important. It's where the original negative meets a pair of scissors and if there is too much pressure in terms of schedules, needing to see answer prints and check prints... let's say it's probably not desirable to put pressure on at this stage.

We would then print it, taking into account the comments that were made at the cutting copy show. We would look at it internally - the grader would assess it, to see if he had the result on screen which he anticipated getting - the result of the colour changes, modifications he'd made. He would probably put it back in for a reprint, once or maybe twice, in order to make sure he was confident with what he had and then he would be in a position to show that to the production. We would then screen that first answer print for the production. If there are any problems, we'll do a reprint, fixing the grading that the production isn't happy with - the production doesn't pay for this extra printing. The problem for us here is when you have four people all saying different things - *I want more blue - No, more red - I want lighter - I want darker* - you end up getting into a loop that you can never get out of. Everyone should be present or just one nominated decision maker for the production and the decision should be binding - it's important to avoid both Chinese parliament, repeat screenings or discussions, simply because one key person couldn't make it. That can cost time and is frustrating.

Q - Leaders can be a problem, i.e. they can be BBC or Academy - can you supply the leaders that you prefer to be used?

Brian - Yes, we would normally supply leaders on negatives and duplicates. The Academy count down leader is standard for independent productions. We could also supply the BBC leader, but it's important to nail down exactly which type of leader is going to be used throughout the production. For the matching sound leaders, simply use the Academy leader which can be bought on Wardour Street or wherever.

Q - If the master sound mix has been done, is it possible for that mag to be sunk up and the film screened with sound?

Brian - Absolutely. It can be run with separate magnetic sound (sep mag). However preferably, if the optical sound transfers have taken place, we would produce a married print for the first screening. Remember though, on first answer prints, neither Super 35mm or Super 16mm can have a married optical sound track, but you can run with separate magnetic sound.

Q - What is the optical sound?

Brian - The master sound can come to us in a variety of formats, optical disk, DAT and occasionally nowadays 16mm or 35mm mag. That master will be transferred onto film, with a special lab camera, as an optical representation of the sound. That optical sound can then be printed alongside the picture for a married print. When that print is screened, the projector can read the optical sound and the audience hears it. Digital formats are now well established such as DTS, Dolby Digital, SRD or SDDS, but the old style analogue optical sound always runs alongside it, just in case there's a problem with projection.

Q - How does blowing Super 16mm up to 35mm work?

Brian - Firstly, an Interpositive would be made from the Super 16mm A&B roll cut negative, at the same grading lights as the answer print that has been approved - so all the grading would then be locked in. Then we make a 35mm blow up Internegative from that Super 16mm Interpositive, and from that, 35mm prints. That means we have a 35mm printing master from which we can make as many prints as you want, perfectly graded, without touching the original negative. Alternatively, if you're not looking for many prints, maybe only one, you can make a direct blow-up from the Super 16mm negative. However, producing prints from an original cut negative is a process with which you must take a great deal of care as you don't have any protection should damage occur. Again you're talking about the material where all your hopes and aspirations are lodged. Also, because special care must be taken when printing from an original negative, the costs are much greater. It should always be practice to budget for an Interpositive to be made, at the earliest possible stage, for protection of the original negative - this is regardless of the subsequent handling and printing the original negative may or may not receive.

Q - What happens to the master neg once its been printed?

Brian - It will be vaulted. Most labs will store material, or you can take it out and vault it somewhere of your own choice. However, in the lab, it's secure and the conditions of storage (temperature & humidity) are maintained. It's not a good idea to keep it in your garage or under your bed.

Q - After the first answer print, are subsequent prints cheaper?

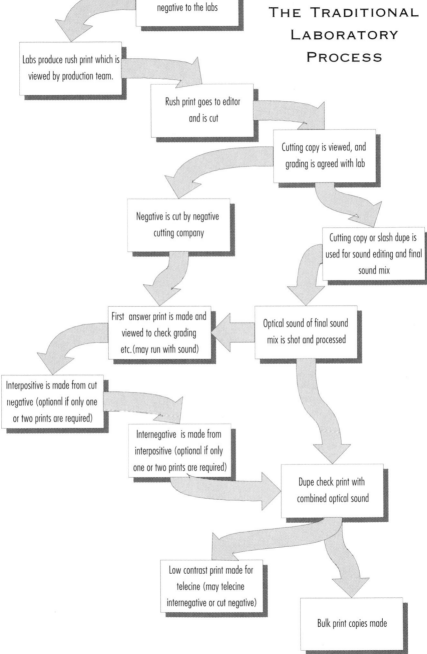

Main shoot sends exposed negative to the labs

THE TRADITIONAL LABORATORY PROCESS

Labs produce rush print which is viewed by production team.

Rush print goes to editor and is cut

Cutting copy is viewed, and grading is agreed with lab

Negative is cut by negative cutting company

Cutting copy or slash dupe is used for sound editing and final sound mix

First answer print is made and viewed to check grading etc. (may run with sound)

Optical sound of final sound mix is shot and processed

Interpositive is made from cut negative (optional if only one or two prints are required)

Internegative is made from interpositive (optional if only one or two prints are required)

Dupe check print with combined optical sound

Low contrast print made for telecine (may telecine internegative or cut negative)

Bulk print copies made

Brian - Yes they are. Any print from the original neg is going to be expensive by comparison with a print from a dupe (internegative). Most labs have a sliding scale of discount, depending on how many prints you are ordering on that dupe.

Q - What is the procedure should the master neg be damaged by the lab?

Brian - If the damage is on the Internegative, we would go back to the Interpositive and make a new Internegative for which the producer wouldn't be charged. If it's the master negative, then things become a little more problematic. I can only speak for this laboratory, but our procedure is to be totally honest with the production company, apologise and accept the ear bashing you're quite rightly going to get. All labs have commercial protection in their terms and conditions which effectively protects them from expensive claims due to accidental damage. A good lab wouldn't hide behind that and would be prepared to talk to you about what can be done to alleviate the problem. The neg should always be covered by other insurance anyway. That insurance would be provided by the producer and not the lab though. It's therefore vital for the producer to insure the negative, right up to the time that you get your Interpositive made.

Q - What is Super 35mm and how does it work?

Brian - Very wide images, commonly referred to as Cinemascope, are usually produced using a special anamorphic lens that squeezes the image when shooting and unsqueezes the image when projected. One problem with this is that the extra glass means you need more light to expose the negative properly and the lens hire itself adds expense. Super 35mm is an alternative to anamorphic photography. The image ratio is 2.35-1 and it's shot on normal 35mm film. You simply shoot the 35mm negative as normal, but with the viewfinder marked up for Super 35mm (so the camera operator knows where the edge of frame will be). As with Super 16mm, more of the film area is exposed (where the soundtrack traditionally lives). The camera operator must keep in mind that the image will eventually be widescreen (2.35-1) and so the top and bottom of the image won't be used - there will be markings in the camera eyepiece so everyone knows what the frame is. You then produce your rush print, grade it, neg cut it, all in the same way as normal 35mm. At the Internegative stage, on an optical printer, you put the anamorphic squeeze in. Then when you make the final projection print, it has the anamorphic squeeze and when it goes to theatre, they unsqueeze it on projection and put it back to wide screen format.

Q - So in the middle there is an optical process which is going to be slow and expensive?

Brian - Yes, but the extra lab costs may well be outweighed by the savings of not having to shoot with an anamorphic lens and don't forget, you use a greater negative area in shooting. It's simply a matter of paying your money and making a choice.

Q - Like the dubbing theatre the labs are expected to perform miracles in terms of grading - you're not able to turn blazing sunshine into the dead of night are you?

Brian - We'd have a pretty good go, but no you're right. There are limitations. However, effects like day for night are achievable, though less necessary with modern, high speed film stocks.

Q - What is the laboratory access letter?

Super 16mm to 35mm Blow Up

Stage 1 - Super 16mm Cut Negative - Once an answer print of this cut negative is agreed from a grading point of view, it moves on to Stage 2.

Stage 2 - Super 16mm Interpositive is made from the Cut Negative - this Interpos is low contrast and contains ALL the gradings agreed by the production company.

POST-PRODUCTION

Stage 3 - Super 16mm Interpositive is blown up to 35mm Internegative. Notice The Super 16mm aspect ratio (1.66-1) has been cropped down with a mask to 1.85-1 for cinema release (optional).

Stage 4 - Check Print is made and agreed by the production.

Stage 5 - Optical Sound Negative is made from master sound mix. This will be combined with Stage 4 to produce a combined, optical and picture Check Print. Note the digital sound encoded between sprockets on the left of the negative.

Stage 6 - 35mm release print, with combined optical sound.

Super 35mm -
Widescreen without anamorphics

Stage 1 - Super 35mm negative is cut - notice the aspect ratio (not on negative but in camera viewfinder). Notice also that more negative is exposed than on flat 35mm.

Stage 2 - Answer print is made to check and confirm grading.

Stage 3 - Super 35mm Interpositive is made from Super 35mm cut negative.

Stage 4 - 35mm Internegative is made up - The image is now optically squeezed, freeing up the area on the left of the frame for the optical sound track. This internegative now conforms to standard 35mm formats and includes the anamorphic squeeze.

Stage 5 - Optical Sound negative is made from master sound mix. It can be combined with Stage 6 to produce a combined, optical and picture, print. (Com Opt). Note the digital sound encoded between sprockets on the left of the negative.

Stage 6 - Combined Optical and Picture print (a check print will be produced before show prints). Note how the image is squeezed, and the optical sound on the left.

Stage 7 - Theatrical Projection - when the print is projected in the cinema, the projectionist uses an anamorphic lens to 'unsqueeze' the image, giving a very wide image.

Brian - It's a letter that specifies who has access to the negative. It could be for different people in different companies, or it could limit the number of prints. It's simply a means of controlling who has access to the material, usually the negative, internegative and optical sound. Typically, sales agents and distributors will need a lab access letter.

Q - Can you achieve artistic effects in the lab, like make Super 16mm colour neg B&W?

Brian - Yes. If you want to end up with a B&W movie, then there's a strong argument for shooting in B&W in the first place. However, if it's a decision that has been made after shooting, the lab can produce a new B&W negative through various intermediate stages although, it tends to look softer on screen than B&W original negative. Then there are the softening and mood effects which can be created by controlled negative exposure. I once talked to a producer about a particular cameraman who was very artistic, where artistic is 1 stop underexposed, very artistic is 2 stops underexposed, and very, very artistic is three stops underexposed. Seriously, it depends on the look you want. People do deliberately underexpose by a stop or so in order to get a harsh, grainy, appearance and overexpose for the opposite reasons although modern film stocks don't always react the way you expect, so you should always do tests. The earlier you talk to the labs the better. You should be shooting tests and viewing them with a grader.

Q - Is the Super 16mm frame the same aspect ratio as the 35mm?

Brian - It depends. If you're going to shoot Super 16mm on 1.66-1, you haven't got a concern. If it's to be blown up to 35mm for theatrical release, you should be aware that cinemas usually project at 1.85-1, so you would need to accommodate extra headroom at top and room at the bottom of the picture. The viewfinder in the camera should be set up this way by the camera hire company.

Q - What are the most common mistakes made by the production team?

Brian - Communication is obviously an essential factor. Not completing the information on the camera report sheets, making sure messages and comments are received, particularly with regard to cutting negative or moving negative about (which is always confirmed in writing). Also, always shoot tests with the camera and stock you have chosen before shooting a film.

Acme Films, 123 Any Road, Anytown, Somewhere, London

To - The Chosen Labs
Somewhere
London W11 5NP
21/11/2013

Dear Sirs,

We have granted to ANY DISTRIBUTOR, hereinafter called "The Distributor" the rights of Film Distribution, video, and television in TERRITORY on the following Film:-

YOUR MOVIE

This communication is your authority to allow the Distributor access to the following materials in your possession, for the purpose of manufacturing the Film and Trailer requirements:

LIST MATERIALS (Negative & SOUND for example)

It is to be understood that all costs in connection with the manufacture of their requirements are at the sole cost of the Distributor.

Also you will not impose any lien upon or against the materials by reason of any charge or obligations incurred by the Distributor. Three copies of this letter are enclosed for signature and return two copies to this office.

A Producer   *the Labman*   *A distributor*

Signed   Countersigned   Counter signed
Acme Film   Laboratories   Distributor

GLOSSARY OF LABORATORY TERMS

A & B CUTTING - *A method of assembling original material in two separate rolls, allowing optical effects to be made by double printing.*

A OR B WIND - *The two forms of winding used for rolls of film perforated on one edge only.*

ANAMORPHIC - *An optical system having different magnifications in the horizontal and vertical dimensions of the image. (Used for cinemascope style effect.)*

ANSWER PRINT - *The first Answer print is the first combined (action and sound) print produced by the laboratory from a cut negative for further customer grading comments. The final Answer Print is a print which has been fully graded and accepted by the customer.*

ASA or EI - *Exposure Index or Speed Rating to denote film sensitivity.*

ASPECT RATIO (AR) - *The proportion of picture width to height.*

CHECKER BOARD CUTTING - *A method of assembling alternate scenes of negative in A&B rolls, used for 16mm which allows prints to be made without visible splices.*

CINEMASCOPE - *A system of anamorphic widescreen presentation. (Trade name).*

CLONE - *An identical copy, usually referring to a digital tape.*

COMBINED PRINT - *A motion picture print with both picture and sound on the same strip of film. Also referred to as COMPOSITE PRINT/MARRIED PRINT.*

DAILIES (USA) / RUSHES - *Daily Rush Prints. The first positive prints made by the laboratory overnight from the negative photographed on the previous day.*

DENSITY - *A factor which indicates the light stopping power of a photographic image.*

DEVELOPING - *The chemical process which converts a photographic exposure into a visible image.*

DISSOLVE - *A transition between two scenes where the first merges imperceptibly into the second.*

DUPE - *A copy negative, short for duplicate negative.*

EDGE NUMBERS - *Coded numbers printed along the edge of a strip of film for identification.*

FADE - *An optical effect in which the image of a scene is gradually replaced by uniform dark area, or vice versa.*

FLOP-OVER - *An optical effect in which the picture is shown reversed from right to left.*

GRADING - *The process of selecting the printing values for colour and density of successive scenes in a complete film in order to produce the desired visual effects.*

INTERMEDIATES - *General term for colour masters and dupes.*

INTERPOSITIVE - *A colour master positive used as protection for the original negative and as a printing master from which the internegative is made.*

LIQUID GATE - *A printing system in which the original is immersed in a suitable liquid at the moment of exposure to reduce the effect of surface scratches and abrasions.*

MAG-OPT - *A motion picture print with both magnetic and optical (photographic) sound track records.*

OPTICAL SOUND - *A sound track in which the record takes the form of variations of a photographic image.*

PITCH - *The distance between two successive perforations along a strip of film.*

REVERSAL - *The processing of certain types of film to give a positive image on film exposed in the camera.*

UNSQUEEZED PRINT - *A print in which the distorted image of an anamorphic negative has been corrected for normal projection.*

WET PRINTING - *(See Liquid Gate). A system of printing in which the original is temporarily coated with a layer of liquid at the moment of exposure to reduce the effect of surface faults.*

WIDESCREEN - *General term for form of film presentation in which the picture has an aspect ratio greater than 1.33:1. i.e. 1:66, 1:75, 1:85, the latter being generally used for cinema presentation.*

POST-PRODUCTION

The Laboratory
New Technology
Paul Collard
of Soho Images

Q - I'm a film producer about to make a picture, I have no preconceptions about what post production route I should take, but I'm working on a low-budget and a tight timescale, and I want to cut non linear because I believe that is the way to go. What are the options I have - I need to end up on a 35mm print and I'm either going to originate on 35mm or Super 16mm and do a blow up?

Paul - You're going to develop your negative, that's definite. You're then going to want some means of viewing that picture and to quality control check what you've shot and also something you can have to edit with. If it's a feature film, it's going to end up on the big screen, so you're going to need, at some point, to check that the images you're getting are going to look good on the big screen. Therefore, it makes a lot of sense to put in your budget an amount of money for your first day's rushes to be printed onto film so they can be projected. You then have your rushes transferred on telecine to Beta SP, which is the most common format for feeding into a non linear editing system. You can then view and edit all your material on the non linear computer, say an Avid. By choosing this route, you save the cost of rush printing all your material, your sound synching can be done at telecine, so you don't have the added cost of audio mag transfers and synching - it's all done to the tape. At the same time as you sync your location DAT to the Beta SP, a copy DAT of all the used audio, with the same time code as the picture, is run off. You can then take those DATs with the EDL (Edit Decision List) you generate once you have edited your picture non linear and do an Audio Auto Conform prior to the final mix. The Audio Auto Conform transfers all the different sound takes used in the film, in sync with the final edit, to either disk or tape. You end up with a digital version of what used to be multiple mag tracks. Almost all films, especially low budget, are post produced this way now.

Q - What about the 24 - 25 fps issue?

Paul - Most features shoot at 24 fps (frames per second) but PAL telecine works at 25fps. There are two main ways of dealing with 24 to 25 frame conversions. The first method is telecineing at 24 fps, but recording onto BetaSP which is PAL at 25 frames. The telecine sorts it out by putting in two extra fields per second, so you end up with 25 frames of video in a PAL domain. A second of what you've shot is still a second of what you are working with. Alternatively, we can telecine at 25fps then Lightworks or Avid can 'slow down' the telecine from 25fps to 24fps playback. If you shoot at 25fps you do not need to bother about any of these issues. For micro / low budget features, yes, it's simpler with less opportunity for error. Things like TV's in shot and some HMI lighting also cease to be a problem. Ther's no reason why you can't shoot at 24fps, but if you intend to cut on a non linear system that isn't say a Lightworks or Avid, it won't be able to handle the 24/25 conversion. So for low / micro budget films, it is still recomended to shoot at 25fps.

Q - What specific problems with telecine should somebody be aware of in advance?

Paul - I think the need for the cameraman to maintain a record of his exposures is important so that we can put the negative onto an analyser and give him a printer light report. Framing is also important and I think it's important to shoot a framing reference test before you start the film. The actual aspect ratio that you shoot super 16 is not quite the same as the theatrical release print, therefore when framing up you must consider you are going to lose a bit of top and bottom. 1:66 (Super 16mm) to 1:85 (theatrical) is a 5% crop at the top and bottom for which you have to allow.

Q - If you are on location, how do you view your rushes?

Paul - There is controversy about what format you view the rushes in. One of the problems with viewing rushes for a feature off a VHS copy of the Beta in a hotel room with a hired TV and video is that you can't see that much. The focus puller is probably tearing his hair out trying to work out if he got the focus he wanted. A better way to do that is to view in a slightly higher format, such as SVHS or MiniDV. We supply all productions a VHS tape with a gray scale, framing reference and colour bars, so that the DoP can line up the monitor (some monitors are dark or too contrasty for instance).

Q - What if there appears to be a technical problem with the rushes?

Paul - If we or the production team see a problem on the rushes tape, we would produce a print straight away, screen it and supply the producer with a screening report.

Q - What are the advantages of this particular method over traditional film cutting?

Paul - In a nutshell, the real advantage is that you can dramatically cut down your post production timescale - time is money. If you have a non linear editing device on location or close by, and you shoot days one and two, by day four, the editor should have a rough cut of days one and two. When the director has spare time, he can have a look. By the time you've wrapped, three quarters of the film is already rough cut.

Q - If you were on the ball, within a week of wrapping, you could have a first cut?

Paul - Yes. It's good for backers as you can fire off very positive progress reports, show them scenes or even make a promo reel very quickly. It's easy to mock the film up and say this is 80% of what it's going to be, or even test it with a small audience to get a feel for it.

SOHO IMAGES

SOHO IMAGES @ SOHO GROUP 8-14 MEARD STREET LONDON W1V 3HR
TEL +44 020 7437 0831 FAX +44 020 7734 9471 MOBILE 07971 444 450
EMAIL paulc@sohogroup.com

PAUL COLLARD DEPUTY MANAGING DIRECTOR

Q - If you decided that you knew that your little low budget movie was never going to be screened on film, what could you do?

Paul - You could master to digibeta only, which means it can only be

NEW TECHNOLOGY TIPS

PLANNING
Always plan out every aspect of your post production route, well in advance. Especially with regard to film speed and time codes.

RUN UP
Always allow five seconds where both sound and camera are rolling before marking and calling action.

VIEWING
Watch your rushes on as high a quality format as possible, at least SVHS or MiniDV.

NEGATIVE
Never touch or cut the negative, especially before it has been logged and telecinied.

STORAGE
Keep your BETA telecine tapes and DAT copies safe. Never work from a dupe copy of your telecine.

screened from a video tape, but it will be much cheaper to do. There are two distinct routes - one is to do an overlength neg cut and telecine the negative whilst doing a fine grade scene by scene. The alternative is to do digibeta 'technical grade' (which is a neutral flat grade) of the rushes as you shoot, then when you 'online' the film you would do a digibeta tape grade. We feel that for ultimate grading, the over length neg cut is better than the tape to tape grade method.

Q - What are the most common mistakes you come across?

Paul - Not allowing enough time for run up on the sound. If they're shooting timecode then they need to allow 5 -7 seconds of the camera running and the sound running before the clapperboard in order to get sync. Another mistake is not testing the kit beforehand. You need to allow yourself a day or two testing, DATS in particular are notorious for creating problems. A lot of people start shooting on DAT and then go over to Nagra as DAT's are not that secure when it comes to time code - if time code jumps all over the place, you can go into post production with all kinds of sync offsets and that costs a lot of money to put right. A word of caution - when you are non linear editing, those original Beta tapes are your one and only link between your original film and your non linear pictures. The time code on those tapes is THE link to the edge numbers on the negative. If somebody messes with the time codes, for instance somebody else needs that Beta, *I'll go and make a copy of it,* and on the copy you use timecode that doesn't mean anything, then you start editing with it, the link between the time code and edge numbers is broken. You then provide an EDL to the neg cutter and nothing works.

Q - But it is possible to dupe that tape and ensure that the timecode is copied?

Paul - Yes, it's possible to clone it.

Q - Clone is the word, so you're asking for a clone, not a copy?

Paul - Yes. The important thing to understand about non linear editing is that there has to be an unbroken link between the timecode that the rushes

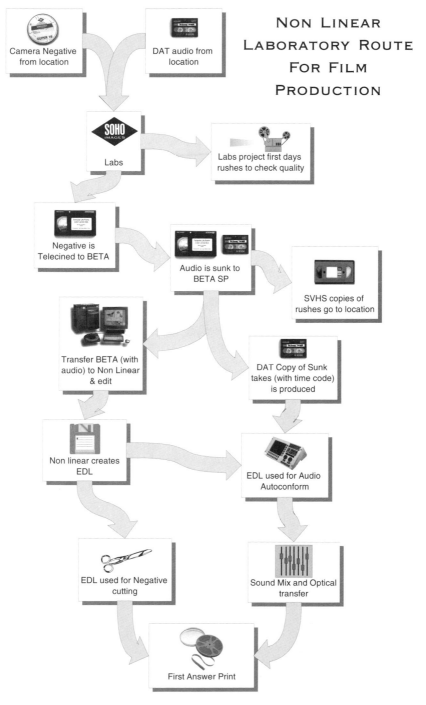

NON LINEAR LABORATORY ROUTE FOR FILM PRODUCTION

Camera Negative from location

DAT audio from location

Labs

Labs project first days rushes to check quality

Negative is Telecined to BETA

Audio is sunk to BETA SP

SVHS copies of rushes go to location

Transfer BETA (with audio) to Non Linear & edit

DAT Copy of Sunk takes (with time code) is produced

Non linear creates EDL

EDL used for Audio Autoconform

EDL used for Negative cutting

Sound Mix and Optical transfer

First Answer Print

POST-PRODUCTION

SHOOTING SPEED - 24FPS OR 25FPS?

This is a very common debate for new film makers - 'should I shoot my film at 24fps or 25fps?' There is a great deal of confusion on this subject. We would say quite adamantly, based on the post-production of three features, that shooting at 25fps is cheaper, easier and makes no discernible difference. If you must shoot at 24fps, perhaps because there is American money involved for instance, then bear in mind you will need an Avid Film Composer that can handle 24fps playback. Almost everyone in the business will say 'if it is a feature, it must be shot at 24fps.' This is wrong, you can and should shoot at 25fps. Shooting at 25fps ensures a cheaper and easier post production process, and again, there is no discernible difference between the two.

As a general rule, no matter what speed you shoot at, always inform all people in the post production process exactly what speed the film is working at so that costly errors are avoided.

Note - these points only apply to the UK and other PAL or Secam countries. If you are post producing in NTSC (in the USA for instance) ignore these points. Also note that many stages in post production have been omitted from the flow chart on the next page, it serves only to illustrate the major implications of post production at 24fps opposed to 25fps.

1. You will use 4% less film stock shooting at 24fps than you will at 25fps.

2. If you are utilising a computer editing post route, you will need to hire a more expensive Avid Film Composer to edit your film on if you shoot at 24fps. If you shoot at 25fps you will be able to post produce on virtually any editing solution, two VHS decks if you like!

3. If you shoot at 25fps, you can take advantage of older and cheaper non flicker free HMI lighting.

4. If you shoot a scene with a TV in shot, that shot MUST be shot at 25fps anyway, regardless of whether the rest of the film is shot at 24fps.

5. When you complete the film, if you cannot afford to do a pitch adjustment on the soundtrack, there will a slight audio discrepancy. If you shot at 25fps, on video it will play at the right speed, in the cinema it will sound slightly slower. If you shoot at 24fps, in the cinema it will play at the right speed, on video it will sound slightly faster. Of the two, shooting at 25fps produces a more attractive compromise.

6. When completing a low budget film, running time will be an issue. Your film will more than likely be short. If it was shot at 24fps and the running time is 83 mins in the cinema, when you telecine onto video tape it will speed up to 79 mins - too short. If you shoot at 25fps and the running time is 83 mins on video, when play in the cinema it will be 87 mins long. There is a 4% trade off, no matter whether you shoot at 24fps or 25fps, so use this trade off in your favour and shoot at 25fps.

7. If you shoot at 25fps, you can compile a picture online from your BetaSP telecine tapes. This will give you a broadcast quality picture that you can show investors and distributors. You cannot do this at 24fps with either picture or sound conversion processes.

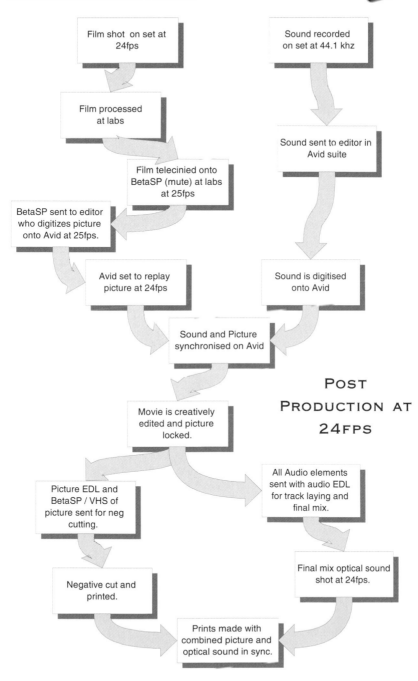

Film shot on set at 24fps

Sound recorded on set at 44.1 khz

Film processed at labs

Sound sent to editor in Avid suite

Film telecinied onto BetaSP (mute) at labs at 25fps

BetaSP sent to editor who digitizes picture onto Avid at 25fps.

Avid set to replay picture at 24fps

Sound is digitised onto Avid

Sound and Picture synchronised on Avid

POST PRODUCTION AT 24FPS

Movie is creatively edited and picture locked.

All Audio elements sent with audio EDL for track laying and final mix.

Picture EDL and BetaSP / VHS of picture sent for neg cutting.

Final mix optical sound shot at 24fps.

Negative cut and printed.

Prints made with combined picture and optical sound in sync.

TIME / FOOTAGE CHART

Time/Minutes	35mm @ 24 fps	16mm @ 24 fps	16mm @ 25 fps
1 mins	90ft	36ft	37.5ft
5 mins	450ft	80ft	187.5ft
10 mins	900ft	360ft	375ft
15 mins	1350ft	540ft	562.5ft
25 mins	2250ft	900ft	937ft
30 mins	2700ft	1080ft	1125ft
60 mins	5400ft	2160ft	2250ft
90 mins	8100ft	3240ft	3375ft
120 mins	10800ft	4320ft	4500ft

16 frames 35mm = 1ft
40 frames 16mm = 1ft

were transferred with and the key edge numbers on the film. That is reliant upon that film roll not being cut or broken down in any shape or form, until it is logged against the timecode of the video tape. It can be broken down after that because it is all now on a computer, it is stored and any timecode we can get to on the edge number. But for arguments sake, if there was damage to the neg, or somebody cut a shot out before it had been logged, the whole relationship just fails. It's very important to appreciate that the non linear edit is not your film, you do not have a product until you've gone back and cut the negative. It is that chain between the key numbers and timecode that is vital.

Q - What basic advice would you offer?

Paul - Always involve your production house and laboratory from the start. You'll get good advice based on the experience of many productions and you will be able to agree a method of attack. If you don't tell them what you're doing, and you reveal the parameters to them after you've started or at the last minute, it could mean that you've taken the wrong route. Try and think of everything you want to do and ask questions. Bare your soul and you'll get good advice.

Q - Essentially put everyone in one room, and nobody leaves until everybody understands the process and knows the route that has been chosen.

Paul - Yes, we've had projects where we've called a pre-production meeting with the camera crew, the sound recordist, the editor, the director, producer and, sound post production company and other representatives of post production. And we say *right, we're going to start this on such and such a date, we're going to do this and this is the way we want to do it.* That couple of hours is worth it's weight in gold.

Q - There is a new technology where the film is post produced entirely digitaly? What is this?

Paul - Our system is called Spirit Datacine. It is a lot like post producing for television, but using the telecine at film resolution. So you get all the benefits of what has traditionally been used for broadcast TV, but at film resolution. In lay terms, we scan the whole film into the computer, put it all together, view it and check everything is as wanted, then scan it back out onto film which then becomes the master negative. Currently, I would guess is that this new route would cost more than the traditional interneg/interpos route. We have done two features from S16, and a third is going through now, so it is already proven that the system works and the quality is very high.

Q - The advantage is that you lose things like interpos / internegs, you don't go through the horrible nightmare of grading opticals that have just been cut into your final 35mm?

Paul - Precisely.

Q - What about grading?

Paul - Film grading is very good, considering how it is done, but it has limitations. Using the Spirit route, manipulation of the image is considerably more sophisticated. It is much more akin to the tools you find in software like Photoshop whereby you can isolate colours, shadows, gamma, or apply an overall look etc. It is very powerful. Things like dissolves and slow motion effects are no longer limited by traditional lab technology, so your dissolves can be any length and we can interpolate slow motion shots so they remain smooth unlike step printing. Also, re-use of footage is not an issue, nor are frame overlaps for A&B roll negative cutting.

Q - Things that were done traditionally like matte paintings were difficult to do in camera or as an optical effect, but this way they become much easier?

Paul - Matte painting is a good example of something that has been enhanced by digital tools. Joins can be made so much better for instance, and colour hues can be matched more easily.

Q - Talk me through the process from step one.

Paul - You shoot the camera negative just as you would shoot any other feature film. You have your rushes delivered to the cutting room on BetaSp, they are digitised into the Avid, then the film is creatively edited and locked off by the editor and director. The editor also knows that he does not have any of the constraints of film post production so dissolves can be any length for instance. The next stage is that the EDL is sent to the neg cutters who break the neg down and do what is called an overlength neg cut - a cut that includes handles on either end of the shots. This cut neg is then put on the Spirit Datacine and it is graded. This grade would take about a week where you have much more power to grade than you would with the traditional film grade. Once you have locked off the grade, there would be a day when the film is actually telecinied and 'digitised'.

Q - When you say it goes onto a Spirit, a Spirit is like a telecine...?

Paul - A Philips Spirit Datacine is a high end CCD type telecine but the main feature of it is that it has the ability to record out to standard definition video and high definition video in real time. But

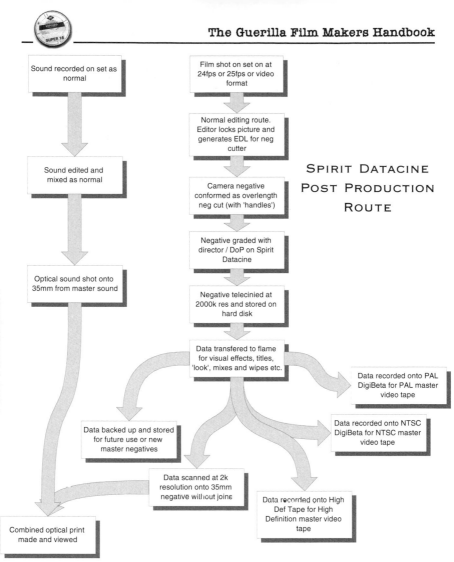

SPIRIT DATACINE
POST PRODUCTION
ROUTE

POST-PRODUCTION

for this scenario, we are looking at features so it records the information out as data which goes down at about 6 frames a second and is put onto an Inferno. Inferno is a very powerful visual effects tool that can manipulate the image as much as time, imagination and budget can afford. It takes so long because the frames are very high resolution (2k) and it is an enormous amount of digital data. So at the start of week two all the data is sitting on the Inferno discs as a complete movie. Then the EDL is applied and all the shots drop in place on the time line within seconds. Then all the effects such as dissolves and wipes are rendered, which could take a few hours. You can then start work on all the effects shots and titles etc. To save money you could prepare a lot of material and instruction on lower end machines and bring it all into this final Inferno stage. Things like title cards could easily be produced using Photoshop, as long as image sizes were correct and

The Spirit Datacine is much like a normal telecine, but because you are working at film res, you are able to work in a way that previously only ever took place in darkened theatres or the bowels of the laboratory.

file compatibility's were checked in advance. You would also create a trailer at this point.

Next the movie is viewed and any final colour tweaks can be made. At that point a lock off is achieved and then the data is then scanned onto 35mm negative, which takes about ten days currently. Remember, as it is coming from one continuous source, there will be no joins in your master negative. It can also output all your other masters, including HiDef, PAL, NTSC, even data for encoding onto DVD. And the quality is superb as it is not derived from another generation of film, then telecine. The data is then backed up and stored away so that if you need to make any new negatives in the future, you can, and they will be as good as the original as they are made from a digital master.

Q - Can you mix formats?

Paul - Yes, you may want a movie where you want to input some DV or Digibeta but also have the benefits of 35mm where you need it. This method is totally flexible in so much as you can input anything at the Inferno stage and it will sort out sizing issues and things like that.

Q - So you make all your masters from that one thing?

Paul - Yes, from your new film negative you can make a check print, multiple release prints, inter-positives and dupe negatives for distribution around the world etc.

Q - How much does it cost?

Paul - Currently it is about 30% more expensive than doing the traditional lab route. However, when you offset that against the quality issues, the headaches of having to make multiple telecines, and the sheer creative freedom this process provides, it becomes a very attractive proposition. Remember though, technology is moving very quickly and it may have dropped in price or changed technologically by the time this is read (Feb 2000).

POST-PRODUCTION

Editor
Eddie Hamilton

Q - What is a Film Editor?

Eddie - The editor is the person who takes the footage shot by the crew and cuts the shots together to tell the story in the best way possible, shot by shot, a scene at a time, making sure the cuts flow smoothly and the audience understands the story and emotions being communicated by what they're watching. They have the responsibility to ensure that everyone's best work gets up on screen – a combination of the best performances, lighting, makeup, costumes, and sets. The editing process is also the last chance to correct any mistakes made during the shoot. If the script has problems, you have to fix them with re-structuring or ADR (lines recorded by the actor in a studio after the shoot). Similarly, if an actor's performance is disappointing, you have to cut around it. You cannot make a silk purse out of a sow's ear, but if there is life in the rushes and you have a good story to tell, taking the time to find the moments that work and then piecing them together to create a movie is very rewarding.

So it's very creative, but it also requires an immense amount of organisation. Every single frame of film has to be carefully logged when it arrives in the cutting room so that it can be found at a moment's notice. Any inaccuracy can cause problems and if not spotted can cost a lot to put right.

The editor is also an ambassador of diplomacy. Sitting in the same room as the director working on their masterpiece for months takes its toll – emotions get charged, especially if there is a producer who disagrees with the director. The editor should serve the director's vision, but must speak up if he thinks the director is mistaken. It's important to try and stay objective and see the film fresh each time. Sometimes you have to be ruthless with the cut to improve the film. It's not personal. Everyone wants the best film at the end of the day.

Q - How do you edit film?

Eddie - Traditionally, cutting film meant having a room filled with rolls of film and magnetic tape (the rushes), looking through these on a machine called a Moviola or Steenbeck, then literally splicing the film together shot by shot with clear tape. The system worked well, but it had disadvantages. It took time to locate a trim (an offcut from an edit) and if you wanted to change the cut it wasn't easy to return to a previous version. Plus, the more you handled the cut reels, the dirtier, dustier and more scratched they became. The advent of fast, cheap computer technology changed all that.

The leading computer-based film editing system is the Avid Film Composer. It is the simplest, fastest and most feature-rich system on the market today. All the rushes reside in digital form on the Avid's hard disk drives, giving instantaneous access to any one of the hundreds of shots that make up a movie. The Avid allows you to keep several versions of a sequence to compare them, and the image quality never deteriorates or gets scratched, it physically can't! Because you work from video, the resolution is not as good as working on film, but this will change in the coming years and the positives massively outweigh the negatives in my opinion. There are other benefits of using a computer to cut a film – you can produce dissolves and other optical effects to see how they look in the cut. For test screenings you can produce an incredibly rich soundtrack with ADR, sound effects and temporary music. Every frame of film has a timecode associated with it and the Avid takes care of that all the way through the editing process (as long as the information you give it in the first place is correct).

Q - What is a good edit?

Eddie - Well, there is no simple answer to this – whole books have been written on this very topic by people who've had a lifetime of experience editing films!

Q - OK, so what makes a cut between two shots work?

Eddie - The cut should be fluid (unless deliberately being obtuse). The flow and rhythm of the cut should not interrupt the audience's passage of concentration. It should feel natural. For me, it's a gut reaction, some kind of instinct. As you play through a take you feel the cut should be HERE, or you sense an edit needs a couple more frames on the outgoing shot. When you watch it back you just intuitively sense if a cut is working or not.

There are some grammatical rules to follow (though these should have been taken into account when shooting the film). When cutting between shots try not to cross the line (the imaginary eyeline between the actors on screen – see elsewhere in the book). If you do, it will feel wrong. Just try it. You can sometimes get away with it if there's no option and you're careful but generally it's a bad idea. If someone or something exits frame right, they should enter the next shot frame left and vice versa. Picture a car chase along a road. If the lead car zips off to the right of the camera, it always enters to the left of the camera (unless you pick up the chase at an entirely different location). Try imagining it the other way. Of course, in some totally frenetic action sequences almost anything goes, but especially on a low budget movie it can look incompetent if you do this the wrong way.

When cutting dialogue I often find a natural place to cut to another character is on punctuation, where there's a natural pause in the delivery. I have read a theory that says it takes at least two frames for the audience 's eyes to travel from one part of the screen to another between cuts. I would tentatively agree with this – if I'm editing a conversation I tend to trim the incoming shot back a couple of frames and find the cut feels smoother. Another tip, all subconcious emotion is shown through the actor's eyes. Even the subtlest movements give away a character's thoughts.

EDDIE HAMILTON

FILM EDITOR

email: eddiehamilton@email.com
website: www.eddiehamilton.co.uk

Pace

Ever seen a film that was too fast? We've all seen films that are too slow. Cut your movie as tight as you can, then cut it some more.

Mechanics

Do the audience actually understand the plot as you intend? It's easy to think you are making something clear but the audience doesn't get it.

Screenings

Hold test screenings to see if your film is working. Ask questions about plot, characters, your title, and invite people to rip your movie to shreds.

JOE BLOGGS PRESENTS...

A JOE BLOGGS MOVIE

PRODUCED BY JOE BLOGGS

Technology

Shoot at 25fps! Make sure you fully understand all the stages of post production so you do not make costly mistakes.

Reshoots

Plan small sequences or cutaways to bridge drama gaps or plug story holes and shoot them over a long weekend with minimal crew.

Take a break

You can get too close. After you complete your first fine cut, try and take some time off to reflect on it and the comments. When you come back to it you will see it with new eyes.

Titles

Put all your titles at the end. No-one is interested in who all your crew are, get straight into the action and drama. But, as the producer / director, do give yourself the first credit at the end.

Effects

Don't go crazy with effects just because the Avid can do slow motions, freeze frames and fancy titles. It will all need to be replicated at the optical house at great expense.

Q - What makes an edited scene work?

Eddie - As you have no doubt discovered when writing or reading a script, most scenes have a beginning, middle and end and are designed to carry the plot forward, developing the characters along the way. This may seem obvious, but you should take it into account when cutting a sequence together. How does the scene start? Where are we? Who's here? Has time passed? Subconsciously the audience will be asking these questions when the scene starts. Unless you're setting out to confuse them, you should try and set the scene as soon as possible so that they can get on with digesting the plot and characterisation. Sometimes, you can start with an exterior of where we are (e.g. a crowd outside the cinema for a premiere before cutting inside to show who's attending). Or maybe start on a detail and reveal the situation, (e.g. a digital counter counting down from 30 seconds, track out to reveal a small bomb under a table, track out to reveal two characters having dinner unaware of their predicament). These are obvious examples but the audience immediately knows what's what.

Now, consider what the function of the scene is. Which character do you want the audience to identify with? Who's story is this? What plot details must the audience understand so that we don't lose them? For example, consider a scene where a woman is asking a man to marry her. She might beat around the bush a bit, nervous. At the start of the scene we might stay on a medium

Backing up your project on a daily basis is essential. If the Avid is stolen or crashes, or the house burns down and you don't have a backup you are, well er, screwed. If you do daily backups you will have only lost one days work at the most. Use Zip disks as they are Mac and PC friendly and will fit the whole project comfortably, unlike a floppy which is too small for a feature. It's a good idea to have two backups in two different places. Yes, I know we are paranoid.

two shot showing both the actors. Then she plucks up courage – do we go in for a close up? Maybe. Do we want to show her extreme anxiousness? Or do we want to see the man getting intrigued about her emotional turmoil? The answers are never clear cut, but if you know what the audience needs from the scene, it can certainly point you in the right direction. All the time you're listening to your gut feeling about whether the flow of the cuts feel right. At the last minute, the woman can't do it. She's trying to win a bet with a friend by getting engaged before the week is out but decides it's not worth it. The scene builds to this moment and without an explanation she leaves. The man is left standing wondering whether it was the garlic he ate for lunch. Do we stay on a close up of his confusion, do we see his POV (point of view) of the woman walking away, or do we cut out to a wide shot of him standing alone and bemused? Any of these will work, depending on what you want to say. But for sure the scene has drawn to a close. We've had a beginning, middle, and end. Very few or even no words have been exchanged, but we've understood and the edited scene has done its job.

Q - What makes a movie work as a whole?

Eddie - When you've finished the first cut of a film, the fun really starts. Just cutting the scenes and putting them in script order is only half the battle. If I'm cutting during a shoot I normally have a first assembly ready a couple of days after the wrap party. The editor and director will watch this and as a general rule it's very average and probably poor – it's too long, the pace is all over the place and there will probably be bits missing such as special effects or second unit shots. But this is to be expected – every editor I've spoken to says the first assembly always looks terrible. However, it's also exciting because it's the first glimpse that all the work so far has been worth it.

First you work through the film with the director getting the scenes how he or she wants them. You've been cutting alone so far, according to what you think works. Of course it's their film and they may have other ideas about how to approach a scene. It's a long process of going through the rushes re-working each scene according the director's taste – with your input where necessary. Then you take a look at the film as a whole. Are the characters introduced correctly? Is the plot working? Does the pace lag anywhere? Is it too fast? As a rule, the film is probably too slow. How many people have seen a film that's too slow? Then ask yourself if you have ever complained about a film because it was too fast or too packed. Sometimes what worked well in the script seems redundant on screen. Sometimes the performances are lacking something. Maybe the relationship between the two lead characters is misfiring somewhere. Maybe a character is unnecessary now. Maybe some of the jokes just aren't funny.

What did you think of the film? Incredible European feel to the film making it unlike anything I have seen from this country. The story + acting was great, but the music was amazing - great purchasan!

Was the film:		Would you recommend the film?	
Excellent	☐	Yes, definitely	☑
Very good	☑	Yes, probably	☐
Good	☐	No, probably not	☐
Fair	☐	No, definitely not	☐
Poor	☐		☐

How would you describe this film to your friends?
As a spooky socialistic story seen from the eyes of a child

What was your favourite bit in the film?
The end - the whole 'Lizzie remembers' bit

What was your least favourite bit in the film?
It would have been nicer to have had more of Kevin + Lizzie

Did you feel disbelief or confusion about any part of the story, if so what?
Why didn't Lizzie's mother defend her to Kevin's mother - they never met on screen?

Which scenes did you like or dislike?

LIKED	DISLIKED
1. Debt collector getting his come uppance	1. Why were the heavies paid off with a cheque?
2. Lizzie unable to sleep - masize cupboard	2. Scientists - they just arrived.....
3. The whole see search - very funny + frightening	3. Why didn't vicar reappear?
4. The vicar - quiet and tense	4. Why mother so quick to trust Journalist - yet another man?

Please tick the box next to each word/phrases below that you think describes this film (as many/few as you like).

Original	☑	Feel good ending	☑	Well performed	☑
Dreary/dull	☐	Unsurprising	☐	Not enough action	☐
Involving	☑	Emotional	☑	Good storyline	☑
Improbable	☐	Stereotyped	☐	Charming	☑
Entertaining	☐	Too sluggish in parts	☑	Not humorous enough	☑
Foolish	☐	Gripping	☑	Predictable	☐
Agreeable	☐	Not my sort of film	☐	Too inaccessible	☐
Perplexing	☑	Has great music	☑	Humorous to watch	☐
Stimulating characters	☑	Credible	☐	Too drawn out	☐

What did you feel about the film's pace?

Moved just right	Moved too fast	Moved too slowly at start

If you think parts of the film moved too slowly, please list which parts or parts they were.
The intro duchy bits - the first 15 mins were very bitty + slow, then it really picked up. Hospital bit a little slow too.

Are you		What is your age?			
		Under 15	☐	30 to 34	☐
Male	☑	15 to 17	☐	35 to 39	☐
		18 to 20	☐	40 to 44	☐
Female	☐	21 to 24	☑	45 to 49	☐
		25 to 29	☐	50 and over	☐

What do you do? Well, work through the problems. Can I move some scenes around to get the pace more even? Can I intercut some scenes? Can I cut out this joke altogether? Can I shoot some pickups to act as clever cutaways or help with the plot? Slowly but surely you'll work out the answers over several weeks of cutting. Then screen your cut to a select audience of people whose opinions you value and who aren't afraid of being brutally honest about the film. You want to fix problems, not hear how wonderful it is when you know it isn't. Watching your film with an audience is like watching it afresh. You suddenly sense when they begin to fidget. You sense when they're gripped. You know if a joke has hit the mark. Ask them questions afterwards. You'll soon find out what the problems are. There'll be comments like – *But isn't he her brother?* – and the characters aren't related at all! The audience will come back with all kinds of comments that you hadn't even thought of because you're too close to the film.

Back to the cutting room for more changes, more careful honing. You will probably have to cut some scenes you love because they just don't "play" to the audience or aren't needed in the film any more. Screen the film again for a larger number of people. Get them to fill in a questionnaire. Read the forms and listen to what they're saying. Don't take them as gospel, but don't ignore them. And gradually you will get closer to the day when you lock picture.

There is a saying that films are never completed, just abandoned. This is partially true because you will never be 100% happy with the end result. The director will have had this vision for the film that can never be matched. You will always have to compromise. But with patience and creativity you will find the movie hiding in those rushes and it will take on a life of it's own. The audience will watch it and forget that they're seeing dozens of cuts flickering across the screen – they will be engrossed in the story being told and then you'll know you've done a good job.

Q - What common mistakes do you see?

Eddie - The way to avoid mistakes is to ensure you understand the entire post production process from the moment the neg leaves the camera right up to the premiere. Make sure you know about processing, telecine, timecode, digitising, neg cutting, opticals, sound tracklaying, mixing, grading and delivery requirements. These are all places where you can trip up and it will cost you time and money to fix, neither of which you will have a lot of, probably. Ask an editor to explain these things to you and if he or she doesn't know, don't give them the job.

Q - What advice would you give to a low budget movie maker?

Eddie - Don't rush into production without really working on the script and developing it until you know it's the best it can be. If in doubt about any technical aspects of film making, ask - people will be happy to explain. Know who the audience is for your film and don't bore them. Have test screenings (even small ones), because they will help you understand where your film needs more work. Finally, if you're shooting anywhere that uses PAL, SHOOT AT 25 FPS. It will save you ENDLESS headaches later in post production. Good luck!

Left - when you hold a test screening, pass out simple questionnaires at the end, invite your audience to be brutal and ask them questions that you want answering about the plot, character dynamics, pace, title etc. Remember, there is opinion 'I liked' or 'I didn't like' which you can't do much about, but 'I didn't understand' or 'I was bored' you can do something about. Have lots of pens at the ready too.

Non Linear Editing
Barry Stevens
of Avid

Q - What is an Avid and how does it work?

Barry - In the past, movies used to be cut on film. Nowadays almost everything is cut on a non linear editing system like an Avid. An Avid is a computer that allows you to digitise video and audio and store it on hard drives. You can then take those digitised clips and arrange them in any order you want, cut them up, add effects etc. When you make an edit it is non destructive, you simply tell the Avid to play a given sequence of shots. This means you can have as many versions of your film as you want, without ever damaging a single frame.

Q - How easy is it to learn to use an Avid?

Barry - Once you have grasped the fundamental concepts behind editing and non linear editing in particular, learning how to use an Avid is quite simple. There are a number of training courses that are very good and worthwhile if you intend to hire an Avid to cut a low budget feature film. There are many layers to the software and a two day intensive course will save you time in the long run as you will spend much less time scratching your head. The basics of using an Avid, simple cutting, checking audio, dissolving video, titles on pictures etc. can be taught in a hour.

Q - Aside from the computer, what other bits of equipment come with the Avid?

Barry - You'll need a machine controllable VTR, probably a BetaSP, so that you can digitise the picture and sound with timecode, your link back to those master tapes and your negative. You'll also want to think about things like a CD player, TV monitor, speakers etc., although most of this should come with the Avid you hire.

Q - There is some confusion about the difference between memory and hard disk storage.

Barry - Yes. Some people refer to the hard disk storage as memory, which is incorrect. The memory is what is used by the computer as part of it's normal operating process. Every Avid has enough memory to operate optimally. However, hard disk space, or storage space, is limited by how much you buy or rent. Usually it comes as external drives, often in 9gb sized drives. You connect it to the Avid and you can then digitise material and store it on the drive. When you run out of storage space you'll either need to get more drives delete or consolidate some of the media to make room.

Q - How much video and audio can you store on an Avid?

Barry - It is dependant on how much hard disk space you have, and at what resolution you digitised. Normally, you would start work at an offline resolution. This means that the image is highly compressed so that it doesn't take up much space. It also means that the image is degraded, however, even high compression rates now give very good picture quality. I would say that for an average micro budget film you would need at least 36gb of storage.

Q - Is the picture quality on an Avid very good?

Barry - It is a little fuzzy at high compression rates like 20:1, although it's good enough to get into the story and performances. At the top end it can handle uncompressed images which are as good as they can possibly be. One of the valuable things an Avid brings to bear is the fact that after you have your cut, you can transfer it to VHS and view it, even with an audience. This way you can see if the overall pace of your movie is working, a problem overlooked by many new film makers. It's easy to see when a scene isn't working, but harder to sense if the whole two hours is working as it should. Remember, you can have as many different cuts or versions of your film as you like without having to use up any more space.

Q - What film rate should you shoot at, 24fps or 25fps?

Barry - If you are post producing in a PAL country, it is easier to work at 25fps as you bypass many of the technical issues thrown up by 24fps post production. You can post produce at 24fps very easily on some Avids, but not all. However ALL will work at 25fps. This is becoming less of an issue but as of today, if money and experience is in limited supply, I would advise shooting at 25fps.

Q - How does my film get from the lab onto my Avid?

Barry - Normally, the film will be processed overnight and telecinied onto BetaSP sometime in the early morning. If you can afford it, and it saves a lot of headaches, you could have your sound transferred and sunk up at the lab (this sound process is not available if you shoot at 24fps). That BetaSP comes back to you, you digitise it, break it down and start cutting. It is very fast to cut non linear and it's possible for an editor to cut a whole days rushes in a day so that the producer and director can see the cut scenes the day after they were shot.

BARRY STEVENS
Consultant Chief Editor UK

Avid Technology Europe Ltd
European Headquarters
Pinewood Studios
Pinewood Road Iver Heath
Buckinghamshire SL0 0NH
United Kingdom
direct tel +44 (0)1753 658464
tel +44 (0)1753 655999
fax +44 (0)1753 658600
mobile +44(0)7768 156661
E-mail barry_stevens@avid.com
E-mail barry@bazza.ftech.co.uk

Q - Can you add sound effects and music?

Barry - The sound quality on an Avid is CD quality. Older Avids have two, four or eight tracks of audio, but newer ones, essentially the ones you are likely to hire, have eight, even twenty four tracks of simultaneous audio. This means that you can add

GFMH
OFFICIAL
SPONSOR

COMPRESSION - PUTTING ON THE SQUEEZE

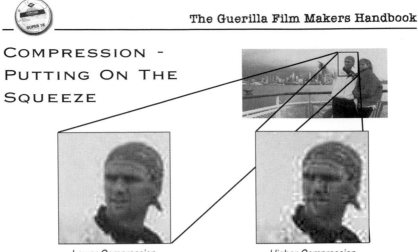

Lower Compression -
Higher Quality but uses more disk space

Higher Compression -
Lower Quality but uses less disk space

sound effects and music easily. I wouldn't recommend mixing a feature film this way, but you could track lay it using an Avid. There are also a host of audio effects tools like expanders, compressors, echo etc., although if you are going to do a mix in a studio it is probably best to let them do that, not because the Avid isn't good enough, but because the editor probably won't have time to be a sound expert.

Q - What happens when you want to make a print?

Barry - When you have locked picture you send an EDL to the negative cutter. You'll need to speak to them to find out what format they want, but it will probably be a CMX 3600. An EDL, or Edit Decision List, is a list of all the edits you have made. The neg cutter can trace back all the editorial decisions you made on the Avid and match the master negative to it. The Avid will detect duplicate frames and any overlaps if you tell it to do so - on film you cannot re-use the same footage without making optical or digital copies. As we move toward entirely digital post production, frame overlap and dupe frames will cease to be an issue.

Q - What happens if you can't afford a print initially?

Barry - You will be able to use your master BetaSP tapes and re-conform the picture at a high resolution. If the Avid you hired doesn't have a high enough resolution, you could take your tapes and Avid project on disk to an online facility, or to an Avid that does have higher resolutions, at least 3:1, 2:1 or best of all, uncompressed. This means that you could have a broadcast quality master of your film for very little extra money. If there are any picture grading issues, you can deal with them, as well as adding effects and titles. This is very useful as you will be able to show your film on video tape in the knowledge that it will look as good as the master. It's worth mentioning that a dissolve on film looks different from a dissolve on video. It has a steeper curve whereas a video dissolve is linear. Some Avid's have film dissolves which mimic the way film emulsion will behave in the lab. It's worth bearing in mind that your dissolves on the Avid may behave slightly differently in the lab, it's especially important if it's a critical dissolve.

OTHER SYSTEMS? BARE ESSENTIALS

There are many semi pro and pro non linear edit systems such as *Premiere, Final Cut Pro, Speed Razor* etc., but can they do the job of post producing a feature film?

Real World Power	**Machine Control**	**25fps**	**EDL Export**	**Storage**
Will the software handle a ninety minute project? It might on paper, but what about the real world? Find someone else who did it and see what problems they encountered.	You MUST get machine control or you won't be able to generate an accurate EDL in order to reconform your negative later.	Of course, if you shoot at 24fps, you will need to use a more expensive 'film composer' which can do the maths. Shoot at 25fps.	You must be able to generate an accurate and rigid EDL. Check for CMX3600 support and make a test EDL for your neg cutter.	Hard disks are cheap now, so it won't cost too much to upgrade. Don't expect your home PC or Imac, straight out of the box, to be able to handle post producing a feature film.

Q - What happens if the Avid crashes, you're burgled or the suite burns down?

Barry - There is an autosave facility so that technically, unless the computer crashes seriously, you should never lose more than a few minutes work. If the computer is lost or stolen then you will be able to recreate the entire programme in just a few hours, that is if you have backed up your project. It's worth carrying a Zip disk around with you so that you can back up your project at the end of each day. You could take that project to another Avid and be up and running from where you were in a matter of hours.

It's worth mentioning about version compatibility as there are many different Avids in the field. If you cut on a v5 Avid, which is very old, then moved onto a v8 Avid, that should be fine. However, you cannot move from a v8 Avid onto a v5 Avid as it won't read the project files.

Q - What about Mac and PC issues?

Barry - As long as the computer can read the disk, and you aren't trying to work backwards in terms of the software version, there shouldn't be too much of a problem. Certainly with newer Avid's this just isn't an issue. However, Avid projects are not compatible with other non linear editing systems, you can't put an Avid project on a Discreet Logic Edit* system for instance, although you can export an EDL and take that into any other professional non linear editing system. There are no guarantees with EDL import/export so do tests.

Q - What about special effects?

Barry - The Avid is capable of sophisticated effects, but you must remember that if you do an

POST-PRODUCTION

Suggested Avid Non Linear Post Production Route

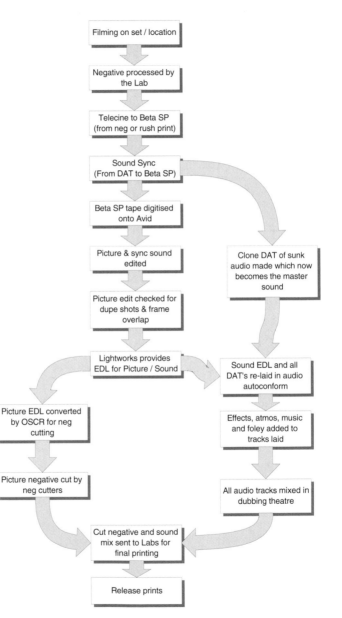

Filming on set / location

Negative processed by the Lab

Telecine to Beta SP (from neg or rush print)

Sound Sync (From DAT to Beta SP)

Beta SP tape digitised onto Avid

Picture & sync sound edited

Clone DAT of sunk audio made which now becomes the master sound

Picture edit checked for dupe shots & frame overlap

Lightworks provides EDL for Picture / Sound

Sound EDL and all DAT's re-laid in audio autoconform

Picture EDL converted by OSCR for neg cutting

Effects, atmos, music and foley added to tracks laid

Picture negative cut by neg cutters

All audio tracks mixed in dubbing theatre

Cut negative and sound mix sent to Labs for final printing

Release prints

POST-PRODUCTION

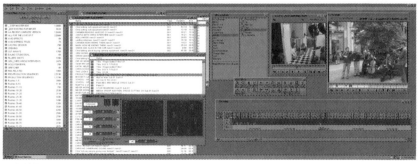

Avid Express, currently the Avid entry level machine. If you shoot at 25fps, Avid Express would easily cope with post production of a feature film.

effect on the Avid, that will probably need to be replicated either digitally or at an opticals facility. This is a costly business. Be aware that simple things like applying a slow motion effect to a shot could be costly (if you want slow motion, shoot it in slow motion on the day).

Q - Could you shoot on MiniDV and digitise it into an Avid?

Barry - Yes, but MiniDV is a domestic format. There are time code problems which mean that you have to be careful when digitising. If the camera was reset halfway through a tape, the timecode might reset and cause problems when you came to redigitise at higher resolutions. Remember you probably won't be able to use your camera as it isn't a controllable edit deck, so you might need to make BetaSP copies or even rent a professional DV deck from which to digitise. If you are post producing from a digital format, when you come to your final online, you must use an Avid with a digital input to ensure you get the best possible quality.

Q - What common mistakes do you encounter?

Barry - Many film makers, outside of editors, don't fully grasp the technology, or indeed, post production. It is essential to ask post production questions, or better still, hire a post production supervisor.

Q - What advice would you offer?

Barry - Preparation. Do as much as you can before shooting. Preparation will avoid so many headaches!

POST-PRODUCTION

Music Supervision
Ian Hierons
of Faber Music

Q - Film music is a complex business, what rights need to be cleared to use music for a film?

Ian - If you want to obtain permission to use a song by a well known band or artist, there are two types of rights you have to obtain. The first are the rights to the composition or song, which you obtain from the music publisher. There are several multi-national publishing companies like EMI Music Publishing or Warner Chappell Music, as well as thousands of smaller independent ones, they grant you the right to synchronise a composition to the film, hence the name 'synchronisation rights'. Secondly you then have to licence a recording of that composition or song, from the record company that owns the recording.

For example "Yesterday" was written by one person, but has been recorded by numerous recording artists. Therefore several record companies may own recordings which you can choose from, but there may be just one publisher. The producer will then pay a fee to both the record company and the music publisher for the use of one recorded song. If however you choose to re-record the song then you would only pay the publisher and you the producer would own the rights to that recording.

If however the song has been co-written by two, three or four writers there may be separate music publishers for each writer, although the larger publishers usually control the world-wide rights to a song. Smaller publishers may only own the song for specific territory and you will have to talk to other publishers who own rights in other countries. The same can be true of record companies who only own a recording for a specific territory, although they may have the right to licence for the world on behalf of other companies.

Obtaining synchronisation rights to one song can sometimes involve building a complex web of contracts from several record companies and music publishers, but thankfully not always. Also don't fall into the trap of only clearing a song for limited territories and then find yourself repeating the exercise months later if the release of your film has grown internationally.

Q - How do you find out who owns which particular rights?

Ian - Either look on the back of a CD or telephone the Performing Rights Society (PRS) in London or the Mechanical Copyright Protection Society (MCPS). The PRS collects performance royalties on behalf of music publishers and can tell you who publishes which song (if you know the names of the writers) and the MCPS can tell you which record company owns which song if you know the performer.

Q - How much does it cost to use a song in a film?

Ian - This is really down to the process of negotiation. The factors that will determine the price are; your film project, how the song is being used and the playing time, who the artist or group is and how famous they are and also how contemporary or popular the song is. As a very rough guide some publishers start at around £1,500 per 30 seconds of use. So if you have two minutes, that's 4 x £1,500 which is £6,000 for the publishing rights only. Then you have to add on top of that the record or 'master' rights from the record company. Some publishers are cheaper than others, however sometimes the larger ones are more expensive. Often if they know you really want a specific song then that may inflate the price. You may also be able to negotiate concessions if you buy a bundle of rights that includes several compositions from one publisher. The rights you usually buy are the rights to put the composition in the film, i.e. to use it theatrically, on cable TV, pay TV, satellite, free TV - in a specific territory, or world-wide and also on a set number of videos.

Q - You said you can get deals by saying I'll use five of your copyrights. Is it possible to get a better deal in return for the rights to release a sound track record?

Ian - Some record companies may be happy to release an album and perhaps include some songs in a package for you to use on the film. Some may pay you an advance and still ask for payment for using their records in the film, others may not. Some may waive their fee in return for the rights to the album. It all comes down to trading the value of each set of rights and sound track album rights can be sometimes hard to value. Record companies are now much more cautious than five or ten years ago, simply because they paid huge advances to film companies for albums that then did not sell. The model works better in America where you have the corporate synergy between record companies and film companies like Sony, Time Warner and Polygram.

A note of caution! - Merely licensing the right to use a record and a song on the sound track of your film does not give you the right to use that song on a 'sound track' album. These are separate rights and are negotiated separately. You can negotiate both sets of rights at the same time but a major record company will not grant rights to you to pass on freely to another record company without prior approval over their identity and without knowledge of their royalty accounting procedures.

Q - You mention royalties, where do they come in?

Ian - Royalties are generated from music performance on radio, television, cinema as well as live performance and also from the duplication of tapes, records and compact discs. These are collected and distributed by the PRS and MCPS and their sister societies world-wide. For a sound track album you will get a percentage of the retail selling price from the record company that releases the album and they will pay a royalty to other record companies who own tracks

Faber Music Limited

ff

3 Queen Square
London WC1N 3AU
Telephone: 020 7833 7942
Fax: 020 7833 7939
E-mail:
ian_hierons@fabermusic.co.uk

IAN HIERONS

compiled onto that album. There is also a percentage of the retail selling price paid to the music publishers of the songs on the album on behalf of the writers of those songs. Royalty accounting can be very complex and it is often advisable to place the onus on the company releasing the sound track to pay any third part royalties directly. You do not want to be obliged to prepare royalty statements every three or six months for a sound track album.

Q - If you want an original score, how do you go about getting a composer?

Ian - Have a look in the sound track section of a record store and talk to agents and managers. The large talent agencies represent composers as do smaller specialist composer agencies. They will send tapes for you to consider.

Q - When is the composer brought in?

Ian - Usually towards the start of post production. Although I would advise talking to a composer as early as possible as it is a common problem that they don't have enough time. Also another problem is that the music budget is often eaten into if the film has gone over budget. I always talk to them very early and try to work to a fixed budget as this can lead to better results.

Q - How do deals with composers work?

Ian - They work for a fee, paid in instalments, usually half on signature of a contract and half on delivery of the score or recorded music. The producer then pays additional sums for the recording sessions in a studio and for the orchestra or musicians. Some composers will work for a fee that is inclusive of their salary, recording and orchestral costs. Depending on the fee a composer may also retain music publishing rights to the music ('the copyright') created as these rights have a value that can be realised at a later date, by selling them to a music publisher. Or the producer may negotiate to keep them as he/she is commissioning the work.

Q - Do they organise the orchestra?

Ian - Orchestral Fixers are used to employ the orchestra and musicians. In the UK they work to very strict union rules with regard to payment and hours worked.

Q - If the composer retains the publishing rights and we sell the film in Taiwan, do we then have to pay the composer a slice of that payment?

Ian - No - you are buying the composer's performance and the right to exploit that copyright with your film. You would pay no more for showing the film in Taiwan unless you did not have the right to do so. The performance of the music in the film would however generate performance revenue that we discussed earlier.

KNOW YOUR RIGHTS

PUBLISHING RIGHTS
Copyright owned by the author or composer of the work, literally the notes on the page. These become public domain 50-75 years after the death of the composer dependent on the country. These rights are controlled by a music publisher on behalf of the composer or author. Where there is more than one writer, then two or more publishing companies may own a share of the work.

RECORD / MASTER RIGHTS
Copyright in the recording of a song or composition owned by either a record company or the entity that has paid for the recording and thus owns the master tape. Different record companies may hold the copyright to a recording in each separate country.

SYNCHRONISATION RIGHTS
Rights granted to a film maker to 'synchronise' the copyrighted music in conjunction with the film. Publishing rights granted for the composition or song by a music publisher on behalf of the composer or author. Record / Master rights granted by the record company to use a recording of that song or composition.

Q - How does a director work with the composer?

Ian - You hire a composer, talk to them, let them read the script, show them a rough cut of the film and then go through a process of spotting where the music is needed. Often in the States, there is also a music editor and a music supervisor who would work out where the music was going to start and end and also what the dynamics and the function of the music is. Sometimes editors will use a 'temp' score (pre-existing music) on a film to give an indication of the style required. Also, by this stage you will have worked out where the songs are going to go and know how much music there is going to be. Composers like as much time as possible, but are usually given 3 - 5 weeks. A lot of composers will do mock up scores, using synthesisers, enabling you to hear what they have done, and discuss changes before you go into a studio and hear it with a full orchestra.

Q - Can you use synthesisers if the music budget is prohibitively tight?

Ian - Synthesisers are as much a creative consideration as a financial one. For example listen to Eric Serra's score for *The Big Blue* (Luc Besson), which is a brilliant mix of electronic score and real instruments. If the music budget is tight then I would tend to suggest that a composer does something more interesting than just trying to recreate an orchestral score with keyboards.

Q - If for instance, you want to release the music on disc a year later and you have that separate fee to pay to the performers, is that fixed in advance or is that something that is renegotiated later?

193

Ian - When you record music with an orchestra you can choose just to pay for the work of the musicians on the film or you can pay a 'Combined Use Fee' which also covers sound track albums. You would also have to pay an album royalty to the composer, generated from the sales of the album. This percentage would have been fixed in their contract.

Q - How much does it cost to hire an orchestra?

Ian - Musicians are paid for each session which lasts 3 hours and are also paid for any overtime. PACT has a very useful booklet on the subject. I would suggest employing an Orchestral Fixer to organise it for you. Many scores are now recorded in mainland Europe as this can save orchestral costs, but then you will have to pay for travel and accommodation.

Q - Who could release the sound track album ?

Ian - Major record companies like Warner Brothers and EMI own sound track labels. There are also several independently owned specialist sound track companies. They would want to know who is releasing the film in each territory, how wide, what the P&A spend is and how can they tie in the sound track in the publicity.

Q - Is it usual for a low-budget film to get a sound track album deal?

Ian - If the film becomes a hit and is seen by many people and the music is good then the album could have a shelf life of many years, think of *The Postman* or *Diva*. There are no rules, but generally if the film is going to have a very limited theatrical release, a sound track album deal is very unlikely.

Q - Something like the Young Americans had a lot of contemporary hit songs in it, how much would the production company get for that album if they sold it to EMI or whoever?

Ian - I don't know the details of that deal. However as we discussed earlier, a record company may pay an advance to the production company, or may agree to provide a certain number of tracks for the film and album in return for the right to release the album. You can negotiate a trade off on a compilation type album. However a lot of score only sound tracks don't even get advances from record companies. Score albums have to be re-mixed and edited (the 'conversion cost') and although that money will be paid by the record company it will be

Composers and their agents will gladly send you copies of their work on CD or cassette if they believe there is a feature film available for scoring.

recouped out of your royalty, so in a way they are paying an advance.

Q - When is the best time to talk to record companies?

Ian - Once you are in production. They are not really going to be interested in talking to people when they are in development because there are thousands of scripts in development that never get made. It's just a waste of time for them.

Q - Where can I get a list of record companies?

Ian - There is a trade publication called Music Week that publishes the Music Week Directory which lists all the record companies and artist's managers.

Q - Am I correct in saying that if a new band is 100% behind the project, they will do it for free in return for the exposure and percentages down the other end?

Ian - The record company and the management company must be 100% committed as well. The agenda of the record company is to market a band and sell records and to recoup the massive cost of recording. If your plans for the film fit their agenda and schedule then there is a basis for a deal. A band providing services for free Is another matter and depends on how a deal is structured and who stands to gain the most from the situation, the artist or the film.

Q - What is library music and how does that work?

Ian - Library music, which also known as 'Production Music', came into existence for companies that wanted pre-recorded off the shelf music, it now covers the whole gamut - rock, jazz, funk, and everything else. The clearances are obtained through the MCPS and cost £280 per 30 seconds for a world-wide licence for cinema, television and video use. You simply register with the MCPS and they send you an information pack.

Q - Can you release a sound track album built from library music or does it just cover synchronisation rights?

Ian - The initial fee only covers synchronisation to the film, you then pay additionally for sound track album use.

Q - For instance, we thought of using some Holst as we believed he was out of copyright, having died over 50 years ago. However, we found that if we wanted to release our film in either America or Japan, he also had to be out of copyright there and therefore dead for 75 years.

Ian - Yes. Up until recently music fell out of copyright (and became 'public domain') 50 years after the death of the composer or writer, in some countries it is now 75 years and some music has therefore come back into copyright. The EC are trying to ratify it at the moment.

Copyright problems can occur in different countries. Under UK legislation, Rachmaninoff, who died over fifty years ago (1943), would now be public domain and out of copyright. Other countries, including the USA have a time limit of 75 years which would mean Rachmaninoff is still in copyright there.

Q - When a composer is out of copyright can you do whatever you want with the music?

Ian - You can do whatever you want with the composition, but not with a specific recording of that composition, because that recording is still owned by a record company.

Q - When we made White Angel, we discovered there was an extra fee we had to pay in America, why was that?

Ian - Performance royalties are generated when film music is played in a cinema. In the US there is no performance income from the cinema so the producer has to pay a fee, by law, to the PRS in the UK for using a UK recorded score in America. (See diagram).

Q - Is that something the sales agent would take care of?

Ian - No, it is usually a delivery requirement from the production company.

Q - What is a music cue sheet?

Ian - A music cue sheet is basically a chronology of all the music that is used in the film. It details how it is used, (foreground or background/front title etc), who the songwriter/composer is, and names the publisher and record company. A cue sheet is then sent to the PRS and one is given to each publisher whose music you have used.

Q - What is the differentiation between background and featured music?

Ian - Background is music heard by the actors, for example, it's coming out of a radio, from a juke box or played in a nightclub. Featured music is music that is not heard by the actors, for example, an opening title song is featured.

Q - On the first film that we did, we got a friend to write the music with a synthesizer, are there any problems doing that?

Ian - There are no problems, but I would ask you two questions. Did you like it? And did it work for the film? Beware of people who haven't scored films before, beware of using songwriters who

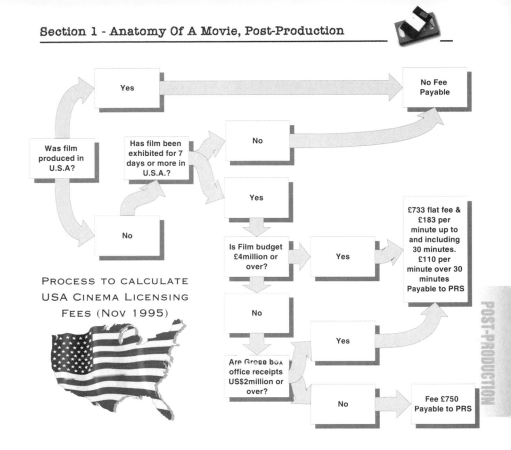

PROCESS TO CALCULATE
USA CINEMA LICENSING
FEES (NOV 1995)

think they can score a film because it is a different discipline. Always look at the composers credentials and the training they have had, and beware of inexperience. If you have a very tight budget talk to composers studying at the NFTS or other film schools. They will understand the discipline better than a friend with a synth. Although there are more composers than work for them to do, so talk to everyone you can.

Q - Do you have any final advice?

Ian - Producing music takes a lot of time and effort to get it right. People always have problems with music either because of inexperience, lack of money or both. Seek advice from someone who has experience and can advise you on the best approach, either a fellow producer, a solicitor or a music supervisor. Also talk to music publishers who may offer a range of services for the film maker.

Music Composer
Simon Boswell

Q - When does a composer first get involved in a film production?

Simon - There's no normal scheme of things, I've been involved from script stage and at the very last minute. However, the most common thing is that the production will concentrate on finishing the picture and it will be very close to a finished edit before they start thinking about music.

POST-PRODUCTION

Q - Do you ever get a phone-call from a producer, saying 'what are you doing tomorrow and for the next three weeks?'

Simon - That's rare, but it happens. I prefer to be involved at the last minute as the nightmare for a composer is things changing all the time, not only from a technical point of view, it becomes a real pain to rewrite for different lengths or for scenes that disappear altogether, but because creatively, it does my head in to have the ambience of the film changing all the time. I'd prefer to be watching it as a punter, if you like, to get a very instinctive response to an almost finished film.

Q - How does a film producer get to a composer?

Simon - Usually they've seen something that I've done that they like, or they've heard from friends or people in the business, then they'll call me direct and we'll just talk about it. Then if I'm interested, the next thing is to talk to my agent about the business side of things.

Q - As a composer, what do you need to actually produce the score?

Simon - I need as near to a locked picture as I can get. A final edit on Umatic videotape with visual SMPTE timecode on it, which also refers to the audio timecode on one of the channels of the audio. I can then synchronise and lock all my equipment to it. Like the majority of composers now, I'm very much computer based so that I actually write locked to picture. My keyboards will record every move I make, every note I play.

Q - If the decision was made to stay with a digital soundtrack, as opposed to a traditional orchestra, do composers have all the equipment to do it?

Simon - I have my own studio, and if I'm doing it all myself, I can finish it here.

Q - How good are synthesisers compared with ones that we all heard in the eighties?

Simon - It's a very personal thing what you actually do with the technology. Whether you're trying to emulate an orchestra, or you're trying to do something original with the technology in a different way. Everyone handles it differently. I've done scores where they simply couldn't afford an orchestra and would say, *please can you make it sound like an orchestra.* Yes, I'll do that. And then there are others like *Hackers* where we don't think a real orchestra is going to work with the film, let's make it as synthetic or as artificial as the environment, which is obviously computers.

Q - How large a band do you need to get a real big orchestral sound?

Simon - A good example would be *Jack & Sarah.* I had done an earlier synthesised version and the production now wanted it with real instruments and a full orchestrated score. We recorded that with 65 players which is an average sized orchestra. The cost of doing that I would estimate at $175k, but that's with a top orchestra and a top studio.

Q - But you could do it for considerably less?

Simon - Yes, you could do it for less if you're prepared to juggle around the components. What you could do is use a much smaller group of musicians and add samples to it. A lot of people do it because you can get a more interesting sound. Or, you can go abroad, which is the other scenario that is always coming up. There are certain orchestras in Eastern Europe where they are much cheaper and you can get a *buy out* deal as opposed to a *residuals* deal.

Q - What you're saying is that you can lay down the basics of the music with samplers and synthesisers and then you can bring in your violin soloist?

Simon - Yes, to give a human aspect to what you are doing. And vice versa, you can use a small orchestra, and then use synth pads to thicken the sound without really being aware of it, just to make it sound bigger. And of course you can use sounds that an orchestra can't do.

Q - How do you deliver the final music mix?

Simon - If they want a lot of control over the music during the mix, then you break the component parts of the music down into separate stereo tracks, for example, if there's a lot of percussion drowning out dialogue, they could be taken down whilst leaving the other elements, such as strings, mixed up. I've done a lot of films where I've just delivered a stereo mix and that's it. Without doubt, that's the cheapest and easiest way to do it. In that case, the final music is usually supplied on DAT.

Q - What are music cues?

Using synthesisers, composers can now 'mock up' the final score. If push comes to absolute shove, then this type of score can be used in place of an orchestra. It doesn't necessarily sound like an orchestra, but as long as it supplies the correct emotive qualities, it can work just as well.

Session musicians aren't cheap, but they do bring that big orchestra feel to your movie. Some orchestras in Eastern Europe are more cost effective, and still excellent musicians. Pictured, Jerry Goldsmith conducts one of his scores.

Simon - Strictly speaking, my job starts when the picture is locked and you have spotted the picture. Spotting the picture means going through the film and saying *we want music from here to here* and so on. 1M3 for instance would be the third piece of music on reel one. Very often they've done temporary music that has been pulled from other films or albums, usually the director or music editor has dug around and found stuff that's pointing the composer in the right direction. Having listened to the temp music, you would then sit with the director and discuss with him what you think is required. How much you're left to do yourself is variable and depends on the director.

Q - When it comes to the soundtrack album, do you have any control over that?

Simon - Yes. I always redo everything for the soundtrack album, not only remix, but rewrite, use bits of dialogue and special effects to make it interesting, because a lot of scores are just lifted from the final mix of the film and I think they're really dull. I try and spice it up a bit as a listening experience and I've been very involved with the albums that I've made.

Q - Do film makers have a tendency to want to overscore or underscore a movie?

Simon - Usually they want you to do wall to wall music and then cut out what they don't want.

Q - Are you involved with the songs that are used in films?

Simon - I'm involved in discussions with the director on a creative, not a budgetary level. Often they hire music supervisors who make legal clearances of tracks and get them as cheaply as

Music software for sequencing and recording is now extremely cheap. Cakewalk for the PC and Mac is an excellent program that could easily be used for the creation of a sophisticated musical score. 'Lite' versions often appear in computer mags, and prices start at £20! Beware though, just because you have the tool, doesn't mean you are a craftsperson able to deliver the goods.

TEMP SCORE	EFFECTS	PUBLISHING	WALL TO WALL
Track lay a temporary score so that you can test screen the film and give the composer a feel for what you want.	*Music and effects often clash. If you know there is going to be a series of loud effects, get the composer to dip the music to accommodate.*	*Try and hold onto as much of the publishing rights as possible, it might represent one of the only revenue streams you'll see from the movie.*	*Avoid too much music as it will deaden the ears of the audience so that when you really need it, the impact is gone.*

possible. It's a very highly developed department in the US and becoming more so over here.

Q - What are the common mistakes that producers make when it comes to the music?

Simon - Producers always under-budget and as a result they ask the impossible. They're incredibly unrealistic. The thing about getting bands and good songs is that it's expensive. Record companies know what they're going to charge these days and it all adds up, I had a phone call today from a production manager who's putting a new film together asking me what I'd advise them to put in the budget. That's quite an intelligent call to make but very rare. The commonest mistakes that I've encountered are to do with the songs aspect, leaving it too late to license the ones you need. That happened with *Shallow Grave*, it's happened with *Jack & Sarah*, and it's happened with *Hackers*.

Q - What can a production do to make your life easier?

Simon - The big thing is not to keep editing the film whilst I'm working on it. I guess having a director who knows what he wants and is very polite and straightforward about it is also good. Aside from that, having a sensible budget. The other thing to remember is that whilst you're watching the film over and over, everyone else is going to see it just once, and very simple things are often the most effective. Music is often thought of as a means of fixing things in a film. There's no question that music transforms a film, but above and beyond that? I think people will say, *this scene really doesn't work - fix it.* And that's very often why scores get thrown out, because music is the very last stage in the production before people have to admit that their film is crap. So if they score it, and the film still doesn't work they blame the music. What can they do? They can't reshoot it, so music has a terrific weight of responsibility.

A videotape of the final, locked edit of the film with SMPTE time code is all most composers require for them to produce an original score.

Production Music
Russell Emanuel
of Extreme Music

Q - What is library, or production music?

Russell - For the last forty years library or production music has been available, initially on vinyl and tape, and now on CD. This is music that can be bought off the shelf at a fixed price and put into a production. It's cheap, fast and nowadays it's excellent quality.

Q – How many library companies are there in the UK?

Russell – There areover 70 in the UK and they are administered by the MCPS.

Q - What is the MCPS?

Russell - The Mechanical Copyright Protection Society represents music publishers and composers, and collects and distributes royalties due for the recording or music in the UK.

Q - How does it work?

Russell - If a producer wants to use library music, they first need to ensure they are registered with the MCPS. This is a straight forward process and completely free. MCPS will send them a pack of information containing all the information on rates and what type of clearance they will need. Once they've registered with them and knowing the kind of music they want, for instance it might be a minute of Bach or twenty seconds of Rap etc., the producer can then call the libraries. Pretty much every style of music is catered for. CD's, which are also free, will be sent out and once you, the producer, have decided what music you will be using, you only have to fill out a licence application form, detailing what you've used, how long the cue lasts and what rights you want to clear. Music is sold in thirty second blocks. If you use twenty seconds, that's still charged at thirty seconds. And obviously, for a feature film, you are going to want to clear world wide rights. The producer is then invoiced for the music used.

It's a good idea to make sure all this paperwork is cleared before you do the final mix for your film, just to make sure you haven't used more than you can afford or there are other problems. You must also remember that all library music must be included in the music cue sheet, with information about the composer, performer and publisher.

Q - How much does it cost?

Russell - Rates are based on a published rate card and are dependent on the exploitation.

Therefore music used in an advertisement is more expensive in corporate video. You should contact the MCPS for a full and current breakdown, but for feature film use worldwide it currently costs £325.37 per thirty seconds. For just TV it gets even cheaper, £129 for world terrestrial TV for instance. If you know you are only going to sell to some territories, you can get the price down even more.

Q - So you can have the Royal Philharmonic Orchestra on your movie soundtrack for that?

Russell – Yes, we have 40 discs of the RPO, not some obscure Czech orchestra. And there are other top artists too. Library music has been accused of being a little dull and grey. What we wanted to do was to bring some fight back into it so we engaged top artists to write for us, artists from Aswad, Whitesnake, Dire Straights etc.

Q - So by using your library music a new filmmaker could access top talent at MCPS rates?

Russell - Exactly.

Q – And because it's digital, you can just drop it straight in to your cut?

Russell – Yes, the CD's we are sending you are essentially clones, not copies, of the masters.

Q – If the film was a hit and then they wanted to release a soundtrack album, the producer doesn't have clearance to use the library music - what should they do?

Russell – They would come back to us and we would cut a new deal. The last feature film that we did was *Everybody Loves Sunshine*, which starred David Bowie and Goldie. I would say that 80% of the music in that film was ours. I don't think people realise that a lot if it was library music and we are getting calls now to release a soundtrack album. It's funny when you read reviews and they say that the soundtrack to this film was awesome - and it's our library music!

Q - What advice would you offer a new film maker?

Russell - Speak to us before making any decisions because the music you are looking for may already exist in our library, or another library, and you won't have to go through the hassle of paying for composition, perform-ance, recording, contracts etc. It's a one stop shop with us.

russell emanuel

The Extreme Music Library Plc
Greenland Place
115-123 Bayham Street
London
NW1 0AG

Tel: 020 7485 0111
Fax: 020 7482 4871
email: russell@xmusic.co.uk

MCPS - 29-33 Berners Street, London, W1P 4AA
Tel: 020 7 306 4500 Fax: 020 7 306 4300

Sound Design
Paul Hamblin of Boom

Q – What is sound design or sound editing?

Paul – Essentially, sourcing sound effects, either from libraries or custom recording, then track laying them against the picture. On a more aesthetic level it is about looking at the picture and making it shine, enhancing the light and shade through sound. The soundtrack should always move the story on in an elegant and clever way.

Q – Isn't sound just dialogue, sound effects and music?

Paul – Not at all. Of course it is those things, but it is so much more. The main role of sound is to make a scene run in real time as opposed to all the bits of dialogue that get joined together. It can smooth the edges. It also tells the story outside the picture frame, creating a world that you can trust and believe in.

Q – From a low budget filmmakers point of view, sound can be used to create production value?

Paul – Yes, you can have helicopters passing over, or bullets flying everywhere when on the set there was just an actor in an army uniform having dust thrown at him.

Q – Is the pacing of the sound important?

Paul – Without question, you can be economical in order to create contrast. *The Matrix* was masterfully handled from this point of view, often there was a great deal of stuff going on in the image where there was little sound, but enough to keep it alive. By keeping it kind of empty they achieved great clarity and character whilst allowing the hard bits to have real impact. They also had a good idea about focus and the sound can focus the story. In life, your ear will guide you to any individual thing that you want to listen to at any particular time. You should try to achieve that balance in your film. Use the sound to guide the story, perhaps a scene where one character is talking to another, but really listening to another who is behind them for example. You could drown it out in the mix, or subtly mix it so that the audience understands, from, their own personal experience, what is going on.

Q – What is interesting here is that when you listen to the soundtrack of a movie it sounds so effortlessly mixed?

Paul – It is often a massive amount of work with enormous attention to detail. It takes a lot of effort and is labour intensive to make something seem simple.

Q – Where can you source sound effects?

Paul – The sound effects libraries give you a lot of choice. It is also easy to go out and record your own, but not in London as the skyline is generally too noisy. A lot of people now have DAT recorders or even minidisk recorders that produce excellent quality, provided they have a half decent microphone.

Q – What should a new film maker do if they have little or no money for sound editing?

Paul – If they have any acoustic appreciation about them they could do it on basic computer equipment using semi professional software like Adobe Premier. This will allow you to lay multiple tracks alongside each other and against a digitised picture. However, you need to go in to a dubbing theatre and mix it in the end as you need to produce an optical soundtrack for cinema, but in terms of putting the sounds in the right place, pulled off CD or recorded yourself, as long as you spend enough time, you could create an excellent soundtrack.

Q – How long will it take to track lay a low budget feature?

Paul – I would give yourself as much time as you could. I wouldn't be thinking of three weeks or something if you are going to do it properly and by yourself.

Q – What are the common sound mistakes that you come across?

Paul – Preparation - people put good sound effects in place, very abstract sometimes, but they put them on one track, or break them up in a disorganised way. It's important to keep effects separate so the mixer can do their job. For instance, keep gun shot sound effects on one track, telephone or RT effects on another so that each go on a seperate fader. The channel on the mixing desk can then be equalised to get the optimum effect from that type of sound.

Q – What about things like sound and music fighting?

Paul – The tendency with big scenes which have dynamic music is to go for big sound effects. If everything fights, it can make the sound mushy or hard. Advice to the sound editor who puts the sound effects in place is not to be too precious about whether it gets used in all its glory or not, because the film should have an organic and natural feel at the end.

Another common mistake is to do with sounds off screen, when the sound is telling the story outside of the image. If you have got a tram in vision coming right at you and you have a poor sound effect, the combination of sound and picture will make that sound effect work. However, if you don't have the tram in shot, the lack of

TRACK GROUPS AND WHAT THEY MEAN

Dialogue Tracks (mono)
Keep dialogue tracks clean and bright, where needed use ADR (dialogue replacement), but be mindful that ADR can sound pretty bad.

Sound Effects Tracks (mono and stereo)
Track lay an effect for as many things as you can. Differentiate between effects that will stay mono and are from the perspective of the characters (such as doors and switches), and effects that will be in stereo and add acoustic punch (such as police sirens and thunder claps).

Atmosphere Tracks (stereo)
Don't be afraid to lay several thick atmosphere tracks and mix them as they can provide a very attractive stereo image. Use atmospheres to help create continuity during a scene, and also to help illustrate that a scene has changed by switching to a different atmos track.

Foley Tracks (mono)
The movement of the actors in the scene need to be brightened by a foley artist, a person who will add these with expert precision and clarity. Don't be afraid of going a little over the top, very rarely do you make a loud swishing sound when you turn your head but you do in the movies.

Music (stereo and mono)
Always in stereo (except when it comes from a prop in a scene such as a TV) and sparingly placed. Avoid drowning out your sound mix with music and use it only when you really need it.

Tools
A dubbing mixer will have tools like echo and reverb (used for churches, canyons etc.), a noise gate (that can kill sound below a certain level, excellent if you have too much reverb), a notch filter (to help get rid of continuous sounds such as a fridge or the camera). Don't let these tools lull you into a false sense of confidence, get it right in the track laying.

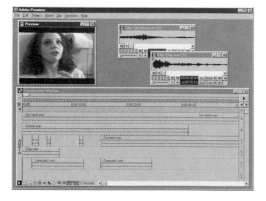

You can track lay the sound in your film with a number of semi-pro and domestic computer tools such as Adobe Premier. Using either SPDIF digital input / output, and by pulling effects directly off CD, you can stay 100%, maintaining acoustic excellence without a silly price tag.

Story - Use effects like a dog barking to imply danger or a clock chiming to imply a passage of time. Be creative, be oblique.

Atmos - Go for thick and rich atmosphere tracks. Don't rely on just a quiet room unless your scene is intimate.

Orchestrate - After a loud crash bang whiz scene, bring it down. Think of your soundtrack as a passage or music with loud bits and quieter bits.

Think Gobal - Look at the scene and the world and fill in as much acoustic texture as your budget can afford. Don't be afraid to drop them in the mix if they don't work or fight with other effects.

Bridges - Use outgoing sound effects to seamlessly flow into the next scene. Play Hollywood movies through a big sound system and listen to the way sound is used creatively.

character in the sound effect can make it hard to identify. Sounds off screen create fantastic atmosphere when they are good and can distract when they are not.

Q – What advice would you offer new film makers?

Paul – Try and make your film in a way that gives you time to pay attention to the detail. You said at the beginning of this chat that the difference between four weeks sound editing and having seven weeks is amazing, especially considering what it costs. The difference it can make to the film is massive because it is not just about doing obvious stuff, it's about what else is happening off screen, the details, having time to reflect on how well it is working and then to make the necessary adjustments. You know the way an artist will break up a straight line by something really rather clever, well we are doing the same sort of thing with sound, and that is when it will feel like a natural thing. People have more of an idea about sound than they imagine, provided they are remotely musical.

What I feel is that the main role of sound is to provide the focus for the film. In places it can stand on its own right in a high fidelity or ballsy kind of way, and can reach out and touch you. But mostly its role is to guide the ear and the eye through the film, and I guess a good camera man would say the same about the way that they frame.

Sound Effects CDs are an excellent source for very high quality stereo recordings of pretty much everything you could imagine. If you can't afford to buy the disks, try asking the dubbing theatre where you plan to do your final mix and see if you can use their CD library. Be creative with sound and try and fill your soundtrack.

POST-PRODUCTION

Sound Mixing
Tim Cavagin of
Twickenham Film Studios

Q - What is the final mix?

Tim - It is where the dialogue, music and sound effects meet each other and get mixed into what you hear in the cinema. Hopefully the director, editor and producer all want the same thing and don't have different ideas and will stomp their feet and refuse to budge from those ideas.

Q - What materials do you need to do a final mix?

Tim - Normally we have a BetaSP for the picture so that we can run the sound alongside it. With regard to the sound element, it's important to check with the theatre in which you are mixing to see if they can handle the digital audio format you have chosen. Common formats include Magneto Optical Disks, hot swappable hard drives, Jazz drives and DA88 using a Hi8mm video tape. The Tascam DA88 Hi8 system is used all around the world and it is probably the cheapest and most efficient way to do it, especially on a low budget. It can take up to eight tracks of simultaneous digital audio and can hold the length of an average feature film on one tape. However, we prefer the sound to come to us on disk because there is more flexibility with hard disk recording than there is with tape recording. You will also need dubbing charts. Even though we could take them digitally, a dubbing mixer will always prefer paper charts because he still has to mark down on that chart where he has put things in various pre-mixes.

Q - Let's talk about the different types of sound that there are, firstly dialogue tracks?

Tim - The dialogue that is recorded on location will never be bettered in terms of performance. Provided the background sounds are not atrocious I would always advise the director to use this production sound. However, there are times when you can't use the production sound, because of background noise such as aircraft, in which case you are going to have to use ADR. This is where you replace the dialogue, but invariably, it lacks the sparkle of the original performance as the actor isn't giving the same energy levels, so it's best avoided. Every sound effect and every atmosphere in a room can be put on afterwards, the most important thing, especially with a low budget movie, is to make sure that your dialogue is as clear as possible. The sound recordist should spend all of his time concentrating on that fact. Forget about the door slams in the background, forget about the atmospheres of the room, forget about multi-track recording, just get the dialogue between the people in front of the camera, as cleanly and simply as possible.

Q - One of the things we did on Urban Ghost Story is that whenever we had an ADR scenario, as soon as we called 'cut' we would take the actors to a quiet room that was padded with duvets and ask them to re-perform it. They were not looking at any picture for sync, but nine times out of ten it would fit and the energy level would be there.

Tim - If you can get an actor after he has finished shooting the take to go off to your little room that you may have sound proofed then I think that that is a very good idea. As you say they are fresh from the shoot, the lines fresh in their head, and they know what they have just done so they can give a very similar performance.

Q - What happens about sound effects and atmospheres?

Tim - Sound effects are the colouration of the film, they enhance the production track which can be very flat, you need to spike up the sound. There are obvious effects such as doors closing, cars starting, but they can be used creatively to enhance the drama and story. You can get effects from CD libraries, or record them yourself. Atmospheres, a continuous sound that runs through a scene, are also used to enhance production sound, but you have to be wary of over egging the pudding. When you pre-mix your production sound you spend a lot of time sucking out the noisy backgrounds. There's no point in layering new atmospheres to create a mushy sound. Unless of course you are creating an other worldly or spooky atmosphere in which case you can use creative licence. If it's a normal contemporary atmosphere I think that it is very dangerous to put too many atmospheres down as the ear can only take in a few things at a time.

Q - What about music?

Tim - If at the end of the day you think about the sound track to a film as a bucket, you can only fit so many things in that bucket. Once it's full, everything else becomes a waste of time. The dialogue is obviously very important, then the music and then the effects. In say a large sci-fi movie you want the sound effects upfront, you also want the music upfront and you also want the dialogue upfront - something has to give. So you to start chipping away at things to find the right balance otherwise you have a wall of noise that is unintelligible.

Q - In terms of quantity of music is it common to over-score?

Tim - A good score will really help the film and a bad score will really drag a good movie down. Too much music will suffocate a film, you have to allow for it to breathe, to allow the dialogue and the effects to have their space, otherwise you are in danger of swamping everything with music, a common problem especially with inexperienced film makers.

Q - What tools do you have at your disposal, other than the mixing desk?

Tim - We have a variety of tools. For the dialogue we use compressors which keep the dialogue within a certain dynamic, cutting the top off the loud bits and bringing up the quieter bits. If you raised the dialogue track to raise the whispers, then a shout would almost deafen you, so the compressor raises the whispers and catches the shout so they sit happily on the ear. We have dynamic equalisers which you can tune into a certain frequency, so if your dialogue has a noisy background, you can tune into the 'noise' frequency and this machine will just suck out that frequency in between the lines of dialogue. This can help clear up a noisy track. We also use reverb to match dialogues and to give sounds greater space. If two people are talking in a room and you want it to sound like a cathedral you can add reverb. A common problem with dialogue is a thing called 'essing'. When people pronounce their s's the sssss is annoying at times, and can start to hurt the ear.

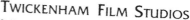

TWICKENHAM FILM STUDIOS
St. Margaret's · Twickenham · Middlesex · TW1 2AW · England
Tel: +44 (0)20-8607 8888 Fax: +44 (0)20-8607 8889

Tim Cavagin
RE-RECORDING MIXER

So we have a de-esser, which tunes into the frequency of that person's s's and decreases them.

The sound for your film can be encoded onto the print in several formats. Each use a form of surround sound, but you can mix in simple stereo.

Twin Analogue Tracks *containing a stereo mix. Can use encoded Dolby or DTS SVA mix to gives left, centre, right and surround. This is the cheapest and universal format. The quality is very good. If money is tight, this sound format alone will be more than adequate.*

Dolby Digital *- Surround digital mix with left, centre, right, left surround, right surround and sub bass channels. Encoded and stored between the sprocket holes on the film.*

SDDS *- Sony's digital format. Eight channels, left, centre left, centre, centre right, right, left surround, right surround and sub bass. Encoded and stored on the extreme left and right of the film. If one side is damaged, the other side which is offset, will drop in to ensure the sound never disappears.*

DTS *- Surround system recorded onto CD Rom with left, centre, right, left surround, right surround and sub bass channels. A time code like signal is encoded on the print which controls a CD Rom with the audio stored on it. One print can be used with different sound mixes being supplied on different CD Roms.*

We also use exciters. If somebody is talking and they are not projecting very much, as long as the background isn't too high we can make it more dynamic and punctuate it with an exciter. We grab certain levels and raise them just to make it a little bit more dynamic. There's a tendency to over use these tools because they are so great and you think *isn't that a fantastic machine! I can suck out all this* and then you hear your soundtrack back you think *Oh No! I have sucked all the life out of it!* It's always a compromise, you want to suck backgrounds out but you do not want to suck the life out of your dialogue.

Q - What is Foley?

Tim - Foley is performed by a Foley Artist, a person who stands in front of a screen and watches the film, then re-enacts the footsteps, door openings, glasses being put down, clothes rustles, leather creaks etc. They are important to enhance the location sound, but their primary job is for M&E used for foreign sales. If a film gets sold abroad, any sync sound with dialogue is unusable, so that is when foley becomes very important.

Q - What is the M&E mix?

Tim - It's the Music and Effects mix for the foreign markets, of great importance to world sales. It is everything in the final mix minus the sync dialogue so that abroad they can re-voice their dialogue into it. If you don't do the M&E properly it bounces back and you have to do it all over again.

Q - If you forgot an effect, could you drop it in there and then?

Tim - It depends on the dubbing theatre, but on the whole, as long as it is simple, yes. Check with the theatre though as they may not have an effects library. Instead of slowing the dub down it would be better for your editor to go off, get those sounds and come back once he has those sounds in synchronisation to the picture. We could then drop them into the mix. Because it's costing a lot of money, it's best not to slow the mix down. The most important thing to get right is the dialogue because without that you are lost. Proportionally, the time spent mixing in a four week mix would be four days spent pre-dialogue mixing, two days Foley pre-mixing, five days effects and atmos pre mixing, then six days final mixing. If you then said that you had a one week mix I would say decrease those amounts by four times.

Q - As digital audio tools on a computer are getting cheap and common, how much work can you do at home?

Tim - We had a film with a very low budget. I pre-mixed the dialogues, then they had already done all their work at home on their digital system for the effects and atmospheres. They had done an effects and atmospheres pre-mix and I sat here with sixteen faders set at zero, just making the odd adjustment. It was a very fast way to work. Aside from the computer you'll need a way to monitor the sound at home. It doesn't need to be superb, just a good amplifier and speakers, a way to listen to all the effects in relation to each other.

Q - How does the final mix get from your master tape, say a DA88, onto the print?

Tim - Your lab will take the master mix and shoot an optical version of it which will then be married to your print. Aside from the analogue stereo tracks, there are several other digital formats that you can use but you will have to pay a separate licence fee for them. As long as your film is not going to be distributed theatrically, you can use the Dolby SVA surround system for free. If you do get a

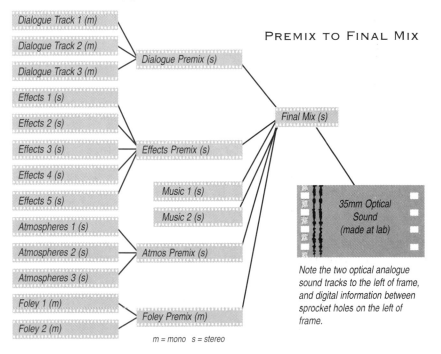

PREMIX TO FINAL MIX

Dialogue Track 1 (m)
Dialogue Track 2 (m)
Dialogue Track 3 (m)
Dialogue Premix (s)

Effects 1 (s)
Effects 2 (s)
Effects 3 (s)
Effects Premix (s)
Effects 4 (s)
Effects 5 (s)

Music 1 (s)
Music 2 (s)

Atmospheres 1 (s)
Atmospheres 2 (s)
Atmos Premix (s)
Atmospheres 3 (s)

Foley 1 (m)
Foley Premix (m)
Foley 2 (m)

Final Mix (s)

35mm Optical Sound (made at lab)

Note the two optical analogue sound tracks to the left of frame, and digital information between sprocket holes on the left of frame.

m = mono   s = stereo

211

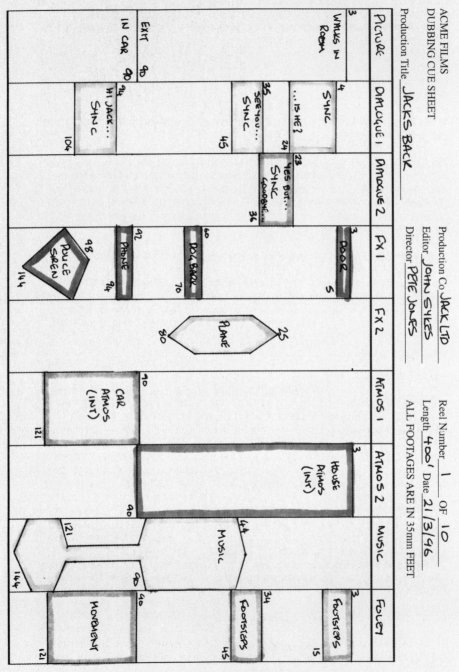

The Dubbing Chart

The Final Mix - a time and a place where all the elements of a film come together. Make sure all your creative decisions have been made in advance.

deal for a theatrical release you will then have to pay the licence fee to Dolby.

Q - Who should attend the final mix?

Tim - In the theatre I'd expect to see the picture editor, sound editor, director, and producer, no more. Any more and you'll have a constant cross pollination of ideas as everyone has their own little agenda, everyone wants to hear their own little things and it is just not possible.

Q – How do you get the best deals?

Tim – When a dubbing theatre is busy you're not going to be able to match the £300ph that fully funded productions pay. What you can do is agree to come in during downtime. You might have to have a day here, then not mix for a few days and you might be pushed out by a paying job. Most theatres are accommodating because they might as well be earning some money than nothing at all. If they've done a deal they probably won't let the tapes out without the money upfront.

Q – What are the most common mistakes that you come across?

Tim – On a low budget film the most common mistakes I come across are in fact over track laying. People who have far too many tracks for the time allocated, it is all right coming in saying I have got thirty two tracks but if you have only got two days you are not going to be able to mix those tracks, it's just not physically possible, you have to cut your cloth accordingly. Another problem is when people bring in their own tracks and they do not give you any separation, they do not checkerboard the sounds or dialogue. This means that I can't get in and apply an EQ or mix easily. This can make the final mix much longer or force creative compromise. I would say to all editors who are laying up tracks, think where you are laying them and *if I was me mixing it, would I be happy with what I have here?* Indecision is a common problem too because the dubbing stage is the last stage before the film goes out. The dub is the point where you have to make up your mind about all those things you have been putting off and a lot of people are uncomfortable about that. Come in with a firm idea of what you want. If you have a firm idea of how you want things to be, don't be afraid to tell the mixer. It's much better than a director turning to the dubbing mixer and saying *it's not how I want it, I can't tell you how I do want it, I can just tell you that it is not how I want it.* That's the worst thing in the world. Often they haven't had enough time, *we haven't slept for seventy-two hours* they say. It happens on the low budget films, it happens on the big budget films. Give yourself enough time. If you think it's going to take four days allow six. Give yourself time and a half and you can't go far wrong.

Q - What advice would you offer a new film maker?

Tim - Many low budget films come in and you can see that they would be so much better if the editor and director had been ruthless and cut aggressively instead of leaving it long and baggy.

Titles & Opticals
Alan Plant of
Howell Opticals

Q - What does a producer supply you with in order to make their titles?

Alan - A typed script of all the titles, setting them out exactly how you require them in frame with what type-faces and style of lettering you want. We then produce a proof to approve, then produce acetate cells which we film to make the final titles. If it's simple white titles on a black background then it's just a question of shooting them on a rostrum camera. That's also the cheapest way of doing it. It helps if producers set out their titles on a computer, showing the position, font and spelling exactly. Then we're not involved in the headache of design, we can just make up the acetate from the provided text and shoot the titles.

Q - What's the procedure if the titles are colour on black?

Alan - If it's just one colour, then we put a coloured cell underneath the title on the rostrum. If the title is multi-coloured, then you need to have that made up by a designer as a piece of camera ready artwork. With regard to animated titles, most of that has moved into the computer world.

Q - How is the end roller produced?

Alan - Pretty much the same way, if you want it just as white text on black we would produce the artwork on one long black acetate cell which we lay on the rostrum camera and the cell is physically pulled across the lightbox as it is filmed frame by frame. The film maker will say the roller needs to run for so and so seconds, but it's also dictated by the speed that an end roller can run. If it runs too quickly it will strobe.

Q - What's the procedure if titles need to be put on top of picture?

Alan - It's exactly the same process as far as producing the artwork is concerned, so the artwork is presented to us in the same way as if the titles were going to be white on black. We film those titles on high contrast stock and, without getting too entangled in technical details, combine that with the original negative on the optical printer. At the end of that you'll have a new negative of the sequence with the titles in place. If you start to put titles over picture area or backgrounds, then you can probably multiply the cost of producing simple white on black titles by three. Remember, your sales agent will need the original negative of any sequences where we have combined it with titles - they need it for foreign countries who will put titles in their own language on it.

Q - What materials do you need, aside from the acetates of the titles to achieve that?

Alan - Once the titles are shot on high contrast b&w stock and we have access to the lab materials, such as the neg/interneg, and a cutting copy or a workprint where the editor has marked up in chinagraph the points that he requires the titles to come in and go out, we can make up the titles. If you have cut non linear the neg cutter will supply us with frame counts for the titles and a VHS as a rough visual guide. If you're talking about producing half a dozen titles over a couple of scenes at the front of the film, with perhaps a small end roller that was just white on black - if all went well, I would say five to seven days. If it's just straight black on white titles, it could be shorter.

Q - How does it affect you if the film originates on super 16mm?

Alan - We always shoot title elements on 35mm. These will then be cut into the 35mm Internegative by the neg cutter.

Q - What other kind of opticals are common?

Alan - The most common opticals are the basic ones - slow up a scene, speed up a scene, freeze a frame on a scene, do an optical zoom in on a shot to lose something like some scenery that shouldn't be there, reposition frames, reversing the action, flopping (mirroring) the action, complex montage sequences with images laid ontop of each other. Wipes are rare. Dissolves tend to be done in the lab as part of their service. If you want a unique dissolve that the lab cannot handle as part of their standard service, then it will have to be produced as an optical effect. The labs are governed to set frame lengths, they can do 8, 12, 16 frame dissolves, also 20, 24, 32, up to 96, the maximum they can do on their printers. On our optical printer we can do anything from 2 to 999 frames and any number in between. We can also do straight Super 16mm to 35mm blow ups, and sometimes, offer better deals than you get at the labs.

Q - Is it fair to say that because titles are at the end of the production process, the money that's supposed to have been allocated has often been eaten up by earlier problems?

Alan - Yes, and not just that, the time factor is always a problem - people come to us saying, '*I've got to have this done, will you do it in the next three days?*' - and it's something they've been working on for six months!

Q - What common mistakes do you come across?

Alan - Spelling mistakes. The guy who does the graphics for me is excellent, he doesn't make mistakes, he produces the artwork in the form that the proof has been supplied and approved. We've just done a Scottish job where the main title is in Gaelic - and they have just found out after it's been screened at festivals, that they spelt the main title incorrectly. This kind of unforeseen cost is a problem for production companies. Also, inexperienced film makers often supply us with a scrap of paper with a list of titles and no idea of fonts, sizes or positioning. That can be very difficult.

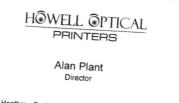

HOWELL OPTICAL
PRINTERS

Alan Plant
Director

Heathrow Business Centre, Technicolor Limited
Bath Road, West Drayton, Middx UB7 0DB
Tel: 020 8664 0329 Fax. 020 8564 8705

Negative Cutting
Mike Fraser of Mike Fraser Ltd

Q - What is the negative cutting?

Mike - Whenever you shoot a film, you always edit it on what is called secondary material, you never touch the master until the final conformation of your film, be it on video tape, be it on film, whatever - you only ever touch a copy. The negative cutting is the final conform of the master negative to match the final edit you have decided upon. The final edit usually comes to us either as a film cutting copy or some form of edit decision list (EDL).

Q - Am I correct, in saying that once a film is neg cut you can never go back and rejoin a cut?

Mike - Certainly on 16mm there is no going back, but on 35mm we have a method whereby you can extend shots without loss.

Q - How long does it take to neg cut an average feature film?

Mike - An average feature film, lets say 110 minutes long with say 800 cuts would take 2 weeks or so. It can be done quicker, and it depends on how many people you have working on it.

Q - Are there any special requirements when cutting super 16mm?

Mike - Yes, stability is important because it's single perf only. Super 16mm is often blown up to 35mm so the joins have to be very smooth and seamless. It is vital to find out if the negative cutter has worked with Super 16mm before and that he is set up for it, otherwise you could end up having to go to great expense and re-neg cut the whole picture. Super 16mm is cut A and B checkerboard. Every shot is on an alternate reel so that the joins don't show and you can have dissolves etc. With 16mm and Super 16mm you have to have an overlap which effectively destroys the frame before and after every shot. The important thing to remember about 16mm when in the cutting room or edit suite is that you must always lose one frame at the beginning and one frame at the end of every single shot of your film - that's the absolute minimum requirement. Also, laboratory printing machines can only do dissolves at the rate of either 16, 24, 32, 48, 64, 96 frames. They can't do anything else - if you want it done at any other length you have to have it done optically which will produce an interneg. Also when you're doing A and B roll, you have to leave on 16mm at least 20 frames between a cut and the beginning of an optical or the end of an optical and a cut, and you must always leave a minimum of 4 frames between the end of one optical and the beginning of the next.

Q - What do you need from the production team to enable you to cut the negative?

Mike - We need to have logged the negative in the first place, we need either a cutting copy if it's edited on film, or an edit decision list if it's been edited on non linear. We also need full instructions if there are requirements other than what is shown on the cutting copy or EDL.

Q - What happens to the negative when it's cut?

Mike - The cut rolls are sent to the laboratories where they are graded, frame cue counted, cleaned and printed, and you get a first mute answer print. If you are going to blow up to 35mm it is important to check with the lab the maximum roll size they can handle on their optical printer. It's usually either ten minutes or twenty minutes, including leaders.

Q - What happens to all the unused negative?

Mike - It stays with the negative cutters, until such time the producer says *junk it* or *store it* or *can I have it back?*

Q - How does non linear computer based editing affect negative cutting?

Mike - For feature films, regardless of how you edit it, you still need to neg cut. Non linear editing affects neg cutting in a very specific way in so much as you no longer have a cutting copy to check your neg against. As non linear is digital, we do not get any kind of cutting copy to physically check against the picture, shot by shot. All you have to work with are numbers. Therefore it is absolutely vital that those numbers are generated by something you have total confidence in. If the numbers are wrong and you cut the negative you're in a lot of trouble. There are various ways of doing it, but the way we've pioneered has always been the most frame accurate and in our view, the most comforting. We use software called *OSC/R* which in itself, has never let us down, it always produces the goods.

There are other ways of doing it, other systems such as Excalibur, Computer Match, and also Lightworks and Avid have their own ability to produce key neg cutting lists - the only problem with that is that the negative cutting list produced out of a Lightworks or Avid is only as good as the information that the Avid and Lightworks received in the first place. If the telecine reader head has read the Key Kodes incorrectly or has been offset incorrectly it could be a disaster - and remember, there is no visual guide, no cutting copy to check it against.

Q - What's the telecine head reading?

Mike - The telecine machine must be fitted with a Key Kode reader which translates the Key Kode to numbers. On the edge of new negative stocks is a bar code - Kodak call it Key Kode, it's their trademark. All manufacturers carry this type of 'bar code' now and they are all completely compatible. Everyone refers to it as Key Kode but it is actually edge numbers in a bar code form.

MAKING SENSE OF
POST-PRODUCTION

Mike Fraser

Mike Fraser Ltd., Unit 6, Silver Road, White City Ind. Park, London W12 7SG
Tel.: +44 (0)20 8749 6911 Fax.: +44 (0)20 8743 3144
E-Mail: mike@mfraser.demon.co.uk

16mm & Super 16mm A & B Roll

CHECKERBOARDING

The A & B roll cut negative rolls are printed to produce a single positive print. A & B rolls must be used in all 16mm formats as there is no room in between frames to make a clean join between two shots. By using two rolls with black spacer, a whole frame can be used for the join. The black spacer covers the join and creates a 'window' for the incoming shot on the alternate roll.

COMBINED IN LABS

"A" Roll   "B" Roll   Answer Print

16MM NEGATIVE JOIN IN DETAIL

← **Exposed negative frames** - the frame directly before and after a shot is used to join the negative to the black spacer.

← **Overlap Frame** - used to join onto black spacer and effectively destroys the frame.

← **Black Spacer** - used to create unexposed windows for printing A & B roll checkerboard negative.

CUTTING COPY MARKINGS FOR THE
NEGATIVE CUTTER
(16MM & SUPER 16MM)

All chinagraph instructions should be written on both the cell and the emulsion sides of the cutting copy. Markings for 35mm are the same.

Dissolve
(Shown is a 24 frame dissolve). Dissolves can be 16, 24, 32, 48, 64 and 96 frames in length. A minimum of 4 frames must be allowed between the end of the dissolve and the start of another. A minimum of 20 frames must be allowed between a cut and the start of a 16 frame dissolve and 20 frames between the end of a 16 frame dissolve and a cut.

Fade Out
(Shown is a 16 frame fade out) See fade notes below.

Fade In
(Shown is a 16 frame fade in) Fades can be 16, 24, 32, 48, 64 and 96 frames in length. A minimum of 20 frames must be allowed between the start of a shot and the start of 16 frame fade out. A minimum of 20 frames must be allowed between the end of of a 16 frame fade in and the end of a shot.

Jump Cut
Used when only a few frames are cut out. Marked to ensure the neg cutter doesn't mistake it for a rejoined cut.

Unintentional Cuts
Used when only a cut has been rejoined. Marked to inform the neg cutter to ignore it.

35MM
NEGATIVE
CUTTING

35mm is marked up for neg cutting in the same way as 16mm.

35mm is neg cut as a single A roll.

There is no B roll unless there are dissolves or fades in the film. If there are dissolves, then a B roll is made up which comprises mainly of black spacer. The only negative on this B roll is the second half of any dissolve, or the clear spacer for a fade.

To the right are rolls A and B with a 16 frame dissolve. Please note that a 16 frame dissolve needs 20 frames outgoing (not the 6 that are shown).

At the far right is a wider view of the 35mm negative. Roll A has several shots, roll B is black spacer except for the negative of the second half of the dissolve.

Note - some labs only use the B roll for the second part of a dissolve.

35mm
Cutting Copy

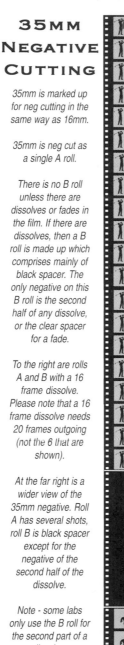

COMBINED IN LABS

35mm
Neg Roll A

35mm
Neg Roll B

Shot 1
Shot 2
Shot 3
Dissolve
Dissolve
Sh 4
Shot 5
Shot 6
Shot 7
Shot 8

35mm
Neg Rolls A& B.
Wider view

ANATOMY OF AN EDL

TITLE: Reel 4 neg cut   FORMAT: CMX 3600 4-Ch

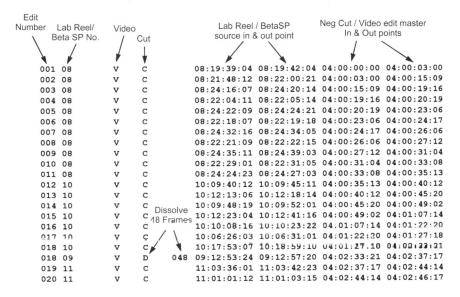

Edit Number	Lab Reel/ Beta SP No.	Video	Cut		Lab Reel / BetaSP source in & out point		Neg Cut / Video edit master In & Out points	
001	08	V	C		08:19:39:04	08:19:42:04	04:00:00:00	04:00:03:00
002	08	V	C		08:21:48:12	08:22:00:21	04:00:03:00	04:00:15:09
003	08	V	C		08:24:16:07	08:24:20:14	04:00:15:09	04:00:19:16
004	08	V	C		08:22:04:11	08:22:05:14	04:00:19:16	04:00:20:19
005	08	V	C		08:24:22:09	08:24:24:21	04:00:20:19	04:00:23:06
006	08	V	C		08:22:18:07	08:22:19:18	04:00:23:06	04:00:24:17
007	08	V	C		08:24:32:16	08:24:34:05	04:00:24:17	04:00:26:06
008	08	V	C		08:22:21:09	08:22:22:15	04:00:26:06	04:00:27:12
009	08	V	C		08:24:35:11	08:24:39:03	04:00:27:12	04:00:31:04
010	08	V	C		08:22:29:01	08:22:31:05	04:00:31:04	04:00:33:08
011	08	V	C		08:24:24:23	08:24:27:03	04:00:33:08	04:00:35:13
012	10	V	C		10:09:40:12	10:09:45:11	04:00:35:13	04:00:40:12
013	10	V	C		10:12:13:06	10:12:18:14	04:00:40:12	04:00:45:20
014	10	V	C	Dissolve	10:09:48:19	10:09:52:01	04:00:45:20	04:00:49:02
015	10	V	C	48 Frames	10:12:23:04	10:12:41:16	04:00:49:02	04:01:07:14
016	10	V	C		10:10:08:16	10:10:23:22	04:01:07:14	04:01:22:20
017	10	V	C		10:06:26:03	10:06:31:01	04:01:22:20	04:01:27:18
018	10	V	C		10:17:53:07	10:18:59:10	04:01:27:10	04:02:33:21
018	09	V	D	048	09:12:53:24	09:12:57:20	04:02:33:21	04:02:37:17
019	11	V	C		11:03:36:01	11:03:42:23	04:02:37:17	04:02:44:14
020	11	V	C		11:01:01:12	11:01:03:15	04:02:44:14	04:02:46:17

CMX 3600 is the most common and robust cross platform EDL that we have come across. Make sure that when you supply your EDL it is on the correct format disk, most cutters use DOS format. Note also that a CMX 3600 can only handle 999 cuts.

Edit Number - this is the chronological number given to each and every cut.

Lab Reel / Beta SP number - this is the direct reference back to which Lab roll / BetaSP tape each shot was taken from.

Video - As it's a picture only EDL, each of these will be V for video.

Cut - This describes the way the shot is handled, mostly this will be C for Cut. Note toward the bottom of the EDL, D for dissolve with the dissolve length in frames.

Time Code Column 1 - this is the Lab reel / Beta SP source in point - the time code where a shot actually begins.

Time Code Column 2 - this is the Lab reel / Beta SP source out point - the time code where a shot actually ends.

Time Code Column 3 - this is the point on the assembled master negative time line where the shot begins.

Time Code Column 4 - this is the point on the assembled master negative time line where the shot ends.

NEGATIVE CUTTING 35MM / 16MM

35mm contains enough space between frames for the negative cutter to actually cut the negative and join it up as one single roll.

16mm and Super 16mm is considerably smaller with virtually no space between frames. This forces the negative cutter to conform using A&B rolls.

DUPE DETECTION & FRAME OVERLAP

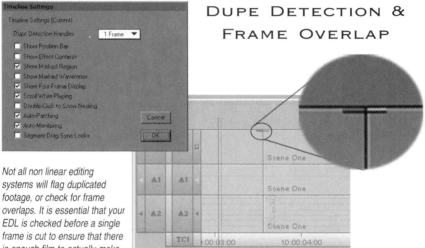

Not all non linear editing systems will flag duplicated footage, or check for frame overlaps. It is essential that your EDL is checked before a single frame is cut to ensure that there is enough film to actually make up the master negative. Avid Film Composer will make this check for you, but most other systems won't. If your software doesn't check, send your completed cut EDL to the neg cutter who will then check it for you.

It reads those bar codes and converts them to edge numbers. You're not always able to read the Key Kode because the negative may be fogged, certainly around ends, dissolves and splices etc. Problems can arise. For instance if a reader head goes through a splice and the next roll of material (with different Key Kodes) is fogged for the first 10, 20, 100 feet or whatever, the first thing that the telecine reader does is to stop reading. It merely accumulates the previous numbers which are incorrect because the neg has changed. It also flags the operator but if the operator doesn't notice, you're going to get 10,20, 100 feet of negative where the edge numbers have been incorrectly read.

Q - In the telecine, how do you check that the Key Kode that is being read is correct?

Mike - You can't. There is no practical way of checking that the Key Kode that is being read is correct. That is why we do not log it that way - we log it on a bench, with a Key Kode reader. These numbers are later fed into the computer and should match the telecine timecode numbers, that is unless there is a problem. Either way, you are aware of the problem before the damage is done.

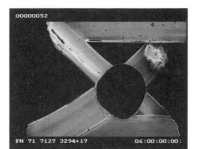

The punch hole at the start of each lab reel represents the absolute point from which all negative cuts are calculated. In this instance, this frame is from lab roll 52 (top left) with a time code starting at 06:00:00:00 (six o'clock). Note the Key Kode details in the bottom left of the frame.

Beta SP rushes frame. Lab roll 52, Timecode frame 06:05:58:24, Key Kode reference bottom left of frame.

Q - What methods of post production are available to a producer?

Mike - Currently, there are several methods of producing an end result. Firstly is the traditional film edit where rush prints are sunk and cut by the editor. The final cutting copy is sent to us where we re-cut the neg to match the cutting copy. The cut neg goes off to the labs and is printed. This is the most tried and tested method that has worked for decades, but it is a little labour intensive on behalf of the editor. There is a general trend to non linear editing systems now and traditional film cutting may become a thing of the past. Method 2 - after the telecine of the rushes negative, you stay on tape, and you don't come back to film. During the telecine you do a 50-80% grade of all your rushes, transfer them onto whatever final conform tape you want, Beta, D2 etc. That footage is then digitised from tape onto hard disk in your Avid or Lightworks - you edit the movie. Then you conform the final picture purely on tape - the final grading is done in the edit suite and you never go back to cut the original negative. There are advantages there but obviously the completed production can only ever exist on tape and unlikely to be projected in a cinema.

Method 3 is pure non linear, where the rushes are telecinied and digitised into a system like Lightworks or Avid. The movie is edited and the computer produces an EDL. We use the EDL to cut the negative and the final neg is then printed at the labs. Both Avid and Lightworks have got ways of getting around the problems of productions shot at 24fps which can entail slowing down and speeding up - it's all tried and tested but it's something of which to be aware. There are other systems and without doubt new systems will have been developed by the time you read this. The system to opt for is the one your post production team has the most experience with, or with which they are happiest

Q - As traditional editing was mechanical, the speed at which film was shot was

"academic' with regard to the negative cutting. Is this the same for non linear?

Mike - No. It's important if you are shooting a theatrical release, i.e. if you are shooting at 24fps that you are aware of how you are going to post produce as your film is 24fps and will be using 25fps timecode. If you shoot at 24fps and telecine transfer at 25fps, your picture is going to be shorter than your sound. The only way to get them in sync is to do something to either the picture or the sound, and you don't want to do that. You want to keep the sound at the proper speed the whole time - AND the picture at the proper speed the whole time. One of the ways of doing it is with Avid - you shoot at 24fps, transfer at 25fps and take it into Avid. Avid can then slow down the picture to 24fps so that it will match your sound. Now you edit and send the final EDL to us and we do the neg cut. Lightworks has a similar method to combat this problem too.

Q - White Angel was shot at 25fps to avoid technical headaches so it is possible to shoot a feature at 25fps and not 24fps.

Mike - Every feature film that's been shown on television here for years was shot at 24fps and transferred at 25fps yet few know the difference. Nobody watching television knows that the *Guns Of Navarone* or *The Magnificent Seven* has been speeded up by 4% to be transferred at 25fps instead of 24fps. It is fair to say that if you shoot at 25fps there are less headaches, especially if you cannot afford a Film Composer and are cutting with a cheaper non linear editing system. I would advise micro budget films to always shoot at 25fps.

Q - What are the most common mistakes made by a film maker that you encounter?

Mike - Not preparing the post production route in the early stages. Producers tend to think, *Oh well, we'll get that done later when we go into editing* and they simply don't give it enough thought, planning and preparation.

Q - What extra things can a production team do to make your life easier?

Mike - The most important thing is for the neg cutter and the editor to sit down and talk about how

The huge negative storage warehouse at Mike Fraser Ltd.

Key Kodes are checked on the bench before the actual negative cutting, just to make sure there are no mistakes.

Neg can be telecinied directly to tape with 'Key Kodes' linked to timecode. The picture can then be edited non-linear or on tape before being conformed, either as a film neg cut or purely on tape for TV broadcast - & all under one roof!

he's going to do it. We're talking film editing now, the way the cutting copy is marked up is vital, so it must be marked up in either a standard way or a way the neg cutter understands the editor's wishes. With non-linear editing you do not have a film cutting copy to check against. Therefore you are cutting to a neg cutting list, which has been generated by the translation of timecodes from an EDL (edit decision list). Therefore the translation has to be absolutely frame accurate.

It's very important that an editor on a non linear system understands the logging in of his material so that he gets the right tape numbers and so forth. If you're using something like OSC/R it doesn't matter, because OSC/R will sort it all out. On a more basic and cautionary level, always put plenty of leader at the head and tail of any reels, if you are going to blow up Super 16mm to 35mm, check with the labs that you have made the rolls up to the right length, label all your cans with as much information as possible - it's amazing how quickly material accumulates and people forget what's in a can. That often leads them to the last point, NEVER handle your negative - get it sent straight from the labs to the neg cutters and have your problems checked out by professionals in the right environment. Remember absolutely everything you have worked for is contained in that negative.

Q - What is the future of film with regard to post production and neg cutting?

Mike - Sometime in the next 5 – 10 years show 35mm prints as we know them will be replaced by satellite delivery and digital projection. Although the pictures will still be acquired on 35mm/S16mm for the foreseeable 5 – 20 years, the film handling will diminish rapidly.

Already there are two new methods of getting to the show/release prints from the negative without going through the painful process of fine neg cut, grading for approval/answer prints etc and all the handling that that incurs. The first is the Digital Film Lab route which requires a Long Handled Neg cut scanned on a Spirit telecine at 2K resolution. Final effects etc composited on inferno and the final completed production recorded out to 35mm neg. This route is particularly cost efficient for S16mm features with lots of optical effects. The second is still in the throes of it's first feature. It works like this. We telecine transferred and sunc the 35mm rushes to BetaSp for the offline. At the same time we produced Clone anamorphic Digital Betacams of the rushes. These digibetas were conformed and digitally projected on full size screens for viewing and decision making. Then we long handled neg cut the final EDL and it is, as I write, being scanned by an Oxberry at between 2 and 4k resolution to inferno where all the effects are being composited. The entire movie will be recorded back to 35mm film of a quality indistinguishable from the original rushes neg. These methods are in their infancy and may require modification as they advance.

Digital Effects
Dennis Michelson
Visual Effects Supervisor

Q - What is the basic concept when it comes to computer / film, and manipulating a 2D image?

Dennis - The broad concept is that you have this moving image, a series of 24/25fps, each one a single image on film - with computers you can control the colour, the saturation, the contrast, insert objects, remove objects, distort the image - the possibilities are limitless (aside from budget and time). Only recently have computers got to the level where they can handle the volume of information that film contains within it. The smallest unit of data that film contains is a grain - a pixel on a computer is now of that scale, and even smaller, so computer manipulation enables us to do work with film, down to the most minute detail. In theory, given time and money, you can do anything - colours, shapes, people's exploding eyes, turning sunset to day, morphing, also repairs - there have been shots where blemishes on actor's faces have been fixed for instance, that can never really be foreseen.

Q - How does it work?

Dennis - You send the facility house the negative of what you've shot. They scan that in - by scanning I mean, the technicians put it on a machine that rolls the film through a frame at a time, and as each frame is held in the gate, it is literally scanned and turned into digital bits, millions of bits. Once you've entered that domain, the manipulation begins, be it effects, removing wires, darkening skies etc. The work is then approved by the producer and the image is then put back on 35mm film using a Film Recorder - again a frame at a time. They then give you the negative to cut into your cut negative.

Q - What are the most important issues to be considered in advance when you know something is going to involve some kind of digital manipulation?

Dennis - The critical thing is for the people on set to be aware of what the effect they want actually is, because any given visual element interacts with other visual elements. If you do a shot of a table and want them to add an angle-poise light to it, not only will they have to put the light in, but also the light it casts, the reflections and the shadows - all elements affect all other elements - if this isn't done properly, the unschooled eye knows something is wrong. It may not be able to say what it is, but it can tell - then you have a bad effect. Recreating those lighting effects in a computer can be costly and time consuming. If on the day, the lighting cameraman had lit the area of table that was to be illuminated by the lamp (that would be inserted later on computer), everything would become easier, the effect would be better and cheaper. Always consider the lighting implications of any elements to be inserted, be it props, casting shadows, even lightning.

POST-PRODUCTION

Q - If you're not going to storyboard the whole film, it's essential to storyboard the sequences with the effects?

Dennis - Yes, it's essential. That way the technicians would know what the angle of the house that is being lit by the lightning is, if the camera is moving or not, what elements cross in front of others, what has to happen etc.

Q - Currently, can Super 16mm be used with computer technology and what type of stock can be used?

Dennis - Yes. A rule of thumb regarding film stock is not to shoot grainy, fast, film-stocks for effects elements. Technicians have some issues with DOP's who say *we're shooting the rest of the film on it...* it makes sense from the point of view of the DOP that you would maintain continuity that way, but that betrays a complete misunderstanding of what this process is all about, because they can make the end result look like the film stock the DOP shot the rest of the movie on. The technicians need to start off with the highest resolution image they can get.

Q - Say we have a shot of a landscape and a horseman rides past - we need to replace the sky as we want a sunset - what things make this easier or harder to achieve?

Dennis - If it's a clear, constant, sky, they can do that in an instant with the software tools we have. If, for whatever reason, the sky is cloudy, or the horseman goes in front of the sky, then it becomes more difficult and therefore more time consuming. People have to be aware of this so that they can make creative choices on set - so it's a question of educating people, to know that these are the factors involved, this is what will impact your budget - it may be acceptable to have the horseman pass by a rock instead of across the skyline for instance.

Q - If the budget was low you would be able to advise the producer of certain elements to avoid with sequences that involved any form of digital manipulation?

Dennis - Exactly. A more economical way to achieve an effective result.

Q - Technicians also spend time fixing problems - what kind of things can they fix?

Dennis - It ranges from things like a camera scratch, which is often an insurance claim - previously the only option had been a re-shoot, now they can simply fix it, even if a line crosses an actor's face, they can paint it out. A blemish on an actor's face, a microphone boom can be taken out, depending on what it crosses, we can darken bleached out skies, stabilise camera shake, smooth out pans and tilts. This is where I see the greatest potential in the future for digital technology, actually changing the quality of the film in term of its overall colour balance, the level of blacks, the contrast throughout etc.

Dennis Michelson
visual effects supervisor

lunarfilm@quista.net

DO IT ON YOUR DESKTOP
USING A DOMESTIC PC OR MAC TO EMULATE HOLLYWOOD EFFECTS

Desktop effects (left and below) - Relatively inexpensive software & hardware can now create images & animations that are technically good enough to be used in low-budget feature films. Autodesk 3D studio was used for certain effects in T2 & Lightwave created almost all the effects for Babylon 5.

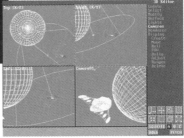

(left) An appreciation of the way certain software tools work in programs like Adobe Photoshop strengthens the understanding of what is actually possible using computers and film - without breaking the bank.

Q - How much does it cost?

Dennis - I can't give you a formula, but generally, a stationary shot will be cheaper than a moving shot. Well shot bluescreen will be cheaper than poorly shot bluescreen. The fixed costs are scanning and recording, plus the laboratory costs. The field is moving so quickly you need to make a call to find out how much it costs right now. The big variable is how much time needs to be spent making the effect work. These variables are the number of elements and complexity, the larger one clearly being complexity. It's practically impossible to define complexity in financial terms. The bottom line is that digital compositing and effects aren't as expensive as people think.

Q - Who are the most important crew members aside from the producer?

Dennis - If there's an effects supervisor they will liaise with production. If not, the cinematographer, editor and director.

Q - CGI (Computer Generated Images) - going back to the shot we discussed earlier, the valley and the sunset, the director decides he wants a UFO going across the sky, how would you go about doing that?

Dennis - Depending on complexity and detail, it's probably best now to create the model in a 3D program. Once it exists you can do anything you want with it in a computer, unlike a model where you will need crew, bluescreen, cameras etc. If you want to blow it up, then that's still better to do with a model.

Q - Correct me if I'm wrong, that kind of CGI effect could be done on a very low budget?

Dennis - I'd say it can be done quite economically if you choose the right people. If it was very low budget, you could approach people with PCs with software like *3D Studio, Lightwave* or *Electric Image* on the Mac. It's quite possible to produce high quality, high resolution images and animation using this lower end technology, although the processing time is greatly increased.Computers are getting faster and cheaper all the time, the software is getting more sophisticated, cheaper and more accesible. There's no reason why you should not access that technology, but be aware, rendering times at full film res is still VERY long. Programs like *Commotion* are state of the art and used in major effects companies around the world, yet you can buy it and install it on your laptop computer.

Q - You mention 3D Studio - this is a £2k program that you can buy and run on a fast PC on your desktop. With it, you can create anything from a whizzy logo to a number nine bus, at the pixel resolution required for 35mm film, dump it onto DAT or CD, bring it to you and you can then comp it into the final shot?

Dennis - Yes, it's certainly do-able. A friend of mine is part of a CGI team, he does all the effects animation on his MAC at home, so this is already being done. I like the idea of putting something together for a release print in your bedroom!

DIGITAL COMPOSITING
(THE NUTTY PROFESSOR)

Shots 1 and 2 - Eddie Murphy is shot against Blue Screen. Shot 3 - the two shots are composited on computer, along with a separate background shot. The final sequence would then be output back to 35mm negative to be cut into the film.

DIGITAL
COMPOSITING
BASIC
TECHNIQUES
(THESE IMAGES
WERE PRODUCED
USING ADOBE
PHOTOSHOP ON A
DESKTOP PC)

1. Original stock has unwanted elements removed.

2. The sky is keyed out and a new cloudy sky, shot separately, is comped in.

3. Visual effects elements are added. This time, a shot of a plane, again, filmed separately. This could easily be a CGI plane against a blue screen.

2. The final composite with added CG (computer generated) sun and a little lens flare.

POST-PRODUCTION

DAVID LEAN CROWD SHOT - DIGITAL EFFECT STYLE

1. A group of extras are photographed several times (2) and eventually, all the separate shots are composited to turn a small group into a vast crowd (3)

Q - What about camera movement, if you have a sequence with an actor who is playing twins and we need to move the camera?

Dennis - That would have to be motion control. Motion control is basically a camera on a motorised head/dolly that is computer controlled. It enables you to perform a camera move, the computer records the move, then the same move can be automatically replayed, but with the actor in a different place for instance - then they can combine the two shots and you've got twins.

Q - Do you have any basic advice to offer inexperienced film makers?

Dennis - Visual effects occur in two stages - it's both an *Art* and a *Craft* - the first one being in the concept stage, in the story-boards, what does the story need, what propels the narrative at this point - there we can be part of the creative team. Once that's nailed down, they put on the problem solving hat. I also think that the mystique and propaganda about digital has been too effective, people think anything can be done with digital effects - that's why people feel confident of coming in after the effect saying *wave your hands over this and make magic*. Then questions of time and expense come in and they may have problems. Involve the digital effects facility or the supervisor as early as you would your production designer and cinematographer to avoid costly mistakes.

Q - Any final words?

Dennis - Most important is preparation. If you are looking for a company to do your effects, don't get fazed by their equipment. Whetever they have, the effect will only be as good as the driver of the equipment. Seek out the artists with the right vision, not necessarily the company with the most up to date equipment. Last year's state of the art is still very powerful and considerably cheaper than today's. Lastly, don't assume your effects need to be realised with digital technology. Many old style effects, such as force perspective models, are just as good and probably a lot cheaper.

Telecine
Sam Hollingdale
Colourist at 4MC UK

Q - What is telecine?

Sam - It is the transferring of film onto videotape. It's sometimes referred to as the TK.

Q - What materials do you need and how much does it cost?

Sam - The film itself - a print, negative, inter-positive, inter-negative, 35mm, 16mm, 8mm. The sound often comes to us on formats like mag, DA88 or DAT. We don't use the optical sound for mastering, although we can use it as a guide track. Often the sound is dealt with separately in the sound department. You can get a deal, but it depends on the operator and the telecine machine you intend to hire. It can cost anywhere between £100 and £600 per hour. As a rule, you should get the best you can afford, it's not a stage you want to compromise. If you want to save money you can bring your own stock.

Q - What's the best all round route for a low budget film?

Sam - A low contrast 35mm (blow up from S16mm) print would be the simplest route as all the elements such as opticals and titles are integrated and it should be fully graded. It's on one print so it should simply be a case of one and a half times the running time of the film to do a telecine. The print should be new and must never have been projected. If the print has some dirt from a previous telecine you could have it ultrasonically cleaned here. Often, especially on low budget films, the telecine is rushed, the print is a little dirty and little care is taken, then it gets rejected by broadcasters and you have to do it all again but this time with more care and attention. The closer you can get to that original camera negative, the better. For S16mm this might mean a low contrast S16mm fully graded print. But remember, all your optical effects and titles will be missing in that S16mm print so you will need to bring those in from 35mm or recreate them in an online video edit suite.

Q - What format of videotape is the best to use?

Sam - Technically D1 is the best although DigiBeta is better all round as the quality is superb, it is universally used and is considerably cheaper. In the real world, you can't see the difference between D1 and DigiBeta.

Q - What is grading?

Sam - If you assume the film we are going to telecine is from a final graded print from the lab, there might only be minimal grading needed. Grading in the telecine is where I can make adjustments to the picture, darkening, lightening, colour satuation etc., in order to make the picture consistent for veiwing on demostic tv's. I must also make sure that the picture remains legal for broadcast. I have a waveform monitor and vectorscope and I keep my eye on it to make sure that the video levels don't drop too low or go to high. We have a legaliser so that the video levels can't go too high or low, but if a director is pushing it lighter or darker, it can crush detail into solid colours that look very unattractive. I also have a PPM meter for the sound and I make sure that the sound never peaks over six, or +8db over reference tone.

Q - What is pan and scan?

Sam - If a film is shot in widescreen, when you zoom into the picture to do a TV sized (4x3) telecine, you will lose picture to the left and right - you might find a vital piece of story isn't actually in the shot anymore, so we would *'pan and scan'* left or right to accommodate it. This can take a very long time to do and is very subjective. If you telecine in wide-screen, clearly this isn't an issue.

Q - What is DVNR?

Sam - DVNR, like MNR11, is a noise reduction system that can help with sparkle, scratches, grain, and generally clean up the picture. It isn't a panacea to all problems though and you can't expect it to work miracles. Using a wet gate in telecine can also help eradicate scratches and general damage. Bring a roll in for us to look at before booking a full session as we can check to see if you will need DVNR or a wct gate as this alters the price.

Q - What is TV safe?

Sam - We need to compensate for the fact that domestic TVs crop a lot of image. *TV safe* is a guide that you should keep in mind when framing a shot so that you don't loose any information on the edge of a frame. We can put a grid up on the screen which shows areas within which your titles, and your action must fall.

Q - What are the different television standards?

Sam - In this country we work on a TV standard called PAL, in America it is NTSC - the two are not compatible without conversion. So you need to make more than one master, you need to make a PAL master and an NTSC master. There are others too, SECAM, which is very much like PAL. The world is peppered with different standards and you must deliver tapes to those countries in the formats that they can use and broadcast. You should make all your masters at the same time as it saves a great deal of time later. If you spend a day grading it will only take 2½ hours to lay it off onto DigiBeta. Accordingly, it will only take another 2½ hours to lay off a second copy in NTSC. You would not have to re-grade for NTSC, the information is the same, you just have to switch the machines over and then run the film again. Most people tend to make four or even six masters, they will make a 4x3 master which will be your *pan and scan* version, the original letterbox version so that you are getting

SAM HOLLINGDALE

Film House   142 Wardour Street
London W1V 3AU
tel 020 7878 000   fax 020 7878 7800

COMMON FORMATS - VIDEO DELIVERY

1" - *Analogue reel to reel format, industry standard of the 1980's. Called 1" because tape is 1" wide. Commonly used in foreign territories for delivery of masters. Not suitable for mastering.*

Betacam SP- *Cassette analogue component format. See Digital Betacam. Commonly used in foreign territories for delivery of masters. Not suitable for mastering. Maximum running time of approximately 110 mins.*

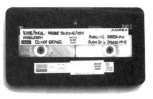

D1 - *Currently the ultimate digital videotape format with no generation loss. Digital component quality means it is ideal for mastering. High tape and running costs. Maximum running time of 90 mins.*

D2 - *Composite digital videotape format. High quality tape format, D2 is vastly superior to 1", but not superior to D1. Commonly used in foreign territories for delivery of masters.*

Digital Betacam - *A 'compressed' digital version of Betacam SP - made by Sony. Common format that is ideal for mastering as tapes can easily accommodate a feature film. Robust and has a relatively low tape and running cost.*

Domestic Formats - *Low Band Umatic, HiBand Umatic, VHS, SVHS, 8mm and Hi8mm can all be requested at various stages of production and are commonly used for preview tapes and sync tapes.*

MiniDV and DVCam - *Digital, semi pro formats ideal for micro budget video production. Superb picture and sound in relation to the cost but not suited to mastering and archival for video masters.*

DVD - *High density CD look alike disk that stores around two to three hours of video in MPEG2 video format (dependent on video compression / quality). Ideal for distribution to consumers as quality is superb. If you can master your movie onto DVD, you can hook it up to a VHS and run off VHS dupes whenever you need them.*

POST-PRODUCTION

VIDEO FORMAT FACTS

Analogue	*Digital*	*Composite*	*Component*	*Compression*
Technically inferior to digital. Picture noise is introduced when tape copies are made. This 'generation loss' can lead to unacceptable quality.	Technically superior to analogue. Virtually eliminates generation loss as information is recorded as a series of numbers.	The 3 basic components of a TV signal (red, green & blue) form one combined signal. Good for transmission/ distribution as only one cable is needed.	the 3 basic components of a TV signal (red, green & blue) are kept as separate signals. Vital to post production applications like D1 editing, chroma-keying, & computer graphics.	A complex mathematical technique that condenses digital picture information to make it take up less space on a videotape. Compression gives longer playing times, similar to the Long Play function on VHS.

everything that your director intended, and then a 16x9 version all in PAL and then you do them all again in NTSC. You can choose not to do all these at the same time, but if you do, you might have to come back later and start from scratch.

Q - What about an 'edgy' look?

Sam - Some directors want to create a look that may be too dark or too bright. This is a problem because some territories will just fail the tape as it looks so extreme, even if it is a creative decision. If you use a Super 8mm home movie look for instance, you will need to specify this on the report sheet with the telecine as they might reject it saying that it is too grainy and scratched. With a film we did last year the director wanted a very dark picture that was the look and the mood that he wanted, but the people distributing said *that's too dark we won't be able to sell it like that.* So they did two versions in the end, the director's cut with his grading and the distributor's version which was lifted slightly. In a theatre you might be able to get away with very dark and moody images but your average viewer sitting at home with his VHS and his wife reading under a light on the left hand side of the room is not going to be able to see a thing.

Q - What common mistakes do you see and what advice would you offer?

Sam - From a low budget point I would say that most producers are unwilling to spend money to do the job well and end up spending more fixing it than it should have cost in the first place. Sometimes producers expect to get a great telecine from a normal contrast projection print and don't get a low contrast print made up and the results are usually very poor. Play it safe with exposure and framing. If you frame it too tight when you film it then there is nothing you can do with it. If you shoot a wider picture than you need then that gives you room to manoeuvre later. The same is true with exposure, if you underexpose and want to make it lighter it will just go grainy and milky. If you overexpose, we have more latitude to get the look you want.

TELECINE ASPECT RATIO FOR S16MM / 1-1.85 PROJECTS

Original Ratio Letterbox
The transfer of the whole image in the ratio the director intended with the relevant letter box blanking (example in 1.85:1). Commonly referred to as Widescreen.

4x3 Pan And Scan
The telecine operator zooms in to fill the 4x3 frame. Note how creative decisions have to be made, like dropping the girl on the left of the full frame. The process can be long.

16x9 Anamorphic
A squeezed version of the letterbox, which is un-squeezed when broadcast or viewed from other sources such as DVD.

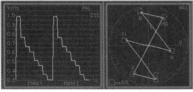

The waveform monitor and vectorscope are used to measure the video on a technical level. The video level must not peak over 1v or under 0.3v or it will be rejected. Many software editing tools come with software scopes, like this one from an Avid Online. Generally, these are a guide and are not as accurate as a dedicated scope.

Bars, of which there are 30 seconds before your picture starts, are used to line up the levels on the scope. The white to the left is just under 1v, the black to the right is just over 0.3volt.

The PPM meter is used to measure the sound. It must not peak over 6 on the scale, or it will become an illegal signal. Generally, voices should burble around 5, gunshots at 6, quiet scenes at 2 etc. At this stage, you should have processed your final mix and M&E mix through a compressor limiter in order to squeeze the sound into a narrower band for TV.

The clock is needed so that the tape can be cued up for broadcast or duplication. Normally the clock will countdown from 30 seconds to 0 (the start of the show) and will fade to black at 3 seconds before the start of the show.

TV Safe and Title Safe - the TV safe area, the outer box, is used as a guide and your drama must stay within it. Many TV's will crop off right up to TV safe. Title Safe, the inner box, is a guide for the maximum extent to which you should place your titles onscreen.

VIDEO TERMS GLOSSARY

BITC - *Burnt-in-time-code. Time code numbers recorded from camera tapes and visually displayed on screen giving a frame-by-frame picture reference. BITC is used on reference copies of rushes, which in turn will be used for the off-line edit.*

BLUE SCREEN - *Foreground subject is shot against a plain blue screen, on film or video, so that background images can be added electronically in post production. Blue is chosen as it is the least naturally occurring colour in flesh tones. (see Chromakey)*

CHROMAKEY - *Technique which allows a vision mixer to substitute a saturated colour (usually blue or green) in a picture for another picture source. (see Blue Screen)*

DVE - *Digital Video Effects. Devices such as ADO, A53, Encore and Kaleidoscope, for picture manipulation.*

DVTR - *Digital Video Tape Recorder. Multiple generations or passes on DVTR's (see D1/D2) do not suffer from tape noise degradation associated with analogue tape formats.*

DROP OUT - *Momentary loss of signal on a video tape, showing up as randomly occurring white spots on the picture, present in worn or poor quality tape.*

525 - *This is the standard, specifying the number of horizontal lines that makes up the TV picture. 625 being the U.K standard and 525 being the American.*

FIELD - *Area of a TV screen covered by alternative lines. 2 fields are equal to 1 frame i.e. picture. (see Frame)*

FRAME - *Single television frame or film image. In European television 25 frames per second are scanned to give an illusion of continuous movement. Each frame is composed of 2 fields.*

HUE - *Colour tone of a picture.*

KEY - *Effect that allows a picture to be superimposed over a background.*

LUMINANCE - *The black and white information of a video signal.*

MATTE - *An area blanked off within a frame in order to include additional material or remove unwanted material.*

MOTION CONTROL - *A computer assisted camera and rig with multiple moving axes, enabling high precision, repeatable camera moves.*

N.T.S.C - *National Television Standards Committee. Colour standard used in USA, Canada and Japan.*

OFF-LINE - *A pre-edit used to establish edit points for the on-line edit, usually on non-broadcast standard equipment.*

ON-LINE - *The main edit during which mixes, effects and audio are brought together using broadcast standard equipment in order to create a 'master' edit.*

PAL - *Phase Alternate Line. Colour system used in Europe (not France), Scandinavia, China, India, Australia, South Africa etc.*

PAL M - *A version of PAL standard, but using a 525 line 60 field structure. Used only in South America.*

PIXEL - *Smallest picture element on a television display.*

Q-LOCK - *Device for synchronising audio with video machines.*

R.G.B. - *Red, Green, Blue. Primary television colours before encoding to a composite signal if required.*

RESOLUTION - *The definition of a television picture, and the ability to determine small objects.*

625 - *This is the standard, specifying the number of horizontal lines that make up the TV picture. 625 being the U.K standard and 525 being the American.*

SECAM - *French and East Europe, USSR colour television standard. Stands for Sequential Colour with Memory.*

STANDARDS CONVERSION - *The process of converting between different TV transmission signals. Usually refers to conversion from and to PAL and NTSC.*

T.B.C - *Time Base Corrector - device required to correct time base errors of a VTR which build up during operation. Needed in dubbing, particularly for poor quality material.*

TELECINE - *Device for transferring film to video tape. Film can be colour graded during this process.*

TIME CODE - *Binary Code recorded on video and audio tape recorders which uniquely identifies frames. Used for synchronising recorders and editing.*

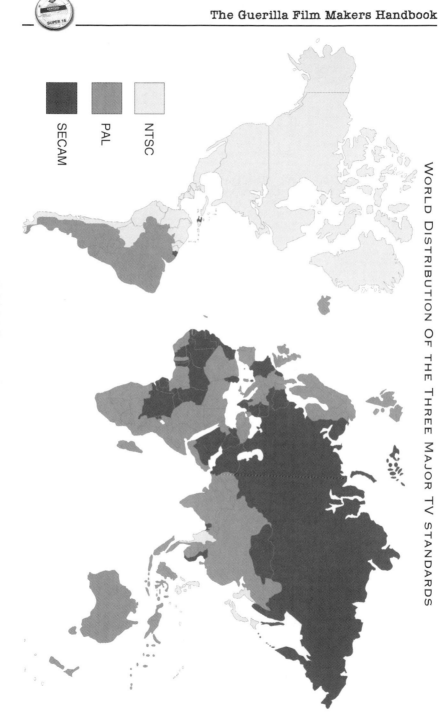

WORLD DISTRIBUTION OF THE THREE MAJOR TV STANDARDS

NTSC

PAL

SECAM

POST-PRODUCTION

TELEVISION STANDARDS - BY COUNTRY

Abu Dhabi - 625 PAL
Afghanistan - 625 PAL/ SECAM
Albania - 625 SECAM
Algeria - 625 PAL
Andorra - 625 PAL
Angola - 625 PAL
Antigua - 525 NTSC
Argentina - 625 PAL N
Australia - 625 PAL
Austria - 625 PAL
The Azores - 625 PAL
Bahamas - 525 NTSC
Bahrain - 625 PAL
Bangladesh - 625 PAL
Barbados - 525 NTSC
Belgium - 625 PAL
Belize - 525 NTSC
Benin - 625 SECAM
Bermuda - 525 NTSC
Bolivia - 525 NTSC
Bophuthatswana - 625 PAL
Bosnia/Herzegovina - 625 PAL
Botswana - 625 PAL
Brazil - 525 PAL M
British Virgin Isles - 525 NTSC
Brunei - 625 PAL
Bulgaria - 625 SECAM
Bukina Faso - 625 SECAM
Burma - 525 NTSC
Burundi - 625 SECAM
Cameroon - 625 PAL
Canada - 525 NTSC
Canary Islands - 625 PAL
Central African Republic - 625 SECAM
Chad - 625 SECAM
Chile - 525 NTSC
China - 625 PAL
Colombia - 525 NTSC
Congo - 625 SECAM
Cook Islands - 625 PAL
Croatia - 625 PAL
Cuba - 525 NTSC
Curacao - 525 NTSC
Cyprus - 625 PAL/ SECAM
Czechoslovakia - 625 SECAM
Denmark - 625 PAL
Djibouti - 625 SECAM
Dominican Republic - 525 NTSC
Dubai - 625 PAL
Ecuador - 525 NTSC
Eire - 625 PAL
Eqypt - 625 PAL/ SECAM
El Salvador - 525 NTSC
Equatorial Guinea - 625 SECAM
Ethiopia - 625 PAL
Faeroe Islands - 625 PAL
Fiji - 625 PAL
Finland - 625 PAL
France - 625 SECAM
French Polynesia - 625 SECAM
Gabon - 625 SECAM

Galapagos Isles - 525 NTSC
Germany - 625 PAL
Ghana - 625 PAL
Gibraltar - 625 PAL
Greece - 625 SECAM
Greenland - 625 PAL
Grenada - 525 NTSC
Guadalope - 625 SECAM
Guam - 525 NTSC
Guatemala - 525 NTSC
Guinea (French) - 625 SECAM
Guinea - 625 SECAM
Guyana Republic - 625 SECAM
Haiti - 625 SECAM
Honduras - 525 NTSC
Hong Kong - 625 PAL
Hungary - 625 SECAM/ PAL
Iceland - 625 PAL
India - 625 PAL
Indonesia - 625 PAL
Iran - 625 SECAM/ PAL
Iraq - 625 SECAM
Israel - 625 PAL
Italy - 625 PAL
Ivory Coast - 625 SECAM
Jamaica - 525 NTSC
Japan - 525 NTSC
Jordan - 625 PAL
Kampuchea - 525 NTSC
Kenya - 625 PAL
Korea (North) - 625 SECAM/ 525 NTSC
Korea (South) - 525 NTSC
Kuwait - 625 PAL
Laos - 625 SECAM/ PAL
Lebanon - 625 SECAM
Leeward Isles - 525 NTSC
Lesotho - 625 PAL
Liberia - 625 PAL
Libya - 625 SECAM
Luxembourg - 625 SECAM/ PAL
Macedonia - 625 PAL
Madagascar - 625 SECAM
Madeira - 625 PAL
Malawi - 625 PAL
Malaysia - 625 PAL
Maldives - 625 PAL
Mali - 625 SECAM
Malta - 625 PAL
Martinique - 625 SECAM
Mauritius - 625 SECAM
Mexico - 525 NTSC
Monaco - 625 PAL/SECAM
Mongolia - 625 SECAM
Morocco - 625 SECAM
Mozambique - 625 PAL
Namibia - 625 PAL
Nepal - 625 PAL
Netherlands - 625 PAL
Netherlands Antilles - 525 NTSC
New Caledonia - 625 SECAM
New Zealand - 625 PAL

Nicaragua - 525 NTSC
Niger - 625 SECAM
Nigeria - 625 PAL
Norway - 625 PAL
Oman - 625 PAL
Pakistan - 625 PAL
Panama - 525 NTSC
Papua New Guinea - 625 PAL
Paraguay - 625 PAL M
Peru - 525 NTSC
Philippines - 525 NTSC
Poland - 625 SECAM
Polynesia - 625 SECAM
Portugal - 625 PAL
Puerto Rico - 525 NTSC
Qatar - 625 PAL
Reunion - 625 SECAM
Romania - 625 SECAM
Rwanda - 625 SECAM
Sarawak - 625 PAL
Samoa (Eastern) - 525 NTSC
San Marino - 625 PAL
Saudi Arabia - 625 SECAM
Senegal - 625 SECAM
Seychelles - 625 PAL
Sierra Leone - 625 PAL
Singapore - 625 PAL
South Africa - 625 PAL
South West Africa - 625 PAL
Spain - 625 PAL
Sri Lanka - 625 PAL
St. Kitts & Nevis - 525 NTSC
Sudan - 625 PAL
Surinam - 525 NTSC
Swaziland - 625 PAL
Sweden - 625 PAL
Switzerland - 625 PAL
Syria - 625 SECAM
Tahiti - 625 SECAM
Taiwan - 525 NTSC
Thailand - 625 PAL
Togo - 625 SECAM
Trinidad & Tobago - 525 NTSC
Tunisia - 625 SECAM
Turkey - 625 PAL
Uganda - 625 PAL
United Arab Emirates - 625 PAL
United Kingdom - 625 PAL
Uruguay - 625 PAL M
USA - 525 NTSC
Former USSR - 625 SECAM
Vatican City - 625 PAL
Venezuala - 525 NTSC
Vietnam - 625 SECAM/ NTSC
Virgin Isles - 525 NTSC
Yemen - 625 PAL/ SECAM
Former Yugoslavia - 625 PAL
Zaire - 625 SECAM
Zambia - 625 PAL
Zanzibar (Tanzania) - 625 PAL
Zimbabwe - 625 PAL

POST-PRODUCTION

Tape to Film Transfer
Geraldine Swayne
of the CFC

Q - What is tape to film?

Geraldine - The transfer of images from video-tape onto film. There are now a few ways to do this but in terms of *price* there are either cheap low-resolution transfers (off monitors), or expensive high-resolution digital methods. Digital transfers can be done using a CRT scanner or an Arri-laser recorder. The video image is interpolated from 500 odd lines to aprox. 2000. The necessary digitisation of images during this process allows for re-racking, digital sharpening and grading and title compositing to take place before shooting. Low-res transfers are much faster but a film-camera is literally just grabbing images off a high-definition monitor.

Q - Why use tape to film?

Geraldine - Tape to film saves money for commercials producers because they can shoot on film, then telecine to tape, then do their effects at video res (i.e. cheaper), show the piece on telly, and *then* go straight to cinema by simply transferring the finished piece digitally. And in this way they won't have to rebuild the whole job using the original camera negative which is very expensive. In the features world tape to film is necessary for directors who've shot their film on some kind of video tape, for example DigiBeta or DV (*Festen, Blair Witch* etc). The digital high-res route is always preferable because of image quality but for longer work a low-resolution transfer is more affordable. For a low budget feature, stick to S16 if possible, (you can always telecine later). However if the project was shot on DV, then a later tape to film transfer may be needed for certain presentations. Things like grading, special effects, fades etc, can be cheaper and faster to do at video resolution, but remember shooting on tape with a view to a later transfer is not a cheap route. Even a low-resolution transfer is expensive and it won't be as pretty as film.

Q - How long does it take?

Geraldine - Shooting on a low-res system is done more or less in real time, with very few changes being made to your piece. The negative is then processed as normal at the lab and a rush print made. Shooting on a digital devise is slower. Each frame is treated in its various colour components, and the images are also digitised prior to transfer, then usually re-racked, re-sharpened and anti-aliased. It can take two to three days to set-up and out-put a few minutes of tape.

Q - Can I shoot it off a monitor myself and do my own video to film transfer in my bed-room?

Geraldine - Absolutely. Why not? There is no cheaper way to get video onto film at the moment. Although if its done without care you could end up wasting a load of money, so take technical advise. e.g. you won't be able to use your domestic telly, you'll need a broadcast monitor. You will also need a professional video player, such as a Digi-Beta. You should shoot straight onto 35mm, with a blast of colour bars at the head of each roll for the grader at the lab. You will also need to break your film into 9min chunks as that is the maximum that a 35mm camera can handle. Lastly you must ensure that the camera and monitor are 100% in sync or you might find an unsightly buzz bar creeping up into frame five minutes in.

Q - What happens about picture grading and the sound?

Geraldine - It's best to make all your visual creative choices before you do your tape to film transfer. This also takes advantage of the fact that you are doing post production on video, probably an Avid or other non linear system. DO NOT oversaturate your video with colour in your post-production grading stage as it can cause banding in the film which is very ugly. For the sound, with us it is all part of the deal, but if you were doing your own cheap transfer *'in your bedroom'* then you'd need to send the sound to an optical sound transfer facility like Warwick Sound in Soho. They would shoot a 35mm optical sound for you. Remember, you will need to break your sound up into the same chunks as the picture or you won't be able to sync it up later.

Q - If you are making a science fiction film at PAL video res, you can use software like Adobe After Effects or 3d Studio Max to achieve breathtaking results?

Geraldine - Yes - on a monitor the results can be great. But then transferring the work to film may have its own problems. Video artefacts and poor matte-lines etc will tend to stand-out. Remember watching a 24in TV is very different from a darkened theatre with a 22 foot screen, and cinema projection is very unforgiving. With effects you should render everything at as high a resolution as possible. The same thing applies to titles too.

Q - What are the most common mistakes?

Geraldine - Some colours just don't transfer well, fluorescent and other artificially forced colours may look good on video but on film it might just look terrible - avoid oversaturated colours. Some effects like artificial grain could cause nasty effects, so seek advice before applying any radical effect to your project. If you intend your project to be screened in a cinema, make sure you shoot the correct aspect ratio, probably 1.85-1, otherwise you will lose picture at the top and bottom of the frame and any mistakes like overexposure or poor focus will scream at you in the cinema.

Q - What advice would you offer?

Geraldine - Be absolutely clear why you want to shoot on tape. When shooting video, avoid areas of high contrast, and hard edges which will emphasise video aliasing. If you're using a monitor at the shoot, unless it is properly calibrated do not expect it to represent what is going on in the camera from a colour point of view. Err towards under, rather than over-exposure and remember video colours are very different to film colours, so there will be changes between the video, as you know it, and the final print. You can foresee these changes in a stable, calibrated, digital suite but of course this will cost money. Don't shoot with auto-focus on and be hand-held as seldom as possible. Remember that a cinema is blacked-out and the screen is huge and unforgiving. The least thing will show up. Lastly, if you can afford it, shoot on film.

CF|C

Geraldine Swayne
Senior VF Operator

The Computer Film Company

19-23 Wells Street
London W1P 3FP
Tel (020) 7344 8000
Fax (020) 7344 8001
gerry@cfc.co.uk

Post Production Notes - See next four flow charts.

Post production is the area where most new film makers make the biggest and most expensive mistakes. Here are a series of flow charts that provide a solid, tried and tested route, plus a brief explanation.

On set, the camera team shoot Super 16mm negative at 25fps. The sound recordist records on DAT at 44.1 khz. Both the unexposed rushes and the DAT tapes are then sent to the labs, along with camera report sheets and sound report sheets.

Overnight, the negative is developed and transferred on a telecine machine onto BetaSP with timecode. The sound is then synced to the picture and laid off onto BetaSP as a guide, and clone DAT tapes with timecode that matches the picture are run off. These clone DAT tapes now become the master sound elements.

The following morning the rushes are sent to the cutting room. The editor files all the notes and report sheets, then stores the clone DAT tapes in a box on a top shelf. The editor will come back to these clone DAT tapes later.

The editor then digitises the footage from the Beta tapes, taking care not to digitise unwanted sound or two tracks of audio when the sound was recorded in mono. This will save time later, and storage space now.

Once the footage is digitised, the editor can now start creatively cutting the movie. Each day more rushes will appear and each day these scenes will be cut, until all scenes are cut together. The scenes will then be joined up and the film makers will watch the first assembly.

The first assembly is always awful. Don't get depressed. Fix it. Re-edit, re-cut, re-shuffle... Extra shots or cutaways will probably be needed and the producer will arrange for a weekend shoot to cover these. After inserting these new shots and a lengthy re-edit, show the film to an audience. Try to find a small screening room or theatre with video projection and screen the fllm. Ask the audience of non film makers (who don't know you) what they thought and establish if there are any plot issues that just don't work. If there are, re-cut and re-shoot if needed.

Once everyone is happy, the editor can lock picture and cut the movie up into 35mm length reels (max 2000' including leaders). Look for ends of scenes in which to make these breaks, or during slower sequences without music. These breaks represent where your reel changes will occur and the film can get very damaged at these places - you don't want a four second chunk of your movie to disappear in the middle of a crucial scene just because a projectionist at some far flung festival didn't care about your print. The editor will generate a CMX 3600 EDL (or preferred EDL for the neg cutters)

Continued...

POST-PRODUCTION

POST PRODUCTION FLOW CHART

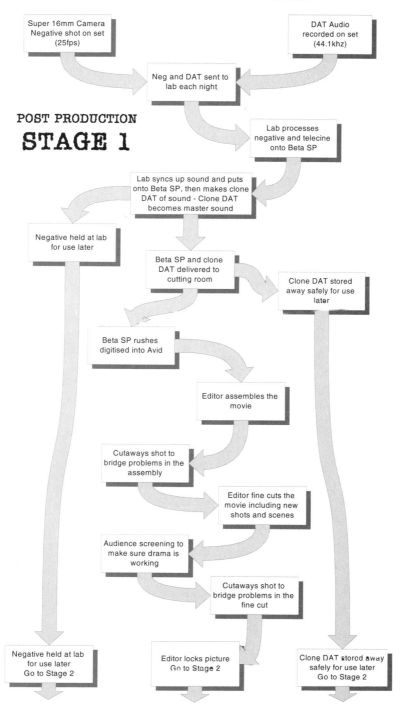

Super 16mm Camera Negative shot on set (25fps)

DAT Audio recorded on set (44.1khz)

Neg and DAT sent to lab each night.

POST PRODUCTION
STAGE 1

Lab processes negative and telecine onto Beta SP

Lab syncs up sound and puts onto Beta SP, then makes clone DAT of sound - Clone DAT becomes master sound

Negative held at lab for use later

Beta SP and clone DAT delivered to cutting room

Clone DAT stored away safely for use later

Beta SP rushes digitised into Avid

Editor assembles the movie

Cutaways shot to bridge problems in the assembly

Editor fine cuts the movie including new shots and scenes

Audience screening to make sure drama is working

Cutaways shot to bridge problems in the fine cut

Negative held at lab for use later
Go to Stage 2

Editor locks picture
Go to Stage 2

Clone DAT stored away safely for use later
Go to Stage 2

POST-PRODUCTION

POST PRODUCTION FLOW CHART

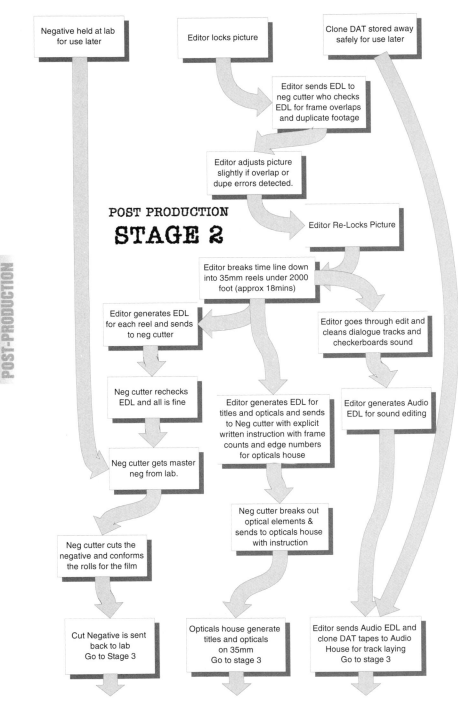

Negative held at lab for use later

Editor locks picture

Clone DAT stored away safely for use later

Editor sends EDL to neg cutter who checks EDL for frame overlaps and duplicate footage

Editor adjusts picture slightly if overlap or dupe errors detected.

POST PRODUCTION
STAGE 2

Editor Re-Locks Picture

Editor breaks time line down into 35mm reels under 2000 foot (approx 18mins)

Editor generates EDL for each reel and sends to neg cutter

Editor goes through edit and cleans dialogue tracks and checkerboards sound

Neg cutter rechecks EDL and all is fine

Editor generates EDL for titles and opticals and sends to Neg cutter with explicit written instruction with frame counts and edge numbers for opticals house

Editor generates Audio EDL for sound editing

Neg cutter gets master neg from lab.

Neg cutter breaks out optical elements & sends to opticals house with instruction

Neg cutter cuts the negative and conforms the rolls for the film

Cut Negative is sent back to lab Go to Stage 3

Opticals house generate titles and opticals on 35mm Go to stage 3

Editor sends Audio EDL and clone DAT tapes to Audio House for track laying Go to stage 3

POST PRODUCTION FLOW CHART

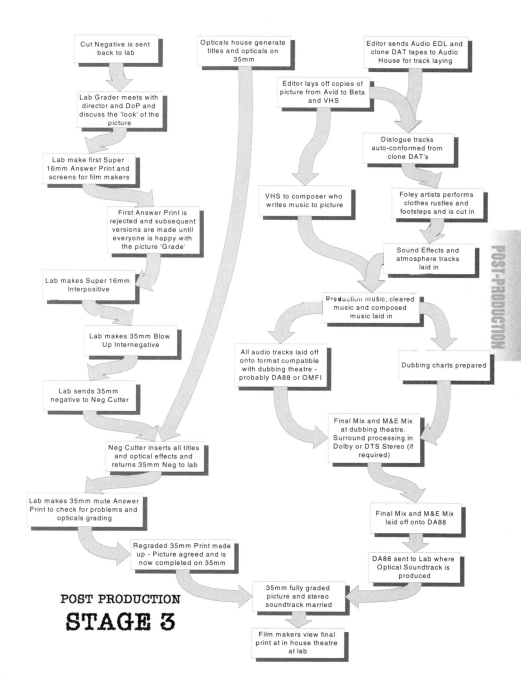

Cut Negative is sent back to lab

Opticals house generate titles and opticals on 35mm

Editor sends Audio EDL and clone DAT tapes to Audio House for track laying

Lab Grader meets with director and DoP and discuss the 'look' of the picture

Editor lays off copies of picture from Avid to Beta and VHS

Dialogue tracks auto-conformed from clone DAT's

Lab make first Super 16mm Answer Print and screens for film makers

First Answer Print is rejected and subsequent versions are made until everyone is happy with the picture 'Grade'

VHS to composer who writes music to picture

Foley artists performs clothes rustles and footsteps and is cut in

Lab makes Super 16mm Interpositive

Sound Effects and atmosphere tracks laid in

Lab makes 35mm Blow Up Internegative

Production music, cleared music and composed music laid in

Lab sends 35mm negative to Neg Cutter

All audio tracks laid off onto format compatible with dubbing theatre - probably DA88 or OMFI

Dubbing charts prepared

Neg Cutter inserts all titles and optical effects and returns 35mm Neg to lab

Final Mix and M&E Mix at dubbing theatre. Surround processing in Dolby or DTS Stereo (if required)

Lab makes 35mm mute Answer Print to check for problems and opticals grading

Regraded 35mm Print made up - Picture agreed and is now completed on 35mm

Final Mix and M&E Mix laid off onto DA88

DA88 sent to Lab where Optical Soundtrack is produced

POST PRODUCTION
STAGE 3

35mm fully graded picture and stereo soundtrack married

Film makers view final print at in house theatre at lab

POST-PRODUCTION

POST PRODUCTION FLOW CHART

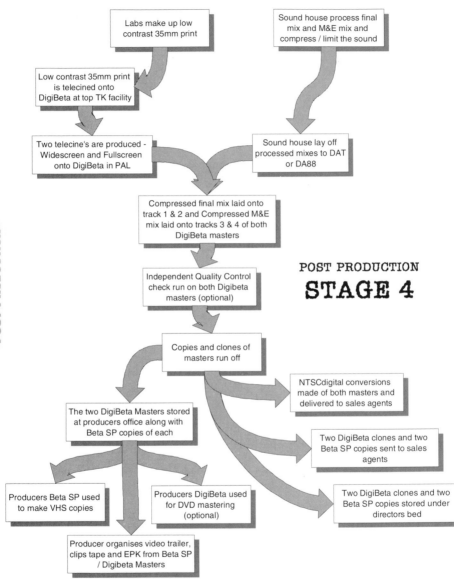

Labs make up low contrast 35mm print

Sound house process final mix and M&E mix and compress / limit the sound

Low contrast 35mm print is telecined onto DigiBeta at top TK facility

Two telecine's are produced - Widescreen and Fullscreen onto DigiBeta in PAL

Sound house lay off processed mixes to DAT or DA88

Compressed final mix laid onto track 1 & 2 and Compressed M&E mix laid onto tracks 3 & 4 of both DigiBeta masters

Independent Quality Control check run on both Digibeta masters (optional)

POST PRODUCTION
STAGE 4

Copies and clones of masters run off

NTSCdigital conversions made of both masters and delivered to sales agents

The two DigiBeta Masters stored at producers office along with Beta SP copies of each

Two DigiBeta clones and two Beta SP copies sent to sales agents

Producers Beta SP used to make VHS copies

Producers DigiBeta used for DVD mastering (optional)

Two DigiBeta clones and two Beta SP copies stored under directors bed

Producer organises video trailer, clips tape and EPK from Beta SP / Digibeta Masters

POST-PRODUCTION

and send it to the neg cutter. The neg cutter will then check for duplicate footage and cuts where overlap frames have not been left. If there are any problems, the editor will have to re-cut to fix them. Once all negative issues have been resolved, these new EDLs, along with a VHS of the picture, will be sent to the neg cutter.

The neg cutter will then get the master film negative from the lab and conform it to the EDL cutting list and VHS tape you supplied. This will be an A and B roll Super 16mm negative cut. Once the neg has been cut, it is sent back to the laboratory.

As soon as possible, a VHS with burnt in time code (and audio time code on Ch2 of the VHS audio) will be sent to the composer who will write music to picture.

At the same time as the negative cutting and if the editor has time, the editor can clean up the dialogue tracks and checker-board them for tracklaying. Once this is complete, the editor will run off a BetaSP of each reel, with burnt in timecode on the picture. The editor will also generate an audio EDL for all the sound. This Beta, the EDL's and the clone DAT tapes will be sent to the company who is doing the audio track lay, the Sound House. The sound was recorded at 44.1khz and it's important that everyone - sound house, musician etc. - works at 44.1khz so that the entire audio post production process remains 100% digital throughout (or as close to).

The sound house will re-conform the dialogue tracks from the EDL and clone DAT tapes. They will then continue to improve the sound, add or replace dialogue if needed (ADR). Once done, they will add sound effects, atmosphere tracks, spend a day with a foley artist spotting the film, and generally brighten the acoustic quality. Once the music is available that will also be track laid in.

Once all the sound is in place, the sound house will prepare Dubbing Charts, or contact the dubbing theatre to see if they have software that can read their EDL's. The Sound House will then lay off all the sound onto a format of media compatible with the dubbing theatre, probably DA88 or OMFI media files.

Note - it is possible that the sound hHouse of your choice will also produce the final sound mix, thereby negating the need to move to a separate Dubbing Theatre.

Note - with all digital media not on tapes, such as EDL's and OMFI files, it is a good idea to perform tests to make sure everyone can read and write each other's formats, disks and software.

At the same time as the audio track lay, the lab will begin work on the print.

The lab will make a Super 16mm first answer print. In this print, the Grader will have made all the shots work in terms of density and colour balance. The DoP and director will watch this print and discuss the changes they need. Generally, there will be several attempts until these elements are entirely locked down - DO NOT move onto the next stage unless you are 100% happy with the picture grade, even if the lab attempt to coerce you.

Once you have locked the picture grade, the lab will produce a Super16mm Interpositive. Then they will produce a 35mm Internegative. These two stages will probably take a month, regardless of what the lab promise.

Once the Internegative is complete, it will be sent to the negative cutters, along with the Optical effects and the Titles from the opticals house. These new elements will be cut into the 35mm Master negative. The 35mm Negative will then be returned to the Lab where it will be printed - this is the 35mm Check Print, or Mute Answer Print. Again, the film makers will watch this print and discuss any changes. Generally, these will be minor as all the grading hard work has been done, although there may be grading issues with the titles and optical elements.

At the same time, the Dubbing Theatre will probably be mixing your final sound. It takes a long time to mix and it is expensive. It is important to make all your decisions before you go in and know exactly what you expect from the dubbing mixer.

Note - at this stage, and indeed all stages, it is worth stating that the project was shot and is being post produced at 25fps, and that the sound was shot and is being post produced at 44.1khz.

You will premix two elements separately, dialogue premix, then the atmospheres and effects premix. You will then do the final mix, adding foley and music to the pre mixed dialogue tracks and atmos and effects tracks. This will be the final mix. If you have chosen to mix in Dolby or DTS Stereo, this is the stage where you will process the sound accordingly.

After you have done the final mix, you will do a second mix, the M&E mix. The mixer will remix the film, but pull out the dialogue tracks.

These two mixes will be put on a clearly labelled tape, probably a DA88. This DA88 tape will be taken to the lab where they will shoot an optical version of the sound onto 35mm film. This sound will then be combined with the 35mm negative and your first print will be produced.

This print will then be screened with full sound and picture. Hopefully all goes well and it's time to go down to the pub... but not for long.

Once the theatrical version of the film has been produced, you will need to make video masters.

First you will need to process the sound. Cinema sound is too dynamic for TV so it needs to be compressed. Take the master DA88 sound mix, both full sound and M&E, back to the sound house and they will pass it through a compressor limiter. This will 'squeeze' the dynamic range, making the quiet bits louder and the loud bits quieter. These compressed mixes will then be laid onto DA88 or DAT (with timecode) and will become the Video Master Sound Mixes.

The lab will produce a low contrast 35mm print which you will take to the Video Mastering facility. Do not use a cheap company, go to the best and pay the rate or you will be back doing multiple telecines.

Take the 35mm Low Contrast Print and Video Master Sound Mixes to the Video Mastering company. They will lock up the 35mm picture with the sound. The picture will then be graded for TV and recorded onto video tape, probably Digital Betacam (DigiBeta) from a telecine machine. At the same time, the full sound mix needs to be copied onto tracks 1 & 2 of the DigiBeta tape, and the M&E mix onto tracks 3 & 4 of the DigiBeta.

You will need to do several versions, to some degree at your discretion.

1. PAL Widescreen Video Master - this is a version of the film where there are black bars at the top and bottom of the screen (1.85:1 aspect ratio).

2. PAL Full Screen Video Master (Pan and scan) - this is a version where the picture is zoomed in to fill the television screen (1 - 1.33 aspect ratio).

3. PAL 16-9 Full Height Anamorphic - Similar to the Widescreen version, but fills the picture area by squeezing the image. Typically used for DVD mastering.

On top of these three masters, you will probably need to do them again but in NTSC.

After completing your masters, each should be cloned for the Sales Agents, Distributors, relevant creatives such as DoP / Director / Editor etc. As the producer, NEVER let the master out of your hands.

Note - it is essential that all video masters contain the full mix and the M&E mix on the audio tracks. It is essential that the video masters are technically 'legal' - that is the video element does not exceed 1v or drop below 0.3v and that the audio never exceeds PPM 6.

Note - film making creates a lot of 'junk'. Find a box where you can store things like DA88 sound mixes, EDL's, Beta tapes etc., and store it away, probably forever... but you never know. Remember, the lab will also be holding onto anywhere between 50 and 100 cut up original camera rolls, 30 DAT tapes, umpteen various interpos / interneg elements. After the first year you will have to pay for this storage, or find a relative with a spacious, air conditioned loft!

IMPORTANT - There are 1001 ways to post produce a film. This is a generic route that works, although at every stage, there are other ways of post producing with a view to extreme economy. Companies have different kit and different ways of working. The best way to approach post production is with as much planning as possible, make your contacts, do your deals, then meet and talk through every detail - don't leave anything to chance or what you feel was implied will bite you where it hurts and when you least expect it.

International Sales Agent
Andrew Brown & Billy Hurman of Winchester Films

Q - Is there a type of film that sells the most?

Andrew - Big names transcend all genres. If you don't have that cast, which you probably won't on a low budget film, then a genre that tends to be more bullet proof than others is thrillers. *Lighthouse,* for instance, sold all over the world, getting a US theatrical and there were no names in the cast. Comedy is the next genre that sells well.

Q - US Indies are often very successful, why aren't Brit Indies more successful?

Billy - The American Indies have more of an edge and appear to be more quirky. The very fact that they're US made seems to act as an endorsement of quality because in the minds of many international buyers - US equals Hollywood. Many British Indies are much more dialogue heavy whereas US Indies are much more 'action'. When an Indie here in Britain works, it's when it's being brave and the film makers are taking a risk.

Q - What do you need from a producer to sell a movie?

Billy - Some kind of marketing hook so that when a buyer says to us *who's the cast?* and we can't give them a big name, we can give them other elements. Nobody gives you brownie points for saying *I'm a poor film maker and my movie cost next to nothing and it took 20 years to make.* The audience won't hear that and say *OK, well we won't go and see the latest Tom Cruise film, we'll see yours instead.* It doesn't work that way. Once you've made the film you're up there with the big boys, fighting for screens, editorial and an audience.

Andrew - It also helps if the producer can shoot on 35mm. We've had trouble with people shooting on S16mm as more and more buyers are getting picky, especially in Germany, where they're getting stricter with quality control.

Q - Can a film maker come to you with their screenplay?

Billy - Yes, we read everything that comes to us. We don't do development but we do invest our time if we like a project. The only thing we're interested in is getting the best possible project to sell. We hope that the producer has already acted as a clearing house, so they've come to us with their final draft, they've got some sort of finance, not necessarily in their pocket, but they've been to see other people who're interested and they've had discussions with agents and they have a wish list of talent.

Q - Technically, what do you need to sell a movie?

Billy - We have our own delivery company called First Service and there's a whole list of delivery items that the producer has to legally and technically deliver.

Q - Is there anything on that list that regularly causes problems?

Andrew - Stills. A lot of people forget this. Producers can be so busy with the actual process of the film that something like stills, which are so imperative to the marketing process, are forgotten and we're left with substandard materials. It doesn't do the film any good and it makes the job a lot harder for us. Get a stills photographer involved from the beginning.

Q - What kind of deal does a producer get with a sales agent?

Billy - Every deal is different, it depends on what's happening in the financing. Whether the film is just a pickup, i.e. we've seen it, like it, we'll sell it and take a commission, or whether we've put money in or put the strands of money together and acted as an Executive Producer. Standard commissions are 20 - 25% outside the US and 15% within the US but it's negotiable.

Q - What about expenses?

Billy - When the producer comes to us, we sit down and look at the film year, through the three main markets. We agree on a marketing budget which depends on the budget of the film, but a standard amount for a low budget film is $150k. This includes us going to the 3 major markets, advertising in trades, doing posters, screenings, a contribution to our travel expenses and to the offices in the markets. The marketing overhead costs like flights and offices are split between the amount of films that we're representing. If the budget doesn't appear to be enough and sales are going well we will only increase it with written permission from the Producers. We might also set up pre screenings, for instance with *Shooting Fish* we went to New York preceding Cannes. It's very difficult to get all the Americans in one room at one time so the idea was that we'd have one hit, on home territory with them and then we'd screen the film two or three times. This worked wonders - a buyer from Fox Searchlight saw the film in New York, then another one of their buyers in Cannes and all the decision makers finally saw it and they bought it. Once we start to do sales from the film, our expenses come out first.

Q - How long does it take to see returns on the film?

Andrew - It's difficult to sell low budget movies as a lot of distributors do regard marketing as *names on a poster*, but I think that if you target the right audience with the right film, then you're going to get a good reaction and return. If a film is looked after, nurtured with very targeted marketing, you could get bigger returns than on a film with bigger

FOUR MEDIA COMPANY
2820 W. OLIVE AVENUE, BURBANK CA 91505-4455   818.840.7100
QUALITY CONTROL REPORT

Part 1 of 1

Title: White Angel   Eps. #:   4MC ID. #: LS700724
Series:
W.O. #: 134615 P.O. #: 370   TRT: : 95 : 26
Client: Colimar Ent.

☐ PASS ☒ Fail ☐ Hold Comment: AUDIO TICKS ON CH 3&4

QC Date: 6/18/96   Record Date: ☒ Full QC   ☐ Spot Check
QC Vtr #: 22   Record VTR #   ☒ Video   ☐ Film
Stock Mfg: Fuji   Vendor: Soho601   ☒ 2 ch Audio   ☐ 4 ch. Audio

☐ D-1	☐ D-Betacam	☐ Transfer Master	☐ Letterbox	☐ DFTC
☐ D-2	☐ NTSC	☐ Protection Master	☐ Pan Scan	☐ NDFTC
☐ 1" C	☒ PAL	☐ Edit Master	☒ Flat	☒ EBUTC
☒ Betacam	☐ Conversion	☐ Clone	☐ Scope	☐ ASTC
☐ DCT	☐ DEFT	☐ Dub	☐ 16 x 9	

11.4	Horizontal Blanking	1.4	Front Porch ☒	RF Envelope	☒ Format
0	Setup	19/21	VITC	Control Track	☒ Slate
300/300	Sync Burst		CC	Channel Cond.	☐ Labels
26	Vertical Blanking		VITS	Tension	☒ Tape Wrap
	Serrations		VIRS ☒	Tracking	☒ Shipper

PROGRAM VIDEO LEVELS   Luminance Avg 300   Luminance Peak 700   Chroma Peak (Flat) 700

Audio Specifications

Levels   NR   Tones

Channel	Track Content		Avg	Peak	Dolby	100	1K	10K
								0
1	English Stereo Comp		0	+13				0
2	English Stereo Comp		0	+13				0
3	Music Mono		-9	+12				0
4	Effects Mono		-17	+16				
Cue								

General Comments

Line up tone under bars are down 5DB when left in unity.
Time code not set at regular format picture starts at 00:03:00:00
Copyright 1993 Living Spirit Pictures Ltd. Failed because audio ticks are only on ch 3&4.
At childrens party scene the back ground music is on both ch 3 & 4 should only be on ch 4 as an effect

Inspected By: Valerie Moore-Porter

WHITEANGEL.DOC REV07/9/89 PM

The Quality Control (Q/C) on delivery items can be stringent. Dust particles, scratches, bumps - anything technically imperfect could stall a deal. This company actual found a negative scratch on White Angel that Living Spirit had never seen in 62 screenings!

names. We sold most of the major territories for *Lighthouse* on the strength of it's trailer at MIFED, then cleaned up in Cannes which culminated in the US deal. So it can happen very quickly. If something doesn't happen in the first year then you've got a problem, you've then got to start looking at alternatives, say packaging the movie for instance.

Q - So the territories are bought for a certain length of time?

Billy - Yes usually they buy a licence for between 7 to 10 years, paying a minimum guarantee with a possible royalty share a couple of years down the line. Our job is to reach an arrangement with a distributor where they feel they've been given a term which is long enough for them to recoup. After that license period we can resell the film.

Q - What is the shelf life for a film before you've exhausted everything?

Andrew - You've got your initial burst of life, which is the market year including the 3 main markets, then you start getting into packaging and library material. The real physical life of a film continues indefinitely. After the agreed licence the film reverts back to us and/or the producer and if it's a film that isn't dated, sometimes you can resell it as a library item. There are more and more ancillary markets opening up, especially now with the Internet.

Q - What's the likelihood of an advance for film makers?

Andrew - We don't offer advances except for when we are talking to Hollywood producers where you really have to have the capital to make an offer otherwise you're not going to get the movie.

Q - What are the main markets and how do they work?

Andrew - There are three main markets, AFM in February, Cannes in May and MIFED in October. But increasingly for guerilla style movies, the Berlin Film Festival, Toronto Film Festival and Sundance are becoming important venues. As a producer you could be working abroad for a whole year doing markets and festivals because there are so many!

SALES

Q - What do you need from a producer to help you with those markets?

Billy - On a technical level we need a print and stills. We don't take on any film that we feel we can't market. The marketing campaign is devised by us, all the publicity materials are done in house although we also consult with the producer and director.

Q - Does it help if a film makers go out to any of these markets?

Billy - When producers have come out to Cannes for instance, they've been great in helping drum up publicity, fly posting and getting an audience into theatres. We advise directors not to come out because no matter how many times you tell them how buyers go in and watch their movie for 5 minutes, then walk out, they just don't believe you. Film makers believe, quite rightly, that they have the best film that he or she can make and we will endeavour to sell that film to the best of our ability. Sometimes they can be over zealous but it is good from our point of view because ultimately we benefit from the positive attitude.

Q - Do you send out tapes in between markets?

Andrew - Yes we do but the markets are the best environment to sell, you've got the buzz going around the film and everyone's there to buy.

Q - What are pre-sales?

Billy - Selling the movie before it's been made which is all down to the marketing of the film. If buyers like the script and it captures their imagination then you can get pre-sales, especially if the elements fit together quite well. It comes down to whether you've built up a desire for these people to buy the film or not. We have good relationships with buyers around the world which is important to the point that some buyers will even buy over the phone.

Q - Is there a possibility for a low budget movie to make pre-sales?

Andrew - Yes, but it's getting harder at the markets, people have been burnt before when they

During Cannes week, sales agents and distributors descend on the south of France and take over any free space where they could promote the films they are selling. It's worth going down to Cannes, even if you don't have a project, to experience the Insanity that is international sales.

Not all of these items will be needed by a sales agent, but most will. Some items, like the E&O policy can be negotiated around as it is usually only needed for the USA. The cost of making up this extensive list of items could feasibly cost more than the production costs of an ultra low budget film. Speak to your sales agent and negotiate an exact list, with a budget for making up that list, BEFORE you sign any sales agreement.

Release Print - 35mm com/opt print (Combined optical print). This is used by the sales agent to screen the film at markets in a cinema environment.

35mm Interpositive and 35mm Internegative - made from the original negative. You have already made this in order to produce your final print, and will be held at the lab.

35mm Optical Sound Negative - made from master sound mix. You have already made this in order to produce your final print, and will be held at the lab.

Sound Master - master sound mix, probably supplied on either DA88 or time coded DAT. Some agents may request a 35mm sound master which you should avoid. This sound mix will also be on the DigiBeta on tracks 1 and 2.

Music & Effect Mix (M&E) - master M&E sound mix used for foreign territories to re-voice the film. Supplied on either DA88 or time coded DAT. Some agents may request a 35mm sound master which you should avoid. This sound mix will also be on the DigiBeta on tracks 3 and 4.

Textless Title Background - 35mm Interneg / Interpos / print of sequences without title elements. Used by territories to re-title in their native language. Video versions of the textless backgrounds will also be needed.

35mm Trailer - Including access to interneg, interpos, optical sound, magnetic sound master and M&E mix. It is common now to produce the trailer on DigiBeta and digitally copy the video onto film. The quality isn't as good but it may be adequate and certainly cheaper and easier to produce.

Video Tape - Full screen (not widescreen) perfect quality Digital Betacam of the film, including stereo sound (on tracks 1&2) and M&E (on tracks 3&4). You may want to make widescreen versions and 16-9 versions too, but these will probably be subsequent to the full screen version. You may need to supply a BetaSP so that the sales agent can make VHS copies.

Video Tape Textless Backgrounds - Full screen (not widescreen) perfect quality Digital Betacam of textless background sequences, including stereo sound (on tracks 1&2) and M&E (on tracks 3&4).

Video Tape Trailer - Full screen (not widescreen) perfect quality Digital Betacam of the trailer, including stereo sound (on tracks 1&2) and M&E (on tracks 3&4). Digital Betacam is currently the preferred format. You will also need a trailer with textless backgrounds too.

Stills set - 100 full colour transparencies will be requested but you can get away with 20 as long as they are good.

Screenplay transcript of final cut including all music cues. This isn't your shooting script, but an accurate and detailed transcription of all the dialogue and action. You will need to sit down with your PC and a VHS and do it from scratch.

Distribution restrictions - statement of any restrictions or obligations such as the order in which the cast are credited etc.

Music Cue Sheet - an accurate list of all the music cues, rights etc. See the music cue sheet later in the book. Used by collection agencies to distribute music royalties.

US Copyright Notice - available from The Registrar of Copyright, Library of Congress, Washington DC, 20559, USA.

Chain of Title - information and copy contracts with all parties involved with production and distribution of the film. This is needed to prove that you have the right to sell the film to another party. Usually the writer, director, producer, musician, cast and release forms from all other parties involved.

Certificate of Origin and Certificate of Authorship - available from solicitor. You go in, pay a small fee, swear that the information is correct, they witness it and you have your certificates.

Certificate of Nationality - available from the Department of Culture Media and Sport, Dept., of National Heritage, Media Division (Film), 2/4 Cockspur Street, London, SW1Y 5DH.

Credit List - a complete cast and crew list, plus any other credits.

Errors and Omissions Insurance Policy (E&O) - a policy that indemnifies distributors and sales agents internationally. Available from specialised Insurers (approx. cost £4-10k). You may be able to negotiate around this, agreeing to supply it if and when it is needed by any specific distributor.

Lab Access Letter - a letter giving access to materials held at the lab to the sales agent. Remember, if you haven't paid your lab bill yet, they may not give you this letter.

Press and reviews - copies of all press and reviews. Don't give them the bad reviews.

EPK - Electronic Press Kit - betacam of interviews with actors and principal crew. Shots of crew at work, plus clips from film and trailer. You will also need a split M&E version so that interviewees voices can be dipped down allowing a translation to be spoken over the top.

Mini Documentary - more common now and seen as a sweetener. Essential if you want a successful DVD release. Ensure someone shoots some DV footage on set.

SALES

AFM

The American Film Market, held in Feb., taking place at the Loews Hotel in Santa Monica. You pay to get in. Contact the AFM, 10850 Wilshire Blvd, 9th Floor, Los Angeles, CA 90024 USA
Tel: 1 310 446 1000
Fax: 1 310 446 1600
Contact: Jonathan Wolf
email: jwolf@afma.com

Cannes Film Festival

Held in May in Cannes, west of Nice. Free to get in but costly to attend. Contact Cannes Film Festival, 99 Boulevard Malesherbes, 75008 Paris France,
Tel: 33 1 45 61 66 00
Fax: 33 1 45 61 97 60
Contact: Gilles Jacob
www.Cannesmarket.com
www.festival-cannes.fr

MIFED

Held in Milan in Oct. You need a pass to get in. The market is like any other trade fair and sedate in comparison.
Contact MIFED, E.A. Fiera Milano, 20145 Milano, Largo Domodossola 1, C.P. 1270 - 20101 Milan, Italy
Tel: 39 02 4801 2920
Fax: 39 02 4997 7020
Contact: Elena Lloyd
www.fmd.it/mifed

thought they'd take a chance. Now they feel they don't have to and they'll wait for a finished film.

Q - How does a first time film maker get a sales agent?

Billy - Many films we see are at screenings. At this stage of the game there's nothing we can do with the film. Only when the film's exceptional or with a great marketing hook would we do a pick up. More often if the producer had come to us before shooting we could have possibly brought some creative element to the table to make it work better. The sales company has a much better idea of what the end user wants and we know the trends, one year thrillers might be the vogue and horror the next. Ask yourself do you want to make your vision come what may, or do you want to bring in people who spend their daily life speaking to buyers about what they want to buy? We don't want to stifle creativity but we can help. For instance we can organise targeted test screenings before the film goes out and make any relevant changes if there are problems, before it's too late.

Q - How important is it to launch a film at film festivals?

Andrew - Festivals are really important as you can get a buzz going about a film, which can make our job a lot easier. Sundance is a prime example where you can find tiny films that capture the imagination, everyone knows that huge deals can be done there and everyone's waiting for that big cheque from Miramax. For the really small budget, Slamdance is a great one too.

Q - Do you sit down with the producers and work out a film strategy?

Billy - Yes. One of the most important things is that we have to make sure we're all talking about the same film. The director might see it as one kind of film and *we* might see it as another. We have to discuss what the genre is, which is not always as easy as it seems, then we discuss the marketing of the film, *are we going to do merchandising or change the title of the film?* With *Shooting Fish* for example, we changed it's name from *Entrepreneurs*, a decision taken before the markets. We thought *Entrepreneurs* sounded too Wall Street, too 80s, whereas *Shooting Fish* was an expression that many people didn't know what it meant and it had them asking, *what does it mean?* The next thing you know it's caught on like wildfire.

Q - How often do you report back to the film producers?

Billy - We report two weeks after every market and in between if something happens. Film makers ring us often, I can't think of a week that goes by that we're not in contact with them. We work as a team.

Q - If nothing really happens after the three main markets, is contact lost?

Billy - No, we sit down with them and look at it sensibly from their point of view and ours. We give them a marketing report which gives them all the information of what we've done with the movie, for instance, we've gone to Cannes, taken out ads, posters etc, spent this here and this there. We look at the sales figures, form a conclusion and look at what can be done in the future. Then our accountant does another report which is purely financial, listing territories sold, amounts owed, amounts paid etc. The buyers will tell us why they don't buy, *I didn't like it, it wasn't funny enough, it's not for them, it's difficult for my territory* etc. Maybe we would wait for good reviews and even if people had passed on it, we would still go back for another go with the positive reviews requesting they bring in their video and TV people. Then if all of that fails we package it with other films.

Q - How does packaging work?

Andrew - If we have unsuccessful lower budget films we package them together making them more attractive, particularly for the TV buyer. We get as much as we can for the package but sometimes there is a certain film in the package that will have acted as the catalyst for the distributor to buy, so we'd want to apportion more money to that film.

Q - What common problems do you encounter?

Andrew - Stills, always stills. Also music. So many times we've seen a thriller which has a great bit of music in it, but the film maker hasn't got clearance. Music, like post production, seems to be the last thing for producers to think about yet it's so important. Clearances can be expensive, you could be looking at £10k for 60 seconds. The blow up from 16mm to 35mm is often problematic too. Creative issues like a director with a dark look to their film might mean it gets rejected, because it's too dark.

Q - Any advice for a first time film maker?

Billy - The only way to answer this is with clichés. The script. There are so many films we've seen where it's not been a budgetary problem that's ruined the film, but an underdeveloped script.

Domestic Distribution
David Nicholas Wilkinson of Guerilla Films

Q - What is your job?

David - I distribute films in the UK, getting them in cinemas, video shops, retail outlets, TV companies etc., then collecting and distributing the payments back to the film maker, should there be any left. I am different from the large distribution companies as I am mainly interested in the low-budget (sub £500k) end of the film market and therefore I have to work in unconventional ways. I am in my 5th year of selling my films via the Internet and believe that I was the first UK distributor to use the medium for selling films. I have sold films around the world to an audience that I would have never reached any other way which offers great opportunities for filmmakers.

Q - When should a producer come to you?

David - The best time for a producer to come to me is when they have completed their first rough assembly. I can usually tell from that point what is going to be the reaction to the movie. The real acid test though is it's screening to the sales agents and distributors, when you find out what they actually think of the film. I can make a decision on a film by looking at the box office grosses of films that are similar. No one can hide the cinema figures any more. Years ago when a producer lied and said that their movie *took £300k at the UK box office* you had to believe them because there was no way of disproving them. I have just had someone come to me with a film about the Oxford and Cambridge boat race. I looked up how the Film4 boat race film performed (*True Blue*) and other similar films and discovered none have done at all well. Even though I feel that his script is very good, I won't take it on because I know that the audience is just not there. This is a very powerful tool for me and for smart producers.

Q - Do you ever offer any kind of advance?

David - I don't have the money nor would I feel comfortable giving money to a first time film. It is hard enough persuading cinemas to take it on and very expensive to make up prints, pay for BBFC certification, master DVD's, make posters, pay for advertising etc.

Q - What is P&A?

David - It is an industry term for Prints and Advertising, in essence, the cost of releasing your film to the distributor. It can mount up very quickly as so many items are unmovable.

Q - Say I did a 5 print release which took £150k at the UK box office, how much of that will I see as the filmmaker?

David - Of that, 17.5% VAT in the U.K. goes to the government and then what's left, a percentage, usually 25%, will be paid from the cinema to distributor. If the film does really well you might hit the house nut figure in which case you will start to see considerably more, perhaps even 90%, but this is very unusual, especially for independent films. Out of that 25% from the cinema the distributor will deduct their fee, usually around 35%, then whatever is left pays off the P&A. I don't know of a micro-budget film in ten years that has paid off its P&A and made a profit.

Q - So in reality theatrical release is really to raise the value of the film, like a very expensive marketing exercise that will lead into the real money that is in TV, video, pay per view, overseas sales etc?

David - Yes, it is very important. Overseas sales are where the real income is found.

Q - How do sales to video rental work?

David - There is now a shared revenue on video rental. You used to just sell the video to the store for a fixed price and that was it, now the theory is that for every £1 the video rental store takes, 50% goes to the store, 40% to distributor and 10% to whomever organised shared revenue. This is fine if your video is *The Matrix* because you will receive considerable income. In the past video companies paid an agreed fee (this practise is still around but seems to be going out fast) which meant that you would get a definite return. In the future it will be down to whether or not a particular film rents well. Generally low budget films do not appeal to a mass audience. Your local video shop should be able to give you details of how various similar films have performed. Talk to them as their advice could be invaluable and on the whole they're very helpful.

Q - Talk me through a deal for say a £50k film?

David - I would want a licence on all UK and Irish rights for 15 years. We would take a 35% commission for cinema and also charge a movement fee for every time the print moved from one cinema to another. There are cases when you only get £20 from the cinema because it played so badly, which isn't even enough to move the print. Any P&A that we had put up we would get back from the net income and that is usually about 65%. We pay a royalty of 25% of the net dealer price for video rental and 12.5% for sell-through and DVD. With TV we charge a commission of 35% unless the producers have provided some or all of the P&A. This is up for negotiation. If there are any unpaid losses from P&A from the theatrical release this will come out of the producers share of the revenue of video, DVD and TV. This is the BIG problem that all low budget British films face. They have a very difficult time making the P&A back let alone making their distributor a fee to cover their overhead. There are many films I have wanted to take on but cannot because of the losses we would incur with just the P&A. We always expect to lose money in the cinema on low budget films and hope to make up those losses from video rental / sell-through and DVD. However with shared revenue becoming the norm it is making it more and more difficult to do well on video for low budget films. TV becomes vital for a company like mine. Sadly with a number

★

guerilla films

David Nicholas Wilkinson

Tel + 44 (0)208 758 1716   Fax + 44 (0)208 758 9364
david@guerilla-films.com   www.guerilla-films.com
35 Thornbury Road, Isleworth, TW7 4LQ, England

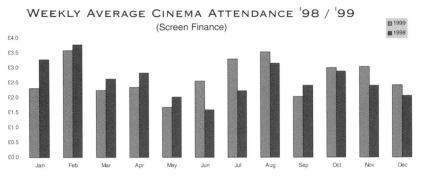

WEEKLY AVERAGE CINEMA ATTENDANCE '98 / '99
(Screen Finance)

of the films we wished to distribute we sent copies to all the UK broadcasters but none agreed with our view that they were good films. We had reluctantly, to turn them down. Before you start your film your need to know what a UK film is worth. Study the gross box office figures for British films, it can be quite distressing to find out just how little some films actually took. For more up to date and in-depth figures you should look at Screen Finance which you can find at the BFI Library. Search out a UK film that is similar to yours and work out how well it actually did.

Q - What materials should a producer bring to you?

David - I would love everything including a 35mm trailer, otherwise I have to pay for one to be made. I have in the past paid £17k to get a trailer cut and I don't want to do that again. I want access to the negative at the lab, the digibeta masters of the telecine, ideally in pan & scan and widescreen. I need lots of stills. It is the single biggest mistake I see repeated again and again, people come to me with 5 stills and expect it to be enough. I need lots. Producers don't seem to have any idea of the importance of having the actors available for promotion. I want the leading actors, the director and the writer available for promotion and if they have disappeared it makes it very awkward. The press will take a greater interest if they can interview someone who is reasonably well known.

If your leading actor refuses to be interviewed then you are in real trouble, journalists are always looking for a story that is different to the one that you want to give them. You must remember that they are used to *Sleepy Hollow* and *Notting Hill* where they can interview the lead, because it is part of the lead's fee to promote the film around the world. So they will not read the best into your film if you can't provide them with your actor who used to be in *Emmerdale*. You should have a

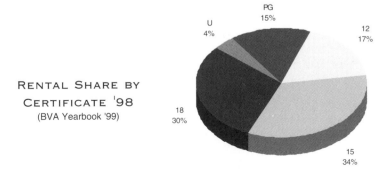

RENTAL SHARE BY
CERTIFICATE '98
(BVA Yearbook '99)

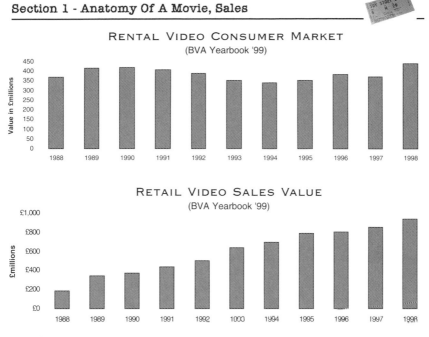

RENTAL VIDEO CONSUMER MARKET
(BVA Yearbook '99)

RETAIL VIDEO SALES VALUE
(BVA Yearbook '99)

clause in your contracts with your actors for publicity. You must not blow your chance with doing publicity while you are shooting because it could be two years before your film reaches the cinema. Journalists will not give you a second chance. You can ask them to hold their piece until your movie comes out but they may not. For low budget films free marketing is vital.

Q - How important was it for a movie like Lock Stock to have someone like a major soccer star playing a part?

David - I think that casting Vinnie Jones was the most brilliant marketing I have seen in a long time. It got them so many thousands of pounds worth of marketing and advertising for free. If he had been crap then they would have had a real problem, fortunately for them he was excellent in that role, it seemed to have been written for him. Vinnie Jones however, would have been wrong to cast as the lead role in a light-hearted romantic comedy as audiences expect something else from him. That said I am tired of films that don't use professional actors as they are a hopeless waste of time and money. If you, as the audience, don't believe the actor is the person that they are playing then the whole film falls apart. There are not many that can make the change from soccer star to movie actor as well as Vinnie Jones did.

Q - How often do you do your accounts?

David - Every three months. After two or three years I tend to drop that to every six months. Of course if a large cheque from TV comes in I will pay that out straight away.

Q - What is the SFD?

David - The Society of Film Distributors. They look after us, make sure we behave and organise

261

UK Films Gross Box Office '98
(Source - Screen Finance)

Title	Budget (£)	No. Of Prints	Wks on release	Box office Gross (£) UK
A Soldier's Daughter Never cries	£6,200,000	9	6	£37,896
Amy Foster	£9,200,000	39	3	£27,627
Babymother	£2,000,000	8	6	£61,929
Big Swap, The	£640,000	11	5	£30,852
Bride of War	£1,700,000	3		£1,610
Bring me the Head of Mavis Davis	£3,000,000	59	3	£63,949
Cousin Bette	£5,000,000	75	3	£105,814
Dad Savage	£3,500,000	19	2	£14,249
Dandy Dust	£30,000	1		£482
Designated Mourner, The	£1,000,000	1		£1,371
Different for Girls	£1,400,000	2		£11,760
Disappearance of Finbar, The	£2,500,000	1	6	£4,752
Divorcing Jack	£2,700,000	107	8	£471,627
Downtime	£1,900,000	42	1	£28,135
Elizabeth	£13,000,000	198	35	£5,358,514
Girl with Brains in her Feet, The	£1,000,000	14	3	£19,332
Girls Night	£3,000,000	56	13	£653,115
Governess, The	£2,800,000	8	7	£111,976
I Want You	£3,500,000	6	2	£16,236
James Gang, The	£1,600,000	38	2	£23,342
Kurt & Courtney	£500,000	7	5	£96,758
Land Girls	£5,000,000	101	21	£1,461,924
Life of Stuff	£2,000,000	1		£1,214
Lock Stock and Two Smoking Barrels	£2,600,000	215	32	£11,621,664
Love and Death on Long Island	£2,700,000	24	12	£393,857
Love is the Devil	£1,000,000	16	11	£267,321
Martha, meet Frank...	£3,000,000	197	10	£2,641,174
Mojo	£2,200,000	6	4	£73,665
Monk Dawson	£1,000,000	3	1	£2,765
My Name is Joe	£2,500,000	51	18	£916,267
My Son the Fanatic	£2,000,000	16	9	£159,361
Oscar and Lucinda	£7,600,000	26	12	£232,260
Razor Blade Smile	£350,000	6	1	£3,225
Real Howard Spitz, The	£4,600,000	8	3	£16,309
Respect	£80,000	1	3	£3,633
Resurrection Man	£3,500,000	5	5	£85,882
Scarlet Tunic, The	£750,000	13	12	£70,871
Secret Agent, The	£4,000,000	4	2	£8,387
Sliding Doors	£6,880,000	280	19	£12,298,655
Something to Believe In	£9,400,000	60	1	£27,903
Stella Does Tricks	£450,000	4	3	£28,861
Stiff Upper Lips	£3,930,000	87	4	£151,367
Still Crazy	£7,000,000	211	5	£896,295
Up 'n' Under	£2,000,000	204	5	£3,126,317
Twentyfour/Seven	£1,400,000	77	6	£235,126
Velvet Goldmine	£4,500,000	77	8	£454,683
Wings of the Dove, The	£8,700,000	81	23	£2,072,168
Winter Guest, The	£5,000,000	28	7	£250,583
Wisdom of Crocodiles	£3,500,000	25	1	£19,856
Woodlanders, The	£4,000,000	18	7	£165,424

SALES

BBFC Certification	Prints	Posters	Advertising
Approx £1k for cinema, and £1k for video / DVD. Your trailer will need certification too.	*Approx £1k per print. How many did you say you wanted?*	*Approx £2k for design plus £2k for printing. Be aware that your own design might not be good enough.*	*As much as you want to spend. You could easily blow £20k and get very little.*

Shipping	Fly Posting	Screenings	PR
Moving prints and posters around is costly, budget £1k.	*It's illegal but you can pay people to plaster your poster everywhere. Budget £1k.*	*Outside of the SFD screenings you will need more for the journalists who missed it. Budget another £1k.*	*Trannies and press packs, duplication and delivery upon request. Budget at least £500.*

your screenings for the press. They schedule the official press screenings. It is then up to the distributor to organise and pay the costs. These are official SFD screenings which no one can clash with so that no distributor can arrange a competitive screening at the same time.

Ten years ago three screenings would be fine but now you have to screen the movie perhaps 10 times to make sure everyone sees it. The journalist's workload often makes them request the movies on video, clearly the wrong medium to see the film. Sometimes I arrange a special screening just for one person as I would prefer them to see it in the cinema than on video.

Q - How much do things cost, like the BBFC, posters etc?

David - Big distribution companies spend a lot of money here, I try to spend as little as possible. On a movie that I am working on at the moment the producer has found someone who has designed the poster which is great. I won't pay him very much for the design as this is his opportunity to get his work out there. If I went to one of the big companies to get them to design the poster they will probably charge £2k and that does not include the printing of the poster. The video sleeve usually costs about £500. I also like it if the film maker comes with the trailer. The big companies do not normally request this, as they want to cut the trailer themselves.

Q - How big is the UK market on a global scale?

(left) UK theatric revenues are, on the whole, shocking. And remember, these figures have VAT at 17.5% in the U.K. deducted, then the distributor at say 35%, then the P&A recoupment, which unless the film is in the top few percentage, will be completely eaten up. Source Screen Finance.

EXAMPLE UK THEATRIC RELEASE FOR LOW BUDGET FEATURE

Basic Costs	
BBFC Certification	£1,000
Prints	£5,000
Posters	£4,000
Trailer	£4,000
PR	£4,000
Advertising	£5,000
Shipping	£1,000
Fly Postering	£1,000
Misc	£500
Balance	£25,500

Gross Box Office	£150,000
Minus VAT at 17.5%	£127,659
25% returned to distributor	£31,915
Minus distributors fees at 35%	£23,640
Minus Expenses Above	-£1,860
Balance	-£1,860

This example is for a fictitious film where everything has been done cost effectively. It is for a five print release, and quite frankly, it's done astonishingly well at the Box Office. More than likely it will have taken maybe £10, instead of £150k. If that were the case, you can see how much money would be owed at the end. Any distributor would offset losses at the box office with sales to video and TV in all their various forms.

David - Europe is broken up into three types of territory, big, medium, small. These definitions are based on how well films do in these territories. The head of the EU Media Film Programme told me last year that she now considers the UK to be a small territory. British films do best in Europe, however you can have a British film, with a British cast, crew and money, it can sell to every country in Europe except for the UK! You must not be put off by this. The UK is only 5-10% of the world market. Unfortunately if you have not released in the UK people seem to think that there is something wrong with your movie.

Q - What mistakes do you see regularly?

David - I have been a producer myself and have made so many of these mistakes. It is a general perception to think that all you have to do is make a film and it will be sold / distributed / screened on TV etc. Every year every distributor in the world is offered far more films than they could ever take on. Last year I looked at 39 low budget British films and I have taken on 2 of them. Very few of those other ones have been picked up for the cinema. The large and medium distributors will have invested, co-produced or pre-bought a number of films before they are made. A great deal of their time and funds will be tied up with these films and much as they might like your completed film most will just not have the resources to get involved with it. Most first time low budget films will be lucky to obtain a theatrical release. In 1997, of the 1000 non-studio films made in the USA, 60 had a theatric release and only 14 of those had a substantial release. In other words 940 either went straight to video / cable / TV or else they did not have any release.

I have just put together a deal on a film called *Small Time Obsession* after I saw a rough-cut of the film and really liked it. The producers could not finish it, as they had no more funds. I raised the finishing funds as well as the P&A I needed, from an investor and now take a small slice of it's

Small Time Obsession, a film which David at Guerilla Films liked and was able to secure additional funding so that it could be completed as a full theatrical release was paid for. The upshot is that international sales will also be enhanced.

international sales. I have always resented the fact that our time and money releasing a film here in the UK boosts it for the sales agent in overseas markets. A UK release results in deals that would have not have happened if we had not put it in the cinema. So often we have ended up with a loss and a very small commission for providing this unique selling point. I have seen 3 excellent low budget British thrillers in the last 12 months. They are no better and no worse than what you see on TV and that's their problem. TV produce/screen well over a hundred thrillers -films & series every year. Why is someone going to get in their car, go out and pay to see what they have for free in their own home? If they had thought more about marketing at the pre-production stage I am sure they could have enhanced the film's value.

Q - What advice would you offer a new film maker?

David - Perseverance is the most important thing that you need to get your project off the ground. I have just managed to sell a movie to a TV company and this has taken me nine years. They took it eventually just to shut me up. I think the reason why a lot of really bad films reach the market-place and the cinemas is because the people involved have not let go of it and pushed and pushed and pushed to get it out there. Every film has an audience even if it is only your mum and dad, so you have to be realistic. You have to step back and look at it for what it is. Put it on a shelf for six months and come back and hopefully at that point you have managed to distance yourself from it and you can see where the inherent flaws are. Make sure that your Brit flick is not so full of topical British issues and very British jokes because these will not travel to Taiwan. Try to see the bigger picture.

As a filmmaker you must absolutely believe in your film, however you also need to be realistic about it. Try to look at it as an outsider. Watch videos of similar films to yours, then watch your film or read the script. BE HONEST. Why will anyone pay £5 to see your film? At the time of this interview there are 29 films being released in the cinema in this month alone. There are a number of films being held over from previous months. Even the most ardent film fan will only see a small percentage of them.

Screening Rooms
Andy Young
of Mr Young's

Q - What are preview theatres?

Andy - Preview theatres or screening rooms are theatres which are for hire to show films provided by the customer for commercial purposes - i.e. to sell a film to sales agents or distributors, or to do test screenings or press screenings. It's a place where you can professionally present your work to a group of people you invite. We can screen 35mm in all it's aspect ratios, with full Dolby and Dolby Digital. We can also project video, usually off BetaSP. The smallest theatre costs £80 an hour, the medium £100 an hour and the largest £110 an hour. There is an extra £20 per hour for all theatres after 6pm. The smallest theatre seats twenty five people, the medium sized one forty-one and the largest forty-four. Most preview theatres are about these sizes. If you want larger you can hire a cinema on a Sunday morning for instance.

Q - What times are best for distributors?

Andy - Mid morning and mid afternoon are the best times for distributors. However, press shows and test screenings fare better at lunch time or early evening, when you can offer the viewers something to eat or drink.

Q - What about food and drinks?

Andy - We supply both food and drinks on request, with a little warning. You can bring your own food and drinks if you like.

Q - What are the common technical mistakes that you encounter?

Andy - Missed reel changes due to a print not being 'spotted'. It's also worth remembering that prints get dirty quickly, especially if they have been used at film festivals, so don't expect it to look crisp and clean if your print has been around the block (although it can be helped a little by ultrasonic cleaning).

Q - What advice would you offer a new film maker?

Andy - Don't start filming until script is absolutely right, we often see disappointed film makers who only realise they didn't work hard enough on the script when the sales agent walks out ten minutes into the screening.

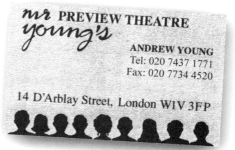

mr PREVIEW THEATRE
young's

ANDREW YOUNG
Tel: 020 7437 1771
Fax: 020 7734 4520

14 D'Arblay Street, London W1V 3FP

SALES

Deal Tracking
Paul Madigan of ETS

Q – What is ETS?

Paul – Since '93 we have tracked where and when films and programmes play on a daily basis on 144 channels in twenty countries. So we would be able to tell you if and when your feature film or programme had played in one of those twenty countries.

Q – So you can track if your film has been screened or sold without your knowing?

Paul – Yes, it's an independent source of information that enables you to go to your sales agent and say *'I know that this played on television in Switzerland on Jan 11th 1993 at 9.45pm'*. You can also ensure that you get your collections from other agencies such as the PRS or the DPRS. It also enables distributors to know when the programme is available to re-sell because it has played its contract through. For instance if you sell three screenings over two years, if the film is screened three times in the first month, it is available for re-sale and you don't need to wait twenty three months. Remember, the TV station won't volunteer this information. We have a 157 publications come into the office on a weekly basis, typically TV guides. Our translators go through them all and enter the details of all the shows into a huge database, currently holding 600,000 titles and 5 million entries since '93. With regard to costs, $200 gets you a report for a year - a print out of when and where your show screened (also available from June on emstv.com).

Q – How often do producers get their report and say "Oh, my god, I did not know that it was showing there"?

Paul – It is not uncommon. A lot of producers never know what happens. They just sell it and don't follow through. They don't look upon it as an asset. Asset management is not perceived as part of the producers job.

Q – What common mistakes do you encounter?

Paul – The inability for creatives to realise that they own assets, they just don't see what they do as assets. A film is like building a house, it has to be built correctly, you have to maintain it, you have to follow through and of course if you get it right at the start you then have an asset that buys you many lunches over the years. Some never wake up to it. Some wake up to it who have been out there for years and they get quite a surprise when they get their money.

ESSENTIAL TELEVISION STATISTICS

Paul Madigan
Managing Director

Pinewood Studios Iver Heath Bucks SL0 0NH
Tel: +44 1753 656762 Fax: +44 1753 630860
e-mail: ets-ltd@netcomuk.co.uk

Festival Attendance Geraldine Higgins at The British Council

Q - What is the British Council's job when it comes to feature films?

Geraldine - There are two sides to our feature film operation. One where we acquire feature films on 16mm for non-theatrical use overseas which means screening on British Council premises (we are based in 110 countries) and certain educational establishments. The second operation is where we support and organise film events around the world i.e. film festivals, film weeks, retrospectives, European Union film events etc, utilising 35mm prints borrowed from distributors and production companies. The organisers of these events approach either the local British Council office or Films and Television Department direct for help in selecting films. After the films have been selected we collect the prints and any publicity material and despatch them overseas. Sometimes we arrange for a director or actor to go out in support of the event, therefore it can be in the interest of smaller production companies to let us know about any new feature films they have made.

Q - What kind of British feature film does the British Council help?

Geraldine - We promote a wide range of feature films from established directors such as Mike Leigh, Ken Loach and Peter Greenaway to young directors who have just made their first feature, i.e. Lynne Ramsay, Jasmin Dizdar and Damien O'Donnell.

Q - How does a producer engage your services and what does that producer need to supply you with?

Geraldine - Basically we need to know about new features. There are so many films being made these days, it is impossible to have contact details on all of them. We produce the annual British Films Catalogue, which contains information on new British features and shorts. Work begins on the catalogue each autumn for publication the following January. This catalogue is distributed at markets such as Berlin and Cannes. A copy of the film on video together with a basic press kit, just a few typed sheets on the film, cast and crew list and some photos, are useful for sending to festival selectors for preview purposes.

Q - Would it be advantageous for the producer to invite you to an early screening of the film?

SALES

Geraldine - The earlier we see the film the better. We are handling feature film events all the time and we may miss a film that might be ideal for an event simply because we do not know it exists. So yes, the earlier we know about a film, the more festivals/events we can submit it to.

Q - If a film is selected to play in a festival abroad and the director or producer is invited, can the British Council help with finances?

Geraldine - All our offices around the world have a small budget for travel grants. If a film was selected for a festival, we would contact the office in that country and ask if they would be prepared to offer a travel grant for the director to attend. It really depends on the budget of the local office and if they support films. But yes, you can theoretically get a travel grant.

Q - And the shipping of prints etc?

Geraldine - Once we get involved in an event, we will take on all the administrative work i.e. sending out preview cassettes, publicity material, entry forms and ultimately the films selected. So we will do everything.

Q - Will the festival ever help out?

Geraldine - If the British Council provides a travel grant we would expect the festival or event organisers to pay all onshore costs i.e. hotel and meal allowances. This is the normal practice.

Q - Can the British Council help with attending commercial markets like the AFM or the Cannes Film Festival?

Geraldine - The British Council is not a commercial organisation. Any financial support we are able to provide is for filmmakers to attend the screening of their film, give lectures or conduct workshops.

The British Council can be enormously helpful. It's worth giving them a call in advance of the completion of a film just to let them know that it's going to be around soon. They can work wonders but do need plenty of time to be truly effective.

See the yellow pages for a full list of film festivals.

The British Council

Films and Television Department

Geraldine Higgins
Programming, Events and Acquisitions

The British Council
11 Portland Place
London W1N 4EJ

Tel +44 (0)20 7389 3066
Fax +44 (0)20 7389 3041
geraldine.higgins@britishcouncil.org

www.britishcouncil.org

Image
Chris Fowler
of The Creative
Partnership

Q - What does a producer need to do in order to exploit their film?

Chris - The basic rule of thumb to getting a film out to the public and making them aware of it, is the earlier you start the better. It's common, particularly with first time filmmakers, that somewhere along the way they kind of forget the reason for making the film in the first place - they start with *I know I want to make a film about a talking horse* and by the time they've been through this incredible learning curve, they hate the film and say *can we bury the talking horse?* What we do is deconstruct the film and take it back to the pebble of why they wanted to make the film in the first place, back to what the public would be interested in seeing.

Q - So it's important to latch onto a single concept in order to exploit the film?

Chris - Yes, people are not waiting to be told how wonderful your film is, they don't give a shit. If they see a trailer for it, it will be by complete accident - they will be more concerned with putting their coat somewhere safe and getting popcorn. If they get a handbill thrust into their hand for it, it's another piece of paper they don't want. It's common for new film makers to naively believe that the whole world is just dying to see their film and the world really isn't that interested.

Q - So does this go as far as suggesting new titles for a film? With our film White Angel, we felt, in retrospect that a title like Interview With a Serial Killer would be better?

Chris - I'd be the first person to tell you to dump *White Angel* as it tells you nothing. The conjunction of the words *White* and *Angel* suggest a U certificate aimed at kids, they're very soft words, it feels wussy - not the image you want to give. We retitled *The Crying Game* - originally it was called *The Soldier's Wife* which gives off two things, a happily married man, boring, and a soldier, which at that time was a massive turn off. We ended up going through the Book of British Singles - *The Crying Game* doesn't mean anything except there's some kind of tension about it, a game, mischief, it feels like there's more to it. So it starts with the title and some kind of strap line. Even though you might not end up using the strap line, it's a good idea to establish it in the crew's mind.

Q - How do you go about designing the poster?

Chris - The subject matter will suggest itself. For example, we did a film for Marc Samuelson, an entirely British financed production called *Wilde*, the biography of Oscar Wilde. The first thing you think of is Oh! flowery lettering - Merchant Ivory, lovely and pretty. Then you hear that Stephen Fry and Jude Law are the leads and it's much more modern, so we scrap the idea of it being flowery and think, we'll go for a very modernistic approach. So your design is decided by the flavour of the script as much as the subject matter of the film. It's all about the subject matter and the approach

SALES

of the director. Ben Ross, on the film *The Young Poisoner's Handbook,* had a very specific agenda. The script read like True Crime and it had actually been filmed once before for the BBC or ITV as a one hour show. But he wanted to play it as a black comedy and this is the sort of stuff only the director could tell you - it's not always there in the script. We were then able to say *let's not pull any punches* and we did a series of very black posters - we did it like a kid's chemistry set with all those fifties happy families on the front and he's making poison to kill them all. So first the script, and then the director's view of the script.

Q - How do you go about creating a good trailer?

Chris - Usually, there are two trailers, one for the UK, and another for overseas (that's also used by the sales agent). We did Mike Leigh's *Secrets and Lies* for both the UK and International territories, and took two different approaches. The UK one deals with people who know Mike Leigh, so it's very much on personalities. His films are character studies, but the international trailer requires more of a story, more setting up. The first rule is that the trailer can't lie - you have to reflect the film directly and these days you have to do it harder and faster. We did the *Trainspotting* trailer and it was very much in your face but it also used techniques of the film, freeze framing, captions, talking to camera, things like that. So it's a distillation of the film.

Q - When do you normally get involved in a film?

Chris - We handle anything from small films to blockbusters, and lots in between. We do an awful lot of nurturing of new talent, but we are happier working when the film has been sold or it has a sales agent. Often, we are the first show of faith, but there's only a certain amount we can do.

Q - Am I correct in saying that the service you offer should be looked on as being as important as the solicitors or accountant's advice?

Chris - For most of it's 100 year life, advertising a film has been an after-thought. The gestation of a film is so long and slow that by the time the film comes out, the subject matter is no longer appealing to the film makers or public. But if we're there from the beginning and see it through, we can actually help solve problems. In the last fifteen years people have become aware that without advertising and publicity, a film is dead in the water. At the other end of the scale, you can't keep chucking millions at a film - you get a good first weekend, then 30% drop off for the second week, and it spirals down from there. There is an argument that we're all firm believers of here, that is to keep one single idea in everybody's mind so that when you do come to the end of it, you have a very clear campaign that you can nail into somebody's head - go see this film.

Q - How much of the success of Shallow Grave was the result of your input rather than the film on it's own?

Chris - This is one of those chicken and the egg things that we argue about in the pub all the time. The film is undeniably superb, I loved it. We came in very late, we weren't

creative PARTNERSHIP

LONDON   HOLLYWOOD   HONG KONG

CHRIS FOWLER

13 BATEMAN STREET   SOHO   LONDON   W1V 5TB
Tel: 020 7439 7762   Fax: 020 7439 1467
HOLLYWOOD 7525 FOUNTAIN AVENUE HOLLYWOOD CA 90046 TEL (213) 850 5551 FAX (213) 850 0391
HONG KONG SHOWREEL G/F MANDARIN COURT 16 ARBUTHNOT ROAD CENTRAL HONG KONG TEL 524 8316 FAX 521 8798

(left) Pitch - Teen mag image designed to display the piece as a bright summer feel good movie. FFD (Film Four Distribution) Response - Liked very much, but it didn't quite take in the whole picture. Nice try though.

(below) Pitch - Teen nightmare image. We wanted a far more abstract and menacing visual and this was the outcome. FFD Response - The whole image smacked of druggy violence. Very clever though and not without merit.

(left) Pitch - Troubled people living in difficult life of urban decay. The in your face 'if you don't like it, tough' pitch. FFD Response - Oh dear! Not our film at all. Never really a contender.

(below) Pitch - The relationship feel. Something more intimate. Urban but openly hopeful and good natured. FFD Response - Really liked it, but just a little messy. Getting to the place we wanted to be though. Loved the rainbow.

(left) Pitch - The urban, joyous, funny, sunny happy ensemble campaign. FFD Response - Getting there but a tiny bit awkward.

POSTER PERFECTION

Film Four movie, 'Beautiful Thing' had two campaigns. As the film had a gay theme, it was decided to target the gay media, but also push the mainstream media with a different campaign. Many poster images are mocked up for the distributors in order to find the image to sell the film to the right audience in the right way.

This was it. Bold, in your face and aggressive. This would lead the 'gay' media push.

The final agreed mainstream image. Much better organised than its predecessor. Really bright sunny and feelgood. Translated wonderfully to press ads too.

photo by Donald Milne

273

The image may be familiar but it's one that could not be used to promote 'Reservoir Dogs' here in the UK. It was used unofficially with fly-posting, but the spattered blood was a big no no for the SFD.

involved in *Shallow Grave* early at all - I believe that it was a really simple and strong idea to put the shovel on the poster. I can't remember who came up with the shovel idea, it was probably someone at Polygram video. There was a wonderful trailer for it which we cut - it reflected the film beautifully because it got the humour in there. If you take the title out of context - *Shallow Grave* - it sounds like a horror film. But it's a horror film with funny bits in it, it's shot very kinetically, it's been made by young people - wow! so it was a novelty. So you put all these things together and you get a very good trailer. We also had the age old problem of having no stars and a very good film, that without careful handling, could get lost between the cracks. It's true in this industry nobody knows anything as films do often die. *Reservoir Dogs* dropped dead in the States because they had a traditional campaign. We did a poster with the guys walking and lots of blood - very in your face - it really took off and the time was right for that. The American campaign for *Shallow Grave* is very different, it's got the three actors and a spiral staircase. The spiral staircase hints at mystery, three friends says warmth and friendship. It flopped in the States. I think the signals you give off with a poster are very limited, you can only really make it look one thing. We've just done the poster for *Things To Do In Denver When You're Dead* - it's a hip film, there's not much else to it other than it's hipness, so it's a very hip poster.

Q - The Reservoir Dogs poster had blood spattered on it, did that cause problems?

Chris - There is a committee called the SFD who give a yes or no to posters. One of the things they dreamt up was that you cannot have anything on a poster that a lonely woman on a deserted train platform at night might by upset by. It's true a poster is in the public arena, but few people are disturbed by them, beyond the Benetton type of poster. There are very few images on a film poster that are very shocking, but it still causes us major problems. You can't have a gun facing out for instance, or blood. We certainly had a problem with *Salvador* which had a silhouette of two people, one pointing the gun at the other. We said *they're silhouettes*, and they said, *well yes, but if they're silhouettes, what sex are they?* I said *they are no sex, they are silhouettes.* And they said, *so one could be male and the other a female.* I said *yes.* They said, *then the victim could be the female and the other the male.* I said *yes.* They said, *it's banned.* That evening I spent the entire night with two helpers licking and sticking panels over the offending images, all 25,000 of them.

Q - What does a producer usually supply you with for you to do your job?

Chris - Ideally a set of stills. It's a good idea to allow a day for a stills shoot. If you don't, there's a good chance that most of your stills will be crap, through nobody's fault, just from the messiness of the shooting process and actor availability. So a special shoot with the actors is a good idea.

IMAGE	*TRAILER*	*STILLS*	*TITLE*
Be clear about what you have made, what story it is telling, and who you have made it for. Audiences want to make a decision and if you don't know what it is, they won't go and see it.	*Don't promise too much in the trailer, you might not deliver. Be honest and don't misrepresent the movie, it will just piss off buyers.*	*At the risk of being laborious, stills, stills, stills!*	*Make sure your title is the right one for your movie. Just because you have had it all the way through production doesn't mean you can't come up with a better one.*

Q - What should a producer do for a low budget campaign?

Chris - Stills are absolutely essential, and there's no use taking pictures of the crew at work, because no-one wants to see them - they want the leads in action. Next is the mindset - if they have a clear, lucid way of explaining how, where and why they see this film being made then it's an enormous benefit. It would be good to do a flyer, a colour image on one side, the synopsis on the other. The image can be built up from either a scene you've shot or a special shoot. It shouldn't be expensive because somebody will have access to a computer and Photoshop and they can put it together themselves and save the time and expense of someone like us doing it for them. If they're smart, they can do me out of a job and do their own trailer. However, film editors rarely cut good trailers because they are too close to the film - the director is standing there saying put the bit in where we blew the car up, it cost money to do that bit - it may have cost money, but it might not be the thing that appeals to the audience.

Q - What are the most common mistakes you've experienced from producers?

Chris - From my point of view, it's a lack of clarity and vision, fuzziness of who they see the film aimed at. It's often the case they don't see the film aimed at anyone in particular. Communications are a massive problem. You can't believe we're in a communications industry from the way people fail to tell each other the most basic things.

Q - What basic advice would you offer a low-budget film maker?

Chris - Don't do it! (laugh) I would say be aware that you're probably not going to make money. Don't do it because you think you're going to be rich, or become famous. Don't overestimate people's interest in you and your film. We won best British short film of the year in 1993, we got theatrical distribution, TV distribution in the UK and around the world, and we've yet to break even on it. Most people I know that keep going kind of have another job. Make sure you have time to do it. When I worked on a short film and I went to follow it up and do a feature, the three of us couldn't find time to do it - we couldn't even get meetings together because we have our day jobs. So if you're going to take it seriously, you have to allow for the fact that A, you're not going to make money from it and B, you're probably going to lose money from doing it by not doing other jobs.

Nigel Floyd
Freelance Journalist

Q - What is your job?

Nigel - I review films and write features about films and the film-makers.

Q - What is unique to low budget films from your perspective?

Nigel - If you are an independent film maker and you think that your film should be given an extra star just because it cost £100k as opposed to £100m then you are barking up the wrong tree. To some extent you get brownie points for having gone out there and done it, because most critics have never made a film. But in the end you have got to judge the film as a film. It is hard because you have split loyalties - I want to encourage film makers because I know how hard it is for them to make the film and I want them to succeed; but you also have a responsibility to the readers, especially if you write regularly for a publication like *Time Out*. The readers need to know that the reviews are consistent so they can make a judgement about which film to spend their time and money on.

Q - Film makers complain that making a low budget film isn't a level playing field. But the minute that you get it on the screen, it is a level playing field because the audience responds to it purely as a story and they don't care about the budget.

Nigel - Yes, take *Following,* it's a very strong, nicely played, well constructed film, and the reviews were very good. It wasn't because it was made cheaply that the reviews were good, it was because it was an interesting take on something new and the ideas were up there on the screen - not handed down clichés, but of fresh and original ideas. On the other hand, the new Schwarzenegger film is appalling and it doesn't matter how much it cost or how much publicity money the distributors throw at it, it will not get any better. As a critic I would prefer to see *Following* rather than *End of Days* and I would give a better review to *Following* because, to me, it was simply a better film. So in that sense it is a level playing field.

Q - What should a film maker give to you to make your job of reviewing their film any easier?

Nigel - This is an area where people fall down very badly. The three most important things for any independent film are STILLS, STILLS and STILLS. Most independent film makers think that if they spend long enough making the film it will sell itself. Films don't sell themselves, they have to be sold, and one of the things that sells a movie, and particularly the way that magazines and websites are constructed now, is images of your movie. These should be taken by a professional photographer during the shoot. When the art director at *Total Film* or *Time Out* sits down to lay out the page, if they have four crappy B&W grainy images from a little independent movie and one monster pic from the latest Schwarzenegger, with shades, sparks flying, hardware and muscles, then they are going to choose the Schwarzenegger pic. They don't think in terms of film or story telling quality, they think about how a picture is going to look on the page.

You can get the press involved early on, get them on set and get them involved in the idea of what the movie is about. You may spend a year editing without any money, but if journalists were on board at the beginning, then there is a likelihood that when the movie is screened they will look more favourably upon it because they are somehow involved.

Q - *It's human psychology that you would be inclined to be more favourable if you like someone, and more damning if you don't like someone?*

Nigel - Yes. Personalities ought not to be an issue but the fact is that when you do an interview and you get on with the film maker, they are making an effort to engage with you and talk about the film, then there is a tendency to feel more positive towards them and their film.

Another common problem is poorly organised screenings. If you can afford it, employ someone to organise screenings on your behalf. If not then hire out cinemas early in the morning and get people along.

If I receive two invitations and one of them comes on a scrappy photocopied piece of paper and the other comes on a nice printed ticket, the chances are that I am going to think to myself, *I need to go to this one, this is the one that look's like it is going to do the business, this is the one that is actually going to be out there.*

You need people saying hello as you come in, getting names and phone numbers, so that afterwards you might have a ring round to ask people for their opinion, or send them an email asking for a few words about their reaction.

Journalists also need well presented, reliable and detailed information about the characters, actors, principle crew. Also background information on how and why the film was made. This is usually in the form of a press pack, and it must be professionally presented. If I receive a press kit for a small independent film and it looks like they have taken the trouble to use some computer graphics or a still or something on the cover, or to use an icon like the *Blair Witch* stick man, then I have a sense that they are involved in selling the film to me. You don't want to plead *please feel sorry for us, because this only cost £3k* but you can be factual and put in interesting stories and anecdotes, stuff that journalists might pick up on. Then when they do an interview they can say *that was an interesting story about that night when you were trying to do the big effects scene and everything went wrong.* So in a sense you can lead journalists into areas you want to be given exposure.

Current release

inside her womb? Long on atmosphere but sho n momentum, the meandering plot is fleshe ʳ by Theron's delicately nuanced perfor- nce. Ravich's slick direction, meanwhile, fills interiors of the couple's apartment with a ʳing menace. Sadly, this slow-burning sus- se is rapidly extinguished when too much is aled at just the wrong moment. (Nigel Floyd) ‹ E: Plaza

THE PRESS PACK

COVER	SYNOPSIS	CAST & CREW	NOTES	REVIEWS
Movie title, contact, press quotes, credits and film festival awards.	The story of the movie, with a few pics to spice it up.	Biogs of main cast and crew, with pics and brief quotes about the making of the film. Also, full cast and crew listing.	The story of how the film got made, where, why and when.	Copies of all your good reviews that you have collected so far. Don't include bad reviews!

One thing that is guaranteed to make journalists feel good about your work is to offer them a drink at the screening, nothing heavy, just a beer or coffee, and perhaps a few sandwiches. In a way it is a lot like art direction, you shouldn't notice the hospitality, but when it is not there, you notice it immediately.

So you wander in, are greeted by someone, get a drink, watch the movie - which starts on time and is well presented - then at the end people are standing around thanking you for coming - it is very simple manners. Then you get home and look at the press kit and you go *oh, yes, I see, so that's the guy, oh yes he did this, oh yes, he was involved in that other movie.* And when you sit down to write your review you have it all at your fingertips.

Q - Do journalists talk to each other?

Nigel - Yes. Naturally you gravitate towards the people that share your likes and interests. Word of mouth within that community is almost as important as the word of mouth out there in the audience at large. Again, if people have a choice between three screenings in one evening and they have heard that there is this really interesting low budget independent film that has good word of mouth, they might be inclined to see it above the two bigger competitors.

Q - If your film is going to be released by a small distributor, or if you are going to distribute yourself, how can you get as much good press as possible?

Nigel - You can't start early enough. In a sense, you need to cultivate the journalists, not schmooze them or be sycophantic, because that can be counter productive, just act professionally. I have seen many low budget independent films pissed away because they made a pretty good film, with a few problems, but had no idea of what to do when it came to being presented.

HOSPITALITY	INFO	HOLD BACK	QUESTIONS
Give your journalists some food when they come to your screenings. They'll be more disposed to enjoy your film if they're not hungry.	Make journalists lives easier by giving them as much information as possible. In some instances, you can even control what they write about by 'giving' them the story.	If you don't want it printed, don't say it. It's easy to let slip something that you regret later. If you don't want to answer a question, politely decline and don't expand on why you decline.	Not all journalists will be prepared, so you should be. Have a list of ten questions to which you have meaty, interesting answers. Politely offer it to them and they might bite.

It's important to have a hook - something that captures the imagination of the journalist, a background story, an interesting tale that happened during the making of the movie, something that might make it stand out as a story. If the arts editor of a TV show says *we have got to do something about films this week,* and they look down the list and there are a couple of sub-titled movies which they can't do because it's breakfast TV and then they say *Oh, there's this little independent movie,* like yours perhaps, *there's a story here.* Not every film is going to have that magic ingredient, that built in hook, but it is up to you to find one.

Some new directors tend to present themselves and their movie in such a way as to antagonise people - *here's my film, it is brilliant, I am the best film maker that has ever been* - it's not surprising then that if the movie is on the edge, critics will tend to lean toward a bad review. It's also important to make yourself and your cast available to journalists.

Q - Should you approach everyone with your film?

Nigel - New film makers tend to hit everyone, which is counter productive and wastes energy and resources. For instance if you have a low budget horror comedy then you are not going to target *Sight and Sound* or the *Sunday Times,* you are going to target the sort of publications that are sympathetic to that kind of movie. Similarly if you have made an action picture you are more likely to get coverage in *Total Film* or *Empire* than you are in *Women's Realm.* You have to think about which publications you will target.

Q - What is the SFD?

Nigel - The SFD co-ordinates the times and dates of screenings for journalists. They try to organise things so as to avoid conflicts, such as two screenings of different films, both for

"IT'S THE DOG'S B*LL**KS"

TIME OUT

a comedy of families,
a chip shop...
and a very randy dog.

eASt is eASt

AT CINEMAS EVERYWHERE NOV '99

www.eastiseast.co.uk

East is East presented the simple problem of how to get a multiplex audience in to see what is primarily an Asian film, with Asian issues. The campaign was extraordinarily successful, and it's simplicity doesn't even hint at the hours of work put into it's conceptualision and design. Almost all successful campaigns are bold and simple.

magazines but at the same time. They organise separate screenings for magazines, TV and radio, London and suburban newspapers, and the national press. As an independent film maker you are not part of that club, so unless your film is being distributed by one of the majors, finding a slot is going to be a major headache, but not impossible.

Q - What is lead time?

Nigel - It is the time between a journalist seeing a film, writing about it, and then the magazine actually going to press and hitting the streets. You have to understand that the lead times for different publications are very different, so if you are dealing with a glossy magazine that is published monthly, like Maxim, the lead time can be as much as two months. Magazines like Total Film and Empire have slightly shorter lead times, and daily newspapers will just want to see the film a week or so before it's release.

Q - What is positioning a film all about?

Nigel - It is a cynical word, but movies are 'positioned' and a lot of thought goes into it. The campaign for *East is East* took a low common denominator approach, *it's the mutt's nuts* and *it's the dog's bollocks*. It was a brilliant campaign as it side stepped what the movie was really about and got people to go and see it. I know that they spent months working out how to position an Asian comedy in a multiplex environment. You need to figure out who your audience is, how to get to them and what will make them want to see your movie.

Your movie, *Urban Ghost Story,* is not an easy film to position. On one hand it addresses social issues but on the other hand it appears to have some kind of supernatural element. You don't want people coming expecting a ghost story, but at the same time you don't want to overplay its social realism because then people will be equally misguided. Not all films have a single *Star Wars Episode One: The Phantom Menace* kind of simplicity about them. In some ways this is where journalists can help and if they like the film they can get behind it.

You can also think in terms of an icon too, which will normally be derived from the movie concept and probably some stills. *Blair Witch...* the image of the stick man became a kind of icon. Show that image to anyone now and they will say *The Blair Witch Project*. The Pi symbol from the US

SALES

Indie film *Pi* also became synonymous with the movie.

Q - What about the Internet?

Nigel - *Blair Witch* was clearly helped by the swell of support from the Internet site and the build up before it came out. It is very cheap to set one up and is a good way of getting information to journalists. Always put your website address on posters and press kits, and make sure it's easy for a journalist to send you an email.

Q - Is there a list of journalists to see my film?

Nigel - Someone once phoned me, someone that I hardly knew and said *would you let me have your contacts list of all the journalists in the film industry* and I said *yes, if you pay me £2000.* Information is power. Those details are held on databases at PR companies and are very valuable to them. It is a major part of their business, knowing who is who and who can do what for you.

If you don't have a PR agency working for you, you will have to go and buy all the magazines and newspapers, write down where they are and then contact each of them. There is no guarantee that you will get to the right person either, whereas a PR company will already have a relationship with the right journalists and know exactly who is right for the project, I would advioc approaching a major PR company if you are a low budget film. They know they will not get blood out of a stone, but if you are professional and they like you and the movie, they may be inclined to help and do a deal with you. If you can't afford to employ them, then maybe you can buy an hour of their time and say *can you give me some pointers here, because I don't have any money, but what sort of things could I do?*

Q - What final advice would you offer?

Nigel - It all comes down to stills, stills and stills. Then the press kit, then screenings, in that order. The stills you have got to do while you are shooting, the press kit has to be prepared before you get to the screening, and the screening has got to be run professionally.

Internet web sites are a great, inexpensive and professional way to present your company. You can have full colour pictures, text, video clips... and it can all be put together by you on your desktop PC.

DPRS
Suzan Dormer

Q - What is the DPRS?

Suzan - In essence, as a Director you may be entitled to payments from European companies irrespective of what contracts you signed in order to get your film made or sold. The Director & Producer's Rights Society was set up by a group of directors to collect payments that were due to directors for the re-use of their work under European regulations. In mainland Europe, directors have been legally regarded as owners of rights in their work, the rights of authorship. The three main re-uses where royalties may become due are cable re-transmission, video rentals and private copying.

Q - So nobody else can touch your royalties?

Suzan - Under the UK law which came into force at the end September '96, the director of any work made on or after the 1st July 1994 is co-author of the work itself with the producer and co-first owner of copyright of the work with the producer. The other authors, including the scriptwriter and the composers are authors of their underlying work but the work itself is for the director and the producer.

Q - How much money can it generate?

Suzan - It varies. If your work was shown in Holland as a feature film and it was privately copied you could be talking £50. If it was shown on Canal+ in France again with private copying you could be talking £6k. The most we have collected for an individual director now is going on for £90k. The biggest payment that we have got going out at the end of next month to one director is £20k.

Q - How much does it cost?

Suzan - It costs £30 to register. Thereafter we take a 12.5% commission. We are a non profit making organisation.

Q - I joined the DPRS because I found out that there was £2,800 waiting for me as my share from a German deal. White Angel also sold to Sky in the UK - how much would I as the director get for that Sky screening?

Suzan - Screening in the UK won't generate a penny. You have to remember that although the rights exist under UK law, there are no rights to remuneration.

Q - What is the deal for producers?

Suzan - Producers are also entitled to money from the revenue that is collected from Europe. However, they do not come to the DPRS for those rights, other collection agencies exist such as ComPACT. Generally speaking, producers are due twice what the directors get. Switzerland for example has over 20 cable channels and the rights are divided 25% to the writer, 25% to the director and 50% to the production company. The problems with collecting for producers is that they have often signed their rights away to a broadcaster. Therefore the money from some countries in Europe would be due to the broadcaster. We now recommend a clause be put in all directors' contracts. It reads...

> "Nothing in this agreement shall prevent the director from
> being entitled to receive income under collective agree-
> ments negotiated by recognised collecting societies but the
> director shall have no claim to payment by (COMPANY NAME)
> in respect of rights collectively licensed."

Q - What other organisations would you recommend a new film maker contact in order to get as much out of their film as they can?

Suzan - Certainly the DPRS in terms of their directors, the ALCS for the writer (which also covers books). The producer is difficult and it depends very much on the relationship with the distributor, but they could contact ComPACT.

Q - What advice would you give to a new film maker?

Suzan - Register with the DPRS now. There are countries in Europe, irrespective of the contract that the director signed, where payment for the re-use of his work is due. It's therefore essential that new directors register with the DPRS as soon as they have completed some work so that we can register with a network of collection agencies.

Other contacts
For Authors...
ALCS - The Authors Licensing & Collecting Society
14-18 Holborn, London, EC1N 2LE
Tel 020 7 395 0600 Fax 020 7 395 0660

For Producers...
ComPact Collections Limited
Greenland Place, 115-123 Bayham Street,
London, NW1 0AG
Tel 020 7 446 7420   Fax 020 7 446 7424

The Directors'
& Producers'
Rights Society

DP®S

Victoria Chambers
16-18 Strutton Ground
London SW1P 2HP
Tel: +44 (0) 20 7227 4757
Fax: +44 (0) 20 7227 4755
email: sdormer@dprs.org

SUZAN DORMER
Secretary General

SALES

British Board Of Film Classification
Michael Vizard

Q - What is the BBFC?

Michael - The British Board of Film Classification (BBFC) was established in 1912 under the Cinemas Act to operate as an agent for local authorities in the regulation of film in a nationally consistent way. The authority to licence films remains with local authorities though it is rare for any of these authorities to act independently. In 1984, the Video Recordings Act established the Board as the regulator of video works, accountable to the Home Office. On average, the Board classifies 3-4000 works a year. The Board's essential activity is the classification of films, videos and some computer games, according to their suitability for viewing. The classification tariffs are *U, PG, 12, 15, 18*. In the case of the *U* and *PG* any child may be admitted to the film or be able to hire or purchase a video unaccompanied by an adult, however, *PG* warns parents that some scenes may be upsetting for younger children. In the case of the other categories, no person under the age indicated will be admitted to a cinema or be rented or sold a video. In its certification and classification of films and videos, the Board can exercise its authority, where necessary, to censor contents or, in rare cases, to refuse a licence. Such actions would be taken where it was necessary on legal grounds (e.g. Obscene Publications Acts 1959, 1964; Protection of Children Act 1978; Cinematograph Films (Animals) Act 1937; Video Recordings Act 1984). Other aspects of legislation may also be relevant, such as the Race Relations Act and the laws relating to blasphemy and libel. The European Convention on Human Rights is to be integrated into British law and Article 10 guarantees the right to freedom of expression. If the Board cuts or rejects a work, it must justify such a step by reference to the test contained in this Article, as well as to the requirements of UK law and to issues of offensiveness. In particular, the Video Recordings Act requires the Board to make judgements about potential harm, directly to the viewer or indirectly to society.

Q - How long will it take and how much does it cost?

Michael - From submission to certification, it varies according to the workload of the Board but it should be around two to four weeks. A problematic work requiring cuts and/or several examination viewings will take longer than those which are straightforward. The fees for certification are on a price-per-foot basis and reviewed annually. Supplementary fees are payable where the Board incurs additional costs, for example, foreign language films where an interpreter is required. The Board's web site contains details of fees. Clients may apply in writing (with supporting documentation) for a discretionary concessionary rate if, for example, they have produced student films which are not to be distributed for private gain or they have been produced by a registered charity.

Q - What about trailers?

Michael - Trailers and advertisements also have to be classified by the Board. The tariff of classifications is the same as for film and video works, the exception being advertisements for theatrical release where there are only two classifications, U or 15.

Q - Where can you get information?

Michael - The Board has a website (www.bbfc.co.uk), email helpline (helpline@bbfc.co.uk) and a phone line (020 7287 6977). The website contains a wealth of information about submission procedures and other relevant details.

Q - What common mistakes do you see?

Michael - Failure to approach the Board until the eleventh hour means it may not be possible to accommodate all the client's wishes. Films and trailers must be booked in as early as possible once an answer print is to hand and must be accompanied by a submission form. If a film is not viewed until close to the proposed release date, there may be problems if amendments are required. The Board needs as much time as possible and release dates should be noted on the submission form. Videos do not need to be pre-booked but, similarly, must be accompanied by a submission form. Sometimes a client doesn't appreciate that the film may need some work in order to receive the desired certificate, this a probelm especially when time is pressing. There are guidelines that you can refer to which draw attention to potentially problematic legal areas. This does not happen too frequently but if time is pressing there may not be enough time to make the required changes. Cuts are inadequately made. The Board specifies cuts as precisely as possible so as not to damage the film's narrative or aesthetic qualities. An experienced editor with experience in cutting to BBFC requirements can get around this. Cut videos must be resubmitted in full with the cuts made. Resubmission forms must accompany resubmitted works in both media. Sometimes clients send us the only copy of their work. Don't do this! The Board is legally obliged to maintain a statutory archive of all classified videos and these aren't returned (unlike film prints). The Board can only classify work in the form in which it is to be released so don't submit until it is completed. This means the titles must appear on screen, the music track etc., must all appear.

Q - Where can you get the BBFC guidelines?

Michael - The Board's website, or by contacting the Board by telephone, fax, e-mail or letter.

Q - What advice would you offer a new film maker?

Michael - Contact the Board at the earliest possible stage so that anticipated problems can be addressed and assessed as early as possible.

Pricing Guidlines - 35mm film costs £10.20 per minute for the 1st hour, £7.50 per minute for the 2nd hour, £5.60 per minute thereafter with a 10 minute minimum charge. Video costs £11.68 per minute for the 1st hour, £7.75 per minute for the 2nd hour, £6.48 per minute for the 3rd & 4th hour, £5.15 per minute thereafter, with a 10 minute minimum charge. All prices plus VAT (circa March 2000).

3 Soho Square
London W1V 6HD
Telephone 020 7439 7961
http://www.bbfc.co.uk

BRITISH BOARD OF FILM CLASSIFICATION

Michael Vizard
Examiner
mvizard@bbfc.co.uk

Getting An Agent
Charlotte Kelly of
Casarotto Ramsay

Q - What is your job?

Charlotte - I represent writers and directors. In terms of what I do, it's both creative and practical. From the creative viewpoint it's about advising, guiding and focusing clients on their strengths. We also introduce people who might be useful eg. producers, financiers etc. From a practical point of view it's about doing deals and contracts, sometimes we help with packaging.

Q - Because of your position you have your finger in pies that a new film maker might not have access to?

Charlotte - Yes. Production companies often don't have time to seek out new film makers and can be inundated by new hopefuls. So many people think they can write a screenplay, so the agent acts as a filter. A development executive is likely to take you and your project much more seriously if you have been forwarded by an agent.

Q - How do film makers get an agent?

Charlotte - Obviously you need to have made a film to showcase your talents. If you're at film school, then you will have a graduation and usually they'll invite agents. We see new film makers at film festivals and more often than not, you get to hear a buzz about a film, read something that gets you interested, or get a recommendation from someone in the business who you trust.

Q - What if somebody sends you a showreel saying 'would you represent me'?

Charlotte - We do look at unsolicited tapes but the best way to get agents to see your work is to set up a screening. Present your work seriously and professionally. Agents are looking for professionalism and talent, but mostly originality. Obviously I need something that I can sell, but that doesn't mean it has to be overtly commercial, although I need to feel that I know where and who I can sell the particular talent. Personality counts for a lot as eventually a writer or director will have to sell themselves. An agent can only get them into the right place at the right time. A lot of agents want to build longterm relationships, so you want to enjoy working with that person and get on with them. I think the most important thing is originality.

Q - We made two commercial films for what we perceived to be a commercial market place and then we made Urban Ghost Story with the attitude that we didn't care about the commercial marketplace. The movie itself might not have been very successful, but it really opened doors to new opportunities.

Charlotte - Yes, because it's fresh and original. It's a unique film with a unique voice and that's what people are looking for. Second guessing in my experience doesn't work - you have to remain faithful to your belief in the story, it's really important to try and retain your integrity.

Q - Part of the psychology with people who finance films, especially at the studio level, is that they're still going to make the same movies but they want to find people with different voices so they look like new or different movies?

Charlotte - Absolutely. I think there's always the Holy Grail of what will clean up at the Box Office this year. I guess we're going to see thousands of Blair Witch Projects and the thing about *The Blair Witch Project* was that it's completely and utterly original and because it's micro budget they just did it. But you won't be able to repeat that.

Q - What kind of agent would you recommend to new film makers?

Charlotte - It depends on your personality. If you're new you may want somebody who's going to work with you, give you time and help you make the films you want to make.

Q - How does the commission work?

Charlotte - I believe there are variations but we usually take 10% plus vat of all the money earned by a client. Any agent or manager asking for money up front should be avoided.

Q - You don't actually have cash to give film makers straight away?

Charlotte - No, we aim to help clients get jobs that pay but we also work with clients to help raise finance for their own projects for example by introducing them to potential sources of film finance.

Q - Do producers have agents?

Charlotte - Yes, sometimes. A producer is most likely to have an agent to do a deal for them - for example, with a studio or a financier.

Q - What are the advantages and disadvantages of having an agent?

Charlotte - I'd have to say I can't see any disadvantages unless you're with the wrong agent. The advantages are that you've got somebody out there talking about you, focusing on you, bringing you into a world that you might find difficult to get into, protecting and advising, and always trying to get the best deal. In many ways it's a partnership.

CASAROTTO RAMSAY & ASSOCIATES LIMITED

Charlotte Kelly

National House 60-66 Wardour Street London W1V 4ND
Telephone: 020 7287 4450 Fax: 020 7287 9128
Email: charlotte@casarotto.uk.com

Q - What is the most important selling tool once you've signed a client?

287

Charlotte - If you've made a film, people need to see it and I'd much rather people saw it on the big screen but often this is not possible so you will then target the ones who didn't make it to the screening by sending out tapes; so plenty of VHS tapes, both PAL and NTSC are useful. For example, with *Urban Ghost Story*, having a print in LA was important. It means producers, agents, lawyers and executives can screen the film whenever they want to see if you are suitable for a project. They all have access to 35mm theatres so they will get to see it on a big screen too. If you can afford it, have more than one print of your film. It's also a good idea to know what your next project is (ie. what you want to make - it doesn't necessarily have to be in script form) because everybody will want to know about it. To an extent you also have a "sell by date"; it doesn't mean that if you don't get your next film off the ground within the year that you aren't going to make another, but you should take advantage of being hot.

Q - Is it common for new film makers to have unrealistic expectations and become disillusioned with their agent?

Charlotte - A lot of this business is about personalities. It's also about communication. If you're not happy with how things are progressing with your agent, do something, talk about it, work with your agent, have a brainstorming session, come up with ideas. This is a partnership. However sometimes the fit is wrong. You can always change agents - it happens on both sides.

Q - Going from micro budget film to the professional world where you get paid is a shock - how much can you earn?

Charlotte - Yes it can be shock but a very nice one! Mostly the budget will dictate what a writer or director can earn. There are many variables but as a very rough guide, you might command between 2 and 4 % of a film's budget plus a share of the films profits (eg. if it's a £3.5m feature and you've made one good film already, you could be earning anywhere between £75k and £100k plus a share of the film's profits). In any case there will be a ceiling on the fee. It obviously makes a huge difference if your film has been a real hit at the box office, for example *Blair Witch*. So it's a hard question to answer but the likelihood is that you could personally earn more on your second film than it cost to make your first!

Q - Do film festivals and awards help?

Charlotte - They help immensely to raise the profile of a filmmaker, especially festivals like Sundance and Cannes. If you win an award at either of those you're likely to become hot property. Other festivals are good too and any award might get you a few inches in Screen International and Variety. But beware, you can become a festival junkie as well, so it's important to keep focused on your next film and not on travelling the world on other peoples expenses.

Q - How does the LA thing work, you're a UK agent but there's the rest of the world?

Charlotte - We're not just agents for the UK because we represent clients from all over the world, including Canada, Australia and Europe; we deal directly with producers, studios and TV companies worldwide. We co-represent some clients, mainly with LA based agents. In that case, we split commission (usually higher than 10%) with the other agent and work together for the client. As well as agents we also work with lawyers and managers, particularly in the US.

Talent - the agent can get you in and cut the deal, but YOU have to deliver on the promise and at the top, it's uncompromising.	*Deal Maker - agents make deals day in and day out, they can negotiate harder and better than you, so let them do it and don't scupper the deal.*	*Reel - cut yourself a good showreel to showcase your work. Make sure any VHS copies of your reel or the movie itself are top quality.*	*Contacts - use your agent, they know many people who could be helpful and will be able to get you into places you couldn't get to before.*	*Focus - projects land on your desk thick and fast, so focus on what you want to do next. Remember, people are watching to see if you deliver on the promise of your first film.*

Q - Do you have any comments for a young film maker who made a hit movie with a DV Camcorder suddenly finding themselves on the set of a $15m studio picture where the crew are seasoned professionals, perhaps twice the age of the director?

Charlotte - That's one of the daunting things that's easy to forget. That's why you need to have a really good producer who knows what they are doing and who is going to support and back the film maker all the way. I remember one film maker who's just made her first big feature saying she got to set the first day and saw 00 people standing there and she was thinking *Oh My God they're here for me!* The pressures can be enormous.

Q - What are the common mistakes you come across?

Charlotte - I can think of three mistakes in particular that we've come across here at Casarotto... Firstly, directors or writers who are hungry to make their film, make agreements without thinking about it and more often than not, find that they've signed something away that could have been of benefit to them. If you're going to have an agent you might as well use them and let them do the deal for you. A new film maker might have creative talent but sometimes they don't fully appreciate their true market value. Secondly, two people work on a screenplay together without making an agreement as to how they will split any payment that they might receive. This can be the end of many a friendship so put everything in writing even if it's just a simple letter setting out your mutual understanding. Lastly, many a micro film maker promises their cast or crew a position on their next film. However, if it's a financed feature you might not be in a position to fulfill that promise so be careful about making promises. This obviously doesn't mean that you should forget those who helped you when you started out.

Q - What advice would you offer?

Charlotte - Make the film you really want to make. It's the only time that you won't have people interfering with your vision and it's the only way anyone's ever going to get to know what your voice is like. So have faith in yourself and your instinct on the one hand and on the other hand, do remember to ask yourself is anyone going to want to finance this film and is anyone going to want to watch this film?

IE GERSH AGENCY

Hollywood Agent
Lee Keele
The Gersh Agency

Q - What is your job and how does a new film maker get represented?

Lee - I'm a literary and feature film agent which means I represent writers and directors for theatrical films. The management phenomena has blossomed in the last five years based on the rational that at the bigger agencies clients just didn't get the personal and business attention that they feel they deserve and managers are able to fill in the gaps. Of larger issue, the attractive part about being a manager is that you can produce. There are movies that I have put together where I certainly could have taken producer credit, but because I am an agent I couldn't. The problem: There is an inherent conflict of interest in producing someone's films and managing their career. However, it's an attractive prospect to a lot of agents and there is now an argument that deregulation may happen with SAG and DGA where agents may be able to produce and invest in production companies. With regard to getting representation, I'm open to unsolicited material, meaning it doesn't have to go through an attorney or manager. Occasionally, I attend festivals to see new film makers' work. More often than not, I receive recommendations from friends in the business. What I look for is material that shines. The Agency would take 10% as a commission from the film makers fee per job, law firms generally take 5%.

Q - What makes talent shine out?

Lee - First and foremost it is the work itself — the quality of the film or screenplay. It's a hard competitive business so we're quite ruthless in our assessments. We also look for personalities that are good for Hollywood, for instance, some writers are extraordinarily talented, but don't do well in a room. For a writer, the performance art-ability is less important, but it can be helpful, particularly in selling pitches. More importantly, a director should have a strong presence in a room. Personality is important because executives want to be able to feel they can work with you and know that as director you could be the captain of the ship and they can trust you with a $m's to make a movie. With screenwriters, we look for an original voice - the characters, dialogue and premise leap off the page. Film is collaborative and at the studios you typically do not have that much control, so you have to be able to gauge the political waters and work with a lot of different people. The more skilful you are at manoeuvring the waters, the more you can get what you want to maintain your vision.

Q - What kind of projects can you get a first time film maker?

Lee - If they've made a terrific movie that's received a lot of attention, the market place is quite open and you may get high profile offers. The pendulum is always swinging. Right now, it's open to video commercials and first time feature directors. Studios desperately want something fresh and new, yet the very process the 'new talent' is subjected to at the studio can often silence that fresh voice.

Q - What are open writing assignments?

Lee - A studio or producer will have a possible project where they are looking for a director and/or writer. They'll call up the agencies to find out who we'd have that would be right and available. Often, the have their own wish list in mind.

Q - Is it a good idea to have a screenplay ready after completing you first movie?

Lee - Absolutely. It's best to go into rooms ready for the executives to ask what's next? Pitch me. They're looking to find a creative meeting ground where they can be in business with you. They themselves may also have projects that they can throw at you. Usually this project is of a similar tone to what you have just proven you can do. If you want to establish a quick commercial career in Hollywood, it's easier if you follow up with a similar genre, for instance if you made a comedy, pitch a romantic comedy. However, there is no use churning out staid romantic comedies which are not going to sell because your heart is not in it.

Q - Can you help with funding?

Lee - It depends on the commercial viability. I may read a screenplay and think it's perfect for Warner Bros. as they are looking to do this sort of high concept political thriller right now. If you do a dark character piece then there may be a few of the mini majors or independents that we can go to. A lot of studios are on a wait and see basis particularly if it's a character piece. *We'll wait and see how the film turns out and then we'll acquire it.* It may be amazing material but not what they're looking for. Even the places that traditionally did more independents are now doing genre pictures.

Q - What kind of money can a film maker earn out here?

Lee - The sky's the limit. For first time film makers on a studio picture you're typically looking at a director's guild minimum plus 10%, usually about $150k. If you've already made a movie I would shoot for $250-$300k. It depends on a number of factors like where you go, which studio, who is starring in it and how far you can push that. It's all driven by the box office success of your previous film. The studio can have a horrible experience with you but if your movie performs well at the box office they will be eagerly lining up to fund your next project.

Q - What common mistakes do you encounter?

Lee - Hollywood is a complex web of personalities and hidden agendas. You need to understand studio politics and have good communication skills otherwise you will have a miserable experience as the studio does tend to take over. It's about learning, being open, smart and savvy. How can I best make this work for me? Opposed to defining yourself in black or white absolutes, i.e., an unbending attitude - *I am the Director and everything you (the Executive) say will be of no importance* - puts a lot of people off. You mustn't take everything personally, you have to let go of whatever so and so did to you yesterday because the chances are that so and so will be the person you are going to make a movie with tomorrow. It is a small community and you have to continually cleanse your mind and spirit.

Q - What advice would you offer a new film maker?

Lee - Be a film maker for the joy of being a film maker. Some people like the idea of being a film maker, because of some imagined glamorous lifestyle, which it certainly isn't. Ultimately, that isn't going to inspire or drive those around you and it certainly won't create happiness in your own life. There are going to be highs and there are going to be lows. There's a copycat syndrome in Hollywood, where they're always looking for the next *Blair Witch* which was it's own original phenomenon. What foreign directors do well is come to Hollywood with something new and different. The studio wants to do that, but in their own controlled studio way which the film maker may not be happy with. One sure way to win the Hollywood game is if you can convey great emotion to the audience with your work. However, there really is no right or wrong way. One day you are nowhere, the next day you are the cause to celebrate.

THE GERSH AGENCY
LITERARY AND TALENT AGENCY

LEE KEELE

232 NORTH CAÑON DRIVE, BEVERLY HILLS, CALIFORNIA 90210
PHONE: (310) 205-5827   FAX: (310) 274-4035

MGM Studio Executive
Elizabeth Carroll
Senior Vice President - Production

Q - What is your job?

Elizabeth - My job is to look for new projects for the studio, either in screenplay or book form or by way of a pitch or remake idea. We either option or buy the ones we get excited about. If the material is not ready right away then we begin the development process. We usually do a couple of drafts with the original writer, or sometimes we hire a new writer if we want a different take on the writing. When we're happy with the quality of the script, we begin to attach a director, cast etc. Then we have a budget made. If it's a movie we ultimately want to make, we "greenlight" it. From then on, I supervise the pre-production and production processes, making sure we stay on the agreed budget and schedule. After principle photography ends, the director works with the editor to create his or her cut of the film. After we see the director's cut, the film is tested in research screenings which may determine if and how the film is re-cut. Finally, the film is marketed and distributed, I'm less involved at that point of the process, as we have departments internally that handle those aspects.

Q - What size projects are you looking for?

Elizabeth - It's hard for us to make movies for $6million and below because of the unions and because our overhead goes into the budget. When a major Hollywood studio says "low budget", it usually means $8 - $20million. More of the movies we do fall into the $50-$60million range with the occasional $90-$100million film.

Q - What do you look for in new filmmakers?

Elizabeth - I look for someone who can tell a story. I see a lot of music videos, commercials or shorts that are flashy and stylish. The director may use cool lenses and neat special effects but not possess the ability to tell a good story. I need to know if that filmmaker can hit all the dramatic beats and draw in an audience. It helps if I can see a feature the new filmmaker has made. While dramatic structure is a priority, it is also important that the filmmaker be able to pull good performances out of the actors. When watching a sample film, I am less concerned with production value because most films by new talent are made on such meagre budgets.

Q - How do you see their movies if you've heard good things?

Elizabeth - When an agent or a colleague that I trust asks me to take a look at a filmmaker's new material, I will have them send me a tape or set up a screening. And since I'm constantly flooded with new material, I remember the projects that really stand out.

Q - What mistakes do new filmmakers hired by the studios make?

Elizabeth - Studios don't hand a new filmmaker a cheque for $8million and say *OK, go make your movie.* Filmmakers must understand that there is a certain amount of bureaucracy they will have to contend with when making a film for a major studio. When we make a movie that will open on 1000 or more screens, a certain level of casting is required to attract such a large audience. This is not to say that a director cannot fight for a certain actor but he or she should keep the studio's casting interests in mind.

New filmmakers must realise that a studio wants to reach a very wide audience. While we don't want to discourage individual style, we need the filmmaker to be aware of what type of material is or isn't commercial. We often see independent filmmakers who prefer a darker sensibility to give a film mood and texture or who use film stocks that are not necessarily right for studio pictures. However, independent fimmakers can also bring a lot of special qualities to a project. They tend to know many creative tricks and shortcuts and tend not to have as bloated a sensibility as many Hollywood directors do.

Q - Should a new filmmaker pitch a film that is in the same genre as their independent feature?

Elizabeth - If he or she directed a successful independent horror movie, the studio will moot likely look at that film as a sample for the horror/thriller genre. If this filmmaker wanted to do a romantic comedy however, his or her past work won't be of much help. The director should consider directing a romantic comedy independently to show his or her range.

Q - What advice would you offer?

Elizabeth - When making your first independent feature, worry about creating a dramatic and focused story, more than anything else. A good story rises above flashy production design or unique look. Many new filmmakers make the mistake of choosing style over substance. Be careful when signing with an agent. Find someone who believes in you and has the time to promote you. Realise that as a first time director for a studio, you're still going to be working on a limited budget. While the budget will be more than you're used to in the independent world, it still won't be the big Tom Cruise vehicle. It's important to understand the studio's sensibility. While our aim is to produce movies that appeal to a large audience, we don't necessarily look for ordinary material. *American Beauty,* for example, was a unique film and was also very successful. A film, which achieves this sort of balance, is what the studio ideally wants to produce.

METRO-GOLDWYN-MAYER PICTURES INC.

ELIZABETH CARROLL
SENIOR VICE PRESIDENT - PRODUCTION

A METRO-GOLDWYN-MAYER COMPANY
2500 BROADWAY STREET, SANTA MONICA, CALIFORNIA 90404-3061
(310) 449-3445 • FAX (310) 449-3024 • E-MAIL: ecarroll@mgm.com

WHAT NEXT?

Anonymous
Where to next?

Q – So you've made your first film and you've come out the other end feeling emotionally drained and you really need to get into the world where the 'real' film makers live. Where should you start to hang out, what clubs should you join?

Anon – Off the record, I am not a member of any club, although I will say that I do frequent many clubs. There's Soho House - I used to get in by saying my name at the door with great conviction, sometimes kissing the cheek of the door-lady. One time I got called up on it - *are you a member?* and I said *yes, of course,* so they said, *well, can we see your card?* and I say *sorry, I forgot my card* and they said *can we look you up on the computer?* and I said *sure* and I told them my real name. Of course I wasn't on the system though someone did share my last name so I pretended that he was my brother. That didn't quite work and then they said *well, what colour is the membership card?* and because the membership card in Cannes was silver, I said *silver* and they said *ah, no* so I said *well what colour is it?* and they said *purple* and I said *well, mine's silver.* In the end it was really embarrassing, especially as I had three actors in tow – I made up a story *look, I have been shooting till 5am this morning, I just want to come to a nice quiet place to drink with my actors,* and the long and short of it is that I got booted out. The up side is they now think I am a member because they recognise my face, but don't quite remember from where. I could join if I wanted to but it's terribly overpriced, I just have an aversion to paying for something when I know I can get it for free. Paying to go to a pub just seems such a waste of money although some might argue that it is the place to meet people in the industry.

Q – What about the Groucho Club?

Anon – Groucho's is slightly more up market, more A list celebrities and important industry people. Groucho's is hard to get into unless you know someone. And you can't buy a drink in Groucho's unless you are a member. Beware, the average price of drinks at both places is more expensive than normal pubs.

Q – How do you get invited to those all important media parties where deals get struck?

Anon – For the first two years in Cannes I wasn't invited to anything. I don't know who gets officially invited, nor how they get invitations, it's a mystery to me but it is important to go. Normally I would have to blag my way in any way I could - scaling fences, crawling through windows, elaborate scams pretending I was related to the film maker. Another very simple way which seems to work every time is approaching the doorman in great haste and saying *oh, I'm terribly sorry I left my coat inside* at which point they usually let you in. What you want to avoid is being escorted in by some six foot beefcake to look for it. The way that I usually dealt with that was to go to an empty chair and shout, *oh, my God my jacket's missing! My friend must have taken it, let's look for him togethe*r. So he gets really bored and after a while says *when you've found it come on out.* Once you are in the party there is another queue inside trying to get into the VIP lounge. The jacket scam is very good for that one. Hopefully you will have started to rub shoulders with executives, solicitors, agents and the like. You need to develop relationships with these people as they have a direct line into the business and they can keep you informed of who is doing what. They also tend to get invited to all the top functions and sometimes have spare tickets. Even so, when you get into a party, if you don't know the people in the first place it is hard to know who to go up to and speak to. I find the best way of meeting people in Cannes for instance, is to stand outside the Petit Carlton and the Petit Majestic at 3am in the morning where you find yourself stood next to drunken acquisitions executives from big studios and the like.

Q - What trade magazines should you get?

Anonymous - The most popular UK trade magazine is Screen International, which at £2 a pop can be pricey - hey, you can always read it at the newstand. Screen tells you what is happening in the business right now, what films are in production, plus lots of fluff about the business in general. Screen Finance is also a very good publication, aimed at the financial section of the market. It is a well-constructed newsletter created through an arm of the Financial Times, but it's really expensive, so find someone who subscribes and raid their offices after they have read it. You must arm yourself with knowledge – so read the trades and become familiar with who's doing what. A problem that is very apparent at Cannes is that people just turn up and call themselves 'producers' when they don't know a thing about how the industry works. We all have ambitions and dreams of doing It and you have to start somewhere, but if you are going to call yourself a producer, then at least know how a film works.

Q - Have you ever gate crashed a premiere?

Anonymous - Many, although one stands out in my mind. I had seen *The Mask of Zorro* while at the Deauville Film Festival. I enjoyed the film and the party afterwards was an event in itself. When I heard about the big London premiere, followed by a swank party at the Criterion, I though it might be fun to try to blag my way in. I thought I'd give it a try so I called the London press office and announced with great conviction that I am a film maker, and I would like tickets to the party. Without a moment's hesitation I was refused. There's nothing like rejection to fuel one's perseverance. I now had a mission - to get tickets to this party. I needed a way of approaching them where there would be no possible way of them turning me down - and how

Keep on top of what is happening in the business by reading the trade press, or better still, reading somones else's. Screen Finance (0207 453 2800), Screen International (0207 505 8056), Variety (0207 520 5222).

Late night drinking clubs are a haunt for film makers. Hard to get membership, hard to get into, but a place where important people hang out. This inconspicuous doorway is Soho House (upper left) at 40 Greek St, 0207 734 5188, and the Groucho Club (lower left) 45 Dean Street, 0207 439 4685.

could they turn me down if I worked for the company? Not only that, but what if I was actually an executive from the upper echelons of the studio in LA? A while back I had sent a script to Universal in Hollywood with the hope of someone actually reading it. Several weeks later the script was returned with a rejection letter. I had kept the letter, so scanned the letterhead in colour and made a replica. I also had a database of executives working in Hollywood, found one, the "Executive Vice-President of Business Affairs", filled in his name and personal phone extension number and wrote a letter which read something like...

"Dear Maggie - I am writing on behalf of Mr Smith, Executive Vice-President of Business Affairs for Universal Studios here in Los Angeles. Mr Smith will have a brief stopover in London on his way to Paris this Thursday. Please could you arrange for his name to be placed on the guest list for the post-premiere party of The Mask of Zorro. Should you need to contact Mr Smith blah blah blah..."

I printed it out. It looked perfect. I had to be careful of what time I faxed the letter due to the time difference and from what machine I faxed it as most fax machines send out a fax ID. Also, I didn't want the press officer contacting the LA office, so I gave a convenient London fax number, my mum's! With these things solved, I sent off the fax and sat back, thinking I'll just show up at the party. Imagine my surprise when that very day a fax came for me from the London Press office!

"Dear Mr Smith - your secretary faxed me yesterday and told me you would be stopping in London for business. We are delighted that you will be coming to the post-premiere party. Would you also like to come to the Gala Charity premier in the presence of HRH, the Prince of Wales? Unfortunately, your secretary forgot to mention what hotel you were staying at. However if you contact me, I can arrange to have tickets biked over. Yours faithfully..."

OK - firstly I am not staying at a hotel and secondly, I'm not who I say I am. How in hell was I supposed to get her to bike these tickets to a legitimate hotel like the Dorchester, for a fictional guest that would not be arriving? I have a friend with a public school accent who I convinced to help me out. Luckily he is a member of an exclusive club in Mayfair, so I got him to call the press office in his best Queen's English...

"Yes, I am the general manager of the 'blah blah' club and I'm calling on behalf of Mr. Smith who is tied up in meetings all day. He's asked me to call you to confirm that he would be attending the Gala Premiere and asked if you could send the tickets to his suite here..."

"Sure, we'll bike them over..." Nervously I turned up at my friend's club, of course he wasn't the manager, he was the doorman. And lo and behold, the tickets had arrived.

WHAT NEXT?

I went to the premiere in black tie and when I arrived there were film crews everyone relaying the video to the screens inside the cinema - where hundreds of studio executives were watching everyone's entrance. Simultaneously there was a man commentating on all the entrants, and pointing out the well known faces and executives. At any moment I was waiting for the announcement, *and coming in now is Mr Chuck Smith, Vice-President of Business Affairs for our LA office.* Thankfully, that didn't happen. I had great seats, several rows up from Prince Charles and the Sultan of Brunei. I also noticed that the tickets were numbered by the press office - and the seats were assigned - which presumably meant that someone, somewhere, had a list of where everyone was sitting. Again, I nervously waited for a lady with a clipboard to come up to my seat and introduce herself, *Mr Smith, how nice to finally meet you and put a name to the face, when are you off to Paris? By the way, I called your office today and how funny that you're still in LA...*

Q - Isn't that immoral, no illegal?

Anonymous - Yes, it is illegal to pretend to be someone else in order to get into a party. Morally it was wrong, but have you ever tried to get invited to one of those things, it's damn hard. At the end of the day I wasn't trying to defraud anyone of anything, I was just seeing how far I could get. You have to be prepared to do almost anything at times. My first feature had a very small budget. I did everything I could to save costs. I remember one incident when an agent asked me to bike over the script so her celebrity client could have a look. *Oh, sure, I'll bike it over today* would be my normal response. Of course I couldn't afford to bike over a script every time an agent asked me, so I got into the habit of dressing up as a bike courier and delivering it myself. I dress up in all the kit, have shades and clip board and put on an Ozzie accent. The things you do!

Q - What is the key to survival in the industry?

Anonymous - You must have passion for your craft and ask yourself why you are in this business. Ambition is all very well, but a grounded sense of passion and commitment to the art itself is the single most important quality you must have. Yes, the drive for money, success and power might be ramifications, but commitment and belief in your art should come first. You have to be determined and thick-skinned and eventually your perseverance will pay off. Someone, somewhere will recognise your talent...eventually. Don't give up!

Decide if you are a person who is into the business for the fun, if you are, leave now - or if you are a person in the business for life - recognise it's a marathon. No-one really knows what's good. The single biggest problem is that people don't have faith in their own judgement of what is good. It's easier and less of a risk to just say no. Know you can do one of two things – continue to try and convince somebody to take an interest in your project, or you can take control of your destiny and go do it yourself. And why not? My suggestion is, be motivated and do it yourself. On my first feature I went straight to a company I knew had money and got them to write me a cheque – that cheque funded my film and I did it without going to the BBC, Ch4 or any of the usual suspects that end up rejecting projects from people they don't know. Like everyone else, I have a huge file of rejection letters, and if I gave up during all those times, I'd be flipping burgers by now.

WHAT NEXT?

12
The ~~Ten~~ Low Budget Film Commandments

Thou shalt cast out of thine mind, the phrase 'it can't be done'.

Thou shalt shoot at 25fps in the UK, no matter what anyone tells you.

Thou shalt never work a crew more than 12 hours a day, 6 days a week.

Thou shalt ask if in doubt. If not in doubt, thou shalt ask anyway.

Thou shalt make a film through the legal mechanism of a limited company.

Thou shalt never shoot standard 16mm, thou shalt shoot Super 16mm or 35mm.

Thou shalt shoot hundreds of high quality stills of the actors and action.

Thou shalt get the best deal by paying cash upfront.

Thou shalt always shoot two takes of every shot possible.

Thou shalt disregard friends and colleagues ridicule at your ambition.

Thou shalt only shoot when thine screenplay is Oscar winning.

Thou shalt cut, then recut, then recut, then recut, then recut.

Section 2
Case
Studies

CASE STUDIES

The Living Spirit Story

Prologue

Chris Jones and Genevieve Jolliffe met at Bournemouth Film School in 1989.

Chris, born and bred in the North of England, had started making amateur horror films on Super 8mm many years earlier. His first triumph, an unashamed homage to the films of George Romero and the *Evil Dead*, was an immense success at his college. After 'bluffing' his way into film school, he began work on what he believed would be his greatest film yet, *Rundown,* a sci-fi thriller.

Genevieve was inspired and terrified at an early age, by the black & white classic, *Dracula. Star Wars* quickly followed and she knew that she wanted to make movies. She started out working in the industry, attending markets such as the Cannes Film Festival and dabbling in animation before travelling the world with her Nikon and Super 8mm camera. When she attended film school, she quickly became frustrated by the lack of inspired leadership and was eager to make a movie.

After meeting, Chris and Gen decided to make *Rundown*, Chris' graduation film, but too many obstacles were put in their way. They decided to leave the film school, Chris after two and a half years, Gen after only six months. Neither of them made a movie or shot a single frame of film whilst at Bournemouth film school.

Note - The interviews in this section were performed between 1994 and 2000.

First Assistant Director, Lisa Harney on 'The Runner'. Photographed after five weeks shooting at 3 a.m. in a Manchester ghetto. It's all a bit much.

Q - How did Living Spirit Pictures Ltd. come about?

Gen - Film School, at the time, was about making depressing TV style drama, full of pessimism, about minority issues - anything that involved a social problem. They didn't want to do anything that strayed from that formula, there was no variety, just one particular kind of film and if you didn't fit into that, then you didn't get a film made. Therefore, when we came out of film school we just wanted to get into the real world and do something that was BIG. The frustration of film school had built up in us to such a degree that when we considered what to make, there was one thing we really wanted to do - blow everything up! We were both great fans of *Aliens* and *Die Hard*, so we knew that we wanted to make an action thriller.

Chris - I was in my third year at Bournemouth Film School.

Image Copyright Jon English

Game Shows on which the contestants are killed - Rundown was at a very developed stage when Chris and Gen left the film school. However, due to problems with special effects, and the Schwarzenegger vehicle, The Running Man, the project was eventually binned in favour of 'The Runner'

Gen was in her first. We teamed up and decided to make a film school project together. I was taken onto the film school course as a director and I was supposed to be directing a film that year. I put forward a script that I had written in my first year and had been developing ever since. It was about a game show in which contestants were killed and after endless script development meetings with the staff, it became apparent that this was not going to happen in the form that I wanted. It wasn't going to be the sci-fi action-adventure that I wanted to make. Gen felt the same.

One night we sat down and thought - What would happen if we didn't actually make this movie at film school? We'd worked out a budget of around fourteen thousand pounds. We went down the list and calculated that the film school offered us a crew (which in any case we could persuade to work with us) and equipment (which would cost us four thousand pounds if we had to hire it). So, in reality, all the film school could offer was a few thousand pounds worth of equipment hire and some serious headaches (and they got to retain the copyright!)

"A verbal contract isn't worth the paper it's written on"
Samuel Goldwyn

We still had to raise fourteen thousand quid and if we could raise fourteen, we could raise eighteen and make the film outside the film school. It was ludicrous and we decided to leave film school, go on the enterprise allowance scheme (a government small companies incentive scheme that existed at the time), set up our own company and make the film the way we wanted. We worked out which county would provide us with the most grants for setting up a business, and eventually settled on Cheshire. London was out of the question as it would just be too expensive to live there.

Q - Is that when you approached the Princes' Trust?

Chris - We found that we were eligible for the PYBT (The Princes' Youth Business Trust, an organisation headed by HRH Prince Charles which helps eighteen to twenty five year olds who have the ideas, guts and determination, but no seed money). We put our application through and got a soft loan of three thousand pounds and a further two thousand a year later. This enabled us to get all our business equipment, computer, fax, letterheads, all that kind of stuff. And so Living Spirit Pictures was born.

Q - Why the name Living Spirit Pictures?

Gen - We wanted a name which expressed the way in which we were going to run our business and make movies. Everyone seemed to like it, even the strange people who still ring us and ask if they can join our religious cult! (no joke)

Q - Did you start a formal company?

Gen - Yes, we were no longer in the playground. We took an accountant's advice and started a Limited Company. There is so much to running a company that you can never know until it goes wrong, and it's very expensive. You can waste a lot of money if you don't know what you are doing. Read some books on starting a company, they're a lot cheaper than advice from a solicitor or accountant.

Q - After you began trading, what was at the top of the agenda?

Gen - The movie. We were at home, planning the film, looking at the reality of the project. We had a script for a forty-five minute film costing about £18k and had sent off details to potential investors informing them of the project. We weren't sure what to expect, maybe one or two replies. Every single one wrote back to us, offering finance, saying - if you make a feature, we will put in more money.

Short v Feature

The obvious starting point when making a low budget film is to make a short. Whilst your short may be a great movie, it isn't a feature and you will have terrible problems trying to sell it to get your money back.

1. A feature film is a saleable product which will generate interest from buyers. A short will generate virtually no interest.

2. A feature film is three or four times longer than a short - therefore three or four times more work (not exactly true, there is a sharp learning curve.)

3. Don't expand a short screenplay into a feature. This almost always produces a very padded out, slow feature version of a short idea. Start from scratch.

4. If a feature film is a success, you could find yourself at the helm of a Hollywood feature. If a short is a success, you will collect an award from a bizarre film festival from a place no-one has ever heard of.

5. Shorts are excellent for learning the various technical crafts of film making - editing, sound, directing the camera and actors etc.

6. The structure of a short film is entirely different from that of a feature. Just because you can tell a story in ten minutes does not necessarily mean you can tell a story in ninety minutes.

7. If you make a great short, you could get an Oscar nomination, in which case, your career is seriously boosted. Brits get short Oscar nominations every year.

8. Shorts are good to make up a showreel of the work you have done.

303

Starting A Company

1. There are several ways of operating, each with their own advantages and disadvantages - sole trader, partnership, co-operative, limited company etc. Take advice as to what is best for your purposes.

2. Accountants and solicitors are very expensive. Buy a good 'business start-up' book, 95% of your questions will be answered in it.

3. If your turn over is high enough, you will become VAT registered and reclaim the VAT on your purchases (currently 17.5%).

4. Limited companies cost a lot to run. You need to supply information to Companies House and if your turn over is high enough, you will also have to supply audited accounts (expensive). However, they do offer some 'limited' liability in case of problems.

5. Some film makers opt to start a limited company for each film. This protects all their projects should one turn into a disaster.

6. Don't underestimate how much of a pain and how time consuming doing your accounts will be. Teach your mum or brother to do book keeping for you.

7. Don't get hung up on being a limited company before you need to. It just wastes time and money. But do start a limited company before you shoot, this will give you just what it says... Limited Liability in the event of disaster.

We started thinking, maybe they're right. Eighteen thousand is a lot of money for a short - why don't we double it to make a ninety minute film costing thirty six thousand quid. Naively we believed that to be the equation. We're not going to sell a forty five minute film. But we could sell a ninety minute film and suddenly, a much larger market was opened up to us. No longer would we be confined to television - but now the feature market, which included, the cinema, video, television and now the booming satellite market.

Q - Were you nervous about skipping the short film stage?

Chris - Yes of course, but we were no longer in film school, we had to pay the rent and put food in our stomachs. We weren't going to get rich making a short film, that's for sure. I have spoken to so many film makers who say - *I'll make a feature film next but I've got to do another short and learn a bit more*. And I say - *What do you need to learn? - You'll learn three times more if you make a feature film and regardless of how much you mess up, you'll still be able to sell it. More than likely you'll make back your money. If you don't, so what! Make another one*. You've just got to go for it!

Gen - I think you've got to be prepared to take the risk - we were prepared to do that, to plunge in head first. We realised that if we wanted things to happen, we couldn't wait in the hope that Hollywood would give us a call and offer us *Jurassic Park 3*. Those who play safe, who want everything to be hunky dory, problem free, are going to be sitting on the sidelines for a long time.

Q - Have you chosen the projects you have undertaken on commercial viability?

Chris - It's strange, we've talked endlessly about how we chose the stories we make into a film. Anyone who has seen both *The Runner* and *White Angel* would agree that they are poles apart. We're aware of commerciality, we have to be. No matter how much we ever thought we were being hard nosed business people, it all boiled down to one thing - what did we want to make?

When we made *The Runner* we were into movies with serious muzzle flash, semi automatic weapons and lots of explosions - and we did just that. It turned out to be a pretty dreadful

10 Ways to Raise Money

10 Ordinary Ways To Raise Money

1. Get a bank loan - (!?)

2. Get venture capital investment.

3. Speak to the British film funding bodies such as British Screen, the Lottery Franchises and Film Four Lab. The odds are astronomical but you MUST try this.

4. Pre sell your film - almost impossible if you have no track record, unless you have big names attached.

5. Knock on the door of every single person in the film industry and ask if they will fund your dream.

6. Approach other production companies, or TV companies for capital in return for joint production status (dodgy).

7. Product Placement. Get large companies to pay you for putting their products in your film. They won't be very interested unless the production is mainstream commercial, or you have a star. They will often give you the products, but no money, which could help out in the catering budget.

9. If your script is good, and a star is in place, a distribution company may put some money in. You will have no track record, so it is unlikely.

10. Organise a European Co-production knowing that you'll spend your development budget on lawyers and accountants, but at least your movie will be made before you retire.

Give up on this lot and move onto Extraordinary Ways To Raise Money

10 Extraordinary Ways To Raise Money (not recommended)

1. Get accounts with all the facilities houses you need to hire or buy from and work on credit.

2. Get a credit card with a big limit. If you use it a lot and make regular repayments, the credit card company will ask you if you want an increased limit.

3. Get friends and family to invest a little seed cash and use it to shoot a two minute trailer. It will greatly increase your chances of getting investment as the film will no longer be words on a page, but a moving image with sound (and hopefully quite good too).

4. Get friends and family to invest a little more and get your movie in the can (and worry about the debts later). It's possible to shoot a feature film for £10,000.

5. Approach ANYONE with money and invite them to invest (you will need a good prospectus).

6. Approach ANYONE and ask them to invest, regardless of whether you think they have money or not. Many people have a little stashed away and may be prepared to gamble. If you get money off friends and relatives, make sure they understand they could lose it all (likely).

7. Turn to illegal acts (not advisable at all).

8. Let a bored, rich person pay to play a small role in the film (and then cut them out if they are bad).

9. Sell your body to science. Worked for Robert Rodriguez.

10. Write a brilliant script, sell it to Hollywood, get sacked as the director but take the money and make a new movie with your fee.

In order to convince investors, some pretty dodgy artwork was created. We couldn't afford a model, so Gen had to step into the role for these shots.

movie but we blew a lot of things up. I guess in context, *The Runner* is a knee jerk reaction to the inhibitions of film school. It felt VERY decadent.

Q - Did you have problems talking to people at the top?

Gen - To begin with we did - it depends on your approach. Many young film makers, particularly those fresh out of film school, are arrogant, they assume that they have an unwritten right to freebies, discounts and will get offered the best projects. We didn't feel that way and chose not to be arrogant. We reasoned that we were more likely to get help if we asked politely.

Q - In general, how did people in the industry react to these two young upstarts?

Chris - At the time, the lottery didn't exist and the industry was depressed and didn't seem to understand what we were doing, we were so far removed, we were almost a cottage industry. It was obvious that if we wanted to make movies in the UK, then it was up to ourselves to generate our own projects. We've just had to do it with the limited means at our disposal, with whatever talent that we had, and on a micro budget. Risk it all and hopefully at the end of the day it will all come together, and no matter how bad the movie is, it will still sell. We were in a *need-to* situation.

Q - Are there any film makers who have been a source of inspiration?

The Runner - a movie with lots of blue light and "serious muzzle flash"

Low Budget movies to see...

THE EVIL DEAD - The grandfather of the modern micro budget film which hit the horror movie market just at the right time. Made by teenagers with $50k, guts and determination and buckets of blood. Director Sam Raimi, is now a top Hollywood player.

EL MARIACHI - The now legendary movie made for $7k, financed by the director selling his body to science. Shot entirely from the hip and a good example of what can be achieved if you ignore everything and just shoot film with a bunch of friends. Check out the DVD with excellent commentary and additional footage including Rodriguez's 10 minute film school.

DARK STAR - John Carpenter's first feature film which was an expanded short (stars screenwriter Dan O'Bannon). Sets were built in Carpenter's kitchen and garage. Check out the plank Dan O'Bannon is lying on in the elevator scene. This has to be one of the best low budget films ever.

CLERKS - Offbeat American comedy shot on 16mm B&W over weekends and in evenings at the convenience store where the director worked. Budgeted at $27k and originally titled Inconvenience. Picked up by Miramax after screening at Sundance.

THE BROTHERS MoMULLEN Now York tale of three brothers, financed by director Ed Burns' family and shot over nine months on 16mm for $24k. Fox Searchlight picked up the film after screening at Sundance.

Pi - A bizarre and unique high contrast B&W thriller about a genius mathematician, shot for $60k. Picked up by Artisan after winning Best Director at Sundance in '98. Took $3m at the US Box Office.

GO FISH - A grainy B&W lesbian romantic comedy shot on 16mm for $60k with a largely non professional cast. Screened at Sundance in '94 and snapped up. Partly financed through Christine Vachon's Killer Films.

LOVE AND OTHER CATASTROPHES - Australian Emma Kate-Croghan's screwball comedy debut shot for $37k in 17 days. Takes place in the space of one day on a college campus. Another hit at Sundance.

SLACKER - Richard Linklater's debut and a seminal event for US indie film making in '91, produced on a budget of $23k. Apparently half of the finance came from the director's mother whom he persuaded to give him the same amount of money that went toward his sister's wedding on the theory that he wouldn't be getting married.

PUBLIC ACCESS - Bryan Singer's debut shot for $250k and shot in 18 days. Singer's next film was the $5.5m Oscar winner The Usual Suspects.

FESTEN - The second film from the Dogme series directed by Thomas Vinterberg. Although fully funded, this is a film that through the conditions of the Dogme scheme could have been shot on a very low budget.

MUTE WITNESS - Anthony Waller's low budget debut shot in Russia. Look out for scenes with Alec Guiness. The Director asked him if he'd like to play a small but key role in his next film but Alec Guinness told him he was tied up for the next year and a half. So he suggested they shoot the following morning before his return flight to England which they did and the rest of the movie was shot ten years later! Waller went on to American Werewolf in Paris.

CASE STUDIES

To prove to EGM that Living Spirit had what it takes, they produced a short two minute action packed trailer. This was a very successful course of action to take as it convinced everyone the picture was going to happen.

Gen - We knew the story of Sam Raimi, the director of *The Evil Dead.* And when we saw *The Evil Dead* documentary on *The Incredibly Strange Picture Show* hosted by Jonathan Ross, we heard how he shot a promo on Super 8mm. He then went round to the houses of doctors, dentists etc. He would get out his 8mm projector and pin a bedsheet to the wall, and show these potential investors what he wanted to make - and these people put money in. He was only eighteen. We thought - Wow! Maybe we could do this.

Q - You tried getting investment for The Runner from several sources, but because you had no real track record, you didn't get very far. How did you eventually get things going?

Director Sam Raimi was the inspiration for both Chris' early horror movies, and Genevieve's business plans for Living Spirit. He produced The Evil Dead at the age of eighteen, with a budget of $50,000

Chris - We met a company called EGM Film International, a Cardiff based production company. We said - *Hey! We're young film makers and we've got this idea for a film.* We showed them a promo tape of films (made by other people) and they were very impressed. Now, we had a one page synopsis which we had written the night before because we thought that we should look like we knew what we were doing. And they said - *We'll make this but we need to shoot in three weeks time. If you're not going to be ready then the whole show is off.* And we said - *Of course.* - We're all poised. - And we walked out of the office thinking; - *Great! We've got this chance to make a feature, but what are we going to do?* We're shooting in three weeks time *and we don't even have a script!*

Like most things on *The Runner*, the script was written on a need-to basis. We'd been floundering about, trying to make this great movie and just never got around to putting words on paper. Now we had a real big problem.

Gen - We said we'd fax them the budget, so we had to go out to Dixons and buy a fax machine! EGM had said, *we don't want to spend over £40k,* but we knew it would cost more. We said, *we need £140k* and they said, *We'll give you £40k.* We said *Okay, we'll send you the budget tomorrow.* We consulted our figures and saw that we really had to have at least £100k. They said - *No! No! We'll give you £60k.* We realized then that once they committed funds, they would have to finish the film. Besides, they were supposed to be executive producers and should have known that it costs a certain amount just to expose negative and feed a crew.

Now, we didn't really waste a lot but it actually cost a certain amount of money to blow up half of North Wales, so we spent a lot on pyrotechnics and bullets and all sorts of things - the budget escalated to £140k, exactly what we thought.

Q - *With only three weeks pre-production, no money, and no script, how did you manage to get everything going?*

Chris - We rang a few friends and asked, - *What are you doing for the next couple of months? Do you want to come and live at our house and make a movie?* - Everybody said yes and moved in. About thirty people in all. It was great. There were very few problems. Lots of relationships sprung up between various crew members, perhaps because the work was so crisis ridden, everyone needed a shoulder to cry on and it all got rather steamy at various points.

I suppose there was a tremendous sense of camaraderie, that no matter what was asked of anyone, they would do it. It was very bizarre. I've often felt as if I knew what kind of team spirit troops must feel before they go into battle for the first time (not that our job is anywhere near as demanding).

Q - *The screenplay usually takes months of development?*

Chris - Yes - We had to write a script, good, bad or indifferent. We had to have ninety pages of words to give the actors, to say on the day. Neither Gen nor myself could

Making a Contract

A contract is an agreement between two or more parties. It can be a verbal agreement, but a piece of paper which clarifies the terms of the contract, who will do what, when, how etc. is much better. The contract is really there so that each party knows what they have to do - it's written there in black and white. It also protects you if things go wrong.

1. Remember, a contract is just a piece of paper and if someone is intent on doing something which breaks the contract, there is nothing you can do short of legal action (which you may not be able to afford).

2. If money is involved, get it up front, preferably on signing. If not all up front, as much as possible. You don't know what might happen a little down the line - your investor might die, go bankrupt, get bored.

3. ALWAYS make a contract for everything, even when friends do work for you. If your movie is ultra successful, all those freebies and favours will cost you. At the same time, don't get hung up on huge wordy and over the top contracts.

4. When entering a deal with a company where they will supply you with goods or a service make sure they put the quote down on paper and fax you. We had one deal fall through because the chap we struck it with had died - his predecessor wasn't interested and we had no proof of the prior deal.

afford the time to divorce ourselves completely from the much needed three weeks of pre-production.

Mark Talbot-Butler, the editor of the film, seemed to be capable of writing a screenplay, so we commandeered him. He did a commendable job when you consider that this was his first screenplay, and the timescale involved. There was simply no development process. When it came to the point where we were shooting, I would walk on set, be given my pages of the script, hot from the photocopier, and read it for the first time. I'd think, - *Oh!, so that's what we're doing!* - and Gen would read it and see that there were three helicopters needed - she'd say to me - *Give me three hours* - and off she would go and come back with three helicopters. Really, she did get three helicopters. It was incredible.

There were so many cock-ups because we were totally unprepared. It was a serious crash course, and I emphasise the word crash, in how not to make films. We learnt so much. At the end of the day the film was pretty bad. It looked and sounded great, and consequently sold, but it's five years on we still haven't received a penny, and I don't think we ever will.

Q - How did you get a cast crazy enough to become involved in this movie?

Gen - We put an ad in the actors newspaper The Stage and received sack loads of mail, CV's and photos. It really was sackfuls. The postman once brought three sacks up to the front door and then he informed us that he wouldn't deliver to the door but would leave it all at the back gate. We sifted through these replies and thought, there can't be this many actors in the world, let alone Britain - It was hopelessly

5. Follow your instincts - if something is too good to be true, it probably isn't true.

6. Always sign a contract before any work begins (especially actors).

7. It's obvious, but read and understand all the text of the agreement, including the infamous fine print. Never sign straight away, take the contract home with you and sleep on your decision.

8. If it comes to the choice between signing a dodgy contract and getting to make your film, OR not signing and not making your film, sign, take the money, make the movie and get ripped off. You will walk away with a very valuable experience and showreel at someone else's expense.

9. If in doubt consult your solicitor.

10. If you are going to get a solicitor involved, make sure that both you and they absolutely understand how you will be charged. Some charge by the half hour, so you may get a £70 bill for ringing and asking one question. Ask if you can be charged for work on contracts only, and not for infrequent advice.

3 choppers for free in as many hours...

overpowering - we just didn't have enough time to sift through all the details, so we sorted them into two piles, *Looks OK, Doesn't look OK*. Then sorted the *Looks OK* into two piles, *Done Film Work, Haven't Done Film Work*. It still took a few hours to short-list, and the list wasn't very short, but it did cut down our work load.

LOW BUDGET BRITISH FEATURE FILM

Lead actor and actress required for low budget action thriller feature film to be shot in North Wales. Please send a recent photo and CV. Tel 0270 71411

Q - So what did you do about the lead actor?

Chris - Tough man Jack Slater had to be played by a star - but we couldn't afford a star - so we got the brother of a star.

Gen - We rang up a few agents, told them who we were and that we were affiliated to The Prince's Trust (which made people see us in a different light).

Advertising for cast is often a good idea, but prepare your postman, and NEVER EVER print your phone number - actors are persistent and will make your life hell.

One agent came back to us and said, - *I've got this guy called Terence Ford* - we'd not heard of him - *Well, he's been in Dynasty and Dallas and guest appearances in similar stuff* - still we weren't impressed. *Then she said - he's the brother of Harrison Ford*. We thought great! Apparently Terence had read the treatment and liked it, so he rang up. Chris would speak to him about the part over the phone because we couldn't afford to fly out to audition him - *He sounds OK* said Chris.

Chris - They sent us his CV which was pretty unimpressive with regard to feature film work, but his photo was good. He looked like a younger, more rugged version of his brother. We felt we had found our lead actor. He was Harrison Ford on a budget. We offered Ford a fee of five grand. EGM took over at that point. We said Harrison Ford's brother's interested. Their ears pricked up and they gave him the job.

Gen picked him up from the airport and brought him to the studio (which was actually our garage). When we first met, I feared we might have problems as he had lost a lot of weight and his hair had silvered. His photo had portrayed him as a much more rugged and tough looking actor. As he was Harrison Ford's *younger* brother, we all imagined someone like Harrison Ford ten years ago. In fact, they were only separated by a few years so looked about the same age.

"The hardest thing about directing a film, is managing to stay awake for nine weeks" Michael Winner

Gen - We didn't have much choice. We'd spent loads of money on his flight over here and were about to start shooting. We'd have to change him a bit. Dye his hair for a start.

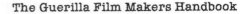

CASE STUDIES

*Screen hero Jack Slater as
portrayed by Terence Ford...
The Man, The Myth, The Legend,
The Brother...*

Chris - We had cast another guy in the role of the villain, he was an American living in the UK. A week into shooting, he didn't turn up. We thought, *where is our villain?* Gen got on the phone to his agent and found out that he was on holiday in Turkey and didn't want to come back.

Chris - So, here we were, I was on set and Genevieve came up to me and said - *We have a problem with shooting McBain tomorrow* (the villain), *well, he's on holiday in Turkey and he's not coming home.* - and I said, - *Fine, OK.* - because I had become used to this kind of crisis every twenty minutes. I relied on the company slogan - *Gen'll fix it!* - Anyway, that night I returned to the production office and there were two photographs on the production office wall, one of this rather delicate looking actor from Amsterdam and the second, slightly less delicate, living in London.

Gen - They both looked like models.

"Actors
are Crap"
John Ford

Chris - The one in London was an 'associate' of the lead actress and she suggested him as he could play American, so we decided to interview him. We asked him to take the train up to Cheshire and we gave him an interview. This is an interview that took place at two-thirty in the morning after a long day's shooting, with the whole crew asleep in this house.

We had twenty bunk beds in our living room and there I was in one of the bedrooms with fourteen people farting and snoring giving an interview to this guy who must have thought - *oh my God! What am I doing here?*

Gen - The other actor from Amsterdam had said - *Whatever happens, I will come over from Holland for an audition* - And I said, - *Well. Look, we can't afford to pay for you to come over. And if you don't get it, then I'm sorry, it's your tough luck!* - And he said - *That's fine. I'll get it! I'll get it!* - and I said - *Okay. Fine.* - And so I drove to pick him up from Manchester - he didn't have enough money to fly, so he had spent thirty hours on a ferry and train. It was about two thirty, maybe three o'clock in the morning when we got back and it's straight upstairs to do the audition.

Paris Jefferson and Andrew Mitchell - Heroine and Villain. Andrew gave such a psychotic interview that Living Spirit nearly rejected him - as it happened, he turned out to be one of the best things about the film.

Chris - He was quite good looking and very pleasant. We took him into a room full of bunk beds and asked, *'what would you like to read for us?'* He replied in a strong Dutch American drawl. - *Okay man. I don't want to read no words. I've prepared my own interpretation of the part. Do you want to hear it?* We agreed and he exploded into this incredible, violent, one-man play about killing babies in Vietnam. I was sitting on the bed thinking - *we cannot employ this guy, he will murder us in our beds. In fact, I'm going to double lock my bedroom door tonight.* Mark, the editor and writer, was sitting next to me and he was equally terrified whilst watching this performance with dinner plate eyes. We left the room.

I said to Mark - *Oh my God. What are we going to do? This guy's completely insane.* And Genevieve is hyper, saying - *He's great. He's so energetic* - So we had a real conference. What should we do? The actor from London was a little more bankable, a little more secure. We knew he would at least

Keep the cast in their place with a firm hand, and an automatic weapon

CASE STUDIES

Casting

1. No-one is out of reach. Make a list of people who could play the parts in your picture and approach their agents. Actors can often have a bad year and be eager for feature work, or may have a soft spot for the decadence of low budget film making. If you don't ask, you'll never know - and they may say yes.

2. Agents are all difficult. Their sole job is to protect their client, hustle as much money as they can and moan and groan about conditions. Agents often neglect to inform their clients of the potential job as the money is likely to be bad. Agents are paid on commission, and if the percentage is poor, why spend time and energy on negotiations if there isn't a pot of money at the end?

3. The agent's flip side is that if you have an exciting project, you are honest and upfront, then they may see your movie as a positive opportunity. Deals can be struck; for instance, a named actor is supplied along with four new faces for the experience.

4. If you have a way into an actor, bypass the agent and get the script to them. No agent will be able to stop an actor who is determined to be involved in a project. Be aware that some actors hate this approach and enjoy the protection their agent gives them from a barrage of wanabe film makers.

5. Get a copy of THE SPOTLIGHT, a book with all the Equity actors in Britain listed with pic. Spotlight 0207 437 7631. Fax 0207 437 5881. They are also on the web at www.spotlightcd.com, and the database can be bought on CD ROM.

read the words on the page (when they were eventually written).

Then there was the method maniac who might have been a little more exciting on the screen, but I just couldn't get over the paranoid thought that he might actually kill us all.

We couldn't decide so we promised to tell them in the morning after sleeping on it. So, the Dutch actor had to sleep on the kitchen floor, since there was no space anywhere else.

In the morning, we decided not to give him the part. We said, *'We are really sorry. You can't have the part. We're going with the other actor'* - he was absolutely devastated. He was so shocked.

Gen - You shouldn't admit this.

Chris - It's fine now - but for some reason, something said - *this man's not as loony as I thought he was.* It was something he was projecting in the hope of getting the role and I had this gut feeling - *Hire him quick!* - So I dragged Gen out of the room and said - *I think we should take him* - she said - *You've spent all night saying we can't* - and so we had another debate and decided to go with the psycho Dutchman.

I went out and told him - *Andrew, I'd just like to tell you that you've got the part. That was just a test to see how you would react* - and he bought it. He really believed me.

Q - How did you go about crewing?

Gen - Most of the crew were very young, and everyone was inexperienced. I suppose we were all cheap labour. The crew got nothing but a five pound donation from EGM, halfway through the film. One day, Geoff, one of the partners in EGM, came in with a brown envelope full of used fivers. He handed them out on set. Actually, he ran out, so a few crew members didn't even get a fiver.

Q - With thirty five people living in your house, what was it like?

Chris - Everyone was living in this one cottage. There were at least eight people to a room, mixed accommodation. We sectioned off half of the main room. That was the office.

Windmill Cottage - Living Spirits' base in Cheshire. Served as hotel, kitchens, locations, studios, indeed everything for the thirty strong crew and production of The Runner. "We were evicted three weeks after shooting, but at least we got the movie in the can."

The other half was the bunking quarters. One bathroom, one loo, no shower, no washing machine and we shot like this for over one month. We ran out of locations, so we built a lot of them in the garage, in our back garden. And it was hell on earth. But it was great and everybody loved it. We could ring everyone of those crew members up tomorrow and say - *there's a reunion* - and everyone would be there. The only way I can explain it is like this.

Sometime during the shoot I remember being driven around North Wales, I'm not entirely sure where and I'm not entirely sure how many hours we'd been out there, I just sat in the van, looking across this dark landscape and tried to remember what it was like to sit down in front of the TV at night. I had completely lost contact with that side of my life. And it felt that we could do anything we wanted to. Really, seriously weird.

Q - How did you deal with preparing locations with so little time?

Gen - Because we were so eager to get going, we didn't have any pre-production time. The general method of business was - *What are we going to do today? We've got to do this or that scene and we'd better do this tomorrow* - And so we'd sort out the locations a day in advance, two days if we were lucky. The money situation just made things worse - on the first day of principal photography the backers didn't turn up.

6. You can get international casting information from the links on the Spotlight web site, including America, Canada and Australia.

7. There are several casting services where ads can be placed very cheaply, or even free. PCR and SBS for instance.

8. Videotape auditions, it will help you put a face to the hundreds of hopefuls you will doubtless see.

9. Be honest and up front about money and conditions - preferably on the phone when arranging an audition. It's better to know then rather than on set if there are going to be problems.

10. If you are paying below Equity recommended levels, don't shout about it. Equity can be rather aggressive and tip the cart a little. Remember, that no matter how much Equity scream and shout, we live in a free world where people can do as they like. Just lie low.

11. Where should you hold auditions? Many agents and casting facilities have rooms for this purpose, but you can hold them in your front room if you like - we did.

12. Once you have cast a part, sort out ALL financial arrangements in a contract, before you shoot.

13. If you can afford to run with the Equity / PACT registered low budget scheme, do so. It will cost you some money, just over £500 pw and just over £100 pd, but agents love it and there are no contracts. Pretty much equals minimal headaches.

Working From Home

1. Working from home can reduce your overheads and maximise your time. You won't have to rent offices and you can start work the moment you get out of bed (no tubes or traffic queues).

2. Working from home can decrease your work time - it's all too easy to sleep in or get distracted into fixing the kitchen sink etc. It is difficult to separate business and pleasure.

3. If you intend to shoot a movie from home, rent a very big house - and we mean BIG! Preferably in the country where you can't disturb neighbours. A call to the police from an angry neighbour could shut down production and force you to relocate.

4. Inviting a client or investor into your living room can have two effects. It can either make you look very amateur, or it can make you look home grown and honest. People do like home grown talent and this is an angle which could be very effective. Just look as professional as possible and stress that working from home is a way of minimising overheads.

5. If you mess around too much, be prepared to be evicted - landlords DON'T like the self employed. Keep it quiet.

6. Mum and Dad may say that it's OK to make your film at home, just remember, they don't expect 50 people to move in!

We had to carry on without them but we didn't have any money to get the food. We had no advance. A week later they turned up on set and said -*Do you want some money?* - And so we got our money, and quickly bought some food.

Occasionally, we ended up in deep trouble - I remember one time, we drove for hours, a whole crew and cast in convoy, to a mine in the middle of Wales. When we got there, they wouldn't let us in. And that was one of the times when we had actually *got* permission!

Chris - That's right. We were about to do the final scene in the film - the climax of the movie. As usual we were trying to set up the shoot the day before and Gen was flying (she'd given up driving) across North Wales to find a mine in which to shoot. She found a brilliant one in Llan-something. We got to the mine/power station and took all the kit in.

It was like driving into a Bond set. The middle of this mountain had been quarried out. There were houses, office buildings, everything *inside* the mine. Roadways, traffic lights and cars parked inside the mountain. We shot for two days without any problems, and on the third day we had to film in another location. Come the morning of the fourth day, we returned to the mine and there was a new guard on the gate who said - *You can't go in.*- We protested. - *We've clearance.* But it was clear we weren't going to get in, no amount of bribery could budge this guy.

It transpired that the original guard had been sacked for letting us in as part of the mine was a top secret, Ministry Of Defence, nuclear air raid shelter. It was so high level that even the guard who had let us in didn't know it was there!

Gen thinks - *Okay we've been filming in a high security establishment and we're not getting back in. We've got to finish our movie. What are we going to do?* - So, she gets back into the car and zooms off to find another mine - she did! However, it was in some horrendous place.

The next day, the convoy drove a hundred miles into what seems the heart of hell. It's raining like a waterfall - all we can see is wet black slate. It's so depressing. We arrive at the mine entrance and unload the gear. Everyone is soaking.

Quickly we check out where we can film - and it is a half mile walk underground with the equipment. We have twelve hours to shoot the last fifteen pages of the script of our action-packed adventure, the most action-packed sequence in the whole film. And I'm thinking - *Let's go for it. Lets go for it!* We're going to finish it.

The mine in Wales - a great location, but unfortunately, it turned out to be a secret Ministry Of Defence Nuclear Air Raid Bunker.

Five hours later, we're still lugging *IN* all the gear. Eventually it's all in. We're about to go for the first shot. It's taken five hours to set up. Terence is there. Lead actress, Paris is there. I rehearsed. I called for silence... Then we realised there were no guns. This was the big shoot out. The armourer says - *I'll go and get them.* Fifteen minutes later the guy comes back looking kind of sheepish and says - *I don't know how to tell you this, but the guns are in the back of the prop girl's car.* And I said - *Fine, then get them.* Then he says - *But the prop girl has gone back to Cheshire twenty minutes ago.* The props are four hundred miles away and we have got six hours to shoot the climax to our movie!

The next thing I can remember is being woken up by Jon Walker, the DOP. Apparently, I'd just fallen asleep on a large rock. Both body and mind had gone into retirement - for a short time I was in a vegetative state.

Gen - Then it got worse. We had a massive argument with the cast. It became apparent that we weren't going to finish the film that night. Also we had been rushing to finish the film because the lead actress, Paris Jefferson, had said she had to fly off in the morning so that she could get to another shoot somewhere in Europe.

Things got pretty nasty on set.... A good rule was, 'Never argue with the director when he has a gun...'

Shooting on Location

If you have no budget, shooting on location is probably the only option for you.

1. Shooting on location can be a major advantage as you will have to do minimal set work, merely dressing.

2. Space can be a major problem as even the biggest of rooms will become sardine like with a full crew.

3. Shooting outdoors can be a problem as there is no way to control the weather. Consider shooting in a place like Spain where there are long days with great light. The locations will be cheap too.

4. Always try and get permission to shoot wherever you intend to be. Sometimes, if you can foresee problems, it is best to simply dash in, shoot, and get out as quick as possible. If someone turns up to find out what is happening, try to get them interested and involved, and claim complete ignorance.

5. Getting to and from difficult locations can be very costly in terms of time - one hour travelling is one hour less shooting. Don't underestimate the chaos of moving thirty cast and crew just one mile down the road.

6. Use movement orders. This is a piece of paper with photocopied map (the route picked out with highlighter pen), explicit directions and mobile phone numbers for those who get lost.

We knew this was the last day we had with her. We knew we were running out of time, and we'd lost the guns - it was absolute hell. Then Paris says - *Well, why don't we all come back tomorrow?* - *But you're not going to be here tomorrow!* - we reply - *Oh, no. I can be here if you want me to be* - Shocked, we blew up at her and had a massive argument with all the actors. Everyone took sides, mainly against us. It all got pretty heavy and many enemies were made. I think most of us made up later, but there are still a few grudges floating around. In retrospect, Paris was quite within her rights, it's just the insanity of low-budget film making creates a crazy atmosphere.

Our executive producers, John and Geoff, had gone off to America. We didn't know where they'd gone. We couldn't contact them. So, we decided to pack it all in for the night and come back in a month when we had the guns, the mine and the actors. Then we'd finish *The Runner*.

Chris - It has to be said that a lot of the time the actors were quite right. There was such hell going on, they couldn't help but snap, because they spent ninety percent of the time just waiting for us to decide what to do. And everybody was ill. Everyone had flu. However, one day we had a real medical shock.

I was shooting on set and Gen comes up to me and says...

- Have you heard?
- Heard what?
- Terence is dead.
- What!
- He's dead. He's just been air lifted to Bangor Hospital. He's dead. What are we going to do?

We'd got so used to problems that the concept of our leading man being dead was simply another obstacle to be overcome. What had actually happened was that Terence was ill, the doctor had given him a sick note and sent him to bed. By the time we heard about it, the Chinese whispers had changed it to - *Terence is dead* - It was something out of Fawlty Towers. The entire production was thinking - *What is going to happen?* whilst Terence is wrapped up in his bed with a hot water bottle and a Lemsip. That was a bad day.

Gen - I remember my state of mind at that time. I had been told that Terence was in the morgue - it was some kind of Welsh joke by the hotel owner. So I was racing through the narrow winding roads at a hundred miles an hour, thinking of ways we could write him out of the story without it looking crazy. I wasn't bothered that he might be dead - all I wanted was to make sure that the film didn't suffer! That is the degree to which we were all affected by the insanity of low-budget film making. It gets into your blood and takes over your soul, I guess that's why it feels a little like going to war.

We were staying in a tiny Welsh village, where the villagers thought that this kind of joke was really funny. The other joke they played on us was potentially more serious. Someone rang the hotel telling them that they had planted a bomb as they hated the Americans. So we had the police round searching everyone's room. I remember being in dreaded fear that the police were going to check my room, because that morning I had just taken delivery of a crateful of semi automatic weapons from our armourer, AND a fake bomb for the bomb scene. Luckily they didn't check my room.

Q - The Runner has many action sequences with one breathtaking highfall. How did you get stuntmen involved?

Gen - The week before filming, we received lots of phone calls because we were trying to find actors and crew. I got a call from a guy called Terry Forrestal who said he was a stunt man and wanted to help. I said - *Yeah, great, great.* - thinking he was another karate expert from down the road who wanted to get into the business.

Terry said - *I've been working on Indiana Jones, this, that and the other and I used to do James Bond.* He reeled off a list of a hundred A movies. So, I asked for his CV and said I'd get back to him. You have to understand that we had taken so many weird phonecalls from so many wacky people that we were very cautious. Then his CV arrived, and I looked at his list of movies - it looked like my video collection! I realized - this guy's for real! Immediately, we rang him up and arranged to meet up. He was so keen and wanted to do everything he could to help us out. Everything was possible. In fact, he was so enthusiastic that he wanted to do more stunts than were in the script!

Chris - Terry had read the script and saw the bit about the

7. Facilities for the crew on location can be a problem - a place to eat and sit will be needed, and a loo must be provided - you can't ask your star to squat in the bushes.

8. Closing down streets in the UK is difficult. The police will be as helpful as they can, but they have crimes to stop and don't relish the thought of holding the hand of a crawling producer.

9. When choosing a location, don't forget the sound. There isn't much use shooting a period drama next to an airport (unless you can post sync the dialogue).

10. Film crews trash locations. Try and clean up after yourself, leave muddy boots outside, ban smoking inside etc. Remember, you may need to return to the location if there is a problem with the negative - try not to burn your contacts.

11. Think creatively - many locations can double for several different parts of your story. This will minimise the time you waste moving between places.

12. Shooting in London is tough as many councils have got smart and will charge you just to take a camera out on the streets. Be aware that parks, streets, schools and the like will probably all carry a price tag that is small to your average production, but crippling to a micro budget movie. Avoid paying at all costs.

Stunts and Pyrotechnics

There is a certain gung ho approach when shooting stunts and effects. Everyone knows that what is happening is potentially dangerous and could result in tragedy.

1. Stunts are dangerous. Don't push a stuntman to do his job quicker, or with less safety equipment. Remember, they are putting their life on the line for you, and the last thing anyone wants is a repeat of the Brandon Lee tragedy on the set of The Crow because the producer was hurrying everything along.

2. Stunts aren't as expensive as you may think. A good stunt can make the film look like it cost much more than it actually did. °

3. If a stuntman or pyrotechnician is eager or very willing to reduce safety standards, be wary. They may not be fully qualified and therefore a liability. Don't mess, get a qualified person to do the job.

4. Be careful with blank firing weapons. Although they fire blanks, there is still a possibility of injury and even death through misuse.

5. Try and organise all your stunts into one shooting block. This will minimise time wastage by dedicating the production to stunts and effects during this period.

6. There are many books on the subject of home made (safe) effects and cheats, some of which are excellent and safe. This approach could save you lots of money. For example, a helicopter flying over in the dusk can be achieved by panning a bright light over the set and mixing the chopper sound over it.

high fall - *How are you going to do this? - Well, we'll probably dress the actor up and jump off a low point onto some cardboard boxes. Ten feet or so. You know, we'll cheat it. It'll look all right.* - And he said - *No, no. You need a proper stunt.* (These guys are perfectionists). *I'll do a high fall for you* - And I said - *How high is high? Fifteen or twenty feet?* - *Oh no,* - he said - *I'll do a ninety foot high fall for you* - And he pointed to this house in the distance which seemed pretty big and explained - *It's about that, and a half again.*

I was stunned. So we went on this recce in North Wales to find a cliff from which he could jump without killing himself. Finally we found a cliff. On the day he just turned up with his airbag man, blew the bag up and jumped off the cliff. Well, in fact there were two high falls. We co-ordinated this with Terry. The first one was off the cliff into the airbag. The second, the more dangerous was off the cliff into the water. On each stunt attempt we had three cameras. Two would have done the job but we really wanted three. So we had three cameras set up and shot each stunt twice. We ended up with six separate shots, all in slow motion so that they would cut together to make it look like the fall lasted for ever. Well, the actual high fall lasts for nine seconds in the movie - a serious amount of screen time for somebody to be hurling towards earth at two hundred and thirty five feet per second. So it gave the impression of an immense fall which really did get gasps in the theatre.

To be honest, one of the best things about *The Runner* is that stunt and even Terry considers it one of the best falls he's ever done. I think he means in the way it comes across on screen. He's done other, more dangerous falls, much higher but somehow they do not look as dangerous. Perhaps the circumstances were never quite as wild as on one of our shoots. We were totally into Sam Peckinpah and action movies, so we wound the slow motion dial until it wouldn't go any further - no

Stuntman, Terry Forrestal, considers the jump he is about to make.

matter how fast the film was whizzing through the gate, Terry still went flying through frame.

Gen - And there really was, as with all stunts, a real sense of danger. When Terry jumped into the lake he said - *If I don't come up after five seconds, either I've hit my head on the bottom or I'm dead. It was a very long five seconds.*

Q - Once you had the film in the can, was it all down hill?

Chris - Not really, we had to fix all the problems we had given ourselves during the shoot. A good example is the firing range scene - there are shots in that sequence from five different locations, shot at seven different times, with up to seven months separation - piecing it together was a logistical nightmare.

Mark Talbot-Butler edited the film after we finished shooting. Unfortunately, we were evicted from our house for having thirty five people living there which broke the terms of our tenancy. This meant that we had to put most of the work in Mark's court - he had to go off and do a lot of the cutting on his own, locked in his attic. It was all very rushed.

EGM wanted the film ready for the MIFED film market in Milan which took place in October and we therefore made sure it was done. This really compromised the movie. We only had about seven weeks post-production. A great deal of energy was spent getting the picture to look good, the audio to be full and rich, and to make sure the cuts flowed. But at

7. Sound is a major consideration with stunts and effects. A good 'whack' sound in a fist fight can hide a dodgy stunt. Track lay these sequences with extra care and attention.

8. Digital effects are now very cost effective and techniques such as wire removal for high falls may well be within your budget. Ask for a quote.

9. For large stunts you may be required to supply a fire engine and ambulance. It's not cheap but there are dedicated film companies for this, they can charge by the hour and are usually very receptive to a plea for help on a low budget movie.

10. Actors are comforted when a stunt man is around for potentially dangerous scenes. It says to them that they are protected, that you take their safety seriously, and that you are professional. If the situation is relatively low impact and merely involves a degree of physical acting, try a trainee stuntman to lend a hand on set.

11. Stuntmen and pyrotechnicians know hundreds of cheap ways to achieve what may seem impossible to you as a new film maker. Ask for advice.

12. Stuntmen are members of Equity.

13. Before embarking on an expensive and time consuming stunt or effect, ask yourself if you could actually cut away from it or cut out of the scene just as it is about to happen. For instance, see the lead up to a car crash, then hear the impact over a shot of the face of a grieving relative at the funeral. It's a lot cheaper if you don't have to film it.

321

> "Making a film is like going down a mine - once you've started you bid a metaphorical goodbye to the daylight and the outside world for the duration"
> John Schlesinger

no point do I remember sitting down to ask whether the story was actually working. This neglect meant we had a good looking, great sounding, boring movie. And even then, the sound was rushed with effects still being edited whilst we began dubbing.

Mark didn't even have an assistant. He was in his Mum's attic with a Steenbeck (editing machine) working a good eighteen hours a day. No pay, no nothing. Each time I saw him, he began to look a little weirder - not surprising really.

Whilst Mark was cutting away, we were working on the score with an old school friend who had done the music for my amateur Super 8mm Zombie films. He had gone on to play in a local band and was excited by the prospects of being involved in a *real* film. He had to fake an illness and take time off work to spend seven days at his keyboard. There was no music budget, so we had to create that big orchestra sound with some synths and an Atari computer locking it all together. It worked out really well, the music was pacey and dynamic - and recorded in our front room.

When John Eyres came to view the final cut, he wasn't particularly happy. He wanted some stuff cut out. We agreed but never cut the scenes out. He wanted to remove the helicopter rescue at the end of the film, because it said RAF on the choppers (giving away the fact that the film was shot in the UK and not in the USA as claimed).

Q - How was the premiere?

Chris - Everyone clapped, but it was hollow polite clapping. I

The score for The Runner was conceived, composed, performed and recorded by an old school friend, Gary Pinder, in the Living Spirit living room!

The Living Spirit team - Left to right, Chris Jones - Director, Genevieve Jolliffe - Producer, Mark Talbot Butler - Screenplay & Editor, Andrew Mitchell - Actor and Jon Walker - Cameraman.

Cast and Crew of The Runner at the London Premiere - A great night!

think people were amazed that we had managed to get it made, a film that looked and sounded good. But what a dreadful story.

Gen - It was the achievement, rather than the actual film that was applauded. The audience were saying well done for getting this far. We were caught up with it all. We didn't get nervous. We just enjoyed it.

Chris - In our opinion, it was the best movie ever made. We were like old time moguls. It was terrific. We were not aware that we had actually made a really crap film. But at the time, that didn't matter - it was OUR premiere!

Gen - However, we do have people coming up to us who saw The Runner, saying how much they like the movie, how they've gone out and bought their own personal copy of the film. I think the film is an example of what low-budget film makers who want to make Aliens or Die Hard can look to. It's nothing like Leon The Pig Farmer or Soft Top Hard Shoulder, some of the other low budget films made at the time. It's not the type of quirky movie that is so often labelled Low-budget British Film.

Q - How much did The Runner make you?

"Pictures are for entertainment, messages should be delivered by Western Union"
Samuel Goldwyn

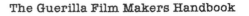

> "Experience is the name every one gives to their mistakes"
> Oscar Wilde

Chris - To date, not a single penny. Living Spirit did not make the proverbial 'fortune' out of *The Runner*.

What happened to us, and what happens to most first time feature makers, is that we got caught with a standard distribution deal. Basically, EGM financed the film and acted as the sales agents. They received thirty-five percent commission plus all expenses before they started to recoup their investment. This meant that they got all their money back, plus thirty percent commission, plus expenses, before we would even see a penny. It means we will never get paid, never ever, which means that we'll never be able to pay our cast and crew which means it's a bit of a downer really. This is a very common story that many film makers tell.

Gen - You see, we were very naive when we took the film on. Our attitude was - *Let's do the film, We've got three weeks. Let's just do it, get our foot in the door rather than just sit on our arses.* So, when the contract came, we had a lawyer go through it, and he advised us not to sign it. But at the end of the day, we thought, well, we have a choice here. If we sign it, there is a possibility that we could get ripped off. If we don't, the film may never happen. So we went with it. I am very glad we did, it gave us a track record and a showreel. Most important was the experience, *that* was invaluable. If you have nothing to lose, just go for it. The younger the better.

The International Sales booth for The Runner at the Milan Film Market 1991

Q - How do you feel about it all now that it is ancient history?

Chris - We went with it and got the chance to make a film. We got to go mad in North Wales, with Hollywood stuntmen, bombs, guns and a bunch of actors - it was a fair trade off. My only regret is that nobody got paid - I guess and hope that everyone was rather philosophical about it. For many of the crew the experience was worth more than the money.

Gen - A lot of the crew members were either still at film school or had just left and had never worked professionally on any kind of film. I remember at the first production meeting, Chris asked who had worked on a film set before. It was quite a shock when only two people put their hands up. The average age was 19/20. There was even a fourteen year old - I felt old at 20.

Q - Can you protect your rights as film makers on the first film?

Gen - The main problem you're facing is that it IS your first film. You are so desperate to make it that you will sign anything. If it comes to the crunch, I would advise anyone to sign because what is important is that you make the film. Just make sure you invest none of your own money or money that you are responsible for and therefore reduce your losses. If you can make your first movie without losing anything, then go for it because nobody is going to give you free money and nobody's going to invest in you because you've never made a film before. It is easy to be completely shafted, everyone from Tobe Hooper to Steven Spielberg has been ripped off, and not just on their first films. I think it is the nature of the business.

Once we had finished *The Runner*, we had a lot less trouble making *White Angel*. We had more control and simply refused to sign anything unless we had total control.

The final poster for The Runner, complete with splendid action movie style chromed logo and blazing background.

Q - I believe you are in the Guinness Book of Records.

Gen - Yes, as Britain's youngest producer for *The Runner*. I was 20, not so young when compared with American film makers.

Q - Because of your connections with the Princes Trust, did you invite the Prince of Wales to the screening?

Chris - We actually won an award - the PYBT/Readers Digest Editors award for being a tenacious business. There was a special award ceremony with a screening of The Runner at the BAFTA theatre in Piccadilly. HRH came along and presented the award. We had a chat afterwards and I will say that the Trust is terrific. I would recommend it to anyone but don't think that it is an easy ride. They are tough business people, though they're not in it to make money, and they make sure that they don't lose it. You can't approach it

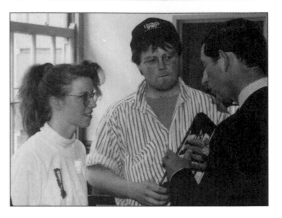

Living Spirit are presented to HRH Prince Charles after receiving their award.

feeling that they're a soft pushover and I'm going to walk out of here with three grand. You might as well forget it because it's a fight all the way. Bit like the real world.

Q - Did HRH see the film?

Chris - He saw some of it but he couldn't watch it all because he had other appointments on the schedule. He said it looked a little too violent for him.

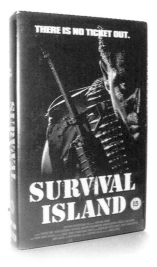

The Runner has been released across the globe. It is released in the UK under the alternative title, SURVIVAL ISLAND and in America as ESCAPE FROM... SURVIVAL ZONE.

Q - How did White Angel come about?

Ellen Carter fights Steckler in the climactic scenes of White Angel.

Chris - Obviously, after *The Runner*, we wanted to make another film. *The Runner* had crippled us so much, that we didn't have any funds at our disposal. The only way we could possibly get out of the great financial hole we were in was to make a another movie. We decided to make what we considered to be the most commercial film possible with the least amount of money.

White Angel was conceived the same day that we saw *Henry, Portrait of a Serial Killer,* in an extremely seedy cinema with an audience of seedy looking men. We thought it was a great movie but it was offensive, at least my mother would think so. However, we thought we could make something with the same feel, but not quite so graphic - turn it into a taut Hollywood thriller.

Q - What research did you do for White Angel?

Gen - We also saw *Silence of the Lambs* and felt that we could do something similar, that was contained, but not awash with gore. Also we didn't think that Hannibal Lecter gave a true portrayal of a serial killer - sure, he was a terrific character which the audience had a love hate relationship with - he had been glamorised for Hollywood. We researched British serial killers, reading lots of books, for example

"All first drafts are shit"
Ernest Hemingway

327

CASE STUDIES

> "95 perecent of films are born of frustration, of self despair, of ambition, for survival, for money, for fattening bank accounts. Five percent, maybe less, are made because a man has an idea which he must express"
> Sam Fuller

Dennis Nielson's biography, *Killing For Company* by Brian Masters. We became fascinated by the British serial killer and his peculiarities.

Admittedly, most of our research was very lightweight, we didn't want to start making psychological assumptions, merely chart the actions of a killer. The closest that we came to real research was through my uncle who worked at the top security Parkhurst Prison on the Isle of Wight. He would tell us of his encounters with the Yorkshire Ripper. We also saw some home movie footage of Dennis Nielson which gave us the idea of using video taped interviews.

Chris - Everyone has a morbid fascination with death, and especially the serial killer. The motivation seems so meaningless, and it's now a bit of a cliché, but it could be the person next door. Audiences like to dip into horror, to experience the shocks and come out the other side unharmed and emotionally purged.

Q - What are you looking for in a no-budget script?

Gen - We knew the limitations of our location, so we developed our story from that single point. We were looking for containment, to keep the majority of the story in one place. The production office would be there, all the facilities such as makeshift changing & make-up rooms, a kitchen and equipment store. The location chosen was inside the M25 around London, at the end of the tube line, we could see the tube station from the front door of the house. This meant that the cast and crew could be given a monthly tube pass and therefore their travelling expenses were minimal. The location was also close to many shops, parks etc., all the other locations required in the screenplay were within five minutes walking distance. It worked quite well.

The house that was used for the primary location in 'White Angel' had to double up as both production office and set. Ruislip outside central London was the perfect location and was steeped in suburbia.

Chris - Where we went wrong with *The Runner* is that the production was sprawling, shooting in locations that were hundreds of miles apart. That would eat up our shooting time. We had to put people up and pay for hotel rooms, catering, travelling etc. The number of principal cast was five, far too high. This in itself was very expensive which is why we limited the principle cast in *White Angel* to two, with Don Henderson bobbing in and out (we actually only shot for two days with Don).

Q - So The Runner was a good exercise in how NOT to make a low-budget film?

Chris - Yes, after *The Runner* we sat and looked at the budget to see where the money went. A lot of money was wasted on American actors, flying them over, making them comfortable and getting them in front of the camera. So, we said, *what has Britain got to offer?* And we made a list. Now it is true that we have wonderful landscapes in Scotland but we couldn't use them. We didn't have the resources. But in Britain, we do have great actors and we knew that if we could find a really good actor who was willing to do it for virtually nothing on the assumption that they will get paid eventually (and also receive a percentage), then we were made. We made a conscious decision to try and get a really good, classical actor and Peter Firth filled that bill.

On the other hand we felt that we had to have a North American in the film, or we would be in the position where the Americans don't understand the film because it doesn't have the appropriate accent in it. And we've all heard the stories of *Gregory's Girl, Trainspotting* and *Mad Max* being dubbed for the American market. We knew that *White Angel* had to sell in the states as in financial terms, the American market represented a huge slice of world sales. In retrospect, we were being over cautious. If we could have persuaded a great British actress like Helen Mirren (*The Hawk*) to play Carter, I think it may have improved sales and I think it would have been a better film. The American character of Ellen Carter (played by Harriet Robinson) felt inserted into the story, which she was. Having said all that, Harriet does have a quality that people like - I don't think we could have made a better choice with a North American.

Q - Why genre subjects?

The Story So Far...

Ideas are cheap and easy, it's implementing them that is difficult.

1. Decide what kind of film you will make - a commercial film, or a film for yourself (which could also be commercial). A commercial film is the kind of picture that sells, that the video shop rents. No matter how much you like your idea, it doesn't necessarily make it a commercial one. There is nothing wrong with being commercial or non commercial, each have their advantages, but it is essential that you know what it is.

2. Other movies are a good source of stock ideas. Get two successful pictures and mix the concepts. 'Outland' for instance is 'Alien' meets 'High Noon'.

3. Anything written by an author who died over 75 years ago (50 years in some countries) is out of copyright and now Public Domain. For example, if you want to adapt a Dickens novel, you won't have to pay to do so.

4. Speak to a sales agent, they will tell you if your idea is commercial or not, and give you an idea of what kind of cast will help.

5. Without doubt, if you want to be noticed by the Miramax's of this world, you need to make a unique movie, expressing your unique voice. Clones of other movies may sell but they won't impress the big boys who could finance your second picture.

6. Read lots of good books on screenwriting "The Writers Journey" and "Story" are both excellent.

CASE STUDIES

Peter Firth and Don Henderson - great British actors are worth every penny or percentage you pay them. They will bring quality and experience to any production.

Chris - Most low-budget film makers chose a genre, not because they've sat down and clinically thought, *'now if we make a sci-fi thriller the Japanese market is going to like it'*. I think most first time film makers make the kind of film that they really want to make. Either that works or it doesn't. With *The Runner* we wanted to blow as much up as we could - we wanted to throw as many people off cliffs as possible - we wanted to create mayhem because we loved *Die Hard* and similar Hollywood movies. Low-budget film makers seem to be products of their youth. In terms of myself, I was raised on John Carpenter, horror movies etc.

However, because of our dealings with EGM and visits to trade markets, we knew that certain genres at certain times were not saleable. Horror movies went through a rough patch in the late eighties. Some couldn't be sold at all. The market was so flooded with cut off the head and let the blood flow movies, or teenager lovers axed to death in the barn by deformed brother movies etc.

More than anything, on your first film you get the chance to do whatever you want. More than likely, the money will come from someone who knows nothing about film making. You've got so little money at risk that you can go out on a limb and in retrospect, we could have been more daring with some aspects of *White Angel* - to arouse a little controversy.

"If you want art, don't mess around with movies, buy a Picasso"
Michael Winner

Q - The script idea is strongly rooted in the idea of a very British murder?

Chris - We said let's make this film British. As British as *The*

Long Good Friday. The intrinsic Britishness emerged during script development. We didn't start off saying, let's make a film about a VERY British serial killer. We said let's make a film about a serial killer in Britain and the true British angle came out when we started on the research and also with the involvement of Peter Firth. He manipulated the script in the way that we wanted him to. The scripts that we've produced are functional. They get from A to B without showing *too many of the footprints in the wet paint.*

> "Insecurity, commonly regarded as a weakness in normal people, is the basic tool of the actor's trade"
> Miranda Richardson

Peter Firth took the screenplay and changed Steckler from this mid Atlantic, non-existent psychopath and brought the character into the English home. Many of the mannerisms in the film were invented by Peter. A number of people have been surprised by this. They think everything in the film comes from the director or writer, when in essence, the director, writer and producer are merely the people in control (hopefully) of the creative talent. Actors have the last say by virtue of their own performance.

We felt Peter's ideas were good. You know on set whether something is working or not and we agreed with Peter to use the cup of tea as a main prop in the film. It was there in the script but Peter made much more of it - each murder was followed by a cup of tea. Even the way Steckler dresses, the top button being fastened was Peter's idea.

There was a conscious decision to make Peter this *out of date character,* in so much as the film is set in the nineties but everything about him is stuck in the late sixties and early seventies. He wears those trousers and that tie that only weird people still wear. He was very much stuck in that vein and of course Oxfam was the best place for him to shop. This is what people of quality bring to a production. An experienced and talented actor, or star will bring so much to any production, it is worth moving heaven and earth to engage their services. From a marketing point, everyone always thinks that big actors cost big bucks. This isn't necessarily so, and their mere presence in a film will raise it's value.

Gen - We had seen so many American movies about serial killers - but nothing that really explained why they do what they do - so we wanted a more realistic approach, looking into what urges these characters to do it - Hollywood had shown those killers in a kind of glamorous light - never

Peter Firth as the mild mannered serial killer, Leslie Steckler. Peter's experience brought a new dimension to an otherwise run of the mill screen killer.

"I never had a goddam artistic problem in my life, never, and I've worked with the best of them. John Ford isn't exactly a bum, is he? Yet he never gave me any manure about art"
John Wayne

exploring why. We thought that the British serial killers were more interesting. In the States, the serial killers use all methods of murder that are quite violent - for example with guns, axes, chain saws, etc. and they were into cannibalism. They also had that weird look about them - one eye, seven feet tall, a limp - strange characteristics that you expect from a James Bond movie. But in the UK, the frightening thing, was how these killers really blended into society - how normal they looked... what fascinated us most was - could it be the guy living next door to you?

Q - The killer next door seems to be a concept which keeps coming up?

Chris - Yes, we decided that the screenplay should take the serial killer living next door right to its logical conclusion, to create a killer who is actually very likeable as a human being. We never see him murder except in small details*, and when it does happen, it has a kind of humour to it rather than horror. Therefore, apart from his memories of various crimes, we never experience Steckler, the serial killer. But we do see Carter kill and she is not the serial killer, which in turn is an interesting slant.

Several people have mentioned that Carter was a bit of a cold character and that they liked Steckler. Yes! This is exactly what we wanted. A lot of people seem to like this

Polaroid photos are one of the only times we see Steckler's victims. It is amazing how multi talented your crew can be when pushed.

* In order to secure deals later, extra scenes of sex and violence were shot and added.

completely different slant on the killers. At the end of the day if you get two killers together in a house and get them to talk about killing it's going to be strange, it's going to be funny, it's going to be horrifying and it could get very nasty. We wanted to get that seething atmosphere into the house, lock the doors and see what happened.

Some of the elements from the screenplay we lost. For instance, the heating was supposed to have gone insane during the film so that it was always hot in the house. We wanted a pressure cooker. We wanted claustrophobia. That is something that harks back to the needs of a low-budget film. You need to look at what you've got and turn that into an advantage. We had a small location, so we thought, let's make it claustrophobic.

Q - Had you seen 10 Rillington Place?

Chris - We saw *10 Rillington Place* a long time before we made *White Angel*. After *White Angel* was completed, we saw the film again and were pleased and to some extent shocked by the similarities. I don't think there were any major conscious similarities when we were making it. I don't know whether Peter had seen it but he had done research into serial killers and we watched some quite shocking home videos of Dennis Nilson.

I remember Harriet asking Peter whether he had a defined idea of how he was going to play the character and he said no, *I don't have a clue, I'll tell you how I'm going to play it on the last day of photography*. And it is interesting as he didn't know, you could see it sometimes when he was unsure how Steckler was developing. He had in him that ability to say, *I'll try this out and if it doesn't work, then fine*. This was a very valuable asset to have.

Q - A serial killer moves in with an undiscovered murderer. Where did that idea come from?

Chris - I don't know really, I guess by a process of development from a single concept. What we do is play around with this single concept. For example, we want to make a film about a serial killer. We have to make it in one house. We can't have him just going out and killing people because that would be boring so we introduce a woman to get a male/female thing going. What could she be? Well, if she

Costume

1. Keep a tight reign on your designer, don't let them go over budget.

2. Actors can be persuaded to use their own clothes, but beware of damages.

3. Charity shops are a great source. If you can return the items, you could negotiate a good deal.

4. Film & TV costume houses are not as expensive as you think. Give them a call and set up a meeting to view their warehouses, it's astounding what they have. Everything is negotiable.

5. Work out your story days and build these days into your screenplay and schedule. Story days are the actual days on which scenes take place, not the period of time over which a story is set. For instance, a film may be set over a month but the story is told over three specific days. These will be your three story days. Minimise story days wherever possible.

6. Remember you may need clothes for re-shoots so keep hold of them after the wrap.

7. Minimise the amount of times a character changes clothes. A designer will want a costume change with each story day. Wherever possible, avoid this, but don't go too far or your cast will end up looking cheap.

8. Some sequences, especially stunts or scenes with water or rain, may need stand-by clothes for a 2nd or 3rd take. Ensure these scenes use cheap clothing so as not to double up on expensive items that may not get used.

CASE STUDIES

"If it aint on the page, It aint on the stage"
Anon

knows he's a serial killer, maybe it's his wife, but then it's not original. Maybe she can be a crime writer, an expert on serial killers and he wants her to write his story. That's good. But why would she do it? Well, maybe she murdered her husband, bricked him up in the wall of the house and got away with it. Maybe the serial killer finds the body and blackmails her? Then, they're both murderers. Hey! That's a good idea. Before you know it you have a structure.

Gen - Then you write the first one page synopsis, give it to your mates and ask what they think - *well, this is good, this is crap* - OK. Turn it into a two page synopsis. You keep building and building. What we like to do is to write it as a novella first or at least a thirty page short story. When that reads well, then you've got something. It is structured very heavily. We have two plot points which come thirty minutes from the beginning, thirty minutes from the end and we have a sixty minute centre section.

So, we have act one at thirty minutes, act two which is sixty minutes and act three at thirty minutes and in addition, in the middle of act two we have a mid point. If you watch any good Hollywood feature, you'll see that they stick to this. When editing, what usually happens is that you end up cutting some of the junk out of the middle where it gets too wordy and slow and it ends up around ninety minutes.

Q - What are the plot points in White Angel?

Chris - We spend the first ten minutes setting up the various stories which combine to form the main plot and characters. Ellen Carter has killed her husband and hidden the body - she

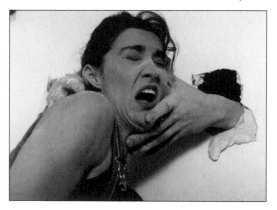

In a scene cut from the final film, Ellen Carter has recurring nightmares about her husband's body trying to escape from it's living room wall tomb.

The fingerprint computer creates the timescale for the movie. It is a time bomb ticking down, and ready to go off. A little artistic license was used - a real fingerprint computer could produce results in minutes - but I guess that's the movies!

has 'got away with murder'. She is a crime writer who studies serial killers. There is a serial killer in London killing women who wear white, and the killer may also be a woman. Mild mannered Steckler is probably the serial killer, he cuts up newspapers and has dead bodies in his living room. He moves in with Carter as a tenant. The police are closing in as they have a fingerprint on a hammer.

The plot is completely set up, we had a framework in which to work, and the fingerprint is the time bomb waiting to go off. This gives the movie the sense of impending doom and momentum.

Plot point one is where Steckler says - *I am the White Angel and I want you to write my story*. Up until that point he has been getting on with his life, Carter has been getting on with hers. We've been setting up various parts of the story. But at that point the film changes direction. It sheers off at ninety degrees. Carter's life is totally destroyed. Steckler's is totally fulfilled because he's got the writer he wanted to do his book.

We then spend the next forty minutes of the movie exploring this theme of writing the book and what Carter is interested in. The mid point of the film is where Carter interviews Steckler and he says about his wife - *she deserved to die, the world is a better place without her.* In the same scene, Steckler turns the interview around to Carter and she says of killing her husband, *he deserved to die. The world's a better place without him* - And she realises that she has said the same thing as Steckler, therefore it questions the differences between them.

It's a very subtle mid-point but it is a character point when Carter suddenly realises that she is essentially the same creature, a human being with the ability to kill.

> "I know audiences feed on crap, but I can't believe we are so lacking that we cannot dish it up to them with some trace of originality"
> Darryl F. Zannuck

The original premise for White Angel explored the differences between murder and manslaughter through the eyes of two killers.

Therefore, the rest of act two continues with the plot and develops this theme - her attempts to poison him etc. Plot point two is where Carter finds out (wrongly) that her friend, Mik, has been killed by Steckler. She finds the glasses covered in blood - that's a pinch point - just before plot point two.

The exact position of plot point two is where she sees the blood and the knife in Mik's flat and comes home to find Steckler burying the body in the garden. Again, at this point, the film sheers off at ninety degrees. Carter is no longer interested in writing the book. She has one thing on her mind and one thing only. To kill Steckler. To get him off the face of the planet. She can't turn him in to the police because she'll go down for murder. So she makes an elaborate plan which the audience discovers as it happens. This leads us to the exciting climax and twist in the tail. Most people like a good twist, it lets them leave the theatre feeling fulfilled in a strange sort of way. However, it can often backfire and make the audience feel cheated.

We are not saying *White Angel* is the greatest screenplay ever written, but it does work as a thriller. Most people say the story was 'gripping', which is a real compliment when considering the constraints under which the film was made.

Q - So the treatment was extremely detailed before you wrote the script?

Gen - Absolutely. *White Angel* wasn't a short treatment. I think that the final version was twenty five pages. It is important that you can write a thirty page treatment and you know the structure (page eight is plot point one and on page

The hammer in White Angel was the device which provided the plot and twists. This evidence would eventually lead the police back to the killer, and straight back to Ellen Carter for the final twist in the plot.

22 you have plot point two, with the mid point on page fifteen). We structure everything, so when writing, you don't lose control of your characters nor will the story lose its direction. Every scene has got to move the story onward to its final conclusion - otherwise you will be boring your audience. You have around 2 hours to get everything across, and leave no loose ends.

Chris - Screenplays and stories are all about mystery and exploration. Hollywood is obsessed by character - let's stop the movie and have a talky scene where the character confesses that he's shot a kid in a back alley ten years ago - this is often resolved later in the film, it's divisive and obvious.

What a movie is really about is getting on to the next scene. One of the interesting things that we did on *White Angel* was when we finished the first rough cut we went back and started to cut the end out of every single scene and some of the middle. So, what originally was a very well structured scene now felt unbalanced, not finished. The audience felt there was more, that they were not being told everything. This is not a hard and fast rule. But a good rule to stick to is not to tell your audience everything, it keeps them wanting more. This is something I learnt during *White Angel*.

Q - There is a great deal of video footage used. Was this in the script?

Chris - Yes. There were two reasons for the inclusion of video tape footage in the film. I am from the amateur film making scene and whilst I started on Super 8mm, VHS soon became a medium that was very accessible.

I loved the way that in science fiction movies of the eighties, video footage was heavily used, eg. *Aliens*. It always looked grainy and really gaudy and I thought it was great. What an image. So, wouldn't it be great to get Steckler's monologues on video tape because that is a format that is much more 'real'. People believe what they see on TV. They understand that a film is drama but the news is 'real'. People believe video images.

In the film, Steckler gives interviews, and I thought, if we can do the interview on tape, then we have a five minute take in one. It would look really shocking and real, which is

Cutting Ratio

The cutting ratio is the amount of film stock you shoot in relation to the final length of the movie. The less stock you shoot, the lower the ratio.

1. Save stock wherever possible. It is expensive to purchase, and expensive to process.

2. Work out a system between sound, camera and clapper loader so the camera starts turning over at the last possible moment. Just a couple of seconds wasted at the head of every shot will accumulate on a feature shoot.

3. Don't get too anxious to call cut - often in the cutting room, you will need that extra second on the end of a shot. When you feel the shot has ended, wait a beat before calling cut.

4. Most features are shot at 24fps because of tradition. In todays non linear and video orientated post production world, it's essential you shoot at 25fps. No matter what anyone tells you, shooting a feature at 24fps involves more headaches and will cost you more in the long run.

5. Know in your heart if you have got what you need in your first take. Takes that are not needed waste time as well as stock.

6. If you get a hair in the gate you should re-shoot. If stock is very short and you are having to get everything in one take, don't bother to reshoot, (unless the hair is massive - many major features go out with hairs in the gate.) In the cutting room you will always use the best take, regardless of technical problems that camera operators will moan about, such as hairs, flare, soft shots and wobbly camerawork.

CASE STUDIES

7. *Rehearse as much as possible, block the scene for the cameraman so he knows what is going to happen and when. If the scene could be spontaneous in terms of performance from the actor, allow the cameraman to widen the lens so there is more space in frame to accommodate the unexpected. This will avoid losing the frame or focus, forcing a retake (which will probably be wider anyway).*

8. *If you are shooting 35mm, you will only develop and print the shots you want. If you shoot 16mm or Super 16mm, you will print everything.*

9. *Storyboards will often help, but it is likely that too many shots will be boarded and that when it comes to shooting, the shots will not be possible due to the location being different, or a script re-write.*

10. *Shooting on tape formats such as DV often means that directors will say 'leave it running whilst I just...' - this can mean hours and hours of wasted footage that doesn't cost much in terms of tape, but will cost you severely in the cutting room in wasted time and frustration. Whatever the format, remain disciplined about shooting absolutely no more than is needed.*

11. *Depending on your story and budget, you should aim for anywhere between a 4-1 and an 8-1 cutting ratio.*

what everyone has come back and said. The other important reason is that five minutes of the film translates to about seven percent of the final product. We had fifty five rolls on which to shoot this film. I was fully aware that to get a five minute monologue in one film take, which is what I wanted, was going to be difficult. So we shot it several times on video tape which is reusable and then transferred the final result to film. So you have a chunk of your film finished with a cutting ratio of one to one which is pretty damn good. The cutting ratio is how much stock you shoot in comparison with how long your film is. If the film is to be one hundred minutes long and you shoot one thousand minutes of stock, then you would have a cutting ratio of ten to one. Most feature work is between eight and twelve to one. I think we shot *White Angel* on four and a half to one. It's all about preventing waste. Don't do endless takes. I learnt on *The Runner* that take one is often very similar to take fifty five.

Often in the editing room your can hear your voice calling *"Take four. Loved it darlings!"* and you wonder why you got that far - there was nothing wrong with takes one to three. If you've got the shot and your cameraman says that it's fine and the gate's clear - go with it. It saves you time and it saves you stock and it saves you money.

Gen - We had seen the effect of video images in films like *Henry - Portrait of a Serial Killer* - where it was pretty nasty (they watch a video of massacring a family) - and the reason it was more horrific than seeing the other killings on film, was simply because it was shot on video tape. It was real. Its like seeing the news nowadays - the images can be shocking. Also the video camera had been used in *'sex, lies and videotape'* - as a tool to get into the minds of a group of people - and it worked. It was exactly what we wanted for *White Angel*.

Q - Some writers chose an imaginary cast when working on a script, to give characters life. Did you do this?

Chris - Yes. This sounds really bizarre. When Steckler's character was formed, I had two people in mind. There is a guy in Romero's *Dawn of the Dead* who turns into a zombie at the end. I always thought of him. I don't know why. And I also thought of Jeremy Irons and for Carter, I only had one person in mind. No chance of getting her, of course. Jane Fonda.

Q - When you started pre-production you had very little money, why didn't you wait until you had your full budget in place?

Chris - Mainly because we would have had to wait forever. We had worked out that it was possible to make a feature film for less than ten thousand pounds and we looked at how we made *The Runner* and where the money went. There were obvious things like film stock, processing, camera gear, things that you cannot avoid. You can get a good deal, you can get discounts, you can get some things for free but there is always going to be an expense. There are however, other expenses that you can avoid or minimise. The reason why *The Runner* went over budget was the fact that it was set in lots of locations, so out of a twelve hour shooting day, you'd spend a quarter of it, or thirty percent, driving between A and B, and then twenty percent getting the cameras out and the lighting set up. I guess we lost thirty to forty percent of our time through location changes. *The Runner* was filled with events that just wasted time through ignorance or lack of forward planning. *White Angel* was going to be different.

Gen - The rules for low-budget scripts are all cost related. Money is the one thing you have little control of because on a no-budget film, you don't have it. The big expense we had on *The Runner* was crew and accommodation expenses. That

> "Talk to them about things they don't know. Try to give them an inferiority complex. If the actress is beautiful, screw her. If she isn't, present her with a valuable painting she will not understand. If they insist on being boring, kick their asses or twist their noses. And that's about all there is to it"
> John Huston

When creating a character it helped a great deal to visualise a certain actor playing that part.

"You spend all your life trying to do something they put people in asylums for"
Jane Fonda

took fifteen to twenty thousand quid out of our budget. On *White Angel* we decided to shoot in London and buy everyone a tube pass. It cost about twenty five quid a week to get cast and crew on location and often, on time.

White Angel was based in one house and there are very few scene changes - this minimised time wastage and allowed us to finish the film in eighteen shooting days as compared with nearly forty on *The Runner*. From *White Angel's* point of view the two golden rules we had were, minimise locations and get your cast and crew in a position where they can spend the night at home. This saves money in other ways. For example, if you wrapped early, you did not have to provide a meal in the evening. So, we'd not need catering that night. Catering is one of the areas where basic expense can't be avoided and it is actually a bad idea to skimp on it. If you feed your cast and crew well, you'll get twenty percent more out of them. You have to feed them something so why not make it good! Catering is another area that must be done correctly. It must be good. A low-budget shoot needs good food to look forward to. Out in the rain, or the cold, good food keeps the spirits up.

Q - What would be an average menu?

Gen - We didn't supply breakfast because everyone lived in London and we looked at it as coming to work. Lunchtime, we would provide sandwiches, rolls, very easy food that could be served from a cardboard box anywhere. For the evening meal, always something hot, baked potatoes, stews, shepherds pie. Warm, stodgy food with plenty of carbohydrates to keep people going. We'd also send out chocolate bars to break up the times between meals and

Food is always an issue. More than likely, you won't be able to afford a food wagon. On top of good food, remember cast and crew will need tea, coffee and water at all times, and a warm dry place to sit down and eat.

All the night-time sequences for White Angel were shot during the day with the windows covered by black bin bags. A routine is very important if the cast and crew are going to perform to the best of their abilities with limited resources.

Catering

A film crew looks forward to only one thing - lunch time. It is best not to engage their wrath by providing dodgy grub, or too little.

1. A film crew works better on a full stomach - especially if they are out in the cold. Tea and coffee should always be available, with someone making sure that the key personnel (who are working harder than others) have their drinks brought to them.

2. Feed a crew as much food as you can.

3. Film caterers are very expensive but they do provide a wonderful service. Try negotiating them down to a price per head that you can afford.

4. If you can't afford a film caterer, find someone who is used to catering for large groups and employ them full time for the duration of the shoot. They may bring their own equipment and will certainly have good ideas. Catering students can also be a good option but they will be inexperienced and unprepared for the barrage to which they will be subjected.

5. Large bread roll sandwiches are a good lunch time filler, easy to prepare and distribute. Beware of crew boredom with this simple culinary treat. Try and make up a simple menu (also catering for vegetarians) and give people an option. This will prevent arguments and give them something to look forward to.

6. Actors are more fussy than crew and often expect to be treated better than you can afford. Be aware of this very important factor.

persuaded a local bakery to give us all their cakes that were left unsold at the end of the day.

Q - What happens on a late shoot?

Gen - Not often, maybe once a week, we provided beers afterwards. It is the same idea as getting chocolates etc. You give people beer and they think, *this isn't so bad* and it holds the team together.

Q - Where were all the meals prepared?

Gen - There just wasn't room in the kitchen, so Mark Sutherland, the set constructor, found a skip outside a pub which was being refitted. He pinched the old bar and set up *'Steckler's Diner'* in the garage. Meals were prepared and consumed in the garage, it was pretty squalid - the caterer had a simple gas fired stove, but still managed to feed thirty mouths, twice a day. I guess the crew named it *'Steckler's Diner'* because sometimes we just didn't know what was in the stew!

Q - From a production point, what advantages did White Angel present?

Gen - We had a film set in suburbia, a location that would be cheap to shoot in, which would be near central London so that we could get the cast and crew to it easily. It was set in the present, so actors could wear their own clothes, or we could buy stuff from Oxfam, down the road. I'm not joking. We

7. Sweeties and beers after a hard weeks shoot can offer a good emotional bribe to get back in favour with a disgruntled cast and crew.

8. Concentrate on foods that are easy to prepare, cheap to produce, and fast to distribute and clear. Draw up a list of meals and outline them in the schedule. This will allow certain meals to be rotated.

9. If possible, give your crew a small amount of money each day and ask them to feed themselves. This works well if you are close to shops, a canteen or cheap pub that serves meals. This way, they get a choice, you get zero catering problems.

10. Product placement is always a good source for a couple of boxes of chocolate bars or crisps.

11. Some cast and crew will expect breakfast. It's your choice, but as soon as you give it to them, you will have to cater for this extra meal every day. Ask them to eat their cornflakes and toast before they leave home.

12. If cast and crew are away from home for a location shoot, you will need to cater for all their needs, breakfast, lunch, dinner and supper for night shoots. This quickly becomes VERY expensive.

13. It's obvious, but if you are shooting in a confined place, avoid farty foods for lunch.

had a deal with Oxfam. It cost us fifty pounds for all our costumes in the film. And it worked. At the end of the day, when you have ten thousand pounds to make a film, two and a half goes on film stock, one and a half on cast and crew because you've got to give them something. Before you know it, the whole budget has gone on essentials. Therefore fifty quid for costumes.

At each production meeting, Mark Sutherland, our production designer, would proudly announce that out of his total budget of one hundred pounds, he was going to spend another forty pence on nails. He couldn't get them for free and was quite distressed about this.

Chris - He became notorious for going around skips. The skip is a production designer's supply base on a low-budget shoot. Another man's junk is a production designer's dream.

Q - How detailed was the budget?

Gen - Very, we had to know where every penny was going to go. We worked out what we thought the entire production was going to cost - everything down to petrol and telephone bills. Then we started to work out what things we actually needed to pay for to get the movie in the can - we just couldn't raise the entire budget before we shot, so we concentrated on getting the movie shot.

Eventually, we narrowed our list of essentials down to around £11,000. We knew we might need more than this, but once the snowball is rolling down the hill, it is difficult to stop it.

Chris - That's right, it is weird but you spend months just trying to get this thing going, and then a few days before the first day of principal photography, the production runs itself - it's as if you have built a huge machine, and all you need to do now is maintain it to ensure it doesn't stop working. If you get to the first day of photography, you will probably make it all the way to the finish line.

Gen - First of all, we concentrated on getting the right house that was cheap. Then we could start sorting out everything else. We rented the house in Ruislip and based the production there. Most of the film would be shot there and the production office would also operate from one of the upstairs bedrooms. Then we visited all the hire companies and I spoke to them about the film and of course, getting free deals. I told them who we were and what we were trying to do - *"...to make a career for ourselves - we are young film makers, the film is very low-budget, and we need the best deal ever - please, please, pretty please..."*

Remember that any initial deal is the quote they give anyone. 30% discount is just standard. No one pays full price. Tell them how little you have. Get a quote. Look at your budget and decide what you can afford. Then ring them back and try to make a deal. They can only say no. I used to ring up, say a lighting company and say - *Look, I've got five hundred pounds. Can you do it for that?* It is also important to pick a time to shoot your movie when you know that there is less work around in the industry. Then you will receive better discounts. Usually December - January - Feb - March.

You must make sure that you tell them exactly what you want and for how much. *This is all I can afford, and I need an all in deal, all the kit, all the accessories, all the gel, all the spun - ask if there are any hidden extras, or if you pay extra if you go overtime.* And get a quote that lays everything out in detail. The best deal to get is always an 'all in' deal.

"We must choose material not only on the basis of whether we feel deeply, but on whether or not anyone's bloody well going to see it"
Richard Lester

Q - And what about cast and crew?

If money is tight, the basic Super 16mm Camera, Tripod, Lens, Nagra, Mic and stock is all that is needed to make a cinematic quality feature film... Oh and a script and cast and...

Pic - Jane Rousseau, camera operator for White Angel.

343

How To Get Deals

1. Everything is negotiable. Every list price you will ever be quoted will have another figure next to it which is what the person you are negotiating with is allowed to go down to. The trick is to find out what that figure is.

2. Find out from friends what kind of deals they got - it's a good yardstick.

3. Set up an account with the company and stretch the credit as far as you can. It is cheaper than a bank loan. Always keep in touch with the company you owe money to, never lie and never ever try and get away without paying. Good will can be stretched if you are civil, have a good reason for not paying, and can offer a schedule of payments within a set time frame.

4. When approaching people for deals or freebies, be polite and DON'T try and hustle. Most people who are in the Industry have been in it for many years and can spot ignorance and arrogance a mile away. Both these qualities are not desirable. Go to a person for help and advice - everyone likes to help someone out, it makes them feel good inside. Follow up thank you letters will often get a repeat performance if it is needed.

5. Many things can be begged, borrowed or stolen. If there is any opportunity for a companies logo to be featured on screen, they will probably supply you with free samples of the product. Cars, costume, cigarettes etc. These can all reduce your budget. They may even pay (product placement).

Gen - You've most probably started thinking about who would be an ideal cast for your film, and you may have been speaking to agents who have been asking the kind of money that is completely impossible - tell them that you need help and they will be helping the British film industry. Again, it is best to be straight with these people and not to attempt to deceive them. If an actor likes the script and wants to do it, their agent will probably be unable to stop them. Some actors will only work for money, so don't get disheartened if they tell you to stuff off.

Q - How did you budget for crew wages?

Gen - We put the crew on deferred payments. We agreed to pay their expenses so that they wouldn't be out of pocket. The film was shooting in London so we concentrated on people who could get the tube rather than paying petrol expenses which are harder to estimate before shooting. Also, we always over budget for expenses because there are tiny elements that you just don't expect. Somebody can't get the tube. The shoot runs after tube hours or someone rings up and has to get a taxi for some reason. That money has to come from somewhere so it is best to over budget on transport.

Q - Crew members need to eat and pay the rent, how do you deal with these very serious problems?

Chris - What we did on *The Runner* was very different from *White Angel*. On *The Runner*, we couldn't pay anybody anything and we didn't want to do this again, because people have to live. So, what we did on *White Angel* was cover everyone's expenses, a tube ticket everyday and everyone received £50 a week, to keep them in beer and fags. On top we offered a deferred payment so that when the film was sold, they would receive their wages. This would be more than they would have got since they have to wait two years or more for it - and don't kid yourself by promising money in two weeks. There is also a very good chance that they will never get paid. Selling a film is a long process. You've got to be straight with people. This is the money we've got - they can say yes or no. And make sure you pay it to them and reward them with good catering.

Q - What's in it for them?

Chris - As we speak there are few films getting made in the UK, so there is an experience value (the situation has somewhat improved since this interview). Most pro film-makers earn money through commercials, television etc. but they usually want to make movies. There are also a lot of new students being turned out from colleges - take advantage of their enthusiasm and give them responsibility. In my experience, most people will deliver if you give them the opportunity to do so. There is a great debate over deferred films - are they ethical? Well, almost all big budget features take advantage of free labour by taking on free runners - we are doing the same, but giving them more opportunity and experience, and a possible fee if it all works out. At the end of the day, everyone can say no. As a rule, if you can pay someone, do it, you will get a better worker, and no nasty phone calls two years down the line if you were not able to pay as promised.*

Q - What shooting elements proved a problem later?

Gen - Something hit us when we were doing the effects on *The Runner.* The sheer quantity of stock needed to shoot action and effects. So on *White Angel*, we deliberately had very little stunt work or effects.

By remaining in London, there was another saving. Because we were near the facilities houses, anything could be dealt with by a phone call and a quick trip in the van. For example, if a camera went down - it was easy to get a replacement without costing much in time and therefore money. Also, we were close to the labs and could view rushes every day and make sure there were no problems.

When we were shooting *The Runner* up in North Wales, the camera did go down and it was a serious problem. We had to ring up London to get a new camera delivered - and then wait for them to courier it up by train. With transport on location, always expect your trucks to break down or worse. They always will. Either they'll get stuck in mud, stuck in snow, completely fail or crash. We had a few crashes - no-one was hurt, seriously at least. People get in too much of a hurry. This is one of the major problems of low-budget film-making. Safety. Everybody knows there is a limited time scale. The

6. Be thorough, ring around and get the best quotes. You will get a feel for who will be able to help you.

7. Many companies, not related to the film industry will often render their services for free just to be involved in the production (for the fun) or for a credit on the end titles. Tickets to the premiere can be a good bribe.

8. Go into negotiations with a maximum you will pay and don't go over it. If you are prepared to walk out without making a deal, you are in a very strong position.

9. If you can pay cash on delivery, you can push harder for a bigger discount. This is the best way to get the biggest discounts. Avoid doing non VAT declared deals (cash in hand) - it may be good at the time, but when Customs & Excise or the Inland Revenue ask you where the money went, you may have problems (you should be VAT registered anyhow in the UK).

10. If you can't get a discount, get something thrown in for free.

11. Remember to say thank you afterwards. If you can, send a bottle of booze or even chocolates and flowers. Whatever the gift, it will be appreciated.

12. Take whoever you are doing the deal with out for a drink and build a relationship. After your shoot, start taking the credit controller out for a drink, as you probably can't afford to pay and you need to extend good will to as near breaking point as you can.

*NOTE - UK Law now dictates there is a minimum wage. BECTU believe that making a deferred film may be deemed as unlawful.

During the shooting of The Runner it became obvious that special effects and stunts cost time which translates to money. White Angel was tailored to contain as few effects as possible. Even the body in the wall of the house was created by a (at the time) non professional, Phil Mathews, who is destined to go on to greater things.

production team is rushing to and from the set. Props must get to the set or the crew is sitting about waiting - so the foot goes on the accelerator and you speed along winding roads of North Wales. On *The Runner*, I remember nearly losing my life when I was driving at about 100 mph on a busy winding road on my way to the set. A truck pulled out in front of me at the last minute and the brakes made a horrific noise - luckily I am still around. It is incidents like this, when you realise that although it's important, is it really worth losing your life?

Q - What about insurance?

Gen - You always think - do we need insurance? Can we get away without it? But you can't. You certainly need car insurance and make sure that whoever is driving is definitely insured to drive that vehicle, because things will happen and they could be quite serious - and if you are not insured, you are liable because you are the employer. You must also insure the equipment from the hire companies - you have no choice since they will not let it leave their premises unless it is covered - they will ask for a copy of the policy. You can take out a policy with the company, but this will cost far more than purchasing a separate insurance policy. A good broker can get a reasonable deal for you. We went to a local firm and it worked well.

"A producer shouldn't get ulcers, he should give them"
Samuel Goldwyn

Negative insurance is something that costs a fortune and that we have never done. It covers damage or some delays in shooting. Say for example your camera goes down or you are transporting your neg to one of the laboratories, the van blows up and you lose all that work, all those hours of shooting. Neg insurance will cover your re-shooting everything that you have lost. There is a lot of money involved and therefore it is not cheap.

The E&O policy is the Errors and Omissions Policy which is something that as a low-budget film, you will only come across at the distribution end and probably for America only. It will cover legal suits brought against the film for any reason from breach of copyright to contract errors. It is there to protect whoever buys the film but you will have to pay for it. This could set you back ten grand!

> "You don't need to pray to God any more when there are storms in the sky, but you do have to be insured"
> Bertolt Brecht

Q - What was the total you needed to make White Angel?

Gen - The grand total was £85k. We didn't raise all the money at once. Initially we could only raise £11k and we thought - either we hang around waiting for all the rest or we take a risk and shoot it with what we have. The cast and crew were working on deferments and we could just about do it if we shot for eighteen days.

Once we had the movie shot, we could show investors what they would be investing in, and it worked, it was much easier to get people to part with money when they could see where the other money had been spent. A lot of people think they need the full budget to make the movie but I would say, if you can't raise it all, and it's your first movie, just go for it. Once you've got something there, then people are more likely to put money behind you because they see you are not just talking about it but actually doing it. We both know a lot of people who have been waiting years to get their first movie off the ground because they haven't managed to get their two million budget yet - Dream on!

Investors in White Angel were given simple contracts that were one page long. Good for us and good for them.

Q - How do you approach investors?

Gen - We decided to go to private investors so we could maintain control - on our previous film, a distributor had come in at the beginning to provide the finance before we actually got round to fund-raising ourselves.

"Money is better than poverty, if only for financial reasons"
Woody Allen

With *White Angel* we knew that we did not want a distributor to become involved right away because we would lose control. So, we approached people who we thought might have a bit of money stashed away, and asked if they were interested in investing it.

Also, people who might be specifically interested in investing in films. Lots of people want to be a part of the film business, it's something to talk about over drinks. Starting with the local area, we made a list of doctors, dentists, lawyers etc. and sent letters off to them, working our way from A-Z. Obviously this can cost a lot of money, sending out letters etc., so we decided to make a short-list of firm contacts, people who we'd met or people to whom we could get an introduction.

Also, news of *White Angel* travelled by word of mouth. We would meet a lawyer and he would be really keen so we'd send a full package of information. We'd have a second meeting and he'd say - *I've got this friend and she's interested. Would you like the number?* We had more success that way, rather than by cold calling.

The original artwork on the cover of the White Angel investment proposal. With virtually no material, we tried to make it look as much like a shocker of a movie as possible.

LIVING SPIRIT PICTURES
Present

WHITE ANGEL

EVERYONE HAS A DARK SIDE

Q - What's in an investment proposal?

Gen - We would put a package together that would include a synopsis of the film, a brief of the budget, a breakdown of their investment and the returns that they could expect. The returns were calculated on the *cost* budget rather than the *total* budget. For example, if we were making a movie for £200,000 but only needed £100,000 to cover all immediate cash costs on the film (the remaining £100,000 would be on deferred payments) the investment percentages would be calculated from £100,000. This meant the deal was even more interesting and showed we didn't want to waste a penny.

Once initial investment monies are recouped i.e. all investors get their money back, deferments are then paid (cast, crew, facility houses etc.) Once the film has broken even (paying back the total budget of £200,000) then all monies received from that point are deemed to be profit. Monies are returned and are split 50/50 between the production house and the investors.

Therefore, the investors provide £100k and the deferred cast and crew provide the other £100k. The first sales would

WHITE ANGEL Schedule Breakdown

1991

October
Commence writing screenplay. Begin to attract finance.

November
First Draft Complete.

1992

January
Approx. £16,000 raised. Decision to shoot in February is made. Casting and pre production move into top gear.

February
Principle photography begins and lasts 21 days.

March
Begin editing, continue day jobs and continue raising production finance.

May & June
Several small reshoots to patch some of the holes left in the main shoot. More investment comes in.

September
First fine cut complete.

December
Fine cut complete. Begin track laying sound and music.

1993

February
Final mix at dubbing theatre. Negative is cut and labs begin very long process of printing.

March
Labs damage the master negative. Living Spirit recall cast for reshoot of damaged stock. Re-mix quickly.

April
First Prints viewed. Publicity gearing up for Cannes. London based sales agents view the film. No-one bites.

May
Cannes - meet several companies who all express an interest.

July
Re-edit film and remix as it needs tightening and there are some sound problems.

August
Pilgrim Entertainment signed as sales agents for one year.

September
Premiere at the Montreal Film Festival. Goes down well. German, Korean and US companies express interest and negotiations start.

October
UK premiere at London Film Festival. Plan for an April theatrical release using money expected from Germany, Korea and US to fund it.

December
Korean and German deposits paid.

1994

Jan - March
Publicity for theatrical release.

April
Theatrical release. Film performs badly due to opening on bad weekend. Deals with US and Korea fall through. PANIC.

June - December
Pilgrim fail to deliver any deals. Publicity works a bit too well and Chris and Gen spend short time in police cells. Chris and Gen lose home.

1995

January
Labs threaten court for monies owed. Living Spirit sack Pilgrim. Feature film comes on board to handle the video release.

Feb - March
Video release begins publicity. New version with more sex and violence is edited to help bolster sales.

April
A song, performed by local band, is included in the new edit. It's later discovered to be owned by the Elvis Presley estate and carries a price tag of £1m. Re-edit - AGAIN!

May
Video release.... Film performs poorly.

September
Living Spirit approach and secure new sales agent, Stranger Than Fiction. They are confident of making sales.

1996

February
White Angel is sold to Benelux, Italy and several far Eastern territories. Monies as yet have not been received.

1999

January
White Angel is recut after the experience of 'Urban Ghost Story', taking out seven minutes of 'nothing', tightening the action and drama. The first director's cut in history to be shorter than the original.

CASE STUDIES

> "I felt like an imposter, taking all that money for reciting ten or twelve lines of nonsense a day"
> Errol Flynn

repay the investors back their £100k, then the deferred £100k would follow. The remainder would be split 50/50 between the production company and investors - an investor who put in £10k would receive 10% of the 50% split (5% of total profits).

Q - How do you confirm an investment?

Gen - We would provide a very simple contract, two or three pages and as long as they were happy, they would sign it. We would have all the control. The only thing that they would be doing is putting their money in and receiving reports from us on the progress of the film. For them it was a risky investment but they knew it and wanted to do it. We will see if they are ultimately satisfied with the results.

There are many payments that must be met whilst in the sales process, all of which eat into any potential returns, such as making delivery and marketing. These figures need to be nailed down wherever possible. Obviously, they will be deducted from any sales and will push the investors profits further away, but there is nothing that can be done about this. Without your delivery items, you won't be able to *give* your film away - it's like a car without an engine.

The involvement of TV and Film faces such as Don Henderson help solidify the project in the eyes of potential investors.

Q - Do investors give the money up-front?

Gen - We don't cashflow the payments because our budgets are so small, but if someone wished to invest a larger amount, say fifty thousand pounds, then we might link that in with a cash flow prediction. We didn't do this on *White Angel* because the money was raised in instalments anyway, so there was no need. We were almost doing a cashflow without knowing it.

As soon as we had shot something we invited the investors down to the set, showed them around to prove that we were filming something and they met the lead actors. It creates the buzz and raises more money in itself. Once the filming finished we then concentrated on raising money to finish the film. We cut a trailer and showed that to investors - we kept the trailer short and punchy, left them wanting to see more - I think it only ran sixty seconds.

Q - How long did it take to raise all the money?

Gen - One of the big problems with no-budget film-making is that if you raise money in instalments you often take time off from finishing the film, so the film takes longer to produce. We were still raising money nearly a year after we shot it.

Q - So, you must finish shooting?

Gen - Yes. It is vital to cover the screenplay as thoroughly as you can. You don't know if your lead actor could die, get awkward, move to the States. This could cause major problems. Even if you have to drop close up cut-aways during the shoot, do it in order to cover the main action and the screenplay. I know several other movies that were shot over, say ten consecutive weekends, but I guess the cast must have been made up from either friends or actors who lived locally. I wouldn't like to do it that way, but it is an option.

Once we had completed shooting *White Angel*, we had no problem raising money for post- production. People could see what was there on film. They could watch it to see how it was working, see it was working well and put more money in. Not rushing the film allowed us to have a few test screenings, reshoot the ending and polish the feature as a whole. To check that everything was in place and that the story was going as planned - and that people were going to be gripped. It's better to do this than rush the post-production, only to discover your problems when you are sitting in a cinema with a crowd of a hundred on the day the movie opens.

Q - Control is important. Why?

Gen - On *The Runner* we had given the final cut to the distribution company, they had a lot of say in the picture because they had put all the money in, in one lump sum. At the end of the day the film was not the film we wanted to make. The producers kept changing the film, trying to force the material to be more commercial, sacrificing the characters and the story - we ended up with a film that didn't make too much sense. With *White Angel* we didn't want a situation to arise where people whose opinions we didn't agree with had a creative say in the process - *"Wouldn't it be a good idea if her head exploded?" etc.* - We wanted to keep full control so that it would end up as the movie we wanted to make. That's not being possessive. It comes back to the

Keeping Investors Sweet

1. *Where possible, fulfil any promises made. It may not always be possible to fulfil a promise (one of the disadvantages of low budget film making), but make it a priority to do so at almost any cost.*

2. *Regular updates need only be a photocopied sheet of information which keeps the investor in touch with what is happening. If the line of communication goes cold, so will the investor.*

3. *Press - this is great for keeping people happy. Everyone associates press coverage with success, but beware, this may produce a false sense of financial returns on the part of the investors. If press coverage has used artistic license, let investors know.*

4. *Several low budget pictures have allowed investors to act in the film in return for cash. It works and everyone is happy. Beware of problems if their scene is cut - make this possibility known in advance.*

5. *Send them a VHS tape of the final film & invite them to the premiere.*

6. *If things are going badly, let them know. As long as there is trust and they can see that you have done everything possible, Investors have no real come back (check your agreements though). Investors would rather know things are going badly than hear nothing at all.*

7. *Give them a credit on the end of the film.*

"All you need
for a movie is a gun
and a girl"
Jean-luc Godard

writing stage where we will involve quite a few people to discuss the project, and screenings where we ask the audience to criticise the final result.

From a financial point it is also important - any changes cost money. If an investor or executive producer wants to screen the movie with all the scenes that you have cut, put back in, it will cost money and time - and when you have neither, this becomes a serious problem.

Q - Did you have any experience with British Film companies and institutions?

Gen - Yes, but limited. When we set up Living Spirit, we approached several companies and Institutions who were set up to help and aid British Film Makers. They would read our ideas and the first thing they asked was - *This film seems very much like a Hollywood project - do you see it as commercial?* - and we said - *of course - we hope it's going to be commercial, make money etc so that we can make another film.* They said - *I'm sorry. We can't support this kind of film because it's not alternative. We only support films that aren't commercial.* We were dumbfounded by this. Thankfully, things now seem to have changed dramatically, but there are still some frustrating problems for new film makers.

Q - What were your main legal questions?

Gen - The main contracts are for your actors and your crew. Especially, with the actors, you have to make sure that everything is in there. You have to have total control, to make certain that you can do anything that you want with the picture, reshoots and with the publicity afterwards. You do not want an actor refusing to do something because it's not contractual and they then request more money. The price that you have agreed to pay includes everything. The music contract is also very important to nail down. The composer composes the music and you have permission to use it in the film. You think everything is fine, however, there are other *hidden* problems.

There are mechanical and synchronisation rights along with publishing/performing rights that all have to be cleared. Various societies may have the right to collect royalties on behalf of the composer if you do not obtain a complete buyout of all such rights. Mechanical reproduction is perhaps

White Angel publicity shot - Sexy girl, big gun, blue light - this kind of image is about as far removed as possible from the attitude of many (but not all) UK based production companies and institutions. This was a problem for Living Spirit as we couldn't afford to hire a model, so Louise Ryan, from set construction, kicked off her overalls and dockers, and slipped into something slinky...

Product Placement

Product Placement is a form of advertising. To place one of their products in a film, large companies will provide certain items for the use of the film company. Their argument is that if you have a prop, namely their product, you will use it in favour of buying one. Taking it further, some companies will pay for their products to be featured. The companies who arrange this have several clients and can offer a variety of options.

1. What can you get? Cars, computers, office space, soft drinks, alcohol, cigarettes, courier services. In fact, anything that needs advertising and is useful to the production. For some items, you can even get hard cash!

2. What do they want? The companies are not doing this for free. They want advertising. First, they want a credit at the end of the film. But the real desire is for them to see their car, their cigarette, their toothbrush on the screen, preferably in very close proximity to the lead actor / hero / heroine. You more you can achieve this, the better the odds of success.

3. Time period. Is it set in the present day? This makes things easier. If your lead character does not drive a car in the script, add that scene to the script. A car manufacturer will want that space. Every room, every street, every prop offers the possibility of product placement. In Urban Ghost Story, Daewoo supplied the production with a car on the understanding that Jason Connery would drive it in the movie.

If your film is a period piece, it is more difficult but use your imagination. Some companies did operate in the nineteenth century so with a bit of research, their product can appear in its original form and show the logo.

If your film is set in the future, there should be no problem. All props should carry logos of the relevant companies. Space shuttles with 'Ford' stamped on the side etc.

4. Morality. There are a few catches. The product placement companies will require a good look at your script. If your film centres on a character who eats children, do not expect a queue of advertisers wishing to get involved. They are looking for middle of the road, standard fare.

5. Star. The better your star, the greater the desire for the product to be placed. A photograph of the established actor, driving, smoking, drinking the product is useful for inhouse publicity. It is evidence that the placement company is doing its job. Seldom do the clients see the film, but they might see the photo.

6. Costs. Product placement does cost money. It is possible to acquire a fleet of cars to shuttle actors and crew around but you might be responsible for insurance for instance.

7. When you do a deal, make sure that you deliver on the film. Provide what you agreed to provide. If you say that there will be a close up of a cigarette packet, make sure it is there. You will have to make another film, one day.

8. Don't waste too much time chasing money. Unless you have a star, it's unlikely you will get any cash. But you can get as many props and products as you like. Chocolates, sweets and crisps are always good as they can be used for the crew after featuring.

When To Shoot

1. Traditionally, January and February are slow times for hire companies. It may be to your advantage to shoot during these months as you could get better discounts.

2. If your film is set at night, it will take longer to shoot as every shot will need to be lit. If you shoot during the day, it's possible to get away with little or no lighting. Shooting from the hip during daylight is the best way to cover a lot of ground when you don't have much time and money is really tight. Consider the possibilities of moving the production outdoors as much as possible during the hours of daylight. It is easier to manage an outdoor location, and there is less to damage.

3. If shooting outdoors, remember British weather. Consider shooting abroad in southern Spain or Portugal - it isn't as expensive as you might think. Days are longer and brighter as well.

4. Crews and actors (especially), don't like being cold and wet. Try and work around bad weather, or if the script calls for it, control the weather by creating it with wind and rain machines.

5. Be aware of day and night length - it can get very dark or very light alarmingly quickly. Keep an eye out for the clock being moved forward or back and inform all the cast and crew.

6. Avoid Christmas if possible, everyone just goes silly. Summer months are filled with important people going on holiday.

the most important for low-budget films since a good deal of money is recovered through video. If a buyout is not agreed, money is payable on every single copy of the video reproduced worldwide and it comes out of the producer's pocket. On *White Angel* we covered all such rights and no further payments are to be made. Anyone buying this film will ask to see these contracts and not having them in place might prevent any sales occurring.

Q - Did you use a lawyer?

Gen - We used a lawyer on *The Runner*, but not an entertainment lawyer. This was a problem because the film industry is very specialised and needs a legal expert, which is expensive. But, again, you may be able to come to some kind of arrangement. If not and you shoot anyway, just read carefully through any contract before it is signed. With *White Angel,* we were in a more fortunate position since we had gone through the process once and had copies of all the contracts. Ultimately, we didn't use a lawyer and it hasn't caused us any problems yet, but it could well do. I would strongly advise consulting a lawyer at some stage, if only to put your mind at rest.

Q - What did the schedule for White Angel look like?

Gen - The schedule for White Angel was twenty days with a day off each week, so that gave us seventeen shooting days. We made sure we never had more than a twelve hour day. If you start running into long hours because you are trying to cover ground, you will pay for it further down the line. A crew can only work so long and we said, no more than twelve hours a day. Only the producer works longer. In fact, the producer never sleeps! When I schedule, I look at locations first, making sure I shoot all the scenes around a certain location at the same time. This saves time getting in and out of a location. Try to bunch an actor's scenes together so you use them for the least possible time. It's not possible to make everything work, but minimising waste will save money. It's like putting a massive jigsaw together when you don't have the cover of the box to tell you what the picture looks like.

If you have a star who is costing you real money, then there is no doubt that they should become the priority.

After producing The Runner, the production of White Angel ran smoothly and without hiccup.

We also decided to shoot in February as this was a lean time for hire companies and were able to get great deals.

Q - What was the worst day?

Gen - I can't think of a 'worst day' on *White Angel*. I can think of several on *The Runner* but you see, *White Angel* profited by the disasters on the first film. We learnt from our considerable mistakes. On *White Angel*, we knew the ropes - we knew how to shoot a movie for little or no money. In a way it was quite boring because from a production point of view, we got it right.

We did lose one location and had to make a bank out of absolutely nothing. There is a scene in the film where Carter goes to a bank where all the evidence against her is locked in a safety deposit box. So Carter gets through the reception and into the bank vault. We had planned to use a real bank which was agreed but they pulled out at the last minute, the day before we were due to shoot. Someone found an empty gutted out bank that we could use. There was nothing in there and it was like a warehouse, but it did have the vault door intact. We decided to paint deposit boxes on the wall and we all worked on it, painting away through the night and half an hour before shooting in the morning it was finished. The paint was still wet in the shot. To be honest, that was not a real disaster. Film-making breeds this kind of situation. If you can't handle that, you shouldn't be making films.

Q - Were there any problems shooting on location?

"It's true, hard work never killed anybody, but I figure, why take the chance?"
Ronald Reagan

The bank vault was nothing more than a metal door with cardboard security boxes painted grey. Little white stickers were added at the last moment to give the impression of key holes.

Gen - Nothing above the run of the mill stuff like weird people hassling the cast and crew, or the weather. One thing to consider when looking for locations is the sound. Film making is always biased toward the image, but we had real problems with one or two scenes because we shot near an airport. We also had real problems in a flat where kids were running about upstairs - this really held us up.

Q - How do you find working with actors?

Gen - Actors tend to flock together, as do the crew, and sometimes this can generate a *'them and us'* situation which is very unhealthy. There were a couple of incidents that proved a bit problematic for the production team. For example the lighting for the scene might take a little longer than expected and the actor might have gone for a walk or something. We did lose all our actors on one occasion. We had told them that the set up was going to take a little time so they decided to go off together. We had a room for them but they weren't there. The whole crew had to search Ruislip High Street, looking for them and they were finally found having an Indian in the local restaurant. They were just having coffee and wouldn't be long. It all got sorted but it was a bit of a heart stopper at the time.

On *White Angel*, none of the actors really put pressure on us, they were all great. But on *The Runner*, we did have terrible problems with the cast, clashes of interest, egos, impatience, frustration - all combined to create a volatile pot of angry energy.

Q - How do you go about casting a movie?

Chris - We never finished the screenplay to our satisfaction

"I've done the most awful rubbish in order to have somewhere to go in the morning"
Richard Burton

and were still rewriting the script on the set, but when it was in a position where we felt - *this will work* - and we had our eleven thousand pounds in the bank we had to start casting.

First, we put an ad in *The Stage* and *PCR* (Professional Casting Report). As usual, we received sackfuls of mail. The ad said - *'Wanted. Sophisticated Psychopath'* - we got some very strange letters back. One from a guy who had pasted a reply from pieces of newspaper and enclosed a photograph of himself, hooded in black, holding a carving knife. It read - *Give me the role or I will kill you* - I looked quite hard for the sophisticated angle in this guy's approach but I couldn't quite see it. We also had photos of naked girls saying - *give me the role and I'll make your dreams come true* - It's very strange. People are desperate. I even had one woman come to the house and offer to take a shower with me in exchange for the lead role. Dead serious.

So, you have to be careful how you deal with actors and be as fair as possible. We broke the replies down into a short list of fifty, then to twenty five and initially interviewed them all. We found a church hall in Shepherds Bush, which cost ten quid for the day and was heated by a thermo - nuclear burner in the centre of the room. It had two settings. Off and meltdown. You couldn't hear yourself shout when it was on. So, we spent the day alternating between ice and fire. We ran through the actors and they were all slightly inexperienced, professionals but no weight. We realised that no-one had what it took to fill the role so we started thinking about classic, British actors.

We knew that we needed someone with quality and ability. So, we went to the top. We approached top British agents. We liked the idea of Michael Caine but he wasn't available or interested, and another famous actor we approached seemed to warm to the idea. We said that we were young film makers trying to make British movies, we needed support. He liked the idea so we sent him the script. Two days later we received a phonecall and he absolutely destroyed us. *The script is complete crap. What you are doing is immoral. You're destroying the British film industry by making this sort of crap.* He just decimated us. We were shattered. This great British actor who I'm not going to name, poured cold water over our entire concept.

Eventually I said - *well, it's obvious that we're not going to*

Getting Good Sound

Sound is an area that is neglected by most inexperienced film makers "We'll fix it in the cutting room" usually means several thousand pounds of post production (opposed to 3 mins. on set, for another take).

1. The best way to get good sound is to hire the best sound recordist you can. Inexperienced sound recordists may be paranoid and request further takes when they are not needed.

2. Everyone is a perfectionist. Learn to recognise when the sound is good enough.

3. When looking for locations, bear the sound in mind. Traffic and planes are usually the worst culprits. Most natural sounds can be covered up and disguised in post production.

4. Don't believe anyone when they tell you that it is possible to filter out the camera noise. It is possible to filter most out, but never all. A heavy atmosphere track could cover this problem.

5. Post sync dialogue is a pain and expensive. Try and avoid it.

6. Good track laying in post production doesn't cost the earth and makes the film sound much more expensive.

7. Final mixing should be done at a features studio & not a TV theatre used to mixing local news. This is the stage which shapes your final sound and if you mess around, you will only have to spend more money fixing it at another studio.

Peter Firth liked the screenplay very much and had experience of low budget films - he accepted with little hesitation. Harriet Robinson was a little more unsure - she had no experience of low budget film making, but once she heard Peter was involved, it tipped her mental scales in our favour.

be working together - and he said - *why don't you make something beautiful and wonderful like Baghdad Cafe?* and I said *What's Baghdad Cafe?* I'd no idea what he was talking about. I wanted to make *The Fog* or *Halloween* or *Return of the Living Dead Part IV*. He asked - *Why are you making this kind of film? - Because I like it.* We went around in circles. - *Why can't you adapt a Shakespeare play? - Because, I don't know anything about Shakespeare.* I still don't understand why you have to conform to succeed in Britain.

Q - How do you approach an agent?

Chris - Agents exist to protect actors and to negotiate for them. The problem with agents is that they have opinions. In other words, if the agent doesn't like the script then it might not get to the actor. That is when you are in a problem area. It is not in the agent's interest to have a client attached to a no-budget film and it is not worth their while to go through the contracts and take a client off their books for ten percent of nothing. Even the actors will be aware that another job might turn up and they don't want to commit to your film, especially if Spielberg is considering them for his new project. The trick is to get the script to the actor rather that going through the agent but not to intrude on the actors privacy. That is the easiest way to piss off both actor and agent.

g**i**Ve **m**e t**h**e j**o**b o**r** el**s**e... C**a**ll P**a**ul on ⌐⑩⑩ 555 ⌐⌐⌐⌐

Q - Can an agent stop an actor from doing a low-budget film?

Chris - By virtue of not even telling an actor a film is being cast, an agent can stop an actor getting involved. However, the bottom line is that if the actor wishes to do a film, then they will do it regardless of anything else.

Some actors can get a little too involved in the role when applying for the job.

You have an advantage as a no-budget film-maker. Your screenplay should be different from typical British scripts popping up from British Screen, Channel 4, the BFI and other similar institutions - more than likely it will be rough around the edges, maybe contain some dire clichés but it will hopefully have a bit of energy about it. At the end of the day, actors want to work, to stretch themselves artistically, even experiment. They like to do things that are different, things that might win awards or get some attention and low-budget productions are famous for this.

Q - What about approaching the top actors?

Chris - Actors are more available in the UK. In America we wouldn't get anywhere as near as we could here. Always start at the top. Do not start at the bottom because you will undersell yourself. We tried Michael Caine and got a resounding *NO*, but at least we tried.

Q - And how did Peter Firth get involved?

Chris - His agent was helpful although we never told anyone what the budget was. We always said that it was under a million. The fact that we had eleven thousand pounds in the bank was a closely guarded secret.

When ringing round agents, Peter's agent mentioned his name - I'd seen *Lifeforce*, possibly one of the worst movies

"They ruin your stories. They trample on your pride. They massacre your ideas. And what do you get for it? A fortune."
Anon

ever made, where Peter Firth runs through the streets of London and saves the world from a plague of space vampires. I was aware of his Oscar nomination for *Equus* and his work on *Tess*. We also knew of the low-budget film *Letter to Brezhnev* that was a huge success. We were interested. His agent offered us the usual £25,000 per week deal and I said - *would it be possible for Peter to just read the screenplay?* - he was sent the script and he called me - he liked it - he understood what low-budget meant, and after a discussion over the treatment of the violence in the film, he agreed that he would like to be involved.

I filled the agent in on the fact that we didn't have any money. A certain chill entered the negotiations. She said - *I have to say that this is not what we are in to.* Then I got this phone call from Peter who said - *whatever my agent says, I do want to do this movie. You guys just work it out with my agent and come to an agreement. I just want to do it.* That was great because we knew we had to pay him something but we had a very limited amount of money. We paid him what we could afford and gave him a deferred payment and a percentage so he will get more, once the movie was sold - his agent was fine.

Q - Don Henderson came in. How?

Chris - All we did was try to fill all the big roles with as big 'names' as possible. There was another role we tried to get Barbara Windsor for, but we ran out of time. Don Henderson was originally thought of as the gangster, Alan Smith, from whom Carter gets the gun. The role of Inspector Taylor was available and one night I suggested to Gen that Don should be Inspector Taylor. Now, we paid Don more than we could really afford but his agent was being a real stick in the mud and we ran out of time. But Don was a great chap. He's the best.

One of the great things about British actors is they just get on with the job. Harriet is from the American school of acting and needed a lot of direction - *Am I doing it right?* etc. I guess this kind of acting can produce some dazzling results, but when time is running out, you often want one take wonders like Don and Peter.

I never really had to direct Peter, he just hit his mark and delivered the goods. Occasionally he would look to me to

"Acting, it's not a field, I think, for people who need to have success every day: if you can't live with a nightly sort of disaster, you should get out"
John Malkovich

When trying to attract a star cast on a low budget film, the screenplay is without doubt the most valuable asset a production company can offer an actor

see if he was going down the right alley, or I would ask him to emphasise something, but that's about it. There was one scene with Peter and Don. What a dream it was. One take. Perfect. It was that simple.

Q - So, it's a false economy to use method actors?

Chris - It can be. If time is very short and there just isn't money to get it right, it's better to get a scene covered badly than half the script covered well - half a script doesn't make a feature film. Peter didn't need to immerse himself in the character to play Steckler - he didn't need to keep a knife in his inside pocket, or follow women home from work, just to see how it felt.

It's great if you're Daniel Day-Lewis in a multi million dollar movie. Time is a luxury we did not have. People who have lots of experience in front of the camera know what it takes to play the lead in a film, they know about pacing a character, knowing when to say - *no, we don't need another take.* I remember a scene with Don Henderson - I ummed after a shot and he said - *no, that was fine.* I'd never come across an actor who didn't want more screen time. Don knew that he couldn't give any more so why waste time and money doing another one.

Q - Stars often won't sign until the last minute?

Chris - We were shooting before Peter actually signed.

"You could heave a brick out of the window & hit 10 actors who could play my parts. I just happened to be on the right corner at the right time"
Boris Karloff

This isn't a desperate attempt to raise much needed funds, it's the multi talented crew helping out as the cast!

"The principal benefit acting has afforded me is the money to pay for my psychoanalysis"
Marlon Brando

Principal photography had started. Peter only became involved two days before we began his scenes. It was very tight. That is a problem but it is one of the burdens of having no money. You have to keep a reserve in mind in case your star can't or won't do it.

Q - Did you have to wait until the last minute?

Chris - If an actor says - *I want to do this film* - there are usually a couple of provisos. They might want the dialogue altered to suit them, or a say in the co-star. You have a choice then, to say yes or no. They will only sign at the last moment, just to make sure they don't get that call from Spielberg after they are signed to some low-budget thing. As you get close to shooting the chances become more remote of that call coming and your chances get better.

Q - Main cast professionals. Minor cast are friends?

Chris - Absolutely. Every single crew member of *White Angel* appears in the film. Genevieve actually plays four different characters. A classic example - we were shooting a late night scene with an actress who was to play a prostitute, but she didn't turn up so Gen put on the wig etc and did the scene. I'm in it as a forensic expert. It's unavoidable, but it makes the film very personal and saves you a whole heap of money. Why employ the services of a professional 'extra' to stand around or to hold up a hammer and say - *I found it sir* - I'm not trying to knock actors but often, it's not too demanding, esepecially if it's just a face in a shot. That doesn't mean give the job to anyone though. When you've got ten grand, you're not going to waste even ten quid when anyone can do it. Get friends and relatives. Get them to pay to be in it. Get them to invest money in the film and you'll give them a role. One guy paid a thousand pounds to play one part in *White Angel* (unfortunately, we had to cut him out). But be aware that they might be crap, so audition them and see if they can act. Have a backup plan, don't rely on non professional actors to be able to deliver.

Not all performances require highly skilled thespian abilities...

Q - Did you give him back his thousand pounds?

Chris - No.

Q - What about crew. How do you get the best people possible?

Chris - The initial crew was myself (the director), and Genevieve (the producer). Jon Walker, the DOP who shot *The Runner,* was also very involved with the script for *White Angel and* we have a very good working relationship with him. For the rest of the crew we sent the feelers out - people who knew people who knew people. We had some experienced professionals come in. They said how much they wanted. Then, we'd say - *I'm sorry - Can you do it for this?* Sometimes we got a yes, but mostly a no.

We had very few industry names involved. What we did get was intense dedication from a crew of relatively inexperienced people. Everyone who was there, wanted to be there, and that got us through the rough. Our experience in production pacing also saved the production from disaster.

On a film school project, the crew could work anywhere between three and ten days, and for 24 hours a day. That's fine for film school, but you can't work people like that for anywhere near as long as it takes to shoot a feature film. You can run a film crew into the ground in the first week but by the third week you will pay severely.

When we made *The Runner* the crew had even less experience and I had never made a feature. I didn't think - *let's run the crew into the ground* - but I did think - *Whatever it takes to get the shot* - On the first day we shot for twenty hours and everyone had two hours sleep. The next day another twenty hours - it was okay for the first few days because everyone was high on adrenaline and the buzz of making a movie.

Then, two weeks into the film everyone got the flu, and on virtually the same day. It closed the production. People could work four hours, maybe six, and only at half speed. Treat your crew professionally. Never work more than twelve hours. Never work more than six days a week. If you treat them professionally, they will act professionally. Actually, there's not a lot to film-making if you have the right team behind you. The heads of department should lead. If you have the right producer, DOP, Assistant Director etc the crew need not be as experienced. They will be told what to do.

A classic example is the production designer on *White Angel,* Mark Sutherland. He'd never been near a movie in his life but he became famous for getting the job done. Sometimes he'd

Using Friends as Actors

Actors cost money. Even if they offer to work for free they will at some point probably ask for money for train fares etc. It is almost essential that your principal cast are pros, but if push comes to shove, friends and relatives are an option. If casting a friend or relative...

1. You will still need a contract. Always make a contract with everyone that appears in front of the camera - carry release forms that can be filled in on the spot. Not only will this protect you legally, but the sales agent will require these documents.

2. Unless you are sure of their skills, don't give them any important role. Be aware that they could be spectacularly awful. They may also be unprofessional.

3. It is more likely that they will endure hardship and abuse than an unpaid actor - so if you need 'a body in the lake', ask a relative (you will still get earache, but you will be able to persuade them).

4. Equity, the actors union won't like you making a non union film - beware.

5. Friends and relatives are great if you need a crowd - they will even come in costume (but beware of damaged egos when a costume is terrible).

6. Always consider an actor over a non actor, even if the actor in question has little or no experience. They want to be there and will have some training. There are thousands of actors just waiting for a break. Contact SBS, PCR or the Stage.

The Skip

A Production Designers Dream. One man's rubbish is another man's treasure. And a skip can be a treasure chest for the production designer who has to build the impossible with a budget that would barely buy lunch.

1. Skips are often filled with wood, the main material needed in construction. Don't be proud, scavenge.

2. Don't buy materials from a DIY shop, find a local timber merchant, or building supplier where you can buy at trade prices.

3. Everything is reusable. Don't be tempted to get a skip! Keep everything in storage until the shoot is over. It is guaranteed that if you junk something, the next day it will be needed.

4. Keep a close eye on tools, they are expensive & have a tendency to go walkies.

5. When it comes to the person who is going to oversee the construction of any sets, find someone who is ready to 'go for it'. The construction supervisor is like the caretaker - at the end of the day, whatever they say, goes.

6. Think about re-using sets & locations. Although White Angel is set in a large house, we only shot in one room. A few posters, different curtains, a false plywood wall & a lick of paint all created the illusion of different rooms.

have stupid deadlines. The house where we shot *White Angel* was a three up, two down semi-detached in Ruislip. Now we had three bedrooms upstairs, one of which was the production office, one of which was a bedroom for the production team and the other was make-up and wardrobe. So, no bedroom scenes could be shot upstairs. Downstairs there was a living room and a back room. The backroom became the store room. So, apart from the hall and kitchen, we had one room in which to shoot - this room would have to change, when required, into the front room, backroom, all three bedrooms and anything else that was needed.

Day one - it was dressed as Steckler's bedroom. Overnight, Mark tore that down and built Carter's bedroom. Day two - we shot Carter's bedroom. It was torn down overnight and replaced with the living room including one huge hole in the wall. Virtually, the entire film was shot in that one room and we never waited for the set to be finished. Mark always got the job done on time and under budget. Everybody would muck in and pick up a paintbrush. Once a film begins shooting, it's like a rolling ball - difficult to stop - It's just a matter of how quickly and how well it will be done.

Another example of Mark's flexibility came when we had finished the film and we had a test screening where the audience offered suggestions. The one thing that was clear is that the ending was wrong.

In the original ending, Steckler shuffles in after being stabbed, shot, bashed etc, straps Carter into a chair and starts drilling into her head with a dentist drill. It was a great bit of *Friday 13th* style movie hokum, but everyone seemed to say that it felt like the end of a different movie - it just didn't fit. So we decided to re-shoot the end. We returned to the house where we shot the original footage. Unfortunately, in the interim, American drug dealers had taken over this house and wouldn't let us within a thousand yards of it. So, Mark Sutherland came up with the idea of a set. But where could we build it? In our garage of course. So, we built the hallway and part of the living room in the garage at the front of our house.

We painted the walls, put wallpaper up, built false windows and re-shot the whole end section of the film. The actors were very good and never said anything, I guess they were used to our peculiar ways. I must admit that when I said to

Peter - *let's go to the studio* - I think he was expecting something different from our garage. I remember him walking in - he was very impressed and said *this is fine*. But he did say it was one of the strangest places he'd ever had to shoot. No-one ever knew and we got away with the cheat.

Q - Everyone does everything?

Chris - People like to put film-makers in boxes. This person is an editor, that person is a designer. Most film-makers are just that. People who love making films. Everyone would like to direct but most don't expect to be doing that to start with. So, you get this crossover where everyone can do everyone else's job. One day the sound man was ill so Jon Walker took over and recorded sound as well as lighting the film. That's a tremendous asset. Whatever shit happens (and it always does) you can deal with it.

Q - Did you ever overcrew?

Chris - We just made sure there was enough crew to do the job. For instance, we had two make-up artists which was a conscious decision. The film is about two characters who were needed for shooting almost every day - with two make-up artists we were ready to shoot half an hour earlier every day. That was worth it.

Q - You say it was a small crew, but the credits do seem to be quite extensive?

Gen - Yes, if you have a low-budget picture it's a

> "In my own mind, I'm not sure that acting is something for a grown man to be doing"
> Steve McQueen

Because the location where White Angel was shot appeared to have been taken over by American drug dealers, the house had to be rebuilt in minute detail - in the garage! - Inset above, how the garage looked in the final film.

CASE STUDIES

Employing Crew

1. Wherever possible, hire the best person you can get.

2. Ask around your industry friends & crew (who are in place) if they know anyone who would work on the film.

3. Crew up in advance, especially the main departments like sound, camera, design. If you don't, you may find yourself on set wthout a sound recordist. Don't put an amateur at the head of a department like photography or sound.

4. Film schools are a good source of cheap & cheerful labour. A dedicated student will work wonders.

5. Try & pay everyone, if only a little. People work better with cash in their pockets.

6. Try & avoid deferred payments and offer everyone a buy out deal for a lesser amount.

7. Get production staff in as early as possible. They can start solving simple but time consuming problems. Again, a dedicated film student would excel in this area.

8. Always cover travel expenses & feed the crew. This will avoid rebellion when you least need it.

9. Treat everyone with fairness & honesty. Never lie about the money or the conditions. That way, no-one will ever have cause for complaint.

10. Avoid working more than 12 hours a day & 6 days a week. An exhausted crew becomes demoralised & ineffective.

11. Contact CrewsNews and place an ad. (see yellow pages at back)

good idea to make up about fifty fictitious names in your titles especially if you only have 15 or maybe 20 people working on the team - it makes your movie look more expensive. A few extra credits can also stretch the length of your film if it is a little on the short side. Chris edited the film and I edited the sound. We chose to use pseudonyms to make it look as if we could afford an editor and sound editor.

Q - Was the main reason for editing the film yourselves financial?

Gen - Yes, it was mainly because we couldn't afford to get anyone to cut it for us, so we thought why not do it ourselves. Plus the fact, we wanted to learn the process of editing.

Q - And are you pleased that you did it in the end?

Gen - Yes, because we saved ourselves money and learnt a lot in the process.

Q - What were the main difficulties in editing?

Chris - Objectivity. Staying objective on something that firstly, you wrote, then directed, saw the rushes, sunk up, rough cut, fine cut - It's like the third part of a triathlon. Just being objective about material, *'should that scene have gone or should it have stayed?'* - and keeping the energy up whilst being wracked by paranoia. Technically, we didn't know what we were doing, we'd never cut anything before, so we just had to start on day one, with *oops how do we edit film*, and learn by our errors.

Q - Did you find there was trouble keeping the story-line running through it?

Gen - No, it was obvious when things either weren't working or when the pace was slower than a glacier. We actually didn't shoot too much, our cutting ratio was 4 or 5 to 1 so we didn't have too much material with which to go crazy.

Q - Did you storyboard?

Gen - No, we thought it to be a waste of resources for a low-budget picture. If you have a good storyboard artist and you can afford the time, then great, but otherwise you don't need

it (note *Urban Ghost Story* utilised storyboards). *White Angel* was also restricted by the locations and many times, the rough shooting script that Chris had worked out had to be scrapped because it just couldn't be done in the location we found, or because we just ran out of time and money and ended up shooting the scene in a single wide shot just to cover the action and plot.

The crew for White Angel looks large when everyone is standing together, but every department was honed down to the absolute minimum required to get the job done quickly and efficiently.

Q - Why Super 16mm?

Chris - Super 16mm is different from Sstandard16mm in so much as the negative houses a larger picture area. It's pretty much standard 16mm stock with the right hand redundant sprocket hole dropped. This allows the picture area to expand giving a larger negative AND it maintains roughly the same

The Arriflex BL (right) is perhaps the cheapest camera that can be considered. Solid, robust and often somewhat noisy - and hey, it looks like a real movie camera

The Aaton (left) is the Super 16mm low budget dream camera. Lightweight and easy to operate - just throw it on your shoulder and you're away.

CASE STUDIES

Choosing a Lab

1. Lab contacts are usually very friendly. It's a good idea to go and look round a lab just so that you know roughly how everything is done.

2. Keep in contact with the labs and try not to run up a serious debt without funds to pay. When the film is ready for delivery, the lab could withhold the neg until payment is made. This is a big problem and should be avoided. Find out who the accounts person is and keep them sweet.

3. Try and get an all in deal where you agree a fixed price for a fixed amount of footage, including all sound transfers, stock, even couriers dropping off the stock and rushes.

4. Don't always believe what a lab tells you. Their staff can be ignorant and stubborn. Your cameraman can be a useful source of information here.

5. Get some figures from other production companies to see if the quotes you are being given could be bettered.

6. You will probably edit on a computer non linear system. Make sure the labs telecine your footage with ALL the technical information onscreen such as roll number, keycode, time code etc. Ensure they know what film speed you shoot at (25fps), the sound sample rate (44.1 khz) and aspect ratios (1.85 -1 for Super 16mm). Our recomendations in brackets.

7. Labs are often a source of a good free lunch!

aspect ratio as 35mm. This means that when blown up it creates an image that is roughly 40% better than if it were blown up from normal 16mm. It costs just as much to blow up normal 16mm as it does Super 16mm, and it's expensive, but there is no denying, it is cheaper to get a movie in the can on Super 16 than 35mm.

Q - How does it technically work?

Chris - Firstly you shoot Super 16, that is expose super 16 neg. That neg is then rush printed, the rush print is cut by the editor, the final edit is agreed and the original Super 16mm negative is cut. That cut is then printed onto Super 16mm stock and when everyone is happy with the way it all looks (the grading), it gets blown up to 35mm interpositive then from that 35mm interpos to a 35mm interneg. That interneg is now the final master 35mm negative from which all the prints are made. (Both the 35mm interneg and interpos need to be present for delivery to the sales agent). It is possible to do a direct blow up from the Super 16mm to 35mm print, but it is hellishly expensive and kind of pointless. If money is tight, you could produce a Super 16mm interpos and blow up at the interneg point - I've never done it but I have heard of other films doing it.

Q - How did you decide the final cut for White Angel?

Chris - We had about 95 million different final cuts - this is going back to being objective, because you're so damn close to the thing. We were really happy with our first final cut and had begun track laying and getting ready for the dub when our cameraman, Jon Walker came round and took a look at it. We were saying *Isn't it brilliant*...but he reckoned we could lose some stuff. We went through the film slowly and Jon's point of view made us sit and think about it differently. We ended up cutting about 12 minutes out of what we thought was our final cut - we neg cut, printed it at a running time of 99/100 minutes and we went to the Montreal Film Festival and watched it with a full audience - they enjoyed it but it was quite obvious more needed to come out.

When we returned to the UK, we thought let's have another fine cut - we went back and cut another 6 minutes out, called that the final movie - re-premiered it at the London Film Festival and everything was going swimmingly. Then only 5 to 6 months later, we decided that we had to do yet another re-cut for the international market, to make the film more sexy and violent. We cut out 10 minutes, put some other stuff back in - all this is about 3 years after the film was shot in the first place! We needed more 'oomph' so we re-shot stuff, got Harriet back, with a completely different hair cut and reconstructed the film yet again. All the new stuff was shot on Hi8 video and helped give it a much more seedy and voyeuristic look - we are kind of pleased with it now.

Gen - We also had an audience test with our first rough cut. We arranged a screening at some offices where the staff agreed to stop behind to watch the film - they were all complete strangers and we wanted to see what effect it had. They came back with - *well we thought it was great in this part, but maybe too slow in the middle* - so we decided we could chop out more in the middle. That was also the dreaded point when we discovered that the ending of the film was wrong and we had to go back and reshoot that.

Q - The music is a strong part of White Angel. How did you decide on a theme?

Gen - There were certain composers whose music we liked a lot, for instance Bernard Hermann who did most of Hitchcocks' movies, and we felt that *White Angel* needed a Bernard Herman type score, with mystery, intrigue, suspense and a big orchestra feel. When we initially started out, we were going to have computer synthesised sounding music - then we found Harry Gregson-Williams who could pull off a brilliant 'orchestral sounding' theme and we jumped on him. He could take a few musicians and turn them into what sounded like the London Symphony Orchestra.

> "Editing is crucial. Imagine James Stewart looking at a mother nursing her child. You see the child, then cut back to him. He smiles. Now Mr Stewart is a benign old gentleman. Take away the middle piece of film and substitute a girl in a bikini. Now he's a dirty old man"
> Hitchcock

Harry Gregson-Williams wrote the score for White Angel. He then went on to write the scores for Antz, Armageddon and Enemy of The State!

The Final Cut

It's likely that at some point, you may need to get involved with another company. If this happens they will more than likely demand 'final cut'.

1. Try not to give up the final cut. However, listen to what people tell you. If they say they are bored, it is likely something needs to be done, cutting scenes down for instance.

2. If you do have to give up the final cut, fight for your version in a diplomatic way. If you don't & things get nasty, you'll be sure your opinion will never be heard.

3. If you hate the final cut, don't worry. Five years down the line you'll never think about it, & if you see the picture, you may well agree with the re-edit!

4. Often, directors will cling to scenes when they need to go. The final cut isn't an attempt to ruin the film, merely make it more palatable to the audience. In general, everyone has the film's best interest at heart. Remember this & don't let things get out of hand.

5. If the worst comes to the worst, then take action if you have to. James Cameron allegedly crept into the neg cutting rooms on 'Piranha 2 the Flying Killers' & re-cut the movie AFTER the executives had agreed on the final cut.

6. As a director or producer it is likely that you have less objectivity & more emotional investment in the film than anyone. Listen to other people's comments.

Chris - At various stages during the editing, we cut a lot of music from other films into *White Angel* in order to make it feel more like a finished movie. We used a lot of *Basic Instinct* - that had the right feel and pace. When it came to the music being composed by Harry, we said, listen to this, this is kind of what we want - and then he took all of what that music was 'saying' and regenerated it in his own original way and worked in his own theme and composition. At the end of the day the music doesn't sound anything like what we originally wanted, it sounds better as it is a completely original interpretation of the film. Dubbing on other music just helped everyone focus on what we were aiming at.

We also considered using out of copyright music because it's free. You don't pay copyright on the music, only on the performance. There were loads of music libraries and we could have used anything, from Brahms to Beethoven with a full orchestra for about £250 per thirty seconds. That's world-wide rights. The problem was finding the right music to fit the scenes. If you're doing Amadeus Part 2, then you're fine, but not a UK based serial killer thriller.

Q - Sound mixing is where it all comes together, how did that go?

Chris - Most of the sound in *White Angel*, apart from the dialogue, has been recreated in the studio, and by the studio, I mean our front room, not a several thousand pounds a minute studio. Most low-budget films suffer from poor sound and we were determined that *White Angel* was at least going to sound good.

Q - How does the dubbing process work?

Chris - We ran through the whole movie and we added an effect for every single little thing that happened, be it somebody putting a cup down, somebody scratching their face, whatever it was, we add an effect - all those sound effects were then track laid onto different pieces of magnetic film (which is the same size as picture film, but instead of pictures it's got a magnetic coat) - you can cut and chop it about any way you like.

We ended up with I guess about 12 - 15 tracks of sound - 2 music tracks, 2 dialogue tracks, 3 or 4 effects tracks which would be stereo as would be the music, 2 Foley tracks, 2 or

3 atmosphere tracks - which would be background sound, and then on occasion 1 or 2 extra tracks for when we had problems or when there was a heavy sequence. All those tracks are then premixed, we mixed the 2 dialogues into one, the 2 music into one, the effects into 1, the atmos into 1 - we end up with 4 or 5 different pre-mixed tracks being atmos, music, dialogue, effects whatever, and those were finally mixed into one Dolby (surround) master, which is when it sounds great.

Q - What is Dolby stereo?

Chris - There is a lot of confusion about this, Dolby produce several noise reduction systems which are free to use, but Dolby, often referred to as surround sound, carries a license fee to use in cinemas, but free for TV and festivals. If you just complete you mix for TV, video and festivals you don't pay, then if you sell to a theatrical distributor you pay the fee then. Dolby is a type of encoding that creates a four track mix - left, centre, right and surround speakers. It's clever because it encodes those four tracks into two to make it backwards compatible with pretty much all the sound equipment in the world. Now there is a big push to use the digital formats like SDDS or Dolby Digital. Great but they carry a license fee, and in reality, to low budget film makers, it makes little difference. I'd save your money and put it onscreen. When we made *White Angel*, I think there was a licensing fee of about £3k, which was a lot of money, and they wouldn't budge on it. *The Runner* was not dubbed in Dolby and it can be argued that *The Runner* has a better soundtrack than *White Angel*.

Q - How did you prepare for the dub?

Chris - We had a hell of a time as we weren't ready for our dub. We had a new computer system on which the sound was laid and three days before the mix we found out that it was all out of sync. We had to start from scratch and re sync every effect. We worked solidly for three days and nights, I had never done that before, and I hope never to do so again. We were still cutting hours before the mix but we got there. Fortunately we had been good about track laying and everything was pretty much covered so there weren't any panicked cover up jobs.

Q - What was it like in the dubbing theatre?

The Final Mix

This is when all your sound effects, music & dialogue are mixed into one. It's the most exciting moment of the whole process as your movie seems to leap into life.

1. Sound studios are expensive. Make sure you are prepared, your charts are clear & any creative decisions have been made.

2. Mix in stereo. You can opt for analogue Dolby which is a surround system, free for TV, video and festivals, but you pay for cinema. There are other digital formats, each with a fee for use. Stick to Dolby.ypes of surround encoding which are cheaper, such as DTS.

3. Dolby 'A' and 'SR' are noise reduction systems. It's advisable to do all your premixes with some kind of noise reduction. Dolby 'SR' is superior. This isn't such an issue now as Digital is common and doesn't suffer from tape hiss.

4. Get to know your dubbing mixer. Push them to be satisfied with 90% and don't waste time trying to get that last little effect absolutely perfect. Often a film will mix itself, so avoid trying to get that last 10% out of the mix, it will cost you 90% of your time!

5. It's possible to mix a feature film in 3, 4 or 5 days (with M&E - see point 7). Don't let the mixers persuade you into 3 weeks.

6. If camera noise is a problem, most of it can be filtered out, but not all. Either post sync the dialogue or lay a heavy atmos track over it, eg. a plane flying over, or a printing press.

CASE STUDIES

7. A good foley artist (footstep) works wonders. A foley artist is the person who adds the rustles, footsteps etc. Spend a good 2 day session here and you will have a much livelier sound track.

8. Cheap computer software and hardware can be used. Most PC's can record in 16 bit digital stereo. Sound effects can be recorded and cleaned up in programs like Cool Edit Pro (free download from the web) and editing programs like Premiere can be used to track lay sound effects. This isn't ideal and presents a few technical headaches, but it is possible.

9. Produce a Music and Effects mix (M&E) at the same time as your master mix. The M&E is a mix of the film without any dialogue, to be used for dubbing in foreign territories. This is essential and you will be unable to sell your film without it.

10. Work out what kind of stock you need for you master mix and buy some before you go to the studio. They will try to sell you the tapes at an increased price. Alternatively, do a deal including all stock. Don't underestimate how these charges can mount up.

11. The Dubbing Theatre is the best environment you will ever hear your film. What may seem like an over the top sound effect may be to subtle on a TV speaker. Make sure all plot sound effects or dialogue is clear and correctly emphasised.

Chris - Great, it's where everything comes together. It's dark, it's loud and there are lots of plush sofas and free coffee. The only down side is that it's so expensive and there is always this urgency to get to the end of the picture. There is absolutely NO room for perfection in a low-budget dub. We paid about £200 per hour and mixed for two days, the second day we went late into the night. Big overtime, so I guess we needed three days. I would recommend a minimum of three days and five is better, that would give you time to cover the M&E mix as well. If you're not prepared, you're going to have a terrible time so have everything track laid, know your movie inside out, and just go for it. Good charts are also vital.

We had some pretty bad camera noise which the mixer managed to filter out - not all of it though, so we added a printing press over the top. Don't ever believe that you can get rid of 100% of a noise, unless you're prepared to cut it out completely (dialogue and all). There are amazing things possible at the dub but it all takes time, if you have a 2 hour movie, it takes you 2 hours just to go through it, and you have to go through it at least twice, once for pre-mixes and then your final mix, so you've lost 4 hours just in screen time, never mind changing reels. All this and there's still only 8 hours in the working day.

Q - What is the M&E mix?

Gen - The M&E is the Music and Effects Mix. When you're selling overseas, the buyer will want a copy of the soundtrack without the dialogue so that they can dub over in their own language.

Chris - To actually do the mix is easy, all the mixer has to do is to pull the dialogue tracks out - if you've properly track-laid it and there's good foley, there shouldn't be any problems. The problems with the M&E mix come when you're deciding on what format to mix. Full M&E in stereo or split Music and Effects? We did both in the end but the one we use most, if not all the time is the traditional split Music and Effects, music on track one, everything else on track two.

We also ran headlong into a problem at the telecine. Whilst the video format we chose could take four tracks of sound, (the full stereo mix on tracks 1 & 2, the M&E mix on tracks 3 & 4), we couldn't lay it all down at the same time as the telecine machine could only handle one set of 16mm magnetic sound at a time - we had two separate mixes, two separate sets of mag. We ended up having to telecine it once and then re-run the whole lot for the M&E mix - that doubled our telecine budget straight away, and like the dub, it's damn expensive to start with. Now you could do the sound off DAT but even then you'd have to do it twice, to monitor to ensure that nothing went wrong.

Probably the easiest way to deal with this now is to separate everything. Get the telecine down onto DigiBeta and just concentrate on getting the picture right. Then go to a sound facility, or even the sound department at the TK house, and get them to transfer your full stereo mix to tracks 1&2 of the DigiBeta, then the M&E to tracks 3&4 of the DigiBeta. You'll also need to ask them to pass both mixes through a compressor limiter as the mix you have may well be too dynamic for TV and video. Just make sure they keep the audio levels legal.

"In a good movie, the sound could go off and the audience would still have a perfectly good idea of what is going on."
Hitchcock

Q - By the time you do the dub do you have a sales agent?

Gen - We didn't, but we did speak to a sales agent to see what they would want. By that time you should have sales agents interested enough for them to explain to you what they would require.

Q - What happened about foley?

Gen - We had an amazing woman called Diane Greaves do

The dub can be a harrowing event and there is no space for perfection. Make all creative decisions in advance as a five minute discussion about a bird sound effect could cost you £30!

CASE STUDIES

TV Standards

If you buy a video in the USA, it won't play back in the UK. This is because they have a different TV standard - NTSC. We operate on PAL. When you look at the world there are many different TV standards for which to cater.

1. When sending out a VHS for viewing, it is acceptable to send a PAL copy. Most companies now have multi standard VHS players.

2. PAL is a superior system to NTSC. If you intend to master a video tape, but also have to supply the tape in NTSC or SECAM, produce in PAL & make digital systems transfers to NTSC or SECAM. It is possible to do a separate NTSC telecine but this may well cost too much.

3. SECAM and PAL tapes are partly compatible. If one is played back on the other system, the picture will go black & white, but it is still viewable.

4. Some domestic video recorders can play back NTSC & SECAM. There are some pro VHS decks which can playback & record PAL, NTSC & SECAM, the Panasonic WV1 for instance.

5. A blank tape can be used for any system. A blank tape from the US can be used in the UK for recording and will last slightly longer as the tape speed is different. Be aware that tape lengths and timings are system specific. A VHS 90 minute tape from the UK will not accommodate a ninety minute film recorded in NTSC (it's about a quarter longer).

the foley - the foley, or footsteps as it is sometimes called in the UK, is where someone adds all the sounds that an actor makes just moving around. She would add the leather creak in a jacket, the footsteps on gravel, the sitting on sofas. Diane would make a sound for pretty much everything that happened on screen. She would watch the film through and then do all the foley in one pass! She truly was amazing. We foleyed the whole picture in one very long day and it made all the difference in both the full dub and especially the M&E mix.

Q - What was the first print like?

Chris - The first 35mm print we saw wasn't great - the sound disappeared half way through, it was really dirty and it was a bit of a nightmare as some cast members were present.

At the very last stage there was an accident in the lab and our neg was ripped. We didn't have any insurance so had to go back and reshoot! Thank goodness there were no actors in any of the shots that were damaged or that could have turned into a complete nightmare.

Q - What was it like seeing the print for the first time?

Chris - It was fine, we just knew it was going to be another uphill battle to get it all fixed.

Q - Did you have any problems with the telecine?

Gen - Yes, firstly we produced a widescreen telecine which no distributor could use, so we had to do another. We mastered to D1 and the film was supposed to fit, but the tape ended fifteen seconds before the final end credit, so we had to recompile on another D1 tape.

The sound was not compressed in advance so we had to do another sound dub and lay the M&E down at the same time. The first print we got out of the lab was too dark so we had a battle with the lab to make up a new Super 16mm print with the printer lights increased to give a brighter image. So yes, we had some problems, it all got fixed eventually but it cost an arm and a leg in both time and money.

Q - What was the first thing you did once you completed the film?

Gen - Slept for a week.

Chris - Yeah but when we got our own VHS of the film we literally drove home at 100mph ran into the living room, put it on the telly and watched it. We'd spent the past two years seeing this film in bits and we didn't know what it looked like all strung together.

Gen - We didn't know whether the film worked as a thriller or not. We never saw it in one continuous stream and this was the first time we could watch it from beginning to end.

Q - What was it like?

Gen - Quick, it seemed to fly through. It was brilliant.

Q - How did you approach selling the film once it was completed?

Chris - We didn't have a sales agent or a UK distributor on board. Miramax had made a few phone calls to ask

> "The movies today are too rich to have any room for genuine artists. They produce a few passable craftsmen, but no artists. Can you imagine a Beethoven making $100,000 a year?"
> H. L. Mencken

The final telecine is an invigorating yet terrifying experience. It is the very last stage of production and once traversed, the film is technically completed. However, it is hellishly expensive and fraught with potential technical errors.

Your Negative

All your efforts as a film maker are sealed in the neg which is exposed on set. It's therefore a good idea to treat your neg as though it were gold dust.

1. Make sure it is processed as soon as possible.

2. On the whole, unless your ASA is very high, X Ray machines don't present too much of a threat to exposed neg, so don't attempt to bribe any official in a weird banana republic when entering customs - just let it pass through the machine!

3. Your sound is as important as your neg. Store your tapes or DATs in a safe place.

4. Neg doesn't last forever and should be stored someplace cool and dry. For a small fee the lab will store your neg in a vault at the correct temperature and humidity.

5. Don't ever throw away or erase your Beta SP telecine masters if you have chosen to cut non linear. They are the only way back to your master negative edge numbers.

6. Don't underestimate just how much stuff a feature film generates. 100 rolls of unused cut neg, 5 rolls of A&B roll cut neg, 5 rolls of S16 Interpos, 5 rolls of 35mm Internegative, 5 rolls on 35mm negative, prints, 50 master sound tapes, 50 master BetaSP tapes, 5 rolls of 35mm optical sound, master sound mix tapes, optical effects and titles negs and internegs... You get the picture.

what this strange film called *White Angel* was about, and a few of the big American players like Paramount and 20th Century Fox faxed us at three in the morning, which was quite fun, but essentially we had to start from scratch. Firstly, we set up meetings with five UK based sales agents and sat them down to watch *White Angel* - the idea was that we would then field the offers from those meetings.

Gen - We couldn't afford screenings at a theatre where everyone would sit down and watch together, so we decided it would be better to give everyone their own individual screening in a small studio - we set up a really good sound system and monitor, dimmed the lights and let the film do the job. We sat outside, between the door and the lift so there was no chance of them making a swift exit.

Chris - The reactions we got were mixed. First of all, Manifesto didn't turn up and we had to drop a tape off with them, Majestic watched it and left 5 minutes before the end saying it was too long and didn't have enough scope for them, Mayfair saw it and would get back to us, The Feature Film Company saw it and liked it but ummed and aahed. Finally, Miramax saw it and visibly liked it a lot - obviously Miramax is THE biggest distributor and sales agent of low-budget independent features in the world, and the fact they were interested was very exciting.

Gen - Their UK acquisitions rep sat and watched the movie and thoroughly enjoyed it. She told us that she believed *White Angel* could be a hit at the up-coming Cannes Film Festival - Peter could win awards and we would win Best First Film. She was sure Miramax could do a great deal with it. We talked about advances etc.

Chris - Yes, we were very specific about what we wanted - a big cash advance to cover the budget and pay the cast and crew, and that was all we wanted. We said we needed an advance of £450,000 against all rights, which was double what we needed, and that we wanted an answer quickly. She said, *No problem, I think we can probably do that and I can give you an answer in 48 hours.*

Gen - She told us that she was flying to New York for the weekend to see Bob and Harvey, and that she would like to take a copy of the film, and get back to us on Monday. She did get back to us, telling us that they had seen it but they

The Haymarket in central London on the wet Friday morning of the theatrical release for White Angel.

hadn't got an exact answer yet - '*but we're all really positive about it*'. She was very hyper about it, and again, we thought it was great.

However, as we ran up to Cannes the channels of communication dried up, even after this amazing amount of interest and promises. When we tried to contact her, our calls would either be directed somewhere or she was 'out of the office'. This was a little weird after she had been so positive. Then we got a letter in the post, saying *Thanks very much, we're not interested. Goodbye*; pp'd by somebody else.

Remember, this was after the intimation that we were going to get a very large cash advance with world-wide distribution, and we would pretty much win the Palm D'Or.

Chris - The basic message is to take everything you hear with a pinch of salt, keep your options open, hassle for the money, and don't let the situation rest, pursue it. If you can't speak to the person, and they say they are still thinking

> "The Future. That period of time in which our affairs prosper, our friends are true and our happiness is assured"
> Ambrose Bierce

377

ORION
PICTURES CORPORATION

VIA FAX: #011-44-

September 13, 1

Genevieve Jol
Living Spirit
The Old Pict
Throughpam, S
Stroud, Glo
England

Dear Ms.

Thank
Unfortu
We are
for M
Angel
my
(fax

T
B

Paramount Pictures

SENT BY: JOHN FERRARI

MOTION PICTURE GROUP

June 7, 1993

Ms. Genevieve Jolliffe
Living Spirit Pictures
FAX: (44-285) 821-843
Dear Ms. Jolliffe:

I recently read about your film WHITE ANGEL and would like to discuss
it with you at your earliest convenience.

Would you have a print of the film available for me to screen here at
Paramount in Los Angeles?

I look forward to hearing from you soon.

Kind regards,

JF

JF/db

A Paramount Communications Company

Midnight faxes from Hollywood did prove to be a tremendous giggle and ego boost, but ultimately bore no sales. However, it was good to establish contacts and worth noting that even small obscure British productions do get noticed by the major players of LA.

about it, then you are in an awkward situation - they may still be thinking about it, or they may be giving you the run-around. However, if they really are interested they will come up with an offer within 7 days, and anything over 7 days, then I think you have to say, *well thank you for the interest but really we want to show it to somebody else now.*

Q - Six weeks later you went to Cannes - did you take a print with you?

Chris - No, we didn't have a print then, remember we had shot on S16mm and making the 35mm blow up was going to be costly and we didn't want to incur any extra costs yet. We took 40 tapes of the film (telecinied from the S16mm answer print) and 40 tapes of the trailer that we had cut the night before. We also put together some sales literature that was literally cut and pasted together and printed on a colour laser photocopier before being laminated - it cost us about £100 to do 50 of these brochures, but they looked really good. When we got to Cannes, people were very impressed and thought we had spent thousands on the marketing!

Q - How do you gain entrance to the festival?

Gen - You are supposed to apply in advance, but most people end up leaving it to the last minute. The easiest way to gain access to the market is to turn up with a business card and two passport photos (just in case). Go to the festival accreditation, stand in a hot sweaty line, call yourself a producer when it's your turn and after a bit of pushing, you'll get a pass which will get you into everywhere you need to go.

Q - So if you had to sum up Cannes in one sentence what would it be?

Gen - Hot, blisters, hard work, expensive, bullshit, pornography, free drinks, little pieces of strange food on plates which you eat lots of because you can't afford the to eat properly.

Q - Did anyone show an active interest in the film?

Chris - Yes, we rented an apartment outside Cannes and drove in every day which worked out quite well as it was quite cheap to do that. We targeted every single world sales agent, visited all the hotels and every stand and told them that we had made this feature film called *White Angel* which was terribly good, *and* would they want to see the trailer, *and* would they like to keep a copy, *and* would they like a copy of the sales literature, *here you are and thank you very much,* gave them a business card and took one of theirs.

> "It's much easier to do a $4m deal in Hollywood than to get a film on the BBC for $10,000"
> Nick Marston

Gen - We felt we had to see exactly who was who, and what kind of films they did, so we knew precisely who to target. Obviously it was difficult to see the top people like Fox, Paramount or Universal etc., but everybody else who would have been impossible to see if you walked into their offices in LA, would be willing to see you in Cannes, especially if you have a film.

Q - So Cannes is a great place if you have a film to sell?

Chris - Cannes is an experience which brings the film sales business into sharp focus.

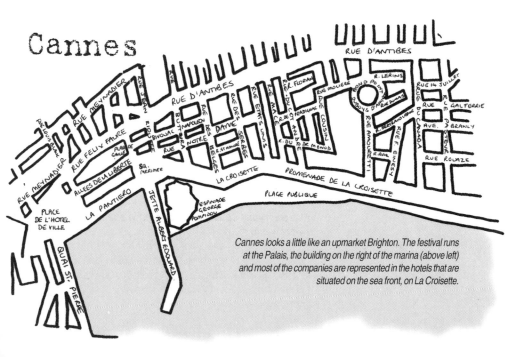

Cannes looks a little like an upmarket Brighton. The festival runs at the Palais, the building on the right of the marina (above left) and most of the companies are represented in the hotels that are situated on the sea front, on La Croisette.

Glossy sales brochures were out of the question so a full colour A3 sheet was pasted up with photos and a synopsis of the film - the torn paper effect was in keeping with the serial killer theme. The results were colour laser copied and laminated. They turned out to be both cheap and effective.

Gen - It is also about finding out which companies do what, learning the marketplace, meeting people either in their sales suites or at parties.

Q - What happened when they saw your trailer?

Gen - We would walk in to their suites, chat to them about the film, show them the trailer and get some feedback - yes, no or maybe. Those who were interested asked to know if we were going to have a screening back in LA after Cannes. No company made an offer there and then.

Chris - The main problem is that sales agents are not at the market to acquire product but to sell their product so it's actually one of the worst places to go to get a sales agent. Cannes is about the only place a film maker can go to and know that anyone who is anyone in the film industry is within one mile from where they are standing. That in itself can make getting a meeting doubly difficult and you do have to be very persistent - most people are booked up before they even leave for the airport to go to Cannes!

Gen - Out of the 100 people we saw, 80 of them were not the type of people who would pick up *White Angel* - they would go for schlock horror, movie rip offs, ninjas or porno - it's pretty sleazy. Films of quality seem to be sold independently, behind closed doors or not at the market at all.

We saw a bunch of Middle Eastern guys who saw the film and were interested, but we suspected they could be terrorists and decided not to do a deal with them. There was also an American company who thought it was wonderful and were very interested, but the thought that we would sign our film to a sales agent who was on another continent was quite terrifying in terms of keeping tabs on them and how much they were spending.

The only company who showed a real interest was Beyond Films. Being an Australian company they felt more in tune with our way of thinking, and because we knew that they had picked up another low budget UK film we felt there was more of a connection. Also at the time, they had done incredibly well with the sales for *Strictly Ballroom*. A week after Cannes we set up a screening for them in London - we felt everything was riding on this so we hired a screening room in Soho and sat their rep down to watch it in a theatre. He liked it. Beyond made an initial offer of something like £8k and then upped it to £25k and finally up to £75k, which was structured over a period of three years. The delivery requirements were quite horrendous and they wanted the film for a term of fifteen years.

We were concerned because of our experience on *The Runner* and the idea of handing the film over to Beyond for fifteen years with a staggered (over years) advance that wouldn't cover our minimal budget didn't sit too well. We had immediate debts that needed to be met so we offered them a £300,000 buy out for all rights but they didn't go for it.

Q - In retrospect, would it have been a good idea to take the deal?

Chris - Now that we know what we know and don't forget they were leaving the UK to us, perhaps it would have been

> 'All television ever did was shrink the demand for ordinary movies. The demand for extraordinary movies increased.'
> Clive James

The British Pavilion at the Cannes Film Market - a hotbed of moaning film makers basking like beached lobsters in the sun.

CASE STUDIES

Cannes -
A Survival Guide

1. The Cannes film market can be daunting. It brings the business of film sales sharply into focus and for that alone, it is a valuable experience.

2. If you are of a sensitive artistic nature - Don't go!

3. To gain entrance to most sections of the market you need a pass. The pass is free but you need to get to the registration area at the Palais during office hours with a business card and two passport photos. Get your photos at home or get ripped off in town.

4. All the companies have suites in the hotels along La Croisette (the front). It's a hot, long and hard trudge to do them all.

5. Book your meetings before you go and be prepared to be shuffled around without notice.

6. When you arrive at the airport, get a train or the bus into Cannes as a taxi will cost you £50.

7. Arrange your accommodation in advance. There are villas and small holiday flats which are quite cheap but are a good drive out of town. Staying in town is very expensive. Sleeping on the floor and sharing with twenty other film makers is also an option worth considering.

8. Everyone now uses mobile phones and you may end up with a huge mobile bill at the end.

9. Don't gush if you meet a star, it gives you away as a new-comer.

a good idea - just to get rid of the film. The thing to remember is that we were acting in the best interests of the investors and the company, we felt at the time that we couldn't accept what we considered a low offer when the film had only just been completed.

The other thing is that we did believe in the film, we were confident we had a very high quality low-budget film. It is a very hard decision to make and I guess one gets more experienced - what do you do if you believe your product is worth much more than your initial offers? How long can you wait before you have to take one? There are no hard and fast answers, only retrospective wishes. I don't think you can ever get it totaly right, but you can let go and move on to your next film.

Q - When you were faced with delivery requirements, was there anything that you didn't know about?

Chris - We knew about basic delivery requirements because we had done *The Runner,* so we knew about the immediate things like the Music and Effects mix or colour slides and that kind of thing. What we weren't prepared for from Beyond was the 25 page fax of the most unbelievable requirements, even down to things like alternative out takes on original master negative. Half of these we just didn't have and couldn't get - I'm sure they thought it was necessary but for a low-budget picture, some of the requirements were totally out of the question. Most companies had this kind of list, some differing slightly - but when it comes down to it, if they wanted the film, they would compromise as long as the main elements are in place, and that's no mean feat!

Gen - The one thing that we didn't know about at the time which came as a big shock was the Errors and Omissions Policy - an insurance policy which insures the producer and distributor against all sorts of weird legal actions, such as a person in America saying that the film is based on their brother - the only thing was that this would cost around £7k!

Q - So the best thing to do, is to have a good idea of what you need to deliver and say there it is, take it or leave it?

Chris - If you can't afford to make *full* delivery, then essentially yes, but you do have to be sure of what the sales agent really does need to sell the film. There are a lot of things that don't actually cost a lot that are on the delivery list, like having the proper contracts with every one involved, waiver forms, release forms, chain of title, legal documents proving country of origin. All of these are cheap to get together, but they do take time.

A delivery list will usually say 75 high quality B&W photographs and 75 high quality colour photographs. With the best will in the world you're not going to have that many good quality pictures on a low-budget film, it's just not going to happen - some lists require as many as 500 high quality photographs.

Q - Apart from Beyond, was there any other interest?

Gen - At Cannes we went to a solicitor's party and started chatting to two brothers, Simon and Andrew Johnson (of Pilgrim Entertainment), who had made a film called *Tale Of A Vampire*. They told us how they had sold the film themselves to a US company, turned a healthy profit and managed to hold onto the UK rights. We felt they were on our wavelength. It appeared they had gone through the same process we were going through but had frustratedly decided to do it all themselves, and they had come out on top. They were very interested in teaming up with us, because we all shared the same goals.

Chris - At the point of us turning down Beyond, Simon and Andrew of Pilgrim told us that they could guarantee deals with America and Japan through their contacts. They only wanted a three month window and ten percent so we decided to let them have a crack of the whip, after all they had been very successful with their film. Sure enough, within months we did have several deals on the table including a deal memo from Trimark who wanted the US rights plus Canada for US$120k advance plus extras which would top it up to roughly $250k.

Q - How did the American deal come about?

Chris - Michael Cole from Trimark acquisitions had seen the film at the Montreal Film Festival in September where we had four totally packed screenings. Michael Cole sat in on our last and best screening with an amazing audience who loved it, and negotiations began.

10. Eating out is very expensive. There are lots of cheap food joints if you are prepared to search in the backstreets. Try and get somone else to pay for lunch.

11. Parties are the lifeblood of Cannes - try and get as many tickets as possible. They are also a good source of free food and drinks. Whenever there is free food, eat it as you never know when your next meal is coming.

12. The European Pavilion offers a free message service for producers who don't have a base.

13. Cannes isn't a place where deals are signed, it is a place where contacts are made and negotiations are opened. Almost all your business will be done when you return, so don't expect to return with a napkin contract.

14. Remember why you are there and don't get too side-tracked by the glitz or the nightlife. Go with a clear objective, even if it is just to soak up the atmosphere and learn how it all works. This way you won't get too distracted. Sure, enjoy yourself, but remember, EVERYTHING is business.

15. There's always a TV crew waiting for a story. Embellish your position, get creative and get yourself on TV - it's easy, fun and shows you just how easy it is to create a buzz around your project.

16. You'll be high as a kite when you get back to the UK, try not to come down with too hard a bump and keep as much of the movie magic Cannes has left with you as long as possible.

The hotel corridors at Cannes are packed sales booths all adorned with hard sell posters for a dizzying array of low brow B movies.

"Shooting a film is like taking a stagecoach ride in the old West. At first you look forward to a nice trip. Later you just hope to reach your desination"
Francois Truffaut

Because of their previous relationship with Trimark we allowed Pilgrim to take over negotiations and they came up with the deal memo. Because of the Montreal screenings we started to get a lot of offers, Germany came in as we stepped off the plane from our return. We had to decide what to do, whether to extend our agreement with Pilgrim as sales agents or to carry on the negotiations ourselves. Because of the Trimark deal, we decided to extend the agreement and to leave all the negotiating to Pilgrim. The German deal happened and we actually got some money.

Q - How much was Germany?

Gen - Roughly £62,000 which was paid in three lump sums. Pilgrim took a slice off the top, about half was used to pay off some immediate debts and running costs which had piled up and the remainder was used to finance our UK theatrical release. Korea also came in at this point with an offer of $35,000 which we took. So at that point, we had nearly $350,000 signed, sealed but not delivered.

Q - How quickly did things happen?

Chris - Firstly it would take weeks and weeks to negotiate a deal. The one thing that was really infuriating was that somebody would make an offer, and then you wouldn't be able to contact them until they came back from their 3 week holiday or whatever - time just goes by. And because you can't sit across a table from these people, you had to call and get through their secretaries who weren't speaking the same language - certainly, in Korea, I know that became a real nightmare. Whatever we did, we just couldn't get an answer.

Q - Were you ready to deliver once a deal was signed?

Chris - Aside from making up the 1" dupe tape, and patching up a few problems with the M&E, yes we could have delivered. The problem we had with the states is that Pilgrim negotiated what they called minimum delivery i.e all you need to sell and exploit the film. Trimark agreed and signed in a deal memo, and then changed the goal posts in the long form agreement. They asked for additional items that we didn't have, so we then had to go back to them saying we don't have these, and we've already agreed that you don't need these. Because we only had a one page deal memo that was not specific, they simply stood firm and stated that the detailed delivery list must be completed if they are going to take delivery. One major problem is that in the delivery list they mentioned the master 35mm negative - of course, we had shot on Super 16mm. Whilst this obviously made no difference to Trimark in terms of quality, they could use it to completely stall the deal.

Q - Did Trimark have a copy of the film?

Gen - They had a copy for about five months - it's a tricky situation because they said that everyone in the company needed to see it for them to finalise. They could have used that time to show the film to their prospective buyers and field the responses - basically get a commercial assessment of that product. Ultimately we couldn't agree on the delivery items and they refused to take the film.

Q - What happened with your Korean deal?

Chris - After paying the £6k deposit the company who aoquircd the righls jusl disappeared otf the face of the earth for six months - Pilgrim just couldn't get hold of them. After the American Film Market they got back to us and explained that the film had been banned as it had 'immoral social values' - they faxed through the certificate of 'banning' (which for all we know could have been an insurance form) and asked for their deposit back. We told them that we had spent it and it was their problem if the film had been banned. So now, not only had we gone stale on the US deal but we had also lost the very considerable balance of the Korean deal.

Q - If you made another film, what could you do differently, how would you overcome this problem?

Chris - You can't. The only thing you can do is make a film that will make the buyers go mad i.e. make a good film, give it to the sales agents and let them go for it. Hopefully you can trust the sales agent, but at the end of the day you can never really be sure - if a sales agent screws up, there's very little you can do as you have assigned the rights to them. I've never heard of any film maker being really happy with their sales agent on their first film.

Gen - I suppose try and get a reputable sales agent and build

Delivery List

This list is by no means comprehensive, it is what we believe is the absolute minimum needed to deliver a film. Sales agents may add to this, or cover the cost of producing some items (deducting from any advance).

1. 35mm theatrical print with optical sound.

2. 35mm Internegative.

3. Master sound mix.

4. Music and Effects mix.

5. Broadcast telecine probably on DigiBeta. M&E mix should be split off onto separate channels.

6. Stills - at least 30 good shots, you can never have enough stills.

7. Contracts with ALL artists both in front and behind the camera. This is to prove that the producer actually owns the copyright of all aspects of the film.

8. Certificate of origin (proving where the film was made and by whom).

9. Full transcript of all the dialogue and action.

10. Errors and omissions policy (may only be needed for a US deal - will cost around £7-10k).

11. Lab access letter (from your labs). This lets the buyer have acces to the neg so that they can make prints. Sometimes a problem if you haven't paid the lab.

CASE STUDIES

12. Textless backgrounds (for shots where you have laid titles over images).

13. Trailer on both 35mm and tape (plus internegs and sound mixes and trailer M&E).

14. Music cue sheets.

15. Continuity Report - like the transcript but in much greater detail writing down every single word, lyric, action, cut and shot.

16. Copyright notice for the USA.

17. Title research report (full US title search report).

18. Full cast and crew list.

19. Press pack with biographies and synopsis.

20. Billing requirements and restrictions (actors billing for instance).

21. Press clipings if you have any.

22. It's a good idea to make masters of all your delivery items and put them in a box. No matter what happens, never give your masters away. Make copies or clones. You may not do anything with your movie for five years, then a sale appears and you must be able to make delivery - then you remember you put evertthing in that one box.

up a relationship to make them want your next film.

Q - So you make a loss on your first film in order to make your second film and get it right then?

Gen - I think our problem was that because we didn't get any money back from *The Runner*, we just didn't trust any other international sales agent with *White Angel* - that was the main reason why we went with Pilgrim. In retrospect, it was a mistake.

Chris - The basic problem is that selling a British film is very difficult. There is a lot of 'quality commercial' product out there, satellite and cable are making prices drop with only the real hit films getting the premium sales. A good example is *Death Machine* which was handled by *Victor Films* - it was a sci-fi thriller, very unoriginal, but very slick - it was also relatively cheap, certainly no $25m budget - yet the buyers went ballistic for the picture. That was a good position to be in - Vic Bateman could hold out and get the best deal and everyone's happy. But when you're making deals to territories for a few thousand dollars, those few thousand dollars are instantly eaten up on expenses.

What could end up happening is that the basic sales merely cover the cost of attending markets in the first place - it's a vicious circle. There really is very little you can do except make as good a film as possible and maybe speak to an agent before setting out - find out what they think they will be able to do with the project before it is committed to film.

Gen - You can either make a movie like *Death Machine*, or go completely the other way and make an offbeat picture like *Clerks*, which Miramax picked up at Cannes when we were there with *White Angel*. However, I guarantee the guys who made *Clerks* haven't seen anywhere near the money Miramax will have made. I guess the fact that they are now several pictures down the line and working with major studios is payment enough.

Q - How do you get a film into a festival?

Chris - First of all you need to find out which are the best festivals, and where they are, when they are and apply at least 3 months in advance.

Gen - For Cannes, which is really more of a market, there is a guy who comes over from Paris and watches all the British submissions one after the other and then decides which will be put in for competition. You can contact him either in Paris before he leaves or in the UK when he comes over.

Obviously he will be booking the films into his schedule so it is important to contact him as early as possible. He turned down *White Angel*, but a few months later faxed us and offered us another place at another festival in France. You can also hire a theatre in Cannes when you get there - many low-budget films do this to generate a buzz about the movie.

For a festival like Sundance you have to make sure that they have seen the film by the end of July and obviously the earlier the better. So really you're looking at nine months in advance before applying. You should be scheduling your film festivals before you start principal photography.

Is this the Korean equivalent of the BBFC's certificate banning White Angel from public viewing, or is it an insurance form, or even the back of a Korean cornflakes box?

The film only ever has one world premiere so it's important to use that on the best festival you can get - pass it around and field the offers - a good sales agent will advise you which are the best festivals to go for. In some respects we blew the premiere of *White Angel* at the Montreal Film Festival. If we knew more about it, we would have premiered at the Toronto Festival (which followed on from Montreal) as it has a reputation for being a buyers festival whereas Montreal is a bit more arty.

Q - Do they pay for you to attend the Festival, how does it operate?

Chris - Send a VHS tape with the application form to the festival co-ordinator, they will then come back to you with *no we don't want it thank you very much*, or *yes, we would like to invite you to attend the Festival*. They will then invite the film and probably one member of the film making body which is usually the director, and may possibly invite an actor or the producer as well.

Normally the Festival will cover the hotel bills of anybody who can get to the screenings (who is directly related to the film). They should also cover the flights for one person, sometimes they will do it for two, but not too often - it depends on how high profile the film is at the festival (the festival will also pay for all shipping of the prints). Essentially the film maker should not spend a single penny to attend a festival.

Gen - Watch out for small print - sometimes a festival will say that the producer must take care of the return shipment of the print, which can prove to be expensive.

Chris - We got inundated with requests to attend festivals and it became impractical to attend them all. At a festival in Puerto Rico we met a top UK sales agent who charges $300 on top of ALL expenses. If a festival comes to us now and we don't want to go, they can have the film for $300 plus all expenses.

Gen - I wouldn't recommend adding a fee if it's a festival you want to attend, particularly if they've agreed to pay for your flight, accommodation and a weeks stay in their country. But if they are asking to screen your film, and they're not going to accommodate you, or you don't really feel as though their festival is going to do much for the film - it's a small festival in the middle of nowhere - then, if the festival wants your film, they will have to pay for it.

Q - Did you find Film Festivals to be useful in the process of selling films?

Gen - Yes, it's a FREE showcase for your product and it can create a profile for your film. If you enter a film and win Best Film or Best Actor, it creates a bit of a buzz about the movie, you get publicity and it becomes an 'award winning film'.

Q - Which Film Festivals has White Angel attended and has it won any awards?

Gen - White Angel has attended 13 Film Festivals around the world - Montreal, London,

𝔍antastic 𝔅urgos 1994

WHITE ANGEL

Premio Feliciano Vitores
Mejor Opera Prima

With the aid of the British Council, White Angel attended several festivals and picked up several awards. Each time Living Spirit would use the award for publicity, even if neither Chris or Gen attended the festival. Below is a picture of Gen taken in her back garden as she accepts a best 'production' award. The picture made it to several magazines.

Ankara, Sao Paulo, Puerto Rico, two in Rome, Mannaheim, Emden, Valenciennes, Burgos... and we won two awards - Best First Film at Burgos Fantastic Film and Best Actor for Peter, at Valenciennes.

Chris - The people that you need to speak to are the guys at the British Council Films Unit - get them involved as soon as possible, as they can help pay for you to go to Festivals. The other major thing to consider is that Festivals are a very good source of free holidays. I did more travelling last year than I had done in the rest of my life combined, and it was all expenses paid. Make a film just for the holiday! But be aware that you should be developing your next film whilst traveling.

Q - What was the weirdest festival you went to?

Chris - I remember I got a phone call from the British Council about a terrific film Festival that I should attend,

White Angel premiered at the Montreal Film Festival where it was very well received. The festival paid for the shipping of the print, one flight and accommodation for four in a five star hotel.

International Film Festivals

1. There are hundreds of film festivals around the world - be selective.

2. Use your World premiere wisely - you only get one.

3. Choose the festivals with competitions, you may walk away with a prize.

4. The festival will cover ALL costs like flights, accommodation and shipping of the prints. Do not pay for any of these yourself.

5. Contact the British Council Films Department as they will offer assistance.

6. Make your application as early as possible and send a press pack with stills (including a shot of the director).

7. Send a pile of press packs to the festival in advance, they will then set up interviews with their press. Take a BetaSP tape with clips (in both PAL and NTSC). Don't leave that tape at the festival or you will never see it again!

8. Remember, it's a free trip, so go for a festival where you actually want a holiday - we spent a week in the Caribbean, all expenses!

9. Don't get tied up going to festivals. You can just go to what feels like a few and before you know it, a year has gone by, you are no longer a hot new film maker and you have blown your window of opportunity.

give some lecture, go on telly and generally be a high profile British film maker. I said fine, where is it - *'Oh, it's the Gaza Strip Film Festival'* - there was a very long pause. Eventually I was persuaded to go - I was even going to be sneaked across borders with guards being bribed! The whole trip got called off a few days before because some tourists were murdered and the Gaza Strip was closed down. That was pretty weird.

Q - Do the festivals expect you to promote the film?

Chris - Yes, usually local press and radio, sometimes TV. The worst TV interview I had to do was in Turkey where I had been lined up for an interview at the local station. When I got there I was more than a little concerned as it was surrounded by razor wire and I had to pass through metal detectors and sniffer dogs to get in - I realised they were looking for bombs and weapons! Suddenly, it dawned on me, I was going on state TV - exactly the kind that was hated by extremist terrorists. I was then informed that my interview was going to be live, and it was the equivalent of the Turkish Wogan show going out to 47 million homes!

The interview was nerve racking as it descended from chit chat about movies to hard hitting political rhetoric - I kept saying, *'I'm sorry but I don't know anything about the political situation in your country'* - which was then translated into a three minute speech! The last thing I wanted to be was a Westerner telling the natives what to do in their own seemingly fundamentalist religious country.

After it was over, both Gen and myself were thanked, passed back out, through the metal detectors, past the sniffer dogs and razor wire before being dumped on a dark and cold Turkish roadside.

Gen - Did you ever see *Midnight Express?* That sums it up.

Q - When and how did the London Film Festival come about?

Gen - The London Film Festival is the major UK festival. There is also Edinburgh, but London occurs in November and it's more of a showcase for British Films over a period of 2 weeks. *White Angel* was selected to play as the 'centrepiece' of the festival and was up there with *Remains of the Day* and

Farewell my Concubine. We sent them a print of *White Angel* and they were very enthusiastic about it and wanted to push it. Eventually it was screened at the Odeon Leicester Square and it was great.

Q - Was this good for the film?

Chris - Yes, it was fabulous for the film. At the time it seemed to crystallise what we thought - firstly, we've got a fabulous film, and secondly, it was very commercial. This small film was suddenly put right up there, right next to *Remains of the Day* in Leicester Square. We got a lot of press and a very high profile. Suddenly we felt that it was all going to happen right here and right now. We felt very confident that the film was going to be a hit.

Gen - And remember, at this time we were negotiating with America, Korea, and Germany - signed deals were on the table, it's just the money still hadn't come through.

Q - What about the UK theatrical release?

Gen - The theatre manager of the Odeon Cinema at Leicester Square told us that he liked *White Angel* - *'it had an amazing effect on the audience'* - and that he would like the film to be screened at his theatre. He told us that if Rank Film Distributors picked it up then he would get it - he had a few colleagues at Rank (who were around at the time) that he would put us in touch with and put a good word in for the picture. We decided to get in contact with Rank Film Distribution who requested a private screening there at their offices. They laid on sandwiches and wine, all the razzma-tazz, and had four or five of their people viewing the film. They told us they loved it, thought it could work very well and they wanted it.

> 'To refuse awards is another way of accepting them with more noise than is normal.'
> Peter Ustinov

Film Festivals are a great place to win awards. This gets distributors, broadcasters and sales agents interested, and as a bonus you get to collect strange figurines mounted on marble blocks.

391

Chris - After we screened the film, we sat down and they made an offer of something like £25k advance against a UK theatrical plus half of the UK video. After several discussions and haggling we got that up to I think £65k. In reality we believed that if we took that deal we would never see more than the £65k offered, and I still believe that, although it was still a very good deal.

Rank guaranteed to do a P&A spend of around £70k which again sounds a lot but it's not huge. It would have ended up going out in five theatres with a lot of advertising. We did the maths and felt we could make more if we did the release ourselves, so we turned down the deal which I think was a shock for them. In hindsight we should have taken the deal, we still wouldn't have broken even but we would have been a hell of a lot closer. Out of everything we ever did, I feel that turning down that deal was the only real and stupid mistake we made.

Gen - That said, the money Rank were offering would mean that we still would be unable to pay the cast and crew. As the German, Korean and US deal which totalled $350k were about to come in, we thought that we could afford to take a risk to make more by self distributing. Pilgrim did their own release with *Tale of A Vampire* and did extremely well, certainly better than Rank's advance. We watched *Tale of A Vampire* and in comparison, we felt *White Angel* was a superior film and

UK 1993
Scr: Chris Jones, Genevieve Jolliffe
Leading players: Peter Firth, Harriet Robinson, Don Henderson, Anne Catherine Arton
Rt: 92 mins
UK Dist: Living Spirit Pictures

White Angel heralds the arrival of two young, talented filmmakers: producer Genevieve Jolliffe and director Chris Jones. More a film about serial killing than about a serial killer, *White Angel* offers a novel and very British view, whilst dealing with the complex (subtle?) differences between manslaughter and murder. Leslie Steckler (Peter Firth) is a soft-spoken dentist who rents a room in Ellen Carter's (Harriet Robinson) house. She is a successful writer on criminal psychology who is being hounded by the police in connection with her husband's

15 MON 16.00 & 21.00 ODEON WEST END 1

White Angel
Dir: Chris Jones

disappearance. Meanwhile, London is in the grips of a serial killer, 'the White Angel', and the dentist and the writer become entangled in a dangerous game of blackmail. The plot is full of surprises, twists and turns (all best left untold) that keep you on the edge of your seat, relying on powerful psychological devices and avoiding unnecessary gore. In many ways it's a first in its chilling (fictional) portrait of a very British way of serial killing. Mesmerizingly good, and a triumph of British independent production. *Rosa Bosch*

Great reviews a plenty at the London Film Festival, helping create a false sense of security.

would therefore do better. It doesn't actually work like that as we later found out. It's more to do with marketing, the type of film and timing - but at the time, we didn't know that.

Q - So you decided to release your film theatrically, so what is involved in doing that?

Gen - Firstly we had to decide how wide we were going to release, on how many screens and work a budget out accordingly. Because of Pilgrims experience with *Tale Of A Vampire* we took a lot of their thoughts on board and they wanted to open quite wide. Initially we were going to open in three theatres only, but they had a screening with the exhibitors who offered them more screens - everybody liked it which meant that it would be picked up by the multiplexes. So our three screens then developed into fifteen scattered around the country in the major cities which increased our advertising budget. The other thing we had to do, was to get hold of a theatrical booker to actually get the film in the theatres, someone who knew how the system worked.

Q - Who is the booker?

Chris - The booker is the person who engineers and schedules the booking of screens and the moving of the prints. For instance, they will tell you the dates where your film will be screened, and the dates that the film is moved from one theatre to another. So with 15 prints we would move from 15 theatres to another 15 theatres, moving around the country until, hopefully, we had covered every major city and town.

Q - What happened about publicity?

Chris - We had to hire a publicist, but a lot of the publicity we did ourselves, and eventually became quite good at getting newspaper interviews, radio and TV. We discovered that telling the occasional white lie or even complete outright lie would always be good for publicity - always managing to get a good column in a newspaper. That was a good way of generating interest around the film.

Q - Did you arrange a press screening before the theatrical release?

Chris - Yes, there's a thing called the SFD (Society of Film

'When producers want to know what the public wants, they graph it as curves. When they want to tell the public what to get, they say it in curves'
Marshall McLuhan

CASE STUDIES

HAYMARKET
(Piccadilly Circus Tube) **071· 839 1527**

ADVANCE BOOKING
081-970 6016 (Bkg fee)

KALIFORNIA (18)

In Dolby Stereo
Sep Progs 2.15, 5.15, 8.15

RESERVOIR DOGS (18)

In Dolby Stereo
Sep Progs 1.20, 3.45, 6.10, 8.40

WHITE ANGEL (15)

In Dolby Stereo
Sep Progs 1.50, 4.10, 6.30, 8.50

Distributors) which sets up special screenings for journalists. We set up several in the 'local' towns and cities as well as the major screening in London. We went to the one in London and introduced the film to a bunch of famous journalists who were shocked and seemed offended that I actually turned up to introduce the film. One guy actually wrote that I came out begging for a good review. We seemed to get universally bad reviews from that screening which, sour grapes aside, I think was rather unfair. Surely it's not THAT bad a film?

Q- Do you think the London Film Festival's good press had an effect?

Chris - Obviously they all had their own opinions about the film, but I think it's fair to say that having the London Film Festival putting us on a plinth and actively using the phrase "Mesmerisingly good and a triumph of British Independent Production" perhaps nurtured a false sense of quality in our film that actually may not have been there. It certainly raised the expectations of the critics as what they actually got was a standard, commercial, ultra low-budget thriller. One interesting thing is that almost ALL the magazines gave us fair to good reviews whilst the 'dailies' unanimously slaughtered us. Maybe that has something to do with youth culture, I don't know.

Q - In retrospect, would it have been a good idea to take some of these people out to dinner and tell them how you made the film, win them over so to speak, instead of hyping the film out of proportion?

Gen - Yes, because the journalists who we did sit down with and have long chats with were the people who gave us favourable reviews and all of them were loyal enough not to mention the budget. The problem here was that we were in essence sitting between two goal posts and we were stretched to the limits. We didn't have the financial resources to schmooze people, nor did we have the contacts in the first

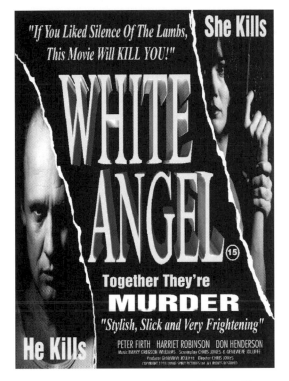

There was so little money for the release that the film's poster had to be put together on a PC.

place. We didn't have the power to demand a favourable or non committal review (or we'll pull £10k worth of advertising from your mag for instance), and you read a lot of non committal reviews. Quite simply, we didn't have the resources to do the job properly within the set time frame. That's the job of a distributor.

Chris - I think the problem with the *White Angel* release was the film itself. I think we aspired to a big budget style film with very little money. When you see a thriller up there on the screen, people expect Bruce Willis, blue light and a lot of gloss. We didn't have all that. What we had, was a TV style film that was a competent thriller and we were actively marketing it as an 'A' movie super duper thriller.

Chris - To some degree, a film appears to be valued at it's perceived cost. If you go down to a used car salesman and say *how much is this car?* and he says *£1,000.* Then you ask *how much is this other one?* and he says *£10* - they may both look the same but you'll think there is something wrong with the £10 one. And it's the same with films. Why go and

> 'Asking a working writer what he thinks about critics is like asking a lamp post what it feels about dogs'
> Christopher Hampton

'White Angel is stylish,
slick and often very
frightening - everything
you don't expect from
British movies"
SELECT MAGAZINE

see a film if it only cost £50,000 to make when you can go and watch Bruce Willis in a film that cost $40m, or another film that has been critically acclaimed. Why bother going to see this small British thriller? That was the double edged sword we were on. So on the one side of the coin you want to get on top of the building and shout *you won't believe what we made this film for* but at the same time you know when you do that you devalue the film, which is exactly what Barry Norman did on Film '94.

"Unpretentiously gripping
and solidly commercial,
White Angel deserves more
than a little glorification"
Mark Wyman - FILM REVIEW

He criticised the film, which is fair enough, he's a critic and it's his job. But one particular comment absolutely destroyed us. And that comment was *This is no more than a 90 minute student film* - Why bother going to see a 90 minute student film, when you can go and see a 90 minute *'real'* film. If he had panned the film it would have been alright as people do have opinions, however he put a value on the film and consigned it to the bargain basement. That's the problem you're up against with a low-budget film.

"A chillingly
impressive film.
White Angel is so
scarily sinister, it
makes Psycho look
like an old Ealing
comedy."
Sam Steele
NME

Also, low-budget films were fairly passé when we released *White Angel - Leon The Pig Farmer* had previously done it very well and there were a couple of other films that had done it, and nobody seemed interested in yet another low-budget British film.

Q - So you claimed not low-budget, but fairly low, you claimed to have made the film for just under a million?

"A cracking thriller with
plenty of edge-of-the-seat
tension. and more twists and
turns than a Dune sandworm"
VIDEO WORLD

Chris - The phrase we used, was that the film cost less than a million.

Q - In retrospect, do you think you should have been straight?

'In the arts,the
critic is the only
independent source of
information. The rest is
advertising'
Pauline Kael

Chris - I don't know. I think a lot of critics may have thought where did all the money go, but then again, we never said it cost a million, just under a million. It is impossible to gauge how much of an effect the bad reviews had, they sure didn't help, but I'm not so sure they damaged us terribly. Most people seem to ignore critics. There were probably other factors other than the reviews that helped the film fail at the UK box office.

Gen - There were other things, like when we booked our opening weekend, we didn't have six months leeway to book in reviews with the big glossy magazines, so we lost a lot of publicity there. The youth magazines could fit us in as they had a much quicker turna-round, and luckily we got in there with some great reviews. And we just couldn't afford TV advertising.

"this occasionally laughable and often inept British thriller from young hopefuls. hard to take seriously"
Wally Hammond
TIME OUT

Q - Would it have been a good idea at the time of production to have got more journalists involved?

Gen - We did attempt to do that. *Empire* were interested, they came on set for a day, took another day taking photos - it seemed to go well. But nothing came of it. They never used it in the magazine. Unless you have Liz Hurley and she's wearing 'that dress', most journalists aren't interested. You need a good sensational angle.

"It's crass and amateurish, and looks as if it was shot for about threepence-ha'penny."
DAILY MAIL

Q - In terms of the prints & advertising, how important do you think the poster is?

Chris - The poster is the only point of sale that the film actually has. Posters are expensive, they're a couple of grand, but that's for as many as you could ever really want. I believe they are absolutely vital. It's the only point of sale where you can make your movie look like all the other Hollywood major movies - we made the name as big as we could on the poster so that people remember it.

"I had a bad feeling about this one even before the opening credits had rolled because its young director, Chris Jones, gave a grovelling speech at the premiere begging us to like his movie"
Julian Brouwer
HARINGAY INDEPENDENT

"aaaaargh!"
Alexander Walker
THE TIMES

Two small ads were placed in the Evening Standard, probably two inches by 3 inches over the weekend of the release, which cost us around £5k (and the Evening Standard isn't even national). 5000 A1 full colour posters cost us £2k. You can see how cost effective posters are.

Q - You had a fairly wide UK release with the film but it didn't go very well, what happened?

Gen - The big thing that went wrong, was that we released on a dreadful weekend, one of the worst weekends in the year. We had no control with the theatrical booker and were naive about the distribution side of the industry. We only found out

'Take heed of critics even when they are not fair; resist them even when they are'
Jean Rostand

CASE STUDIES

afterwards by actually visiting the theatres, usually to help promote the film, and talking to the managers. They all said, *why did you pick this weekend? This is traditionally one of the worse weekends in the year.* Oops.

Q - What weekend was it?

Gen - It was the weekend immediately after the Easter Break. Everybody had gone to the cinema the week before and there were box office records, but the following weekend, our weekend, they were all going back to school, back to college, back to work after their Easter break. Unfortunately nobody wants to open on that weekend, but because we didn't know, there we were in that slot.

The old 'director pointing' press shot - it was actually taken a week before the London Film Festival in a front garden.

Chris - Again, if we had gone with a reputable distributor, that distributor would have said, we're not having that weekend, forget it. So again we learnt. But in retrospect we now know all these things, which we wouldn't have found out if we had gone the other way.

Q - It occurs to me that films have a short shelf life?

Chris - The film only gets one premiere, people can only hear about it for the first time once - that's the point to hit. If the American deal had been made through a reputable sales agent, the sales agent would, firstly, have a relationship or, secondly, the clout to say 'put up or shut up'. If that deal hadn't happened, something else would have come into place. But because it hung about on the shelf, nothing happened and *White Angel* was old news.

Q - So the belief you had in the film from the London Film Festival was one of the downfalls?

Gen - It inflated our perception of the value of the film. In our own minds we believed it was worth much more.

"The length of a film should be directly related to the endurance of the human bladder"
Hitchcock

Q - Do you feel that sales agents, international buyers etc, are out there to rip you off?

Chris - It's not that they're out to rip you off, but again, it's the inherent problem of having a low-budget film. It's not worth very much, and it's not worth anybody's trouble to sell it. And even if they do sell it, they'll never make enough money to make any real profits, and at probably just cover their own expenses.

The advice I would extend to a new film maker is to get to the best sales agent you can, get to the best UK distributor you can, get as much money up-front as you can, and write the rest off.

Do not assume you'll ever get anything else back. Try and get an advance that covers your debts because your investors may never get paid anything else. The rest is really up to the performance of the film and whether the sales agent is honest. If you cling on to it you're dead in the water anyway. Psychologically, write it completely off the moment you have completed the film, don't hang around, get going on your next picture or your first film will become a millstone around your neck. That's what happened with *White Angel*.

Q - What other problems did you encounter?

Gen - We had unexpected events that occurred after our theatrical release which delayed our entire process.

Chris - Basically the film was released and the press were saying how amazingly well we were doing and that we were making loads of money. In real terms we were doing terribly badly. At that point we also lost the US deal and the Korean deal. Suddenly, from having around $350k coming in to us we found ourselves high and dry owing £30,000 from the losses on the UK theatrical release, which was pretty much paid for by the German deal. Not only had we lost all our deals but we had also lost all the money that we had made.

At this very point (long pause) - we had a bit of bad luck. We had just got back from the Cannes Film Festival and at seven o'clock in the morning the doorbell rang. Three of us were living in this house. Myself, Gen and another friend. I went downstairs and eight policemen barged in, and arrested all of us, searched the entire house, drawers, shelves, floorboards - you name it, they searched it - and impounded all our Living Spirit files, floppy disks and equipment.

Gen - This also included sifting through my underwear, reading my diaries, looking through photo albums... They discovered the fake gun that we used for the film and there

The Press

1. Try and get a PR agent on board. If you cannot afford one, go ask for advice and do it yourself.

2. Doing press for a film is pretty much a full time job, especially in the run up to a release - don't try to take on too much.

3. A press pack is vital. It should contain a synopsis, cast and crew biogs, production notes and four or five good stills, including one of the director.

4. Work out the unique selling angle of your film and play on that. If the film is controversial, stir it up even more.

5. An electronic press kit is also helpful - a copy of video taped and loosely edited interviews with cast and crew with long clips from the film and shots during production. Usually supplied on Beta SP.

6. Journalists will almost always hunt out the story - if you don't want it to be printed, don't tell them - EVER.

7. Magazines work with long deadlines, contact them as early as possible.

8. Your story will probably only break once, so try and time it for maximum effect i.e., the weeks leading up to your release.

9. Local press, TV, newspapers and radio are easy to get and can help solve pre production problems.

10. Avoid talking about the budget and focus on the film and it's unique selling point.

CASE STUDIES

602 | 3

EPK - The electronic press kit contains shots taken during filming, very roughly edited interviews with key cast and crew plus several clips from the completed movie. It should be delivered on Beta SP and is vital if any TV coverage is to be expected.

was a flurry of excitement... "Weapons possession..." I entered the office to see three policemen holding the gun on the end of a pencil, examining it in every detail. I pointed out that it was a replica used for the film - "oh yes, of course, we knew that"...

Chris - Basically, they believed we had been making lots of money without declaring it. At that point we had applied for housing benefit as we had absolutely no money, especially with everything falling through. They had read all the press and seen the publicity and believed that we were not entitled to that benefit, firstly because the newspapers said we were doing well, and secondly, they couldn't believe that a film company could make and release a film and be broke. Obviously if they read this book they may see things differently. Anyhow, we were taken down to the police station, shoved in a cell, belts and shoelaces taken off to make sure that we couldn't hang ourselves, read our rights - the works.

Gen - That was if you were wearing a belt and shoelaces, and not still in your nightshirt like myself.

Chris - They closed the cell door and it felt like they were throwing the key away. That was it, kaput. We asked them to call a duty solicitor which they finally did, and a few hours later, which felt like days, the solicitor turned up. He asked what was going on as he was used to representing murderers and rapists - and we certainly didn't look like the murderers or rapists he usually dealt with. It was really bloody horrible at the time. We didn't know what the hell was going on. He told us he would sort it out and we would be out immediately. It didn't quite work that way.

'All publicity is good, except an obituary'
Brendan Behan

Gen - Eventually we were given our interrogation where all our positive attributes as film makers, bullshit, bending the truth, running through the wet paint etc, became indicators of criminal intent. They were quite sure that we had committed serious criminal fraud and continued what we felt were ludicrous lines of questioning. And remember, at this time we are surrounded by a bunch of pretty hefty police officers in a room with a tape recorder and pretty much being shouted at. When you hear about it, you always think I would do this or that, but until you have been put in a cell and had your entire life and home opened up in minute detail, you just can't appreciate what it's like.

> 'I'm not against the police; I'm just afraid of them'
> Hitchcock

Anyhow, we were released on bail to appear in one month for an interrogation, sorry, interview. We couldn't leave the country, so it was a damn good thing we had no festivals to attend and in fact, as everything to do with the film or Living Spirit was in the police station, we couldn't actually do very much apart from watch our future go down the tubes. Our bank managers and investors got letters from Thames Valley Police, asking for information relating to Living Spirit, ourselves and fraud. Our poor friend who lived with us, and who has nothing to do with making films, was considered to be an accomplice in our big operation. They went and interrogated our landlord, not surprisingly we ended up leaving a few weeks later. We were all in this together according to the police. It was astounding.

Q - So how did this all happen?

Chris - Quite simply, they had seen some of our press, wondered what on earth a big film company's directors were doing claiming housing benefit, put two and two together, got three million and decided to jump on us. They even had press clippings we didn't have, so they must have done a lot of research. They confused off shore bank accounts belonging to my brother, who at that time lived in Germany, with me - they also confused Gen's father's credit card with me - they thought I had about six different identities! Slowly, it became apparent that what they thought was a big fraud operation was actually a couple of people who were completely broke trying very hard

Long Arm Of The Law

Lets hope you never have to spend an evening in a cell - but if you do...

1. When you are arrested & taken down to the station you are offered a phone call & a solicitor. Use them. The solicitor is independent - you do NOT have to pay him as he's supplied free, by the state.

2. If things look difficult, refuse to answer any questions until you have spoken to your solicitor. You don't know what angle the police are looking for so keep stum.

3. You can have your solicitor present during interviews and can stop the interview to talk to your solicitor.

4. Assuming you are innocent, or at least relatively, co-operate as much as you can, but always with the solicitors 'say so'. Remember, the police are very powerful - don't antagonise them.

5. Unless you are charged, they cannot take your photo or prints.

6. Stay calm & listen very carefully to all the things they say to you - this isn't the movies, you have rights & they have rights.

7. Remember, you are innocent until proven guilty in a criminal court. You have to be proven guilty beyond all reasonable doubt (unlike civil).

8. Don't panic, unless you have committed a serious offence you will be out in under 24 hours.

9 . A civil offence is NOT a criminal offence - there is a world of difference between the two.

to make the best of a very bad situation - and they had just made it infinitely worse.

Q - How long did it take them to solve this case?

Chris - About four months to assess everything and to say *'No, we're not going to press any charges'*. Two months after that we got all our information back. So all in all, six months, during which we got heavily fined by the VAT office for not having completed our return in time.

Gen - And that was the end of it - but it had created a ripple effect that, combined with the failure of the film at the Box Office and the falling through of all the international sales, crippled us for twelve months or so. During that twelve months, Pilgrim Entertainment did zero business - we couldn't chase them because our plate was more than full just picking up the pieces. One month after we were in the clear, Rank to whom we still owed £30k, sent us a letter saying pay us within 48 hours or we will force you into liquidation. We then had to start negotiating how we were going to get out of this hole. At that point, we decided the best thing to do was to terminate the agreement with Pilgrim Entertainment and take the film ourselves to find new UK distributor and international sales agent. Within days we had The Feature Film company on board to handle the UK video, satellite and TV through Polygram. We had some interest from some international sales agents but couldn't nail anything down. But the UK video was a new source of real cash that could come in for us.

We had been made homeless and had absolutely no money. We were entitled to benefit but just didn't want to take it as the last time we did, we ended up in a police cell. We ended up living with my parents for nearly a year.

Q - When was your video release?

Chris - We had to do yet another re-edit of the film to put more sex and violence in which would make the film a lot more commercial and had even thought of re-titling the film for the international sales market as *"Interview with a Serial Killer"*. With a new edit and a new title, we could in some respects re-invent the film for international sales. But with regard to the UK video, it didn't perform particularly well, I don't think that's a reflection on anything apart from the fact that the market is particularly depressed. We did business, I think we sold somewhere between 2,500 to 3,000 units but at the end of the day we will only get around £7k which doesn't do much more than put a dent in Living Spirit's debts.

Gen - The only thing we hope for now is for the video release to raise the profile of the film to get a better satellite and terrestrial TV deal. The UK satellite, television and sell through video may just about bring the film back to zero, that is if some people will accept deals. If we can then do something internationally we could start to pay back the investors - but it doesn't look good.

When Rank sent us the solicitor's letter giving us 48 hours we decided to fight, to work as hard as we could to make good the debts. Pilgrim also owed Rank from the UK release but they decided to simply go bankrupt.

Q - In all of this you could have opted for bankruptcy, why didn't you do that?

Gen - We felt a moral responsibility to everybody involved, particularly the investors. When this whole thing happened with Rank, our first reaction was fair enough we'll go minus £27k to zero overnight. What a really good way to clear your debt. But it was also a big slap in the face, a big failure and failure doesn't make you sleep well at nights. Not that we've had a great deal of success either but we didn't want to accept failure and lie down and die, they would have to kill us off with extreme prejudice. We were legally advised to fight it and let them force us into liquidation, but the real reason was that we didn't want to write that letter to our investors and have to say *Dear investor, thanks for your money, by the way, we've given up on it, and we've gone into liquidation.* That would have been too difficult a letter to write. That may not be good business sense - maybe a good businessman would say, *Oh well, it's a bad deal, get rid of it and move on.*

Q - In either of your past lives do you think you did something that meant that White Angel went through what you could say is the most unlucky curve of all -

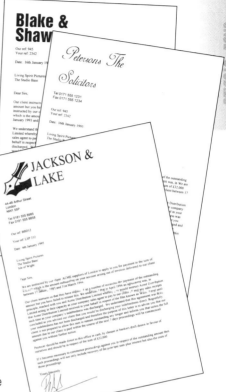

And so the floodgates opened as solicitors, undersheriffs and bailiffs made Living Spirit their business...

CASE STUDIES

'The toughest
thing about
success is that
you've got to keep
on being a
success'
Irving Berlin

*not only were you practically made bankrupt, your
release went totally wrong, you spent time in prison -
but then a real life situation was discovered within 20
miles of where you made the film?*

Chris - The first we heard of Fred West was when we were
on the plane coming back from the Ankara Film Festival, just
a few weeks before the film's theatrical release. We heard
rumours of a serial killer in Gloucester and my first thought
was 'Great PR, the film must be really getting out there' - I
thought it was people talking about the film and didn't realise
that it was a real serial killer. When we found out that it was
reality, it was a huge shock.

Initially, Fred West was only accused of two murders, but
then the body count started growing and we began to worry
that the press would jump on us. The story did break on
Easter day '94 - a lot of the big newspapers carried a small
column about it, but we played it down. It was a very bizarre
occurrence. I think what is most bizarre, and this book will
reflect this, is that many of the interviews in this book have
been conducted over a period of years (before Fred West
was caught). When you refer back to when we talk about the
screenplay and what we say about why people find serial
killers fascinating, that *it's the man next door...* well for us, it
pretty much was - we used to park our car outside his front
door when we went into town! That was very chilling and
brought everything into sharp focus - as we were making a
piece of fiction, only a mile or two away it was happening in
reality.

MOVIE OF HORROR

SERIAL killer West visited
a film set - to watch scenes
from a movie about a mass
murderer.

And there are bizarre
coincidences between
White Angel and the real-life
mass murderer whose wife
Rose is now facing 10 murder
charges.

Scenes were filmed just

PAT CODD
Showbiz Editor

yards from West's front
door in Cromwell Street,
Gloucester, six months
before his arrest.

Director Chris Jones said:
"It's chilling, particularly as
the coincidences were
stunning - bodies buried

in the wall of the house
and garden, 12 young
female victims and family
members being murdered."

And in the film the killer
writes his biography.

West penned his own -
eerily entitled I only Ever
Loved An Angel - before
his suicide in jail in
December.

What was frustrating is that we were being accused of being sick 'cash in' film makers by the people who were printing the story saying Sick West Film made in Front Garden. Actually, the only people making any money out of this story were the people selling the newspapers. We pointed out that the film had been completed and premiered at the London Film Festival before Fred West was known to anyone other than his milk man and neighbours.

We had to defend the film and say *'well it's not that sick and nasty'*, which diluted the impact for the theatrical release of the film. I couldn't say, *'it's a real shocking, real blood and gutsy thriller'*, because the press would say, *'isn't it a bit sick releasing the film the same time as all these revelations about Fred West?'*. What could we do? We couldn't afford to put off the release, we were 4 weeks away and it was all moving - we were in a no win situation.

Q - Why did you decide to write this book?

Gen - First of all, we wanted this kind of book when we started up, a book that gave other people's experiences - showing where they got it right, and where they didn't. Obviously there's nothing better than your own experience, but hearing somebody else's experiences really helps and I'm sure we've had a few bad experiences that can be avoided by other film makers.

Chris - I think the other reason why we wrote the book is that it's about the only way we can make money out of our experiences now. That's the tragic reality of the whole situation.

Q - What basic advice would you give to somebody about the attitude it takes to make low-budget films?

Chris - There are two kinds of new film makers who will go out and attempt to make a film. One is somebody who thinks they want to do it but will cop out, the other is the kind of person who actually believes, quite literally, that they are a genius and that they have no possible way of failing.

Quite honestly when we started out we believed ourselves to be mini geniuses, it was absolutely impossible to fail - that is intrinsic to a low-budget film makers psyche, it's the only thing that will get you to do these ridiculous things that will

Going Under

When that letter from the solicitor comes & you can't pay, there are several things you can do.

1. Make a deal - if your creditor thinks they won't get paid, offer them half or even less & they may take it, but you will have to pay there & then.

2. Offer to pay it off at a small amount of money per month. If it is vaguely reasonable, they will accept.

3. No-one wants to force you to go bust, it costs a lot, takes a long time & often, no-one wins out.

4. If you do want to go into insolvency, let them push you into it. They will then have to pay the liquidator or receiver rather than you.

5. If you do go into liquidation, you will have to supply all your books & records which will be scrutinised. Make sure you didn't do anything illegal or undeclared.

6. If serious negligence or fraud is discovered, you will be barred from being a Ltd company director again.

7. Hopefully you will have made your film under a Ltd company as if you didn't, you can be made bankrupt and everything you own can be taken, bar the tools of your trade.

8. If things get bad, let it go & move on. Liquidation may not be avoidable & is a good way of washing your hands of a serious problem.

9. Keep talking to your creditors & it may not even get that far.

10. Seek legal advice immediately - let's hope the company forcing you into liquidation isn't your solicitors.

CROMWELL S

It could be the man next door - in Living Spirit's case, it literally was, in the form of serial killer Fred West.

destroy your life and financial standing.

Gen - Most new film makers, ourselves included, are never prepared for the chaos that will happen after having made the film - making the film is actually the easy thing, dealing with it afterwards is the difficult thing. My basic advice would be, if you can pay yourself, pay yourself and don't put your own money in. Not because you don't believe in the project, but because if it all goes wrong you won't be left so high and dry that you cannot function for several years. I'm not saying abandon the project at all, I'm just saying don't be so financially screwed that you cannot operate if it all goes wrong.

Chris - The other thing is to get out as quickly as possible and start on the next project - don't be too concerned about quality, turnover is much more important. Quality will come later, with experience and serious development budgets.

Gen - For a first film, you should make the kind of film you want to make as later you will not have that luxury - many other fingers will be in your pie, each with an opinion.

Q - So to make a film you need to be an optimist, but also a realist?

Gen - Not to make it but to deal with it after it is completed. You need a vast quantity of optimism, dedication, self will, self motivation, and I believe, honesty and integrity. Those are the things that allow you to get it done properly. The moment you finish the film, take off your director/producer cap, and put on your sales agent cap, or *'now I have to go and make this business work'* cap, then you need to dash your optimism and replace it with pessimism and realism - put on your accountancy cap, look at the figures and take as much money as you can, as and when you can, and as quickly as you can. Treat it as a hundred yard sprint. After a hundred yards, kick it into touch and move on, because after a hundred yards you're not going to get any more.

Q - What would you advise the balance between the budget for the actual film production and film sales be?

Chris - It's inevitable that new film makers are focused on getting to day one of principle photography and aren't too concerned about things like screenplays or casting - it's just get the movie shot. It's an insane desire to shoot vast quantities of 35mm negative and then deal with the chaos that you have created for yourself. With the best will in the world, I don't think that a new film maker is going to say, *well I've got my £100k to make the film, but I'm not going to make it now, because I need another £100k to sell the film afterwards.*

All I can suggest is be aware of it, know that you are going to have problems and say *I know that I can make the film for £100k, but the real budget is going to be £200k after I have fixed all the problems, paid my rent, been to a few festivals and made delivery to a sales agent.*

If at the end of the day the film doesn't sell you'll never make any money, you'll never pay your investors back and you'll have this millstone around your neck for several years. At which point either everyone will get bored and go away or they'll sue you and you'll be made bankrupt.

Gen - Get your screenplay to a sales agent and say *I have this screenplay, this is the cast I'm thinking about, this is the budget I'm thinking about, what are your ideas* and they'll give you a fair appraisal of the films commercial value.

Q - So test your idea out first and be aware that if you are going to make any money you've got to sell it afterwards?

Gen - When we talk about making money out of it, it's nothing to do with profit. We would all love to have our own yacht in the Caribbean - what we're talking about is making enough money to pay people back what they have put in and to pay for your rent and food. Any film is going to take 12 to 18 months of your life. Who is going to pay for those 18 months?

Chris - Nobody would buy a house for £200k if they didn't know they could pay the mortgage - making a film for £200k is like buying a house and you've got to know that you can pay that mortgage, or you'll lose that money and get repossessed. It's a hard reality. It's naive to blindly assume you're going to make a lot of money. However, if you are prepared to enter the arena and say, *well I'm going to lose it*

Your Credit Rating...

As we move into a more computerised age, every detail of your financial history can be bought and sold by money lenders. The upshot is that if you have abused money, you may find it tough to get a mobile phone, credit card or even a mortgage.

1. Always make good your debts and always get a letter to prove that you have made good your debt.

2. Credit agencies hold details of your credit status and rating. Their details are available from Citizens Advice and if you write to them, they have to supply you with your details.

3. When researching your credit status, remember to check all your previous addresses over the last six years.

4. CCJ - County Court Judgements are a pain. If you get one, it's a big problem. However, if you pay up immediately or can settle out of court, no CCJ should be lodged against your name on your records.

5. If you started a limited company and the company goes into liquidation - it's not you that has been made bankrupt and you shouldn't be affected. But...

6. If you ran the company from home and you get a CCJ, it's almost as big a problem as CCJs are held against an address too (even though it may have nothing to do with you).

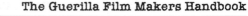
'Stylish, Slick and Very Frightening...'

Living Spirit Pictures
Present

WHITE ANGEL

PETER FIRTH   HARRIET ROBINSON   DON HENDERSON
Production Design MARK SUTHERLAND Costume Design SHEENA GUNN
Sound PAUL LORD Special Effects PHIL MATHEWS Editor CHRIS JONES
Music HARRY GREGSON WILLIAMS Screenplay CHRIS JONES & GENEVIEVE JOLLIFFE
Producer GENEVIEVE JOLLIFFE Director CHRIS JONES
© 1993 Living Spirit Pictures Limited

all, and if I do, I don't care, then great go for it. *And if I lose it all, I can still survive and start again.* I guess that low-budget film making is designed to launch careers, it isn't about getting rich quick.

Gen - However, I think we've been spectacularly unlucky.

Q - Maybe you are just talentless?

Chris - I think we had better end the interview here.

End of interviews 1996

Chris and Gen completed White Angel and after being arrested, spent two years as freelance journalists whilst they worked themselves out of debt. It was during this time that Living Spirit worked on the screenplay for their third feature, Urban Ghost Story.

It's worth noting that in the few years between White Angel and Urban Ghost Story, digital technology has moved on so far that non linear editing is common place and digital features are being made on considerably smaller budgets than the £11k it cost to shoot White Angel.

Q - How did the idea of Urban Ghost Story (UGS) come about?

Chris - I had seen a documentary on TV about a real poltergeist case and it was really scary. We had always wanted to do a ghost story but the genre felt overpopulated, so we decided to make this ultra real version of a paranormal tale. We originally said it would be like *The Exorcist* if Ken Loach had directed it. We wanted to capture that spooky feeling of late night ghost stories, where not too much happens, but because it's real, its that much scarier.

'The surest way to succeed is to be determined not to fail'
Anon

Gen - I had some experiences with the paranormal as a kid, my grandmother was a medium, and I loved horror, so it seemed like an obvious choice. Right from day one we wanted 'real' poltergeist stories and experiences to be the focus of the drama in the movie.

Chris - Yeah, we even spent time hanging out with spiritualists and ghost hunters. It was heaps of fun.

Q - You swapped roles - why?

Gen - Yes, Chris directed *The Runner* and *White Angel,* and I directed *UGS.* It's simple, when we left film school we agreed that we would split everything down the middle, directing and producing. We'd both wanted to direct and it's just the way that the chips fell that Chris directed *The Runner* and *White Angel.* So after producing twice I felt ready to direct.

Chris - In some ways it was a real problem for us. We had two movies behind us, and this book which was doing well, but when people read the script for UGS and liked it, we then had to say oh, *and Gen is directing...* This was usually a problem as Gen had no real directorial experience, she was young and female, which all seemed to go against us.

Gen - This was all compounded by the fact that a lot of people didn't 'get' what the story was about. We had one American company who was interested but wanted to change the end so the tower block was built on a gateway to hell - we just had to say, *guys, you just don't get what we want to do...*

Chris - One of the problems we just haven't managed to get over is that of development. We have searched high and low for scripts written by new writers and they are either crap, or already snatched up by a bigger production company. That means we have to write ourselves, and that means we have to fund that too. And I don't care what anyone says, writing a great 120 page script takes months, maybe years if you can't work on it full time.

The original image put together by Chris with Photoshop conveyed Urban Ghost Story as a horror movie. Printed on 1000 postcards for £100 it gave the film a glossy but cost effective presence in Cannes prior to shooting.

Gen - We were disillusioned about what we had made too. *White Angel* and *The Runner* were both genre films, and whilst *White Angel* was quite good, it still pretty much failed commercially. So we decided to just make a movie that we wanted to make, throw caution to the wind, stick two fingers up to everyone and just do it.

Chris - In some ways it has failed commercially again, but

CASE STUDIES

Just photocopying a 120 page screenplay on a low budget feature is costly, time consuming, not to mention back breaking. DoP Jon Walker helps out just weeks prior to the shoot.

this time it's been a critical success which has meant some very exciting things are now happening.

Q - How much work did you do on the script?

Chris - We spent about 18 months writing but at the same time, we both had to do other work to keep afloat. It was a hard film to write because so much of it was just feel and not plot, it never was a film about a ghost being exorcised. The big problem was always audience expectation of a ghost story. We knew the film wouldn't deliver the shocks that a mainstream audience would expect and that it was too paranormal for your average art film fanatic. So we just said, to hell with it, we fall between two posts, but it's a story we want to tell.

Gen - It was so frustrating to have sales agents tell us that there just weren't enough 'blue light' scenes, or effects. That said, all the actors loved it because it had rich characters for a film that still had a commercial slant.

Chris - We were also taking a big risk making the lead a 13 year old. What if she couldn't act? What if we ran into age restriction laws?

Q - Why in a tower block?

Chris - We wanted an oppressive and interesting backdrop and a tower block just seemed like the obvious choice. It's cold, dark and scary.

Gen - Glasgow seemed like a good location as the accents are so much more lyrical than say Surrey. I also liked the landscape, it felt dramatic, fresh and new. Setting the movie in southern England/BBC land would have been disastrous, it needed an edge.

Q - Where did the money come from?

Gen - We had produced a budget for £800k, set a date, and said whatever we had on that date, we would shoot with. We tried all the usual places but got nowhere - the usual answers were; *we don't get what it's about... It's too paranormal for us... It's not paranormal enough for us... Who's directing? She can't do it, she has no experience... What about Chris directing instead, then we'd finance it.*

I asked Marlon Brando why he hadn't read the script of Superman and he said, "Well, they pay me a lot of money to do this, and if I read it, I might not want to do it, and I really need the money" Terence Stamp

Chris - It was really hard standing by your agreement when someone is offering you the money if I just cut Gen out of the loop and direct myself. It got Gen down a lot because she felt so devalued. So we stood by our guns, and no industry money came our way.

Gen - Just when we were about to crumble we got this call out of the blue from one of the investors in *White Angel*. His name is Dave and he said that he felt we had been in training on the other two films and now it was time to do it properly. He got a few of his friends together and collectively they put in about £220k. This was great, we worked out that we could shoot the movie for that, quite easily actually, but continued to try and get more industry money. Dave then became our Executive Producer.

The tower block was conceived as a character in the movie, with a life of its own, organic and mechanical. It wasn't in Glasgow, but a short drive from the studios where Living Spirit were based.

Chris - The money also meant that we could take an office at Ealing Film Studios, which then meant we were taken seriously by the business... *yeah, it's Chris Jones here from Living Spirit, we're at Ealing Film Studios and blah blah blah* - it just made us sound so much better. The room we hired was very cheap and about the best value we have ever got out of anything. I know most of the other studios hire offices too, and it's just a great way to look bigger and more serious than we might be.

Q - Why didn't you get money from the Lottery?

Gen - We tried, we put in all the forms, but we had shot the film before we received the notification from them that they were processing the paperwork. It was ridiculous.

Concept paintings by Alex Fort helped convince all parties at the table that the production was being helmed by a creative team with vision.

Q - Did you take the project to Cannes before shooting?

Gen - Yes, Chris did some artwork on the PC and we did some postcards and printed up a pile of scripts. We hawked it around but again, no-one seemed to understand what we were making and why. The best thing that happened was that we met David Thewlis and Amanda Plumber at a party, who were weirdly enough, the two actors we wanted for the two adult roles. They both turned the film down eventually, but we did get the script to them and they did read it.

Chris - Cannes was great for getting in the mood, but for actually getting the film made, it didn't really help.

Q - What happened when you took the office at the studios?

Chris - We had a friend called Carmen who had worked as a production co-ordinator on *White Angel* and she was between jobs. We convinced her to come and help out in the office for next to nothing and that made a real difference. Living Spirit suddenly had a consistent voice on the phone and it sounded like we had a secretary. Carmen acted as a filter, making sure we didn't get distracted by unimportant calls, and she also arranged heaps of production things too.

Gen - Because we had set a date, we had some cash and a script we believed in, we absolutely knew the film was going to happen. The only questions left were exactly how much money we would have when we got to photography, and just how good the movie would end up being. The freight train started to move down hill and we both knew it wouldn't be long before it would be impossible to stop it.

"I remember that someone once said that the whole thing is to keep working, and pretty soon they'll think you're good"
Jack Nicholson

Chris - It was a great time.

Q - How did you get the cast involved?

Gen - I spent months interviewing people. A friend, Cathy

Arton who had worked on both *The Runner* and *White Angel* helped out. She dealt with agents brilliantly which meant I only needed to see if the actor was the right person for the job.

Chris - What was most interesting was that Gen seemed to make really good short lists, but because she was so close to it all, when she came to make the final decision on who would be the best person for the part, she just couldn't tell. I wasn't as involved in the casting, so when it came to decision time and there was a lot of *umming and ahhing* going on, I usually had a gut feeling based on fresh new impressions. Although Gen did make a brilliant choice with Heather, the young girl from Glasgow playing the lead.

Dave Hardwick, Executive Producer for Urban Ghost Story, was the only person who believed in both Chris and Gen and the movie itself.

Gen - I went up to Glasgow on the overnight bus, never again I can tell you, and met about 100 young actresses. Heather was the 7th girl I saw and she just shone out immediately. Her dad was a cameraman too, so there was no need to explain how the business worked, they understood.

Chris - We had discovered that all sorts of laws exist for working with kids, all of which were a pain in the arse, so we moved the shoot forward so that we could shoot in the summer holidays and set a shoot date, August 18th. Then we discovered that Scottish kids go back to school weeks before English kids - on August 18th, so we were just as screwed. So we had to adhere to all the laws and get a professional minder and all the rest of the stuff, which was very expensive.

Months of casting and sending out screenplays led to the very best cast we could have imagined. Left to right, Nicola Stapleton, James Cosmo, Heather Ann Foster, Jason Connery, Billy Boyd, Stephanie Buttle, Andreas Wisniewski and Elizabeth Berrington.

Q - Did you have any problems with unions?

Chris - Astonishingly yes. BECTU, the technicians union

Working With Kids

1. There are strict laws about using children in films - the hours and consecutive days that they can work is governed by the council and you will need to apply to them for the licence. If they have done a lot of work recently, the council may decline the film.

2. If you are shooting in the holidays you may not need a licence.

3. If you are shooting during term time you will need to employ a tutor / chaperone so that they don't fall behind in their school work. They are not cheap.

4. Try not to exhaust the children, if they are happy, enthusiastic and energetic, you will get more out of them and faster too. Tired children don't work well.

5. Use a double. Many scenes or even shots in scenes could be done without the child at all, but with a young looking adult of the same build and appearance.

6. Whilst we have never had problems with kids, other film makers have and you should consider carefully how much you are opening up yourself to the take 37 scenario.

7. You will probably have to accommodate at least one parent, and probably pay them for the time they are losing from their job. In rare occasions, the parent could also be the tutor / chaperone.

8. Swearing, horror, blood, sex, racism etc., may be part of your story and plot, but a concerned parent won't want their child exposed. Work out ways to protect the child wherever possible.

blacklisted us. Even after blacklisting, they couldn't tell us why we had been blacklisted, even though we were named for months in their magazine. I have asked them to substantiate their position, but they haven't. It didn't really cause much of a problem for us, just made us look like crooks.

Q - How much did you pay the crew?

Chris - £100 a week, plus food. It's not much I know but everyone did it because they wanted to be there, everyone was getting a break - art directors got to production design, gaffers got to operate camera etc. And because everyone was on the same money, there were no squabbles, no-one felt less or more important than anyone else - DoP, production designer, runner, editor - everyone got the same deal and there was a real team spirit.

Q - But those aren't BECTU rates?

Chris - Who said it was a BECTU film? And what right does a union have to blacklist a company without backing up any claims?

Gen - Then the thing with the agents happened.

Chris - We were about a week from shooting when an agent called me and said to me - quote, *you've just fucked yourself! I'm pulling my actors and you'll never work in the industry again - goodbye.* I couldn't believe what I was hearing. How arrogant to think that they had the power to tell anyone whether they could work in 'their' industry or not. Then it happened with another agent and another. In the space of an hour, we lost most of our cast, except for Jason Connery's agent who stood by us.

Q - What was wrong with them?

Chris - After storming into the offices of the PMA who just happened to be on site at Ealing Film Studios, I discovered it wasn't this PMA, the Production Managers Association, but another PMA, the Personal Managers Association, a group of agents who meet regularly behind closed doors. What transpired was that they had got hold of a letter written (for prospective investment) by our investor, Dave, in which he said Low Budget Films don't pay their deferred fees. It's a fact, deferred fee movies don't work. That's why we decided not to make UGS with deferments, but that just didn't matter. I couldn't even get hold of the PMA, they seemed to me to be more like a secret society than a group of agents who want to encourage new film makers. Anyway, the agents just didn't believe that we were not crooks and insisted that we make the film using the PACT Equity registered low budget scheme. I just want to say clearly and categorically that because we were forced to use the PACT Equity registered low budget scheme, we ended up paying the cast 35% less than what we had anticipated. Even so, I was humiliated by the arse licking that I had to go through in order to get our cast back - but I did it.

> "The art of acting is not to act. Once you show them more, what you show them, in fact, is bad acting"
> Anthony Hopkins

Q - What's the PACT/Equity registered low budget scheme?

Gen - Ironically, it's a great idea if you have any kind of budget. Without getting into all the rules, you pay a flat fee of about £500 pw or £120 pd., pay 0.25% of your budget to PACT and then get simple pink forms for hiring your actors. It's great, much simpler and easier than negotiating loads of individual deals with agents.

Chris - I just found the whole exercise ridiculous. Agents all argued that they wanted this scheme so that profit shares would be dealt with properly, this was *an honest, respectable and professional way to work* they argued. I then discovered that of the hundreds of films that had passed through the scheme, only two had ever made a profit - *Wish You Were Here* and *Trainspotting,* so the whole profit situation was kind of a moot point for us. To crown it all, a top agent who represented a major actor whom we had agreed would play a part in UGS then said, *yes I know it's registered low budget, but... don't tell Equity and hire my actor as a producer then you can give them a £40k deferred fee as well.* I had already been in hot water with Equity and was damned if I was going to jeopardise it all again, so I just let it slide. Weeks later, this guy wrote to me with all sorts of wild accusations, again telling me that I would never work in the industry in the future. Where do they get these people?

The beginning of the compromise. An unhappy Genevieve argues for her shots, against Chris who constantly says 'no, it's a half page scene, we don't need to do it in eleven shots!'

Q - Did you get your cast back?

Chris - Yes, and you can imagine their faces when we told them that Equity, Agents and the PMA had collectively forced us to effectively negotiate their fees down by 35%!

Q - How did you find working with actors?

Gen - Because the production ran so smoothly, nights were early and days relatively short, tempers never frayed. Initially I was a bit daunted by directing and thought that it would be obvious that I had never done it before, but no-one noticed so it was fine! I spent a lot of time talking to them about their characters and they seemed to get the idea that there was a cohesive idea behind what I wanted to get. And because everything had been storyboarded in great detail, I didn't need to spend so much time working on the camera.

Q - Did storyboards help?

Chris - We had never storyboarded before but this was a great experience. Weeks before shooting we could argue out the best ways to cover a scene. Gen would normally *say I want to do this*, I would say *no we can't afford it, why not do this*, then she would say *how about that way then,* and before you knew it, we had the most creative and cost effective way of shooting a scene on paper. This didn't happen on *The Runner* or *White Angel* and I think it shows.

Gen - Alex Fort drew many of the story boards, but we ran out of time and stick figure sketches with camera placement diagrams took their place. It's amazing when you look at the boards then at the shots, just how closely they match. There were times when I turned up on location without any idea of what the location would look like. So I'd have to make it up there and then and looking back, these scenes didn't work as well as the ones that were storyboarded, they just weren't planned out.

Q - Did you shoot on location?

Gen - We couldn't afford to shoot in Glasgow, so we shot all the tower block scenes just down the road in Acton. We used our tried and tested rule of finding as many locations as possible as close to the main unit as practical. Then we shot all the interiors on a set at the studios. Because we were shooting in London, the local council wanted thousands of pounds for us just to stand out on the pavement with a camera.

Storyboarding

1. Storyboards help you, and your cast & crew, visualise the whole movie.

2. Don't be afraid to drop your boards if time, money, locations or miscellaneous nightmares make them too difficult to shoot.

3. Stick man storyboards are perfectly adequate, they are simply a means of conveying shots and spatial positioning.

4. Use overhead camera diagrams to show where the camera and actors will move during a scene, this will speed everything up on the day.

5. Storyboarding allows you to think creatively, without pressure. Making it up the day before, or even in the car on the way to the set is hardly conducive to creative thinking.

6. Don't underestimate how long it will take to board your film, you are talking about 700 - 1000 hand drawn pictures with descriptions, all of which will need photocopying.

7. If you can afford it, buy one of the dedicated Storyboard programs for your computer. It will speed up your work and present a more professional image, unless you can get a professional artist.

8. In the absence of storyboards at least have a detailed shot list for your first assistant director.

URBAN GHOST STORY STORY BOARDS
Sketched by Alex Fort

SCENE 7 - INT. NIGHT - LIZZIE'S BEDROOM
Lizzie sits up and looks around bedroom as she hears noises in the dark.

SCENE 7 INT. NIGHT - LIZZIE'S BEDROOM
Lizzie walks past Alex who is sleeping (wipes frame).

SCENE 54 INT. NIGHT - LIVING ROOM
Close up of Lizzie as she watches John - listening to music on headphones.

SCENE 42 INT. NIGHT - LIVING ROOM
Slow motion dolly into Lizzie and Alex sit on a sofa as a policeman kneels down to question them.

Artist Alex Fort worked with Gen and Chris to storyboard Urban Ghost Story. The storyboards allowed Gen to communicate to every member of the cast and crew, just what was needed throughout each day. It also ensured that what was shot would actually 'cut' once in the edit suite. Overhead camera diagrams were also used to illustrate where actors and the camera would move during a shot. Management of anywhere between 500 and 1000 storyboard images is an issue not to be underrated.

CASE STUDIES

SCENE 44 INT. NIGHT -
KATE'S BEDROOM
Kate looks over her shoulder
as she is undressing. She
hears a banging noise from
the kids room.

SCENE 5 INT. NIGHT -
HALLWAY
Lizzie walks down the grim
hallway in the tower block.

SCENE 5 INT. NIGHT -
HALLWAY
Lizzie goes to her flat door
and looks over her shoulder
as she hears a noise from the
end of the hallway. Slow dolly
in to close up.

SCENE 65 EXT. DAY - WALL
Lizzie angrily walks along
whilst reading the newspaper.

SCENE 12 INT. DAY -
KERRIE'S FLAT
Lizzie and Kerrie look down
into the cot where little Jack is
asleep.

Chris - Being someone who pays my council tax I would have thought I had a right to stand on the pavement with a camera and shoot film as long as I wasn't a nuisance, but the local council had a different idea and wanted £hundreds a day. It was utterly ridiculous. Every time we made a request, they would quote us so much money that it became impossible, so we just lied, told them we weren't going to do any shooting, then just did it. No one ever had a problem and there was not a single complaint.

Stage 4 at Ealing Film Studios, an effects stage with no real sound proofing. Ideal for Urban Ghost Story as it was based at a studio facility, came with green rooms, production offices, storage, parking etc., was cheap and BIG.

Q - How did you find working on a set?

Gen - First of all it was Stage 4 at Ealing which isn't a sound stage, more like a big shed. And some days we were on the flight path with Heathrow airport so that every 90 seconds we'd stop shooting for a plane, then when it rained we couldn't record sound because it had a metal roof. Other than that it was great. We cut a great deal with the studio which got us the stage, green room, production office, changing rooms etc., and there were on site loos and a canteen so catering wasn't an issue. From a production point of view it was a dream come true. The actors liked it too because there was parking, they could go somewhere quiet to relax, and there were virtually no night shoots. Very civilised.

Q - What happened about catering?

Chris - Because we were shooting at the studios we were able to give everyone £5 per day and they could feed themselves at the canteen. On the very odd occasion when we were on location, one of the production team would go to

> "The difference between fiction and reality? Fiction has to make sense"
> Tom Clancy

419

CASE STUDIES

Tescos and buy sandwiches and buffet type food and everyone was happy. Aside from tea and coffee, we always had cold water on tap because the stage wasn't air conditioned and it was the height of summer. With all the lights turned on what was supposed to be a freezing cold Glaswegian flat was more like a furnace and dehydration became a really serious issue. In retrospect it's amazing how much we spent on water, nearly a thousand pounds.

Q - Who built the sets?

Chris - When Gen was casting, I was crewing. I met this wild guy called Simon Pickup who seemed to me to be bonkers. But he had extraordinary passion and a vision. I wasn't too sure about his vision, if it was doable, but I felt that if we were going to build sets, they should be as unique as possible. Simon designed a fantastic set for the film, and gave every ounce of energy in his body to make the film as good as possible. Mark Sutherland, from *White Angel,* came on board as the construction manager, and together they made it happen. A BBC designer came on set one day and proceeded to tell us that what we were doing wasn't the way to do it, it couldn't be done for the money we had, and it was impossible. Well Simon and Mark proved him wrong.

It may look convincing on film but it is just plasterboard, plywood, paint and wallpaper.

Gen - The level of detail in the sets meant that we could shoot anything, and in close up detail. Walls could be moved, and there was a floating ceiling so lights could be suspended from above. The big problem was that it took

Shooting on a set meant an incredible degree of control over lighting, additional space, flying walls and ceiling for better access. In the pictures, the walls look laughably thin and you wouldn't ever believe that in the movie they look convincingly like two foot thick concrete.

We also had a little help from the neighbouring, bigger budget skips that were on the studio lot. Many of the sets in UGS were built from junk pulled from BBC drama skips.

longer to build than we expected so they were still hammering weeks into the shoot. Just as they completed the build we had to rip it all down. One problem we found was that you need lots of space around your set so that you can get lights or a skyline backdrop far enough away to be acceptable. We built the set right up to the wall at times and that was a mistake. The more I think about it, I can't think of a single drawback to shooting on a set. I guess if there isn't time to paint and dress it properly, it might look a bit crap and then it's self defeating. Because you make the sets, everything is bigger, which means there is more space to work in and the actors aren't so restricted. If you look at UGS, it has to be the biggest council flat in the history of Glasgow! One big problem, literally, was Andreas, who played Dr Quinn, was just too, well big and his head would pop off the top of the set all too often. We had a cunning solution which was to put him in a wheelchair, but that was a little too mad scientist, so we just got him to sit down whenever we could.

Chris - We also built a few tiny sets, just corners of rooms or walls. Again, this meant that we kept the kit, cast and crew all in one place.

Q - How did you approach the style of the film?

Gen - With *The Runner* we'd gone for a glossy American look, with *White Angel* we'd gone for a social realist look that ended up looking a lot like telly. For *UGS* we knew we would still have a limited lighting budget but more than we'd had before. Myself, Chris and DoP Jon Walker, who had shot both *The Runner* and *White Angel,* all got together and decided on the 'look'. Combined with shooting in a studio with complete control over the sets allowed us to create a style with which we were all happy. It's hard to quantify the look but we wanted it to look a lot like Luc Besson's *Leon.* We wanted it to look cinematic and not televisual, so we used a lot of slow motion, long lens shots, fast cutting and ultimately, although this wasn't planned, put it through a bleach bypass at the labs. The costume and sets were another area that we wanted to control in order to create this look. Simon Pickup and Mark Sutherland, with their crew of die hard set dressers, had created this unbelievably beautifully detailed set that just meant we could shoot in every direction. Early in the shoot a costume for our lead man was a problem. I hadn't had time to collaborate with costume designer Linda Haysman on everything as there

Set Building

1. It isn't cheap to build a set, but if you can afford it, it's well worth it, especially if most of your movie is set in one main location.

2. Make sure you leave enough time to build, it can take weeks.

3. Make sure you have enough skip space for the strike. You should be able to break your set in a day, but it does produce an enormous amount of junk.

4. Get enough tools and the right tools for the job. You might save a bob or two on cheap saws, but powerful electric ones would speed everything up enormously.

5. Raid skips nearby for wood that you can use. Often you can buy the materials from a set that is about to be struck, it's good for them, it's good for you.

6. Watch out for wandering tools. Hammers, drills, nails etc., all just seem to go walkies on their own.

7. Buy from the trade suppliers and not big DIY stores. Get your production manager on the phone searching out the best deals for timber. Get them to deliver.

8. Make sure your set is 8 feet high or you might find tall cast members heads popping over the top. We had this problem with Andreas Wiesniewski on UGS, so you'll notice he sits down for a lot of the movie!

9. The secret is in the dressing. Make sure you fill your set with props, don't rely on the four walls to do it all for you.

10. Build as many flying walls as you can, it makes it easier to shoot and dress.

11. Try and reuse sets. Once one room has been shot in, could it be repainted and dressed to be another location altogether?

A large main unit and smaller second unit ensured that every scene got maximum coverage.

just wasn't time or money. Actors often end up wearing their own clothes which isn't always the best idea as you don't have much control and personal preferences start to come into play.

Chris - On the first day of shooting with Jason Connery it all went well except I was unhappy with his costume. I thought he looked too dressed up and less like the bit of 'rough' I expected. This 'look' had been a compromise between what Jason was comfortable wearing, budget restrictions and what he had brought with him in his bag. As I was not literally at the coal face directing I was able to stand back and note that the costume was just not quite right. Gen had gone through the whole day and noticed the costume but because it was early on in the shoot and there were other seemingly bigger issues, it just didn't seem like an immediate problem. This is where a creative producer is useful because the costume issue didn't seem too dramatic at the time but in retrospect it would have changed the dynamics and tone of the film and was actually very important. Linda adapted the costume that night after persuading DoP Jon Walker to relinquish his trousers, giving the dressed down 'look' everybody agreed was right.

Gen - Ironically we ended up using these scenes in the final cut of the movie to create a new story thread where Jason Connery's character comes back at the end of the film sometime after the main story has finished. The obvious costume difference implied a change in character and a passing of time. Quite funny considering it was a screw up!

Q - You mention bleach bypass - what is this?

Chris - Bleach bypass is a process in the labs where the film isn't put through the bleach bath. It makes the blacks and dark areas of the film almost impenetrable and it adds a kind of rich feel to the image. It's very subjective and is only used in the theatrical version of the film but it didn't half make it look great. *Seven* used it in the cinema.

Q - What did you shoot it on - S16mm or 35mm?

Gen - Even though we had £200k and could have afforded 35mm we chose S16mm. This was primarily because we had

> "What I really like to do best is whatever I'm not doing at the moment"
> Woody Allen

a thirteen year old girl in the lead and we didn't know if she would be a one take wonder or a take 26 disaster. In fact she was fantastic. It was also because we had learnt from our other films that coverage is paramount. It's a lot like the way Hollywood shoots films, we just wanted to burn stock like there was no tomorrow and we knew that if we shot on 35mm we wouldn't be able to do that.

A typical second unit pickup. On the day we were running late, the baby in the scene was tired and crying and it was unbearably hot. We ended up with no reverse shot of the chemist character, so the following day, the actor was brought back in, a tiny set was mocked up and the second unit picked up the shot.

Chris - We reasoned that audiences were not interested in whether a film was shot on S16mm, 35mm Kodak or Fuji, they were just interested in whether the story and characters were engaging. So we let go of the 35mm and embraced S16mm and truly did burn stock. It was the right decision and I know that the film wouldn't have been as good if we'd have shot on 35mm. We would have crisper shots, but fewer shots and diminished coverage.

Q - Did you use a second unit?

Gen - Yes. One of the things that was different with *UGS* from our other movies were that there were an enormous amount of characters. That combined with the fact that our young actress was legally only allowed to work for a few hours a day meant that often we had to have two cameras running on set. The second camera was usually free and roaming and would grab snippets of anything interesting when it could. A lot of the time, Chris would be directing the second unit whilst I was on set doing the main unit which freed me up to forget about doing close ups of newspapers or hands putting a cup down and concentrate on the drama and the actors.

Working with kids could present a nightmare scenerio. Fortunately, Heather Ann Foster was probably the most profesional cast member!

Chris - The other advantage was that I was able to use a stand in for Heather (Niki Ball) and shoot large portions of scenes with her, then Gen would come in with the lead actress, shoot her close ups, then move on. Because we were cutting as we shot I was able to isolate sequences that needed a cutaway to bridge two shots that weren't cutting comfortably and then go and shoot them, or shoot a cutaway to help cut the middle out of a dialogue scene that wasn't quite working - basically invent tiny segments of drama to help with the overall pacing of the movie. Even though we shot for only 4 weeks, because we pretty much had two units going almost all of the time, it enabled us to nearly double the amount of shots that we were able to achieve had there only been a single main unit.

Actress Heather Ann Foster aged 13 (L), with actress double Niki Ball aged 23 (R). We couldn't get a picture of them stood together wearing the same clothes as we only had one set!

CASE STUDIES

Eddie Hamilton got the job to edit UGS because he had so much energy and loved movies with passion. His technical expertise also meant that we could sleep safely in the knowledge that EDL nightmares, optical effects and sound track laying would all be taken care of.

Q - When did you edit?

Gen - Because we had a budget we were able to hire an Avid which we installed in a room 50 yards from Stage 4 where we were shooting. Our editor, Eddie Hamilton, was fresh out of the corporate video world but loved movies. He appeared to have limitless energy and showed us a short film he'd cut called *Hallraiser,* about a mad axe murderer in a hall of residence and shot on VHS. We recognised a kindred spirit who was born from a love of *Star Wars,* so we gave him the job even though he'd never cut drama before. It was a brilliant decision because Eddie's technical expertise, creative knowledge, combined with his almost super-hero like energy levels meant that by lunch time each day he'd already cut the previous days rushes. This meant we could watch the scenes over lunch and plan how we would plug any holes or problems, or just feel damn fine about how good we thought it was looking. We also let the actors look at some scenes which boosted their confidence in what they knew to be a low budget film that might not be working very well.

Chris - You have to be careful with this because one of the actors often become a unconfident after seeing themselves. I don't know why because they were fantastic. The upshot of having this Avid and Eddie cutting away, aside from plugging holes in scenes, was that by the end of the shoot, Eddie had pretty much cut the whole movie. So within a couple of days of wrapping we actually sat down and watched the movie.

Q - How did it look?

Gen - Terrible. It was the most depressing experience of my life. It was a shambles, all over the place, full of holes and it just didn't flow. My directorial debut was a disaster!

"I have ten commandments. The first nine are thou shalt not bore. The tenth is, thou shalt have the right of final cut"
Billy Wilder

Chris - I believe all movies are like that and the editing process is designed to smooth everything out and fine tune the story. Editing is an interesting stage because when you think about it, if there's a problem with the script, the editor has to fix it. If there's a problem with the acting, then the editor has to fix it. Problems with the camera, then the editor has to fix it. And so much of post production is just making something that doesn't work into something that does work.

And after a few drinks, the cut didn't seem as bad as we thought, but we knew we had a lot of work to do. We discovered there were a lot of holes we hadn't seen and we almost immediately planned a quick re-shoot weekend where we shot an extra 50 or so shots without any actors. These were things like exteriors of buildings etc.

Gen - Another advantage of cutting on Avid is that you can put it onto a VHS tape and watch it at home, or screen it to a large group of people which is exactly what we did.

Q - So you held test screenings?

Gen - Yes. The first one was with a few friends and whole sequences were still missing, like the car crash at the end of the movie, so it lacked an enormous amount of punch but we were just trying to find out if people understood the story mechanics that were going on underneath the bonnet of the film. We isolated a lot of problems and did another re-cut, then we had to plan the stunt sequence which Terry Forrestal co-ordinated for us. Once we had this footage and cut it in the whole movie came to life. To be quite honest, none of us expected the crash to be as spectacular as it was.

Chris - So we had another test screening, this time for a large group of 30 or so people who we didn't know. It was quite an eye opener as we discovered that all our friends had been on the whole fairly generous with their criticism. We weren't really interested in finding out whether people liked it or didn't like it. There's nothing you can do about personal taste, we just wanted to know whether the story was working and we discovered all sorts of problems.

Gen - I hated the screening because everything that I knew was wrong with it seemed to glow like a beacon. It was demoralising listening to what people were saying after Chris had stood up after the film and said to the audience *so tell me what's wrong with it?* - after the invitation to tear it apart, they didn't lose much time. In retrospect this was brilliant because all the problems became apparent, and every problem had a solution, so we were able to go back and fix them all. So whilst the process might have been demoralising, in the long run it was the best thing to do.

Chris - We discovered all sorts of strange things. When you write a script and make a film, you create a kind of road map

Test Screenings

1. Showing your film to an impartial audience is a good way to tell if your movie is working or not.

2. You can make a VHS tape from the Avid offline cut. You should add temporary music and effects, and where titles or scenes are missing, put a card up explaining what should be there.

3. There are lots of video projection venues that are cheap to hire. If you can't afford that, find someone with a huge TV and buy everyone pizza one night. Try to create as much of a theatrical experience as possible, so take the phone off the hook.

4. Invite the viewers to be as harsh as possible.

5. Watch the audience as they watch the film. Watch for them fidgeting or getting visually bored.

6. Have a freeform discussion at the end, ask questions about the things for which you have niggling doubts.

7. Draw up a questionnaire and ask them to fill it in anonymously. Have enough pens at the ready.

8. Don't get all your mates or relatives in, let them see it at the premiere. Get people who don't have anything to do with you or the movies, they will be less inclined to be generous.

9. Remember a test screening is all about finding the problems. Don't expect anyone to praise your film, and if they do, ask them what they hated about it.

10. Keep having as many test screenings as you can, and keep re-cutting as tight as you dare. Then cut some more out!

Fine Cuts

1. If in doubt, hack it out. You can always put it back in.

2. Dropping the ends of scenes sometimes helps, it can create a question in the audience's mind - what's going to happen next?

3. Don't be afraid of inventing new scenes, or lines of dialogue, getting the actors back and having a mini re-shoot. If the audience doesn't understand something fundamental you can fall back on the blunt instrument of explanatory dialogue.

4. Try and take a break before locking picture. When you come back to it you will see the movie with new eyes and increased energy.

5. If you are faced with the option of a long dull scene or shot that you can't cut away from, try hacking it with an unusual cut. It might work.

6. Don't be afraid. Fear and uncertainty are the demons with which you wrestle. Some people will like your film, others won't, but everyone will hate it if it's slow and boring.

7. Listen to the audience. Your average person has seen thousands of films, they are expert viewers. They know what they like and don't like, what is working for them and what isn't working. Don't fall into the mistaken position of believing you know better because you are the film maker.

8. Try not to get personal. It's just opinion and at the end of the day, whatever decisions you make, it isn't worth losing a friendship over.

9. Most of all, keep going back and cutting. Keep it lean and mean.

for the story, the idea is that the audience never knows what's round the next corner, the only problem is that sometimes you think they're driving along one road when actually they're off on a completely different road because of the way they've interpreted what they've seen. This happened in UGS with two characters - George was a character who was cut because everybody thought he was the father of the money grabbing loanshark. To everyone involved in the film it was an astonishing revelation that anyone could even consider this, yet there we were with thirty people all saying it to us.

So we had to make some brutal cuts and George hit the cutting room floor. It was an important lesson to learn that no matter how confident you are in your own story, you need to show it to people to test out whether it's working on a purely mechanical level. Do they understand who is who and what relations they have and do they understand where they are being led by you the film maker. If they don't, invariably they get confused and bored and will fall asleep. And we've all seen films where we don't really understand what's going on, or something in the fabric of the story seems very odd, this is probably because you're thinking one thing when the director thinks you're thinking something else.

Gen - We began fine cutting the movie. Even though Eddie was like Buzz Lightyear with inexhaustible batteries, the whole process began to wear his enthusiasm down. Chris and I argued vehemently in the cutting room, often over frames, or the slightly different delivery of lines, and it was very hard work - not just exhausting but it was a spiritual and emotional marathon.

Chris - Because of the fact that three re-cuts of *White Angel* had happened in the past, each time vastly improving the film, I was adamant that there wouldn't be a single frame in the movie that wasn't absolutely essential. This of course flew in the face of what Gen wanted because she was so in love with the nuances and detail that would inevitably require a few extra frames here and there. Eventually we agreed on a cut and after a test screening we felt sure that it was the right one. It felt lean and mean and everyone was happy. I was sure that the horror of re-cuts as we'd had on *White Angel* would never happen. Two months later we had a test screening for some industry people at Polygram. They came out and said it was good but it was too slow. I just couldn't believe it! I'd argued so aggressively to cut, cut, cut! I was sure there was nothing in there that could be taken out. But I knew from experience that even if you're sure, you could be wrong. I went to see Gen, who was recuperating with her family... *they're all wrong* she exclaimed, *but what if they're not?* I argued. For eight hours we fought until Gen dug her heels in explaining that it's her art, her film, and nobody was going to *fuck with it!*

Back in the office I'd secretly arranged for Eddie to drop by to argue the case for a recut of the first 25 minutes, the part of the story with pacing problems. Gen was still opposed to it but at the same time intrigued to see what would happen if we did cut 15 minutes. An hour later and we'd done it. Having been away from the movie for a few weeks it was incredible to see how baggy it was. The three of us sat in the cutting room with our jaws on the floor saying *why on earth did we leave all that junk in? - I can't believe we didn't cut it out before - It's so much better - Oh my God!...* That's the cut that we released, short at 86 mins., but we felt it's better to have a well paced shorter film than a long baggy affair.

> "Art is not a democracy, it's a collaborative tyranny"
> David Cronenberg

Q - UGS uses a famous bit of opera, why and how did that come about?

Gen - We knew we had to get the key sequence at the end of the film right. The car crash formed the pivotal question in the audience's mind *what happened?* - it was also the moment that Lizzie remembered just what did happen, as she faced death falling from a window thirteen floors up in her towerblock.

Chris - We broke this shoot out of the main shoot and did it eight weeks after we wrapped the main shoot. We knew this one would be hard and fast and wanted to have as much energy as possible, plus half of it was a night shoot. It was shot over two days with seven cameras, some running in extreme slow mo. When we got the footage back and Eddie cut the sequence together it was jaw dropping. It was at that moment that I said, *I don't know how or why, but we should put opera over this sequence, how can we do it?* I found an old opera CD that was free from a music magazine and I listened to all the famous tracks, until I heard one that seemed perfect. We put it on the Avid and watched it

George the handyman, a prominent character played by Richard Syms. During a test screening we discovered that the audience believed he was the father of a loan shark character who turned up later. This wasn't the case and we ended up having to cut the character to avoid this confusion.

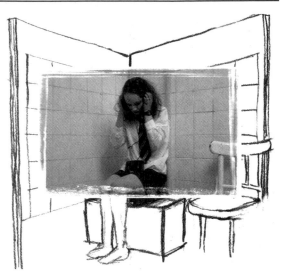

Micro Set - To plug the hole that had appeared because of the opera subplot, we needed to shoot three new scenes with Lizzie listening to her walkman in the loos. The sets had long gone so Chris Burridge built a micro set, simply two sheets of plywood with tiles, a pipe and loo seat that was screwed into a wooden box. The frame was kept tight and the illusion, helped by dripping water sound effects, was sealed.

with the pictures. There was stunned silence as everyone in the room knew that we absolutely must use this opera music.

Gen - The challenge now was to work out a way where we could plausibly use this music without it being self indulgent. Perversely this worked in our favour as part of the screenplay's problem had always been what reason was there for Lizzie to convieniently remember *what happenened in the crash?* at the end of the movie. We used the opera as a kind of acoustic memory that Lizzie has, and when she finally hears it in all it's glory, it triggers a series a mental flashbacks. We then worked in and shot three new scenes to explain it's presence.

Chris - Again this shows that with low budget films as you don't have enough money to write the script and go through as many drafts as is needed, you end up being forced to shoot before you're actually ready. The secret to making this work is to treat the editing as yet another screenplay revision and not be afraid to go back and re-shoot or invent entirely new characters, subplots, scenes etc.

Q - What did you learn directing UGS?

Gen - It's so exhausting! You have to keep your mind on everything all the time, constantly thinking on your feet. The other thing that surprised me was the physical rigours of directing. Unlike producing, you never have a chance to

"You may lose many battles but the trick is to win the war"
George Lucas

stop, there is always a line of people queuing up to ask you questions and the only time that your brain can actually stop is when you switch off the lights to go to sleep, even then your mind is buzzing over the days rushes and thoughts on the day to come.

Chris - There was a funny moment on the first day when I was driving Gen home, She was very depressed and I said *what's wrong?* and she said, *the actors, why couldn't they just act... better?* First days are always dreadful, and actors tend to do things differently from the way you imagined but that isn't necessarily bad work.

Gen - The most disappointing thing about directing is the constant compromise that you have to suffer, camera movements are never quite as good as you visualise, actors deliver performances differently from the way you imagined and there's just not enough time, money or daylight to get what you want. But in a strange sort of way these compromises become your allies because it allows the other creative people around you, as long as you have chosen carefully, to flourish and bring something new to the movie. We tried to work with the most talented creative people we could find and then let them loose within rigid parameters so that they could produce their best work but at all times it stays true to the spirit, vision, story and style of the movie.

There are times when the compromise is difficult to swallow but you have to ask yourself if I go for another take or another shot is it really going to improve what I want or not. It's easy to go for take after take in vain, hoping that the camera move will somehow get better or the actor will somehow do it differently. There's no hard rule here but I learnt to trust my instinct and not to waste time on

> "Wear comfortable shoes. And no matter what you're doing, if you suddenly have an idea for a brilliant shot, get it in and deal with the consequences later"
> Steven Spielberg

Directing is a physically rigorous job. Lack of sleep, mental exhaustion, severe back ache, poor diet and a crisis of faith are all very common.

CASE STUDIES

Nightmare compromise. The chemist heist scene - it's the first day of shooting, it's the hottest day of the year, the location is a tiny chemist with customers coming in and out, there's no air conditioning and the lights make it like an oven, you are behind schedule, the baby is going mad... and it's a really complicated scene. It was eventually shot hand held and the sheer spontaneity of the way in which it was filmed actually helped the scene. Second unit picked up a missing shot the following day and the scene was saved.

"There are no completed films, just abandoned films"
James Cameron

something if it isn't working. I knew that I had a second line of defence in the form of Eddie in the cutting room and he could work wonders with those scenes that I didn't think were working, as long as I had enough coverage to make it work.

Chris - Gen always says to me that there is one scene in the middle of the movie that she hates and regrets the day we shot it because I forced her to shoot it quickly the way that she did because we were so behind schedule. Again with no rules and just opinion, there is no answer aside from the fact that Gen tends to forget about the other times where compromises were made and the compromises didn't show. It's galling but you have to accept that some scenes will be disappointing and you'll end up hating them.

Q - Did directing ever get the better of you?

Gen - Yes, two thirds of the way through the shoot there was a day that I got so overloaded, stressed, hungry and frazzled that I became sick and I had to stop for three or four hours and go and lie down. Fortunately because Chris is also a director and close to the project it was just a matter of him stepping on set and continuing to direct one full scene so we didn't fall behind. Interestingly, although we're not going to tell you what scene it is, you can clearly detect a different directorial style and strangely when I saw it I thought *My God! That scene's great, I wouldn't have directed it that well!*

Chris - Then again when I saw some of the scenes that Gen did I said *My God I wouldn't have done it that way and it works so well*. Interesting how other peoples interpretation is surprising and that surprise makes it better.

Q - How did you approach producing Chris?

Chris - My approach to producing was very different from that of Gen's during *White Angel* and *The Runner*. Gen had taken the weight of production on to her shoulders and had taken every single problem as a personal challenge. I on the other hand, being lazy, decided that I would delegate everything, and I mean everything. I had a really good team of production people around me and I told them that *the only time that I wanted to hear from them was if we were about to be shut down, somebody was going to die or there is some impending disaster*, otherwise, they would fix it. I also developed a peculiar condition called producers cramp which manifested itself in the inability to sign cheques. Because I didn't pay anything until after the shoot I didn't have to keep a track on money and because I didn't have to deal with the thousands of production problems that occurred, my brain stayed clear. Consequently I was able to keep tabs creatively and I became for want of a better description, the cast and crew therapist. Crew members would regularly come to me and bemoan some compromise or condition that they had had inflicted upon them and I would say *there there, I understand and I care.* They'd get it off their chest and we'd get on with it. I didn't realise how important this role was in terms of team building but it meant that everybody's gripe was heard and if something could be done about it, it was.

Consequently from a production point of view, I wasn't stressed, I could deal with *real* problems in a level headed way and everything ran pretty much smoothly.

Q - Were there any major problems?

Chris - I don't know, the production team dealt with it.

Q - How did you do the joy riding car crash sequence?

Gen - Terry Forrestal who was the stunt co-ordinator on *The Runner* came back to do *UGS*. He now had a lot of even bigger movies under his belt and he really did it as a personal favour. There were two sequences - the car crash and the high fall out of the towerblock. From a stunt point of view, the car crash was very dangerous but essentially a fairly run of the mill stunt, a car hits a pile of sand, flips over, skids to a halt and explodes. You could probably see this kind of stunt in a BBC drama. The reason this sequence worked so well in *UGS* and why it looked much more impressive was because of the quantity and the diversity of coverage.

We had seven cameras all running as fast as they could so that they would slow down time on screen (slow motion). The main camera was on a very long lens about quarter of a mile away and this was running at nearly 300 fps, which meant that when the car flew through the air it slowed down so much that visually it looked stunning and smacked of John Woo! It was a very exciting night and even though the crash seemed to happen over just one or two seconds it felt like an eternity before Terry was pulled from the wreckage.

Virgin Directors

1. Don't try to make the greatest film ever. Work hard and be creative but recognise that this one will probably be all about learning.

2. Know your script and let go of as much producers work as you can. Don't get worried about problems that other people can deal with.

3. Cover the scene! Make sure you have enough shots to make it work. Don't believe your screenplay actors and direction is SO good that you won't need to cut it - you will.

4. Keep working. Don't think that when you wrap that is the end of the shoot. Keep shooting new scenes and cutaways as you need them.

5. Don't fixate on the camera, work with the actors and on the story. No-one is impressed by flashy shots, they want a movie that engages and moves them.

6. Rest when you can, get others to get you tea, coffee and food and avoid decisions you don't have to make.

7. Keep a walkman with you so you can listen to music to take you away from the set in order to clear your mind.

8. Rehearse. Work through your script with the actors. If you can't get them all before the shoot, substitute with other actors. It's important to read your script out loud and move actors around in space so that you can get a feel for anything that isn't working.

9. Casting. The most overlooked area of directing is casting, get the script and the cast right and you'll be hard pushed to screw it up.

Even though there were seven cameras on set, it was camera four, running at 250 fps, with a 500mm lens operated by Jay Polyzoides that was the one that produced the shot that gets the gasps in the cinema.

Chris - Then came the explosion with special effects man Dave Beavis. He had a limp which was vaguely worrying considering he was blowing something up for us, but we knew his credentials and felt confident. We set up all the cameras as he rigged the car to explode. Just before we started the cameras I asked him *how far away do we need to be safe?* - he coolly took three paces back and said *here's safe*. So we called action, the cameras started and Dave pressed the button - BABOOM!!! - I was hit by a blast of heat and then my hair stood on end as I watched a wall of flame come at me with terrifying speed. I glanced over to Dave who was casually scratching his chin as though nothing had happened. I looked over my shoulder at the crew but they weren't there, they were twenty yards away, and running! There were a lot of expletives. None of us had any idea how big the explosion was going to be, but whatever we had imagined it was at least three times bigger. It was a splendid experience! As Jason Connery put it, *how unlucky for Lizzie to steal a car only to find that there are 40lbs of semtex in the boot!*

Stunt Co-ordinator Terry Forrestal takes charge (left). To flip the car before hitting the stationary car a pipe ramp was bolted to the floor and greased up. Terry checks the trajectory meticulously as he will be in the car when it hits at 60mph (right).

Gen - The next day we had to do the high fall out of the building. What was supposed to happen here was Lizzie was to be holding on to some pigeon wire attached to the side of

the building thirteen stories up, the wire would give way and then she would drop - again coverage and slow motion made this scene work as well as it finally did. In fact this wasn't as dangerous in terms of stunts because the stunt girl, Danielle, was on a very thin cable and was dropped several floors as the pigeon mesh came away from the building. Still the moment that she came away and dropped was absolutely riveting. Even though you know it's a stunt and she's on a wire, and that there's a crash mat at the bottom, it still looks like somebody jumping out of a twenty story window!

One or two people screamed involuntarily which helped seal the tension on set. There was a guy walking his dog some forty feet away who hadn't seen the film crew and looked round when he heard the commotion only to see what he thought was a young girl falling out of a thirteenth floor window and screaming! We had to stop him ringing the emergency services and calm him down with a cup of tea!

Chris - When we screened the film in Cannes a couple of people came up to me and said *how did you do that stunt? That sequence with the crash and falling out the window that must have cost at least half a million quid.* I wryly smiled and said yes, it was a small portion of our budget that was well spent. In fact this entire sequence, with Equity stunt rates, including paramedic and the emergency services, the fire brigade, six extra cameras, pyrotechnic effects, location fees, cars to crash, special wire rigging etc. all came in under £20k. Sure it's a lot of money but for what we got it was the best twenty grand we've ever spent.

Q - How did you get the music written for UGS?

Gen - Harry Gregson-Williams had done the music for *White Angel* and then went off to Hollywood doing movies like *Armageddon* and *Antz*. As *White Angel* had been Harry's first feature film and because of personal contacts we really wanted Harry to do *UGS* and Harry wanted to do it too. Unfortunately the meagre music budget we had was severely outweighed by Jerry Bruckheimer and *Enemy of The State*, so Harry had to graciously bow out, but did suggest his brother might do a good job.

Danielle Da Costa, stunt double for Heather Ann Foster, wearing oversized costumes and wig, prepares to make her leap from the 13th floor whilst attached to a fan descender.

CASE STUDIES

Sales Agents

1. Consider the viability of your film as a salesman - would I want this film, and if not, why not?

2. First films are usually the fruit of a long held dream. From that perspective, if you feel the desire, don't worry about commercial viability. As long as the film isn't awful, and you don't spend too much money, you should get it screened somewhere.

3. Sales agents are tough to deal with. If they sign your film, they will more than likely want 15 years, 25% of sales, plus expenses and refuse a cash advance. The upshot is that you will probably never get paid. You MUST try to get a cash advance, and one large enough to cover your costs, but be aware that this is unlikely.

4. Keep some territories for yourself. If your sales agent messes you around, this will mean you can approach distributors in a different country and make a direct sale. You will get a lesser fee because you are not a sales agent, but it's better to get 100% of a $10k than 100% of nothing.

5. Alongside your film, you will have to supply a huge amount of delivery items (See Delivery List elsewhere in the book). These are important and often overlooked. Without these items, no sales agent will touch the film, or they will fulfil the delivery list and charge you. Take care of it yourself. Study this list and make sure you know what each thing is, how much it will cost, and where you will get it.

Chris - We decided to have a look at a bunch of other composers but bizarrely enough Rupert, Harry's brother, was indeed the best choice. He tapped in to the style of music that we wanted, something contemporary and upbeat. It was important not to give it a Hollywood thriller sounding score and equally we couldn't just pack it with Brit pack band songs. I think the music is one of the strongest elements in the film because it is so left field from what you would imagine from a movie called *Urban Ghost Story,* set in Glasgow, and yet it seems to work so incredibly well.

Gen - We were also very specific with Rupert about where and how much music we were going to use and in comparison with our earlier films there isn't that much music in the whole movie, probably around 25 minutes. The music was composed of samples, electronic instruments and wherever possible, real performers. We recorded it over Christmas and all of us all got very severe food poisoning from a dodgy curry. The last thing you want to do when you're up against a deadline is to spend a day chucking your guts up, it's not what you call creatively inspiring.

Q - So you completed all your post production. When did you start to talk to sales agents and distributors?

Chris - After Polygram had made their comments and we'd recut the movie we set up a screening in the centre of London with high hopes because we knew that *UGS* was the best film that we'd made. One thing that had surprised me during earlier screenings is that at the end of the movie, people were in tears because they had found the resolution emotionally moving. We never expected people to cry at the end, but the combination of Heather's performance, the lighting, the music and the story worked so well that everybody started sniffling. We were starting to get a sense that the movie we had made actually looked like one thing, ie a ghost story, but was actually another thing, i.e. a story about guilt and redemption. This dichotomy was at the heart of the problems we were going to have as we tried to sell the movie. *Is it a ghost story? Is it a social realist drama?* We always said that it was a ghost story in a social realist world and that was it's unique position.

Gen - So the distributors watched it, all smiled and passed on it because they didn't know what box to put it in. In the absence of any good reviews or press they also didn't know whether people would take to it or not. Only one company was interested, Stranger Than Fiction, who were already acting as our sales agents for *White Angel*. We were very excited because they were about to sign a deal where they were going to have an influx of cash, which meant that they would have a high profile at Cannes and our movie would be their number one product.

Chris - We had run out of cash and the laboratory processing bill meant that we owed the lab about twenty grand. We were eager to get sales so we signed with Stranger Than Fiction and they began putting together all the bits. A top design agency put together a poster for *UGS* which was about as far away from what either of us had imagined, yet it seemed really fresh and original and we liked it a lot. So we went with it. It was bold red and very eye catching which meant that when we flyposted in Cannes, it really stood out. The poster definitely worked for the movie and it also conveyed a sense that there was perhaps more to this than just a simple spooky tale.

Gen - We'd already cut a trailer for *UGS* which we really liked, but Stranger Than Fiction asked for another one but for this time they said *make it look like Die Hard with ghosts*. So Eddie, who is already energetic to start off with, was caffeined up and locked in a cutting room for a day only to emerge eight hours later, eyes bloodshot and hair crazy, explaining *it's done*. We watched it and somehow Eddie *had* made it look like *Die Hard!* It wasn't exactly a fair representation of the film but it was big and ballsy.

Q - What happened when you took UGS to Cannes?

Chris - We wanted a big push at Cannes so decided to take a few friends down with us, all of whom had worked on the film. All in, there were six of us and we were determined to make sure that everybody in Cannes had heard of *UGS*. Every morning we would go up and down La Croisette and fly post anything that didn't move - cars, telephone boxes, railings, Hollywood movie posters. Within a few hours they'd all have been taken down because it's illegal, so in the afternoon we went and flyposted again. The posters were just the red coloured image that we had decided on for the film and its simplicity and boldness really worked in our favour. After a couple of days everyone we bumped into would say, *Oh yeah I've heard of that film Urban Ghost Story*. It was

6. In the UK you will have to get certification from the BBFC. Remember they will produce a certificate card which you have to shoot and cut onto the front of every print.

7. Think about whether you want to shout about how little you shot the film for. Other films have used this tactic successfully but abroad it could damage sales. In the eyes of a buyer, a film is worth what it cost.

8. Attending one of the big film markets like Cannes, MIFED or the AFM will broaden your outlook of sales agents and of how films are marketed and sold.

9. Get a performance clause in your contract, if they don't do a certain amount of sales, you can get the film back.

10. Cap expenses so that they have to get written permission to spend more than you agreed initially. Otherwise they could be free to charge you whatever they want.

11. Be tough from day one. Insist on reports as agreed, prompt payment, accurate information. Make them understand that you will not tolerate complacency. If you make yourself a nuisance, which is well within your rights, they might actually give you what you want.

12. We are moving into a global marketplace. Consider very seriously selling your film yourself. You might not have the contacts or the budget, but ANY sales made will mean cash in your pocket and not the pocket of a sales agent.

CASE STUDIES

HEATHER ANN FOSTER   JASON CONNERY   STEPHANIE BUTTLE

URBANGHOSTSTORY

She should be dead...

Now she wishes she was

The poster for Urban Ghost Story wasn't at all what we expected, but it was different, suggested there was more to the film than just a spooky tale, and it was bold. The red hue made it stand out when fly-posting and everyone seemed to remember the name of the movie.

> "It doesn't matter how new an idea is, what matters is how new it becomes"
> Elias Canetti

very labour intensive and damned hot but worth it.

Gen - We also had three screenings which we tried to sell out, the first was hard, but the second and third were packed houses and the buzz on the street was that UGS was a cool movie. We also approached every company and gave them an invite to come to the screening, again it's really hard work knocking on so many doors, sensing rejection from people then trying to get them interested. But it has to be done.

Q - Did you pitch new projects when you were there?

Chris - One of the fun things we decided to do was to see how far we could get by talking the talk. Myself and fellow film maker Simon Cox decided to give it a try. We went to the Noga Hilton, targeted the companies who make and sell American style B movies, swaggered in, pitched, told them that we had half of the $2m budget already in place. Of course we didn't but it was really an exercise to see how far you could get with bullshit. Within an hour, we had an Anglo-Canadian co-production for a science fiction thriller that we hadn't even written, budgeted at $2.2m, to be shot in Wales and post produced in Canada. Clearly we couldn't pursue this because we didn't have the $1m that we claimed we had, neither the screenplay or even the desire to make it! But it did show how quickly you can put something together if you have something that you want to do and a bit of cash. We also dropped in on Troma, who had their new movie, *Killer Condom*. Over dinner that night we came up with a concept for a new movie for them and the following day went and pitched it. It was called *The Breath of Death the Killer Fart*. We'd already constructed a really strong story with a beginning, middle and end and it held water. The guys at Troma got very excited and again we talked the talk but really didn't want to make an end of the world movie about an evil doctor and his Killer Fart potion!

Gen - One major distinction from our previous Cannes visits is that because we had a film that was screening, we were perceived as credible film makers. We were invited to parties and dinner and got to hob nob with fairly important people on a more level playing field than we'd ever experienced before. One of the reasons we also got a lot of coverage was because Jason Connery also came down to Cannes and worked very hard with us to get as much good press and exposure as possible. It's really important to have positive and constructive support from your cast as they represent the glitz that Cannes is really all about.

Chris, with fellow film maker Simon Cox, try to sell a concept to Troma, agents for Killer Condom. Their movie, The Breath Of Death - The Killer Fart.

Q - Did you sell the film?

Chris - Yes, one far eastern company from a small territory came to look at the trailer that Eddie had cut, the one that makes it look like *Die Hard.* They got very excited and bought the film. A couple of months later we discovered that they were going to do a 15 print theatrical release and we were opening against *Armageddon -* It was *Urban Ghost Story* vs *Armageddon!* I started to wonder whether the guy had actually seen the film. A week later I discovered that he hadn't and when he finally watched it he had a bit of a panic attack because it wasn't the horror movie he thought it was and that even worse *it wasn't even in English but in Scottish!* The next contact I had was when he asked me if I wanted to buy back 15 prints as he was unable to open the film.

Q - Did you premiere the film at a film festival?

It looks great in the photos and on telly, but Cannes is often exhausting, hot, sweaty, and downright expensive.

Gen - We chose Edinburgh as our World Premiere because UGS is a Scottish movie, the people at the festival liked the

437

"I don't know if ANY film will ever make a profit"
Carolyn Lambert

movie, Jason lived quite close and the timing was right. We wanted to make a big impact and from the outset wanted to promote ourselves as film makers as well as the movie. We wanted the whole world to hear about *Living Spirit Pictures, Urban Ghost Story, Chris Jones* and *Genevieve Jolliffe*. We hired a publicist who cost us a couple of grand but in terms of what we got it was well worth spending as we had full pages in daily newspapers, excellent write ups in magazines and plenty of telly.

Because of the work load in the office, Chris decided to stay behind in London for the first couple of days whilst I went ahead to do the press. As soon as I stepped off the plane it was interview after interview and before either of us knew it, the story ceased to be about *Chris, Gen, Living Spirit* and *Urban Ghost Story* and became *hot new attractive female young film director makes startling debut film.*

Chris - Suddenly Gen was everywhere in the press and I was mentioned in the fine print, if at all. It was the first time that either of realised just how the world views the film makers, the producer is ignored and the director is given all the credit. Everybody and I mean everybody, thinks that the director is the only person who made the film. Whether they've heard of the auteur theory or not, they believe it. Sure the actors acted in it, but the producer, writer, editor, cameraman etc - were merely pawns in the director's grander view. It's sad because there is so much creative talent focused on the production of the film and yet only one person is recognised.

Jason Connery was 100% behind the movie and spent much of his time in Cannes promoting Urban Ghost Story. On this occasion he is doing a live link for Sky News. Getting your cast behind your film is extremely valuable because journalists are always up for an interview with an actor, they're just prettier than us film makers!

Every film will have it's premiere. Make the most of it as it will probably be one of the best nights of your life.

Q - How did the screenings go?

Chris - We had a great response and Q&A session afterward. But then something else happened which neither of us were prepared for. As we were being whisked away from the theatre my mobile phone rang. It was an agent who had seen the film and wanted to meet up with Gen. Then the phone rang again and it was another agent again wanting to meet with Gen. On the one hand it was really exciting because this was a fantastic opportunity and at last we were being taken seriously by the business, but on the other hand, it was a real downer as clearly they were only interested in the *hot new attractive female young film director who made a startling debut film.* The positive press had really worked for Gen, but not for me. Whenever an agent would even consider me in the equation they'd take a look at *The Runner* and *White Angel,* then say *well they're nowhere near as good as UGS, clearly Gen is the one with the talent.* Of course they aren't as good, we didn't know then what we do know now and the next film we make will be better than UGS! It's common sense. But they and the industry in general, just kept on coming back saying well we don't care what you tell us about collaboration, Genevieve is *the hot new young attractive female film director who made a startling debut film.*

Gen - It was difficult because we are both film makers and had hoped that one day we would get agents and a chance to move into the bigger playground. Here was this opportunity for me, but it was quite clearly for me alone. It caused a lot of friction between us. Even though we'd made three movies collaboratively, it's always the director who is picked up.

> "If people could deal with one another honestly, they would not need agents"
> Raymond Chandler

Getting An Agent

1. If you're partnered, discuss how you will deal with an imbalance of power / opportunity when success arrives.

2. Invite agents to a screening of your film and explain that you are seeking representation.

3. Don't sign with the first agent. Find a person you like, who understands your tastes and what you want to do. Find someone who will represent you accurately.

4. Don't go for the biggest agent, go for the agent that is right for you and your needs.

5. The agent won't get you work, they will just get you into a room with the people who can offer the work. You have to deliver on the promise.

6. Arm your agent with press clippings, copies of your film and showreels.

7. Listen to your agent. If you have chosen wisely they will mentor you and help you through the new world of the film business. It is not the same world as the low budget one, so open your mind to learn.

8. If you have made a well received first film, everyone will be watching the second to see if you deliver on the promise of the first. A good agent will steer you toward the kind of work that will showcase your strengths and away from work that will be disappointing.

9. Keep in touch regularly. If you haven't spoken to your agent for several weeks, give them a call to remind them of you, to get yourself fired back up and chat about any new opportunities that might have arisen.

Q - So did you sign with an agent?

Chris - After meeting several agents, Gen met up with one back in London and they got on like a house on fire. She really understood what Gen wanted to do with her career and seemed like she could open doors in Hollywood.

Within days and out of the blue a Fedex landed on Gen's desk. It was a big studio werewolf movie budgeted at $15m, and they were looking for a hot shot new director. They'd seen *UGS* in Hollywood as we had a print out there. We can only surmise why they liked it but it's probably because it felt like a unique slant on a ghost story. So Gen read the script and got back to them and before anyone knew it she was on a plane to LA being given the red carpet treatment.

Gen - We put together some concept sketches and asked Phil Mathews, an old effects buddy from *White Angel,* to mock up a werewolf model. Armed with this I marched into the office of the studio head and did the talk. The moment I landed and had my first meeting in LA, I started to get calls from all the other studios wanting to meet me. Hollywood seems to be constantly in search of new talent.

This was about a year ago now and the project still hasn't been made, with either myself or another director. I think this is part of the way of Hollywood movies, so many films seem to so nearly happen but falter before the final hurdle. This has happened several times with other projects too. It's really frustrating because I put all my personal projects on pause whilst I threw everything at these movies and at the end of the day you just have no control over your own destiny. It was also difficult because the opportunities were clearly for me and whenever I tried to bring Chris in, it just seemed to weaken my position.

Chris - When Gen got back from LA we had to have a heart to heart and accept that she was going to go first and that wherever possible I would be standing right behind her on her coat tails. I had to accept that that was the way the business works and because Gen and myself had gone through so much over the last few movies I knew that come hell or high water I could trust her. If you're in a film partnership with another person, I can't stress how important it is that you have a very frank and open minded discussion about what will happen if one of you suddenly gets an unbelievable opportunity but that opportunity excludes the other. Gen and I had many unpleasant arguments which really boiled down to my frustration at the fact that other people were marginalising me as a film maker. It was out of Gen's hands and I just had to come to terms with the fact that we're a partnership and that if she's going to get an amazing opportunity then hopefully I will be there for the next amazing opportunity. No matter how we looked at it we just couldn't turn away from Hollywood over the question of who gets the glory and who gets to go first.

Gen - A few months later we went to LA to present ourselves as more of a team and pitch our personal projects.

Chris - This was an amazing experience because we'd spent so long complaining that we were totally ignored by the film industry and there we were sitting in Dreamworks pitching our movies. It became clear that the only thing now stopping us from making a $40m movie was the fact that we didn't have a fabulous screenplay that was ready to go. If we'd had that 120 page juicy script we'd have finished shooting by now.

Concept paintings by Alex Fort and a six inch high maquette sculpted by Phil Mathews all helped illustrate what Gen wanted to achieve with the werewolf movie.

Q - Did you meet Steven Spielberg when you were at Dreamworks?

Chris - Yes. We had a wonderful chat.

Gen - You said *Hi* and he said *Hi* back!

Q - So is it that easy to get to meet people in LA?

Gen - Yes and no. If you've made an interesting first film you can take advantage of their perception that you might be the next Tarantino or *Blair Witch.* Ideally this is the point at which they will say *so what have you got next?* And you'll put that 120 page script on their desk. They'll have seen the film because they have their own 35mm screening rooms and they'll say *we can see from your film that you have talent but this film is too small for us, what have you got next?*

Q - So you are starting to meet more important people who could help your career in LA?

Chris - Yes, since we've started to schmooze and hang

"Artisan has done a marketing survey for the sequel to Blair Witch and 40% of the people surveyed in the US still think it is real. I am not sure what that says about the US"
Eduardo Sanchez

around with more important film makers we've found ourselves in a strange new world. Once we were taken out for dinner to the poshest restaurant that I'd ever been in. I needed to go to the loo so I excused myself and went to the gents - as I walked in I was hit by opulence, the bathroom was polished marble. Whilst peeing I looked at the urinal and said to myself, *this has got to be the nicest urinal that I've ever peed in, there's all this water sprinkling down, it's made of marble and oh look there's even coins in the bottom.* I look over my shoulder to see a row of normal urinals and realised with horror that I was pissing in an ornate fountain!

Gen - I think you'd had a little too much to drink.

Q - How about people in the UK film industry?

Gen - Before I knew it, I was sitting at a table next to Nik Powell at the First Annual British Independent Film Awards for which I'm nominated as Best Director and Chris is nominated as Best Producer. We're up against films like *Elizabeth, Nil by Mouth,* and *My Name Is Joe.* We had no expectations and we didn't win, but it was another indicator as to how slowly and surely we were working our way into the British Film Industry. The deep irony here is that just as we're breaking into the British film industry both of us can't help thinking about Hollywood.

Q - Did you take UGS around the festival circuit?

Gen - Because *UGS* is an original film it started to get invited to heaps of festivals. Being a hard up film maker, when you get offered an all expenses trip to somewhere like Korea or Australia it's really hard to turn it down, especially if you love travelling. So I've spent a good part of the last eighteen months in airport lounges, sitting at dinner tables with important dignitaries and I don't even know how to pronounce their names. This all sounds great but the problem is that I haven't spent the time I should have spent on writing my next screenplay

Another Hollywood project that appeared was The Crow Part 4. Chris and Gen met with Ed Pressman for The Crow franchise and pitched a concept about a blind samurai nun. They liked it a lot, suggested some changes, and it looks like the project may be written in the summer of 2000. But again, like other opportunities, it may be a wonderful success or the opportunity may completely disappear, and always for reasons beyond your control.

and whenever anybody says *I've just seen Urban Ghost Story, what's next?* I have to fall back on *I'm writing the film at the moment and I'll let you have a copy when it's completed.* I would be in such a good position if I could just drop that screenplay on their desk, there and then.

Chris - It became a running joke. Whenever Gen went to a festival she'd spend the week before pontificating about how much great work she'd do on her screenplay whilst abroad in those foreign exotic lands, writing on her laptop and generally living the lifestyle of an ex pat creative.

Gen - Of course when you're on the plane you're asleep and when you're in an exotic place you want to go out and sample exotic food and drinks, see the world and meet the people. The last thing you want to do with your five days is work hard on that screenplay.

Q - Do distributors see the film at festivals?

Gen - Yes and there's no reason why, if you're so motivated, you couldn't cut some kind of deal. If you want to do this though, you really need to think about faxing all the distributors before the festival, sending them flyers and press packs, even a VHS trailer, then when you get to the festival you'll need to do fly posting, a lot of press and make sure that you have both PAL and NTSC tapes for distributors who missed the screening. Don't leave this to your sales agent or it might not get done. You'll also meet other film makers, I met one producer who may well end up producing my next movie which is very exciting.

Q - Is it hard to keep going?

Chris - Fitting everything in is a real problem because amongst developing your new projects, dealing with sales and distribution, going to film festivals etc. You have to do things like answer the phone, do accounts and empty the waste paper basket. Making a film generates an enormous amount of stuff to deal with and you shouldn't underestimate how much hassle that is. If you can find someone you can trust, delegate as much as you can, because the window of opportunity after you've finished your film can be short and you mustn't be tied down by the hum drum day to day of running a business. You need to be out there pitching and selling yourself as aggressively as possible.

Survivors Guide to LA

1. Rent a car. LA is a city built for the car. You can turn right on a red light as long as the route is clear, park in the same direction as the traffic and don't expect people to indicate when they change lanes. Valet parking is nearly everywhere so don't panic when you pull up outside a restaurant and they take your car keys.

2. Jay walking (crossing the road at a non designated point) is illegal and you could get an on the spot fine.

3. LA is not a late night city. There are late bars but few and far.

4. Tipping is expected. Waiters - 15%, Bartenders - 10-15%, valet parking $1-2.

5. Internet outlets. Very difficult to find, disappearing and popping up all the time. There are several outlets in Venice Beach and there is a 24 hour Kinkos on Sunset Blvd, but beware, it's pricey.

6. Foreign exchange - the easiest way to get cash is from an ATM so don't forget your cards or pin numbers.

7. It's Cell phones not mobiles. Have your Cell Phone turned international or rent one whilst you're out there. Buy a telephone card at the Airport, they are cheaper than pay phones, you can use any phone and they can be topped up at any time from your credit card.

8. Buy the film trade mags. Hollywood Reporter and Daily Variety. Pick up LA Weekly and The New Times Los Angeles, free weeklies that tell you what's going on in town.

CASE STUDIES

LOS ANGELES

Pacoima

Roscoe Blvd.

Van Nuys

Burbank

Glendale

Pasadena

Ventura Blvd.

Colorado Blvd.

Eagle Rock

Hollywood

Hollywood Blvd.

Beverly Hills

Wilshire Blvd.

Dodger Stadium

Sunset Blvd.

Washington Blvd.

Adams Blvd.

East Los Angeles

USC Exposition Park

Downtown

Martin Luther King Jr. Blvd.

Santa Monica

Slauson Ave.

Huntington Park

The Forum

Florence Ave.

Inglewood

Manchester Ave.

Hollywood Park

Watts

Century Blvd.

South Gate

Downey

Los Angeles Intl. Airport

Lennox

Imperial Hwy.

El Segundo Blvd.

Lynwood

Hawthorne

Rosecrans Ave.

Lawndale

Compton

Gardena

Artesia Blvd.

Redondo Beach

Carson St.

Carson

Torrance

Lakewood

Carson St.

Pacific Ocean

Rolling Hills

Pacific Coast Hwy.

Long Beach

1992 MAGELLAN GeographixSMSanta Barbara, CA (800) 929-4627

444

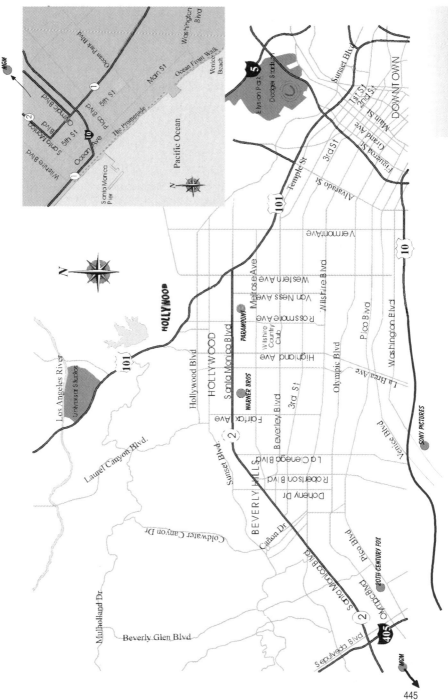

9. Eating is cheap. Shopping malls have food courts with a wide variety of cheap but good fast food. Dining out is also pretty good value unless you want to be ultra hip and trendy and eat in exclusive places.

10. Set up your meetings before you arrive, you don't want to waste any valuable time in LA making phonecalls and setting up meetings for the next few days.

11. Staying in town. There are plenty of motels that are cheap and cheerful, especially mid town. Santa Monica and Venice Beach can be great places to stay but it's pricey.

12. Check out the film bookstores - it's a town for film makers so there are books galore on the subject.

13. Do the LA thing whilst you're there, Rollerblading and people watching on Venice Beach, Universal Studios, Disneyland.

14. Check out the movie theatres. American audiences are much more enthusiastic and don't fear airing their opinions in a theatre. Almost as entertaining as the film itself.

15. Dress to impress. LA is a town where everyone looks great, don't go to meetings in your grotty old jeans and holey T shirts.

16. Flights - shop around for the cheapest as prices vary. It's a long flight, usually about eleven hours, a long time if you aren't used to long flights. LA is eight hours behind the UK, so our late afternoon is their morning.

Gen - This problem is exacerbated by the fact that you'll probably be broke and not able to pay an accountant and you'll have to do that vat return every three months in order to reclaim some money, then meet with the bank manager because you've gone overdrawn. All of this crap is labour intensive, stressful and generally counter-creative.

Q - How has UGS done?

Chris - So far we haven't been able to secure a UK theatrical deal although by the time you read this UGS may well have been released. At Cannes two years ago Germany bought UGS and a few other much smaller territories were snapped up too. Unfortunately our sales agent Stranger Than Fiction haven't supplied us with the financial information we need in order to calculate how well it has done. As far as we're aware the sales we've achieved have been very disappointing and what is more frustrating, Stranger Than Fiction haven't responded to our requests for information. By our calculations (as we go to press) they owe us over £30k and it is very frustrating for us because they won't either confirm or deny this. They just don't make contact, return phonecalls or respond to faxes.

The sales agent/distributor dynamic with new film makers always seems to be fraught. Every film maker we have ever met has complained about their sales agent and distributor. I think it's fair to say that selling a low budget film is very difficult and that unless you make something fiercely original or blisteringly good it's unlikely that your project will financially succeed. Even if you have made such a good film there is still a very good chance that it will fail.

Gen - From day one we have been open to the probability that Urban Ghost Story might not make many sales, but it's unbearably frustrating for us to simply have such little communication for months and months that we just can't tell our investors where we stand.

Chris - One thing new film makers tend to get very upset about is making sure that they have everything contractually tied up. It's just worth stressing that even if you have a strong contract, if somebody wants to breach that contract, or is forced to breach that contract by their own circumstances they can and may well do so. A simple example of this is with our sales agents Stranger Than Fiction who even

though they are contractually obliged to supply us with information, they simply don't. We know that they were paid for our German deal over seven months ago and as we're interviewed here, we still haven't got all the money we are due or even had any kind of communication to explain why we haven't. We've been asked to not comment further because we have been forced to place this whole matter in the hands of our solicitor

The mix of spooky story, urban setting and social realist with a slash of Hollywood treatment made Urban Ghost Story an odd movie. A hit with the critics, film festivals and Hollywood executives, all of whom respond to it's unique qualities, but a failure with international sales as buyers just don't know what label to put on it, Ghost Story or Social Drama.

Gen - Again it's a common story that the film maker ends up in some kind of dispute with the sales agent or distributor. It's very sad when you consider that every other person in the film making process from the camera hire companies to

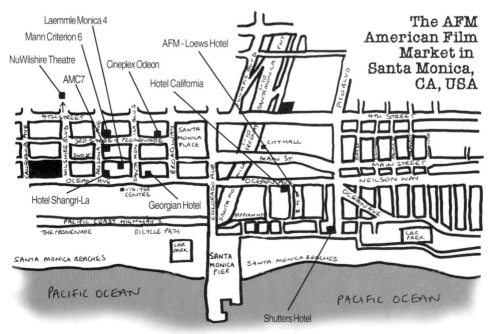

The AFM American Film Market in Santa Monica, CA, USA

Laemmle Monica 4
Mann Criterion 6
AFM - Loews Hotel
NuWilshire Theatre
Cineplex Odeon
AMC7
Hotel California
Hotel Shangri-La
Georgian Hotel
Shutters Hotel

CASE STUDIES

> "The difference between American and European cinema is that in American cinema, entertainment comes first and soul-searching comes second. In European cinema, soul-searching comes first and entertainment second, if at all"
> Milos Foreman

the actors, the caterers to the dubbing mixers, have all bent over backwards with their generosity in order that they help you make your film only for it to end up not getting the exposure it deserves because there are so few sales agents and distributors to go to in order to sell your film. It really does beg the question why not sell the film yourself

Q - You had a documentary crew follow you?

Chris - Yes, video documentary film maker Denise Rose followed us for two years and we allowed her to capture everything that happened, without censorship. She is still cutting but watch our web site for when it will be completed, it's the *Ben Hur* of film documentaries!

Q - What have you learnt from UGS?

Gen - When opportunity knocks you've got to be ready, you mustn't be distracted. If you're in a film making team be prepared to face an imbalance of reward and remember the producer doesn't get the attention. If Hollywood is interested, have your next project ready. Don't have too much fun travelling the world with festivals, get on to your next screenplay and your next movie. We've both learnt that you need certain things, talent not being at the top of the list, but energy and enthusiasm being of paramount importance, original ideas and the ability to tell familiar stories in a different way, but probably the most important factor is your ability to get on with people and nurture your contacts. One strange thing is that you've probably spent years being ignored by the industry, then suddenly you're considered for twenty fully funded films where you'll earn more in ten weeks than you have in the last ten years. Don't accept the first one that comes along, wait for the right one, and that's difficult when you've been struggling for so long. At the same time don't wait too long so people lose interest in you.

Video documentarian Denise Rose followed Living Spirit on their journey for two years as they made Urban Ghost Story. The resulting 80 hours of footage will produce one of the frankest, perhaps even horrifying, documentaries about the making of a low budget feature film. Check out www.livingspirit.com for details of it's completion.

Chris - One important thing is that UGS was a film that we wanted to make, not for a market, but for selfish personal reasons. Therefore it's unique and interesting, and that's what seems to get people excited. They don't want this movie, but they want you to make one for them. We were also very lucky as we found Dave, our Executive Producer who was the only person with the vision and belief and the ability to equip us so that we could make the movie. Without Dave we might still be on the phone and sending scripts out.

Gen - It's been echoed by other film makers that we've interviewed in this book, but if there's one thing you should do, it's MAKE THE MOVIE YOU WANT TO MAKE!

Q - Where to next?

Chris - The only thing that we can truly control is making low budget independent films so we're both working on lowish budget films, mine's called *Rocket Man and Vampire Girl* and Gen's working on a thriller

Chris and Gen in the Hollywood Hills prior to their meeting at Dreamworks.

set in Glasgow and a romantic comedy set in Australia. But we just don't know whether any of these films will happen with 'real' money or if we will have to do them low budget again. It's an exciting time for Living Spirit as Hollywood is continually seducing us, it just seems like we are the right breed of film maker for them, so it's undeniable that we will spend time in La La land making our movies. It's taken us a long time to get to where we are, but for the first time it genuinely feels like we're on the edge of making it and actually earning a descent living out of being a film maker. Then again, who knows?

Gen - Sometimes I wonder if making films is actually a curse. The strange thing and this is something that some people just don't understand, is that we just *have* to make movies. I often think what it would be like to have a more normal job with a regular payslip, especially as water is leaking through my living room ceiling and I've just run out of 50p coins for my electricity meter! We're still broke, credit cards maxed out and still continue to be struggling film makers. But we couldn't and wouldn't do anything else. We have been through hell but whenever I lose the faith I go to the movies and the magic that happens on the silver screen is like a drug, I'm elated and addicted all over again.

Chris - If film making was a sport it wouldn't be football, swimming or the hundred metre dash, it would be a marathon. More than anything, I've learned that going the distance is the most important thing. Some of your friends and peers will be able to run the marathon as though it's a hundred metre dash, the very lucky ones get helicoptered to the finishing line, many of your friends will fall by the wayside exhausted and disillusioned but if you've got the stamina you'll make it to the finish and anyone who makes it to the finish, is a winner.

"You have to get lucky at some point, but you can only get lucky if you are still on the road, and for each of us that road, that journey is a different length. The thing is to keep doing it and doing it, any way you can"
Lawrence Kasdan

Neil Price is in a bad mood.
He got up on the wrong side of the country this morning.

TAGGERE[D]

'Staggered' and 'Sliding Doors' by Philippa Braithwaite

Q - Why did you decide to become a film maker?

Philippa - It was something I always wanted to do, I just loved films. I started off working on commercials and promos before moving into TV. I knew that I wanted to make films but didn't really know how to do it. I read scripts trying to find something to do, and then I thought, even if I find it, I've got to be in with the only funding sources around at that time - British Screen and Channel Four - and I thought I'd never get it funded. As soon as I had read the script for *Staggered*, I thought I should do it. I'd read how Gary Sinyor had done *Leon the Pig Farmer* and decided I'd do just that.

Q - What attracted you to Staggered?

Philippa - My brother's a writer and he came to me with the idea so the project landed on my desk and I didn't have to do contracts with writers I didn't know. He was going to do it with another writer, Paul Alexander who writes for TV, and I thought it sounded like a great idea - they pitched it and I said *Yeah, let's go off and make it.* It was light-hearted and at that time British films were so boring and worthy and I just thought, rightly or wrongly, that those weren't the kind of films I wanted to make, nor did I believe those were the kind of films people wanted to go and see. *Staggered* sounded like a great idea and I thought we could get a good British cast together and just do something that somebody would want to go out and see on a Friday night, no more, no less. I also felt that it would work well outside London in the multiplexes.

Q - Did any UK companies put any cash up front to develop the film?

Philippa - In '92 I had a well paid job but I didn't want to do it anymore. The only way I was going to make a film was to just do it, no-one was going to give me development money for the script, no-one knew who I or the writers were, so I just decided to save some money and leave the job. The only way to get it made was to give up and commit 24 hours a day and take the risk.

Q - What other people were involved in the project?

Philippa - My brother Simon was the associate producer, his enthusiasm was brilliant and he was somebody I could trust. The lawyers, Gouldens, who put together the Business Expansion Scheme package were great. We couldn't have done it without them and they deferred their fees.

Q - How long was it between saying, 'Yes, let's do this', and the first day of shooting?

Philippa - It was the middle of December when we had a two line idea, and we started shooting on August 24th 1993, so it was just over eight months. We then shot for six weeks. We shot on 35mm as I thought that was the only way of getting a good chance of a theatrical release. We shot six days a week, but quite long days. We couldn't afford to go into a studio nor could we afford to pay for locations, so we were all over the place. You just lose so much time running around and also trying to keep up the morale of people who aren't being paid.

Q - Were you entirely deferred?

Philippa - Yes, but I made sure nobody was out of pocket. We paid for travel and fed them, but they weren't paid anything. We did pay the actors a bit up front, 80% of their fee was deferred but I thought there was a better chance of getting actors involved if you can say there's something here. The hardest people to get are always the grips and sparks. It was much easier getting Heads of Department because they obviously wanted to work on features and it's much more valuable for them than for a spark.

Q - How long did it take for you to cut the film?

Philippa - Our editor had a steenbeck so we cut it on film. It took longer than I thought it would as our editor didn't have an assistant, so he was doing everything. We finished shooting at the end of October and had a finished print at the end of February.

Q - Did you have the money in place before you shot?

Philippa - We had the money to shoot but not complete. We raised private finance and it was only by the skin of our teeth that we had it in place in time. I had to set a date for filming and get everything lined up otherwise we wouldn't get the cast we wanted. The extra money to complete the film came in three days before the shoot, so it was hairy and I couldn't tell anybody. The usual producer problems.

Q - Did your finance come from a private source?

Philippa - Lots and lots of private sources. I just rang up everybody I knew and everybody I didn't know. The minimum investment was £500. I received one lot of £10k, a few £5k and a lot of £500. When I was raising the money for the film, we got a good publicist to help place us on the radio and to print interviews. I was doing a live interview on Kaleidoscope on Radio Four and this guy kept pushing me saying *well what else can you offer?* And my mind was just going blank - I had this idea and said *anyone who puts in over £500 can be an extra in the film...* and the phone didn't stop ringing. We got people writing cheques for £501 - it was great because we also got all the extras we wanted, all turning up in their best clothes and all

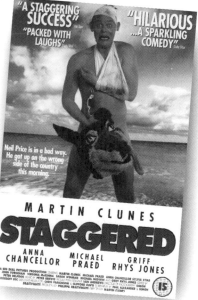

excited. We had a big wedding scene and all the investors were there. It was funny.

Q - Did you go over budget or over schedule?

Philippa - We didn't go over schedule as we had a brilliant 1st AD and Line Producer. They were just so good. They managed to keep things literally on time. We had the £180k to make the film but when we came to post production, I realised that with all the delivery requirements for the sales agent we needed more. It cost another £100k in post, things like the interpos, interneg, answer print and the trailer, which I hadn't even thought about. The budget ended up at £280k.

Q - In terms of production, what were the biggest headaches?

Philippa - Scheduling around actors, who could do what dates. We shot in the Outer Hebrides for a week, getting the crew there and back was a nightmare as we couldn't afford to fly everybody and the only way over is by ferry. When you realise that you're going to lose three days out of your six weeks just travelling you start thinking *well let's just go and shoot it in Cornwall.*

Q - Did you manage to pay yourself?

Philippa - It was difficult even though I had saved some money from my job. I put some money aside for tax from my job and used that - I'm now trying to negotiate with the tax man about it to keep me out of jail. How else? I borrowed a bit. You just do somehow, God knows how.

Q - What were the most expensive things in the budget?

Philippa - The professional catering. Film processing and reprints cost quite a bit too.

Q - How did you get the cast and director involved?

Philippa - It was easier than I thought it would be. I had a lot of people involved before I raised the money so that I could use their names and that was a good lesson in marketing. I rang the agents and sent the scripts and all but one said yes, which just amazed me. And that was through the agents, and still saying things like *low-budget and deferred.* I was very honest as I knew there would not be any real money up front. Some agents were tough and I did have a problem with a few of them, but ICM for instance were really helpful. The cast were all brilliant (hearty laugh!). They really were actually. I had Equity slamming the phone down on me. I got a couple of calls saying they didn't agree with what we were doing - it's like well, who cares?

Q - You had a UK distributor but not an international Sales Agent on board?

Philippa - We had an international sales agent on board before we started shooting but we got the distributor half way through shooting.

Q - How long was it between final print and UK theatrical release?

Philippa - Four months. We were planning the release before we even completed the film,

although I didn't know the exact release until three months before.

Q - Did you find summer a good time to release as you were against the blockbusters?

Philippa -Yes, I don't think there's really a good time to ever release a British film as there's always something big up against it. We had the *Flintstones* and *Maverick* opening a week after us, but those were the only two big films. In it's opening weekend it took £250k which was so exciting. We opened in 108 theatres, it was a nation-wide release and it did very well at the multiplexes. It took a lot more than some of the American films that were playing. They spent a lot on prints and advertising for a low-budget film. However, it was a good decision to make. *Four Weddings* opening so close to us helped too.

Q - In terms of international delivery requirements, did you deliver everything that the sales agent wanted?

Philippa - Yes, but some things came in afterwards which I'd agreed with them. There was one thing that I really argued about. In the contract it was written that they wanted a mono optical sound track and I said, this is ridiculous no one is going to want this, and it was going to cost us £5k to do. Anyway they agreed to delete that. They cover themselves so much though.

Q - Did you cover yourselves with Errors and Omissions Insurance upfront?

Philippa - No, I did that after we shot and it cost £7k. It was a stipulation on the UK distributors part, they needed an E&O.

Q - Has the film performed well around the world in terms of sales?

Philippa - It's made sales. People say to me *You know it's really British and it won't travel, especially the humour* but I've seen it with French and Italian audiences and they've all loved it. We haven't sold it to Japan and I don't think we will. They don't get it, they just don't get it. It baffles them. Germany gave us our biggest deal. UK comedies have always done well in Germany for some reason.

Q - Are you happy with the way the UK distributors and the international sales worked?

CASE STUDIES

Philippa - Not as far as the UK release is concerned, that was handled brilliantly. The international sales were something else - yes, I'd like to have seen more sales, I'd liked to have seen more money, I'd liked to have seen it handled differently when it opened in different countries but unless you've got a big distributor like Polygram managing the world sales, it's hard.

Q - What were your reviews like?

Philippa - Mixed. I knew the high brow critics would hate it and most of them did, although Alexander Walker really liked it. The tabloids loved it and Time Out was incredibly weird.

Q - Are you pleased with the film?

Philippa - Yes because it's done really well and people like it. It tapped into a young audience which is great, and some of them just love it. I'm pleased with the fact that we created this thing out of nothing and we showed everyone we could do it when everyone was saying we couldn't.

Q - Have you made any money, either your company or you personally?

Philippa - No. However I've now got two films that I'm trying to get off the ground (*Sliding Doors* and *Tourist Trap*) both of which look like they will happen. I didn't do it because I wanted to become a big movie mogul and be rich but because I want to make films. I knew making *Staggered* in the way that I did was the only way I'd be able to get to make films - going out on a limb and taking the risk. I can ring up people I want to talk to and now they talk back to me.

Q - In retrospect what do you think are the strengths and weaknesses of the final film?

Philippa - It's very hard as I am so close to it. I'd say the strengths are the acting, Martin is brilliant, and I think the pace works, I've seen it with lots of different audiences and it's interesting that people laugh all over the world at the same things so it obviously works on one level. Not everyone likes it, some people hate it. I think the weaknesses are from the budget. You always think you would go back and do things differently.

Q - What advice would you offer a new film maker?

Philippa - I think they should think very carefully about how they are going to market and distribute the film because at the end of the day, film is a business - how many people will go to see that film - I think too many people don't think of that. They just think of their vision which doesn't necessarily extend to businessmen who are trying to turn that vision into dollars. Be aware of who you are making it for, the audience, be aware that there are people out there who are ready to rip you off every step of the way, it's been written a thousand times, but it's true. Get a good production team around you so you don't go over budget or schedule. Good luck.

End of interview '95. This second interview was conducted in Dec '99 after the success of Sliding Doors.

Q – After Staggered, how did you get the screenplay for Sliding Doors?

Philippa – When I spoke to you last time, the script for Sliding Doors was on about it's 25th draft, so it was pretty well honed. I was working on another project much harder though, it was called Tourist Trap and was written by the same people as Staggered. We had some really good people in it, Christopher Lloyd, Rosanna Arquette and our application for Lottery Funding was turned down. I was furious, I thought it was there for people like us who had made low budget films and proven ourselves and needed help on the next project. I tried really hard to find out why they had turned it down and all I could get was that it was too commercial, so I have given up with the lottery ever since.

Q – So even now you are still out in the cold?

Philippa - Not exactly. I am sure that if I applied for the lottery now they would give me money, that is the thing about the film industry, you have to work and pay your dues and in a way, making a low budget film attempts to skip that part. I have worked really hard to get where I am and what is really weird is that I am becoming part of the establishment. After the lottery turned me down, the American money pulled out and I felt like everything was collapsing. At the same time I was working on *Sliding Doors* with Peter Howitt who had come to me sometime in 1995 with a one line idea - I thought that it was fantastic although I didn't know how we would do it. So he went away and wrote some of it and we went through this really painstaking process of creating the first draft which is probably completely unrecognisable to how it ended up on the screen. But it was such a fantastic idea in which we all believed, so we worked and worked. At one point it looked like it was going to go with private money and sales agent money with Minnie Driver - we had the money then Minnie Driver pulled out and it all collapsed. This, so close to *Tourist Trap* collapsing, was a terrible time for me. So we just kept working away on *Sliding Doors*, all the time re-drafting the screenplay. Everyone really liked the idea, BBC, Channel 4, Granada, British Screen, all the places you go to get things financed in this country, but they did not go with it as they thought that it was such a difficult thing to pull off, they all chickened out at the last minute.

We tried recasting the leading actress but we could not satisfy everyone and we just ended up going around in circles. John Hannah had been on board right from the very beginning. Whilst he was out in the States on another project he just happened to meet Lindsay Doran from Mirage and she asked him what he was up to and he said that he was really holding out for *Sliding Doors* because it was such a good story. She said *it sounds great can I read it?* and he got it round to her that afternoon. She read it, loved it and John called me that night and said she wanted in on it.

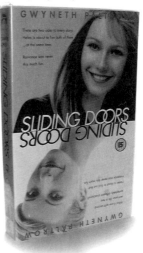

The timing was great as we had just declined a deal to make *Sliding Doors* - it was with a sales agent and private financier, and the deal was just screwing us to the ground. We would have had to make it for nothing and get paid nothing, I just couldn't face that again. I also had such faith in the project and I was not prepared to compromise, so we walked away. And then, through John, we managed to get it financed with Sydney Pollacks company within a week and suddenly we were making the film. Peter, the writer and director, was in the pub getting drunk because the day before I had told him that *Sliding Doors* wasn't going to get made - then I had to drag him out and say you have got to come and speak to Sydney Pollack on the phone and he was like *what?* And from that moment on it was a roller-coaster.

Q - This was money from America - what was it like working with Americans?

Philippa - There are pros and cons to having Americans involved, but overall they showed us the cold light of day and without them I don't think it would have been the huge hit that it was. The main problems came from the British sales agent who had offered us the ridiculous deal that I turned down. They felt we had a verbal agreement with them and there was a standoff for a couple of months, but in the end, we just had to give them some money to make them go away. I learnt a lot from that negative experience too.

The only argument that Pete and I ever had with the Americans was whenever they tried to get heavy with us. Pete and I had been working for 2 years before they got involved and *Sliding Doors* was very much our film, we always stuck it out on a creative level and they did listen a lot of the time. Overall, I found the Americans to be very professional and they brought a great deal of focus to the film, which I believe made it a better movie. Remember, they have an awful lot at stake.

Q – I assume that you had a sensible budget by now?

Philippa - It started off as a fairly low budget British Film, about £2million which really we thought was quite a lot, but they said *well, how are you going to make it for that?* and we said *oh we can make it for that.* Then Pete said he would really like Gwyneth Paltrow to do it. We sent her the script, she loved it, and then the budget just started to rise. It wasn't so much money that we could just throw it around, but we could afford all the little luxuries we had been denied on previous productions. It was great.

Q – How much difference is there between producing on £300k and £6m?

Philippa - Not much in the day to day process of film production. There are the same production headaches, not enough time or money. The big difference is getting Americans involved and having American stars - it makes a difference.

Q – When it came to the release of the film were you surprised by its success?

Philippa – We had an inkling it would be successful because we had the machine behind us, we knew that they were gearing up for a big release, and Gwyneth was pure luck because when she became involved she had not made a hit film, but now she was very much a star. It did really well in the UK, pretty well everywhere else except in the US where it didn't do so well.

Q – Is Hollywood more seductive than the UK now?

Philippa - No, although I think it is important not to ignore Hollywood, we need that marketing machine behind us if we want to make films that people will get to see. You do have to take a bit of a deep breath before you dive in with them - here we go - and you get a much simpler life without them but you know…

Q – What mistakes did you make on Sliding Doors, with regard to American involvement?

Philippa – Getting too emotionally involved. By that stage we were so exhausted and involved in the project but for them it was just business straight down the line. I cannot lose the passion when making a film otherwise I will never get it made. They don't seem to have that, and that was an important experience for me. They also had a different vision of what the film was than that of Pete and myself. If I did it again I would do it in a much cooler headed way. Maybe not say exactly what I thought when I thought it (laughs). At the time Pete and I thought we were doing the right thing, we were protecting our corner ferociously and we thought that they were going to take the power away from us. I don't believe they ever had the intention of doing that, but you kind of feel that you are being bullied by lawyers and such and you don't have the power to fight back the way that they do.

Q – What advice would you offer a film maker who has made one fairly successful low budget feature, with regard to the next one?

Philippa – Get as good a cast / director as possible, get a distribution deal as soon as possible.

Q – And Hollywood?

Philippa – I wouldn't get on a plane until I had made a name here, unless you want to live there and kind of become an American film maker. If you want to play the American game then you have to think like them. I think that there is this myth that we all get treated really badly here in the UK and when we go to the States it is not like that. I have found that to be untrue, you get the same treatment out there as over here, you just get paid a lot more money out there.

Success is a little bit of luck and a lot of hard work. The one thing that I have learnt is to not spread myself too thinly, I try to concentrate on the screenplay now which means I do the job much better. Other people can do the production stuff!

457

From 'Shopping' to Hollywood
Jeremy Bolt

Q - Why did you decide to make films?

Jeremy - When I was 12 I saw *The Elephant Man* and was overwhelmed by the experience. Whilst having a cigarette behind the bike shed after the film I discussed with my friend what we were going to do with our lives, he was talking about running ICI and I thought I'd quite like to make films and thought I'd be a director. When I was eighteen I made a film of the Salome story which was absolutely disastrous, a kind of soft porn epic in Southern Turkey. I realised then that my talents lay in the ability to persuade people to do things, and that my skills lay in production rather than direction. I'm grateful for that experience because I didn't waste any more time trying to be Stanley Kubrick.

Q - How did that film in Turkey lead on to Shopping?

Jeremy - I left University with the goal of becoming a producer and started to work for Ken Russell as a runner, then assistant, then became associate producer on some of the films he made for the South Bank Show. It was an amazing apprenticeship in production. Whilst working for Ken Russell, I went to a party and met a beautiful girl - I was chatting her up, and this other guy was chatting her up. So we were both sort of competing for her interest, but she wasn't interested in either of us and we ended up chatting each other up. I said to him that I wanted to be a film producer, I was a fan of Ridley Scott, *Lethal Weapon* and *Die Hard* and I really loved action movies. He said I should meet this young director/writer called Paul Anderson. I met up with Paul and we got on extremely well, we had the same taste. He had a treatment which was inspired by the joyriding that was taking place in Newcastle, Paul's home town. I said to him, *look I haven't got any money, but if you write the script then you can direct it and I'll produce it*. That's how it began. It took us four years but we managed to pull it off, with a lot of lying and luck.

Q - What was the budget?

Jeremy - £2.3m which was a lot for a first time young director. It couldn't be made for less because there's a lot of action in the film. We had tremendous support from Ch4 and David Aukin, without whom we couldn't have made the film. The money came from Ch4, a German company called WMG, a Japanese company called Kazui and Polygram. Ch4 were the first to be interested and then the others came on board.

Q - And you put that deal together with your limited experience and track record?

Jeremy - Yes. I was persistent and had a desire to learn. I'm very suspicious of the mystique of the producer. There is nothing particularly difficult about doing these deals if you have a reasonable understanding of business. What is hard about this business is the energy level required, the persistence, the will to make the film. It's extremely difficult to pull everything together and you need tremendous self belief to keep yourself going. The rest is your own creative judgement which you either have or you don't.

Q - There are a lot of new film makers thinking of making their first film for £25k for instance. From your experience with Shopping, would you say that it's a good idea to forget £25k and aim for £2m?

Jeremy - It's a good idea to do a low budget film and then work up. When I was 23 I line produced a film for £800k called *Turn Of The Screw*. That was an important part of my education as it gave me the confidence to negotiate deals and to operate in the film world. It also gave Ch4 and the Completion Bond company the confidence to let me produce *Shopping*.

Q - Were there any problems in the making of Shopping that you didn't expect?

Jeremy - Editing. First time directors and producers tend to leave too much in and kill the pace of the film. They should just let the film go and let the editor cut it because they'll probably do a better cut. The final cut wasn't as good as it could have been. Since then, we've cut 15 minutes out and it's a much better picture. You need to give yourself as much time as you can in post production.

Q - How did Shopping perform in the UK and internationally?

Jeremy - Badly. We made a film that was confused as to what it was. It didn't know whether it was a moralistic drama about the dangers of youth-crime and joy-riding or whether it was an out and out action movie. From the beginning, you have to be absolutely clear about who the market is. The classic American distributor comment is *It's not New Line and it's not Fine Line - it's somewhere in the middle.* Well that's really helpful, thank you! I think that's something to do with a lack of confidence to say *I am making a horror film* for example. We had £2m to make something as entertaining as *Lethal Weapon,* and perhaps in retrospect, we didn't have enough confidence in ourselves to state that clearly.

Q - You didn't have the balls to put on the screen what you really wanted?

Jeremy - Absolutely. Now we would say *this is what we're making.*

Q - What happened after Shopping?

Jeremy - We had a truly remarkable experience. We made a film that didn't work but have done extremely well out of it. I think we sold ourselves very well, particularly Paul. We got two very important people, a manager and an agent into Paul's life in America. They watched *Shopping* and saw potential. At The Sundance Festival, Paul's manager, Phyllis Carlisle (also a producer) got him *Mortal Kombat*, a concept film in

459

need of a director. Peculiarly, directors appear to be an amazing rarity in America.

Q - It's advisable after a first film to get an agent and a manager?

Jeremy - Yes, you need a lawyer and an agent, or an agent and a manager, you don't need three. Think about who you want to represent you and why you want them to represent you. The relationship I have with Phyllis has ultimately benefited Impact Pictures, even though I had nothing to do with *Mortal Kombat*. Effectively we had eighteen months apart, but we remained a strong unit, partly because of our friendship and trust, but also because we have people in our lives who want us to be together and present us as a team.

Q - And more importantly you're actually being paid to be filmmakers, whereas most filmmakers in Britain aren't?

Jeremy - Yes, completely right. However, you must be strong enough to allocate time to make the films you want to make and not be completely sold on the money that exists in LA. You must have another life. In fact it makes you more attractive to the Americans. They love it if you say *I'm sorry I'm not available during that period, I'm producing this film over in Europe.* I think it's important for a film producer not to be entirely reliant on one director. I think it takes the strain off that director's talent and it makes the producer feel as though they have value in themselves and that they're not just on the coattails of this extraordinary blazing talent.

Q - Is being English a major advantage in America?

Jeremy - You should be as English as you can. Arrogance is always bad news, but it's important to have an English accent, they like that. What you shouldn't do is try and be American, you should try and maintain your Englishness. For many American film makers, the great directors have all been English, Lean and Hitchcock are the names that come up most in Hollywood.

Q - How did you physically get over to the States to meet agents and managers?

Jeremy - I had a girlfriend whose mother was very wealthy and at that time Virgin Airlines had just launched - if you flew upper class you got a free economy ticket. So her mother kept coming over and giving me these free economy tickets - Paul and I both went to America on my girlfriend's mother effectively. My girlfriend was very important because her mother had this fabulous house in L.A and that's where we used to stay.

Q - How do you relocate over there?

Jeremy - When a company employs you to work for them in America they will give you what's called an O1 visa which is much better than a Green Card. A Green Card means you are taxed in America on your worldwide income, even if you've already been taxed in the UK for any income you've earned there. Whilst trying to raise money, we came in as visitors and could stay for up to six months. There's a huge ex-pat community in LA and somebody's bound to know somebody who's got a floor or a couch - it's completely acceptable in LA to get a call from a penniless filmmaker and put them up for a few days. In those few days you then have to lie. The agents in

L.A are constantly trying to find the next Paul Anderson or Danny Boyle - you just call up and lie, *I've just made this extraordinary film for the BFI, would you like to have a look at it?* cut off the titles, pass it off as your own and go and show them something. You also try and time it so it's around lunchtime so you can get a free lunch. You do that with CAA, William Morris, UTA and ICM and you create a bit of buzz about yourself and get four free lunches. That's how you begin. Then you say *I've got a lot of other films which I've left at home, but this is my latest work* - you must have an amount of charm to get away with it. With Paul, I used to say that he had directed lots of television, *Shopping* was his first feature and that I would send videotapes - but of course you never do, and they never ask for them, they just make a note - *he's done other stuff.*

Q - Should a new filmmaker go to L.A before they have made a film?

Jeremy - They should go to LA to try and raise money because I think the experience of being exposed to the industry there is very inspiring. It's not as intimidating as it sounds and it also makes you want to achieve it more than ever. If you have something to show, it will be a lot better for you. You will get turned down by a lot of places and that can be quite tough.

Q - What are the major bonuses of working in the States?

Jeremy - The money to actually have a life and do what you love and not feel that anybody who gives you money is doing you a favour. Everybody here is so grateful to the BBC and Ch4 when they are given money to make a movie. What they fail to realise is that those companies exist to make product for the public. We almost feel like saying, *well, I'm sorry, but I have to ask you for money,* it's that apologetic attitude. In America it's *Fuck you, I'm going to be the next Tarantino and you should give me money because I'm going to make you money.*

Q - What are the major drawbacks?

Jeremy - People can be insincere in America. It's difficult to identify who in a company has the power to say yes or no. Often you are dealing with people who don't have that power and they're quite frightened for their jobs so they will not commit either way. You tend to get a kind of *yes, maybe,* and you can be strung along. They won't say *No,* because you could be the next *Reservoir Dogs,* and they won't say *Yes,* because you might not be. It's difficult and you have to learn to discriminate between who is really interested and who's not interested. Also, if they think they are doing you a favour they will screw you to kingdom come. You have to make them think that you could go across town to Warner Brothers and do the deal there - you have to use leverage. Fear is the overwhelming atmosphere in LA, you have to make them frightened that they are going to lose the project unless they commit to you. It just doesn't exist here in the UK because there are only one or two companies who do make films, so it's not surprising that you are grateful when one of these companies does give you money.

Q - What do you think are your biggest mistakes?

Jeremy - I think we should have had more courage in our convictions when we made *Shopping,* we should have trusted our instincts to make what we believed in and stand by it.

Q - What do you think were your best decisions?

Jeremy - To keep the machine running, not to stand still, to keep selling ourselves and keep telling the world that we believed in what we made, even when we had made a film that didn't work. Also, we got two people in our lives who could really help us to keep moving.

Q - Do you have any final advice or tips?

Jeremy - At the end of the day, nobody really knows anything, it's all about perception. Even if you have made a film that does not actually work, you must still sell yourself as though you have made the greatest film ever. Don't deny the problems and learn from the experience, just don't apologise for it. The moment that you are perceived as being apologetic for what you have done, you're weak and you sell yourself short.

End of interview 1996. Interview continues Feb 2000.

Q – As Paul was your partner and a 'hot' director, how did you stay attached to Soldier and Event Horizon?

Jeremy – *Soldier* was a film we made with Jerry Weintraub. It was an extraordinary experience as he's one of the largest characters in this industry. From his point of view he did not feel that he needed me in the early stages, he just wanted Paul as the director. Obviously Paul wanted me to work on the film which put me in a difficult position. As a producer with a directing partner you have to get on board the project without upsetting all the other parties who probably don't trust you at first, and that potentially weakens your partner's position too.

Once we had got over the hurdle of me being around he thought that I was a nice guy and competent and I was very respectful of his experience, which wasn't hard when you consider

what he has done. The question was in what capacity was I going to work. After a meeting with Paul he asked Paul to leave the room and he sat down with me and started talking in his thick New York accent which makes him sound like the Godfather, which is very effective because you start feeling that you won't get out of there alive and you will probably end up with the fishes. He said *well, what I think we should do, Jeremy, (Godfather voice) is we should go for a walk on the beach and discuss this credit issue* so at this point I say *Jerry I will take whatever you think is appropriate* and he says *(Godfather voice) good, good, I'm glad you see it my way.* I actually ended up with a co-producer's credit which was actually appropriate and we now have a great relationship.

Jerry is a remarkable man and has taught both Paul and myself a great deal. He was a very necessary part of the process of working at Warner Bros. which is I imagine very much like working at the BBC. It's such an old corporation and nothing is as it seems - there are many layers and it takes time to work out where the power lies and how to get to that power. You really need a Godfather like Jerry Weintraub in your life if you are going to work there.

Event Horizon was a very different experience with Larry Gordon who is also an institution in Hollywood. He was open to me being involved, mainly because we were shooting in the UK and he needed a man in London to run it. Again I had this awkwardness of negotiating myself on board. So I just did the hard work and it eventually paid off when I had this extraordinary phone-call about a month before shooting where Larry made me a full producer with him on the film because he had seen how important it was in the process. He called me up and told me that he felt *just like the Queen knighting somebody, rise Sir Bolt, you are on my card, we are going to share my card, how do you feel about that?* I never imposed myself and I had accepted what was offered me. I think this is the way to play those sorts of situations, let them see how good you are and let them reward that.. and take the risk.

I think that at a certain point your director has to say to the powers that be *I want my partner involved in this process* and he has to say it with some emphasis. Then he is going to have to rely on the personality of the partner to negotiate the part. When we went to Hollywood it was as though we had nothing and we were very grateful and listened as much as possible, talking only as much as we needed and did not swagger. As a result the doors that had opened stayed open. Certainly we came across as guys who were going to be easy to work with. I think that people should listen more than talk in these situations. I came across as somebody who was not going to try to steal Larry's or Jerry's credit, I was going to be working with them in the mix and I was respectful of who they were. At the end of the day I have got forty years of this business left in me, they are probably in their last few movies and there is plenty of time for my glory. You have to keep your ego in check, the minute you start listening to your ego you will probably fall foul of them.

Q - So your partnership with Paul is important?

Jeremy - I think that as a producer one of the ways to juggle as many balls as we need to do in order to survive is through partnership. One of the reasons that our partnership has lasted as long as it has is that there is no insecurity, there is only trust, and it has been proven. A producer director relationship is rather like a marriage, if one party becomes possessive the bond is likely to suffer and break. We are both very relaxed, I don't think he would like it if I got into a relationship with another action director but I do work with other directors with different talents.

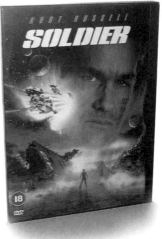

Q – Is it hard existing here in the UK and in LA?

Jeremy – Last year I did 14 round trips and my doctor told me that I was jet-lagged for the whole year. It was at least a trip a month and I would have perhaps one week out of every month where I was stable, so I only had twelve weeks of stable sleep out of the fifty-two. It became very unhealthy and I developed asthma and various

463

other allergies, so I wouldn't recommend it. Actually most of the films that I saw last year I saw in planes which is rather tragic for a film maker, seeing the next big movie on a three inch screen going over Greenland.

Q – How do you feel about Event Horizon and Soldier in terms of how they turned out as movies, how they were received and their performances?

Jeremy – I love them both and am very proud of them. I love *Event Horizon* because of the pull back from the daylight space station which I think is one of the best visual effects ever shot. I love *Soldier* for the final fight scene and people who saw it on Sky and video rave about it.

Event Horizon has become a cult film so I am less harsh on the selling of that because it reached an audience. It didn't cost as much as *Soldier* but I think that the script needed more work and it shows. We had built up this incredible feeling of Evil and then had to deliver on the promise. You spend two hours building this thing up and then – *shit, what is it?* Ultimately the audience was disappointed. I think Paramount should have let us re-shoot the ending and if they had we would have made them another $20-30m. When the audience realised where we were going with it people just lost interest in the third act. Anyway I am very proud of the film, I love it, and I learnt a great deal.

Soldier was mis-sold. It was sold as an eighties action movie, in an eighties movie style, a big head on a poster, it looked like *Universal Soldier* but with Kurt Russell, so the audience thought that they had seen it all before. In fact it was a 1983 script and we didn't update it enough. Again we learnt great lessons. It was certainly good enough to have been theatrically released here but it wasn't because when a movie does not perform well in America, the studios try to stop the bleeding. No matter whether it is a good movie or not, they will just stop the theatrical releases and put it out on video so they don't get the P&A cost. As a result it is doing very well on video and it has not cost them that much. It's not a reflection on the film, it's a reflection of how badly it performed at the American box office.

Q – How easy is it to deal with having made a $70m flop?

Jeremy – Being English I deal with failure better than success, but as Rudyard Kipling said about Triumph and Disaster *treat those two imposters just the same.* You just have to keep focused and try to do good work. I think that if you have not done your own work, or if you have not worked hard then that is your own funeral. For me film is war and I am very comfortable being at war. If it became peaceful then I would probably go into a terrible depression and take up

Paul and Jeremy on the set of 'Soldier'

landscape gardening. So I relish the combat, as does Paul. If you are going to fail, fail huge, because at least then people hear about you and at the end of the day, that's what matters.

Q - How did the studios react to you when it was a failure?

Jeremy - In the industry the perception about *Soldier* was that it was wrongly sold. Although it was our mistake to try to do the thing in the first place as it was an old fashioned concept. Therefore I doubt that we will be making a movie at Warner's for the foreseeable future because of the shareholders - to spend a lot of money again with Paul does not make sense to them. However, Tom Cruise has stuck with us on *Deathrace 3000* which was a project set up before the release of *Soldier*. Nobody pointed a finger at us and said you're irresponsible, bad film makers - we haven't gone to film jail yet. You rise out of it by not being bitter, by not being resentful. As film makers yourselves you know that 90% of this job is war wounds from which you have to recover and pick yourself up, go over the top and hopefully through the barbed wire.

Q - What lessons have you learned from these two Hollywood movies?

Jeremy - Trust your instinct, do not listen to anybody if your instinct says they are wrong. If someone, like your financier, has trust in your instinct but you do not, then not only are you letting yourself down but you are also letting your financier down.

Q - What advice would you offer someone whose first film was moderately successful and they are thinking of going to Hollywood for 'that deal'?

Jeremy - Stick to the ground, or genre, in which you have worked. It will be easier to sell yourself and your project if you have already proven yourself, even if it is only in a small way. For example if you have done short film comedies, make a comedy. If you have done a first feature and it is a horror film, pitch another horror film. Do not move too far away from the genre in which you first proved yourself.

Driven
By Simon Cox

Q - Why did you want to get into movies?

Simon - When I was a kid I saw *Planet of the Apes* and I was inspired. Then *Jaws* and *Star Wars* came along and it changed my life and focused me on the area that I was really interested in - movie making - so I started to make short Super 8mm horror and sci-fi movies with my brother and friends.

Q - How did you make the leap from being a kid with an 8mm camera to being a director of a feature film?

Simon - It was a slow process - when I was about to leave school I asked my careers advisor about working in movies and their advice was *join the army...* I was disheartened because I came from a provincial town where no-one ever worked in the movies, I kind of thought it wasn't for people like me. I wanted to do something important and creative, so I became a chef, something that I could always fall back on. In between tossing salads I started to make pop promos for local bands alongside my continued enthusiasm for home movie horror film making.

Frustration got the better of me so I quit being a chef, packed my bags and headed for London where I believed I could break into the business. I got a job as a runner at a company called Film Fair, made tea for six months, then got into their cutting room and worked my way up until I was the editor on broadcast TV animation shows like *The Wombles*. It took me five years to get there. I was then cutting on film and it gave me a good grounding in the construction of shows and delivery of professional quality materlals for broadcast. During this time, my aspirations to direct were burning and I started to write screenplays - the first of which was awful and the second was *Driven*.

Q - How did you get the idea for Driven?

Simon - I knew that nobody would invest £2m in a first time film director so I decided to make a low budget movie. I went back to the genres that I loved, namely horror - *Friday 13ᵗʰ* came to mind initially - and I thought how can I make a kind of stalker / thriller on a very low budget.

Q - Where did the money come from?

Simon - I made a five minute pilot and took it round to film and distribution companies. I wrote lots of letters saying *can I come and show you my pilot and my scripts?* After knocking on what seemed like a thousand doors I got the money from a small distribution company who basically invested their money in me, not just the movie and idea - it was my energy and enthusiasm that seemed to close the deal.

Q - How much was the budget?

Simon - Well, originally I asked for £40k and they said *you will never do it for that* and gave me £130k. We shot Kodak S16mm and because of the deal I did with the distributor, it was only ever going to be completed as a TV movie so I didn't have to consider blowing up to 35mm, I just stayed on S16mm all the way to final telecine.

Q - How did you go about casting?

Simon - I worked from my front room, borrowed the Spotlight books and started calling agents and actors - when I pitched I would say *look I've got this amount of money, I can't really afford to pay equity rates, but I can afford to pay them something.* A lot of agents just said *No, bugger off* or *we'll think about it,* but some said *Yes, we are really quite interested.* Some came back and said things like *John Hurt's not available but we've got this guy Peter Smith who's available - come and see him.*

Q - As your budget was only £130k how did you pay your crew?

Simon - The deal was that everybody got something. The average wage was £150 - £250 a week, unless they were an actor and their agent had specified that they had to be paid more.

Q - Did you have any problems with cast or crew?

Simon - The cast were on the whole wonderful, although I did have a slight problem with one of them, I think that it was a personality thing. Low budget films are very demanding and there were a lot of late nights - everyone got very tired, so tempers were short. It's pretty much a miracle if you survive a low budget movie!

The majority of the crew were very good, they were there because they wanted to be there. However, there were serious problems with a few people. I took on a guy to help produce - he was a nice guy, very friendly - but when we got into production he suddenly became a "producer" and we began to clash. Part of the problem was that he helped me crew up and he brought a lot of his own friends in. Halfway through the shoot those people teamed up with him and it became a bit of a 'them and us' situation - not very constructive. Being that this was my first film, I was intent on making it the best that I could and I found that some people were not behind me and were there for the ego trip. Looking

back on it, we were tired and under pressure, so I can kind of understand why it happened.

Q - Did the new producer have any comments on the screenplay?

Simon - Yes, I was convinced by this new producer to rewrite the script. I was 12 drafts down the line and I had lost focus so he suggested another writer who would have a better overall view and help focus the screenplay, to do a final polish so to speak. I was unhappy about this but I agreed as I had heaps to do like casting, locations, shot lists... But he didn't do a polish, he went away and did a *complete rewrite!* At the time I thought it was a good re-write, but it had become a much bigger film - suddenly I was on the roller coaster of production with a screenplay I didn't know well. New characters, new locations, big effects... the world ending at the end! But it was too late and we just had to make it - come hell or high water, I got focused and became determined to make the very best of every-thing, script, cast, budget, sets, locations.Once we were going though, the new script just seemed to cause endless problems.

Q - Was one of the problems with the new script that it was worded very well but was not telling such a good story?

Simon - I believe so, yeah. There were lots of phrases like *lightning streaks across the fire ridden sky* which looked beautiful on the page but when you come to the practicalities it was form over content with the script sounding to me much better than the story it was telling.

Q - How long did it take to shoot and did you have a lot of night shoots, locations etc?

Simon - One of the things that I did not take on board when I wrote the script was that making a horror film involves a lot of night shoots. Night shoots are OK when you have a lot of time, but when you do four or five night shoots on the trot and you are not used to it, it has a very odd effect on you. The other problem I had was that I had a lot of locations, far too many and we spent too long moving between places instead of actually making a movie. Often I would turn up in a location and see it for the first time, then work out how to shoot the scene. I think that's common for low budget film makers though.

Simon placed an advert in UK film magazine Empire, asking for people to donate money to make 'Driven'. £1200 dropped on his doorstep which he then used to shoot the promo, which then secured the deal to make the movie.

DoP Gordon Hickie brought experience and expertise to 'Driven', and moral support when it was most needed.

Q - How many days a week did you shoot?

Simon - Six days a week, if we did a night shoot we would have the next day off. We shot for four weeks, 28 days in all.

Q - What were the biggest production problems that you had?

Simon - Money was an issue as I was given it in chunks and when you start paying people £250 a week it soon gets swallowed up. I also found that shooting in London just cost us a fortune, locations especially.

Q - Inevitably the production starts falling apart as there is not enough money or time - because of your friction with the producer and other allied parties, had you become a lone captain of your ship?

Simon - The main people on my side were the DOP, Gordon Hickie (and the camera team), and the Editor, Andi Sloss. I felt like the manager of a sausage factory with a workforce moaning about strikes and wanting to go home all the time - so at that point I became the title of my movie - *Driven*!

Q - How many weeks did you cut for?

Simon - We cut for 8 weeks altogether. That was three weeks during the shoot, and five weeks after. It wasn't enough time, but again, I was under financial pressure to deliver and the film ended up being seriously compromised from a dramatic point of view.

Q - What happened because of that?

Simon - The deal I made with the financier was that I would get the last third of the money when I delivered the film. That meant that I was in the red for the final part of its making and I wouldn't get out until I delivered the completed movie. So I couldn't pay for the editing kit or the labs and the editor. Andi and I worked like bastards through the night trying to get this thing done and we ended up with a cut that was kind of OK. We were both too close to it and there was no objectivity, so we had to go with it. Ultimately, I found myself with a film that I was really unhappy with. It just seemed big, baggy and boring.

It was a year later that I actually got myself into a position to re-cut having had some time to reflect on it. I did a major re-cut, dropping twelve minutes and then went out and shot some more scenes. Just tiny bits and pieces, but it really added to the drama and the momentum in the script. I spent a lot more time re-mixing the sound and building up the soundtrack, because

'Driven' was shot on film but post produced for TV only. This meant that Simon was able to take advantage of cheap desktop effects programs like Adobe After Effects and put together breathtaking title sequences and Industrial Light and Magic style effects for the climax of the movie.

originally we did not have the time or money that it deserved. The new version feels a thousand times better to me, its pace is more even, the shocks are better, lots more digital effects and all the boring stuff is gone.

My advice to a new film maker is give yourself time. Take what you think is your final cut and show it to people that you don't know and they will be brutally honest with you. Get their opinions and then take a little time to reflect because it really will make a difference.

Q - *The original cut had a lot of music - why?*

Simon - Yes, it had wall to wall music. We were under such pressure to deliver that when we mixed the film, I hadn't even heard the music. We just sat there in the dub and said, *yes that sounds great, let's use it.* In essence, the music was helping the film, but by the end, we'd over used it and it became too much. Again, no time to reflect on where we should punctuate the drama with music and where we didn't need it. Musicians will write you more than you need, it will sound great, but you need to learn where you don't need it and just say *no thanks.*

Q - *Because of the deal you cut, you post produced for TV only?*

Simon - Yes, it meant that I could go back to the negative and grade it very nicely. It also saved on the 35mm blow up which we didn't do, and enabled me to do lots of cheap digital effects and a cracking title sequence later, all just using a desktop computer. So it's cost effective and allows much greater control and creativity. The problem was I couldn't submit it to film festivals as they needed a 35mm print - so I missed out there. If you are looking to get an agent or show people in the industry, there are theatres in town that you can project BetaSP. I did a screening a few months ago for some film companies at Mr Young's Preview Theatre and it looked fantastic.

Q - *How did it perform in the international market place?*

Simon - Quite well at the beginning. It sold Germany almost straight away for $205k. The film itself cost $200k so instantly we were $5k up. It also sold New Zealand for $10k, I think and we are still waiting on the UK and the US.

Q - *And how much money did you get out of it?*

Simon - Altogether I made about £3.5k out of *Driven*. And that was the fee that I took while I was making it. I had the idea in 1995 and I finished it in January 1999. Out of sales I've seen nothing and don't expect to see a penny. *Driven* really has been a labour of love, the next film will bring the cash, hopefully.

Q - *What is next?*

Simon - I have several projects going, but it isn't that much easier now I have *Driven* behind me. I thought that having made a feature people would take me more seriously, but in some ways it's just the same. In others it's different because I can say *here, watch my last feature, and here is a script for my next*. On the whole, the doors to the industry are no longer shut and locked and I do have my foot jammed half way in - but they are certainly not wide open.

Q - *What do you think was the biggest mistake that you made?*

Simon - If I could roll back the clock, letting someone else re-write the script was the biggest mistake. *Driven* became a film that I didn't know and I didn't feel comfortable with. You live and learn. You do the best that you can under the circumstances. In retrospect, many of my problems came about because I was making a low budget film, which means you need more time, but with money coming from a company who works in the professional world of TV. So often, we just couldn't say, *hold on, let's wait and figure it out,* because I had to deliver the film. If the money came from private investors, we would have made better decisions under less pressure, but then we couldn't guarantee that it would have done so well in the market place.

Q - *What piece of advice would you give to a new film maker?*

Simon - Follow your heart. Making *Driven* was the hardest thing I have ever done but it was also the greatest thing I have ever done. It is a bit like walking on Mars. When you have made a feature film, no one can touch you. You can approach all the big companies like Working Title and actually be seen as a film director, rather than as a wannabe. You have to take the shit and the knocks - every time a door shuts in your face you are one door closer to the one that is going to open. Stick with it and follow your vision. If you know in your heart that something is right then do it. And never take no for an answer. Don't spend your time complaining how hard it is to make your film or how bad things are. Be positive and energetic, be nice and don't be afraid to ask for what you want.

Human Traffic by
Justin Kerrigan

Q - What inspired you to be a film maker?

Justin - I loved *Star Wars* and *ET* as a kid and I was into painting and drawing at school, so I did a foundation course in art and design. Half way through I started playing around with a friend's second hand video camera and started making really shit films! I was hooked and the idea of drawing for the rest of my life was dead. I applied to film courses but got rejected from everywhere, so I took a year off and after flipping burgers and selling jeans I quit and bought a second hand video camera. I wrote a film about where I was coming from, stuck in Cardiff, no girlfriend, all that kind of shit and made a montage film and it won some awards and I got into Newport Film School.

Q - Was film school a good experience?

Justin - Yes, when I got in I thought, wo*w! this is my chance to do something with my life*, so for three years I just put my head down. There were no holidays or weekends as I had three years to get my act together. My tutor turned out to be my producer on *Human Traffic*, Allan Niblo, we bonded as we were into the same kind of films and I asked him to push me as hard as possible. I worked my arse off, every short film I made I dropped an element that I relied upon to make a film with, i.e. I dropped colour, the next one had no camera movements, doing it in one shot, always trying to learn. I made six short films and five of them got televised.

Q - How did Human Traffic come about?

Justin - At the end of film school I was knackered and wanted to get out of Cardiff and travel. Me and my best mate were talking about packing our bags, going out seeing the world and getting some sort of life. I was still in contact with Allan over the summer holidays and that's when he convinced me that the time was right to make a film. So I thought *why not?* and wrote down everything I knew. The film was very personal, about my sexual insecurities, social prowess, anxieties and frustrations and I just wrote as honestly as I could about me and my friends. One of the characters, Jips, was something that I went through and I wanted to see that represented, I basically made a film that me and my friends wanted to see. I also wanted to see a representation of the club culture in which me and my friends were immersed.

Q - How long did it take to write the screenplay?

Justin - I had a first draft within a few months but I kept on rewriting for about a year.

Q - Would it be fair to say that one of the reasons your film was successful is that you wrote purely from personal experience?

Justin - I guess so. I didn't want to make somebody else's film. The scenes were taken from reality, my reality anyway. I didn't want the film to have a final climax at the end, with a death or something like that, I wanted it to be real.

Q - Did you get support from the industry?

Justin - No, we couldn't get any financial support out of Britain whatsoever, nobody would touch it because it was about recreational drug taking and they saw it as immoral. They wouldn't go near it. They were like, *it sounds great; but no thanks*.

Q - Even though your shorts were televised, still no one was interested?

Justin - Yeah, and Wales made a big thing about it. My graduation film won the D. M. Davies Award, apparently Europe's biggest money award for a short film and they even made a documentary about me graduating from college, but still nobody would touch it man, thinking it was going to be controversial. The irony was that when it came out it wasn't controversial at all. We were expecting a real adverse reaction, specifically with the tabloid press that led the anti rave, anti ecstasy campaign, but we couldn't believe how well it was received.

Q - What was the budget?*

Justin - We had almost no money to shoot it with, so little that we only got two thirds in the can so editing took much longer. I can say that most of the time making *Human Traffic* I was signing on. A bit more money came in during the closing days of editing so we could complete. It was mostly through private investors outside the UK that my exec. producer Renata S. Aly had convinced, who I don't think ever read the screenplay nor saw the finished film. There were a lot of holes in the film and we had to re-jig it, then add some more voice-overs to make it flow. I just know I've not made any money from it.

(* At the time of going to press the producer Allan Niblo declined to disclose the budget as 'Human Traffic' is still being sold internationally)

Q - What happened about casting?

Justin - I didn't want big names to put on the poster to fit into a market slot, the characters had to be right. We had a great response and interviewed up and coming actors for three months. There are also people in *HumanTraffic* who've never acted before, all my friends were in it and all the extras were clubbers - we'd put flyers in clubs and ads in music magazines and we'd get bus loads every day of these clubbers, just off their heads ready to party, it was crazy.

Q - What was it shot on?

Justin - 35mm and there is some video in there as well.

Q - Did you have lots of problems on the shoot, especially with it set in clubs etc?

Justin - Loads of problems all the time man. The end shot when they're walking down the street, that's the busiest street in Cardiff. We did a night shoot on a Sunday and it was pissing down, then it started to clear at about five in the morning. We never had permission to close the roads but we had permission to hold traffic and before we know it, it's Monday morning rush hour and we've got cars everywhere. We're holding traffic on every corner and we start filming *"go, go, go!"* The extras who were clubbers were great, we kept them in clubs for 14 hour days, feeding them sandwiches and promising them a bottle of beer, but it soon started to get a bit dangerous and we'd have half crazed clubbers banging on tables shouting *Beer! Fags! Beer!* So I'd be up on the podium trying to calm them down and at the same time keeping them going for the next clubbing scene by promising *the booze is coming!* It was mad.

Q - There's a lot of music in the film, did you have problems?

Justin - It's almost wall to wall music throughout but that was stereotypical of a weekend with me and my friends. Walking home from work you'd be listening to a walkman, getting into the car you'd listen to a track, you get home and get ready and you put your music on, you go out to the pub and there's music, then to a club and to a party. There's music all the way through, you can't escape it. I started from the basis *is this tune part of the story? is this tune part of the atmosphere? is the tune helping us understand the characters*? so it took ages going through thousands of tracks.

My producers got Pete Tong involved to help with the film. He wanted to be a part of it because it's his scene and he was able to bring in stuff that we needed. He'd come in with a selection of tracks, we'd talk about what I was looking for and listen to the tracks, sometimes they'd work sometimes they wouldn't. When we were dubbing we had new tracks in only a week before the film actually came out, so it was a real rush. We'd dub all day, finish, go upstairs talk to the music editor then we'd come back and dub some more, then crash out in the dubbing theatre overnight.

Q - At the point of post producing the film did you have a sales agent or distributor on board?

Justin - Winging it on self belief man. A rough cut of the film was taken from the Avid, without the proper sound but music was added to it. Everyone, including Madonna and her company, saw it, and everyone turned it down. So I was *fuck!* I knew it was a bad idea to take it over without being properly finished. It just didn't feel right. We took it to all the distribution companies but they all wanted us to take out the drug elements and turn it into a love story. They just didn't get it. We had to cut out ten minutes for the US release as they didn't understand the slang dialogue. For instance like when Trixie talks about Cilla Black, it was Japanese to them. It's full of British culture.

Q - How did Metrodome, the UK distributors, get on board?

Justin - I was ecstatic that we eventually found a distribution company that would take us. I was

Justin Kerrigan directing Human Traffic, his first feature film. It's success is based on it's honest depiction of the club and rave culture without forcing any moralistic issues. Justin was able to write this from his own experience, helping the film resonate with truth.

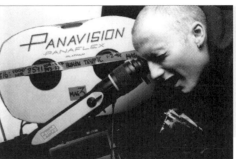

into films like *Buffalo 66* which they were distributing so it was *excellent man, this is going to have some kind of real life!* We were thinking we were going to have a few prints, as up until then their biggest release had been 18 prints, but they started *Human Traffic* on 175 prints! We did loads of publicity but because this film was a big financial leap of faith for Metrodome, when the money came in over the opening weekend they kept it thinking *great, it worked, stay tight*, instead of pouring it back in which we would have liked to have seen. It took about £3.5m.

Q - How does that feel?

Justin - It feels good man!

Q - When you were making the film did lots of people say you can't do it?

Justin - Yeah most people. Certainly funding bodies where decisions were being made by a different generation who wouldn't understand the club culture. At one point we had to write an essay on what differentiates *Human Traffic* from *Trainspotting* and *Loved Up* the TV episode. *Trainspotting* was a great film but it was about heroin addiction. This is the club scene.

Q - You made a film about youth culture, people who were very personal to you, a story that the established industry wanted to change, but you made it the way you wanted to, and now it's a success. Is the secret to stick to your guns?

Justin - I can only speak for myself but yes.

Q - After Metrodome came on board, did you then get a sales agent?

Justin - Yeah, Redeemable Films sold it to North America and Renaissance sold it to the rest of the world.

Q - How did Miramax become involved?

Justin - Two people who deal with submissions at the Toronto Film Festival took a shine to it and said, *yes we'll have it*. This was our opportunity to get our film some kind of distribution, small art house release, at least something. So we went over there, feeling like a real fish out of water, but the day of the screening I went down and Kevin Smith's film was playing at the same time and both his and my movie were sold out. It was a packed audience with queues all the way down the street. I was as nervous as hell but it went down really well.

Afterward, I had an hour's kip back at the hotel, then the phone rang and it was my agent, Duncan Heath, saying *Justin, Harvey Weinstein is watching the film as we speak can you get your arse over there!* I asked him if he was going to be there and he said *no, Harvey wants to meet you alone.* I was *oh Fuck!* I go up there and I was shaking and thinking *whoa, I'm going to meet the Don of the industry.* I had a couple of glasses of wine to cool down, rang him from the lobby of the

Four Seasons Hotel and left a message for him telling him I was down in the bar. A few moments later a man comes down to escort me up to this room. We enter and Harvey comes in, full of praise for the film, he loves it and tells me it reminds him of when he was young. Negotiations began and within two hours they'd bought it! It was amazing to see Harvey in action. Our sales agents were there doing the deal and there was a moment when it looked like it wasn't going to happen and I was thinking *Fuck Man go for it!* then Harvey just said *Oh fuck it, ok we'll go with it* and I just put my hands up in the air screaming *Yes! room service! get the fucking booze in!!!*"

I couldn't believe it! I was ringing up my mates that the film's based on telling them they wouldn't believe what's happened! I spent hours on the phone. I couldn't believe it!

Q - What did you get right in the story?

Justin - Sexual insecurity, the feeling of a weekend, an authentic portrayal of people on ecstasy, the whole course of the up and the down, friendship, paranoia. If I had Jip dying at the end I feel sure that we'd have got financial support, but it would have been a real cop out. If the moral lesson is *if you take drugs you'll die* then it's inaccurate to the clubbing world. People take drugs, they have a good time, they do get paranoid, it's down to the individual whether they use or abuse drugs, and I wanted to fairly and accurately portray that world.

Q - What mistakes do you think you made?

Justin - I tried to do too much. Complicated shots that took too long. Not being able to finish it. Not being able to give it the ending that I was supposed to give it. I learnt so much. But I'm glad it happened. At the time it was like *shit man, this is the only film I want to make, this is it, it hasn't been done before blah blah blah.* I came out gutted at the end.

When I finished it I came down to London and ended up going to a doctor for an allergy problem. I sat in his office and he asked

me lots of questions and then it came to the last one and he asked *how do you feel?* So I told him and went on a ten minute monologue about my film. There was this cold silence. Before I knew it I was being interviewed in a room full of psychiatrists when all I had gone in for was a dust allergy! As soon as I got a distributor I was all right again. I was cured!

Q - You've gone from sitting in film school in Cardiff to sitting in Miramax's office doing deals with Harvey, do you have to pinch yourself or does it feel like a natural progression?

Justin - I think I've been lucky. I've worked very hard but tried to keep my feet on the floor whilst reaching for the stars. It's been a mad turnaround and I remind myself that it could end any day and not to take it too seriously. I've got my girlfriend and friends who also keep me with my feet on the floor. But the film has been my life, it's all I've been doing for the last three and half years!

Q - Have you made any money out of it?

Justin - Fuck all. Not a sausage.

Q - What are you doing next?

Justin - I've got a first look deal with Miramax for two years. It gives me the opportunity to write a script and to consider any they send to me. After *Human Traffic* I was exhausted, I didn't want to do anything, I lost contact with my family making the movie in those three years, and I'm still £32k in debt, no car, no house, nothing.

Q - What advice would you offer a new film maker?

Justin - Don't listen to anyone! (laughs) No, listen to people and take their advice but don't get too led by it so that you think so much about it that you lose focus. Have people around you who help you keep in focus. My Dad used to keep telling me to *keep at it until you get it* and he was right.

Q - How do you feel about the fact that you've created this movie, you've burnt up three years of your life, you're £32k in debt and there are lots of people above you in the pecking order, lining their pockets before you get to see anything?

Justin - Gutted! The people with the money make the money - that's the deal. What blew me away is that cinemas take three quarters of the box office before you see anything. Then the distributor, sales agents, the investors, deferments, and it goes down the line. So is there any chance that you could lend us a quid to get home?

CASE STUDIES

Razor Blade Smile
by Jake West

Q – Why did you want to get into movies?

Jake – I always loved movies and from an early age it seemed to be an exciting thing to do. I loved horror movies and was influenced by directors like Sam Raimi and Peter Jackson. I was inspired by that fact that for low budget film makers, horror was always a good solid starting point for a career.

Q – You are an editor – is that how you got into the film business?

Jake – At film school I edited a lot of people's stuff for them and learnt a hell of a lot through the editing process. That has proved invaluable in the making of my movies.

Q – 'Razor Blade Smile'- it's a black PVC shrink wrapped bare breasted vampire with machine guns thing – how did, um, why?

Jake – I wanted to do a vampire movie in a way I hadn't seen before and to not hold back. I have always been interested in the fetish scene, it's a look that is very striking and when you photograph it, it looks brilliant. Vampires are seductive creatures and a nineties vampire would wear rubber rather than lace or velvet – it just seemed a natural progression of vampire eroticism to take the sexy contemporary clothing and dress them in it. After I decided on a female vampire I asked what would they do with their time? Well they're good at killing people, OK so make them an assassin...

Q – How long did it take to write the screenplay?

Jake – A year and twelve drafts as I knew it was important to get right. To begin with it was funded by the fact that I was editing and directing, stuff like film trailers and pop promos. I had to tailor everything in the story to the fact that I knew I had very little money to make the movie - some of the earlier drafts were better, but I had to cut out some of the bigger set pieces and shrink everything down to a do-able size.

Q – How much money did you have to go on initially?

Jake – It was a 23 day shoot and we shot it for £16k, £12k of which was mine. The rest was split between my Dad and two other film makers, Will Jeffrey at Maverick Media and Rob Mercer. We got it in the can for that £16k although I couldn't afford to process it at that point so we didn't see anything until much later - that was quite scary.

Q – What about the crew and how they worked under pressure?

Jake – It was a small crew, about eight people, sometimes less, all of whom were hard core and I could really trust. There was me, Jim Solan the DOP, James Pilkington the gaffer, my ex-girlfriend did all the costume, make up and bits like catering. Neil Jenkins was the Production Designer, an old film school friend. We had loads of sound recordists which was a pain, and a few days we had to shoot mute as there was no recordist. We had a special effects and make-up guy who didn't work out too well, especially as it's a horror movie, the effects and gore should have been outrageous.

Q – You said your ex-girlfriend – did the movie kill your relationship?

Jake – Yeah it did. I don't think it was the movie, I think that my obsession with film making would have killed it anyway. My first love was film making, and my second love was my girlfriend - I couldn't get any balance on it, I was completely obsessed. On a low budget you answer to no-one and I enjoyed that freedom. You also tend to try to do everything and work as hard as possible, but after a week, or even just a few eighteen hour days, you get very worn down. I was up all the time and just about managed to get through it, but it was a strain on a lot of other people. Because everyone was very dedicated it was ultimately a very enjoyable shoot.

Q – What happened about casting?

Jake – I spent three weeks casting, sifted through thousands of CV's and saw forty people for the lead role of Lilith Silver. Ultimately I chose Eileen Daly as she was both the right actress for the part and incredibly dedicated. She was really fit and up for anything I threw at her, whether it was sex scenes or gunfights. She was fantastic.

Q – How did you approach shooting?

Jake – When working on such low footage ratios, there were times that I had to prioritise - there were some scenes that I absolutely had to get spot on, so I would spend two or three days shooting them, then there were other scenes where we literally spent ten minutes shooting them, often without sound unless there was dialogue. We could only afford a few takes at best, and even then if there was a problem with take one, I would move the camera angle for take two so that at the end I had an enormous amount of angles from which to cut.

Q – What did you shoot on?

Jake – Standard 16mm. We blagged most of it from production companies so we didn't have a choice. It was all Kodak, but we mixed all speeds - even so it looked great in the end.

Q – How long did it take to edit?

Jake – A year mainly because I cut on BetaSP in the evenings and weekends. I did have access to Avid suites but I didn't want to spend my time re-digitising whenever I had to move to a new suite. On tape, all I had to do was collect my tapes and relocate and I could carry on making creative decisions straight away. Usually I would work as an editor during the day, then at night I would cut my movie. So for about six straight months I didn't see anybody. I became like a vampire and was quite sickly. It's not good for you, but I was so dedicated to the project, by any means possible I would get it done.

Q – Did being an editor by trade help?

Jake – If I was a director who didn't have the ability to edit my own film then I don't think I would ever have got it done in the first place - it was always going to be a film with a fast editorial style. Many low-budget films are very slow, master shot after master shot and little or no action. I didn't want to make that kind of movie.

Q - What happened when you completed the cut?

Jake – Before I completed the cut I took two promos to Cannes to raise completion money. At this point we still only believed it would go out on video - never theatrically - so we were only looking for £20k. Finishing on film is a lot more expensive and certain things like a blow-up, sound mix, Dolby licence all cost a fortune - it's a nightmare.

You really have to be ready for Cannes and we made sure we were - we set up all our meetings in Cannes before we went by going through Variety and Screen and highlighting all the companies who liked this kind of movie. We had business cards, flyers and postcards made up, all with the address of where we were staying. I had cut a two and a half-minute trailer and a twelve-minute promo with a temp sound mix. As I had been cutting film trailers for years I really knew how to make what I had look even better - so I cut a world class trailer and I was really proud of it. We spent £1k doing all that stuff.

Q – So you are on the plane to Cannes with your trailers and flyers - what was going through your mind?

Jake – I didn't know what to expect - it was the first time that I had gone with a film and I knew that It would be crazy. I'm quite a social sort of character so I was looking forward to the parties too. I was never embarrassed to talk to people, so even if we did not get the money to finish the film I was determined to enjoy it. I think it was 'don't expect too much, don't be naïve, and keep fingers crossed'. People are always looking for something interesting by new filmmakers and because of films like *Blair Witch, El Mariachi, Bad Taste* and *Evil Dead,* there is a tradition of new filmmakers churning out interesting work even though there are budgetary restrictions.

We put our flyers out in the hotels and all the places where the big companies had their flyers. We used the British Pavilion as a meeting point and place to leave and pickup messages. Most of the people in the British Pavillion weren't very helpful and turned their nose up at a vampire film - they just weren't very helpful with my project. So it was kind of well, *hey guys, if that's your attitude then that's fine.* I was very unhappy about that attitude, so when I did actually get completion money, to a certain extent it was two fingers up to some of those people. There were other people who were really supportive - mostly other film makers who had already made a first film. A lot of the people who had never made films were telling me how I should make the film and I thought *hold on, why am I taking advice from you? What have you done other than corporate videos – I don't think so pal.*

Q - So did you cut a deal at Cannes?

Jake – We did get a lot of interest from a German company but they really wanted to screw us in the deal and were taking too long. Over the following months, simple things like speaking different languages and not having top lawyers really made it hard work.

In the meantime, through Raindance, Elliot Grove had mentioned the movie to Wendy Striech at Manga as she was looking for projects. She saw the trailer, liked it, contacted me and we met. Even though it looked like Manga were going to take the movie, things went really slowly again - we were hanging around for six months twiddling our thumbs, waiting for the contract and money. I hadn't completed the cut so I thought I might as well carry on and finish the movie in the meantime.

Q - So how much did they stump up?

Jake – They needed a detailed budget outlining everything we needed, including the money I and the other investors had already put up. They wanted to do a theatrical release too so that meant a 35mm blow up. That lot came to about £160k. It was very expensive to blow up because I had 250 optical effects, loads more than an average movie. There were also 40 digital effects so there was nearly 300 effects shots in the movie.

Q - This was Jurassic Park on low budget!

Jake – Oh, no *Jurassic Park* had about 500 shots, and they were 3D. Because I had only ever thought the film would exist on video, I did lots of effects which on video are pretty much free. But when you go to film, all those things like making a shot half speed, making colour into black and white, special dissolves and wipes - they all cost shit loads of cash on film. And it took four months of my life too. It was hell. The digital effects were much easier though, done by Cinesite who I had a relationship with because of the promos I had done. They were great.

Q - What happened about the release in the UK?

Jake – The budget we had also included a $50k prints and ads budget. We demanded that money before signing with Manga so that we knew the movie would get out there. Then we knew there would be posters and ads in the magazines. Seeing our posters on the underground was like a fucking dream come true! Too many low budget films get released without advertising which is a mistake. If people don't know a film is released, they won't go and see it. I think it made a small profit of £3k. Even though it went out in some great theatres, it only played late night screens which restricted the audience to hard core fans. I pleaded with the distributors for evening screenings too, but they didn't want to know. I think that was a mistake.

Q – What were the reviews like?

Jake – Mixed - brilliant and awful. The more mainstream the reviewer the less they generally liked the film - and it hurts when you read a bad review. Some of the horror mags were great though, I mean really great reviews - the best I think was in Variety, fucking corking.

The movie was claimed to have cost just under £1m which I believe raised the expectations of reviewers. It's clearly micro budget in places and that just made us look a bit stupid. We felt we should have been honest about the budget and people would then have been more favourable. I mean, shooting a film for less that £20k is pretty special and it doesn't happen very much. People were saying at the time – oh, you had a million pounds for that, you had loads of money – and I'm like 'fucking hell guys, we got it out there, don't complain'.

Q – How did it do on video?

Jake – Good - it got into all of the main video shops with five or ten copies per store. We were number 13 in the video chart! And internationally It's been sold to Japan, France, Australia, a lot of Asian countries. I think that most major territories have been sold.

Q – So, the big question – have you made any money?

Jake – (laughs) The film isn't in profit, no. I'm supposed to get quarterly reports but I have only had one so far, and this was before a lot of the sales had happened. According to the sales agent, the film has to make $500k before it goes into profit. But we did get that small advance so I made my investment back. So investor wise, we have all been repaid and I got back the money that I spent.

Q – Would you recommend deferments?

Jake – If you can pay people up front, even if it's a token fee, then do it. I did deferments because my budget was so small and I only had eight crew members most of whom were friends. Out of the advance they got about 20% of their deferments which is more than I think they expected.

Q – What mistakes did you make?

Jake – I knew that the film was going to be compromised from a writing point of view. Earlier drafts of the script were actually better but I just had to keep dropping the best bits. As soon as you write 'the set blows up' then you are going to have to re-write that scene – this I know! The bits I was most disappointed by were the make-up effects - there should be blood all over the fucking shop, it should be spurting out of people's necks, the kind of stuff that the fans like. I had to cut round it and that really pissed me off. In my mind the film was a lot gorier, and it should have been. One thing that I was pleased with was the lesbian scenes. I made that as strong as I could, without being pornographic - and the BBFC didn't demand any cuts! On the sex front I think I pushed quite hard, I haven't seen a micro-budget film with as much sex in it.

Q - Are you pleased with the way the movie turned out?

Jake – Well, I couldn't ask for any better than it is within the constraints of how it was made. I would throw down the gauntlet and say that I do not think that anyone could have made a better film under the same restrictions. I am sure that I could do better now, with a bigger budget, so for a first step it was all right.

Q - What advice would you give to a new filmmaker?

Jake – Don't do anything until you are happy with your script. It has to be a blueprint of what you are going to do. The other thing is to know how much you are capable of as a filmmaker. I have spent my life making little action movies and horror films on video so moving quickly and shooting entirely from the hip came very easily. Other film makers might have problems squeezing so much in without experience.

I think you need to be obsessed. I have never met a successful filmmaker who was not obsessed by film making. I really think that when you meet people your passion comes across - when you see interviews with people like Steven Spielberg, they are kids. If I am a bit of a geek, then that is all right – hey I have a life too!

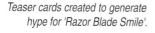

Teaser cards created to generate hype for 'Razor Blade Smile'.

'Hardware', 'Dust Devil' & 'The Island Of Dr. Moreau' by Richard Stanley

Q – I don't want to dwell on Hardware or Dust Devil too much because it's Dr Moreau... that I am most interested in, but as back history, how did Hardware come about?

Richard – I made some obscure shorts in South Africa and wanted to make a feature. I had designed *Hardware* as a commercial film, a simple script, the only time I have written anything that unambitious. I actually set out to create a series of reliable clichés, a catalogue of scenes like gas explosions followed by a cliff-hanger sequence followed by a shower scene. It's riddled with it. It was mostly shot in the Roundhouse in Camden with the very beginning shot in Morocco for a week.

Q – How long did it take you from writing Hardware to getting the finance?

Richard – Like most things in life it was a series of flukes. It was very sunny and I wrote it very fast, with very little thought. As a result it was short and to the point. It was also made at a time when I was chronically disillusioned with what I was doing, making cutesy music videos with kids and animals. So I decided to go to Afghanistan and make a front line war documentary in order to try and shake things up and do something real after all these fluffy animals, which was a catalytic decision because all the *Hardware* stuff happened when I was in Afghanistan. Through a series of flukes, the script found it's way to Palace and Steve Woolley optioned it, which was a problem because I was in the middle of a war in Afghanistan.

Q - Why did they want to make it?

Richard - There were a lot of *Alien* clones at the time, they all seemed to involve a lady locked in a warehouse in the dark, menaced by a monster of which you see very little. Palace got a lot of money from some bizarre sources but at the end of the day the principal source was Miramax who wanted a quickie *Alien / Terminator* kind of thing for £800k rather than $100m. But Palace wanted an *Alien / Evil Dead* knock off that they could own wholly as *Evil Dead* had been a huge hit for them. I don't think it would get made now as people are looking for very different projects.

Q – How much was the budget and did you make any money out of it?

Richard – It cost £800k and I got £12k up front for the original script, nothing since.

Q – And anyone reading this book can go and rent it now?

Richard – Yes, it is widely available despite the fact that it is now owned by Walt Disney!

Q – When did Dust Devil happen?

Richard – Almost immediately. As a script it pre dated *Hardware* by about seven years as I had already tried shooting it in South Africa on 16mm. It was written as a cheap movie that could be shot easily in South Africa as it involves three people in a car and a big landscape. I was in a very bad way at the time and again, had to sign the script away to make it for the money. At one point I was homeless, sleeping and living under the table in the production office.

Q - After shooting, it all started to fall apart?

Richard - Things were pretty disastrous through the post of *Dust Devil* because Palace had been forced into extinction and Polygram who had bought out Palace had no interest in *Dust Devil* at all, I don't think they even knew they owned it. I worked for years to try and get the Head of Film Entertainment at Polygram to actually watch the movie, which I was never able to do, I just could not get anyone from that company to look at the film, so I did something that blew my chances at further employment in the film industry forever. I sought the original investors of the film and I went back to David Aukin at Ch4 and some of the other individuals who had stakes and got their permission on paper to do whatever I could to try and recover the negative of the film and attempt to make delivery. The distributors had never received a master tape and no negative had been cut, it just wasn't completed so it couldn't even be shown. It had just ground to a halt for three years because of the complicated bureaucracy after the collapse of Palace.

Through the support of David Aukin at Ch4 we managed to get back the negative, the cutting copy and the audio. Then we were in a position to edit it but of course we couldn't get any investment to do so as it was a corporate tangled mess, so I just had to finish it myself and I ended up spending £44k that I didn't have. We lost scenes because we couldn't get the actors back to do ADR, and we couldn't do the optical effects that had been planned, so all this made it an much 'artier' movie than was intended. So many times the decisions made in the cutting room were forced because we just couldn't make something work due to a lack of resources. We had to make macabre plot decisions to get from one place to another.

Q – How did you feel about the way that the movie turned out?

Richard – I am happier with this movie than I am with *Hardware*. I think that *Dust Devil* has got more going on in its head and probably works better for a wider section of the audience. *Hardware* tends to alienate everyone above a certain age on account of the very loud soundtrack, the gore and the very fast cutting.

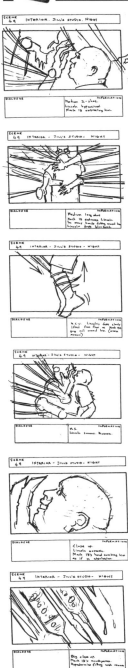

Q – I heard there's more than one version of Dust Devil?

Richard – Yes, there are radically different versions. There are 45 minutes of different footage between the cut that Ch4 put out, which is my version (as is the Polygram tape), and the other common version. Thanks to *Dust Devil's* fractured release it ended up in different lengths and versions all over the world. There are at least two other mutant versions, one of which played in Italy under the name *Demoniaca* which is 82 minutes long. It's almost another movie made from the same rushes as mine.

Q – So after Dust Devils you had to move onto the Island of Dr Moreau?

Richard – Yes, I had to sell *Dr Moreau* as fast as possible to get myself into production to survive.

Q – So the pattern that we are getting here is that you started off as a broke film maker and you consistently find yourself getting screwed in order to pay off how you have just been screwed previously?

Richard – It is called debt bondage. I do not feel that at any time it was ever my decision to make any of the movies I made, although I don't regret them.

Q – So what was your role in the Island of Dr Moreau?

Richard – The script was the only asset that I had on the table at the time and I had exhausted my supply of ready to go screenplays that were lying around. *Moreau* had been a long cherished project that had been kept in a box for ages and at the time I had to try and sell it in order to save my ass. I ended up in a situation where I did not have any political power as one would like to have in order to stay in control of a project. You don't go from nothing to $75m, you simply can't. One needs a bank-able main stream movie behind one otherwise one can be removed very rapidly from the equation. I was going into a situation where the figures were such that I had no way of negotiating my position, they had no reason to deal with me. The only reason I survived beyond the script writing stage to reach production was

Richard Stanley extensively used storyboards, allowing him to create a visually slick and packed 'look' for 'Hardware' despite the low budget.

*Concept paintings helped illustrate
the type of imagery director Richard
Stanley wanted to portray.*

because Mr Brando liked me. I had insisted that I should at least meet him before they got rid of me and I somehow managed to engage with him enough to stay on the project which lasted eight months. I lost touch with the project the minute Brando no longer kept an eye on things.

Q – Right from square one you knew that you were going to be ditched at some point, so you were just holding on? Was it like the bad girlfriend relationship that you know is going to end but didn't know how or when it was going to end?

Richard – I suppose so, but all my relationships are a bit like that...

Q – When they optioned the screenplay were you doing re-drafts? Was it up to you to turn it into the American film that they wanted?

*Richard –*The reality was that I was not American and I do not have a great grasp of what it is to be an American audience, so I couldn't deliver that.

Q – So they took it from you and gave it to another writer?

Richard – Well at this stage they didn't, because it was still optioned to Ed Pressman and Ed is a reasonable guy who is capable of making decent creative decisions. Another writer, Michael Herr got involved, a brilliant writer who I would have killed to get involved with. Michael is extremely cynical of Hollywood and refuses to go there, he lives in total seclusion up in New York State, Syracuse – you need to get a snow-cat to visit him (laughs). He did extremely good work on the *Moreau* script and we worked very closely. I believe that the screenplay that he turned in is one of the best screenplays that has ever been through my hands, I have not read anything better and that is what brought Brando on board. However not one word of that draft was used in the final film.

Q – Were you attached as the director?

Richard – Yes.

Q – At what point did you realise you would be fired?

Richard – There was no single moment when it was clear things were heading for disaster. Brando had been through a lot of bad luck, a film had fallen apart mid shoot, his son was sent to prison and his daughter committed suicide. His problems were so bad that mine were clearly insignificant and I really could not phone him up and say *excuse me, I need your help.* Things really collapsed when Brando didn't arrive which was the moment when the people in charge began their major re-think. I had script notes arriving in reams - *change this, delete, delete, delete, change that,* just a relentless amount. I remember sitting naked on a tropical beach in the middle of the night feeding script notes to the fire (laughs). So things were obviously going wrong and soon after the guys arrived to formally remove me.

Q – Did your agent not fight?

Richard – I was naive at the time and my agent had other vested interests. I was part of the package, just not a very important part.

Q – Are there any shots in the movie that you directed?

Richard – No, although we did shoot some very nice helicopter work at the beginning which they could not use because the script and cast changed so much that they could not match them.

Q – How long were you directing?

Richard – Four days, most of which was sitting in trailers waiting for it to stop raining. Mostly people talked on cell phones to lawyers and agents, it was not really shooting as such.

Q – Did you meet John Frankenheimer, the new director?

Richard - Not as far as he knew (laughs). He never expressed any desire to meet me, so I never attempted to explain who I was. I was an extra disguised as a dogman and I am actually in the film.

Q – How did you do financially?

Richard – They paid me enough so that I will never have to live under anyone's table again. I was given a sum of money and told to leave which is pretty much how it happens.

Q – What do you think of the movie now?

Richard – The sad part is that it is a great story by HG Wells, which has been made several times and now you just have to park the New Line *Dr. Moreau* on the shelf with the AIP *Dr. Moreau,* Sergio Martino's *Island of the Mutations,* the original *Island of Lost Souls* and chalk it up to history as one more duff re-make of the same story. I suppose it also demonstrates why all the other versions didn't quite work, maybe it's just a story that can't be translated to the screen.

Q – What is your feeling towards Hollywood now, would you go back?

Richard – If I got the chance I'd go back, one has to deal with it. It's a ruthless industry and some of the businessmen I experienced are violent people who will do anything to get their way.

Q – How do you make a living now?

Richard – Not easily. People have cottoned on to the fact that I and former associates are prepared to go to places that are outrageously dangerous and shoot nice rushes for them. I've just been to Haiti, and soon I will be doing something on the slave trade in Sudan.

Q – What advice would you give to a new filmmaker who is starting out?

Richard – The only way to learn about movies is to shoot them and then to watch them. Keep the film going through the camera and playing with sound and stuff, don't just stand around talking about it. There is a weird kind of magic that is around when you are trying to make movies. It's like the old adage about riding a horse, if you get thrown off get back on and keep going.

I've had a lot of problems with other people taking control over my master negatives, sometimes simply because I left them in a facilities house where I thought they would be safe. Sleep with your masters under your bed, if you have one. It is your investment. People lock them in bank vaults and store them padlocked in fall out shelters - they are very, very valuable. Whoever controls the master controls the movie.

For film makers like ourselves, the main problem is the lack of a distribution network for our films. How many low budget films have been made and not distributed, even when people want to see them?

I cannot think of a single case of anyone who has actually been happy because of the film industry. Orson Wells, Andrei Tarkovsky, Akira Kurosawa who attempted to cut his own throat after Kagimusha and only survived because he was found in his hotel room by the maid, Kristof Kislowski who died young - I mean you have to be extremely good at what you are doing otherwise you will end up miserable, dead or divorced. Ultimately movies are not life. It's a bit like spending your whole life obsessed with the reflection of something, like a cracked mirror at a rubbish dump, it could be quite beautiful and quite trippy and contain elements of truth, but at the end of the day it is actually not reality.

CASE STUDIES

From Shorts to 'Ratcatcher' by Lynne Ramsay

Q - Why did you start making films?

Lynne - Whilst in my final year of fine art photography, I saw *Meshes in the Afternoon* by Maya Deren and it really affected me, so on a whim I submitted a portfolio of photographs to the National Film School. I was going to go on to do an M.A. in photography at the R.C.A. But I really blew the last interview and didn't get in. I was surprised to be accepted on the cinematography course at the N.F.T.S., I think mostly due to the fact they wanted more camera women. So without expecting to, I ended up in film school. I knew nothing about film making but I'm glad I went without too many preconceived notions and everything to learn.

Q - So did your stills experience help you in your film making?

Lynne - Yes. People who I studied photography with can see the influence of what I was doing in my stills, in the films I make. Through naivety I would do things at film school that people told me were mistakes, like use the same size lens for every shot. Or frame in a particularly oblique way. I started to recognize that these 'mistakes' could change the whole meaning of the scene, that they could be useful if used in the right place for the right reason. In *Gasman* the whole of the first scene is shot without seeing any of the characters' faces, only their body language which I think says a lot more about how this family interact with one another.

Q - So how do people respond to that?

Lynne - We took the film to America where it was screened by the First Film Foundation, and a producer asked if the scene was intentional! She must have thought the camera had slipped or something. I was thinking *My god she must think I'm totally stupid!* But the film has been the most well received of my short films.

Q - So film school was good for learning the ropes?

Lynne - Yes. The first things I shot were absolutely rubbish! But I learnt as much as I could. I hate the attitude of camera people who think great shot, fuck the sound. You have to try to understand as much as you can about every facet of filmaking. So everything works in unison. I actually wanted to move to the documentary course because it was closer to the work I wanted to do, I often find documentary more inspiring than fiction, and on that course you were taught all-round filmmaking. But they wouldn't let me. Bastards!

Q - Two of your films won first prizes at Cannes for the shorts section, how did that happen and did it change things for you?

Lynne - Gavin Emerson, the producer of *Ratcatcher* had the foresight to send *Small Deaths*, my graduation film, to Cannes. When it was accepted I was over the moon, I'd never been to a film festival before, so I took my mates who had worked on the film with me, we had a laugh and blagged our way into all the parties. Coppola was on the main jury who were also judging the shorts. I was just thinking, *wow! this is madness!* When I won the Prix du Jure it gave me the access I needed to make another film, before that it had been a case of *don't call us, we'll call you.* When *Gasman* won the same prize two years later it helped get *Ratcatcher* into production.

Q - Did anything come out of that?

Lynne - I had a few phone calls from American agents but at the time I was thinking, *why do I need an American agent ? I've made a ten minute film and I'm not planning to make a film in America just yet.* If you want to be put together with writers etc, an agent is great. If you generate your own material you can get a lawyer to help sort out the contracts etc. Having said that, I do have an agent!

Q - Our attitude has been to just do it, to go out there and make your movie, but you've gone a different route, making shorts, which do you think is a better route?

Lynne - I think the spirit of what you're talking about was in what I was doing. You don't have to go to film shool to become a film maker. In fact I learned how to direct after I left film school. It's cheaper and easier than ever to make films, if you have a really good idea, then do it.

Q - Did you find that you learnt a lot by doing your shorts so when it came to your feature you were better prepared?

Lynne - I made shorts because I love the short film form, I could take risks and learn as much as I could by trial and error. I explored what I was interested in as a film maker. It was a huge leap from fifteen to ninety minutes. When you get to feature level there's more pressure on you because there's more money involved. I felt some pressure to change the way I worked; *We really liked your shorts but...* You have to be very clear about what you're trying to achieve. I knew the things I had learned had worked and it's a big mistake to try to completely reinvent yourself. If you're doing something really low budget, you don't have the pressure of the financiers on your back so you have nothing to lose and everything to gain from taking calculated risks.

Q - How did Ratcatcher come about?

Lynne - After *Small Deaths* won the prize at Cannes I was approached by a scout/script editor from the BBC. She encouraged me to write a treatment for a feature. I had no idea what she expected having never done this before so I wrote 55 pages, half a feature script. It was bit of a mess, pretty unstructured but she recognised the potential in it and commissioned me to write the script. Coming from having never having earned any money, being a poverty-stricken student and having never held a job down in my life, it was a big deal for me. When they told me they would pay me £25K to do something I loved doing anyway, you could have knocked me over. I phoned my friends and family saying *I'm rich!* which was a big mistake! It took me a year to write, and during that time I made *Gasman,* my last short film.

Q - How long was the process with Ratcatcher?

Lynne - I was very very lucky, almost as soon as I finished the script we went into pre-production. The fact *Gasman* won another prize at Cannes and that there was a small renaissance in the British film industy made for great timing. I was not expecting everything to happen so fast. We started shooting three months after the script had been approved. Two months shooting and about four months post production. The budget was £1.8 million, a lot of money, though considered low budget. It was a co-production between the BBC and Pathe, with lottery money, and pretty much assured distribution in France and Britain.

Q - How was it working on a feature and not a short?

Lynne - I use non-professional actors and a small documentary-type crew. I have to be comfortable as a director and I hate a big machine behind me unless it's necessary for the film. I always worked with the same crew, none of which had ever made a feature before. I spent a year writing *Ratcatcher* and I had a focused idea of how I wanted to make it. But it became clear that the investors were pretty jumpy about all these first-timers and non-actors. I fought and fought to keep my vision intact and work with the people I wanted. I wasted a lot of energy on some battles probably not worth fighting and was already exhausted before I started shooting.

Q - Presumably because Ratcatcher got good reviews you can fight harder for your own way on your next film?

Lynne - You get a little bit more power, but there will always be battles. I fought so hard against compromise on *Ratcatcher* I needed six months to recover.....I'm still recovering!

Q - What have you learnt?

Lynne - To look at your film in terms of how much time you need on everything, and budget accordingly. If you want more time editing, cut down other areas. I could have done with more cutting time on *Ratcatcher* though most directors will say that. I'm more aware of my needs for the next project. Tailor the budget to work in terms of the way you make your film. A lot of money is wasted on things that aren't necessary. Be aware of how, why and where you spend money.

Q - What have you learnt about directing the camera and directing actors?

Lynne - They work best when they work in unison. Knowing when a detail is economical enough to express more about the character than you could do in dialogue. Knowing when to just let the actors roll and not let the camera get in the way. Knowing where the sound will do more work than the images. Cinema is using everything in conjunction with each other until you don't see the joins. I work a lot on instinct. If you feel there is something wrong don't do it, trust your instinct.

Q - You work with non professional actors, is that a choice?

Lynne - Yes. It's 99% in the casting and just as difficult as finding great actors. For me cinema acting differs from theatre in as much as it is about internalising emotion rather than projecting forth, which to me can look really clumsy and overbearing on the big screen. I find working with non-pros exciting, I love the spontaneity and realism it brings to a medium which is all about control. It's a question of taste.

Q - How have you found it being a woman working in a male dominated industry?

Lynne - A few people told me I couldn't be a camera woman saying I wasn't tall enough (I'm 5'2"), but I'd tell them it was a benefit because I could see from a different perspective! It is a male dominated industry, but I think your work should speak for itself. I hate when people refer to me as a woman film maker, or worse, a Scottish woman film maker. You begin to feel slightly marginalised. I think it's great that more women are making films as they make up more than half the population. However that is not reflected in the number of woman directors. It will only make film making more interesting for everybody. The same goes for different cultures who have had little or no access to film making. The bottom line is, variety is the spice of life. I think male film makers can have a lot of pressure on them to be Steven Spielberg and that women in general are more able to communicate quickly if something doesn't work. If I make an arse of myself on a film set I'll accept it and deal with it. Leave your ego at the door. Make a good film.

Q - What mistakes do you think you've made?

Lynne - Wasting energy on battles that were hardly worth the fight. Choose your battles carefully. If something's going to cause you a lot of hassle for little or no gain, don't bother. Appear to compromise, if you have to, but with something that really matters to you, don't budge. Marketing and distribution were big eye-openers for me, remember you should know better than anyone else how to market your film. Go through the whole process even if it kills you. Be prepared for the unexpected - we had to dig up a site and make a canal, on doing so we discovered toxic waste which cost us £10k to dispose of!

Q - Your poster isn't a commercial poster - do you think that's a problem for film makers, misrepresenting your film in order to get bums on seats?

Lynne - My position was - let's take a risk with the poster. I think a lot of films can be badly marketed, by unthinking misrepresentation. What can happen is: in a bid to appeal to the widest possible audience, a bad campaign can alienate your natural audience so you lose both times. Our poster was unusual so it got noticed. Hollywood films have a lot of money behind them which makes it difficult for smaller films to compete. So be different. Get a website together straight away. We're doing that now with our next project.

Q - What advice would you offer a new film maker?

Lynne - Do something you believe in, and see it through to the bitter end. If you believe in it, other people will. Have the courage of your convictions - it comes through on the screen. Have a good idea and make sure its something that you really want to do because it takes a very l-o-n-g time.

CASE STUDIES

Lock Stock & Two Smoking Barrels by Matthew Vaughn

Q – What drew you to movies?

Matthew – I always wanted to make a living by doing something that I enjoyed. So I chose film, and I got myself a job as a runner and enjoyed it so much that I knew that I was in the right business.

Q – How did you get to Lock Stock?

Matthew – I started off as a runner in LA, aged 19, where I learnt about the politics of film making which to me is 80% of the game. Being a producer you can hire people with technical knowledge but unless you know how it actually works and understand the jargon that Production Managers and ADs speak, there's no point being a producer. It's not all about raising the money, it's also about persuading your investors that you know about the other side of the industry, that you know both sides of the coin. After working on several shorts I thought that I'd learnt everything that I needed to learn so I went off to make a film called *Innocent Sleep* which was a £1m feature film. It got a theatrical release in England, but for me, there was no passion in it. I was then aged 23 saying, *I can get a script, I can raise money and I can make a film on budget and on schedule*, so now I can be a producer. As a producer you don't need any qualifications, you can just pick up a screenplay and wing it, the problem is that there are lots of people doing just that.

After *Innocent Sleep* I realised that I couldn't make a film unless I was passionate about it, so it took me three years of reading every script I could and when I read *Lock Stock* I flipped out, rang Guy and said *this is the best thing that I have read it is going to be huge*. I met with him, he wanted to direct it which made my heart sink, but after spending time with him, I realised he was the right man and then all hell broke loose trying to get the film made.

Q – In essence one of the interesting things in what you learnt is not so much 'how' to make films but 'who' is making it and 'why'?

Matthew – I think if you're going to look an investor in the eye and say that this is going to be a great film, you have to be 100% passionate. If you are 1% off, that 1% will be picked up. Now I'm on the other side of the table and people are coming to me for money, I meet so many people who don't seem to have that passion but they're attracted by the glamour of it all which is crazy as the only glamorous thing is the premiere (if that!).

Q – *How difficult was Lock Stock to make considering you had only a £1m budget, an unsuccessful feature behind you and an unproven director/writer?*

Matthew – It was unproven everything! The budget was £960k and it took me two years to raise it. I went through all the traditional routes of film financing, with the sales agents, film companies, every one of them responded with *we love it, go off and get Tom Cruise and then we'll finance it.* You'll know if a film financier is serious when they try and buy the screenplay from you, that's when you know it's good so hold on to it for dear life, be smart and figure out how to stay on board the project. Don't let your ego get in the way, if they say *we'll give you a producer credit but we are bringing in another producer and director and you'll sit side-saddle and watch what happens* - do it because you get a credit under your belt and you can start some good relationships.

After spending a year trying the traditional route, we went around with our begging caps to private individuals. I had been lucky enough to have built up some wealthy and powerful contacts in LA so it was just getting a couple of them to commit. Once we had £4k committed, other people became interested and we structured the deal. I felt we could get this money back pretty much guaranteed from TV and video around the world. It took us a year to raise the money.

Q – *One of the interesting things is the casting, especially Vinnie Jones, how pre-meditated was that?*

Matthew – Very much. We thought we would get a shit load of press getting Vinnie in. We knew that we would not be able to get a big movie star, so we had to think of other ways. In the script the description of Big Chris was that he looks and behaves like Vinnie Jones, so it was kind of, *well why don't we cast Vinnie Jones? There's not that many lines, he looks great, he is a psycho –* and this is before we met him! And then we met him and he was a lovely guy. We did screen tests and he could act and we were like *shit, we're on to something here.* Once he got involved we made the part bigger. He was the only sort of star that we had and a lot of financiers were put off by him, I won't say who but I rang up some film people and said *I've got Vinnie Jones in it,* and they were like *what the fuck are you doing?* There is in England what I call the bullshit star list, where they have these people to put into your film who mean jack shit in the real world. They are great actors but they are not stars. We had all these people to play Eddie but we went with Nick Moran who was unknown. Nick was new and fresh, and I think that if you do a good film with unknown people and they're all interesting then you'll get more press. Film is always going to be a risk and an art form. You have to embrace those two things in order to make a good movie, and if you start trying to hedge your bets the whole time you end up with a compromised movie.

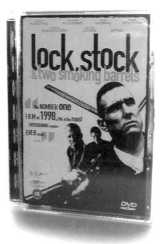

Q – *How much of the success of the film was down to the unique direction?*

Matthew – I think a lot of it was down to the unique writing, the unique style, it was Guy's vision. If you gave the script of

Lock Stock to a more pedestrian director it would have probably ended up like your usual gangster film. One of the reasons why good directors get paid a hell of a lot of money is because they bring a vision.

Q – There is this whole debate about whether you should shoot on 35mm or Super 16mm?

Matthew – We shot Super16mm. The audience doesn't give a fuck, they're not cinematographers, they're happy as long as you're entertaining them. Anyone who focuses on that aspect has either made such a shit film that that is all they can talk about, or people are being pretentious, there is such an ego thing about 35mm or S16mm - who gives a monkey's?

Q – One of the mistakes that new film makers seem to make is that they shoot their movie with a four week shoot, they cut it and if it's not quite working then they say well we've shot it and cut it so that's that. Did you do any restructuring?

Matthew – Fuck yes, we cut forty minutes out of it at one point. We had a leading lady in *Lock Stock* that was not working at all, so we cut her out, which meant that there were huge chunks in it that were not working at all. The final six minutes of the film was a total re-shoot, and there were three linking scenes that we had to reshoot so we had to get all the actors back. The first cut of *Lock Stock* was 50% different from what we now see in the cinema - you wouldn't believe the changes, especially the three new sub-plots.

Q – So in essence script development pretty much finished at the premiere?

Matthew – I think that script development finished about two weeks before the final cut and then we did a test screening and our suspicions about certain things not working were confirmed. We cut them out and yes this left some gaping holes so we went out and filled them with shots, we shot five new scenes then.

Q – And so the lesson here is that...?

Matthew – The thing about making a film is that so many things can go wrong, an actor may not be doing it right, the cinematographer may fuck up, you're trying to get all of these millions of things to fit perfectly at the right moment and if they don't... well. We're about to re-shoot the beginning of *Snatch*, because we think it's good but it's not brilliant. Film making is a lot about compromising, it is just knowing when to compromise and when not to compromise.

The US theatrical release poster. Considering it's success in the UK, the US release seemed disappointing.

Photo - Daniel Smith

Q – As your budget gets lower all those problems that we have just mentioned are magnified?

Matthew – I think low budget film making is good in a way because it keeps you focused, If you've not got money to solve the problem, you've got to solve it in some other way and I like that and I like it when everyone else is thinking on that level. When you have a lot of money the heads of departments think *hey fuck it, let's throw money at it,* the director's like *I don't like that, change it.* You can get into a lazy easygoing attitude. If you look at Hollywood movies, the way they make films is quite frightening. Fuck all happens, they sit around chatting. I think that having too much money is potentially more dangerous than not having enough.

Q – What did it feel like when this project that you had so much faith in suddenly started attracting everyone else? There must have been a moment when it hit you and you thought that it was going to be bigger than anything else?

Matthew – I always thought it was going to be as big as *Trainspotting.* What I couldn't believe was that no one else thought so. When we finished the film we couldn't get distribution and that was when I shat myself and thought I am making a movie that appeals to me but it's not appealing to anybody else. Every distributor saw the finished product and passed on it saying it was crap. That was when my confidence was shaken for the first time, I was thinking I have got this very expensive home video that I love and no one else does. Even when we finally got distribution which was just because of a record deal as well as pure luck, I was still bashing my head against a brick wall. The distributor was like *oh, we'll spend £300k releasing it* and I was like *no, you don't understand this thing will be huge - it's worth spending money on.* Even when we had a good opening weekend, I remember saying to the distributor *this is great, it will go up next weekend* and the reply was *don't be ridiculous, films never go up, it will probably drop 40%.* By the second weekend we were up by 30%. I just knew that if we could get it out there it would tap into the mood of the public.

Q - How did the Lock Stock record deal get you picked up for distribution?

Matthew - Island Records (Polygram owned) had committed to a soundtrack deal assuming the film would be distributed. To their horror and surprise none of the distributors liked it and therefore they were going to lose their advance. They rang their buddies at Polygram Films and told them they were crazy and thank God they changed their minds.

Q – How have you dealt with the zero to hero phenomenon?

Matthew – I'm still sceptical and don't trust many people in the industry, I remember the way they treated us before the film was a hit, they could treat us like that again, very quickly. It will only take one flop to go back. I was shocked at the rise, it was so quick and I was over the moon at the same time, but a fall will be even quicker. So my attitude is keep our heads down and get on with the next film, just keep making good films. This is a tough business and I'm sure there're a lot of people out there who are sharpening their knives, waiting for the moment to plunge them in.

Q – Why do succesful Brit film makers end up in Hollywood?

Matthew – Because that is where they can end up making a seriously good living. When LA treats you well it treats you unbelievably well. Britain always puts success down and always cheers on the underdog. I can't see this changing, just go with it.

Q - How big is your next film and how did the Hollywood element - i.e. Brad Pitt, come on board?

Matthew - For us, it is huge, but in Hollywood terms small. It's about 3 times the *Lock Stock* budget. Brad saw *Lock Stock* and loved it so much he approached us, we got on and the rest is history.

Q – How has Lock Stock performed globally?

Matthew – It hasn't done as well as everyone thinks it has, that is what has been so bloody amazing about our so called 'rise'. It's been a big hit here, in Australia, Japan, Norway and Sweden but it was a resounding flop in America, Germany, Spain, France as well as some of the other major territories. Having said that we did do five times our budget in America so that wasn't so bad, but in England we did twenty times, over $35m world wide now. We've sold 1.2 million video units in England, the album has gone platinum, so yes I guess it's done unbelievably well. Where it was a major hit was amongst the industry.

Q – What kept you going when you were struggling to get the film made?

Matthew – I would have been totally fucked if I didn't get the film made. There was a time when I thought we had the money so I took out an overdraft for £25k just until the money arrived. To me that was a fortune and when the money collapsed, the bank went bananas. I'd borrowed money off close friends as well, so the 3 week loan became a 6 month loan and I was shitting bricks. I believed the script was brilliant, Guy was brilliant and I thought that if I couldn't get if off the ground I should leave the film business because I haven't got a better opportunity to make a movie and I'll never get a script or a director that's better than this. A lot of people said that I should have given up, people begged me to give up, my parents, close friends, I was pissing in the wind and it was time to face the facts and get a proper job because I was doing this every day for at least 8 months. You have to be tenacious, with self-belief and belief in the project. Having got those two things you are certainly over the first and second hurdles, maybe even the third and fourth, although you have got another hundred to go. You've got to be tough and not give up, but make sure that you are on the right horse.

Q – What mistakes do you think you made?

Matthew – I think I made every mistake there was. From the day we got the money there were no real problems, just the usual stuff film making throws at you. I think the biggest mistake I did was that we showed the film too early to Harvey Weinstein of Miramax and he passed on it.

I respect and fear the man at the same time, and in hindsight, even though he had asked to see it, I should have waited and shown it to him once finished. I should have stuck to my guns and gone banging on his door once more saying *look you have got to watch this again*. However we got a huge offer from Grammercy and I was blinded by the money, which we took and ran with. Miramax consequently then saw the film and loved it, they rang us up and were big enough to say *shit, we made a big mistake, great fucking film* .

Q – Any advice for new film makers?

Matthew – Self-belief is my biggest thing, and belief in the project. Know what you are talking about, don't bullshit, you can't pull the wool over people's eyes, try and get people scared to say no, make them feel like they're missing out. The other thing that doesn't work, but it's something that people have done, is to try and play studios off each other, saying *that Fox are really interested* to Warner Bros. but what a lot of people don't realise is that the execs at Fox are friends of the execs at Warner Bros. and they just ring each other up and say *are you interested* and they talk about things. So you look like a bloody idiot when they say *oh we passed on it, it was a piece of shit*. If you're honest because not many people are and you're passionate, those two things mean a lot more than anything and that would certainly make me read a script more quickly. Learn the business, what everyone does, what the agents do, who they represent, what pay or play means, what a negative pick-up is, who runs the studios, know what films have grossed, and understand the economics of the business.

CASE STUDIES

Following by Chris Nolan and Emma Thomas

Q – How did you both get into the film business?

Chris - I've been making films on super 8mm since I was a kid. It's been an organic process, doing whatever I could with whatever was available. Emma and I didn't study film at uni, but there was a great film society where we'd make shorts every year from the proceeds of screening second run films. We had a camera, a roll of 16mm and you'd have to make a three minute film from that. It was much better than film school where you can end up making only a ten minute film after two years.

Emma – We had a budget for five short films a year, so we had a bidding process where people write their scripts and a committee decided who will make them. It was really cool, because there was no discipline, no course tutor, people literally just went out and did it. We made a feature length project in the final year which was about 80 minutes but it didn't get finished as we just didn't have the resources.

Chris - Once I've made a film I move on to the next, usually at the same time I move into a new flat so I can use it as a location, hence I moved a lot!

Q - How did Following come about?

Chris - We made an 8 minute film about a burglary, shot in B&W on 16mm costing us £200. When I wrote *Following*, one of the things going on in my head was *we can make an 8 minute movie for £200 so that means we can make an 80 minute movie for £2k*. As it turns out that was pretty much what we did. With *Following* we tried a much more compromised way of working, black and white, entirely hand held.

Q – How much money did you raise before you started shooting?

Chris – I didn't raise anything, I had a job and I was receiving regular pay cheques for the first time in my life. I would spend half on my rent and the other half on film stock and processing. Whatever I had, I'd work out how much footage I could shoot that week. I shot over 14 weekends, shooting 15 minutes of footage a day. That would be enough, theoretically, to get the film made. I knew that if we ran out of money we could just stop for a couple of weeks. I was not going to process anything because that was expensive, I was just going to keep shooting.

Emma – The key to *Following* was that it was not like any other film, there was not a conventional budgeting stage. We could get the equipment for free, the only thing we paid for was the stock, processing and the odd bit of catering.

Q – How big was the crew?

Emma – There was a core of about 6 to 10 people. Each weekend the actors would be consistent but the crew would be whoever was around. Everyone had worked together in some combination so it worked really well. That was the thing about our group of friends, instead of hanging around drinking coffee all Saturday long, we would just get together and make movies.

Chris – You have to know every job as well as the people that you are working with, then you don't have to fit around everyone's schedules and can do it yourself. One of the things I don't do is work with experienced people on low budgets. I've listened to people who say *you've got to get a good sound guy, you have got to get a really good DoP* - I don't agree with that, we would never have got our film made if we had worked with people more experienced than ourselves, for a start they demand a whole new level of equipment which we just couldn't provide.

Q – What disadvantages were there in the way you shot?

Emma - Finding actors to commit for that period of time, that's why there are so few characters in the film. One of our actors shaved his hair off mid shoot which was a bit of a nightmare.

Chris - I brought Jerry Theobald in as a producer as he's the main actor and in every scene. I wanted him to be part of the process. I wasn't prepared to say to the actors this is a great opportunity, we're going to make it with this one, but instead I said *we're going to have a lot of fun making this film and make it as good as we can.*

Q – How did you cut it?

Chris – It was pretty weird if I think about it. I didn't even sync up any rushes for about six months. We had shot without actually seeing anything, I would check through it and make copies of dats but that was it. I managed to get editing help from my friends from uni, those who had gone into the film and TV business, doing transfers, syncing up, one ended up cutting the movie. I found a place that was prepared to give me a little time to learn the machines for free, and beyond that I had to start paying for it. I rented the machine over a weekend for £100 and over three weekends I did the rough cut.

Q – So how much did it actually cost?

Chris – We finished the film creatively and had a pretty good sound mix. We got accepted into the San Francisco film festival and that's when we started looking for money to complete. We'd spent £3,500 to that point. You can creatively finish your film for literally hundreds of pounds, it's just a question of time and effort.

Emma – The fact that we were in a film festival meant it was a lot easier for us to go to people and ask for cash, so we asked friends to help out.

501

Q – When you finished it on tape did you have a festival strategy?

Chris – We sent a lot of tapes out and one of the judges at a very prestigious festival liked it. Even though we didn't get into that festival she recommended it to San Francisco. My experience this far with the festival world has been that I have never got in to a festival that I have applied for, or where we've had to pay an entry fee, the film needs to be invited.

Q – Did you get good reviews in San Francisco?

Emma – The reviews got better and better. At the time of the first ones we were happy to get even bad reviews! We went to the festival without having thought about publicity, we made the press pack only because the festival asked us for one, we didn't have a particular strategy in mind and I think that we were very lucky that we got the good reviews - actually that we got reviews full stop.

Chris – The only festivals we have ever got into are the ones that had somehow heard of us, then invited us and waived the fee. Festivals have so many submissions a year and there's this belief that if you get your film made, you'll get it into festivals, but it really isn't the case. You need to find some way of getting in there.

Q – So when you got it accepted in San Francisco you suddenly needed a print?

Emma – Yes, the first time we saw our print was the first screening in San Francisco! We were already in America so our lead actor brought it out with him on the plane straight from the lab.

Chris – We had four screenings in four venues and technically each screening was perfect. We then went to Toronto with the same 16mm print and every screening had a problem. That's when I realised that 16mm is a terrible way to screen in Festivals - they roll in their old 16mm projector and you can get terrible sound problems although the picture is all right. 16mm is a very unreliable format for projection, every time you watch it you're on tenterhooks because something could go horribly wrong.

Emma – We managed to create a buzz with our reviews, but afterwards it is a little bit of *well what are we going to do next?* That's when we discovered that there were festival scouts attending all the festivals who then invite you to the next one.

Q - When did Next Wave Films become involved with top up funds?

Emma - We met them just after we did San Francisco and sent them a tape. They liked it and helped us position the film for Toronto and format a strategy.

Chris – I had always wanted to do a 35mm print, partly because we had already seen what could happen with 16mm and also because we wanted to do a good sound mix, so Next Wave came in and we finished the film on 35mm doing the sound mix in London very, very cheaply.

Q – So how much did Next Wave end up putting into the film?

As with *The Blair Witch Project*, one single image was used to capture the essence of what the film is about. Ironically, these pictures often end up being arranged by distributors years after the films are completed.

Emma – We don't really know yet as there are all kinds of associated expenses, the blow up alone cost $40k. They also worked out a festival strategy and organised a publicist which was an enormous help as Toronto is such a huge festival and it's easy to fall between the cracks. Also when we were shooting the film we didn't take stills which was a big mistake.

Chris – They also helped create an image for the film. We went back and took the exact still that we needed two years after filming! You need at least one image that expresses the film.

Q – Isn't black and white stock more expensive?

Chris – There's this myth that it's more expensive but it's not. People talk about using short ends but I insist on buying new stock as I can't accept the risk of the stock being damaged.

Q - Did you change the film in the editing process, from the point of the screenplay?

Chris - Not much, although there's a few structural changes toward the beginning and the end. There's a point where the film stops being a linear story about two thirds the way through. It was scripted in a fragmented way and in the editing we made it less so, to give people time to get into the story. Also I knew that we could stop making the film halfway through and I could make a film from what I had because it doesn't have a conventional story - it could have been a half hour film with certain elements removed.

Emma - Apart from the creative reasons that Chris had for making this story with that kind of narrative, it was actually very helpful to us as we were making this during weekends over a year. So any continuity problems weren't as obvious.

Q - How was the film received?

Chris - The structural element of the film has divided critics, but every now and again, a reviewer will say *it's a good film but it's almost ruined by a pointless structure*. I can see why they might say that but what they're not acknowledging is that they wouldn't be reviewing the film if it didn't have that kind of structure as it wouldn't even exist. Your film has to have something that's different from mainstream to get out there, you have to be adventurous, do whatever it takes to get your film noticed. In our case, it was the structure of the story that seemed to stand out.

Q - They'd probably be more accepting now because of film makers such as Steven Soderbergh hitting the mainstream with films like Out Of Sight and especially The Limey?

Chris - Most reviewers saw the film just before these films came out, and the majority of them liked the structure saying it's an interesting thing about the film. Certainly the American low budget indies realise this but it seems England doesn't and there are a lot of films coming out of the UK where there's still the attitude that you can make a Hollywood movie for $2m but there's no place for them, nowhere for them to go and no one to buy them. We've just spent millions of dollars on our next movie, but in Hollywood terms it's low budget, so it still has be a clever film to be different otherwise it goes straight to video. Nobody's going to give you credit for doing a car chase but more cheaply.

Q - You got a theatrical in the UK and US, how did that do?

Chris - It was a limited release. We released in a prestigious theatre in New York and in the NuArt in LA. We got great reviews but didn't have much money to advertise. Since then we've had three prints playing in various cities around the US. There is a kind of myth that the film will sell itself and people buy into that. In England we got amazing coverage but they did one print and stuck it in a theatre that was a hundred seater, and there was no poster.

Q - Have you made any money from Following?

Emma - No. But doing the Next Wave thing was very good. It was far more valuable for the film, the theatrical has benefited everyone although not financially. For instance Lucy who plays the blond, is now going off to do an Eric Rohmer film.

Q - How did Hollywood react to you and the film?

Chris - Everyone here in the US will watch the film if you can get it to the right people. Getting it into festivals helped getting an agent but nobody's going to offer you your next film, they will send you scripts, but you have to have YOUR next film ready. Before San Francisco I met with a few agents who wanted to look at what I wanted to do next, so I sent them my latest screenplay which I'd spent a year doing and one of them agreed to take me on.

Q - Who came on board with your new film Memento?

Chris - Newmarket are the backers. I can't tell you the budget but it's an awful lot more money than *Following*. All the same kind of problems though. This was a union film and out here I realised that to

make a film for a million dollars is very difficult, because you're in this inbetween world where you can kind of afford certain things but you can't quite afford to pay people properly and you don't have any money to do anything. After *Following* I thought I could make a film for $500k then I started looking at what I could do, and it wasn't enough! It's weird, its easier to sell a $50m dollar movie, people won't go and see a $500k film unless it's exceptional.

The process is exactly the same though, everything we learned making *Following* is tremendously valuable, and despite having what may seem like an astronomical budget, we didn't have enough time to shoot the film. We had to do 40 or 50 set ups a day which is totally unheard of, it's usually ten or twelve, so knowing exactly what I wanted and having planned things the way I did with *Following* was the only way I could work that fast. I managed to get some rehearsal time with the actors which isn't usually done with a film that size.

Q - Previously you've been very hands on, did you find that the studios didn't want that?

Chris - I found a great operator who had become a DP so I was happy not to pick up a camera. They like it if you understand the process well enough to know exactly what you need for every set up and you find someone you can trust to do that - if you just pick up the camera, they'll give you a very hard time. I was given total creative control and *Memento* is quite a wacky film with a quarter of it shot in B&W, and we've got a great cast, Guy Pearce and Carrie Anne Moss.

Emma - It seemed to me that everyone respected the fact that Chris knew what he wanted and was very hands on, but I think the AD's found it difficult because most directors don't run their own set and Chris did.

Q - Emma, did you find it easy to come on board as a producer on your first Hollywood film?

Emma - I'm an associate producer on *Memento*. There are so many experienced producers on it but hopefully the next one…

Q - Any words of advice for new film makers?

Emma - Just do it and don't get hung up on the whole process of the ins and outs of film making, strip back all of that stuff and just concentrate on the film.

Chris - Don't say *we'll fix it in post*. I was once told that you could filter out anything, but you can't. We've just finished mixing the sound on *Memento* here at Universal and you can still hear when there is bad sound and you can't do anything about it. However you have to make a film with whatever resources you have. Treat making that film, however you're making it, not as a means to an end, but as the best film you're ever going to make. If you're making it for money, then you're never going to do it and it's never going to be any good. Do something you believe in, something you love, and enjoy it.

Killing Time, Downtime and The Crow 3: Salvation
By Bharat Nalluri

Q - How did you get into films?

Bharat - I spent a year at the Northern Film School in Sheffield (now in Leeds) as a producer where I produced two short films. When I came out I joined a company in Newcastle and became head of development and drama where I ended up shooting and directing about 15 pilots for them. I met Richard Johns there and both of us realised we had ambitions toward features, so we eloped and formed our own company, Pilgrim Films. We did lots of TV commercials with the idea that we'd make money to pay writers. I did a half hour drama for ITV Films which gave me my directors showreel. Before that I had a company with Paul Anderson, who I'd met at school when we were about twelve, and in fact he wrote *Shopping* in my kitchen. He would act in my films but wouldn't let me act in his! I've still got the footage somewhere which one day I'll dig out...

Q - How did you get Killing Time off the ground?

Bharat - Initially we wrote *Downtime* but realised that it was going to take a lot more resources to make than we had and we needed more time to develop the script. Ch4 and Scala were involved so we decided to do a practice run. We sat down to devise another project and watched lots of videos of chicks with guns running around blowing everyone away and we decided we'd make a Nikitaesque type film. I wrote the original premise for *Killing Time* and gave it to a friend of mine, Neil Marshall who ended up editing it. He wrote the first draft, then we gave it to another writer to enhance the female character. Then we gave it to Caspar, the writer of *Downtime,* and he did the final rewrites. Then we raised the money which was around £100k.

Q - Where did the money come from?

Bharat - We approached Paul Brooks of Metrodome who loved the script and put some money in. The rest was knocking on doors. We had a very good prospectus and in the end we only needed to raise an additional £50k, so we asked people for £5k each. We wrote it in April, May we raised finance, June we cast, July we shot, August we edited, September we sold it to Colombia Tristar. Later we spent another £100k getting the sound right.

Q - How did that big sale to Colombia Tristar happen?

Bharat - We were in Richard's place in Newcastle when a phonecall came in from Victor Films who were selling it saying Miramax want the movie. Then the mobile rings, Colombia TriStar wants the movie. For a small film it was great. They didn't even see the whole movie but a 90 second trailer. We finished it and went straight into prep on the next movie. We thought that this film making business was really easy! (laughs!) We were very naïve.

Q - How much did you sell it for?

Bharat - It was a reasonable figure, all the financiers got paid back, the crew got a good share of their money back, Metrodome did well out of it, the sales company did well, but Richard and I still haven't seen a penny from it, but that's fine as I'm on my fourth movie now. It's still the film everyone knows me for as it's in Blockbusters everywhere. A friend of mine went camping in the Arctic and he went into a wooden hut to buy baked beans and there were three videos in his cupboard and one of them was *Killing Time!* So it's very bizarre, it got everywhere. It's a very Hollywoodesque film so they love it here, but they don't quite get the cynical side to it. Colombia Tristar did a brilliant campaign for it and it got a US theatrical.

Q - Did you find it easy to get the finance for your next picture Downtime?

Bharat - One of the good things about being in Newcastle is that you have to be inventive. Also, we were the only people trying to make films, so we set up a thing called Movies North with sponsorship from Northern Arts. This enabled us to hold film conferences and we did two, the first was called *Going For Bust!* and that got us *Killing Time*. The second was called *Life's a Pitch*, and that got us *Downtime!* We would get a lot of film dignatories coming up from London to give talks and of course there's a three hour train run which is long enough to read a script. We got *Killing Time* like that because we gave it to Paul Brooks and *Downtime* because we gave it to Nik Powell. By the time he got to Kings Cross he'd read it and he rang us up. So the train ride was very beneficial. So Scala came on board. Nik Powell is great to watch in action as he's raising finance, walking around with a plastic bag saying *I've got a script for you!* he's fantastic to watch and everyone loves him. He got Pandora interested and then Ch4 who initially turned us down. It then became a fight between them and the BBC, and the BBC lost out. There were about five companies who made up the budget which was £1.9million, which included the lottery finance of £700k.

Q - How did it do?

Bharat - It sold everywhere in the world bar America because of the Geordie accent. It's had a huge retail success in the UK, so much so they've still not shown it on Ch4.

Q - How did The Crow happen?

Bharat - Downtime was a kind of Ken Loach meets Bruce Willis and it was the Bruce Willis bit that got me into Hollywood. I cut a great reel together which had a 30 second bit from *Downtime.* This alone gets me more work than anything else, everyone loves the action sequences in the States but there's one bit in the movie where a guy gets crushed and they're always squirming in their chairs by the end of it. Paul Brooks knew Ed Pressman who heads *The Crow* franchise and Paul gave him my showreel. Ed watched it and showed it to the creative producer, Jeff Most, who's the originator of the franchise, and they loved it. We met in LA where I accidentally spilt my drink all over him!

Q - When did you get an agent?

Bharat - Jessica Sykes, my agent at ICM, London, saw *Downtime* and loved it. Robert Newman, my agent at ICM, LA, had seen *Killing Time* and had been tracking me since then. So when I came out to LA it was an obvious step to get Robert to represent me.

Q - How different is the US from the UK industry?

Bharat - The difference is that it's a business here, people are geared toward that, they know the world market much better. As a director you tend to have a producer's head too which I've always had. They all want to make good movies and if they feel they're going to get a good movie, they'll let you go back and back and do stuff until you're happy, if they think it's a bad movie, they'll run to the hills. Ed Pressman and Jeff Most were really good to me and they gave me a lot of freedom.

Q - Going from your £1.6m movie to a $12m movie, what differences were there?

Bharat - A lot of the money goes on the franchise. The first thing I learnt was to ask what my below the line was. I was very naïve and thought wow! $12m, I can do so much, the sets I can build, I can shoot for ever. But money goes further here than in England, it's cheaper to film here. They know how to do genre films in Amercia, they look big and they do them all the time. If you want to do a Period movie, go to England. They have great stuntmen here and you seem to get a lot more for your money in terms of action. There are more screen actors here, actors who get more excited about commercial movies. Everyone loves *Die Hard* and *Speed* whereas in England it can be frowned upon.

Q - Was it daunting coming to work on a Hollywood movie?

Bharat - I was scared shitless. I was a director for hire which is how you get your first gig in America. It was very scary especially when I found out what my below the line was, and what I could and could not do with it. But then they gave me complete freedom on casting and crew which was fantastic. There are layers of producers that you have to deal with, having said that I was pretty well protected on this movie. Particularly so after showing the rushes to Miramax and the German investors who loved it.

Everything's targeted into marketing here, they're much more clued up into selling, a lot of thought of how you're going to sell it, where you're going to sell it, who you're going to sell it to etc. There's also a lot of testing and a lot more effort in post. On a normal English movie you might get three months post, our post went on for ten months. The more they saw and liked, the more they'd give me to go and shoot some more extra bits.

Q - So you'd have your main shoot and then cut and go back?

Bharat - I brought the English thing with me, we didn't go over budget and we had a lot of money In our contingency, so once they started trusting me they were willing to spend that. We got a great composer and the soundtrack was amazing, it's a 16 track album with some of the biggest acts in America. I got to choose every single track, it's great, the director is the creative leader here, they will let you have that if they believe in the film. They won't do anything without you, they email you everything, Ed Pressman has worked with many European film makers and likes how we work.

Q - The Crow 3 is very special effects heavy, had you experience with this?

Bharat - No, and this movie is full of digital effects! It was great fun even though we had a very small effects budget. But the movie looks as though it's completely effects driven, we'd go to so many cutting edge effects garages where there are all these kids who have out of date hardware, but only by a year so you're doing effects that they did in *The Matrix*. We took effects that are out there but came up with left field ideas of how to incorporate them, using them in an original way.

Q - Have all the test screenings been beneficial?

Bharat - Yep, it's fantastic. They get about 350 kids who they recruit from shopping malls, they watch it then fill in a questionnaire. It's very clever the way it's worked out statistically. America is driven by these things and it's very impressive to see them in action and it really does work. You take notes, you change, you get another screening, you take notes, you change and then another screening. On a general level it's really interesting, watching 350 people watching your movie and you know when it's working and when it's not. In America they're very vocal, they'll tell you if they hate it or not. I used to video tape the whole thing to capture the audience. The interesting thing about *The Crow 3* is that it's moved out of the cult arena toward the mainstream, the cast are much younger now.

Q - How long did the movie take to make?

Bharat - In the Summer of '98 I read the screenplay and went for the interview. There wasn't a definite yes until August '98. We went into prep in September and we shot in Salt Lake City in January '99 for six weeks, a shorter shoot than *Downtime* but ten times the footage. We used two cameras which was great. We came back in March and started the post which we finished in December '99. They then bring you back for the marketing and keep you informed. I also came back for the promo video of the main song, we have our press tour soon and we expect a release in the States in May.

Q - Is it true that in Hollywood you are forced to shoot much more than you need, so that they could re-cut the movie without you?

Bharat - *The Crow: Salvation* is a kind of Indie Hollywood movie, so if I shot less they were really happy. They'd ring me up on set and ask me if I'm happy, and I'd go *yes I am* or *no I'm not* but they knew it was a tough shoot. But if you're Renny Harlin and you're shooting seven cameras then you'll get loads of footage. They do want coverage but mainly because it's about the star, they always want the close up so that they can cut right in.

Q - Having done a Hollywood movie, do you love it or loathe it?

Bharat - I love a certain kind of Hollywood movie. I've been getting lots of screenplays flung at me and if I get another version of *48 Hours* I'll scream. None of these are offered, they're unassigned projects. But if you get your ear to the ground you can get really good scripts. The English pitch is very different from the US pitch. In England it's a meeting with the financier, producer, director, writer - *we can make a movie. What do you want to see in the movie?*, it's a very collaborative process. America is: *this is what the movie is, this is what's wrong with it, this is how I'm going to fix it blah blah blah.* If you come in with the English attitude you'll find it difficult. They want someone to drive the movie. In England it's very much *let's make movies together.*

Q - Do you have managers and lawyers out here?

Bharat - I have a US lawyer, with regard to managers I end up doing it myself. I think agents are great, they'll open doors that I could never open. A lot of people think *fantastic, I've got an agent, I'm going to do loads of work* but it doesn't really happen like that. It's as much up to you as it is them.

Q - Should a new filmmaker come out to LA to make their first movie?

From Newcastle to Hollywood. Bharat on the set of 'Crow 3 - Salvation'

Bharat - It depends on what kind of film you want to make. When you make your first film you have to be a bit naïve, if I knew what I know now, I might not have got *Killing Time* off the ground. You need naivity, make your first film then come on out here and look around, but just make it.

Q - Is being English an advantage?

Bharat - Both an advantage and a disadvantage. For some reason we resonate in LA, you must be so clever, you're English. I think it's always an advantage being different, being Indian and English in LA is very hip at the moment.

Q - Moving out here for a production, does the company organise a visa for you?

Bharat - Yes, for the length of the production. I'm now known as an alien of exceptional ability. It's easier for directors and actors because you have an individuality.

Q - What are your impressions of Hollywood?

Bharat - My big impression is that Hollywood isn't Hollywood, it's not this decadent, drug taking, three hookers in a Jacuzzi thing that happened in the '70s. I'm sure that happens but in a totally different world. It's a business, it's very serious and the agents are always in bed by ten o'clock, party night is only on Friday night, it's a very hardworking but good fun town that's much less cynical than the rest of the world. Anything is possible and I love that.

Q - Any tips for first time Hollywood directors?

Bharat - My trick is to always cut a good promo within the first two or three weeks. The first shot they see will stay in their heads, so make it a good one. I always shoot the trailer shot, it gets everyone going, they see the rushes and go *Wow!* Then they'll leave you alone! The other thing I do is to do only one take of my first shot. You say *Cut!* and walk away! It scares everyone but the crew then think that they've got someone who knows what they want and they've got to get it right first time.

I get sick of people saying *I want to make a short film* when they should be making a feature, it's just as hard. Just go and make movies, don't expect to earn any money, ever, expect to be poor for a long long, long long time. Making movies is equated with being poor. So do it for the passion. Go and make a movie, set a date and roll the dice...

CASE STUDIES

The Blair Witch Project
By Daniel Myrick and Eduardo Sanchez

(Dan is on a mobile phone on a conference call, going to the airport)

Q - Why did you want to make movies?

Ed - Because we're crazy.

Dan - When I was growing up I was fascinated by films but I didn't realise until I was in my teens that you could actually make a living from it. It was when *Star Wars* came out and Spielberg was making his movies, I grew up on that stuff, those spectacles just made me want to make films and I've been hacking away at it ever since.

Ed - As a kid everything I was interested in had something to do with movies or TV. Dan was living in Florida, I was living in Maryland, and there is no film community in either places, so there's no one to look up to and say *oh my Uncle does it*, or *my Dad's friend is a film maker*. Then we met at film school in '90, at the University of Central Florida, and we started to work together. Whilst there we wrote and co-directed a film which showed us that we have respect for each other's opinions and we realised that we were better film makers together than we were separate.

Q - What gave you the idea of a horror movie?

Dan - It was inspired by old dramatised documentaries like *In Search Of... Bigfoot* and we thought it would be cool to make a horror movie that was formatted like that. We hadn't seen a really scary movie since *The Exorcist* or *The Shining*, films that really really freaked us out, so we thought we'd try this stylistic take on the horror genre. It languished for a few years after film school, until we got back together and thought *let's shoot this woods movie* as we called it then. It made sense because it was just the cheapest thing for two broke film makers to do, we could shoot it on Hi8 and we didn't need any named actors to pull it off. We didn't want a single frame to look as though it was shot by a third person or have a convenient cutaway, it had to look absolutely genuine. We just held onto that realistic line and didn't deviate from it. We weren't sure if it was going to work or not but that was our theory. Conceptually it started with a couple of scenes, we thought *man, wouldn't it be cool if these guys got lost in the woods and all you see is them running with a shaky handheld camera, and everything was shot from the pov from the people who are getting attacked*. We started formulating these scary moments and then said *well, why are these people out there shooting something?* So we created the *Blair Witch* folklore that these kids are documenting and it grew from there.

Q - Technically, how did you make The Blair Witch?

Ed - We cast it in New York and saw a bunch of people to get Heather, Mike and Josh. We shot for eight days during October '97 in the woods near Germantown, Maryland on Hi8 and 16mm b&w. Most of what you see in the film was actually shot by the actors. We sent the actors out into the woods and Dan and I directed them by remote control. We gave them little notes and talked to them every once in a while but tried to keep the contact with them to a minimum because we wanted them to feel lost, hungry, confused and tired. By the end of the shoot we started to give them less and less food, and this all helped in their performance, creating a reality that you can sense.

Q - Directing actors by remote control, isn't that a unique way to do it?

Dan - Yes, I guess so. The first couple of days they were in the town we just had them follow a map - so they were instructed to go to the quickie mart and interview whoever. We'd leave director notes in little canisters on the front seat of their car with new instructions for their characters and also logistics, like go down route 20 to the cemetery. Ed and I had scouted the woods for about three weeks so we knew where everything would happen, the camp sites, the stickmen, coffin rock etc. Once the actors were in the woods we gave them a handheld satellite GPS and we would give them the co-ordinates of the locations so they could find them without our intervention. When they'd get to these check points they'd have a set of directing notes for the next checkpoint and new batteries. They'd leave the exposed film and used video tapes and collect unexposed stock and blank tapes and finally leave a bicycle flag on a milk crate so that we knew they had been there.

We tried to keep them guessing as to what would happen to them and constantly assess what their characters would know and do. We had a tent that was near all the locations as we wanted them to feel safe and they were always within radio contact so they could call us if there was an emergency.

The shoot went remarkably well, nobody got sick, nobody twisted an ankle although all of us were running around for more than a week in the woods, it was pretty miraculous that none of us got hurt.

Q - How did the actors react to this unique approach?

Dan - There was nothing really beyond being uncomfortable which they were all expecting. We told them in the audition process, *don't apply unless you're serious about this.* This is going to be a feature length improvisational film held in the woods and you're going to spend eight days out there, uncomfortable and miserable. The turn out was amazing with over 2000 auditions. The actors looked at it as an opportunity for them to have full creative control over their characters within the parameters of what Ed and I created, but it is improvised. It took an immense amount of trust to allow them to shoot and improvise their lines and to trust our remote control directing techniques.

Ed - The biggest disadvantage with improvising was that we constantly doubted ourselves. We had no idea of what we were doing. Dan and I would be in the woods and we'd look at each other and say *what the hell are we doing?* We would look at the footage and sometimes it was really good and sometimes it was like, *how are people going to sit through this film?* We had no idea what we were doing but we were kept so busy with the machinery of trying to make the film that ultimately we didn't have time to think about it too much.

Q - Did anything ever go missing or go wrong?

Ed - Yeah, we actually lost one of the tapes, it just disappeared for three days. A lot of things went wrong that actually ended up being good. One day it rained so heavily that we, the film makers, fell really behind, so the cast just hiked out of the woods and knocked on someone's door explaining they were shooting a film. There's a really cool moment in the film where they're hiking through the woods, it's raining and they're all miserable. Then they turned off the camera and in reality they're suddenly in somebody's house drinking hot cocoa - funny.

Q - How long did it take?

Ed - We conceived it in '93, sat around for a while, then in the summer of '96 decided we were going to do it. Then we made it in '97 and '98.

Dan - We did about three weeks of pre production prior to principal photography, then we were in the woods for six days and two days in the town. By the wrap party everyone was really high as it had been a great experience to shoot a film this way and we knew nobody had shot a film like this before, it was unique and exciting. We returned to Orlando three months later and Ed and I started editing in between Planet Hollywood corporate videos to pay the bills. In June '98 we built the website, then in September '98 we finished the edit and got accepted to Sundance, went to Sundance and sold it to Artisan.

Q - What was the phase two stuff?

Ed - Our original vision of the movie was for it to be like one of those standard documentaries where we had a lot of third party analysis and interviews with friends and family and the analysers had found the footage. During the edit we shot this phase two footage, interviews with relatives etc, but we realised that we already had our movie and that it was what these kids had already

shot in the woods. Ultimately, that footage was used on the website and integrated into *Curse Of The Blair Witch* that was made for the SciFi Channel. *Curse* was something Artisan wanted to do, a TV tie in with *Blair*. We came up with the idea and it was our chance to make the film that we originally conceived, to completely go the documentary route. It was a lot of hard work for very little money, but it was very rewarding, successful and we're really happy we did it.

Q - Were there any big disagreements in the cutting room?

Dan - I think the biggest thing was that we took two different approaches of how to incorporate this phase two stuff. I was going to try and integrate it through the story and Ed was going to try and build a prologue to the story. Ultimately we realised that neither worked and we just jettisoned it and held firm. That was an agonising decision for all of us at Haxan as you're going on instinct and you're battling the demons of doubt the entire time.

Ed - It's really tough to step back on a movie saying it's not working because take five is better than take three, so much of it is trusting your instincts, debating whether or not your instincts are worth a damn or not!

Q - How much was the Internet really responsible for the Blair phenomenon?

Ed - We'd just shown a clip from *Blair* on a TV show and the show's website got a lot of hits from people talking about the film and asking whether it was real or not. So we decided to put up a website, keeping up the idea that the film was real, that these three student film makers actually had disappeared and people started really digging it. What came out of the website was totally unexpected and I think it's largely responsible for what happened with the film. The film is a good film, I don't think it was a fluke, but the fact that it blew up like that is really a testament to how the Internet can be used. The Internet as a marketing tool for independent film makers is a powerful equalising tool.

Q - At this point did you anticipate how it was going to do?

Ed - We hoped for a success, but had no idea it would be as big as it was. We thought if we get a video or cable deal then that would be great. We didn't expect this to be in the theatres, we thought maybe we could do a limited arthouse run in three or four theatres but as far as opening as big as it did, nobody ever dreamed that anything like that was going to happen.

Dan - Money is always a big obstacle for independent film makers and survival was hard at times. Fortunately, the film itself was implicitly supposed to look low budget so all the weaknesses of low budget films turned into our strengths.

Q - Where did the cash come from and how much did you have?

Ed - From our credit cards, savings and John Pierson gave us almost half the budget that we needed for the initial shoot. We spent $22k to get the film in the can and then kept trying to raise money through private investors. Once we got into Sundance everyone kind of jumped on board and we got the money to take the film to print, then Artisan bought the film, fixed the sound, re-transferred it and did a couple of other things to it. The film you see in the theatres probably cost $500k.

Q - How did you get Blair into Sundance?

Dan - We had a 2½ half hour cut that we screened at our local arthouse theatre in Orlando. We had no idea what the hell we had so we had to show it to an audience and get their reaction. During this screening we met our executive producer Kevin Foxe, who just happened to be producing a movie there, and by fluke came along to the screening. He subsequently hooked us up with our biggest investor and said *You guys are going to Sundance!* and we're like *Oh my gosh, who is this guy?* We had no idea who he was but he seemed for real and he had a couple of films that had gone to Sundance before. Kevin has opened so many doors to people who have been instrumental in our success, publicists, agents, and the success of *Blair Witch*. Following the

The now iconic image of Heather from The Blair Witch Project. This single image conveyed the fear, tone, style and content of the movie. And due to the way the film was made, most of the actors' performances are completely authentic.

movie, three of the top agents at Endeavour flew to Orlando and signed us up. We didn't realise that that was such a big deal, we thought that was just what they did!

Kevin orchestrated a pre publicity campaign and a lobbying group to get into Sundance so that when we sent the tape in, it actually stood out from the pile. We held a screening in New York where some industry people saw it, our website was starting to get a lot of hits, and the news that Endeavour had picked us up - all these things combined made *Blair* an interesting thing and the guys at Sundance wanted to see it. The movie has to work on it's own merit, but it gave us an advantage going in as we were more than just another film submitted.

Ed - Kevin was also the first person to suggest dropping the phase two footage, he said *you guys have ruined the film, take it out!* - and he was right.

Q - After your first screening at Sundance, did Artisan just pounce?

Dan - We screened Saturday night at the Egyptian and there was quite a bit of anticipation for the movie, built up by Endeavour and Clein & Walker (publicists) pushing it, plus the Internet presence. We had a packed house with a lot of distributors who we had met at pre screening meetings. It was a really good sign that 90% of the people stayed and we had a quick Q&A, then our agents talked to three or four distributors who wanted to meet the next day. We were really excited and we all went back to the condo, had a few beers, relaxed and about a hour later Artisan called. They said *we want to get together, right here and now...* So our agents, attorney and producers did an all night negotiating session with Artisan and by 6am the next day we had a deal with them, then the press craziness began.

Q - Do you think Artisan had any idea of how it was going to do?

Dan - They were gauging *Blair Witch* with what they did with *Pi*, which was about $3m at the box office. Because *Blair* was a little more approachable than *Pi* they were hoping it would take maybe $6m - $8m tops. We even made a bet with Artisan, because we're all foosball fanatics, saying that if we break $10m they'd have to buy us a brand new foosball table.

Q - I hope you got the foosball table?

Dan- We definitely got the foosball table.

Q - Did you re-cut the film after Sundance?

Ed - When Dan and I saw it at Sundance both of us agreed we could cut it down so we cut five minutes out. Artisan experimented with the ending, they wanted to make it more extreme, so we shot alternative endings but none of them worked and we ended up with the original ending. Artisan also urged us to do new a sound mix, so we did.

Q - Low budget film makers lament about the distribution nightmare as distributors often act as though they are not accountable to the film maker. Is it any different at your level?

Ed - I can't comment on our experience with Artisan, but just about every film maker, even the big ones, have this same problem. We were recently talking to Barry Levinson and he said that distributors basically rip off film makers and you have to hire lawyers, accountants and you have to do audits - and that's just the way business is done. It's sad and I don't understand why, if you deserve the money, you can't get it as soon as the film has performed. They forget who made the film, that some people got together and sacrificed a lot, putting their heart and soul into making this movie. They forget that this is the reason why the film is in their possession in the first place and the reason that they're making money off it.

Q - Now that the film's done so well, what's the pressure like for your next movie?

Ed - After Sundance we put a lot of pressure on ourselves. For the first time we knew that the film was going to go out to theatres and that's a crazy thing when you're a struggling film maker, there're no more excuses, you've got to deliver. Once the film made so much money I think we were over the whole pressure thing. We knew that we had to continue to make films, the same way we've always made films, from the heart. For our next film we wanted to make a comedy (*Heart of Love*) and didn't want to do a sequel to *Blair* right away, or another horror film. Everybody sent us horror scripts but we stuck to our guns and we said *hey we want to do a comedy*. It's not going to be another *Blair Witch* but it's going to be another film from Dan and Ed and hopefully some people will dig it. There's a lot of pressure but mostly from ourselves.

Q - How did all your friends and family take your success?

Dan - My mum was out of control! It's been pretty good, for the most part everybody's been very excited for us. They say *it's nice to see Dan and Ed now, they're not asking for money anymore, that's a nice change!* Being in Orlando we don't really get bombarded by the fame celebrity thing, if we were in LA it might be different. We try and keep each other on the ground here and stay in perspective.

Ed - It was a conscious decision on our part to stay here in Orlando. There are five of us and we all keep each other down. If anyone's getting out of hand, thinking they're Steven Spielberg or something, there are four other guys saying '*hey, you're not Steven Spielberg, you're the same dork you were a year ago*'.

At this point, Dan gets on the plane and is cut off.

Q - How did you take the fame and fortune?

Ed - Firstly it's not really that much fame! (laughs) To see yourself on the cover of *Time* is kind of

An elaborate history for The Blair Witch was manufactured that captured the imagination of the public and helped seal the illusion that the Blair Witch was a real paranormal phenomenon.

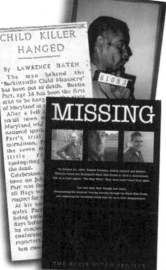

ridiculous. It's like a dream come true, a dream that you never even dreamt. Both of us dreamt of being film makers, winning an Academy Award, but on this first time out to take $140m at the box office was strange. We constantly remind ourselves that we are going to have to make another film and it probably wasn't going to have the success that this one had. We're going to have to do the press tour for our new film (*Heart of Love*) and it's not going to be as big as *Blair*. There will be a time when we make a film and nobody gives a shit. We're still the same people but it's great to have a little money after you've been poor all your life. It's great to help your family and it's great to be, at least for now, financially secure and drive decent cars.

Q - What mistakes do you think you made?

Ed - When we were at film school Robert Rodriguez got the three picture deal at Colombia, that was incredible, that's making it! And that's essentially what happened to us, but having gone through it, I now think that it isn't such a good thing. We got a first look deal for two films from Artisan and I think that kind of deal is to be avoided at all costs, no matter who the company is. First look deals are an excuse for somebody to take your project and hold it hostage. Artisan has been pretty cool with us with *Heart of Love*. They literally greenlit it in July and we still haven't come up with the deal for it, nine months later! The whole three picture deal can sometimes turn into a nightmare because they can turn into films that you don't want to make but you're forced to. We're all creative, at least for now, until we completely sell out. We're motivated by creativity and the first look deal has put deadlines or limitations on our creativity because they need to release a film at a certain time.

Q - What did you get right?

Ed - We did so many things right but it was pretty much out of luck. I built the web site because I didn't have a girlfriend at the time so I had a lot of time on my hands, and that took off. Originally we were going to get rid of Mike, he was the one who was going to end up dying first, but leaving Mike and Heather together formed a nice dynamic and it made the last third of the film different from the first two thirds. We also cut a lot of footage that we loved, the phase two footage, all the documentary stuff, and even though it hurt and Dan and I really had a hard time convincing ourselves to do it, it was the right decision.

Q - What advice would you offer new film makers?

Ed - Go to film school or a college with some practical media course. Learn about editing, lighting, camera, how to work with actors. If you've got a video camera, buy a computer editing system and make movies. It's something that Dan and I didn't have when we were young. Both Dan and I started making things before film school and when we went there, even though there were a lot of talented people in the school, there were only a handful of really good film makers because of the fact that we had already learned so much by making our own little films. I've been editing since I was 16 so I had learned and made my mistakes on a $5 VHS tape. Fellow students who were talented in their own way, were making mistakes on their films that cost them $150. I can't over emphasise this, learn on video, learn how to edit and shoot, then move over to film. You might never move on to film now though as everything is going digital. We're very happy that we made *Blair* when we made it because with the digital revolution that's happening now there are going to be twelve year old kids out there making films much better than *Blair*, and the age of the Hollywood director will plummet. These kids are growing up with Nintendo, 3D graphics on their home computers, shooting their films digitally and editing on their computer. You're talking about ten year old kids who have access to equipment that ten years ago would have cost 1m bucks.

Q - Have you got a big budget for your next movie?

Ed - Instead of raising $30m we're going to raise $10m. It's not going to be hard for us because of *Blair* and if you make a movie for $10m you don't have to make that much money at the box office. We're going to try and keep our films in the lower budget scale because we don't know how to make bigger films! You know, the less you spend on your film the more chance you have of it being profitable, and when it comes down to it, that's all that Hollywood is interested in, that's all that keeps you a viable film maker, how much money your last film made.

Q - So for new film makers, make what you're passionate about?

Ed - Yeah, technically learn stuff on digital video but when you're young and nobody's telling you what to do, make the film you want to make. It's cool to be inspired by certain film makers, like Spike Lee or Kevin Smith, but don't go out and make another *Clerks* or *Pulp Fiction* and don't go out and make another *Blair Witch!* The fact that these films did what they did is because they introduced something new and fresh, something that people hadn't seen ever, or for a long time. So understand that this is the reason why all those films exploded out of Sundance and were a success. John Pierson puts it best, he says *whenever a big independent movie comes out, for the next year and a half I get a hundred and fifty different versions of it.* People are looking for something new, because most of the time Hollywood is not going to deliver that. If you're going to go out there and try and make a Hollywood film on $10k you're NOT GOING TO SUCCEED! So make you're own film and understand that you can't and shouldn't compete with Hollywood. Even if you had an unlimited amount of money, make the film you want to make.

Zero to hero - from low budget film making paupers to multi-millionaires and on the cover of Time magazine.

READ THIS FIRST!

LEGAL DISCLAIMER

The copyright in and to the sample contracts and documents in this book is owned and retained by the originator of the work ("the Owner"). These sample contracts and documents have been created for your general information only. The Owner, the authors of this book and the publishers cannot therefore be held responsible for any losses or claims howsoever arising from any use or reproduction. Nothing in this book should be construed as legal advice. The information provided and the sample contracts and documents are not a substitute for consulting with an experienced entertainment lawyer and receiving counsel based on the facts and circumstances of a particular transaction. Furthermore case law and statutes and European and International law and industry practise are subject to change, and differ from country to country.

This legal section has been compiled with the assistance of Helen Tulley of Hammond Suddards solicitors who wishes to emphasise that the notes and agreements are not a substitute for specific legal advice and are designed for very general guidance only.

Section 3
Film Makers
Toolkit

THE LEGAL TOOLKIT

notes

Limited Company or Partnership?

If you are an independent producer you will need to set up a limited company through which to contract both with financiers and artists in order to give yourself the necessary protection. The limited company can be structured as a joint venture or more usually governed by a shareholder's agreement. You and your fellow producers can effectively act as a partnership in terms of sharing income i.e. profits, if that is what you intend to do. It is a very good idea to enter into an agreement which sets out rules for the conduct of the business of the company as between the directors and/or shareholders. It is particularly important to consider how outside work is to be treated i.e. whether the fees a company director receives for his services on an outside project are to be paid into the company, or to be retained by him personally.

A company is treated as a separate legal entity and it is liable for any contractual obligations, warranties and undertakings it enters into. Therefore, if a company is in breach of any of it's obligations, it and not the company's officers (the directors and secretary) will be liable (unless the company's officers have acted fraudulently or wrongfully). If the company has, for example, an obligation to make a payment under the terms of an agreement and it is unable to do so the company may be wound up by it's creditors. This means the assets of the company are gathered in and paid out to those creditors. But the company's directors will not be personally liable for the company's debts (unless the director has acted or traded unlawfully or wrongfully) and the director's personal property is untouched by the winding up.

This is an important source of protection to the individual. It is particularly useful in the film industry where even though the expenditure on a film may not be high, the liabilities and damages payable to contracting third parties could be considerable.

The downside of having a company is that you must comply with the Companies Acts in relation to how you run and administer the company. In certain circumstances, if you do not comply with the law eg. filing accounts at Companies House, your

company can be struck off the register. It can be restored to the register but not without expense and inconvenience.

If you trade as a partnership, you are personally responsible for the contractual obligations, warranties and undertakings of the partnership. If you or your partners do not meet those financial obligations and they are over £750 you can be made bankrupt by a creditor. If you are adjudged bankrupt your personal property including your home (but excluding tools of your trade) can be sold off to pay the creditor.

As a partner you are jointly and severally liable for the debts of the partnership. Unless you agree otherwise, if your partner binds the partnership to pay money to a third party, the third party can come after you for all of that sum (not just half of it, if for example, there were two partners).

A partnership is governed by the Partnership Act 1890 and there are very few legislative rules regarding the conduct of partnerships.

Company Directors and the Law

Role of Company Director

Directors are agents of the Company and as such occupy a fiduciary position in relation to the Company. All powers entrusted to them are only exercisable in this fiduciary capacity (see Sec. 2).

Since directors have control of the Company's business and assets, the law requires them to act honestly in what they consider to be the Company's best interests, not their own.

If the directors are also majority shareholders or if they represent the majority shareholders, they must not manage the company so as to unfairly prejudice the minority shareholders.

There is also a general duty on the directors to have regard to the interest of employees as well as shareholders.

Directors should also have the interest of the creditors particularly when the Company is insolvent (or nearly so) as well as all (sometimes instead) of the interests of the shareholders.

Fiduciary Duty

The directors are under a fiduciary duty which requires them to act in good faith and with loyalty to the Company (akin to a trustees' position).

They should not permit a conflict to arise between their personal interests and those of the Company and should disclose any interest of any kind, whether direct or indirect in a contract with the Company (including any loans or guarantees).

A director's powers are given to them under the Articles of Association and such powers shall be used for the proper and primary/substantial purposes for which they are given.

They should take proper care of the Company's property and should not appropriate such property, failing which they will be accountable to the Company for any personal gains obtained including from knowledge or opportunities of investment which they obtained as directors (unless the Company agrees otherwise).

There is a general prohibition on companies making loans, guarantees, etc. available to directors over £5000 (or £20,000 in certain other circumstances).

Standards of Performance/Duties of Care Diligence and Skill

A director is under a duty of care, diligence and skill owed to the Company. He must show an acceptable degree of such care, diligence and skill as would be displayed by a reasonable man.

If a director has a certain skill e.g. accountancy, he is required to show proficiency in that skill as would be reasonably expected of a competent member of that profession.

A director is not liable for errors in judgement (but is liable for his own negligence and may be held accountable of any loss arising from such negligence).

A director may accept (without making investigation) information provided by an apparently reliable source e.g. a co-director or senior employee.

He should attend a board and general meetings whenever possible.

Directors as Employees

A director is not necessarily an employee of the Company (although he is liable to Schedule E income tax and National Insurance contributions on his fees.)

A director who is also an employee should not vote at a board meeting to approve his own contact of employment and (unless the Articles provide otherwise) cannot be counted in the quorum for that purpose of that vote.

Accounts and Records

The directors must prepare a profit and loss account in respect of each financial year of the Company with a balance sheet as at the last day of that financial year reflecting a true and accurate position of the company at the relevant date.

The directors must lay a copy of such accounts before the Company in general meeting and file the same with the Register of Companies within certain time limits. The accounts must include directors' and auditors' reports properly signed.

The directors must maintain a register of directors and their interests as well as minutes of all board and general meetings.

Copyright

Copyright is in fact a bunch of rights that attaches to the owner of the copyright in certain types of intellectual property (as defined in the CDPA 1988) i.e. literacy, artistic, dramatic and musical works and derivative works including film, sound recordings and published work. The right of copyright rests first in the author or creator of the work (there are some exceptions to this). To qualify for copyright protection the work must be original to the author and not a copy. The bundle of rights given to the creator of the work are set out in the CDPA 1988 and these rights may not be exercised by another without the permission of the author or owner. The restricted acts are:- copying, issuing copies to the public, performing, broadcasting, transmitting by cable or adapting the work.

523

The rights of copyright rest automatically in the author. There is no requirement of notice or registration. In order to provide evidence of creation, an author may send, for example, a screenplay to him/her self in an envelope which is kept sealed so the postmark on the envelope provides evidence of the date of creation.

Copyright exists in artistic, musical, literacy and dramatic works for 70 years after the end of the year in which the author dies. For Film it lasts for 70 years after the death of the last to die of the director, scriptwriter, dialogue writer or composer of commissioned music for the film. For sound recordings, broadcasts, performances, cable transmissions, it lasts 50 years from the end of the year in which the performance etc. was made or made available to the public. The CDPA 1988 has been amended recently to harmonise copyright duration throughout Europe and important changes, including the revival of copyright in certain works, have been made. Any dealings with Copyright works should be checked with your solicitor.

Options. Licences & Assignments

OPTIONS

An option over a piece of work is an agreement by the owner of the work not to dispose of the work to a third party for a specified period of time in consideration of the purchaser (i.e. a producer) paying a fixed amount of money. This may be a nominal amount of £1 or a commercial sum negotiated between two parties. If the purchaser exercises the option the owner agrees to assign or licence some or all of the rights in the work to the purchaser. An option is necessary for a purchaser so they can develop a project based on a piece of work without the fear that some other party is doing likewise. An option grants the producer the right to develop a project based on the work to see if it is worth acquiring the work or certain rights in the work, or obtaining permission to exploit all or some of the rights in the work.

An option may be taken over a screenplay or more usually over an underlying piece of work such as a novel or a stageplay. The owner of a novel is only likely to grant an option over the work for the specific rights necessary to make and exploit a film or films.

It is advisable to annex the licence or assignment

to the option agreement with the terms set out and agreed. If you enter into an option and do not agree the terms upon which you will acquire the rights in the work, this is an agreement to agree and may not be enforceable. It also leaves you very vulnerable when it comes to negotiating the terms for any licence or assignment.

LICENCES AND ASSIGNMENTS

A licence is a permission given by the owner allowing you to do certain acts without infringing copyright in their work. Frequently, when you are dealing with published literary works the owner or their agent will only wish to grant you a licence to those specific rights in the work that you need to make and distribute the film. You usually need to acquire ancillary rights (i.e. the video, CD-Rom, book of the film) to make the film commercially attractive and viable, but the owner may insist that they participate in income from this source.

A licence fee is payable, usually upon first day of principal photography. This fee can be calculated by reference to a percentage to the budget with a minimum and maximum fee cited. The advantage to the owner of this is that if the film is taken up by a Hollywood studio, for example, and the studio pumps in huge sums for the film, the owner is a direct beneficiary of this. A licence can be for a specific period of time or in perpetuity subject to negotiation. A licence can be exclusive or non-exclusive. If it is exclusive, the owner cannot sell the rights (or otherwise dispose of them) to any one else. If you are making a film you must insist upon an exclusive licence as obviously you (and certainly not your financiers and distributors) do not want a competing product out on the market.

An Assignment is a transfer of ownership from the owner to you. Copyright in a work can be broken down into specific rights and those rights can be sold separately. Therefore, you can buy the film rights in the work and the owner can retain the publishing rights or stage rights (as is usually the case). If you are commissioning a script or treatment or engaging creative talent (directors, actors, composers) then you must ensure you own out right all their copyright in their work or performance and this will be affected by an assignment of rights. As with a licence, it is usual for an assignment to set out those rights which are being transferred.

In both licences and assignments there is usually a turnaround provision which allows the owner of the work to re-acquire it if the film or programme does not go into production within a specified period of time.

Where work is owned jointly by two or more authors/owners you must obtain an assignment from both or all of them, as one joint author/owner acting alone does not have authority to assign rights in the work.

Writers Agreement

If you commission a writer to write a screenplay you must enter into a written agreement with him in which the writer assigns or licences their rights in the screenplay to you (they may assign/licence all their rights or only the specific rights you require i.e. film and ancillary rights). If you do not have this written assignment of rights or an exclusive licence, the writer will remain the owner of the screenplay and could sell the screenplay to another person.

A writer may be a member of the Writer's Guild (of the UK or America) and you should clarify with them in the first instance the status of the agreement i.e. whether it is a Guild agreement or not.

If it is a Guild agreement then you should refer to the appropriate Guild to confirm the minimum payments have been complied with.

A writer's agreement must most importantly contain a waiver of moral rights (see Glossary). Without this it will be very difficult to both raise finance and distribute the film.

Usually the writer's fee is broken down into several payments so that they receive part of their fee on commencement, part on delivery of the first draft, part on delivery of the second draft and the final sum on completion. For a film where many re-drafts and polishes may be required, it should be made clear in the agreement that the fee includes payment for such further re-drafts. A Film Producer will usually want a complete buyout to avoid having to make residual, repeat or fees in the future (the Guild agreements provide for minimum payments for repeats etc.).

The Producer must have the ability to engage another writer to work on the script if the work produced by the writer is unsatisfactory. If you are the Producer you need to negotiate a right of cut off which allows you to engage another writer to write,

for example, the second draft without being obliged to make any further payment to the original writer.

You will need the writer to warrant the screenplay is his and he has not assigned or licensed it to any other person and that it is not defamatory, libellous etc. The writer should give an indemnity to you for any breach of warranty or undertaking provided in the agreement.

It is unusual for a scriptwriter to retain any rights in the work, but where a writer is also an author they will often wish to retain novelisation rights and occasionally the stage and radio rights. As these rights are of little commercial interest to the film producer (except perhaps any "making of " book), producers usually are happy to allow this, provided they retain a participation in any income derived from such exploitation. A hold back on the exploitation of the rights retained for a number of years is often negotiated so that a stage play or book based on the same treatment does not compete with the film.

LEGAL TOOLKIT

Contracts & Agreements

TOP TEN POINTS TO LOOK OUT FOR IN ANY AGREEMENT

Set out below are some very broad considerations which you should give to any agreement. Of course, each circumstance will require more specific attention. If your liabilities under the agreement could involve you in substantial expense, seek legal advice.

1. Ask yourself first what interests you need to protect and are they sufficiently protected.

2. Do you have any existing contractual obligations to other people and if you enter into this agreement are you going to be in breach of those existing contractual obligations?

3. What are your liabilities in this agreement and if things go wrong, what are you liable for? Look out for clauses which make you personally liable even though you may be contracting through a company i.e. are you being asked to give a personal guarantee for a loan which is being made to your company?

4. What is the agreement asking you to do and is it reasonable and within your power to deliver or achieve?

5. If you are required under the agreement to do something ask to change any reference to your using your "best endeavours" to "reasonable endeavours".

6. If you are providing your own original work or any intellectual property owned by you under the terms of the agreement what happens if the project does not go ahead? Do you have the chance to regain or repurchase your property?

7. If you are due to receive any royalties or profit share under the agreement make sure that the other party has an obligation to collect in any revenue derived from the film or project, that they must show you their books and you have the right to audit those books. Check also that your share of Net Profits (as defined in the agreement) is as agreed i.e. are you receiving a share of the Producer's net profits or a share of all net profits?

8. What are the possible sources of income to you from the film or project and are all those sources being exploited and if so are you getting a fair share of that income?

9. What sort of controls do you have over the conduct of the other party? Are the promises they are making under the agreement sufficient to cover your interests? What happens if they are in default of their promises?

10. Remember that if the agreement is being provided by the other side, the terms will be very much in their favour. This does not mean that they are necessarily trying to stitch you up, this is just business.

Option Agreement
(for previous work)

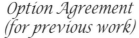

On The CD

This is a guideline only and should not be relied upon without taking legal advice.

THIS AGREEMENT is made as of the .... day of 20.....

BETWEEN

............................(hereinafter called "the Owner")
of .... of the one part

AND

............................(hereinafter called "the Purchaser")
of.................................... of the other part.

WHEREAS

(A) The Owner is the absolute owner free from encumbrances except as hereinafter mentioned of the entire copyright and all other rights throughout the world in an original literary work entitled "..............................." (hereinafter called "the Work") written by........................... (hereinafter called "the Author") which expression shall if the Author and the Owner are the same person be construed as a reference to the Owner.

(B) The Owner has (as is witnessed by the Owner's execution of these presents) agreed to grant to the Purchaser the sole and exclusive option to acquire by way of partial assignment of copyright, the sole and exclusive film and other rights hereinafter referred to for the consideration and upon and subject to the terms and conditions hereinafter contained.

NOW THIS AGREEMENT WITNESSETH as follows:-

1. In this Agreement the following expressions shall unless the context otherwise requires bear the following meanings:-

"First Option Sum" : . ...Pounds (£...................)
"Second Option Sum": ....Pounds (£...................)
"First Option Date" : A date ....from the date hereof
"Second Option Date": A date................following the First Option Date

2. (a) In consideration of the immediate payment by the Purchaser to the Owner of the First Option Sum (the

receipt of which sum the Owner hereby acknowledges) the Owner hereby grants to the Purchaser the sole and exclusive option (hereinafter called "the First Option") exercisable by notice in writing to the Owner in the manner hereinafter mentioned at any time on or before the First Option Date to purchase from the Owner by way of partial (or full) assignment of copyright the sole and exclusive rights in the Work as more particularly specified in the form of the Deed of Assignment ("the Deed") annexed hereto and by this reference made a part hereof for the sums and upon and subject to the terms and conditions set out in the Deed.

(b) The Owner agrees to grant to the Purchaser a further sole and exclusive option (hereinafter called "the Second Option") upon the same terms and conditions as for the First Option provided that the Purchaser pays the Owner the Second Option Sum on or before the First Option Date. Such further Second Option shall be exercisable by notice in writing as aforesaid at any time on or before the Second Option Date.

(c) Not withstanding anything to the contrary herein contained the First Option Period and (if applicable) the Second Option Period shall be extended until such time as the Owner has provided the Purchaser with evidence of it's title to the rights expressed to be granted in the Deed sufficient to enable the Purchaser if the Purchaser should require to obtain errors and omissions insurance in respect of such title upon customary terms.

3. The sums paid to the Owner pursuant to Clause 2 above shall be non returnable in any event and shall be deemed to be paid in advance and on account of the sum payable pursuant to Clause 2 of the Deed.

4. (a) The Owner hereby warrants that the Owner is the absolute owner free from encumbrances (save as expressly provided in the Deed) of all such rights in the Work as are referred to in the Deed.

(b) The Owner agrees and undertakes during the subsistence of the aforesaid option periods not to dispose of nor deal in any way with any of the rights in the Work which are the subject of the options hereby granted.

LEGAL TOOLKIT

5 (a) The Purchaser agrees and undertakes not later than ten (10) days after the exercise of the applicable Option to submit an engrossment in the form of the Deed to the Owner for signature and further agrees agrees forthwith upon signature of the same by the Owner to pay to the Owner in exchange for the executed Deed the consideration therein expressed to be immediately payable.

(b) In the event that the Purchaser fails to submit an engrossment of the Deed to the Owner for signature within the time limited as aforesaid the consideration in the Deed expressed to be immediately payable shall become due and payable forthwith upon the expiration of the said period of ten (10) days without prejudice to the right of the Purchaser to call upon the Owner at any time thereafter to execute an engrossment of the Deed.

6. The Purchaser shall be entitled to write or cause to be written film treatments and/or screenplays and/or adaptations of the Work and undertake so-called pre-production work for the purpose of enabling the Purchaser to decide whether or not the Purchaser wishes to exercise any of the options hereby granted and in connection with the financing production distribtution and exploitation arrangements for the film or films to be based on the Work.

7. The notice in writing referred to in Clause 2 hereof shall be deemed to have been duly and properly served if addressed to the Owner and sent by prepaid post or if sent by telex or if sent by facsimile transmission to the above address or any subsequent address duly notified to the Purchaser and the date of service shall be deemed to be the day of delivery in the normal course of posting if posted or the day of sending such telex if telexed or the day of sending such facsimile if sent by facsimile.

8. The Purchaser shall be entitled to assign the benefit of this agreement to any third party but shall not thereby be relieved of it's obligations hereunder.

9. (a) All sums mentioned herein are exclusive of any Value Added Tax that may be payable thereon.

(b) All sums payable to the Owner hereunder shall be paid to the irrevocably appointed Agent at it's address above whose receipt thereof shall be a good and valid discharge therefore.

10. This agreement shall be construed and shall take effect in accordance with the laws of England and subject to the exclusive jurisdiction of the English Courts.

AS WITNESS the hands of the parties hereto or their representatives the day and year first above written

SIGNED by...
in the presence of:- ....

SIGNED by...
For and on behalf of:-..
(if a limited company)

in the presence of:-..

LEGAL TOOLKIT

Deed Of Assignment
(Original Screenplay)

This is a guideline only and should not be relied upon without taking legal advice.

This Deed is made the .... day of .... 20........

BETWEEN

(Name, address) (hereinafter called "the Owner") of the one part

and

(Name, address) (hereinafter called "the Purchaser") of the other part.

WHEREAS

A) The Owner is the absolute owner free from encumbrances except as hereinafter mentioned of the copyright and all other rights throughout the world in and to the Treatment and Screenplay entitled.........................
(horoinaftor callod tho "Work") written by..........................
(hereinafter called the "Author", which expression shall if the Author and the Owner are the same person be construed as a reference to the Owner).

B) The Owner has agreed to grant and assign the Producer for the consideration hereafter mentioned the (specify applicable rights) rights in the Work throughout the world as hereinafter more particularly mentioned.

NOW THIS ASSIGNMENT WITNESSETH

1.1. In consideration of the payment by the Purchaser to the Owner of the sum of ....Pounds (£..........) (receipt whereof the Owner hereby acknowledges) the Owner with full title guarantee hereby assigns and grants to the Purchaser (specify applicable rights i.e. all rights) (including but not limited to copyright) of whatever description whether now known or in the future existing in and to the Work TO HOLD the same unto the Purchaser absolutely throughout all parts of the world in which copyright in the Work may now subsist or may be acquired and during all renewals, revivals and extensions thereof and thereafter (in so far as may be or become possible) in perpetuity and except as herein expressly provided to the contrary free from all restrictions and limitations whatsoever including (but not by way of limitation of the generality of

the foregoing) free from all so-called "Authors rights" or "droit moral" and any similar right now or hereafter accorded by the laws prevailing in any part of the world (including but not limited to any rights pursuant to sections 77 and 80 of the Copyright Designs and Patents Act 1988) and the Owner hereby expressly waives any so-called "Authors rights", droit moral and any such rights.

1.2. Without prejudice to the generality of the assignment of rights in Clause 1.1 above, the Owner hereby confirms and agrees that the assignment of rights hereby made to the Purchaser includes any and all rights of communication to the public by satellite, cable re-transmission rights and any and all rental and lending rights, whether now or hereafter known or existing in any country of the world, in and to the products of the Owner's services hereunder and/or the Film (as hereinafter defined) and/or copies thereof and/or any part or version or adaptation of any of the foregoing.

2. (a) As further consideration for the rights hereby granted the Purchaser hereby agrees to pay to the Owner (i) upon the first day of principal photography of the first or only film made in exercise of the rights hereby granted and not being part of a television series or serial (hereinafter called "the Film") the sum of (£.............................)

(ii) sums from time to time equal to (...................) Percent (....%) of the Net Profits (as defined below) of the Film.

For the purposes of this Deed the expression "Net Profits" shall have the same meaning as is accorded thereto in the principal production finance and distribution agreements for the Film.

2. (b) The Owner agrees that the consideration payable to the Owner in accordance with the provisions of this Agreement takes into account and includes a payment in respect of all rights of communication to the public by satellite, cable, re-transmission rights and any and all rental and lending rights as referred to in Clause 1.2. hereof and that the said payment constitutes equitable and adequate consideration for the assignment of satellite, cable and rental and lending rights, and constitutes and satisfies in full any and all rights which the Owner has or may at any

time have to receive equitable, adequate or other remuneration for the exploitation by satellite and cable and the rental or lending of the products of the Owner's services and/or the Film and/or copies thereof and/or any part or version or adaptation of any of the foregoing. Without prejudice to the provisions of this Clause nothing in this Agreement shall prevent the Owner from being entitled to receive income under collection and other agreements negotiated by recognised collection societies under the laws of any jurisdiction PROVIDED THAT this does not imply any obligation or liability on the part of the Purchaser regarding the collection or payment of such monies.

3. The Owner hereby represents, warrants and undertakes to and with the Purchaser that:-

a) the Owner is the Owner and Author of the Work which was and is wholly original with the Author and nothing therein infringes the copyright or any other rights of any third party

b) copyright in the Work subsists or may be acquired in all countries of the world whose laws now provide for copyright protection and that the Owner and the Author have not and will not at any time hereafter do authorise or omit to do anything relating to the Work whereby the subsistence of copyright therein or any part of such copyright may be destroyed or otherwise impaired.

c) the rights hereby granted are vested in the Owner absolutely and neither the Owner nor the Author or any other predecessor in title of the Owner heretofore assigned, licensed, granted or in any way dealt with or encumbered the same so as to derogate from the grant hereby made and that the Owner has a good title and full right and authority to make this Deed

d) the Work does not constitute a breach of any duty of confidence owed to any party and does not breach any right of privacy and does not contain any libellous or defamatory statement or matter or innuendo of or reference to any person firm company or incident

e) the Owner will indemnify and at all times keep the Purchaser fully indemnified from and against all actions, claims, proceedings, costs and damages incurred by or awarded against the Purchaser or any compensation paid or agreed to be paid by the Purchaser on the advice of counsel agreed between the parties hereto (and in default of such agreement within one month from the time such

agreement is sought then a counsel decided by the President for the time being of the Law Society) in consequence of any breach, non-performance or non-observance by the Owner of all or any of the covenants, warranties, representations and agreements by the Owner contained in this Deed

f) the Owner will and does hereby authorise the Purchaser at the Purchaser's expense to institute prosecute and defend such proceedings and to do such acts and things as the Purchaser in it's sole discretion may deem expedient to protect the rights granted by the Owner to the Purchaser hereunder and to recover damages and penalties for any infringement of the said rights and insofar as may be necessary in the Purchaser's reasonable view to use the name of the Owner for or in connection with any of the purposes aforesaid and the Owner shall in any such proceeding afford the Purchaser all reasonable assistance the Purchaser may require at the expense of the Purchaser in instituting prosecuting or defending such actions unless the said action is occasioned by some breach or non-performance by the Owner of any covenants or warranties herein contained.

4. For further securing to the Purchaser the rights hereby granted the Owner hereby undertakes with the Purchaser that the Owner will at the request and expense of the Purchaser do all such further acts and things and execute all such further documents and instruments as the Purchaser may from time to time require for the purpose of confirming the Purchaser's title to the said rights in any part of the world and the Owner hereby appoints the Purchaser it's irrevocable attorney-in-fact with the right but not the obligation to do any and all acts and things necessary for the purpose of confirming the Purchaser's title at the expense of the Purchaser as aforesaid and to execute all such deeds documents and instruments in the name of and on behalf of the Owner which appointment shall be deemed a power coupled with an interest and shall be irrevocable.

5. The Owner hereby grants to the Purchaser the right to use and authorise others to use the name, biography and likeness of the Author when exploiting or dealing with the rights hereby granted provided that the Author shall not be represented as personally using or recommending any commercial product other than films or other products of the rights hereby granted based upon the Work.

6. The Purchaser shall not be obliged to exercise any of

LEGAL TOOLKIT

the rights of copyright and other rights in and to the Work or any part thereof granted unto the Purchaser hereunder and if the Purchaser shall not exercise any of these said rights the Purchaser shall not be liable to the Owner in any manner whatsoever.

7. The Purchaser shall be fully entitled to negotiate and conclude agreements for the sale performance licensing and other commercial exploitation of the rights hereby granted upon whatever terms the Purchaser considers fair and reasonable and shall not be obliged in any way to seek the approval of the Owner in connection therewith and the Purchaser gives no warranty or representation as to the amount (if any) of any receipts that may arise.

8. a) In the event of a film or films being based upon the Work the Purchaser shall give the Author a single card credit on all copies of any such film or films issued under the control of the Purchaser in the form: Screenplay written by .... provided however that no casual or inadvertent failure by the Purchaser to accord the Author credit as aforesaid shall be deemed a breach

b) the Purchaser will Incorporate in it's agreements with the distributors or broadcasters of such films as aforesaid a provision obliging such distributor or broadcaster to accord such credits to the Author but the failure of any distributor or broadcaster to accord such credits shall not constitute a breach by the Purchaser hereof provided however that if the Purchaser shall be notified of such failure the Purchaser shall use all reasonable endeavours but without incurring material expense to ensure that such failure is remedied by such distributor or broadcaster (as the case may be)

9. All rights assigned by this Deed shall be irrevocable under all or any circumstances and shall not be subject to reversion rescission termination or injunction in case of breach of the provisions of this Deed by the Purchaser including failure to pay any part of the consideration other than the sum payable under clause 1 hereof. The Owner's remedies shall be limited to an action at law for damages or for an accounting (if applicable). The Purchaser shall not be liable for damages for breach of contract (except for payment of consideration) unless the Purchaser has been given reasonable notice and opportunity to adjust or correct the matter complained of and the same has not been adjusted or corrected within a reasonable time following the notice aforesaid.

10. Any notices required to be served hereunder shall be deemed to have been duly and properly served if addressed to the Owner or Purchaser as the case may be and sent in a prepaid envelope or if sent by facsimile transmission to the above address or any subsequent address of the Owner or Purchaser as the case may be duly notified to the Owner or Purchaser respectively and acknowledged and the date of service shall be deemed to be the date of delivery in the normal course of posting if posted or the date of sending if sent by facsimile.

11. All sums mentioned herein are exclusive of Value Added Tax that may be payable thereon.

12. The Purchaser shall be entitled to assign the benefit of this Deed to any third party but shall not thereby be relieved of it's obligations hereunder.

13. This Deed shall be construed and shall take effect in accordance with the laws of England and subject to the exclusive jurisdiction of the English Courts.

IN WITNESS WHEREOF the Owner and the Purchaser have executed this Assignment and is hereby delivered as a Deed the day and year first above written

SIGNED as a DEED

by:..

in the presence of:..

Executed as a DEED by:..................................... (Limited) acting through it's two Directors/Director and Secretary

On The CD

Actors Agreement

This is a guideline only and should not be relied upon without taking legal advice.

(MAIN AGREEMENT)

Dated:

PRODUCER: ("the Producer")
Address:

ARTIST: ("the Artist")
Address:

FILM TITLE: ("the Film")

ROLE: ("character")

1. Services: Producer hereby engages Artist as a performer in the Film portraying in the role described above (as said role may be changed or rewritten at Producer's discretion).

2. Start Date: It is presently contemplated that read through day will commence on....................and rehearsals will commence on......................and that principal photography shall commence on.................... provided however Artist's services shall commence no later than.....................subject to events of force majeure. Artist agrees to remain available and not accept another engagement which would conflict or interfere with Artist obligations hereunder.

3. Guaranteed Period of Engagement: Term: The term of Artist's engagement hereunder shall commence on the start date and continue subject only to the provisions for suspension and termination set out in Exhibit A hereto for a minimum period of .... (.....) weeks ("Guaranteed Period of Engagement") and thereafter for the period necessary to complete all continuous services required by Producer from Artist in connection with principal photography of the Film. Artist shall perform additional services prior to and after the term in accordance with the provisions of clause 4 hereof.

4. Additional Services: The Artist shall on written notice from the Producer perform additional services ("Additional Services") on .... or such other or additional day notified to the Artist by the Producer in connection with principal photography of the Film.

5. Further Services: If the Producer requires the Artist's services after the Guaranteed Period of Engagement and not for any Additional Services the Artist shall if so requested by the Producer render such further services

("Further Services") which shall include without limitation dubbing and post-synchronisation subject to the Artist's prior professional engagements.

6. Basic Compensation: Subject to the provisions of this Agreement and provided that Artist shall keep and perform all covenants and conditions to be kept and performed by Artist hereunder Producer agrees as full compensation for services rendered and for all rights granted to the Producer hereunder to pay Artist as follows:-

(a) Guaranteed Compensation: For the Guaranteed Period of Engagement, Artist shall receive the sum of .... pounds (£..........) payable as to .... pounds (£.........) following the first week of rehearsals inclusive of the read through day and .... pounds (£..........) following the ....weeks of rehearsals and as to the balance following the end of the first full week of Artist's services in principal photography of the Film. Such payment shall be made to Artist care of (......................). If the Artist renders Additional Services, Artist shall receive.........pounds (£.......) for each day after which he attends at the request of the Producer and renders services hereunder. If the Artist renders Further Services, Artist shall receive a further sum (if any) to be negotiated in good faith between the parties for each day or part day (if any) upon which he attends at the request of the Producer and renders services hereunder.

7. Credit
(a) If Artist shall keep and perform all covenants and conditions to be kept and performed by the Artist hereunder and if Artist appears readily recognisable in the Film then Artist will be accorded credit in the main titles of the Film on all copies of the Film issued by or under the control of the Producer and in all major paid advertising excluding the customary industry exclusions. The size type and placement of such credit shall be at Producer's sole discretion.

8. Transportation and Expenses: From the commencement of principal photography until the expiry of the Term, Producer shall provide Artist with .... transportation facilities (state what these are if any and whether other expenses will be paid).

9. Conditions: Artist's engagement hereunder is subject to Producer obtaining standard cast insurance for Artist at normal rates.

LEGAL TOOLKIT

10. References: The term of Artist's engagement hereunder shall be as set forth in this Main Agreement and in Exhibit "A" attached hereto which is incorporated herein by reference. In the event of any express inconsistency between the provisions of this Main Agreement and the provisions of Exhibit / a the provisions of this Main Agreement shall control.

IN WITNESS WHEREOF the parties hereto have executed the within Agreement as of the date first set forth hereinabove

(insert name of Producer)

BY:..

Duly authorised officers:.....................................

Accepted and Agreed to:

....

EXHIBIT A

1. The Artist hereby
(a) warrants that the Artist is not under any obligation or disability which might prevent or restrict the Artist from entering into this agreement or from giving the undertakings or fully observing and performing the terms and conditions of this Agreement or granting the rights and consents referred to herein
(b) gives all such consents as are or may be required under the Copyright Designs and Patents Act 1988 or any re-enactment consolidation or amendment thereof or any statute of like purpose or effect for the time being in force in any part of the world including but not in limitation of the foregoing all consents under Part II of the said Act in order that the Producer may make the fullest use of the Artist's services provided by the Artist hereunder and furthermore the Artist hereby irrevocably and unconditionally waives all rights relating to the Artist's services in the Film to which the Artist is now or may in the future be entitled pursuant to the provisions of Section 77 80 84 and 85 of the said Act and any other moral rights to which the Artist may be entitled under any legislation now existing or in the future enacted in any part of the world
(c) warrants that the Artist is a "qualifying person" and the performance of the Artist is a "qualifying performance" within the meaning of the Copyright Designs and Patents Act 1988.

2. The Artist undertakes that the Artist shall during the subsistence of and subject to the terms and conditions of this Agreement as where and when required by the Producer:-

(a) perform and record the Artist's part
(b) attend for tests conferences fittings rehearsals and the taking of still photographs and other arrangements
(c) dress, make up and wear the Artist's hair (subject to prior consultation with the Artist) as directed by the Director and generally comply with all decisions of the Producer concerning the manner in which the Artist shall render the Artist's services hereunder and be portrayed and presented
(d) render the Artist's services hereunder willingly and to the utmost of the Artist's skill and ability and as directed by the Producer both in connection with the production of the Film and for publicity and other purposes connected therewith Provided Always that nothing in this sub-clause and sub-clause (c) hereof shall be deemed to require the Artist to recommend or endorse any commercial product other than the Film and any commercial gramophone record of the sound track of the Film or to engage in any publicity or other activities for any such purpose (but without prejudice to Clause 5 hereof).

3. The Artist further undertakes:-
(a) that the Artist will comply with all reasonable and notified directions, regulations and rules in force at places where the Artist is required to render services hereunder (including in particular regulations and rules relating to smoking and the taking of photographs) and will comply with the orders given by the Producer of it's representatives from time to time
(b) to keep the Producer informed of the Artist's whereabouts and telephone number from time to time prior to and throughout the engagement
(c) that the Artist will use the Artist's best endeavours to maintain a state of health enabling the Artist fully and efficiently to perform the Artist's services hereunder throughout the engagement and that the Artist will not take part in any activity which might interfere with the due and efficient rendering of such services or which might invalidate any such insurance as is referred to in the preceding sub-clause
(d) that the Artist shall not at any time pledge the credit of the Producer nor incur or purport to incur any liability on it's behalf or in it's name.

4. (a) The Artist hereby acknowledges that all rights whatsoever throughout the World in or in any way attaching to the Film and all photographs and sound recordings taken and made hereunder (including all rights of copyright therein and in any written or other material contributed by

the Artist and all such rights therein or in such material as are or may hereafter be conferred or created by international arrangement or convention in or affecting any part of the World whether by way of new or additional arrangement or convention in or affecting any part of the world whether by way of new or additional rights not now comprised in copyright or otherwise) shall belong absolutely to the Producer and the Artist with full title guarantee assigns and grants the same to the Producer throughout the World and throughout all periods for which the said rights or any of them are or may be conferred or created by the law in force in all or any parts of the world and all renewals, revivals and extensions of such periods the Producer may make or authorise any use of the same and may exploit the same in any manner but only in and in connection with the Film

(b) the Artist hereby acknowledges and agrees and confirms that the Producer shall be entitled and it is hereby authorised to adapt change take from add to and use and treat in every way all or any of the products of the Artist's services rendered hereunder and to use reproduce and perform and broadcast and transmit the same with or as part of the work of any other persons and synchronised or not with any music or other sounds or motions as the Producer considers necessary or desirable

(c) for the avoidance of doubt the assignment of rights set out in this Clause includes all satellite cable rental and lending rights ("the Rights") and the Artist agrees that the remuneration payable pursuant to this agreement includes and constitutes equitable and adequate consideration for the assignment and exploitation of the Rights and to the extent permitted by the law the Artist waives the right to receive any further remuneration in relation to the exploitation of the Rights.

5. The Producer shall be entitled by written notice to the Artist given at any time to suspend the engagement of the Artist hereunder (whether or not the term of such engagement has commenced) if and so long as:-

(a) the production of the Film or the operation of any studio involved in such production shall be prevented suspended interrupted postponed hampered or interfered with by reason or on account of any event of force majeure fire accident action of the elements war riot civil disturbance sickness epidemic pestilence national calamity act of God or any actual labour disputes (including strikes lockouts or withholding of labour of any kind whether by the direction or with the support of any trade union or other body or otherwise) or illness or incapacity of the Producer of the Director of the Film or any principal artist or principal technician or any cause (apart from those hereinbefore specifically referred to and whether or not similar thereto) not reasonably within the control of the Producer or

(b) the voice of the Artist shall become unsatisfactory in quality or tone

(c) the Artist shall be reason of any illness or physical or mental incapacity or disability be unable in the opinion of the Producer fully to render the Artist's services hereunder or to devote sufficient of the Artist's time ability and attention to such services or

(c) the Artist shall fail refuse or neglect duly to render willingly and to the utmost of the Artist's skill and ability the Artist's full services hereunder or shall fail, refuse or neglect fully to observe or comply with any of the Artist's material obligations under this Agreement or with any of the terms thereof.

6. Upon any suspension of the engagement of the Artist hereunder

(a) such suspension shall be effective from the date of the event giving rise to such suspension and shall continue for the duration of such event and for such reasonable period thereafter as may be necessary for the Producer to make arrangements to commence or resume production

(b) the Producer shall during the period of suspension cease to be liable to make any payments of remuneration to the Artist hereunder (or to pay for or provide accommodation or living expenses if the suspension is due to the Artist's default or refusal) save such instalments of remuneration as shall have become due and payable prior to the suspension and the period of engagement hereunder shall be extended by or (if appropriate) the commencement of the Artist's engagement shall be postponed by and the dates for payment of any further instalments of remuneration hereunder shall be postponed (or further postponed as the case may be) by a period equal to that of such suspension

(c) all rights of the Producer in respect of services rendered by the Artist and in all the products thereof previous to such suspension and the benefit of all consents granted hereunder shall not be affected and accordingly shall be or remain vested in the Producer.

7. The Producer shall be entitled by written notice to the Artist given at any time to terminate the engagement of the Artist hereunder (without prejudice to any other rights and remedies available to the Producer hereunder)

(a) if any suspension under the provisions of paragraph (a) of clause 6 hereof shall continue for 28 (twenty-eight) consecutive days or 28 (twenty-eight) days in the aggregate or more

(b) if any suspension under the provisions of paragraph (b) or (b) of Clause 5 hereof shall continue for 2 (two) consecutive days or 3 (three) days in the aggregate or more

(c) at any time in the circumstances referred to in

paragraphs (d) or (f) of Clause 5 hereof (whether or not the Producer shall have suspended the Artist's engagement under the provisions of Clause 5 hereof) subject to the Artist being given the opportunity to rectify any default if capable of rectification within 24 (twenty-four) hours of the Producer giving notice of such default

Provided however that if any suspension under the provisions of paragraph (a) of Clause 5 hereof shall continue for six weeks or more then the Artist shall be entitled to terminate this engagement by seven days' written notice to the Producer unless by the expiry of such notice the Producer shall have terminated such suspension but the Producer shall not be entitled to terminate this engagement for the same event subject however to the right of the Producer to suspend or terminate the Artist's engagement for other proper cause including but not limited to the occurrence of a different event (even though of the same nature as a previous one) of force majeure in accordance with the provisions hereof

8. In the case of termination of the engagement of the Artist under the foregoing provisions or by the death of the Artist
(a) such termination shall be effective from the date of the event giving rise to the termination or (if there shall have been a prior suspension) from the date of the event giving rise to the suspension from which such termination arose
(b) any claim which the Producer may have against the Artist in respect of any breach, non-performance or non-observance of any of the material provisions of this Agreement arising prior to such termination or out of which such termination shall arise shall not be affected or prejudiced
(c) the Producer's title to and ownership of all copyrights and all other rights in or in connection with the services rendered by the Artist up to the date of such termination and in all the products of such services shall not be affected and such rights shall accordingly be or remain vested in the Producer
(d) payment to the Artist of the instalments of remuneration due and payable to the Artist up to the effective date of such termination shall operate as payment in full and final discharge and settlement of all claims on the part of the Artist under this Agreement and accordingly the Producer shall not be under any obligation to pay to the Artist any further or other sums on account of salary or otherwise

9. The Artist undertakes at the expenses of the Producer to execute and procure the execution of any document which the Producer may consider necessary for the purpose of carrying into effect the arrangements made by this Agreement or any of them including in particular any

documents required to vest in or confirm any rights of copyright or other rights in the Producer

10. The rights and the benefit of all consents granted hereunder to the Producer are irrevocable and without right of rescission by the Artist or reversion to the Artist under any circumstances whatsoever

11. Credit will be given only
(a) if Artist appears recognisably in the Film as released
(b) if this Agreement has not been terminated for the default of the Artist

No casual or inadvertent failure to comply with credit requirements shall be deemed a breach of this Agreement. The sole remedy of Artist for a breach of any of the provisions of this clause or of the Principal Agreement shall be an action at law for damages, it being agreed that in no event shall Artist seek to be entitled to injunctive or other equitable relief by any reason of any of the breach or threatened breach of any credit requirements, nor shall Artist be entitled to seek to enjoin or restrain the exhibition distribution advertising exploitation or marketing of the Film

12. All notices served upon either party by the other hereunder shall be delivered by hand at or sent by pre-paid recorded delivery letter post or by facsimile addressed to the respective addressed hereinbefore contained or any subsequent address duly notified and if delivered by hand shall be deemed to have been served five days after posting and if sent by facsimile shall be deemed served 24 hours after receipt of the facsimile (and facsimile notice shall be confirmed by post). A copy of all notices to the Artist shall be sent to the Agent (if any)

13. The Artist shall treat as confidential and shall not disclose to any third party (save to the Artist's professional advisors whose dissemination of such information they receive shall be limited to use for business purposes i.e. quotes for services or as may be required by law) the provisions of this Agreement or any confidential information concerning the Producer or the Film or it's distributors which may come to the Artist's attention in connection with the Artist's engagement hereunder or otherwise

14. For the avoidance of doubt, it is expressly agreed between the parties that this Agreement and the provision of Artist's services in connection with the Film, is not subject to any collective bargaining agreement or guild or union regulations and the compensation paid to the Artist under clause 6 of the Main Agreement represents full and complete consideration for all of the services of the Artist hereunder and all rights assigned and granted by the Artist

in the products of those services.

15. This Agreement shall be governed by and construed in accordance with the laws of England and subject to the exclusive jurisdiction of the Courts of England.

Accompanying Notes

MAIN AGREEMENT
Clause 3: The Producer needs to ensure the actor is around for a fixed number of weeks and because the actor agrees to make him/herself available for that period the producer must pay accordingly.

Clause 4: Additional services are during principal photography.

Clause 6: Further services are post production services where the artist will be available subject to other prior engagements. Sometimes a producer can negotiate a certain number of so called "free" days (3 is the norm) where the artist will render Additional or Further Services free of charge. This gives the Producer more leeway but is only appropriate on big productions. The fee for Further or Additional Services can be agreed in advance and it is customary for the fee to be a daily rate calculated as a pro-rated amount of the weekly sum.

EXHIBIT A
Clause 4(c): See Glossary of Terms. This may not be legally effective but at present all relevant contracts include such a term.

Clause 7: The periods of suspension giving rise to the entitlement of the Producer to terminate the agreement are subject to negotiation.

Note 1: It should be made clear whether or not the terms of the agreement are going to be governed by the appropriate Equity agreement or not. Many actors, or more likely their agents, will insist on the application of Equity's terms as Equity has negotiated residual and royalty payments on repeats, video etc. with PACT. However if the project is a film intended for theatrical release you should negotiate a complete buy out of the Artist's performance rights wherever possible. A buy out will be expected by most sales agents, financiers and distributors as they will not want the trouble of having to account to the artists and more importantly, any residual payments will be seen as a drain on the revenue of the film.

Note 2: Deferments. If the fee or proportion of the fee is to be deferred, there should be further provisions that should also be mentioned, i.e. that the Deferment will be pro rata and pari passu with all other deferments to persons, providing services to the Film, after which all deferments to companies and firms should be met. All deferred sums are payable in first place from receipts received by the Producer from the exploitation of the Film subject to the recoupment of the production and post production cost of the Film only. It should be emphasised that the Deferment is a contingent amount and is only payable to the extent sufficient receipts are generated. It should also be mentioned that the Producers will use their reasonable endeavours to procure that their auditors or any other firm of Chartered Accountants appointed, will provide an audited detailed statement of all transactions relevant to the production and the income generated which should be made available to the artist and/or representatives by a specified date.

N.B. Due to legislation, BECTU argue that it is possible that using deferred paments is unlawful.

Note 3: A Daily Rate is usually calculated at 1/7th of the weekly rate.

Note 4: If the artist is a so called star they may insist upon a share of net profits.

Note 5: Work exists on bank holidays unless otherwise stated in the contract or accompanying schedule.

Note 6: Credit. The size and placement of the credit (billing requirement) is usually negotiated between the parties.

Note 7: Material. The artist will sometimes ask for the right to select the photographs of themselves to be used and this is usually granted subject to certain restraints.

Note 8: If an actor or their agent is concerned about the ability of a production company to make the payments due to the Artist, they may ask for all the monies due under the agreement to be paid to a third party to be held in an Escrow Account and paid out in accordance with the agreement under the terms of the agreed Escrow arrangement.

LEGAL TOOLKIT

Performers Consent

This is a guideline only and should not be relied upon without taking legal advice.

On The CD

From: *("the Performer")* of *(address)*

To: *(name of company)* *("the Company which shall include it's successors assigns and licensees)* of *(address)*

Dated: *(date)*

Dear Sirs

(Name of film) (the "Film")

In consideration of the sum of (£ *amount*) paid by the Company to the Performer (the receipt of which the Performer acknowledges). The Performer irrevocably and unconditionally grants to the Company all consents required pursuant to the Copyright, Designs and Patents Act 1988 Part II and all other laws now or in the future in force in any part of the world which may be required for the exploitation of the Performer's performance contained in the Film, whether or not as part of the Film, in any and all media by any manner or means now known or invented in the future throughout the world for the full period of copyright protection pursuant to the laws in force in any part of the world, including all renewals, reversions and extensions.

This letter shall be governed by and construed in accordance with the law of England and Wales the courts of which shall be courts of competent jurisdiction.

Yours faithfully

(signature of Performer)

Accompanying Notes

Note 1: The Performer's Consent form is specifically for, and only relates to the Performer and their performance. The performers do not own copyright as such in their performance (there is none) but their consent is needed to exploit their performance.

Note 2: Consideration must be given in any contract. A contract requires an offer, acceptance and consideration. It is a legal necessity. ("Consideration" does not have to be money, it can be provided by, for example, giving up a legal right).

LEGAL TOOLKIT

Release Form

This is a guideline only and should not be relied upon without taking legal advice.

From: *(name of individual)* of *(address)*

To: *(name of company)* *("the Company" which shall include it's successors, assigns and licensees)*

of *(address)*

Dated: *(date)*

Dear Sirs

(Name of the film) (the "Film")

1. In consideration of the sum of £1 (*or any other amount*) now paid by the Company to me (the receipt of which I acknowledge) I warrant, confirm and agree with the Company that the Company shall have the right to exploit any films, photographs and sound recordings made by the Company for the Film in which I feature, or any literary, dramatic, musical or artistic work or film or sound recording created by me or any performance by me of any literary, dramatic, musical or artistic work or film or sound recording included by the Company in the Film in any and all media by any and all means now known or invented in future throughout the world for the full period of copyright, including all renewals, revivals, reversions and extensions.

2. I irrevocably and unconditionally grant to you all consents required pursuant to the Copyright, Designs, and Patents Act 1988 Part II * or otherwise under the laws in force in any part of the world to exploit such performances.

3. I irrevocably and unconditionally waive all rights which I may have in respect of the Film pursuant to the Copyright, Designs and Patents Act 1988 Sections 77, 80, 84 and 85**.

4. I consent to the use by the Company of my name, likeness, voice and biography in connection only with the Film.

5. The Company may assign or licence this agreement to any third party.

6. This letter shall be governed by and construed in accordance with the law of England and Wales and subject to the jurisdiction of the English Courts.

Yours faithfully

(signature of the individual)

* the "Performers Rights"
** the Moral Rights of an author

Accompanying Notes

Note 1: The release form covers any work created by the individual. This form is more comprehensive than the Performer's Consent which does not contain an assignment of copyright (as there is no copyright as such in a performance) and covers an assignment of any artistic material contributed by the individual to the producer.

Note 2: Consideration must be given in any contract. A contract requires an offer, acceptance and consideration. It is a legal necessity. ("Consideration" does not have to be money, it can be provided by, for example, giving up a legal right).

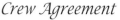

Crew Agreement

This is a guideline only and should not be relied upon without taking legal advice.

On The CD

Dated:

PRODUCER: ("the Producer")

Address:

CREW MEMBER:("the Crew Member")

Address:

FILM TITLE:("the Film")

1. **Services:** The Producer hereby engages the Crew Member and the Crew Member undertakes and agrees to render to the Producer his/her services (hereinafter called "the Services").

2. **The Period of Engagement** shall commence on or about .... (hereinafter called "the Start Date") and shall continue until the earlier of;
a) completion of the Film in all respects ready for delivery to the principal distributor of the Film
b) termination of the Crew Member's engagement pursuant to the provisions of this agreement

3. **Payment:** Subject to the provisions of this Agreement and the observance and performance by the Crew Member of all his obligations under it the Producer shall pay to the Crew Member the sum of .... per week/ day (or a fixed amount), for all services rendered by the Crew Member in respect of the Film and for all rights in the products of such services
b) all sums payable to the Crew Member under this agreement are exclusive of Value Added Tax ("VAT"). The Producer shall pay such VAT as is properly charged by the Crew Member promptly following receipt of the Crew Member's tax invoice.
c) the Producer is expressly authorised by the Crew Member to deduct and withhold from all sums due to the Crew Member all deductions (if any) in accordance with local laws and regulations from time to time applicable
d) all sums payable under this clause 3 shall be paid directly to the Crew Member, whose receipt shall be a full and sufficient discharge to the Producer.
e) the Crew Member acknowledges that the remuneration provided under this clause 3 shall be inclusive of all guild and union minimum basic fees, overtime and all residual repeat and re-run payments, direct or indirect employment and like taxes and state governmental and/or social security contributions.

4. **Expenses:** All payments of pre-approved expenses to the Crew Member will be issued on a weekly basis by the Producer on provision of relevant invoice therefor.

5. **Duration of Filming:** The filming week shall be a 6 day week where the Producer may nominate such 6 days as in any week but the Crew Member shall not be required to work more than 7 consecutive days without receiving the next consecutive day off. A Filming day will not exceed 14 hours inclusive of meal breaks. Any hours worked in excess of the said 14 hours will at the Producer's sole election either be carried over to the following day or a payment of a pro rata hourly rate shall be paid to the Crew Member on the pay day next falling due.

6. **Rights/Consents:** 6.1 The Crew Member with full title guarantee assigns and grants to the Producer the whole of the Crew Member's property right, title, interest in and to the Film and the entire copyright and all other rights in and to all products of the Crew Members services in connection with the Film including all vested future and contingent rights to which the Crew Member is now or may hereafter be entitled under the law in force in any part of the universe for the Producer's use and benefit absolutely for the full period or periods of copyright throughout the universe including all reversions, revivals, renewals and extensions created or provided by the law of any country. The Crew Member undertakes to execute all such documents and takes all such steps as may from time to time be necessary to secure to the Producer the rights in this clause 6.1.

6.2 The Producer shall have the right to make, produce, sell, publicly exhibit, lease, license, hire, market, publicise, distribute, exhibit, diffuse, broadcast, adapt and reproduce mechanically graphically electronically or otherwise howsoever by any manner and means (whether now known or hereafter devised) the Film and all products of the Crew Member's services throughout the universe; to permit any third party to exercise any of such rights in the sole discretion of the Producer.

6.3. The Crew Member hereby irrevocably and unconditionally waives all rights relating to the Crew Member's services in the Film to which the Crew Member is now or may in the future be entitled pursuant to the provisions of Section 77 80 84 and 85 of the Copyright, Designs and Patents Act 0f 1988 and any other moral

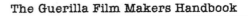
rights to which the Crew Member may be entitled under any legislation now existing or in the future enacted in any part of the world.

7. **Crew Member's warranties**: The crew member hereby warrants, undertakes and agrees that;

7.1 the Crew Member is free to enter into this agreement and has not entered and will not enter into any arrangement which may conflict with it.

7.2 The Crew Member will render his/her services in willing co-operation with others in the manner required by the Producer and in accordance with the production schedule established by the Producer.

7.3 The Crew Member shall not without consent in writing of the Producer issue any publicity relating to or otherwise reveal or make public any financial, creative or other confidential information in connection with the Film or the terms of this agreement or the business of the Producer and will not knowingly commit any act which might prejudice or damage the reputation of the Producer or inhibit the successful exploitation of the Film.

7.4 The Crew Member is in a good state of health and shall use his/her best endeavours to remain so during the continuance of this agreement.

7.5 The Producer shall have the right to make the Crew Member's services available to third parties and the Crew Member will co-operate fully with such third parties and follow all lawful directions and instructions of such third parties.

7.6 The Crew Member shall at all times throughout his/her engagement keep the Producer informed of their whereabouts and telephone number.

7.7 The Crew Member will not on behalf of the Producer enter into any commitment contract or arrangement with any person or engage any person without the Producer's prior written consent.

7.8 The Crew Member shall willingly and promptly co-operate with the Producer and shall carry out such services rendered by the Crew Member as when and where requested by the Producer and follow all reasonable directions and instructions given by the Producer.

7.9 The Crew Member shall attend at such locations and times as are reasonably required by the Producer from time to time.

7.10 The Crew Member shall comply with and observe all union rules and regulations and all the formal agreements, rules and regulations relating to safety, fire, prevention or general administration in force at any place in which the Crew Member shall be required by the Producer to render any services.

7.11 Upon the expiry of earlier termination of the Crew Member's engagement, the Crew Member will deliver up to the Producer all scripts, photographs and other literary or dramatic properties all film materials and all other properties, documents and things, whatsoever which the Crew Member may have in the Crew Member's possession or under the Crew Member's control relating to the Film.

7.12 The Crew Member shall indemnify the Producer and keep it fully indemnified against all proceedings, costs, claims, awards, damages, expenses (including without limitation legal expenses) and liabilities arising directly or indirectly from any breach of the Crew Member's undertakings, obligations or warranties hereunder.

8. **Credit:** Subject to the Crew Member rendering their services under the terms of this agreement, the Crew Member shall be given credit on the Film. The Producer shall determine in it's discretion the manner and mode of presentation of the Crew Member's credit. The Producer shall not be obliged to accord credit to the Crew Member in any other method of advertising or publicity. No casual or inadvertent failure by the Producer or any third party to comply with providing credit, and no failure by persons other than the Producer to comply with their contracts with the Producer shall constitute a breach of this Agreement by the Producer. The rights and remedies of the Crew Member in the event of a breach of this clause 8, by the Producer shall be limited to the rights (if any) to recover damages in an action at law and in no event shall the Crew Member be entitled by reason of any such breach to enjoin or restrain or otherwise interfere with the distribution, exhibition or exploitation of the Film.

9. **Producer's liability:** The Producer shall not be liable for any loss of or damage to any clothing or other personal property of the Crew Member whether such loss or damage is caused by negligence or otherwise howsoever except to

the extent that the Producer receives compensation from an insurance company or other third party.

10. **Waiver:** No waiver by the Producer of any failure by the Crew Member to observe any covenant or condition of this agreement shall be deemed to be a waiver of any preceding or succeeding failure or of any other covenant or condition nor shall it be deemed a continuing waiver. The rights and remedies provided for in this agreement are cumulative and no one of them shall be deemed to be exclusive of the others or of any rights or remedies allowed by law. The rights granted to the Producer are irrevocable and shall not revert to the Crew Member under any circumstances whatsoever. In the event that the Producer terminates or cancels (or purports to terminate or cancel) this agreement or any other agreement entered into by and between the Producer and the Crew Member (and even if such cancellation or termination or purported termination or cancellation is ultimately determined by a court to have been without proper or legal cause or ultimately determined by such a court that the Producer committed any material breach of any such agreement) the damage (if any) caused to the Crew Member thereby is not irreparable or sufficient to entitle the Crew Member to injunctive or other equitable relief and the Crew Member shall not have any right to terminate this agreement or any such other agreement or any of the Producer's rights hereunder.

11. **Insurance:** The Producer may secure in it's own name or otherwise at its own expense life accident health cast pre-production and other insurance covering the Crew Member independently or together with others and the Crew Member shall not have any right, title, or interest in or to such insurance. The Crew Member shall assist the Producer to procure such insurance and shall in timely fashion submit to such customary medical and other examinations and sign such applications and other instruments in writing as may be required by the insurance company involved.

12. **Condition precedent:** As a condition precedent to any and all liability of the Producer, the Crew Member shall at the Crew Member's own expense apply for and assist the Producer in applying for and do all such things as may be necessary in support of any application for the Crew Member's membership of any trade union, labour or professional organisation or guild and/or for passports, visas, work permits or other matters necessary to enable the Producer to make use of the Crew Member's services. If as a result of such application being refused, revoked or

cancelled the Producer shall be unable to make use of the Crew Member's services this agreement shall be deemed null and void and without effect and without liability whatsoever on the parties save that the Crew Member shall repay to the Producer any sums previously paid to him/her pursuant to clause 3.

13. **Suspension:** The Producer shall be entitled by written notice giving reasons for such suspension to the Crew Member at any given time, to suspend the engagement of the Crew Member hereunder (whether or not the term of such engagement has commenced) if and so long as:-

13.1 The production of the Film is prevented, suspended, interrupted, postponed, hampered or interfered with by reason or on account of any event of force majeure, fire, accident, action of the elements of war, riot, civil disturbance, sickness, epidemic, pestilence, national calamity, act of God or any actual labour disputes, or illness or incapacity of the Producer or the director of the Film or any principal artist or principal technician or any other cause not reasonably within the control of the Producer.

13.2 The Crew Member fails, refuses or neglects duly to render willingly and to the utmost of the Crew Member's skill and ability, the Crew Member's full services or that the Crew Member fails, refuses, or neglects fully to observe or comply with, or perform any of the Crew Member's obligations under this agreement.

13.3 Suspension shall commence from the date of the event giving rise to such suspension and shall continue for the duration of such event and for such reasonable period thereafter as may be necessary for the Producer to make arrangements to commence or resume production of the Film.

13.4 During this period of suspension, the Producer ceases to be liable to make any payments of remuneration or provide accommodation or living expenses if the suspension is due to the Crew Member's neglect, default, disability, incapacity or refusal) save such payment Instalments as shall have become due and payable prior to the suspension and the period of engagement shall be extended or the commencement of engagement shall be postponed by an equal period to the suspension.

13.5 All rights of the Producer in respect of the services rendered and products of those services thereof by the Crew Member previous to the suspension shall not be affected and shall remain vested in the Producer.

13.6 If the Producer pays any remuneration to the Crew Member during any period of suspension arising pursuant to clause 13.2, then the Producer may require the Crew Member's services hereunder without additional payment to the Crew Member for an equal period to the suspension during which the Producer paid remuneration to the Crew Member.

14. **Termination:** The Producer shall be entitled (but not obliged) by written notice giving reasons for the termination to the crew member given at any time, to terminate the engagement of the Crew Member hereunder (without prejudice to any other rights and remedies available to the Producer hereunder) if:-

14.1a suspension continues for 3 consecutive weeks or 4 weeks in the aggregate or more, according to clause 13.1, or

14.1b at any time in the circumstances referred to in clause 13.2,

14.1c the Crew Member does not fulfil their respective obligations under this Agreement.

14.2 **In the case of termination** of the engagement of the Crew Member under the foregoing provisions or by the death of the Crew Member

14.2a such termination shall be effective from the date of the event giving rise to the termination or (if there shall have been a prior suspension) from the date of the event giving rise to the suspension from which such termination arose

14.2b any claim which the Producer may have against the Crew Member in respect of any breach, non performance or non observance of any of the material provisions of this Agreement arising prior to such termination or out of which such termination shall arise shall not be affected or prejudiced

14.2c the Producer's title to and ownership of all copyrights and all other rights in or in connection with the services and all other rights in or in connection with the services rendered by the Crew Member up to the date of such termination and in all the products of such services shall not be affected and such rights shall accordingly be or

remain vested in the Producer.

14.2d payment to the Crew Member of the instalments due and payable to the Crew Member up to the effective date of such termination shall operate as payment in full and final discharge and settlement of all claims on the part of the Crew Member under this agreement and accordingly the Producer shall not be under any obligation to pay to the Crew Member any further or other sums on account of remuneration or otherwise nor shall the producer be under any liability whether by way of damages or otherwise for any inconvenience or loss of publicity or other loss suffered by the Crew Member by reason of the termination of the Crew Member's engagement hereunder (but the provisions of this paragraph shall not affect the Producer's rights referred to in clause 14.2b.

15. **Conflict:** Nothing contained in this Agreement shall be construed so as to require the commission of any act contrary to law and wherever there is any conflict between any provision of this agreement and any statute law ordinance or regulation contrary to which the parties have no legal right to contract then the latter shall prevail but in such event the provisions of this agreement so affected shall be curtailed and limited only to the extent necessary to bring them within the legal requirements.

16. **Assignment:** The Crew Member expressly agrees that the Producer may transfer and assign this agreement or all or any part of the Producer's rights under it. The Agreement shall inure to the benefit of the Producer's successors, licensees, and assigns but the Producer shall not thereby be relieved of it's obligations.

17. **Self employed status:** The Crew Member warrants to the Producer that the Crew Member is self employed and is not considered to be an employee of the Producer and the Crew Member warrants to the Producer that he/she is personally responsible for all tax, national insurance and/or other taxes levied by the inland revenue (or relevant tax authority if working abroad). The Crew Member shall provide evidence of their self employed status to the Producer. The Crew Member indemnifies and holds harmless the Producer for any liability to pay local or governmental taxes arising from the Crew Member's engagement.

18. **Notices**: All notices served upon either party by the other hereunder shall be delivered by hand at or sent by prepaid recorded delivery letter post or by facsimile

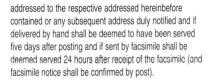

addressed to the respective addressed hereinbefore contained or any subsequent address duly notified and if delivered by hand shall be deemed to have been served five days after posting and if sent by facsimile shall be deemed served 24 hours after receipt of the facsimile (and facsimile notice shall be confirmed by post).

19. This Agreement contains the full and complete understanding between the parties and supersedes all prior agreements and understandings whether written or oral pertaining thereto and cannot be modified except by a written instrument signed by the Crew Member and the Producer.

20. Nothing contained in this Agreement shall or shall be deemed to constitute a partnership or a contract of employment between the parties.

21. This Agreement shall be construed in accordance with and governed by the laws of England whose courts shall be the courts of the competent jurisdiction.

IN WITNESS WHEREOF the parties hereto have executed the within Agreement as of the date first set forth hereinabove

(insert name of Producer)

By...

Duly Authorised Officers...

Accepted and Agreed to:

....

*VAT number or NI no. if applicable:

companies and firms should be met. All deferred sums are payable in first place from receipts received by the Producer from the exploitation of the Film subject to the recoupment of the production and post production cost of the Film only. It should be emphasised that the Deferment is a contingent amount and is only payable to the extent sufficient receipts are generated. It should also be mentioned that the Producers will use their reasonable endeavours to procure that their auditors or any other firm of Chartered Accountants appointed, will provide an audited detailed statement of all transactions relevant to the production and the income generated which should be made available to the crew member/ and or representatives by a specified date.

N.B. Due to legislation, BECTU argue that it is possible that using deferred payments is unlawful.

NOTE 2: Payment. It should be made clear whether or not this agreement is a non guild or union agreement. Clause 3 (e) refers to a buy out.

NOTE 3. Expenses: The travel arrangements to and for the set are usually the responsibility of the crew member. However if on location, the crew member is provided with accommodation and travel expenses depending on the budget of the Film.

NOTE 4: Self employment: It is necessary that if the crew member is self employed, the producer receives written confirmation and evidence to prove their status. Otherwise responsibility falls upon the Producer who could be heavily penalised for not paying on time and be subject to the danger of prosecution.

Accompanying Notes

NOTE 1: Deferments. If the fee or proportion of the fee is to be deferred, there should be further provisions that should also be mentioned, i.e. that the Deferment will be pro rata and pari passu with all other deferments to persons, providing services to the Film, after which all deferments to

On The CD

Composers Agreement
(Original score)

This is a guideline only and should not be relied upon without taking legal advice.

THIS AGREEMENT is made the ....day of ....20....

BETWEEN:.......................................
(hereinafter called "the Company" which expression includes it's successors in title licensees and assigns)

AND...
(hereinafter called "the Composer")

WHEREAS:

The Company is currently engaged in the production of a film called "..............." ("the Film") and wishes to engage the services of the Composer to write compose and arrange the Music and record the Recordings (as hereinafter defined) to be included in the Film upon the following terms.

NOW THEREFORE IT IS HEREBY AGREED AS FOLLOWS:-

1. The Company hereby engages the Composer and the Composer undertakes to make available his services as hereinafter provided (hereinafter called "the Services") on the terms and conditions herein contained:

1.1. The Composer shall compose and arrange the music ("the Music").

1.2. The Composer shall perform and record the Music ("the Recordings") and shall record the Music in a first class recording studio to a commercial and technical quality suitable for the synchronisation of the Recordings made therefrom in timed relation with the Film and for the reproduction therefrom of Records for sale to the public. The Composer shall deliver the Recordings to the Company on or before........................20.....

1.3. The Composer acknowledges that the soundtrack for the Film shall include certain music and recordings thereof ("the Licensed Music") written and recorded prior to the date hereof and owned or controlled by third parties. The details of the Licensed Music are specified in Schedule A hereof and in rendering the Services hereunder the Composer shall take account of such Licensed Music to be included in the Film and such Licensed Music shall not be deemed to be Recordings or Music hereunder. The Composer shall arrange clearance and pay all necessary fees for all Licensed Music.

2. The Composer hereby agrees, warrants and undertakes with the Company that:

2.1 The Composer will render the Services hereunder to the full extent of his creative and artistic skill and technical ability.

2.2 The Music and the Recordings will be wholly original to the Composer and will not infringe the copyright or any other like right of any person firm or company.

2.3 The Composer is free to enter into this Agreement and that he has the unencumbered right to grant to the Company all of the rights and Services hereby granted and that no prior contract or agreement of any kind entered into by the Composer will interfere in any way with the proper performance of this Agreement by the Composer.

2.4 The Composer will execute do and deliver all such acts deeds and instruments as the Company may at it's own expense from time to time require for the purpose of confirming or further assuring it's title to the rights assigned or intended to be assigned hereunder.

2.5 The Composer will indemnify and hold the Company harmless against all claims costs proceedings demands losses damages and expenses arising out of any breach of any of the warranties and representations and agreements on his part contained in this Agreement.

2.6 That no material composed by the Composer recorded on the Recordings will in any way infringe the rights of any third party.

2.7 That the Composer hereby grants to the Company (and it's licensees and assignees) on behalf of the Composer and any person whose performances are embodied on the Recordings the requisite consents pursuant to the provisions of the Copyright Designs and Patents Act 1988 or any similar legislation throughout the world in order that the Company and it's licensees an assignees shall have the fullest use of the Composer's and such persons services hereunder and the products thereof.

2.8 That the Composer and all other persons who have performed on the Recordings hereby irrevocably and unconditionally waive any and all moral rental lending and like rights the composer and such persons may have pursuant to the Copyright Designs and Patents Act 1988 or otherwise in respect of the Recordings the Music and the performances embodied thereon.

3. In consideration of the agreements on the Company's behalf herein contained the Composer with full title guarantee hereby assigns (subject to the rights in the

---

LEGAL TOOLKIT

Music vested in the Performing Rights Society Limited ("PRS") and it's affiliated societies by virtue of the Composer's membership of PRS) to the Company and it's successors in title (and so far as the same has not been completed at the date hereof by way of immediate assignment of future copyright) and for the full periods of copyright and all renewals and extensions thereof throughout the world ("the Territory") whether now or hereafter existing the entire copyright rental rights and all like rights whether now or hereafter existing in the Recordings and the product of the Services and all Masters thereof and the Composer hereby grants to the Company (it's licensees and assigns) the exclusive right and licence to use the Music in synchronisation with the Film and to use the Music as incorporated in trailers therefor and to record broadcast transmit exhibit and perform for an unlimited number of times and otherwise distribute and exploit by sale hire or otherwise in all and any media (including videos) the Music as part of or in synchronisation with the Film or trailers therefor or upon Records incorporating all or part of the soundtrack of the Film for the full period of copyright and any and all renewals and extensions thereof throughout the universe TO HOLD the same unto the Company absolutely throughout the Territory.

4. The Composer hereby grants to the Company (and warrants and undertakes that it is entitled to make such grant):

4.1 The irrevocable right to issue publicity concerning the Composer's Services and the product of the Services hereunder including the right to use and allow others to use the names professional names likeness, photograph and biography of the Composer and all musicians featured on the Recordings in Connection with the Music, the Recordings and/or the Film and the exercise of the rights granted hereunder.

4.2 The right to decide when and/or whether to commence cease or recommence the production of Records embodying the Recordings on whatsoever label and the right to fix and alter the price at which such Records are sold.

4.3 The right to licence grant transfer or assign without having to obtain any further consent from the Composer all or any of it's rights (including without limitation any or all of it's rights in the Recordings and the Music) hereunder and the benefit of this Agreement to any third party.

5. The Composer hereby further authorises and empowers the Company at the Company's expense to take such steps and proceedings as the Company may from time to time consider or be advised are necessary to protect and reserve to the Company all rights hereby granted or

expressed to be granted to the Company and the Composer hereby further authorises and empowers the Company and hereby appoints the Company his Attorney to institute actions and proceedings in the name of the Composer (but in any event at the Company's expense) or otherwise in respect of the infringement or violation of any of the rights hereby assigned or granted or expressed to be assigned or granted.

6. The Composer shall at the Company's request and expense take such steps and proceedings as the Company may require and to execute all or any further documents to vest in the Company and/or to renew and extend any and all rights an/or copyrights assigned or agreed to be assigned hereunder and which are or may hereafter be secured upon the Music and the Recordings or any part thereof and after such renewal or extension to transfer and assign to the Company the rights herein granted for such renewal or extended term. In the event that the Composer shall fail so to do within 7 (seven) business days of receiving a request therefor the Company is hereby authorised and empowered to exercise and perform such acts and to take such proceedings in the name and on behalf of the Composer and as the Attorney-in-fact for the Composer.

7. As full and final consideration for the Services hereunder and for the grant of rights in respect of the Music and the Recordings contained herein and for the physical tapes and for all expenses incurred by the Composer in arranging the Recordings the Company shall pay to the Composer the

7.1 The sum of £......(.......pounds) payable on signature hereof (receipt of which is hereby acknowledged).

7.2 A royalty in respect of Records reproducing only the Recordings sole paid for and not returned and the said royalty shall be calculated upon the Royalty Base Price of each such Record at the rate of 7% (seven percent) ("the Royalty Rate") and subject as hereinafter appears.

7.3 The remuneration payable to the Composer by the Company pursuant to clauses 7.1 and 7.2 in respect of the Services is and shall represent full and final consideration for the Services and the entire product of such Services and the rights granted to the Company hereunder and shall include any and all residual repeat rerun foreign use exploitation and other fees and payments of whatever nature due to the Composer or the Composer by virtue of any guild or trade union agreement and any and all payments due to the funds of any guild or union or other similar taxes and state and government and social security contributions. No further or additional payment shall be due from the Company to the Composer in respect of any of the foregoing or by reason of the number of hours in a day or days in the week in which the Services shall have been rendered or for any other reason whatever.

7.4 The Company shall ensure that mechanical royalties are payable to the appropriate collection society and/or publisher in respect of the sale of Records embodying the Music.

8.1 In respect of a Record reproducing the Recordings and also recordings not the subject of this Agreement the royalty payable to the Composer shall be that proportion of the Royalty Rate which the Recordings reproduced on such Record bear to the total number of recordings reproduced thereon.

8.2 No royalties shall be payable upon promotional Records given away free goods Records sold or distributed under any arrangement for the sale of deleted Records promotional Records Records for which the Company is not paid Records sold at a discount at 50% (fifty percent) or more from published price audio-visual Records.

8.3 If in any agreement made between the Company and the Company's licensees or assigns the royalty payable to the Company by the Company's licensees or assigns or the basis upon which such royalty is calculated shall be reduced (including all reduced rate half rate terminal reductions and royalty free provisions) then the royalty and Royalty Rate payable to the Composer shall be reduced by a like proportion.

8.4 The Composer shall have the first option to produce any soundtrack Record of the Film upon terms to be agreed if the Company in it's sole discretion decides to release such a Record. The costs of editing, remixing and converting the Recordings produced for the Film for the purpose of reproducing the Recordings upon Records shall be treated as an advance against the first recoupable from any and all royalties due to the Composer hereunder pursuant to clause 7.1.

9.1 The Company shall supply to the Composer within 90 (ninety) days after the end of June and December in each year a statement showing the latest information received by the Company during such half year period as to the number of Records sold and the amount of royalty due to the Composer. The Company shall be entitled to establish a reserve for potential returns of Records apparently sold in any half year in a reasonable quantity. The Company's liability to pay royalty to the Composer hereunder shall be limited to the amounts thereof actually received by the Company and the Company may deduct and retain from any sum payable to the Composer hereunder any withholding taxes required to be deducted by any government or law.

9.2 The Composer hereby directs the Company to make all payments due to the Composer to (name of agent if any)

whose receipt thereof shall be a full and sufficient discharge of the Company's obligations in respect of such payments.

10.1 The Company shall accord the Composer on all positive prints of the Film made by or to the order of the Company a main title credit on a separate card substantially in the form "Original Music by".

10.2 The Company shall instruct the distributors and exhibitors of the Film to accord the Composer credit as hereinabove provided on all prints of the Film issued by such distributors and exhibitors but the Company shall not be liable for the neglect or default of any such distributors or exhibitors so long as it shall have notified the distributors of the credit to which the Composer is entitled hereunder.

10.3 The Company shall use it's best endeavours to afford a credit to the Composer upon all paid advertising for the Film subject to the distributor's usual credit exclusions.

10.4 In respect of soundtrack Records of the Film the Company shall accord the Composer a credit in the form "Original Music by" on the back cover and label of the Record save that such credit shall appear on the front cover and label of the said Records if 50% (fifty percent) or more of the Recordings featured on such Record were performed by the Composer and a credit "Produced by Stephen Warbeck" if 50% (fifty percent) or more of the Recordings featured on such Record were produced by the Composer on the back cover and label thereof but otherwise on the same terms and conditions as set out in this clause.

10.5 No casual or inadvertent failure to accord the Composer or any other party credit hereunder shall constitute a breach of this Agreement by the Company and/or the Composer's remedies in the event of a breach shall be confined to recovery of damages.

11. The Composer acknowledges that it and the Composer has prior to signature hereof received independent expert advice on the contents hereof to enable him to understand fully the terms of this Agreement.

12. In the event of a breach of this Agreement by Company the Composer shall not be entitled to equitable relief or to terminate or rescind this Agreement or any of the rights granted to Company herein or to restrain enjoin or otherwise impair the production distribution advertising or other exploitation of the Film the Composer's sole remedy being an action at law for damages if any.

13. For the purposes hereof the following words shall have the following meanings:

"Record" - shall mean vinyl records, compact discs, tapes, cassettes, CDI, CD Roms or any other device or

LEGAL TOOLKIT

contrivance whether now know or to be invented in the future reproducing sound alone (with or without visual images) but excluding videocassettes, videotapes and/or videodiscs embodying the Film.

"Recordings" - shall mean the original sound recordings or combination of recordings recorded hereunder and embodying the Music or any part thereof (whether on recording tape lacquer wax disc or any other material).

"Master" - shall mean a 2(two) track stereo Dolby tape recording fully edited equalised and leadered and of a first class standard suitable for synchronisation with the Film and the reproduction of Records therefrom.

"Royalty Base Price" - shall mean the retail price upon which royalties payable to the Company are calculated by it's licensees and assigns (net of packaging allowances and sales taxes).

"Copyright" - shall mean the entire copyright and design right subsisting under the laws of the United Kingdom and all analogous rights subsisting under the laws of each and every jurisdiction throughout the world.

14. All notices writs legal process or any other documents served under or in respect of this Agreement shall be addressed to the party to be served at the address of that party hereinbefore appearing or at such other address for service as may be notified by each to the other in writing and shall be sent by registered lotter or recorded delivery in which event such notice shall be deemed to have been received 3 (three) days after the posting thereof.

15. This Agreement shall be exclusively governed by English law and the High Court of Justice in England shall be the exclusive Court of Jurisdiction. Nothing herein contained shall constitute or create or be deemed to create or constitute a partnership between the parties hereto.

AS WITNESS the hand of the parties the day and year first before written

SIGNED by.......................................(...............................)
for and on behalf of.........................(...............................)
in the presence of:..........................(...............................)

SIGNED..(...............................)
in the presence of ....(...............................)

Accompanying Notes

Clause 1.3: The Composer (or sometimes the Producer) has to arrange for the use of pre existing music that is incorporated in the soundtrack and arrange and pay for licences to use any such music.

Clause 3: A Composer cannot assign his/her right to receive payment from PRS and they remain the beneficiaries of any income paid to the PRS, which is a collection society for musicians. The Composer must specifically grant the right to allow the music to be played in sync with the film. This is a specific right. This agreement only allows the Producer to use the music for this purpose and does NOT allow the Producer to publish the music.

Clause 5: This gives the Producer the ability to take any legal action to prevent a third party using the music for their film if the Composer does not agree to do so.

Clause 6: A "further assurance" clause is used in contracts where a grant or licence of rights is made. This ensures the producer has all the necessary documents to perfect their right or interests in the licence or grant of rights.

Clause 7.2: A Composer will often get a royalty from any records made whether the Producer acts as the music publisher or whether they negotiate a deal with a third party. This royalty obligation must be made clear to any publisher as the Producer is primarily liable under this type of agreement to make any such payment to the Composer.

Clause 7.4: Mechanical royalties are paid to MCPS and are due when the records are sold.

Clause 8.1: The Composer gets a proportion of the royalty rate according to the proportion of his/her music incorporated on the recording i.e. if there were 6 tracks and only 3 were the Composer's music he/she would get half the royalty.

Clause 8.3: If the Producer assigns the Composer's agreement to a third party (i.e the distributor/financier) and under it's deal it gets a lower Royalty Rate then the Composer agrees to accept that lower rate.

Clause 8.4: The Composer is given the chance to arrange the music for any record produced.

LEGAL TOOLKIT

Location Release Form

This is a guideline only and should not be relied upon without taking legal advice.

From: *(name of company)* of *(address)*

To: *(name of owner of premises)* of *(address)*

Dated: *(date)*

Dear Sirs

(name of film) (the "Film")

This letter is to confirm the agreement with us in which you have agreed to make available to us the following premises (the "Premises") *(specify the premises)*.

1. The premises shall be made available to us on a sole and exclusive basis in connection with the Film on (dates) (the "Dates").

2. You agree to make available to us the facilities in Schedule A on such days as we require on the Dates.

3. We shall be entitled to use the Premises as we may require on the days on giving you reasonable notice and as are negotiated in good faith between us but subject to the same terms as this agreement and on any additional days. You understand that we may need to return to the Premises at a later date if principal photography and recording is not completed on the Dates.

4. We have notified you of the scenes which are to be shot on or around the Premises and you confirm and agree that you consent to the filming of these scenes and you confirm that you will not make any objection in the future to the Premises being featured in the Film and you waive any and all right, claim and objection of whatever nature relating to the above.

5. We shall be entitled to represent the Premises under it's real name or under a fictional name or place according to the requirements of the Film.

6. We shall be entitled to incorporate all films, photographs and recordings, whether audio or audio-visual, made in or about the Premises in the Film as we may require in our sole discretion.

7. We shall not <u>without your prior consent</u> (not to be

unreasonably withheld or delayed) make any structural or decorative alternations which we require to be made to the Premises. We shall at your request properly reinstate any part of the Premises to the condition they were in prior to any alterations.

8. We shall own the entire copyright and all other rights of every kind in and to all film and audio and audio-visual recordings and photographs made in or about the Premises and used in connection with the Film and we shall have the right to exploit the Film by any manner or means now known or in the future invented in any and all media throughout the world for the full period of copyright, including all renewals, reversions and extensions.

9. We shall have the right to assign, licence and/or sub-licence the whole and/or any part of our rights pursuant to this agreement to any company or individual.

10. We agree that we shall indemnify you up to a maximum of £*(amount)* against any liability, loss, claim or proceeding arising under statute or common law relating to the Film in respect of personal injury and/or death of any person and/or loss or damage to the Premises caused by negligence, omission or default by this company or any person for whom we are legally responsible. You shall notify us immediately in writing of any claim as soon as such claim comes to your attention and we shall assume the sole conduct of any proceedings arising from any such claim.

11. In consideration of the rights herein granted we will pay you the sum of £*(amount)* on *(dates)*.

12. You undertake to indemnify us and to keep us fully indemnified from and against all actions, proceedings, costs, claims, damages and demands however arising in respect of any actual or alleged breach or non-performance by you of any or all of your undertakings, warranties and obligations under this agreement.

13. This agreement shall be governed by and construed in accordance with the law of England and Wales and subject to the jurisdiction of the English Courts.

Please signify your acceptance of the above terms by signing and returning to us the enclosed copy.

Signed..

Sales Breakdown

All sales are negotiated and calculated in US$

TERRITORY	Max	Min	Probable	Actual
Benelux	$25k	$10k	$20k	$20k
Canada	$50k	$20k	$20k	$20k
French Canada	$25k	$10k	$10k	$0k
France	$60k	$15k	$20k	$0k
Germany	$75k	$25k	$50k	$50k
Greece	$10k	$5k	$5k	$0k
Italy	$60k	$10k	$20k	$20k
Iceland	$10k	$2k	$4k	$0k
Israel	$10k	$2k	$5k	$0k
Portugal	$10k	$2k	$3k	$0k
Spain	$60k	$15k	$20k	$20k
Scandinavia	$50k	$20k	$20k	$20k
Czechoslovakia	$10k	$2k	$4k	$0k
Hungary	$10k	$2k	$5k	$0k
Poland	$10k	$2k	$2k	$0k
Romania	$10k	$2k	$2k	$0k
CIS	$15k	$5k	$5k	$0k
Former Yugoslavia	$10k	$2k	$3k	$0k
Turkey	$10k	$2k	$4k	$0k
Egypt	$10k	$2k	$2k	$0k
Arg/Chile/Uru/Para	$20k	$2k	$5k	$5k
Brazil	$20k	$7k	$10k	$0k
Colombia	$10k	$2k	$5k	$0k
Mexico	$15k	$5k	$5k	$0k
Peru/Equa/Bol	$10k	$2k	$2k	$0k
Venezuela	$10k	$2k	$2k	$0k
Central America	$10k	$2k	$2k	$2k
West Indies	$10k	$2k	$2k	$2k
India	$30k	$10k	$10k	$0k
Pakistan	$10k	$2k	$4k	$0k
Hong Kong	$15k	$5k	$5k	$5k
Indonesia	$10k	$2k	$3k	$3k
Japan	$100k	$20k	$50k	$0k
Korea	$80k	$40k	$50k	$50k
Malaysia	$10k	$2k	$2k	$2k
Philippines	$15k	$5k	$5k	$0k
Singapore	$10k	$2k	$2k	$0k
Taiwan	$25k	$5k	$5k	$0k
Thailand	$10k	$2k	$5k	$0k
Burma	$10k	$2k	$3k	$0k
South Africa	$25k	$10k	$10k	$10k
Australasia	$50k	$10k	$20k	$20k
USA	$200k	$20k	$50k	$20k
TOTAL	$1235k	$316k	$481k	$269

These figures are based on the sales of a no-star, low-budget, average British film. The figures quoted in the first three columns represent Max., Min. and Probable sales based on the assumption that film is actually sold in a given territory. The fourth column, Actual, is based on what sales are likely to be achieved in total. This fourth column is drawn from Living Spirit's and other production companies' experience. The UK has been excluded due to possibilities of separate sales or buy outs. Genre films also sell more consistently. Remember, it is very possible that you may only acheive two or three sales, say the UK, Germany and Korea. Treat any more sales as a bonus.

TOP 21 POINTS TO LOOK FOR IN A
SALES AGENT/DISTRIBUTION AGREEMENT

The following pagees contain a sample sales agency agreement. It is included to illustrate just how elaborate these contracts can be, and is slightly weighted in favour of the sales agents.

1. An Advance: Rarely given, usually only if the Film needs completion money, in which case the Sales Agent may take a higher commission.

2. No. of Years for the rights to be licensed to the Sales Agent/Distributor: From 5 to 35, standard is 5-10 years.

3. Extent of Rights being requested by Sales Agent/ Distributor: i.e. worldwide, worldwide exc. domestic, worldwide exc. America, etc. to be negotiated between the parties.

4. Fees/rate of commission: Usually between 20 - 25%. Sometimes 30% depending on extent of input by Sales Agent/Distributor and this should be limited so that the Distributor takes only one commission per country.

5. Ownership: Make sure you, the producer, will still own the copyright to the Film - not applicable if you are selling the film to the Distributor. If you are licensing the rights to certain territories you will remain the copyright owner.

6. CAP on Expenses: Make sure there is a maximum limit on expenses and that you are notified in writing of any large expenses i.e. over a specified amount.

7. Direct Expenses: Make sure that overheads of the Distributor are not included in Distribution expenses and will not be added as a further expense.

8. Sub Distributor Fees: Make sure that these fees are paid by the Sales Agent/Distributor out of it's fees and not in addition to the Distribution expenses.

9. Consider you position on Net Receipts: i.e. monies after Distributor has deducted their commission and fees subject to any sales agreements you enter into with a Distributor.

10. Errors and Omissions Policy: See if this is to be included in the delivery requirements as this could be an added unexpected expense.

11. Cross Collaterisation: Where the Distributor will offset expenses and losses on their other films against yours. You don't want this.

12. P & A (Prints and Advertising) commitment from the Distributor: Negotiate total expenses that will be used on P & A in the contract i.e. a fixed sum.

13. Domestic Theatrical Release: Negotiate what print run is expected, and in what locations.

14. Distribution Editing Rights: Limit for only censorship requirements although if you are dealing with a major Distributor this will not be acceptable.

15. Producer's input in the marketing campaign.

16. Trailer commitment: Will this be another hidden additional cost? Make sure theatres have this in plenty time.

17. Release window: Get Distributor to commit to release the film within a time frame after delivery of film to Distributor.

18. Audit Rights: The Producer has the rights to inspect the books re: the distribution of the film.

19. If the Sales Agent intends to group your film with other titles to produce an attractive package for buyers, ensure that your film is not unfairly supporting the other films or that you are receiving a disproportionate or unfair percentage.

20. Make sure that the rights revert back to the Producer in case of any type of insolvency or if the Agent is in material breach of the agreement.

21. Check the Delivery requirements very carefully.

SALES AGENCY AGREEMENT

BETWEEN:

(1) ▮▮▮▮ (the "Sales Agent") of ▮▮▮▮
tel ▮▮▮▮ fax: ▮▮▮▮; Company No. ▮▮▮▮
and

(1) ▮▮▮▮, (the "Producer") of ▮▮▮▮
tel ▮▮▮▮ fax: ▮▮▮▮; Company ▮▮▮▮

RE: ▮▮▮▮ (the "Film")

DEAL TERMS

1. The Producer hereby appoints the Sales Agent as its sole and exclusive sales agent for the Film and the Sales Agent accepts such appointment in accordance with this Agreement.

2. The particulars of the Film are as set out in Schedule A and the Producer undertakes to make and deliver the Film in accordance with such particulars.

3. PAYMENTS : Address for Payments of sum due to Producer:─▮▮▮▮

4. DELIVERY DATE: The Producer shall effect delivery by no later than 07/01/2000 of the items set out in the attached Schedule B.

5. RANK FILM LABORATORY: The Sales Agent shall have full access to all materials delivered to the laboratory in accordance with the Laboratory Access Letter set out in Schedule C.

6. TERRITORY: the World - Holdbacks - none

7. MEDIA RIGHTS GRANTED: the Sales Agent is appointed sole and exclusive agent in respect of all distribution rights in any and all media including but not limited to theatrical, non-theatrical, all forms of TV, video on demand, cable, satellite, all forms of video, and ancillary rights such as airlines, hotels, schools but excluding soundtrack, music publishing and merchandising rights throughout the Territory.

8. TERM: Commencing on the date hereof until the expiry of the end of the year which is 30 years after Delivery of the Film pursuant to this Agreement, that is 2029.

9. Sales Forecasts - attached as Schedule D.

10. COLLECTION ACCOUNT: A sales collection account shall be established by the Sales Agent with Barclays Bank or a third party Collection Agent appointed by the Producer shall open a collection account (the "Collection Account"), from which the Sales Agent shall be paid its Sales Fees and Distribution Expenses in accordance with this Agreement.

11. The Sales Agent is authorised by the Producer to enter into sales/distribution contracts and sign AFM International Rights Distribution Agreements (Short Form Version) (aka "Deal Memos") in the name of and as the disclosed agent for the Producer.

12. This Agreement shall be deemed to include the Deal Terms, Standard Terms and Conditions and the Schedules annexed hereto. In the event of any discrepancy between the Deal Terms and the Standard Terms and Conditions the terms of the Deal Terms shall prevail.

THIS AGREEMENT is executed by the parties hereto this 7th day of January, 2000.

BY: ▮▮▮▮

For and on behalf of PRODUCER

BY: ▮▮▮▮

For and on behalf of ▮▮▮▮

STANDARD TERMS AND CONDITIONS

1. DEFINITIONS

1. The following terms shall have the following meanings in this Agreement:-

"Business Day" - means a day (other than a Saturday) when banks are open for business in the United Kingdom;

"Collection Account" - means the separate trust account held at the Bank pursuant to the Collection Agreement or if no Collection Agreement the bank account opened by the Sales Agent for collection of Collected Receipts;

"Collection Agent" - means the bank selected to manage and operate the Collection Account (if any);

"Collection Agreement" - means the agreement (if any) to be entered into between the parties hereto governing the receipt, administration and disbursements of Receipts;

"Collected Receipts" - means Receipts generated by the exploitation and distribution of the Rights in the Film in the Territory to the extent actually received by the Collection Agent or the Sales Agent net of deduction of any withholding, sales or similar taxes and all costs and expenses of remittance and conversation and less any part or parts thereof which comprise (i) the payment or reimbursement by Local Distributors in respect of the cost of delivery materials supplied to Local Distributors and any freight or insurance costs in connection therewith (ii) prizes, subsidies or aid (iii) cable re-transmission fees (iv) any amounts paid to the Sales Agent by way of returnable deposits or advances or which are otherwise subject to a condition requiring repayment in any circumstances until the same become non-returnable (v) recoveries from infringements;

"Delivery" - means the delivery and acceptance by the Sales Agent of the items listed in Schedule B hereto and the laboratory letter in the form set out in Schedule C produced and completed in accordance with this Agreement to the Sales Agent at such locations as Sales Agent may specify.

"Distribution Expenses" - means the aggregate of all costs, expenses and charges incurred by the Sales Agent in providing its services hereunder including without limitation, the cost of release prints, replacements, re-recording, preparation or trailers, processing, repairing, packing, shipping, transportation, insurance, advertising, publicity, personal transport, living and incidental expenses for promotion, administration and negotiation purposes, printing and distribution to trade, all advertising and screening costs, novelties, personal appearance fees, telexes, faxes, mailing, courier, pro-rated share of convention costs, auditors, photography, all import and export fees, levies, licenses, tariffs, duties, censorship expenses, costs incurred in connection with cuts, editing, dubbing, lengthening, modifying of the Film, attendance at any and all exhibition of the Film, all costs in connection with reparation of foreign versions, amounts allocated in connection with checking accounts, collection and costs of security and maintaining copyright, any royalties or profit or any other financial participation's, reuse fees and transmission fees, cost of delivery materials not provided and costs of taking, defending and settling any and all legal actions, claims, allegations, disputes, controversies, causes of action.

["the Fee" means the finder's fee to be paid to the Sales Agent for finding finance for the Film, of an amount equal to [£   ] payable on completion of financing or first day of principal photography whichever is the earlier in accordance with a Finders/Executive Producer Agreement;]

"Film" - means as described in Schedule A, a film or films or programmes and associated sound-tracks whether made for theatrical release, television or any other media based on the Screenplay;

"Licensing Distributor" - means a distributor or licensee to whom the Sales Agent grants the right to exploit the Film by means of any of the Media in any part or parts of the Territory;

"Local Agreement" - means an agreement with a Local Distributor for the distribution, sale and exploitation by such Local Distributor of the Film by means of any of the Media (as set out in the Deal Memo) in any part or parts of the Territory;

"Receipts" - means receipts to be paid to the Collection Account by Local Distributors and any advance or minimum guarantee on account thereof together with al prizes, subsidiaries or aid, all cable transmission fees, blank tape levies and other similar collections and recoveries from infringements;

"Rights" - the sole and exclusive right in relation to the Film and all parts or versions thereof (now or hereafter existing) in all formats, sizes and gauges, to exhibit, sell, reproduce, transmit, broadcast, project, perform, distribute or exploit in any manner relating thereto in all media now or hereafter known, including the Media (as defined herein) including without limitation theatrical exhibition, all forms of television exhibition (including without limitation network, syndication, cable television, "Pay TV" MDS DBS, pay per view, satellite, toll and closed circuit television and referred to as "Television Rights") video-on-demand, video cassettes or discs, videograms, laser discs, 8mm cassettes, and all similar electronic or mechanical devices (whether now known or hereafter created and referred to as "Video Rights"), non-theatrical exhibition including without limitation use of exhibition in aircraft, military and government establishments, libraries, schools, hospitals, churches and other institutions (referred to as "Non-theatrical Rights") and to make arrangements and enter into agreements with sub-licensees, sub-distributors or any other third party in respect to any or all of the above rights, and the right in the Sales Agent's sole discretion to do or authorise others to do the following with respect to the Film:-

(a) make foreign language versions and cut, edit and insert dubbed and synchronised versions of the Film; and

[(b) use the title and insert the Sales Agent's logo and credit onto the Film and to change, revise, cut, edit and adapt the title and Film as Sales Agent shall determine in its sole discretion; and]

(c) advertise, publicise and promote the Film with other materials or alone and to have sole discretion as to the content, design and frequency, advertising/publicity agency and other such arrangements and for these purposes to publish synopses and excerpts and use all and any copyright material included in the Film and to broadcast for promotional purposes by radio, television or other means parts of the Film and to create, exhibit, and distribute trailers incorporating material from the Film and to use the names biography reproductions of the physical likeness and photographs of any person contributing to or performing in Film and to use exerpts of the Film on the internet for promotional purposes;

[(d) grant and permit the exercise by third parties of the right of first negotiation and matching last refusal in relation to the right to make remakes, serials, prequels and sequels based on or derived from the Film;]

(e) enter into, alter and conclude and cancel all contracts for the distribution, lease, licence, exploitation, exchange, rental, sale, sub-distribution, grant, authorisation, barter or assignment of all or any rights granted herein to Sales Agent and to collect payments adjust and settle disputes relating thereto.

"Sales Fees" - means [twenty five per cent (25%)]of Collected Receipts;

2. APPOINTMENT
The Producer irrevocably appoints the Sales Agent through the Territory for the Term as the Producer's sole and exclusive agent to exhibit, distribute, broadcast, licence, subdistribute, market, exploit, sell, advertise, publicise, perform, dispose of, turn to account and otherwise deal in or with the Film and the soundtrack thereof and to license such rights to others and/or any part thereof or rights therein or thereto in such manner and in and by such Media (now known or hereinafter devised) as the Sales Agents may in its sole discretion determine.

3. SALES AGENTS OBLIGATIONS
Subject to this Agreement the Sales Agent agrees to use its reasonable efforts to distribute and exploit the Film throughout the Territory in its sole business judgement. The Sales Agent shall use reasonable endeavors to sell the Film for the prices set out in Schedule D provided however the Sales Agent makes no representation to the Producer or any third party that such prices are attainable.

4. DELIVERY
The Producer shall deliver those items listed in Schedule B namely: the completed Film, free of any and all liens, claims and encumbrances (other than any customary lien by a Completion Guarantor to secure payment of amounts expended to complete production of the Film) fully cut, edited, scored and ready for release in all respects, and complying in all respects with all of the material specifications, approvals, terms and conditions, shall be fully delivered to the Sales Agent or to the laboratory as the Sales Agent shall designate, at the Producer's sole cost and expense on or before the Delivery Date, time being of the essence. Delivery shall not be deemed complete until all items in Schedule B have been delivered which items shall be of first class technical quality suitable for commercial exploitation.

5. PRODUCER'S WARRANTIES
The Producer warrants and represents with the Sales Agent as follows:-

(a) that the Film and all material delivered hereunder shall be of first-class technical quality suitable for exhibition, broadcast, transmission, distribution and dissemination to the public throughout the Territory;

(b) that upon execution hereof the Sales Agent shall be the sole and exclusive agent in respect of the Film throughout the Territory and all obligations and commitments which in any way affect the exploitation of the Rights shall have been fully paid and satisfied;

(c) that the Film will not violate or infringe upon the rights of any person, firm or corporation including without limitation, copyright, moral rights of authors, performers rights, trademark rights and such use or exploitation shall not constitute a libel or slander upon any person, company, entity or from material delivered hereunder, shall not contain unlawful material and the Producer warrants it has conducted a title search and know of no reason or adverse claim which would prevent or cause liability by reason of the use of the title;

(d) there are no claims and no litigation is pending or threatened which will adversely affect the Rights and the Producer has not granted and will not hereafter grant any licence, assignment, charge, lien, mortgage or encumbrance whatsoever to any person, firm or corporation in respect of the Rights or material or rights granted hereunder to Sales Agent and will not appoint another agent or otherwise dispose of or deal with the Film in any rights therein in the Territory and the Film and Rights are free from all charges, mortgages, liens, claims and other encumbrances.

(e) the Film shall be based on the Screenplay and the Producer shall upon the Sales Agent's request supply to the Sales Agent copies of all agreements forming the chain-of-title by virtue of which the Producer has acquired the rights in the Screenplay and the Film;

(f) that all persons contributing copyright material used in the Film have waived their moral rights;

(g) that there are no third party restrictions that may be imposed in respect of the exercise of the Rights granted hereunder nor any residual, reuse or use fees or payments due (including without limitation profit participation) or that can be claimed other than those disclosed to and approved in writing by the Sales Agent before Delivery;

(h) in respect of any musical recording or composition used or recorded in the Film the Producer has obtained and will throughout the Term maintain irrevocable assignable rights and licences to record, reproduce, transmit, perform and exploit the same alone and in synchronisation with the Film throughout the Territory for the full period of copyright payments for recording the dialogue, sound effects and music in the Film and for the use of the Rights therein has been paid by the Producer on or before Delivery save for monies payable to performing rights societies;

(i) copyright in the Film and in all copyright material incorporated in the Film or upon which the Film is based is and shall remain valid and subsisting throughout the Term in the Territory;

(j) the signature and execution of this Agreement has been authorised by all appropriate persons on behalf of the Producer; and

(k) On reasonable notice from the Sales Agent at any time, the Producer shall supply the Sales Agent with all documents and other information required by the Sales Agent in its discretion with respect to evidence of compliance or otherwise by the Producer of its warranties, undertakings or agreements contained herein.

6. PRODUCER'S UNDERTAKINGS
The Producer hereby undertakes with the Sales Agent as follows:-

(a) at their own expense to effect Delivery of the Film including without limitation all items listed in Schedule B hereto, fully titled, synchronised and ready for immediate exhibition not later than Delivery Date;

(b) at the request of the Sales Agent to do all such further acts and execute all such further documents as may from time to time be required by the Sales Agent for the purposes of assuring to the Sales Agent the rights granted hereunder. If the Producer fails to execute the said documents within seven (7) days the Producer hereby authorises the Sales Agent to execute such documents and all costs incurred by the Sales Agent pursuant to the execution shall be borne by the Producer;

(c) to defend, indemnify, save and hold harmless the Sales Agent, its assignees, representatives, successors licensees, affiliates, subdistributors, employees, officers, directors, shareholders, agents and independent contractors from any and all loss, damage, liability and expense including without limitation, reasonable legal fees and court costs (whether or not litigation is actually commenced), which may be incurred as a result of or in connection with any breach or alleged breach of any representation warranty or undertaking of the Producer hereunder;

(d) upon signature Producer shall supply to the Sales Agent originals duly executed of the following documents referred to in Schedule B:

Short Form Assignment;
Certificates in French;

(e) to pay the Sales Agent upon or within 10 (ten) days of a request therefor the Sales Agent's reasonable costs of performing any other services which the Sales Agent may perform at the Producer's request;

(f) that the Sales Agent shall be entitled to include its customary presentation credit on the negative and all positive copies and/or prints of the Film and all tracks and promotional material in respect of the Film, and to authorise its agents, licensees, subdistributors, designees and assignees to include their respective presentation credits and logos in a like manner in their respective territories;

(g) to effect a world-wide Errors and Omissions Insurance Policy for the Film with an insurance company acceptable to the Sales Agent for such sum as the Sales Agent shall consider appropriate and effective for a minimum period expiring 3 (three) years from the Delivery of the Film to the Sales Agent, such insurance shall not be cancellable without notice to all loss payees and additional insured parties and shall name the Producer and the Sales Agent and any third parties notified by the Sales Agent including any relevant distributors and their bankers (inter alia) as additional insured parties.

7. CREDIT

(a) Producer shall deliver to the Sales Agent for approval a full and detailed list of final screen and advertising credit requirements and the Sales Agent shall comply therewith provided that the Sales Agent shall not be liable for any error, neglect or default on the part of the Producer in the preparation and delivery of such list and the Producer shall defend, indemnify, save and hold the Sales Agent harmless against any loss, liability, damage, cost, debt or expense incurred by the Sales Agent, its affiliates, sub-distributors, licensees, assigns, representatives, agents, employees, officers, directors, shareholders and independent contractors as a result of or in connection with any such error, neglect or default.

(b) No casual or inadvertent failure by the Sales Agent nor any failure by its licensees or assignees to comply with the provisions of this clause shall constitute a breach hereof and in any event the Producer's remedy and the Producer shall ensure that any remedy of any third party providing services or goods (including initial limitation copyright) shall be limited to damages and the Producer nor any third party shall be entitled to equitable (including without limitation injunctive relief) relief or termination of this Agreement.

8. COLLECTION

8.1 The Sales Agent shall collect all initial distribution deposits payable by distributors under Licensing Agreements and will retain these until the production financing is agreed. It will be at the Sales Agent's sole discretion to release this deposit to the production at any earlier date. The Producer shall not be liable, responsible or accountable for such deposits whilst they remain under the control of the Sales Agent. [As part of the production loan documentation, the Producer shall arrange for a Collection Account to be set up into which all such deposits shall be paid to the extent that they have not be applied towards the cost of production of the Film and into which Collection Account Receipts shall be collected from the sale, exploitation and distribution of the Film and from which all the financial entitlements of the Film shall be administered and disbursed to all interested parties pursuant to the terms of the Collection Agreement.] or [The Sales Agent shall set up a Collection Account into which all Receipts shall be collected and monitored in accordance with this Agreement].

8.2 It is acknowledged by the parities that all Licensing Agreements shall provide for the payment of all monies and other consideration payable thereunder directly into the Collection Account. In accordance with the terms of the [this Agreement/Collection Agreement,] the Collection Agent shall pay directly to the Sales Agent the Distribution Expenses, Sales Fees and reimbursements it is entitled to receive hereunder out of the Receipts actually received and deposited in the Collection Account provided that no sums shall be disbursed from the Collection Account before a completion guarantee has been issued in connection with the production of the Film or, if earlier, commencement of photography of the Film, without the written consent of the Sales Agent, and the Producer. In the event that the Producer or the Sales Agent receives any sum which constitutes Receipts directly, the Producer or the Sales Agent (as the case may be) shall hold such sums in trust and shall immediately deposit such sums into the Collection Account.

9. ACCOUNTING

(a) Sales Agent agrees to keep available during normal business hours for inspection all usual books of account relating to exploitation of the rights in the Territory and all costs and expenses incurred for a period of 2 (two) years after monies relating thereto are contracted and the Producer's authorised accountants shall be entitled to inspect such books not more frequently than once in any calendar year upon reasonable notice and at Producer's expense.

(b) Sales Agent shall prepare statements of account made up to the end of every calendar period, which period is defined as every month for the first two (2) years from delivery and every quarter for the next two (2) years and every six (6) months for the next two (2) years, and thereafter six (6) monthly only when sales income is received, (herein referred to as "Statements") and shall send such statements to the Producer within thirty (30) days following the end of the period to which they relate.

(c) Statements shall be deemed conclusively true and accurate if not disputed in writing by Producer within one (1) year after being delivered to Producer.

10. APPLICATION OF RECEIPTS

Subject to Clause 8 above Receipts shall be paid into the Collection Account and together with any interest thereon shall be paid and applied in the manner and order set out in Schedule E hereto (which shall be reflected in the Collection Agreement, if any);

11. EDITING AND TITLE

The Sales Agent shall be entitled throughout the Territory during the Term to authorise others:

(a) to use the Film's title or any translation thereof of the Film in connection with the distribution exhibition exploitation advertising and any others uses thereof to change the said title and to use any other title in any language to designate the Film but no warranty of Producer shall be applicable to (any of) the said changed title;

(b) to arrange or commission the subtitling and dubbing of the Film in any language spoken in the Territory and make subtitled and dubbed language versions of the Film for use in the Territory;

(c) to make such changes to the Film as may in the Sales Agent's good faith judgement be necessary for censorship and other regulatory purposes for time segmenting purposes for airline versions and for the interpolation of commercial advertising. If the Producer is available (having strict regard to the Sales Agent's distribution exigencies) to undertake such changes then the Producer will (at their own expense) be offered the first opportunity to undertake any such changes;

12. PRESS AND PUBLICITY
12.1 The Producer will fully co-operate with the Sales Agent to assist with any and all promotional activities including co-ordinating the presence of the cast and director, subject to their availability.

12.2 Each party shall have the right to release individual corporate publicity releases without the consent or approval of the other, but agree to show such releases prior to their distribution.

13. BREACH BY PRODUCER
In the event that Producer is in material breach of any of its obligations hereunder which is incapable of remedy or is in material breach of its obligations hereunder including failure to deliver the Film to the Sales Agent in accordance herewith and fails to cure correct or remedy such breach within thirty (30) days after service of notice specifying the same or in the event that at any time prior to the Delivery Date the following events occur:-

(a) liquidation or bankruptcy proceedings are commenced against the Producer and are not withdrawn within twenty one (21) workings days;

(b) the Producer shall petition for or consent to any relief under any bankruptcy reorganisation receivership administration, and administration receivership liquidation compromise or arrangement or moratorium statutes whether now in force or hereafter enacted;

(c) the Producer shall make an assignment for the benefit of its creditors or;

(d) the Producer or any other party shall petition for the appointment of a receiver administrator, administrative receiver liquidator trustee or custodian for all or a substantial part of the Producer's assets and the Producer shall not cause him to be discharged within 60 (sixty days from the date of appointment hereof.

14. EFFECT OF BREACH
14.1 The Sales Agent shall be entitled to terminate this Agreement with immediate effect by giving notice in writing the Producer provided that such termination shall not affect or prejudice the rights and remedies of the parties here arising prior to the date of such termination. Such termination may relate to this Agreement as a whole or only to the country or countries of the Territory in respect of which the breach complained of occurs as the Sales Agent in its discretion may elect.

14.2 If the Sales Agent terminates this Agreement pursuant to any right so to do, the Sales Agent shall be released and discharged from all further obligations under this Agreement; provided, however, that the Sales Agent shall have the continuing right to receive and collect all and any Sales Fees, Distribution Expenses, Fees, Profit Shares or otherwise to which it is entitled, and if it shall so elect, to service any or all subdistribution or license agreements with respect to the Film or any rights therein or thereto entered into by the Sales Agent with Local Distributors or third parties prior to the date of such termination. Subject to any claims or damages from the Sales Agent, the Producer shall be entitled to receive its share of Receipts, if any, therefrom for the remainder of the term of such agreements (and for so long thereafter as Receipts if any, shall continue to be derived therefrom).

15. BREACH BY SALES AGENT
This Agreement may be terminated in whole by the Producer if:

(a) the Sales Agent acts in material breach of the Sales Agency Agreement or any other agreement relating to the production of the Film and fails to cure such breach within thirty (30) days of the Sales Agent's receipt from the Producer of written notice of such breach;

(b) the Sales Agent makes an arrangement or composition with its creditors;

(c) if any judgement is obtained against the Sales Agent which substantially affects its credit and financial standing in relation to the Producer and is not discharged without thirty (30) days of such judgement being obtained unless the Sales Agent (as appropriate) shall appeal against such judgement within the time allowed for appeal;

(d) if any distress, execution, sequestration or other process is levied or enforced upon or sued against any chattels or property of the Sales Agent and is not discharged within thirty (30) days;

(e) if the Sales Agent is unable to pay its debts within the meaning of Section 123 of the Insolvency Act 1986 or any statutory modification or re-enactment thereof for the time being in force;

(f) if a petition for liquidation is presented or an order is made or any effective resolution is passed for winding up the Sales Agent except a resolution for reconstruction or amalgamation the terms of which have previously been approved in writing by the Producer (such approval not to be unreasonably withheld or delayed) or an order for the winding up of the Sales Agent which is paid off or otherwise discharged within thirty (30) days;

16. EFFECT OF TERMINATION BY PRODUCER
The Producer shall be entitled to terminate this Agreement with immediate effect by giving notice in writing to the Sales Agent provided that such termination shall not affect or prejudice the rights and remedies of the parties hereto arising prior to the date of termination and the Sales Agent shall continue to be due any outstanding Sales Fees, Distribution Expenses or Fees. Such termination may relate to this Agreement as a whole or only to the country or countries of the Territory in respect of which the breach complained of occurs as the Producer in its discretion may elect.

17. EXPIRY OF TERM
Upon expiry of the Term or upon termination of this Agreement the Sales Agent shall enter into no further arrangements licences or contracts for the exploitation of the Rights or any of them and the Rights shall thereupon revert to the Producer provided that rights of agents, sub-licensees, sub-distributors and exhibitors (sub-licensees) under agreements entered into by the Sales Agent prior to the expiry of the Period (sub-licensees) shall remain unaffected and shall continue until the expiry or exhaustion of the rights granted to them under the sub-licensees and the Sales Agent shall remain solely entitled to collect and account for all further Receipts and to retain the Sales Fees and Distribution Expenses.

18. NOTICES
Any notice required to be served on either party hereunder shall be in writing given or delivered in writing personally by registered prepaid first class mail or by telex or fax to the said party at its address aforesaid or such other address of which it may hereafter give notice to the other party in writing. Any notice sent by registered prepaid first class mail shall be deemed served forty eight (48) hours after it shall have been so sent. Any notice sent by telex or fax shall be deemed served upon telexed or faxed answerback or acknowledgement of receipt.

19. PARTNERSHIP
Nothing herein contained shall constitute a partnership between or joint venture by the parties hereto. Neither party shall hold itself out contrary to the terms of this clause and neither party shall be or become liable by any representation act or omission of the other contrary to the provisions hereof.

20. ASSIGNMENT
The benefit of this Agreement shall not be assigned in whole or in part by the Producer without the prior approval of the Sales Agent.

21. WAIVER
No waiver express or implied by one party hereto of a breach by the other party of any of the provisions of this Agreement shall operate as a waiver of any preceding or succeeding breach of the same or any other provision of this Agreement.

22. PRIOR AGREEMENTS
This Agreement shall supersede and cancel all prior arrangements and understandings between the parties relating thereto whether oral or in writing. No modification hereof shall be valid or binding unless in writing and executed by both parties hereto.

23. FORCE MAJEURE
Notwithstanding anything to the contrary contained in this Agreement if for any reason beyond the control of either party either party shall be delayed in or prevented from performing any of its obligations under this Agreement then such non-performance shall be deemed not to constitute a breach of this Agreement. If this Agreement cannot be enforced or performed according to its terms for a period in excess of six (6) months it shall be deemed to have terminated at the end of such six (6) month period provided that if any such reason shall apply in respect only of one or more countries of the Territory such termination shall apply to such country or countries only.

24. LAW
This Agreement shall be governed by and construed in accordance with the Laws of England and the parties hereby agree to submit to the non-exclusive jurisdiction of the English Courts.

SCHEDULE A

Film Title:
Running Time: 120 mins
Language Recorded in: English
Director:
Principal Cast:
Calendar year in which Film is to be completed:
Screenplay by:
Budget:
Delivery Date: 04/09/2000

SCHEDULE B

DELIVERY REQUIREMENTS

FILM ELEMENTS TO BE DELIVERED:

A.	FILM ELEMENTS	
1.	Release Print	Deliverable Item
2.	Original Negative	Access Item
3.	Internegative - 2 copies	Deliverable Item
4.	Interpositve - 1 copy	Deliverable Item
5.	Sound Negative	Access Item
6.	Dolby or Ultra Stereo	Deliverable Items. If picture is to be exhibited with a Dolby or Ultra Stereo soundtrack, the following materials, items 6a to 6e must be delivered in additionto all other materials.
a	One 35mm four-track magnetic master of the final stereo domestic dub.	Access Items
b	One 35mm optical Dolby two-track Dolby master from the final domestic dub.	Access Items with Interpositive
c	A copy of the executed license agreement between the Producer and Dolby or Ultra Laboratories	Deliverable Item
7	One 35mm four track magnetic master of the final stereo domestic.	Deliverable Item
8	One 35mm optical	Delivery Item
9	Six (6) Track Stereo Soundtrack	Access Item
10	Check Print/Answer Print	Deliverable Item
11	Video Mastering Print (aka Low Contrast Print)	Deliverable Item
12	Magnetic Sound Master ("Three Stripe")	Access Item
13	Textless Title Backgrounds	Deliverable Item
14	Music Tapes	Deliverable Item
115	Coverage Materials	Access Item

TRAILER ITEMS (90-270 seconds duration):

1.	Compositive prints - 3 -	Delivery Item
2.	Negative prints -	Access Item
3.	Textless internegative print	Access Item
4.	Mag sound master	Access Item
5.	Mag M/E track	Access Item
6.	Other trailer materials	Access Item

VIDEO AND AUDIO MATERIALS

A.	NTSC master - Digital Beta and/or D1*	Deliverable Item
B.	PAL Master - Digital Beta and/or D1*	Deliverable Item
C.	Viewing Cassette - PAL and NTSC	Deliverable Item
D.	Reference Cassette	Deliverable Item
E.	Music and Effects Audio Track	Access Item

PROMOTIONAL MATERIALS

1. "PROMO REEL"
   Promotion cassette master - Beta SP or 3/4"
   (i) Promotion cassette consists of 3 to 15 minutes summary of the film (with dialogue and/or narration) or
   (ii) series of sequences from the Film, which capture the "flavour" or "essence" of the film

2. PROMOTION CASSETTES
   20 PAL VHS and 10 NTSC VHS copies

3. ELECTRONIC PRESS KIT (EPK)
   (approximately 30 minutes duration)
   Master Digi Beta (PAL and NTSC) and
   2 Beta SP PAL and 2 Beta NTSC and
   20 VHS PAL and 20 VHS NTSC

   EPK consists of at least two of the three items listed below:

   (i)   Trailer
   (ii)   Promo Reel
   (iii) Interviews shot on camera with
          - 3 to 6 of leading actors
          - director
          - producer
          - special guest artistes (if any)
          - DOP/writer/music/novelist

4. 4 - PAGE BROCHURE 4 COLOUR
   (layout and content according to Sales Agent's approval)

5. POSTER (portrait size)

6. Campaign for print advertisements

7. Free access to art work for items (4) and (5)

RECORDS AND DOCUMENTATION

A.	Records and Documentation	
1.		Deliverable Item
2.	Combined Dialogue and Action Continuity	Deliverable Item
3.	Final Footage Record	Deliverable Item
4.	Final Main and End Credits	Deliverable Item
5.	Title Materials	Deliverable Item
6.	Paid Ad Credits	Deliverable Item
7.	Video Packaging Credits	Deliverable Item
8.	Dubbing and Subtitling Restrictions	Deliverable Item
9.	Residuals Materials	Deliverable Item
10.	Music Licence	Deliverable Item
11.	Music Licence Materials	Deliverable Item
12.	Synopsis	Deliverable Item
13.	Cast and Technical Personnel List	Deliverable Item
14.	Publicity Materials	Deliverable Item
15.	Promotional Materials	Deliverable Item
16.	Black/White Stills and Negatives - 10 different scenes	Deliverable Item
17.	Colour Still and Negatives and Colour	Deliverable Item
18.	Rights Agreement	Deliverable Item
19.	Service Agreements	Deliverable Item, if requested
20.	Rating Certificate	Deliverable Item, when available
21.	Certificate of Origin - 10 copies	Deliverable Item
22.	Final Certified Statement	Deliverable Item, if available
B.	Certificate of Insurance	Deliverable Item
C.	Chain of Title Documentation	
1.	Title and Copyright Reports	Deliverable Item
2.	Copyright Reports	Deliverable Item
3.	Anti-piracy Documents	Deliverable Item

RECORDS TO BE DELIVERED OR ACCESSIBLE TO THE DISTRIBUTION IF REQUESTED

A.	Script Supervisor's Notes	Access Items, Deliverable upon request
B.	Editor's Line Script	Access Items, Deliverable upon request
C.	Daily Film Code Shoots or Book	Access Items, Deliverable upon request
D.	ADR and Wild Line Recording Logs	Access Items, Deliverable upon request
E.	Conductor's Score of all music recorded for the Film	Access Item
F.	Music Scoring Logs	Access Item
G.	Music Re-recording Cue Sheets	Access Item
H.	Sound Effects Re-recording Cue Sheets	Access Item
I.	Dialogue Re-recording Cue Sheets	Access Item
J.	Negative Cutter's Key Sheets	Access Item

PROTECTION ELEMENTS

A.	Picture Elements	Access Item
B.	Sound Elements	Access Item
C.	Video Masters	Access Item
D.	Audio Recording, Tracks and Masters	Access Item
E.	Other Film Elements	Access Item
F.	Work Materials	Access Item

SCHEDULE C

Laboratory Access Letter

SCHEDULE D

Sales Forecasts

SCHEDULE E

Recoupment Schedule

As witness the hands of the duly authorised officer on the day, month and year first above written.

SIGNED
BY: ███████████████

███████████████████████

For and on behalf of PRODUCER

SIGNED
BY: ███████████████

███████████████████████

For and on behalf of
███████ LIMITED

Glossary Of Contract Terminology

ABOVE THE LINE - *the portion of a film budget that covers creative elements and personnel i.e. story, screenplay rights, producers, directors and principal members of the cast.*

ACCRUALS - *the accumulation of payments due.*

ANCILLARY RIGHTS - *other subsidiary rights i.e. the right to make a sequel, soundtrack, computer game etc., merchandising, video, novelisation.*

ACQUISITIONS - *purchases.*

ARBITRATION - *an informal method for resolving disputes (by finding the middle ground) which is usually quicker and less expensive than litigation. Usually an arbitrator is agreed in advance by the parties or chosen by the head of an appropriate professional body i.e. Institute of Chartered Accountants etc.*

BELOW THE LINE - *accounting term relating to the technical expenses and labour involved in producing a film.*

BREACH OF CONTRACT - *failure of one party to fulfil the agreement.*

BREAKEVEN - *the point when sales equal costs, where a film is neither in profit nor loss.*

BUY OUT - *this term is used in relation to the engagement of artists where no repeat, residual or other fees are required to be paid to the artist in relation to any form of exploitation of the film or programme.*

BEST ENDEAVOURS - *means you have to do all you can including incurring expense in order to carry out your relevant obligation under the agreement.*

CAP - *a ceiling, upper limit. Try to cap expenses in sales agents agreements.*

COLLATERAL - *assets pledged to a lender until the loan is repaid. i.e. with a bank loan a house can be put up for collateral.*

COMMISSION - *a percentage of specified amount received for services performed.*

CONTINGENCY - *money set aside for unanticipated costs.*

CREDITOR - *one to whom monies are owed.*

CHAIN OF TITLE - *contracts and documents that hand down the copyright to the present owner.*

CROSS COLLATERALISE - *this is where a party, usually a distributor, will offset losses in one area against gains in other areas. If you are a producer you will want to resist this.*

DEAL MEMO - *a short version of the contract, giving the principal terms of the agreement which can be legally binding - check carefully if this is the intention.*

DEFERRAL - *delay of payment of a fixed sum which is all or part of payments for cast and crew and other services, usually paid out of receipts from the film after the distributor or financier has taken their commission/fee/expenses or been repaid their initial investment (plus a %).*

DISTRIBUTION EXPENSES - *there is no set definition for this term but things to watch for are that the expenses are reasonable and relate directly to the film. It should not include the distributor's overheads and any expenses payable by the distributor to third partioc chould bc negotiated on the best commercial terms available.*

DISTRIBUTION FEE - *this is usually between 30-50% of income received. You should try and negotiate a sliding scale for the fee which reduces as the income from the film increases.*

ERRORS AND OMISSIONS - *insurance protection covering against lawsuits alleging unauthorised use of ideas, characters, plots, plagiarism, titles and alleged slander, libel, defamation of character etc.*

ESCROW - *monies or property held by a third party for future delivery or payment to a party on the occurrence of a particular event or services rendered.*

EQUITY - *the interest or value an owner has in a property but where they have no legal ownership in the property.*

FAVOURED NATIONS - *meaning that the contracting party will be given treatment on an equal footing with others that the other party deals with. i.e. could refer to placement of billing requirements, or profit participation.*

FORCE MAJEURE - *this term is usually defined in the agreement. Generally it means any event which is outside the control of the parties to the agreement i.e. act of God, fire, strike, accident, war, illness of key persons involved in the production, effect of elements etc.*

LEGAL TOOLKIT

GROSS DEAL - *a profit participation for the producer or others in the distributor's gross receipts (unusual).*

GROSS RECEIPTS - *this term is usually defined in an agreement to mean all income received from the exploitation of the film by the distributor before any deduction of the distributor's fees and expenses but sometimes it is expressed to include the deduction of such fees and expenses.*

INDEMNIFY - *in essence to secure against loss and damage which may occur in the future or to provide compensation against any loss or damage.*

INDEMNITY - *a promise to make good any loss or damage another has incurred or suffered or may incur. It may not always be appropriate to give an indemnity.*

IN PERPETUITY - *to exist forever.*

INDUCEMENT LETTER - *this is required where a party, usually an artist, director or individual producer, contract through their company (for tax reasons) rather than as individuals. A Producer and/or financier will require the individual to provide personal warranties and undertakings in relation to the ability and authority of their company to state the artist/director/producer will render their services. The letter will also confirm that they have granted the relevant rights to the company which the company then grants to the producer under the principal agreement of engagement.*

INSOLVENT - *where one has liabilities that exceed their assets.*

JOINT VENTURE - *a business by two or more parties who share profits, losses and control.*

LETTER OF INTENT - *a written communication expressing the intent of a person or company to perform whatever services that they provide. This may not be legally binding.*

LIBEL - *a false and malicious publication which defames one who is living (it may not be printed for that purpose - you don't have to show malice in UK libel law).*

LICENSOR - *one who grants a license.*

LIMITED RECOURSE LOAN - *a loan which may only be repaid through specified sources of income i.e. income derived from the exploitation of a film.*

LABORATORY ACCESS LETTER - *this is an instruction to the laboratory to release the negative of the film to*

named distributors and is required where more than one distributor is being used.

MORAL RIGHTS - *this is a general term used to describe a bunch of rights which belong to the author of a copyright work. These so called "moral rights" derive from the European principle, which was asserted most forcefully in France and Germany, that an artist has the right to protect their work even if it is the property of another. England only recognised authors "moral rights" in 1988 by the incorporation of those rights into the Copyright Designs and Patents Act. See ss77-79 The right of paternity (i.e. to be identified as the author), the right of integrity (i.e. for the work not to be treated in a derogatory way), the right to object to false attribution. These rights may be waived by the author and in nearly every case they are. A distributor would not find it acceptable for an artist to be able to prevent the distribution of a film on the basis that their moral rights had been infringed. In France and Germany an author cannot by law waive these rights.*

NEGATIVE COSTS - *total of various costs incurred in the acquisition and production of a film in all aspects prior to release. Includes pre production, production, post production costs.*

NET DEAL - *a distribution deal where the distributor recoups all it's costs and collects all it's fees before giving the producer the remainder of the film's revenue.*

NET PROFIT - *there is no set definition of this term as in every case there will be much debate about what may or may not be deducted from the gross receipts to arrive at the net profit. The definition of net profit in any agreement should be looked at very carefully to ensure inter alia expenses and commissions are not being deducted twice i.e. once by the distributor and again by the sub distributor etc.*

OUTPUT DEAL - *a contract through which one party delivers it's entire output to another party. i.e. a distribution agreement between a production company and a distribution company in which the distributor commits to distribute the films that have been or will be produced by the producer.*

PARRI PASSU - *means on a like footing i.e. everyone is to be treated in an equal fashion. For instance, on distribution of net profits everyone gets an equal amount irrespective of their contribution.*

PRO RATA - *means that, for example, if an artist is entitled to payment on a pro rata basis then if they receive a weekly fee for 6 days work and the artist subsequently works only 3 days the artist would receive half the weekly* fee i.e. the weekly fee would be pro rated according to the amount of time the artists services were engaged.

PER DIEM - a daily payment. It is usually used in the context of an artist's daily expenses.

PRODUCERS SHARE - means the net sum remaining to the Producer after deductions of distribution fees, expenses (or other deductions that are agreed) and after other profit participants have received their share. The producers share of net profits may be shared with other third parties.

PROFIT PARTICIPATION - percentage participations on net profits.

REASONABLE ENDEAVOURS - this is less onerous than best endeavours and simply means you will make a reasonable effort to carry out your obligations.

RECOUPMENT - when the costs and expenses of a film production are recovered from the film's revenue i.e. when production costs have been recouped.

RENTAL AND LENDING RIGHTS - these rights are contained in Directive no. 92 and 100 EEC and have been brought into effect in the UK by regulations which amend the CDPA 1988. The principle behind the changes is that with the development and expansion of video and other similar forms of distribution, an artist should share in the income derived from this commercially important area. However this is of concern to producers and distributors who do not wish to have a continuing obligation to make payments to artists and so all agreements contain a clause stating that the artist recognises that the payment due to the artist under the agreement is adequate and equitable remuneration for these rights and they assign all such rights to the producer. There is uncertainty as to whether such a clause will be legally binding on an artist as the right to remuneration for rental rights is expressed to be unwaivable and this issue has yet to be considered by an English Court.

RESIDUALS - payments for each re run after initial showing. In the case of guild or union agreements minimum residual payments have been agreed.

ROYALTIES - payments to a party for use of the property calculated as a percentage of a defined amount (i.e. net income from video sales).

THEATRICAL RELEASE - exploitation of the film in the cinema as opposed to on television or video etc.

TURNAROUND - e.g. a screenplay development situation where the purchaser or licensee of the property has decided not to go forward with the production or if the production is not screened or does not begin principal photography within a specified time the owner or licensor can serve notice on the owner/licensee so that the screenplay can be re-acquired by the owner/licensor.

VENTURE CAPITAL - financing for new ventures that involves some investment risk but usually offers a share of any profit - there is usually a high premium paid for such investment reflecting the risk taken by the investor.

WAIVER - a relinquishment or surrender of particular rights

WARRANTY - a promise by one party that the other party will rely upon. i.e. in a distribution agreement a producer may warrant that the filming is of a particular quality and standard.

LEGAL TOOLKIT

The Crew & What They Do

Producer - *Head of the production, the first one on the film and the last one off. Generally they are the ones who have found the screenplay and are involved in all aspects of the film making process. They raise the finance for the film, prepare the budget and are answerable to financiers. On a low budget film, more often than not, they will also be doing the job of the Line Producer.*

Executive Producer - *Usually the person who has made the film possible in either putting together the finance and/or creative package. Also used as a credit that is given as a 'big thank you' for funds or services that have made the film possible.*

Line Producer - *Assigned by the Producer early on. One step up from the Production Manager. May prepare budget with Producer. Takes care of main deals with facility houses, keeping control and in line with the budget. Not necessarily needed on a low budget movie where the Producer and/or Production Manager will do the job.*

Production Manager *(PM) - Needed early on. Makes sure the Director has everything he or she needs at an affordable price, keeps in contact with the Accountant. Keeps a close eye on the schedule, makes sure that everything works smoothly. Visits the set daily to be aware of everything that is happening.*

Production Co-ordinator - *Works with PM. Makes sure there is a smooth flow of information between departments both verbal and written. Prepares call sheets with 2nd AD, schedules, progress reports, orders equipment, co-ordinates transport.*

Production Secretary - *Hired very early on by the Producer for secretarial administration skills.*

Production Assistants - *Assistants to the production team, where job varies from being a typist, running errands, carrying equipment etc.*

Runner - *Runs for everything needed, fulfils a variety of chores. From message carrier, miscellaneous buyer, getting tea and coffee etc.*

Production Accountant - *Takes care of monies throughout the shoot. Arranges for payments that need to be made, expenses etc. Keeps an eye on how the shoot is going with relevance to the budget.*

Location Manager - *Organises the recce's (finding locations) and takes care of everything associated with shooting on location. i.e. various permissions, hotel bookings, toilets, car hire, informing police, authorities, residents; to be the liaison on set between crew and location owners. May have location scouts as assistants.*

Director - *Creative decision maker throughout the film making process, directing cast and crew from pre to post production. Responsible to the Producer for transforming screenplay into film.*

Second Unit Director - *Aids Director in shooting certain shots, generally those that don't require sync sound or the principal actors i.e. cutaways, establishing shots, insert shots etc. Receives instructions from the Director of what needs to be shot and how to shoot it.*

First Assistant Director (1st AD) - *The link between the production office and set. Must ensure that everything is available that is needed on the day. Keeps in close contact with the Director and the Production Manager as he/she must know everything there is to know about the script, locations, actors, sets, schedule and how the Director intends to shoot. Aids the Director, keeping up the energy and strength of the crew pushing them within sensible limits to keep the show moving at a good pace.*

Second Assistant Director (2nd AD) - *A good backup to the 1st. Writes the call sheet in conjunction with the Prod. Co-ordinator, arranges cast calls, pick ups, extras, stunt calls, deals with payments to extras and is present when cast arrives and is available to sort out production problems if and when they arise on set.*

Third Assistant Director (3rd AD) - *Assists the 2nd and acts as a Runner.*

Casting Director - *Over sees finding the appropriate cast working closely with the Director. Has a good knowledge of agents and their clients, having built up good relationships.*

Continuity - *Observes and records continuity details such as costume, props, script, makes sure shots match during varied takes and that all shots are completed.*

Storyboard Artist - *Prepares detailed panels of shots as requested by the Director. On low-budget shoots this may not be deemed to be necessary.*

Director of Photography (DoP)/ Lighting Cameraman/ Cinematographer - *Collaborates with the Director to establish the photographic style of the movie. Familiar with camera and lighting equipment and film stocks. Contact person between the lab and production. Head of the camera team.*

Camera Operator - *Operates the camera. Must have familiarity with equipment, camera movement and an eye for framing.*

Focus Puller/1stCamera Assistant - *Loads film, keeps the image sharp by following the focus, changes lenses, sets exposure and fits filters as requested. 'Checks the gate' after each take.*

2nd Camera Assistant/Clapper Loader - *Loads film into magazines, cans exposed film and short ends, fills out camera sheets, keeps records on stocks, lenses, filters and 'f' stops as well as noting any additional info for the labs and production office. Marks each take with clapperboard.*

Grip - *In charge of operating dollies, cranes, laying track, moving cameras, - all heavy work so needs to be strong. If needed they design or construct special rigs and camera mounts. (Key Grip, dolly grip. crane grip).*

Gaffer - *Chief electrician in charge of equipment and connection to power supply. Works closely with DoP explaining and delegating the lighting design. Chooses his own crew of Best Boy, Generator driver and Sparks. Named after a hook for overhead hanging lights.*

Best Boy - *1st Assistant to the Gaffer.*

Sparks - *Move and maintain the lights. Organises power from generator.*

Sound Recordist - *Records production sound, wild tracks, ambience. Will either have their own kit or will hire from sound houses.*

Boom Operator - *Works with the recordist either holding the boom or arranging the necessary mics for a particular scene. Takes care of sound recording sheets which will be used in the editing.*

Costume Designer - *Designs a particular look in with the Director. Breaks down the script, working out how many costume changes are needed according to story days, meets actors individually to discuss requirements. Usually the first people from production to meet the actors therefore they set the whole tone of the production. They must shop, hire, or make the costumes and have good social skills to have a good working relationship with the actor. Can have a Costume Assistant.*

Dresser - *Sets up a working wardrobe. Arrives before actors to set up costumes, supervises their dressing, checks continuity throughout the day. Stands by with wet weather or warm clothing depending on conditions.*

Make Up Artist and Hair Stylist - *Breaks down script for effects, special make up or cosmetic make up i.e. bruises, wounds or shaved heads may be needed. Each artist will have their own basic kit and will take care of hiring wigs, special effects and prosthetics. Keeps continuity notes.*

LEGAL TOOLKIT

Production Designer - Works with the Director, DoP on visual style of the movie. Responsible for sets either in the studio or on location. Ensures the 'look' of the set and props are as desired.

Art Director - Oversees the ideas of the Production Designer, arranging furnishings, liaising with Construction Manager and the art department.

Set Director - Responsible for the selection of props and supervising the dressing of sets. Prepares prop lists and works closes with the Prop Buyer in organising the dressing and striking of sets. Makes continuity notes. On low-budget shoots, the Set Director and Art Director may be deemed to be as one.

Prop Master - Physically puts and removes furniture and props on set. Keeps tabs on all props and looks after them during the shoot.

Prop Buyer - Responsible for finding appropriate props from specialist sources. Purchases, hires and maintains a record of art dept. budget. Organises collections and returns of hired props. On low budget shoot, Prop Buyer and Prop Master may be deemed to be as one.

Prop Maker - Designing, building and operating any props. On low budget shoot this may also be done by the Production Designer and/or Art Director.

Construction Manager - Responsible for building sets within art department budget. Organises materials and extra crew if necessary. Schedules building and striking of sets in conjunction with the Production Designer.

Painters/Scenic Artists/Carpenters/Plasterers/ Runners etc. - Work with Construction Manager with building and striking sets.

Stills Photographer - Shoots production stills for use in press kits, publicity, advertising.

Unit Publicist - Works with Stills Photographer making sure the 'right' shots are taken to publicise the film. Takes care of getting publicity whilst shooting, prepares press kits and makes sure that sufficient material is obtained during the production to publicise the film later on.

Caterer/ Catering company - Oversees all catering requirements on the film.

Drivers - A team of drivers for ferrying crew, cast, equipment. Not necessarily required on low budget film as job doubled up with crew members.

Craft Service Person - Oversees tea, coffee, hot and cold water, snacks etc. on set. On low budget film this job can be doubled up with Runners or PA's or Caterer.

Stunt Co-ordinator - Oversees, plans and executes all stunts and action throughout the film. Co-ordinates with Stunt Performers and special effects. Equity registered.

Special Effects Co-ordinator - Oversees, plans and executes special effects throughout the film - inc. atmospherics (rain, wind, smoke) fires, explosions etc. Works with Stunt Co-ordinator.

Greensman - Oversees the greenery required in film i.e plants, flowers etc.

Post Production Supervisor - Oversees entire post production process. Not necessarily required on low budget film. On low budget film this may be the Editor/Director/Producer.

Editor - Once rushes are received from set, the Editor will assemble the movie. Works closely with the Director.

Assistant Editor - Aids Editor with preparing picture and sound, synchronising rushes if necessary, logging, maintaining good files and records and storage of all movie elements. On low budget film not necessarily needed.

Sound Editor - Assembles production tracks, effects, music, recording extra effects if necessary, transferring other effects from libraries, taking control of Foley and ADR (Automatic Dialogue Replacement). Ensures all location atmos' are covered with wild tracks. Takes Film to final mix with Editor and Director. Should hear and approve the final optical soundtrack.

Foley Artist - Creates Footsteps, sound effects that match the cut movie filling empty scenes.

Composer/ Musician - Hired for the original score of the film and composes music in accordance with Directors wishes.

Music Supervisor - Hires musicians, locates and clears required additional music tracks.

Budget Template

How much can you make a film for? There is no answer to this question, hence we have dropped a budget from this book. Perhaps a more pertinent question is how much money can you get? Maybe that is what your budget will be.

The list over the next few pages is a fairly in depth guide to most things you will have to find, pay for, steal, borrow etc. Many things you can just ignore as they won't be relevant to your film.

Many things you will get for free, but things like catering and travel will always cost you - we've never heard of a petrol station or the London Underground sponsoring a film, but you never know.

BUDGET TOP SHEET / SUMMARY

Development/ Story and Screenplay
Producers Fee
Directors Fee
Principal Cast
Production Overheads
TOTAL ABOVE THE LINE

Cast
Crew
Production Department
Equipment Hire
Costume Design
Make up and Hair
Production Design
Props
Stunts
Special Effects
Location and set facilities
Accommodation and Catering
Transport/ Travel
Stock
Lab and processing
Editing and Post Sound
Music
Film Effects
Professional Fees
Insurance and Taxes
Publicity
Delivery

TOTAL PRODUCTION
Completion Bond @ 5%
Contingency @ 10%
Overhead
Interest
Insurance @ 2.5%

TOTAL ABOVE THE LINE
TOTAL BELOW THE LINE
TOTAL ABOVE AND BELOW THE LINE

LEGAL TOOLKIT

DEVELOPMENT

Story and Screenplay (Rights & Options)
Drafts & treatments
Story Editor & Story Consultant
US copyright and Research
Screenplay duplication and binding
Development finance

PRE PRODUCTION

Producers fee
Directors fee
Exec Producer fee and Other Producer fee
Company fee
Legal - incorporation/contracts and Accounting

PRINCIPAL CAST

List principal cast
Rehearsal hire and per dium

PRODUCTION OVERHEADS

Office rent & power
Secretary/ Pas
Fringe benefits (healthcare, associate fees etc)
Medicine
Trade subscriptions
Maintenance

CAST

List characters:
Per Dium
Extras and stand ins/ voice over artists/rehearsal hire

CREW

Production Team - Production Manager/ Co-ordinator
Assistant/Secretary
Production accountant
Location Manager
AD Team - 1st AD, 2nd AD, 3rd AD
Script Supervisor/ Script Continuity
Casting Director

Director of Photography
Camera team - operator/focus puller/clapper loader
Gaffer/ Best Boy/ Sparks
Key Grip and Grips
Production Sound Recordist/ boom operator
Costume Designer/ wardrobe assistant
Make up and Hair stylist
Production Designer
Art Director/ Set Director/ Set Dresser
Props Master/prop makers
Construction manager
Leading scenic artist/ scenic painters/ carpenters
Runners/ craft servicemen
Tutor/ chaperone / dialogue coach
Storyboard artist
Stills photographer
Driver
Editor/ Sound Editor
Technical advisor. animal handlers/ trainers

PRODUCTION DEPT

Office rent
Phone and Fax
Office equipment/photocopying & printing
Office consumables
Post and delivery/freight and courrier
Computer consumables and stationery supplies
Communications
Transportation for production team
Location Recce
Gratuities and Hospitality

EQUIPMENT HIRE

Camera Department
Camera kit (includes body, mag, filters etc)
Lenses - zoom lens/ set of prime lenses/ distagons
Tripod legs, short/tall & tripod head
Camera filters
Steadicam and operator
Camera tape & Gaffer tape
Consumables and video assist
Lost or Damaged equipment

GRIPS

Dolly etc/ bowl for camera head/remote head
Track, straight and curved/ wedges and blocks
Snake arm/jib - to attach to dolly
Car mount
Camera rig - misc
Grip truck and camera vehicle
Large crane plus op/ cherry picker
Lost or damaged equipment

SOUND

DAT hire and microphones/radio mics etc.
Accessories
Lost or damaged equipment

LIGHTING

Lighting Kit (12K, 6K, 4K, 1.2K HMIs)
5K Tungsten/2k Blonde/1K Redhead
Inky dinks/mizars/sunguns
Generator and genny operator
Stands and tripods
Gels/trace/spun
Lighting operators
Accessories
Lost or damaged equipment

PRODUCTION EQUIPMENT

AD's walkie talkies and headsets
Production walkie talkies

COSTUME DESIGN

Costume hire
Wardrobe purchases & accessories
Cleaning &damages

MAKE UP & HAIR

Wig hire/purchase/make up hire & special make up hire

PRODUCTION DESIGN

Set construction
Construction equipment hire
Materials/ consumables
Set strike/skips
Storyboards
Continuity polaroids/ artwork

PROPS

Prop hire/ purchase/ damages
Special vehicles/greens/paint

STUNTS

Co-ordinator and crews
Equipment/accessories/ stunt players

SPECIAL EFFECTS

Co-Ordinator and crews
Materials
Pyrotechnics/smoke machines/prosthetics
Models/studio hire/camera/lighting/stock/processing
Motion Control/ rig/blue screen studios

LOCATION and SET FACILITIES

Studio stage hire/office hire/facilities/personel
Studio power/on set tea&coffee
Location hire/fees/offices/facilities/security/recces
Location permits/police/contact man/power/phone
Location shipping costs
Location tea&coffee/repairs/office equip. hire
Location cleaning/parking
Location costume/make up/green rooms/wagons
Location wagon fuel and maintenance
Overseas equipment shipment/flight insurance
Interpreters/guides/export/import/custom fees
Location personnel/paramedics/ambulance
Nurse

ACCOMMODATION and CATERING

Accommodation/ Catering plus caterer

LEGAL TOOLKIT

TRANSPORT

Cast/Crew travel
Vehicle rentals/camera/grips/lighting/production
Car hire & misc. trailer hire
Repairs and maintenance
Taxis
Fuel and parking
Oversea flights and misc.

STOCK

Film Stock/ sound stock
Master TK stock and dupes
Non linear tapestock
Polaroids & stills stock
Foley stock, dat stock
Film consumables and Extra stock

LAB & PROCESSING

Neg processing and tape transfer & sync up/
additional vhs
Neg cut
1st Trial print/A&B surcharge/answer print
Interpositive/internegative/check print/optical track
Leaders and misc. special lab work/low con print
Titles/textless title backgrounds/tk to broadcast
Courrier charges
Trailer - Neg cutting
Trailer - trial print/optical sound transfer/titles
Textless titles background
Trailer - opticals/ 1st Answer print/show print.
Trailer low con tk print
Trailer - tk to broadcast/dupe/ntsc

EDITING and POST SOUND

Hire of Avid/ cutting room off-line and on-line
ADR/sfx studio hire/sound transfers
Tracklaying & sound effects
Cutting room supplies and consumables
Premixes,Final and M&E mix, dubbing theatre hire
M&E trailer mix and dupes
Dolby/DTS Fees
Foley
Test screenings
Courrier fees

MUSIC

Composer inc. relevant rights
Perfomer fees inc. relevant rights
Orchestra fees inc. relevant rights
Recording studio fees
Incidental library music
Music supervisor
Existing recordings inc. relevant rights/ licenses

FILM EFFECTS

Consultants/effects/lab processing

PROFESSIONAL FEES

Legal and accounting
Production audit/ bank charges
VAT error/repayment
Insurance and Tax/ company tax

PUBLICITY

PR Company
Promotional material
Stills photographer/studio hire/stills
Artwork image
EPK and clips tape
Preview theatre screenings and gratuities
Markets and festivals
Internet presence
Courrier/delivery

DELIVERY

Vid dupe of master movie & trailer + M&E
Errors and Omissions/ copies of all legal docs
Dupes of master stills/vhs copies/EPK dupe/clip
tape dupe
35mm print release/ 35mm trailer release
Posters/ one sheets/ dat dupe of music
Transcript/ continuties/ misc. certificates
Title research and copyright report
BBFC Certification
Vault rental

LEGAL TOOLKIT

The Production Board and Scheduling

How to use - *The vertical strips represent all of the scenes in the film and contain all the information that is required such as whether scenes are Location or Studio, Day or Night, Length of script pages (calculated as 1/8ths of a page), Scene nos., Scene description, and Cast number. The vertical strips come in a variety of colours (blue, green, yellow, etc.) and are used to represent additional information which is obvious at a glance such as Day / Night / Ext / Int or Ext. Night / Ext.Day / Int.Night / Int.Day. Black Strips are used to separate shooting days or each shooting week. Cast are listed with their cast numbers. The key to the information is recorded on the left hand side of the board.*

How to Schedule - *Scenes of a film are NEVER shot in sequence but in an order that best suits the production, for instance the availability of cast / location / night shoots / stunts etc. There is a lot of shuffling to make everything fit to produce the most efficient and cost effective schedule. Remember to allow more time for action sequences and complicated set ups. Tracking shots do take time. If you're working with children there are only a certain amount of hours they can work; working with animals will take time. Make sure you have a back up plan as things always go wrong. If there's a torrential downpour for your sunny location, perhaps there's a possibility of shooting in an interior location; what to do if your lead actor gets sick? If a location falls through?*

As well as the Film Production Board, there are computer programs that enable you to create your schedule, change it, compare with a variety of scheduling options - all within seconds, as well as being connected to your budget, call sheets etc.

The cheapest method is to schedule on white cards that can be pinned up on the wall, they're cheap and easy to organise.

Production Forms

On the following pages are several documents used in the production office, on set or in the cutting room. They are a guide, not an absolute, and copies of most can be found on the CD accompanying this book. They are saved in MS Word format.

Actors Day out of Days - *This checklist shows when an actor is on set or not. The information is taken from the Production Schedule. It is used for anyone who needs to know which actors are on set on which day. (page 573)*

Call Sheet - *This is handed out to all cast and crew the day before the shoot day it represents. It is created by the 2nd AD and deals with the cast's pick-up, arrival and on-set times and any other relevant departmental information. (page 574)*

Production Checklist - *Created by the Production Office as a checklist prior to principal photography and for putting the budget together. (page 575)*

Continuity/Edit Notes - *Filled out by the Continuity person and should state all and every detail about the shots, usually as a sheet per shot and can include photographs and diagrams. These are later handed to the Editor as a guideline for putting the rough assembly together. (page 576)*

Petty Cash Expense Report - *Must be handed out any time petty cash is issued to keep track of how much money each department is using and how much you have left. It also reminds crew members that they are accountable for any money spent on behalf of the production. (page 577)*

Daily Progress Report - *Completed by the 1st AD and usually sent to the Production Office if the shoot is away from the office. Forwarded to Financiers and the Bond Company. It shows exactly how much has been shot on what day, how long it took and who was involved. (page 578)*

Script Breakdown Sheet - *The 1st AD should break down every scene of the script to extract what is needed, where it takes place, day or night etc. - essentially, everything needed to shoot the scene. (page 579)*

Locations Checklist - *Produced by the Locations Manager, this is a list of things that must be done in advance of the production moving to a location. It also provides useful information for the 2nd AD for the Call Sheets. (page 580)*

Movement Order - *Produced by the Location Manager as travel directions. It should also include train times, whenever possible. Usually attached to Call Sheet for the day it refers to. This is an example only and could include photocopied maps with highlighted routes. (page 581)*

Sample Schedule Page - *A single page from a schedule to illustrate the type of information and layout that works. Programs like Movie Magic make producing a schedule easier and it is available for both Mac and PC. (page 582)*

Sound Report - *Filled out by the Sound Recordist and sent to the lab, copies also sent to the Editor. Details takes, technical problems and other illustrative information. (page 583)*

Music Cue Sheet - *Produced for international sales to detail where and how the music is used in a film, also who own what in terms of publishing and copyright etc. (page 584)*

Production Gratuities Form - *All amounts for miscellaneous payments with regard to 'thank you's'. These must be recorded and kept track of to where, to who and how much. (page 585)*

ACTORS DAY OUT OF DAYS

Date: 17 . 1 . 02

Production Company	Mad Dog Movies
Producer	Claire Roper
Production Title	Bank Holiday
Director	John Oldman
Script Date	6 . 1 . 02 version
Prod. Manager/Asst. Director	Emma Smith / Paul Edwards

Rehearsal - R   Hold - H
Started - S   Travel - T
Worked - W   Finish - F
On Call - C

Day Number: SAT
Date: 17 . 1 . 02
Day of the Week: Monday

No.	Character	Cast Member	M	T	W	T	F	S	S	M	T	W	T	F	S	S	M	T	W	T	F	S	S
1	EMMA DUGGAN	JOSIE FELLOWES	X	X	S	R	C	C	N	W	W	X	C	N	W	W	N	X	X	X	X	X	X
2	CHRIS KERR	HARVEY WILLIS	S	R	N	N	W	C	C	X	X	N	W	C	X	X	N	W	N	N	N		
3																							
4																							
5																							
6																							
7																							
8																							
9																							
10																							
11																							
12																							
13																							
14																							
15																							
16																							
17																							
18																							
19																							

Mad Dog Movies
Bank Holiday

Production office
PM: Emma Smith
23 Movie Avenue
Guerilla Town
KP12 9DR
Tel: 01555 123456
Fax: 01555 123455

Director: John Oldman
Producer: Claire Roper   Mob: 555 2468
1st A.D. Paul Edwards   Mob: 555 4321

Unit office
Loc. Mgr: David Moore
Portacabin 8
Guerilla Indus. Estate
Mob: 555 1234

Date: Monday 17th January 2002
UNIT CALL: 08:00
Breakfast will be on set at 07:30
Estimated Wrap: 18:00

WEATHER: Fine and Dry day, frost in morning,
sunshine, a little cloud in the afternoon, light winds

Location 1: Int of Emma's Office at the Industrial site
Location Contact: Mr Bill Travers Tel: 01555 456123

NO SMOKING ON ANY SET

Scene No	Scri pPg.	Int./ Ext.	Description		Story Day	Day/ Night	Pages	Cast
9	5	Int	EMMA'S OFFICE	Establishing shot	Day 1	Day	1/8 pgs	
3	1	Int	EMMA'S OFFICE	Chris walking towards Emma's office, through window	Day 1	Day	2/8 pgs	1, 2
1c	1	Int	EMMA'S OFFICE	Emma and Chris first conversation	Day 1	Day	1/8 pgs	1, 2

NO:	ARTISTE	CHARACTER	PICK –UP TIME	ON SET TO REHEARSE	M/UP/COST	TURNOVER
1	Josie Fellowes	Emma	08:15	08:30	08:45	09:00
2	Harvey Willis	Chris	08:15	08:30	08:45	09:00
SUPPORTING CAST/EXTRAS						

REQUIREMENTS	
PROPS:	Chris's bag & coat, Emma's mobile
ACTION VEHICLES:	Chris's car
MAKE-UP & COSTUME	As per Charlotte and Zoe
CAMERA DEPT:	As per James
CHAPERONE:	NONE
MEDICAL:	Casualty at Queen Victoria Hospital Tel: 01555 654321
CATERING:	Breakfast on set from 07:30, Lunch at 13:00, Tea break at 16:30
RUSHES:	To be given to Barry to take to Metrocolor drop off

ADVANCE SCHEDULE TUESDAY 18th JANUARY								
Scene No	a.o.b.	Script Pg.	Int./ Ext.	Description		Story Day	Day/ Night	Pages	Cast
1d		1	Ext	INDUSTRIAL ESTATE	Montage of estate for title sequence	Pre-Story	Day	1/8 pgs	
20a (i)	high crane	10	Ext	INDUSTRIAL ESTATE	High shot of Emma & Chris walking through estate	Day 3	Day	1 2/8 pgs	1, 2
20a (ii)	stunt	10	Ext	INDUSTRIAL ESTATE	Fight scene between Chris & guard	Day 3	Day	1 2/8 pgs	2, 7,

Call Sheet No 1 Monday 17th January 2002

On The CD

PRODUCTION CHECKLIST

Date *17 . 1 . 02*

Mad Dog Movies
Production Company

Bank Holiday
Production Title

CAST	✓	KEY CREW	✓
Deal memos	☐	Contracts signed	☐
Contracts signed	☐	Wardrobe - special	☐
Wardrobe fitted	☐	Armourer	☐
Special make-up	☐	Make-up & body make-up - special	☐
Hair/wigs	☐	Hair - special	☐
Dialogue coach	☐	Props - discuss	☐
Stand-ins	☐	Stunt Co-ordinator	☐
Stunt/doubles	☐	SPFX co-ordinator	☐
Musicians in Picture	☐	Action vehicles co-ordinator - Special	☐
Children & licences	☐	Greensman - special	☐
Chaperone/tutor	☐	Script supervisor - script timing	☐
Extras/crowd	☐	Paramedics	☐
		Unit Nurse/Health and Safety/First Aid Box	☐
		Technical advisors	☐
Livestock or Animals	☐	Handlers or Wranglers	☐

CAMERA	✓	LOCATION / STUDIO	✓
Equipment ordered - extra cameras	☐	Dressing rooms	☐
Film ordered	☐	Police	☐
Video assist	☐	Parking	☐
		Firemen & fire permits	☐
SOUND	✓	Location permits	☐
Equipment ordered	☐	Heaters/air conditioning	☐
Stock ordered	☐	Tables & benches	☐
Walkie-talkies	☐	Location facilities	☐
Pa system	☐	Hot & Cold water	☐

GRIP	✓	FOOD & DRINK	✓
Equipment ordered	☐	Breakfast	☐
Generator - special	☐	Lunch	☐
Crane	☐	Dinner	☐
		Snacks	☐
LABS	✓	Tea & Coffee	☐
Contact address & tel	☐		
Rushes drop off/Collection	☐	**MISCELLANEOUS**	✓
Special process	☐	Petty cash	☐
		1st AD Sheets (script breakdown)	☐
VEHICLES	✓	Transportation and Lunch Lists	☐
Motor homes/caravans	☐	Release forms	☐
Vehicles - picture or standby	☐	Call sheets	☐
Honey-Wagons/Toilet facilities	☐	Movement orders	☐
Water wagon	☐	Production reports	☐
Buses/coaches	☐		
Trucks	☐		

On The CD

CONTINUITY/EDIT NOTES

17 . 1 . 02
Date

Mad Dog Movies **Production Company**

Bank Holiday **Production Title**

Page 1 of 1

Production No. 1.

WEATHER Sunny, dry, windy, cold, no clouds	SCENE	SLATE
LOCATION Unit 8, Penzale Indus Estate	14	26

CAN ROLL	SOUND ROLL	Circle whichever appropriate						CAM INFO	
5	7	(INT) (DAY) (SYNC) (WILD)		LENS	DISTANCE	STOP	SP FILTERS		
		EXT NIGHT MUTE (TRACK)		16	5'	T 2.8	Wratten		

SHOT DESCRIPTION

Emma meets Chris for the first time at the Indus. Estate.

TAKE	DUR	REMARKS (if ng)	CONTINUITY NOTES (inlc. Costume/props/dialogue etc)
1	0.55ecs	ng	boom in shot
2	2mins	✓	fine " I'm looking for Emma Duggan"

On The CD

EXPENSE REPORT FOR PETTY CASH

Mad Dog Movies   Bank Holiday   B7610
Production Company   Production Title   Petty Cash Voucher No.

Larry Nash   Art Department   Amanda Roberts.
Crew Name   Department   Issued by

Entered into Accounts	Checked by Accountant	Approved by Production Manager
Amanda Roberts	Amanda Roberts	Clare Roper
Date: 27 . 1 . 02.	Date: 17 . 1 . 02	Date: 17 . 1 . 02 .

Crew Only		Accountant Only	
Petty Cash Advance Received	£300	Receipts Paid	£250
Total Receipts	£250	Cash in Hand	£ 50
(Over or Under)	£ 50	Total	£300

Crew Signed: Larry Nash.	Accountant Signed: Amanda Roberts.
Date: 17 . 1 . 02	Date: 17 . 1 . 02 .

Date			Company/Payee	Purpose	Cash/Cheque		Amount	
31	12	01	SUPER HIRE	KITCHEN FURNITURE	✓		£ 200	00
16	01	02	STUDIO + TV HIRE	PAINTINGS	✓		£ —50	00
							£	
							£	
							£	
							£	
							£	
							£	
							£	
							£	
							£	
							£	
							£	
							£	
							£	
							£	
							£	
							£	
							£	
							£	
							£	
							£	
							£	
							£	
							£	
							£	
							£	

DAILY PROGRESS REPORT SHEET

17 . 1 . 02	Bank Holiday	1	1
Date	Production Title	Page	of

John	Mad Dog Movies	Paul Edwards.
Director	Production Company	1st AD

Started: 17.1.02   Finishing Date: 17.2.02   **Scene Nos:** 14, 16, 24
Scenes scheduled:
Days to date: 1   Location: Perivale   Scenes shot today:
Scenes part shot:
Remaining Days: 27   Weather: Sunny cold dry   Scenes not shot:

TIME | SCRIPT:

Call time: 08.00
1st set up completed: 08.30
Lunch break: 13.00 to 14.00
Supper break: n/a to n/a
Breakfast break: n/a to n/a
Unit wrap: 16.30
Total hours: 7 1/2 hrs

		total scenes:		pages:				
		scenes deleted:		pages:				
		scenes shot to date:		pages:				
		scenes remaining:		pages:				
		No of setups	mins	no of pickups	mins	no of retakes	mins
Prev.							
Today:							
Total:							

ACTORS (s-start day, w-days worked, sb-standby, c-call, s-set, f-finish)   CROWDS

Name	s	w	sb	c	s	f	rate
Josie Fellowes	X						
Harvey Willis							

PICTURE NEGATIVE | SOUND

	exposed	N.G.	Print	waste
Prev.				
Today:				
Total:				

STILLS - COLOUR/B&W:

ARRIVALS:
TRANSPORT:
CATERING:
PROPS:
EFFECTS:
XTRA CREW:
ABSENTEES:
REMARKS:

SCRIPT BREAKDOWN SHEET

17·01·02	Bank Holiday	1	1
Date	Production Title	Page	of

John	Mad Dog Movies	Clare Roper
Director	Production Company	Producer

17	Chris takes Emma's dog out
Scene Number	Scene Description

CAST NOS	CAST/CHARACTER	INT/EXT	DAY/ NIGHT	W/R	M/U
1	Josie - Emma	INT	NIGHT	As per B	Chris sweat
2	Harvey - Chris				

STAND-INS	CROWD	LOCATION	ART DEPT/CONSTRUCTION		GRIPS
n/a	n/a	Outside Indw in Emma's Hse	Dress Emma's kitchen and hall		Long track hall

CAMERA	LIGHTING	EXTRA EQUIPMENT	ACTION VEHICLES

TRUCKS/TRAILERS	EXTRA CREW	PROPS/ANIMALS	SFX/WEAPONS
		Emma's Dog called Bertie	

MISC

"Bertie" will be on set from 14·00hrs. While he is here he will be the most important person on set. Best behaviour, as as soon as he arrives we will need to shoot.

On The CD

LOCATIONS CHECKLIST

Production Company: Mad Dog Movies
Producer: Claire Roper
Production Title: Bank Holiday
Director: Ben Selman

Date 17.1.02
Location Manager: David Moore
Prod. Manager/Asst. Director: Emma Smith / Paul Edwards

Location	Contact Tel & Fax No.	All Dates Required	Release Form Issued	Release Form Returned	Schedule A Issued	Police Informed	Movement Order	Nearest Hospital Casualty	Meter Readings	Elec. Source	Rooms & Green Room	Parking
Int. Church	Rev Michaels	13th Feb 02	Yes	Yes	Yes	Yes		Ealing 5670728	n/a	main church	Yes	very limited

On The CD

580

David Moore
Location Manager

Date **17 · 2 · 02**

Mad Dog Movies
Production Company

Bank Holiday
Production Title

16 · 1 · 02
Script Date

Claire Roper
Producer

John Oldman
Director

Emma Smith
Prod. Manager

Movement Order No 3...

Location 1: (*story location*)

Address: Flat 7, White Angel Road, Guerilla Town KP3 1PD.
Tel: 01555 123333
Contact there: Mr. Jones.

Directions by Car: (see attached map)

This is off the A3, take the Guerilla Town turn off and the road is the second on the left, and on the right hand side.

Trains:

Paddington : 07.30   07.45   08.00
Guerilla Town: 07.45   08.00   08.15

Buses:

The number 37, please call london travel line on 0345 484949.

Parking:

Generator: In car park, in bay no 7.
Catering Truck: In car park, in bay no 8.
Dining Bus: In car park in bay no. 10
Honey-Wagon: In car park, in bay no 1.

Facilities:

Toilets: Cast to use ones in flat 7. Crew use honey wagon.
Green Room: The second bedroom in flat. look for signs.
Crew Room: The fourth bedroom. Look for signs.
Dressing Rooms: First bedroom in flat.
Make-up/Wardrobe: First bedroom in flat.

NO SMOKING, FOOD OR DRINK ON SET PLEASE!!!!!!

On The CD

A. O. B. | sdc - Steadicam | indpt unit - unit works seperately | 2nd unit: Works simultaneously | ngt shoot: night shoot | Day 3a - Extra story day

Shooting Schedule No......

Movie Title

Scene No A.O.B	Scrpt Pg	Int/Ext	Description	Story Day	Day/Night	Pages	Cast
15	9	Int	Boys' Flat LIVING ROOM — Joe comes back from pub, smokes joint, leaves room	Day 1	Day for Night	1 6/8 pgs	2, 4
18	12	Int	Boys' Flat LIVING ROOM — Bob relights joint, having put Joe to bed	Day 1	Day for Night	1/8 pgs	4
68a*	54	Int	Boys' Flat LIVING ROOM — Lady 1 in business attire. Long stare then slaps Bob.	Day 5	Day for Night	1/8 pgs	4, 25
52	43	Int	Boys' Flat BATHROOM — Douglas experiences the mirror	Day 3	Day for Night	1 pg	3
107	79	Int	Boys' Flat BATHROOM — Joe flossing, Bob discussing Alison	Day 10	Day for Night	1 1/8 pgs	2, 4
130	94	Int	Boys' Flat BATHROOM — Alison and Joe being coupley and cleaning teeth in harmony	Day 15	Day	3/8 pgs	2, 5

End of Day 1   4 4/8 pgs (4.5 mins)   Monday 23rd August 2002

Scene No A.O.B	Scrpt Pg	Int/Ext	Description	Story Day	Day/Night	Pages	Cast
25	16	Int	Boys' Flat LIVING ROOM — Joe tells Bob that he hallucinated last night	Day 2	Day	1 4/8 pgs	2, 4
32	24	Int	Boys' Flat LIVING ROOM — Sitting in flat with their angels, having cups of tea	Day 3	Day	4/8 pgs	1, 2, 3, 4
42	29	Int	Boys' Flat LIVING ROOM — Bob teaching Audrey what dancing is, interrupted by Joe	Day 3a	Day	2 4/8 pgs	1, 2, 3, 4
50a	41	Int	Boys' Flat LIVING ROOM — Reaction shot of Audrey hearing this news through Joe's head	Day 4	Day	1/8 pgs	1
75	57	Int	Boys' Flat LIVING ROOM — Joe and Alison sit, she talks of newspaper story	Day 6	Day	7/8 pgs	2, 5
84	62	Int	Boys' Flat LIVING ROOM — Joe tells them all that Audrey has gone, reactions	Day 7	Day	1 2/8 pgs	2, 3, 4, 5

End of Day 2   6 6/8 pgs (just under 7 mins)   Tuesday 24th August 2002

Scene No A.O.B	Scrpt Pg	Int/Ext	Description	Story Day	Day/Night	Pages	Cast
49a	41	Int	Indian restaurant (mocked up in house) — Bob admits to Joe that he thinks that he is in love with Audrey	Day 3a	Day	4/8 pgs	2, 3
50b	41	Int	Indian restaurant (mocked up in house) — Joe's reaction, battle to order with Waiter 1	Day 3a	Day	1 4/8 pgs	2, 3, 10
50c	43	Int	Indian restaurant (mocked up in house) — Finally order with Waiter 2	Day 3a	Day	4/8 pgs	2, 3, 11
50d	43	Int	Indian restaurant (mocked up in house) — Joe and Bob fooling around with the orange peel, waiters reactions	Day 3a	Day	4/8 pgs	2, 3, 10, 11

End of Day 3   3 pgs (3 mins)   Wednesday 25th August 2002

SOUND REPORT

ROLL No.

PRODUCTION COMPANY	PRODUCTION TITLE	PROD. No.	DATE

TAPE SPEED

3.75	7.5	15

DOLBY NOISE REDUCTION

A	B	C	SR	OTHER OR NONE

RECORDER MAKE & MODEL

CAMERA FORMAT

35mm	16mm	VIDEO

PILOT Hz **NR TONE**

50	60	

TONE REFERENCE LEVEL

RECORDING FORMAT

CAMERA SPEED FPS

24	25	30	PAL	NTSC

DIGITAL SAMPLE RATE **USER BITS**

44.1	48		:	:	:

USER BIT COMMENTS

AUDIO TIME CODE PPS

24	25	30	29.97

TRANSFER TO:

35mm	16mm	R-DAT	OTHER

RECORDER MAKE & MODEL

SLATE	TAKE	FOOTAGE or TIMECODE	MONO or STEREO	CHANNEL 1	CHANNEL 2

On The CD

PRINT CIRCLED TAKES ONLY

mcps PPL PRS
GIVING MUSIC ITS DUE

LICENSOR APPROVED MUSIC CUE SHEET

Important Note

The correct completion of this cue sheet is a strict condition of the granting of the broadcast licences by the various copyright owners and agencies. The shaded sections indicate essential items of information which **must** be supplied in all cases. The unshaded sections signify information which should be supplied if it is available.

Please turn to the reverse side of this form for explanatory notes, a key to the standard codes, and helpful telephone contacts should you require any further assistance.

Production Details

Film Title	AN URBAN GHOST STORY	Production Co.	LIVING SPIRIT PICTURES '97 LTD	Country of Origin	UK	Trailer /Promo/ Full Programme (T/P/F)	F
Episode Title	-	Production No.	-	Production Year	1997	Tx Time	
Episode No.		Director	GENEVIEVE JOLLIFFE	First Tx Date		Film Duration	90'
Film/Item No.		Principal Actors	Jason CONNERY	Channel		Music Duration	28'40
Alternative Title(s)			Heather Ann FOSTER				
			Stephanie BUTTLE				
			James COSMO				

Music Details

1. Music Cue Title and ISWC No. (if known)	2. Composer(s) Author(s) Arranger(s) CAE No(s) (If known)	3. Publisher(s) CAE No(s) (If known)	4. Performer(s) / Video/Record Title	5. Catalogue No. and Label	6. ISRC No.	7. Music Orig. Code	8. Music Use Code	9. Music Cue Dur.	10. Video Clip Dur.
"Vesti la Giubba" from "I Pagliacci"	Leoncavallo	Public domain	Cornel Staura World of Opera	2120.2007-2 Electrecord/ Selected Sound Carrier	-	C	F	0'18"	-
1M1 The Day I Died	Rupert Gregson-Williams CAE: 263121401 Guy Edward Fletcher CAE: 161847559	Living Spirit Pictures 97 Ltd/ Trackdown Music Ltd CAE: 269 127 448	Rupert Gregson-Williams Guy Edward Fletcher	-	-	X	B	0'30"	-
Clyde 2 Jingle	Muff Murfin	Happy Face Music	Muff Murfin Clyde 2 Jingle	-	-	?	F	0'05"	-
1M2 Suicide?	Rupert Gregson-Williams CAE: 263121401	Living Spirit Pictures 97 Ltd/ Trackdown Music Ltd CAE: 269 127 448	Rupert Gregson-Williams	-	-	X	B	0'24"	-

Page 1 of ..6....   Cue Sheet Compiled By ..LIVING SPIRIT PICTURES 97 LTD...Cue Sheet Supplied By . TRACKDOWN MUSIC   Date Supplied ....

PRODUCTION GRATUITIES FORM

Bart Holiday   12th Feb 02.

Production Title   Date

Date	Item	Amount
9th Feb	Payment to gym next door to location use of power	£40.00
11th Feb	Payment to neighbour of location uses of power + water	£50.00
20th Feb	Bottle of whisky for use of location	£15.00
1st March	Wrap party misc.	£100.00

On The CD

LEGAL DISCLAIMER and LICENCE

You may not alter, merge, modify, or adapt the Screenplay program in anyway including disassembling or decompiling. The Screenplay software is distributed AS IS. HARD COPY DISCLAIMS ALL WARRANTIES ON THIS PROGRAM INCLUDING, WITHOUT LIMITATION, ALL IMPLIED WARRANTIES OF MERCHANTABILITY AND FITNESS. IN NO EVENT WILL HARD COPY BE LIABLE FOR ANY DAMAGES ARISING OUT OF THE USE OR THE INABILITY TO USE THIS PROGRAM.

THIS PROGRAM IS NOT SUPPORTED. IF YOU REQUIRE SOFTWARE SUPPORT, YOU MUST PURCHASE IT.

On the CD accompanying this book there are several files that you might find useful.

Production documents are saved in a directory / folder called *Production Documents*.

Contracts are saved in a directory / folder called *Contracts*.

These documents are saved in MS Word format. You will need a copy of MS Word, either v6, 95, 97 or 200o for the PC, or 96 / 98 for the Mac.

The screenplay formatter is saved in a directory called *Screenplay*. It is also compatible with the above versions of MSWord.

There are also several shareware utilities that should be registered with the authors should you find them useful and continue to use them. These programs. There is a sound demo which you can play back from your CD player and a short video documentary.

Updates and links are available from our website at www.livingspirit.com.

Section 4
Film Makers
Software

Screenplay

Writing a screenplay is hard enough without having to worry about the complicated technical formatting required by the film industry. *Screenplay*, which runs with Microsoft Word (versions 6, 95, 97 and 2000 for Windows and versions 6 and 98 for Mac) does all the hard work for you, freeing you to spend time on your script and not on your formatting.

It's worth looking at the sample *Screenplay* layout page supplied to see just how specific it needs to be, then load up the software and start working.

Benefits of using *Screenplay*

Screenplay uses *styles* to quickly layout your script without you having to do the hard work.

Screenplay has four script layouts making it easy to write scripts for film, TV, radio and theatre.

Screenplay does all the formatting of a script i.e. adding scene numbers, breaking pages with MORE and CONT'D etc.

Screenplay is completely customisable, allowing you to format your work any way you like, alongside the predefined professional formats supplied. You could even format your script for printing on Filofax paper and then with a few keystrokes convert it back to A4.

You can change one layout (e.g film) into another (e.g TV) in minutes.

Screenplay will be able to interface with the *Screenplay Scheduling Package* to help in production (available Autumn 2000).

You can import scripts from different programmes to work in *Screenplay*.

You can export your script to enable you to work on your script away from your computer on any other system capable of editing text, then re-import back into *Screenplay*.

So free your mind, get the creative juices flowing and get writing.

Installation

Start MSWord and then open the Setup.Doc file which you'll find in the CD's *Screenplay* directory. Setup.doc will take you through the rest of the installation process.

Screenplay - Quick Tutorial

Screenplay is a powerful script formatter, but it's also simple and easy to use. If you don't want to use it's extended features, you can stick with the industry standard defaults and write your screenplay with ease.

This simple tutorial will get you up and running in minutes.

1. After installation, open your version of MS Word.

2. Go to the *File Menu* and select *New*. The Templates dialogue box will appear. From the files onscreen select *Screenplay* and hit OK (or double click on it).

3. The *Screenplay* splash screen will appear. Follow the onscreen prompts.

4. You are now in the *Screenplay* software. Take a moment to note the new tool bar and menus. Don't worry if you don't know what they do just yet, sit tight.

5. There are several simple styles that you will use regularly when writing. To access these styles go to the *Script Styles* menu, the toolbar, or best of all, learn the keyboard short cuts.

We'll start by writing a simple scene. If you don't want to start with FADE IN: delete it from screen. If you do, hit enter to move down to the next line.

To add a Slug Line type INT. LIGHTHOUSE - NIGHT and press Alt+S. The text will turn blue and upper case and will now be in the *Slug Line* style so that *Screenplay* knows what to do with it when it comes to formatting your final work.

You can also use the *Smart Slug Line* facility which builds a database of locations to speed up writing and ultimately for exporting / importing into the *Schedule Module* (sold separately) when you come to making your movie.

Hit the enter key and start writing some descriptive text. Note that it is coloured dark blue. This is the *Action style*. Press Alt+S and it will turn it into a Slug Line, which is obviously incorrect. Hit Alt+A and it will turn back into Action.

Hit the enter button and type the name Joe. Press Alt+C to change this to the *Character style* (red upper case). Hopefully you are now getting the idea that to change the style of any text so that *Screenplay* knows what to do with it when formatting, is simply a matter of press the Alt button with another key, Alt+C for Character, for instance.

The main styles are - Alt+S for Slug Line, Alt + A for Action, Alt + C for Character which we have just covered. In addition there is Alt + O for Action in Dialogue (simple descriptions below; a character's name or in the dialogue before they talk), Alt + M for Stage or Camera Direction, and Alt + N for Scene Notes (which can be omitted from the final screenplay but used for viewing, planning the overall structure of the story or to remind the writer of something).

There are other styles but for now let's keep it simple, you can get your hands a little dirtier later on.

Write a few scenes and try to get used to using these short cut keys. Alternatively, load the sample screenplay that comes with the software (on the CD) and play around with it.

6. **Saving**. Writing is tough, so save your work regularly. A simple tip here is to hit Ctrl + S (or the Apple Key + S on a Mac) as regularly as you can, then if your computer crashes you will have saved your work recently.

There is a safety copy function in *Screenplay* which when set (from the *File Menu*, select *Safety Copy Setup*) will save your work to a second place at the same time. If you want to use this feature read the manual.

7. Now you are ready to *Format the Screenplay*. Go to the *Format Menu* and select *Add / Remove Script Formatting*, or alternatively hit Ctrl + Shift + F. The *Script Formatting Wizard* will begin.

7 1 Wizard - Title Page
This will build a title page for your screenplay. Fill it out as needed then hit the Next button.

7.2 Wizard - Notes, Shortcuts, Database & TV / Radio
Leave this screen with the default settings for now. If you want to know more about these settings, read the manual. Hit the Next button.

7.3 Wizard - Scene Numbering
This box deals with how scene numbers are inserted in your screenplay. Leave the defaults for now and hit Next.

7.4 Wizard - Page Breaks
When a scene or dialogue drops off the end of a page, *Screenplay* will insert *More* and *Cont'd* to inform the reader of

this fact. You can adapt these settings as you like, but for now, leave the defaults and hit the Next button. See manual for more details.

7.5 Wizard - Header Information
Fill in the title of your screenplay to add the script's name at the top of the page. Leave the other defaults for now. Hit the Next button.

7. 6 Wizard - Footer Information
If you want a copyright notice or other information at the foot of the page, fill in the details here. Hit the Next button.

7.7 Wizard - Page Numbers and Printer Setup
This box deals with the placement of page numbers. Leave the defaults and hit the Next button.

7.8 Wizard - Script Formatting
This is the final box. Hit the *Format* button and your screenplay will be formatted. It will take a few moments, dependent on the length of script, and once completed the screenplay will be 'locked'. You can unlock at any time with the *Key* button on the toolbar. Locking is a simple way of stopping a formatted screenplay from being changed accidentally. If you want to move around your script to see how good it looks, use the mouse. The keyboard keys are disabled when the script is locked.

8. **Printing** - You can now print your screenplay from the *File* menu, select *Print*.

9. You can at any time remove the formatting and continue editing and redrafting. To remove formatting go to the *Format Menu*, then select *Add / Remove Script Formatting*. The Wizard dialogue box will appear. Press the *Remove Formatting* and the scene numbers, page breaks etc., will be stripped out of the script and you can continue to write.

10. There are many other sophisticated features to *Screenplay*. Read the manual, watch the tutorial files on the CD, and write that Oscar Winner!

In brief...

Save regularly and learn the keyboard shortcut keys. Happy writing.

The Basics of *Screenplay*

When you first open *Screenplay* it is set up to write a film script and in this layout all the main styles are set to use the font 'courier new', size 11 point.

There are 6 principal styles within *Screenplay* and 9 ancillary styles. The six principal ones are:

Slug Line - for scene identification
Action - where any action that takes place is described
Character - identifies any speaking person
Dialogue - what a character says
Action in Dialogue (Parenthetical) - action description within dialogue
Camera and Stage Directions - for directorial information; for example, CUT TO: FADE UP: MIX TO: etc.

```
INT. CHURCH - DAY

Lizzie askes who she is…

LIZZIE enters - light streams through the stained glass windows -
candles lit dimly. It's peaceful and serene.

                          LIZZIE
             How do you know who I am?
                          (she Smiles)
             Aren't you going to tell on me?

        CUT TO:
```

Scene Notes - used by the writer to briefly describe each scene. This can be hidden in the final printed draft. N.B. Scene Notes are most useful when producing script breakdowns and in the early stages of script development. This is also useful in the *Outline View* editing mode.

Parallel Dialogue - not actually a style although it appears in the *Script Styles* menu. When you wish to have two characters talking at the same time write their dialogue consecutively and then with the cursor on the first character's name select *Parallel Dialogue* from the toolbar or use the *Keyboard Short Cut* Alt+R. A table will appear that places the dialogue side by side (although you can see the table lines they will not be printed out). To edit this dialogue at a latter date use the *Parallel Dialogue* again which reverts the dialogue back to a consecutive state and then turns it back into *Parallel Dialogue* once you have made changes.

<u>Using Styles</u>
Each of *Screenplay's* styles has a different colour to identify it and a *Keyboard Short Cut* to activate it. This should make using them quick and easy. Changing a line of script from the Action style into the Slug Line style can be done in three ways:

First, from the *Script Style* menu select *Slug line*.

Second click the right mouse button (Ctrl + Click on the Mac) on the script line and select *Slug Line* from the menu that appears.

Third, press the 'Alt' key in conjunction with 'S' (Alt+S). The Slug Line will appear in blue. Some of the styles are 'smart' about what style follows them. For example the Action style will follow a Slug Line and Dialogue follows Character.

It's quicker to learn the keyboard shortcuts than it is to use the mouse. Spend a little time here and you'll save hours later.

The 9 ancillary styles are for things like the Front Page, Title and Act headings and work in exactly the same way as the principle styles but are less frequently used.

You MUST ONLY use *Screenplay* styles or the automatic formatting functions will cease to work.

See *More Information* to find out more about styles.

Screenplay's Script Layouts

Screenplay has four pre-set script layouts (See *Script Page Layout Options*) which automatically re-program the styles to suit their needs. So if you want to write a TV script, *Screenplay* will re-set all the styles to suit this layout. You can create your own layouts by programming any of the styles to look as you want them to look. As long as you change the styles using the *Font and Paragraph Styles* Function, all of *Screenplay's* utilities and functions will work. By using *Font and Paragraph Styles* and *Script Page Layout Options* you can create a limitless range of script layouts and you can perform these processes at any point in the writing process.

Screenplay's Functions and Tools

A working knowledge of word processors and MSWord has been assumed in writing this section. *Screenplay* hides some of MSWord's features (drawing and object imbedding for example) because they are not needed.

FILE MENU

New

Selecting this option will show a list of all the templates available to Word. Selecting 'Normal' creates a new 'blank' document (based on the 'Normal' template). Selecting 'Screenplay' creates a new document/ script based on the *Screenplay* template with all the formatting functions available to write a script.

Open

Selecting this option opens an existing Word document. If you open a document/script that has been created using the *Screenplay* template then *Screenplay* will automatically work at the same time. You do not have to start *Screenplay* separately.

Close

This option closes the active document / script. If you have made changes since you last saved it you will be asked if you want to save them.

Save

If you click on *save* or on the save button on the toolbar, your script document will be saved in its current form. If you have not given it a name then you will be asked to give it one. Pressing 'Ctrl + S' will also save the document. Doing this every ten minutes is a good habit to get into and quickly becomes second nature.

Save As

Opens the *Save As* dialogue box which is predominately used to change the name of the document file you're working on. e.g. you might want to save *Draft1.doc* as *Draft2.doc*. *Draft1.doc* will remain on your disc in its previously saved state and a new file *Draft2.doc* will now exist both on disc and on your screen.

You can also use *Save As* to change the document's file format (i.e. save the script document as a WordPerfect file or Text file). This will be useful if you have to work on your script file on a different computer. N.B. Saving a script document in a file format other than Word 6, 7, 97, 98 or 2000 will lose some information, (e.g. the *Short Cut Database*). More importantly the script's layout may change. (See *Add/Remove Style Prefixes* and *Import Text Clean* for more information about importing and exporting your script file).

The *Options* button in the *Save As* dialogue box opens another dialogue box which lets you select various save options; for example you can set the *Auto Save* function (which makes a backup of your script at a timed interval of your choice in case your system crashes). You can also set a password in this dialogue box so that only you can see and work on your script.

Save Copy As
If, for example, you have named your script document *Script1.doc* and wish to make a text copy, use *Save Copy As*, the subsequent text file (*Script1.txt*) will be saved on your hard disk but *Script1.doc* will remain on your screen unchanged. If you had used *Save As* to perform this function you would have to re-open *Script1.doc* as the file on your screen would now be *Script1.txt*. This function therefore speeds the process of changing a document's file format and avoids confusion. You can also use this function to make backups of your script (also see *Save Safety Copy – Setup*).

Safety Copy - Setup
Opens a dialogue box that allows you to set a back-up location for your work. Once this is set, a copy of your script document will be made in your chosen location (e.g a zip disc) each time you use *Save* or *Save As*. A document file in this location that has the same name as the one being copied will be replaced automatically. MSWord has a number of its own backup facilities that can be accessed from the *Options* button in the *Save As* dialogue box.

Print
Prints out all or part of your script depending on what options you choose from the Print dialogue box.

Print Preview
Shows you how your script will look when printed.

Print Setup (Windows)
Lets you set up the printer you want to use and other printer options.

Page Setup (Mac)
Lets you choose your printer and page options.

Exit
Closes all open documents (asking if you want to save them first if necessary) and shuts down Word/Screenplay.

EDIT MENU

Undo.... And Redo...

If for example you *Cut* and *Paste* some text from one place to another and then realised this was a mistake you can use *Undo* to correct it. *Undo* can't help in all circumstances though, you can't undo some of Screenplays functions using *Undo* because too many operations may have been performed, however most of Screenplays functions can be 'undone' by using them again. Don't use undo if you've changed one style into another for example, just set the style back to what it was originally.

Cut, Copy & Paste

Useful for moving text around. You must highlight the text you want to *Cut* or *Copy* by holding down the left mouse button and dragging the cursor over the text you want to move (holding the 'shift' key and using the cursor keys does the same job). Select either *Cut* or *Copy* and then move the cursor to the position where the text is to be placed – then select *Paste* from the menu. The process can also be achieved without using the menu by highlighting the text as before, releasing the left mouse button and then clicking with the left mouse button on the highlighted text. You can now drag the highlighted text to the new position (holding the 'Ctrl' key whilst doing this moves a copy of the text leaving the original in its place).

Paste Special

May be useful when bringing in text from another application.

Find & Replace

These are MSWord functions that can be used to find specific text and if required replace it with something else. Use *Replace* for example to change all the names of a character in your script from perhaps Mike to Michael. You can search for specific styles and special characters too by using the *Format* and *Special* tools too (see *More Information*).

Go To... and Bookmark...

You can use this function to put bookmarks in your script, so that you can jump to these sections quickly at a later time. This is particularly useful if you have a long script.

N.B. Bookmarks can be removed by using the script formatting tools especially the *Font and Paragraph Styles* tool and by changing the style of a paragraph. To avoid some problems put bookmarks in the middle of a sentence not at the beginning.

SOFTWARE

VIEW MENU

Normal

This view shows the script file in its 'easiest to read' format, by filling the screen.

Outline View

Outline View is an MSWord function that provides a very powerful way of looking at your script. In *Outline View* you can use the toolbar buttons to show you either just the Slug Lines (by clicking '1') or the Slug Lines and Scene Notes (by clicking '2') or everything by clicking 'All'.

If, for example, you want to move scenes around, click '1' to

collapse the script view to just Slug Lines, click on the cross next to the Slug Line of the scene that you wish to move and drag it to it's new position; the whole scene will be moved. Double clicking on a cross toggles between displaying the whole scene or just the Slug Line.

You may find the *Temporary Scene Numbers* function helpful in moving scenes around.

Page View

This displays the whole page (as pieces of paper) on the screen (depending on your zoom setting). For example, this is useful when looking at a formatted script as you are able to see the headers and footers and how the script has been laid out.

Toolbars

Screenplay uses its own set of toolbars to keep all the MSWord functions that you don't need out of sight. You can use

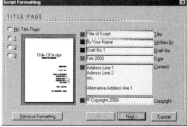

the toolbar function to display other toolbars. In MSWord 6 and 95 the two toolbars that are displayed on start-up are in fact reprogrammed versions of MSWord's Standard and Formatting toolbars. In MSWord 97, 98(Mac) and 2000 the toolbars that are displayed are Script - Standard and Script – Format. *Screenplay* remembers which toolbars were displayed before it was started and re-sets these when it is closed. If you want to open other non *Screenplay* documents it is best to open a new version of MSWord.

FORMAT MENU

Add/Remove Script Formatting

This is the most powerful function of the *Screenplay* software. The script formatting wizard will take you through the whole process of completing your script for final printing out and delivery. The entire process is reversible so you can continue to work on your script without the formatting elements getting in the way.

Wizard - Title Page

Produces a front page for your script. There are four options to choose from; *No Title Page* or a choice of three different layouts. Use the colour codes and the appropriate text box to fill in your script details and a title page will be generated at the front of your script. Of course, you can design your front page independently of *Screenplay* if you like.

Wizard - Notes, Short Cut Database & TV/Radio

Details from Short Cut Database

If you have used the *Short Cut Database* to enter character, prop and location information this information can be printed at the front of your script.

Script Notes

If you have added *Front and End Notes* or *Scene Notes* and you don't want them to appear in your printed script you can hide them (they will re-appear as soon as the formatting is removed).

TV/Radio Layout

While you have been writing, character name and dialogue have been split over two lines, however for some TV and radio script requirements, character and dialogue should appear on the same line. This function allows this process which is reversed when formatting is removed. You can also set an indent for the dialogue if you want the character's name to stand out.

Wizard - Scene Numbering

There are two options; *No Scene Numbers* or *Scene Numbering*. Scene numbers can be any number between 1 and 1000. Use *Number Style* to set scene numbering as either numbers or letters (useful when writing **Pink Pages**) and *Scene Text* to add either a number or a word in front of the scene number (also useful when writing *Pink Pages*). Use the *Position of Numbers* option to decide where you want your scene numbers to appear (for example in a film script scene numbers usually appear on both sides of the Slug Line in the margins). *Hang left scene number* puts the left scene number in the margin and *One scene per page* starts a new scene at the top of a new page.

Wizard - Page Breaks

There are many conventions about how scenes should be broken over pages. *Screenplay's* script-formatting wizard tries to cater for all of them. You may need to experiment to find what suits you. There are a number of things to be aware of. You can change the text in any of the text boxes to suit your needs. But of special note are the...

Top of Page Text

Some film scripts require that when a scene breaks over a page, or more than one page, more information than just (CONTINUED) be put at the top of the next page(s). Sometimes the scene number and the number of the page of that scene need to appear at the top of the page as well, e.g 5 CONTINUED (3) would represent the 3rd page of scene 5. By using the asterisk (*) and hash (#) characters you can dictate where that information appears in the continuation text.

Broken Dialogue Text

When dialogue is split over two pages the script formatter puts the speaking character's name and whatever you have typed in this text box, for example (CONT'D), at the beginning of the second page. Some scripts also require that dialogue by the same character which is broken by a line of action description should have (CONT'D) placed after his or her name in the continuing dialogue. Select the *Broken by Action option* if you want this to happen in your script.

New Act Titles

Mainly for stage plays. When using act titles, (Act 1, Act 2...), you can use this option to make sure that each act always starts on a new page.

Wizard - Header Information

Headers appear at the top of each page. The wizard allows you to either put the same header on each page or a different header on odd and even pages. (Useful for double-sided printing and publishing). If you do want to print the script out on both sides of the paper you might find *Mirror Margin's* useful. If this option is selected pages will be printed out as mirror images; if you've set a *Binding* distance in the *Script Page Layout Options* function this distance will always be set on the binding side, headers and footers will no longer just be left or right they will mirror each other.

Wizard - Footer Information

Same as Header. However, you also have the option of showing the date and the Script's file name in the footer for later reference.

Wizard - Page Numbers and Print Set-Up

Page numbers appear in the footer (the footer option does not need to be enabled) and numbers can be either numbers or letters (useful for *Pink Pages*). *Print from* lets you select the paper tray you are going to use to print your script. (Not available on the Mac – use *Page Set-Up* for this option).

Final Note

Once the script is formatted it is locked so that editing cannot take place. You will need to use the mouse and scroll bars to look through the script as the cursor keys will not work (page up, page down etc). Locking the script is only a precaution to protect the formatted script, it is not a security function. (If you wish to secure your script see *Save As)*. You can easily unlock your script by clicking on the 'key'  button on the toolbar or by using the *Lock/ Unlock Script* function in the Tools menu.

Removing Formatting - Button

To continue writing your script you need to open the *Add/Remove Script Formatting* wizard and click on *Remove Formatting*. This will remove anything added during the script formatting process (scene numbers, page breaks, etc.). Losing scene numbers may be inconvenient when it comes to editing your script or getting feedback from other people, so use the *Temporary Scene Numbers* tool to add scene numbers for editing purposes. These temporary scene numbers remain during the *Script Formatting/Remove Formatting* processes and are easily removed when you want to get rid of them.

Script Page Layout Options

This function provides the facility for changing or setting the basic layout of your script - film, TV, radio or stage play. You can use this function at any time in the writing process and it will actually convert one layout to another. You can also select the paper size and set the margins for the layout (the paper *Size* option is not available on the Mac, so use *Page Setup* in the File menu before using *Script Page Layout*). If you select the *Use Pre-Set Font Settings* the *Font and Paragraph Styles* function will also be activated while *Script Layout* makes changes to your script. Changing the layout of a long script may take some time.

Font and Paragraph Styles

To understand fully what styles are, see the section on *Styles*.

Style To Edit

This lists all the styles used by *Screenplay*. Use this list to choose which style you wish to change; at the top of the list is *All Styles* if you wish to make sweeping changes. Whichever *Style* is selected in this list will be changed when the *Apply* button is pressed.

Font Settings

Set the font, size and options like bold and italic.

Special Settings

Different script layouts sometimes require certain styles to have symbols around them. For example, in a film script *Action Included in Dialogue* sometimes called Parenthetical has (brackets) around it. Using *Special Settings* you can make these brackets appear round this style automatically every time you use it.

Paragraph Settings

Fairly obvious. Some styles need to be set in from the normal margin (for example Dialogue in a film script is narrower than Action and using the paragraph settings you can adjust the left and right indent).

Paragraph Spacing

Sometimes writers use a double carriage return to space out their script, for example before a new Slug Line. *Screenplay* works best if you set a distance in points for this spacing and don't use double carriage returns. The default *Paragraph Spacing* for a Slug Line in a film script is 30 points.

Spell Check Language

Each style can have a separate spell checking language (just one of the many functions of MSWord). Use this function to set the language you require. All styles within *Screenplay* by default are set to UK English. You can use this option to set this to French, German etc.

Default Button

At the top of the *Font and Paragraph Styles* dialogue box you will see an information line i.e. 'A4 paper-Screenplay'; when you press the *Default* button the pre-set settings will appear in all the various font and paragraph options for this layout. For example, if you selected *All Styles* in the *Style to edit* list then press the *Default* button the word 'default' will appear in most of the text boxes. By clicking *Apply* the default setting for each style will be applied to the whole script.

Text Colours On/Off

This function simply turns on or off the different style colours.

Change Case, Underline, Bold and Italic

Can be used to emphasise and highlight areas of the script, but be aware that changing a style from one type to another or running the *Font and Paragraph Styles* function may remove this highlighting.

TOOLS MENU

Script Short Cut Database

This function performs two tasks. The first is a way of storing information about your key characters, props and locations, which will be used in conjunction with the *Script Scheduling Software*. This information can also be added to the front of your script in *Screenplay's* Formatting Wizard. (See *Add/Remove Script Formatting*).

The second function is to program Word's *AutoCorrect* facility. The *AutoCorrect* facility is usually used for correcting typos, but it can also be used to abbreviate long words. For example, you could type 'Es' and spacebar and MSWord could replace this with 'Esmerelda'. So, as well as storing important information the *Short Cut Database* sets *AutoCorrect* with all your short cuts. The advantage of using the *Short Cut Database* is that all your short cuts are stored with your script and should you wish to work on it on another computer all your short cuts can quickly be restored. Another example of how this is useful, is when you have a couple of scripts and you want to use the same abbreviation but with different words, such as 'C' for Claire in the first and 'C' for Chris in the second. Each time you open either script you just need to open the *Short Cut Database*, click on the *Update* button, and your short cuts for that script will be restored.

To make a *Short Cut Database* entry, first type the abbreviation you want to use in the *Replace* text box, then type the full text in the *With* box, select what it is, i.e. character, prop or location from the *Type* list and add a description if you want to. Finally press the *Add* button, and you will see your new entry appear in the *Replace-With* list box. Continue to do this until you have entered all your short cuts and finally click on the *Update* button to confirm all your changes (none of your changes will be kept if you press the *Cancel* button). You can also edit and remove entries.

Smart Slug Line

This function can speed up typing Slug Lines, by having a set of options that you can just click on. If your Slug Line is supposed to read EXT. LONDON – DAY, open *Smart Slug Line* click on the *EXT* option, set the next text box to whatever you want in between (in this case a full stop and a space), then select the location 'London' from the list, then set the next text box to space dash space, then select *DAY*, then click OK. The new Slug Line appears in the script at the cursor. N.B. It is not necessary to change the 'in-between text' unless you want to.

The button *Add/Remove Locations* opens the *Short Cut Database* so that you can add all your location information.

The *Smart Slug Line* function is activated either by selecting it from the Tools menu, or by choosing to use the Slug Line style on a line with no text in it. The *Smart Slug Line* function will not operate if there is already text in a paragraph and you change it to the Slug Line style.

Lock/Unlock Script

Locking the script stops any accidental changes being made to the script as the keyboard is

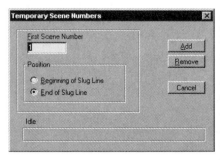

'turned off'. It is not a security feature because, for example, WordPad can still open the script. So if you want to protect your script from other users, use the password function by pressing the *Options* button in the *Save As* dialogue box.

Temporary Scene Numbers

This function adds a number in brackets to either the beginning or the end of Slug Lines and it also removes them. *Temporary Scene Numbers* are seen by the formatting function as part of the Slug Line, and so remain during the *Add/Remove Script Formatting* processes. Use *Temporary Scene Numbers* when you are editing the script and as a reference when other people are also working on the script (particularly useful when using script *Revisions*). You can add your own *Temporary Scene Numbers* by using the same 'number within brackets' format. The *Remove* button will remove any number inside brackets that's part of a Slug

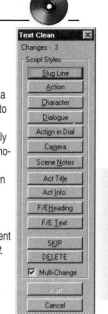

Line, so be careful how you use it.

Import Text Clean

This function is for importing text from a script not written using *Screenplay*, for example, you might have created your own script styles in MSWord or be using a different script writing package. Of course when you *Cut* and *Paste* this script into a *Screenplay* document none of the formatting functions work properly. You will need to convert this text into something that *Screenplay* will recognise. Potentially there are hundreds of possible variations and *Import Text Clean* tries to accommodate them all. *Import Text Clean* can also be used in conjunction with the *Add/ Remove Style Prefixes* function for importing and exporting your script to work on a different platform.

How to use *Import Text Clean*

Either *Cut* and *Paste* the text you want to convert into a new *Screenplay* document or into an existing one, then open the *Import Text Clean* function and press *Start*. The script will be analysed paragraph by paragraph and once a paragraph is found that doesn't conform to one of the *Screenplay* styles, it will be highlighted and all the buttons in the *Import Text Clean* dialogue box will be activated. By using the keyboard (see *More Information*) or clicking on the buttons you can choose what the *Style* of the highlighted paragraph should be. Continue to do this until you reach the end of the script. This is fairly laborious so if you select the *Multi-Change* option, part of this process will be speeded up. For example, if a paragraph is found of a certain style and you change it to a Slug Line, when the *Multi-Change* option is selected all subsequent paragraphs with that same style will be automatically changed to the Slug Line style. If the script you *Pasted* in is all the same style, *Multi-Change* can not help you because once it's changed one it'll change the whole script. If you are not sure how the text you are hoping to convert will respond it might be a good idea to *Cut* and *Paste* a small section (2 or 3 pages) in and test that first. Finally, before using *Import Text Clean* use the *Replace* function in the Edit menu to remove text that should not be there, for example, if there are scene continuations (e.g. *MORE* & *CONT'D*) remove these first.

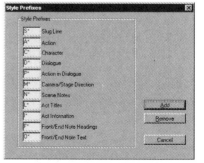

Add/Remove Style Prefixes

This function adds a *Style Prefix* identification to the beginning of each paragraph. You can chose what this prefix is, but, for example the default for Slug Line is S*. What would you use this for? If you want to export your script so that you can work on a different platform (a palm top or WindowsCE machine for example), which does not directly support MSWord files. Used in conjunction with the *Import Text Clean* function style prefixes ensure your script does not lose its layout.

How to use *Export a Script*

Open the *Add/Remove Style Prefixes* dialogue box and click on *Add* (after changing any prefix you might want to). Once this process is complete you will see that each paragraph in your script has had the appropriate prefix added to it. Now go to File Menu and select *Save Copy As,* save your script in the appropriate document/file format for the platform you wish to use, e.g. as a simple text file. After this is done you will see that the script on the screen looks exactly the same and has the same name as before because *Save Copy As* makes a copy of your script in the new format in the background and does not affect the script that you are working on. Once the copy has been made you no longer need the prefixes so remove them, re-open the *Add/Remove Style Prefix* dialogue box and select *Remove* (be aware that any text that looks like a style prefix will be removed).

Whilst you are working on the other platform use the same style prefixes (by just typing them in at the head of each paragraph) to identify what each paragraph is. You can then *Cut* and *Paste* this script back into your script and Use *Import Text Clean* to return it to its correct layout.

N.B. If you wish to use all the information that's stored in the *Short Cut Database* of a script you've exported make sure that you *Cut* and *Paste* your text back into the same script document as you exported from in the first place (deleting the older text first).

Reset Menus
This tool is only available on *Screenplay* running on Word 6 or Word 95. If you find the menus and short-cut menus are not working properly then run this utility to reset them.

AutoCorrect
This is a Word function for correcting typos, for example '*hte*' will be changed to '*the*' automatically as you type. It is this Word function that is programmed by the *Short Cut Database* to speed up your typing of characters names etc. You can use *AutoCorrect* rather than the *Short Cuts Database* but your short cuts will only be available on your computer. Using the *Short Cuts Database* means you can move *AutoCorrect* short cuts with your script from computer to computer.

Revisions
Revisions is also an MSWord function and it allows various people to make changes to the script without losing the original information. Any changes that are made are highlighted so if you add something it is underlined and if you delete something it is shown ~~with a line through it~~.

You can review these changes one by one, keeping or rejecting them until you have a new script. It is worth looking at this function as it is very powerful and saves printing out scripts for people to mark. Use *Temporary Scene Numbers* to aid with editing a script.

WINDOW MENU

New Window
Clicking on this menu item opens up a second, third or more window(s) showing the same active document. Any change made in one is made in the others. You could use this function when moving text around as you can view different parts of a document in different windows.

Arrange All
If you have a lot of document windows open you can use this function to arrange them all on the screen at the same time.

Split

This function splits a document window in half allowing you to see two different parts of the script at the same time. Useful when moving text around. You can even view the split windows differently; one could be in *Normal View* the other in *Outline View*.

List of Windows

You can select which window is active by selecting one from the list.

Pink Pages

Once production has commenced there is often a need to make changes to the script. New scenes are often distributed on coloured paper, which can be inserted into the script. Once you've finished a script and re-writes are required make a copy of your script then delete all the text; this will provide a clean document with all the master script's short cuts and styles. Use this blank document to write your *Pink Pages*. The facility to use letters instead of numbers in scene and page numbering in the *Add/Remove Script Formatting* function should help with duplicated scenes and pages (you can also unlock the script and add your own scene numbers).

Other *Screenplay* Modules

Screenplay is part of a suite of programs that are being developed to help with the film making process. There's a budgeting program and a scheduling program all in development and some other utilities too. *Screenplay* has been designed to interface with the *Scheduling* package to take the grind out of breaking down a script. Also planned is a module to turn a TV script into a multi camera script.

Styles:

Alt+S - Slug Line
Alt+A - Action
Alt+C - Character
Alt+D - Dialogue
Alt+R - Parallel Dialogue
Alt+O - Action in Dialogue
Alt+M - Camera and Stage Directions
Alt+N - Scene Notes
Alt+L - Act Title
Alt+I - Act Information
Alt+F - Front Notes
Alt+E - End Notes
Alt+T - Toggles between the Front Notes
Heading style and information style

Formatting Tools (Windows)

Ctrl+Shift+F - Add/Remove Script Formatting
Ctrl+Shift+L - Script Page Layout Options
Ctrl+Shift+P - Font & Paragraph Styles
Ctrl+Shift+C - Text Colours On/Off
Ctrl+Shift+S - Short Cuts Database
Ctrl+Shift+M - Smart Slug Line
Ctrl+Shift+U - Lock/Unlock Script
Ctrl+Shift+T - Temporary Scene Numbers
Ctrl+Shift+I - Import Text Clean
Ctrl+Shift+X - Add/Remove Style Prefixes

Formatting Tools (Mac)

Command+Shift+F - Add/Remove Script Formatting
Command+Shift+L - Script Page Layout Options
Command+Shift+P - Font & Paragraph Styles
Command+Shift+C - Text Colours On/Off
Command+Shift+S - Short Cuts Database
Command+Shift+M - Smart Slug Line
Command+Shift+U - Lock/Unlock Script
Command+Shift+T - Temporary Scene Numbers
Command+Shift+I - Import Text Clean
Command+Shift+X - Add/Remove Style Prefixes

Import Text Clean – Once utility is working just use the keyboard.

S - Slug Line
A - Action
C - Character
D - Dialogue
O - Action in Dialogue
M - Camera and Stage Directions
N - Scene Notes
L - Act Title
I - Act Information
H - Front/End Notes Heading
T - Front/End Notes Text
E - Delete
K - Skip

Screenplay is incredible value for money - the combined cost of *Screenplay* and MSWord is less than most stand alone script writing software yet you get one of the best word processors in the world and very powerful script writing software for your money.

Registration

If the version of *Screenplay* you're using is not registered, each time you open a *Screenplay* document you'll be asked if you want to register it. To register you'll have to go to the *Screenplay* web site. There are no writing restrictions with the trial version, you can write as much as you like. The only restrictions limit the amount of formatting available. Note that for writing short scripts the software is fully functional.

Also on the CD accompanying this book are all the production forms and contracts. These files are saved in MS Word format. Whilst you can access the files easily from the CD, it is best to copy them to your computer hard drive. The two directories you should copy are FORMS and CONTRACTS.

AN URBAN GHOST STORY — *SCREENPLAY TITLE*

7   INT. KATES BEDROOM - NIGHT   7

A large double bed fills the room - a figure lies sprawled out
on the bed - ALONE

KATE FISHER

A young woman of perhaps twenty seven.   *ACTION*

Her eyes snap open

Looking up she sees LIZZIE standing beside the bed with Alex by
her side…

                    LIZZIE
          It's happening again

                        — *SLUG LINES*

8   INT. BEDROOM - NIGHT   8

KATE, half asleep shuffles the kids back into the moonlit
bedroom - she listens - looking up to the ceiling - DEATHLY
SILENCE but for the evil howling wind

*AUTO
INSERT
SCENE
NUMBERS*
                    KATE
          Looks like Mr mouse has finally gone
          to bed which is where we should all be
          - now into your beds

The kids jump into their beds. KATE tucks in ALEX giving him
his beloved power ranger -
                              — *CHARACTER*
                    KATE
          I'll tell you what - I'll see if
          George can catch him for us tomorrow

                    ALEX
          If George catches him can I keep Mr ___ *DIALOGUE*
          Mouse as a pet?

                    LIZZIE
          What if it's a rat

                    ALEX
              (frightened) —————— *ACTION IN DIALOGUE*
          A rat?   *(PARENTHETICAL)*

                    KATE
          Lizzie!
              (gives LIZZIES a scolding
              look)
          It's not a rat, it's a mouse that has

                              More... ___

          PAGE NUMBERS   *MORE.. & CONT...*

COPYRIGHT NOTICE   Page 3

          © Copyright 1996 Living Spirit Pictures 97 Ltd

The Film Makers Compromise

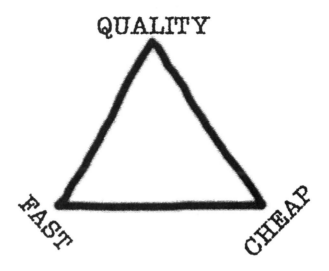

Study this simple triangle. Whatever film making discipline you apply, you can only ever have two corners, and always at the expense of the third corner.

Section 5
The Directory

accountants

101 Film & TV Production Accountants
26 Goodge St, W1P 1FG
Tel 0207 436 1119 Fax 0207 436 8887

ACE Accounting Ltd
25 West Grove Walton-on-Thames
KT12 5PF
Tel: 01932 247292 Fax: 01932 267474

Baker Tilly
2 Bloomsbury St, WC1B 3ST
Tel 0207 413 5100 Fax 0207 413 5101

BBT Financial Services
Wrens Court Victoria Rd, Sutton
Coldfield B72 1SY
Tel: 0121 3554500 Fax: 0121 355 5512

Beecham's Chartered Accountants
3 Bedford Row, WC1R 4BU
Tel 0207 2425624   Fax 0207 405 6287

Clayman & Co
189 Bickenhall Mansions, Bickenhall
St, W1H 3DE
Tel 0207 935 0847 Fax 0207 224 2216

Coopers & Lybrand Media Group
1 Embankment Pl, WC2N 6NN
Tel 0207 213 5353   Fax 0207 213 2411

Deloite Touche Ross
Hill Hse, 1 Little New St, EC4A 3TR
Tel 0207 936 3000 Fax 0207 583 8517

Dover Childs Tyler
15 Manchester Sq, W1M 6LB
Tel 0207 935 7609 Fax 0207 486 6457

Ernst & Young
Becket Hse, 1 Lambeth Palace Rd,
SE1 7EU
Tel 0207 928 2000 Fax 0207 928 1345

Fraser Russell
Fairview Hse, 71-73 Woodbridge Rd,
Guildford, Surrey, GU1 4YZ
Tel 01483 567252   Fax 01483 300081

Hacker Young
3 & 5 St Pauls Rd Clifton Bristol
BS8 1LX
Tel: 0117 973 8926 Fax: 0117 973 0872

Henry Bach & Co Chartered Accountants
15 Broad Court, WC2B 5QN
Tel: 0207 2402834 Fax: 0207 2402813

Ivan Sopher
5 Elstree Gate, Elstree Way,
Borehamwood, Herts, WD6 1JD
Tel 0208 207 0602 Fax 0208 207 6758

Lindford & Co
1 Duchess St, W1N 3DE
Tel 0207 637 2244 Fax 0207 637 2999

Lubbock Fine
Russell Bedford Hse, City Forum, 250
City Rd, EC1V 2QQ
Tel 0207 490 7766 Fax 0207 490 5102

Lucraft Hodgson & Dawes
2-4 Ash Lane, Rustingham,
Littlehampton, W Sussex, BN16 3BZ
Tel 01903 772244 Fax 01903 771071

MacCorckindale & Holton
POBox 2398 Langham Place W1A 2RT
Tel: 0207 636 1888 Fax: 0207 6362888

MacIntyre & Co Chartered Accountants
28 Ely Place EC1N 6RL
Tel: 0207 242 0242 Fax: 0207 4054786

PricewaterHouseCoopers
8th Floor Room 8 107Embankment
Place WC2N 6NN
Tel: 0207 804 9783 Fax: 0207 213 2411

Shipleys Chartered Accountants
10 Orange St, Haymarket, WC2H 7DQ
Tel 0207 312 0000 Fax 0207 312 0022

Silver Levene
37 Warren St, W1P 5PD
Tel 0207 383 3200 Fax 0207 383 4165

The Philip Hills Partnership
3 Quayside St, Edinburgh, Midlothian,
EH6 6EJ
Tel 0131 555 1599 Fax 0131 555 1029

associations, organisations and unions

BAFTA
195 Piccadilly, W1V OLN
Tel 0207 734 0022 Fax 0207 734 1792

BAFTA Scotland
74 Victoria Crescent, Glasgow,
G12 9JN
Tel 0141 357 4317 Fax 0141 337 1432

BBFC (British Board of Film Classification)
3 Soho Sq, W1V 6HD
Tel 0207 439 7961 Fax 0207 287 0141

BECTU
111 Wardour St, W1V 4AY
Tel 0207 437 8506 Fax 0207 437 8268

British Council
Films Department, 11 Portland Pl,
W1N 4EJ
Tel 0207 389 3065 Fax 0207 389 3041

British Film Institute
21 Stephen St, W1P 2LN
Tel 0207 255 1444 Fax 0207 436 7950

British Screen Finance Ltd
14-17 Wells Mews, W1P 3FL
Tel 0207 323 9080 Fax 0207 323 0092

DPRS (Directors' & Producers' Rights Society)
Victoria Chambers 16-18 Strutton
Ground SW1P 2HP
Tel 0207 227 4757 Fax 0207 227 4755

Equity
Guild Hse, Upper St Martin's Lane,
WC2H 9EG
Tel 0207 379 6000 Fax 0207 379 7001

The Irish Film Board
Rockfort Hse, St Augustine St, Galway,
Ireland
Tel: 353 91 651398 Fax: 353 91 561405

MCPS - Mechanical Copyright Protection Society
Elgar Hse, 41 Streatham High Rd,
SW16 1ER
Tel 0208 769 4400/0208 664 4400
Fax 0208 769 8792

MU - Musicians Union
60-62 Clapham Rd, SW9 OJJ
Tel 0207 582 5566 Fax 0207 582 9805

NPA - New Producers Alliance
9 Bourlet Close, W1RP 7PJ
Tel 0207 580 2480 Fax 0207 580 2484

PACT - Producers Alliance for Cinema & Television
45 Mortimer St, W1N 7TD
Tel 0207 331 6000 Fax 0207 3316700

PRS - Performing Rights Society
29/33 Berners St, W1P 4AA
Tel 0207 580 5544   Fax 0207 306 4050

Scottish Screen
74 Victoria Crescent Rd, Dowanhill,
Glasgow, G12 9JN
Tel 0141 302 1700   Fax 0141 302 1711

SFD - Society of Film Distributors
22 Golden Sq, W1R 3PA
Tel 0207 437 4383 Fax 0207 734 0912

The British Film Commission
70 Baker St, W1M 1DJ
Tel 0207 224 5000 Fax 0207 224 1013

Women in Film & Television
Garden Studios, 11/15 Betterton St,
WC2H 9BP
Tel 0207 379 0344 Fax 0207 379 2413

Writers Guild of Great Britain
430 Edgeware Rd, W2 1EH
Tel 0207 723 8074 Fax 0207 706 2413

---

audio post production

Air Studios
Lyndhurst Hall, Lyndhurst Rd,
Hampstead, NW3 5NG
Tel 0207 794 0660 Fax 0207 794 8518

Anvil Post Production Ltd
Denham Studios, North Orbital Rd,
Donham, Uxbridge, Middx, UD9 5HL
Tel 01895 833522 Fax 01895 835006

Broadcast Film & Video Ltd
33 West Park, Clifton, Bristol, Avon,
BS8 2LX
Tel 0117 9237087   Fax 0117 923 7090

Cinesite
9 Carlisle St W1V 5RG
Tel: 01753 630 285 / 0207 973 4000
Fax: 01753 650 261

D B Post Production
1-8 Bateman's Buildings, South Soho
Sq, W1V 5TW
Tel 0207 287 9144/0207 434 0097
Fax 0207 287 9143

D B Post Production Ltd Cinema Sound
27-29 Berwick St, W1V 3RF
Tel 0207 734 9870 Fax 0207 439 2012

De Lane Lea Ltd
75 Dean St, W1V 5HA
Tel 0207 432 3800 Fax 0207 437 0913

Dolby Laboratories Inc
Wootton Bassett, Wilts, SN4 8QJ
Tel 01793 842100 Fax 01793 842101

Essential Pictures Ltd
222 Kensal Rd W10 5BN
Tel: 0208 6967017 Fax: 0208 9608201

FX Rentals Ltd
38-40 Telford Way W3 7XS
Tel: 0208 7462121 Fax: 0208 746 4100

Goldcrest Post Production Facilities Ltd
36-44 Brewer St, W1R 3HP (entrance
no 1 Lexington St)
Tel 0207 437 7972 Fax 0207 439 4177

Interact Sound Ltd
160 Barlby Rd, W10 6BS
Tel 0208 960 3115   Fax 0208 964 3022

London Post
34-35 Dean St, W1V 5AP
Tel 0207 439 9080 Fax 0207 434 0714

M2 Television Ltd
The Forum, 74-80 Camden St,
NW1 0EG
Tel 0207 387 5001 Fax 0207 387 5025
Freephone 0500 220200

Magmasters Sound Studios Ltd
20 St Anne's Court, W1V 3AW
Tel 0207 437 8273 Fax 0207 494 1281

Music Hse
5 Newburgh St, W1V 1LH
Tel 0207 434 9678 Fax 0207 434 1470

NATS Post Production Ltd
10 Soho Sq, W1V 6NT
Tel 0207 287 9900 Fax 0207 287 8636

Pinewood Studios
Pinewood Rd, Pinewood Rd, Iver,
Bucks, SL0 0HN
Tel 01753 656301 Fax 01753 656014

Reel Sound Ltd
Pinewood Studios, Iver Heath, Iver,
Bucks, SL0 0HN
Tel 01753 656372 Fax 01753 653351

Snake Ranch Studio
90 Lots Rd, SW10 0QD
Tel 0207 351 7888 Fax 0207 352 5194

SVC
White City Motion Control 8 Silver Rd
W12 7SG
Tel: 0208 7491600 Fax: 0208 7491700

Twickenham Film Studios
The Barons, St Margaret's,
Twickenham, Middx, TW1 2AW
Tel 0208 607 8888 Fax 0208 607 8889

Video London Sound Studios
16-18 Ramillies St, W1V 1DL
Tel 0207 734 4811 Fax 0207 494
2553/0207 734 0743

Videosonics
13 Hawley Crescent, NW1 8NP
Tel 0207 4822588 Fax 0207 482 0849

West 1 Television
10 Bateman St, W1V 5TT
Tel 0207 437 5533 Fax 0207 287 8621

Yorkshire Tyne Tees Television
The Television Centre, Leeds, LS3 1JS
Tel 0113 243 8283 Fax 0113 234 1293

---

casting services

PCR (Production & Casting Report)
PO Box 11, SW15 6AY
Tel 0208 789 0408 Fax 0208 780 1977

---

crewing services

Awfully Nice Video Company
29 Kingsend Ruislip HA4 7DD
Tel: 07000 345678 Fax: 07000 345679

Crew 2 Services Ltd
5 Albion Wharf Hester Rd Battersea
SW11 4AN
Tel: 0207 2231220 Fax: 0207 2231330

Crewsnews
Tel: 0208 3514157 Fax: 0208 373 7038

---

catering

Busters Catering
65 Thorney Mill Rd, Bucks, SL0 9AL
Tel 0208 961 3525 Fax 0208 759 1824

Clarkson Catering
Tavern Quay, Sweden Gate, SE16 1TX
Tel/Fax 0208 693 6508

Film Cuisine
308 Smithdown Rd, Liverpool, LI5 5AJ
Tel 0151 722 7416   Fax 0151 722 7416

Glenn's Star Catering
94 Cumberland Drive, Chessington,
Surrey, KT9 1HH
Tel 0208 397 7921

Hollywood Catering Services
52 Jeffcutt Rd, Chelmer Village,
Chelmsford, Essex, CM2 6XN
Tel 01245 451051   Fax 01245 359917

J & J Preparations Int
Unit 5, Midas Industrial Park,
Longbridge Way, Uxbridge, UB8 2YT
Tel 01895 232 627   Fax 01895 257 033

J & R Catering
Hey Green Lodge, Waters Rd, Marsden,
Nr Huddersfield, HD7 6NG
Tel 01484 843 842   Fax 01484 843 842

Kennedy's Caterers Ltd
Park Hse, Queen St, Morley, Leeds,
LS27 9LY
Tel 0113 2532867   Fax 0113 2526112

Set Breaks
4 Gleneagles Close, Stanwell Village,
TW19 7PD
Tel 01784 490238   Fax 01784 420347

Set Meals
Unit 7, Tower Workshops, Riley Rd,
SE13DG
Tel 0207 237 0014   Fax 0207 231 8401

St Clements Catering
Unit 25, Argyle Way, Ely, Cardiff,
CF5 5NJ
Tel 01222 598 121   Fax 01222 592 846

---

commissions & local services

Australian Film Commission
99/101 Regent St, 2nd Floor, Victory
Hse, W1R 7HB
Tel 0207 734 9383   Fax 0207 434 0170

Bath Film Office
Abbey Chambers, Abbey Church Yard,
Bath, BA1 1LY
Tel 01225 477000   Fax 01225 477221

British Film Commission
70 Baker St, W1M 1DJ
Tel 0207 224 5000   Fax 0207 224 1013

Central England Screen Commission
Unit 5, Holiday Wharf, Holiday St,
Birmingham B1 1TJ
Tel 0121 643 9309   Fax 0121 643 9064

Eastern Screen
Anglia Television, Prince of Wales Rd,
Norwich, NR1 3JG
Tel 01603 767 077   Fax 01603 767 191

Edinburgh and Lothian Screen Industries Office
Castle Cliff, 25 Johnson Terrace,
Edinburgh EH3 9BZ
Tel 0131 622 7337   Fax 0131 622 7338

Isle of Man Film Commission
Dpt of Industry, Illiam Dhone Hse, 2
Circular Rd, Douglas, IoM, IM1 1PJ
Tel 01624 685 864   Fax 01624 685 454

Lancashire Film & TV Office
Lancashire Enterprises Plc, Enterprise
Hse, 17 Ribblesdale Pl, Preston, PR1
Tel 01772 203 020   Fax 01772 252 640

Liverpool Film Office
Pioneer Buildings, 65-67 Dale St,
Liverpool, L2 2NS
Tel 0151 291 9191   Fax 0151 291 9199

Northern Screen Commission
Studio 15, Design Works, William St,
Felling, Tyne & Wear, NE10 0JP
Tel 0191 469 1000   Fax 0191 469 7000

Scottish Screen
74 Victoria Crescent, Glasgow G12 9JN
Tel 0141 302 1700   Fax 0141 302 1711

Screen Wales
Canolfan Sgrin Centre, Llandaf, Cardiff,
CF5 2PU
Tel 01222 578 370   Fax 01222 578 654

South West Film Commission
18 Belle Vue Rd, Saltash, Cornwall,
PL12 6ES
Tel 01752 841 199   Fax 01752 841 254

South West Scotland Screen Commission
Gracefield Arts Centre, 23 Edinburgh
Rd, Dumfries, DG1 1JQ
Tel 01387 263 666   Fax 01387 263 666

Southern Screen Commission
Production Enquiries, 4th Floor, Baltic
Hse, Kingston Crescent, Portsmouth
PO2 8QL
Tel 01705 650 779   Fax 01705 650 789

Yorkshire Screen Commission
Unit 416, The Workstation, 15
Paternoster Row, Sheffield, S1 2BX
Tel 01142 799 115   Fax 01142 796 522

---

computer graphics

Bionic Productions Ltd
Pinewood Studios, Pinewood Rd, Iver,
Bucks, SL0 0NH
Tel 01753 655886/656980   Fax 01753
654507

Bitsoft Ltd
Black Screen Projection, 193
Hempstead Rd, Watford, Herts, WC1
Tel 01923 237575   Fax 01923 237575

CFX Associates
16-18 Ramillies St, W1V 1DL
Tel 0207 734 3155   Fax 0207 494 3670

Cinesite Europe Ltd
9 Carlisle St, W1V 5RG
Tel 0207 973 4000   Fax 0207 943 4040

Complete Facilities
Slingsby Pl, Long Acre, WC2E 9AB
Tel 0207 379 7739   Fax 0207 497 9305

Computer Arts Specialists 30 Monmouth St Bath
BA1 2SM
Tel: 01225 732330

Computer Film Company
19-23 Wells St, W1P 3FP
Tel 0207 344 8000   Fax 0207 344 8001

Computerised Timelapse Cinematography
27 Birstall Rd Tottenham N15 5EN
Tel: 0208 802 8791   Fax: 0208 211 8286

Digital Arts
9-11 Richmond Bldg, off Dean St,
W1V 5AF
Tel 0207 439 0919   Fax 0207 437 1146

FrameStore
9 Noel St, W1V 4AL
Tel 0207 208 2600   Fax 0207 208 2626

Infynity Ltd
49-50 Marlborough Hse, W1V 1DB
Tel 0207 434 1665 Fax 0207 734 4229

London Post
34-35 Dean St, W1V 5AP
Tel 0207 439 9080 Fax 0207 434 0714

M2 TV Ltd
74-80 Camden St, The Forum,
NW1 OEG
Tel 0207 387 5001 Fax 0207 387 5025

Moving Picture Company
25 Noel St, W1V 3RD
Tel 0207 434 3100 Fax 0207 734 9150

NATS Post Production
10 Soho Sq, W1V 6NT
Tel 0207 287 9900 Fax 0207 287 8636

Peerless Camera Company
32 Bedfordbury, WC2N 4DU
Tel 0207 836 3367 Fax 0207 240 2143

Rushes Post Production Ltd
66 Old Compton St, W1V 5PA
Tel 0207 437 8676 Fax 0207 734 2519

Soho Group
71 Dean St, W1V 5HB
Tel 0207 439 2730 Fax 0207 734 3331

SVC Film Hse
142 Wardour St, W1V 3AU
Tel 0207 734 1600 Fax 0207 437 1854

The Mill
40-41 Gt Marlborough St, W1V 1DA
Tel 0207 287 4041 Fax 0207 287 8393

Touch Animation
44 Earlham St, WC2H 9LA
Tel 0207 379 6247 Fax 0207 240 3419

TSI Video Ltd
10 Grape St, WC2H 8DY
Tel 0207 379 3435 Fax 0207 379 4589

West 1 Television
10 Bateman St, W1V 5TT
Tel 0207 437 5533 Fax 0207 287 8621

costume

20th Century Frox
614 Fulham Rd, SW6 5RP
Tel 0207 731 3242

Academy Costumes
50 Rushworth St, SE1 0RB
Tel 0207 620 0771 Fax 0207 928 6287

Angels & Bermans
40 Camden St, NW1 0EN
Tel 0207 387 0999 Fax 0207 383 5603

Barnums
67 Hammersmith Rd, W14 8UZ
Tel 0207 602 1211 Fax 0207 603 9945

Escapade
150 Camden High St, NW1 0NE
Tel 0207 485 7384 Fax 0207 485 0950

Flame Military Costumiers
Old Victorian Police Station, 31 Market
St, Torquay, Devon, TQ1 3AW
Tel 01803 211930 Fax 01803 293554

Granada Television Costume Hire
Quay St, Manchester, Lancashire,
M60 9EA
Tel 0161 827 2020 Fax 0161 832 8809

Gwen & Janette
19 Acre Rd, Colliers Wood SW19 2AL
Tel/Fax 0208 544 1092

Hairaisers Ltd
9-11 Sunbeam Rd Park Royal
NW10 6JP
Tel: 0208 9652500 Fax: 0208 9631600

Laurence Corner
62-64 Hampstead Rd NW1
Tel: 0207 8131010 Fax: 0207 813 1413

RSC Hire Wardrobe
Timothy's Bridge Rd Industrial Estate,
Stratford-upon-Avon, CV37 9UY
Tel 01789 205920 Fax 01789 265609

The BBC Costume Store
172-178, Victoria Rd, North Acton, W3
Tel 0208 576 1761 Fax 0208 993 7040

**The Contemporary Wardrobe
Collection**
The Horse Hospital, Colonnade,
Bloomsbury, WC1N 1HX
Tel 0207 713 7370 Fax 0207 713 7269

The Costume Group
12 Wolverton Gardens, Ealing, W5 3LJ
Tel 0208 752 1247

The Costume Studio
Montgomery Hse 159-161 Balls Pond Rd
Islington N1 4BG
Tel: 0207 275 9614 Fax: 0207 8376576

distributors

Artificial Eye Film Company
13 Soho Sq, W1V 5FB
Tel 0207 437 2552 Fax 0207 437 2992

Buena Vista Home Entertainment
Beaumont Hse, Kensington Village,
Avonmore Rd, W14 8TS
Tel 0207 605 2400 Fax 0207 605 2793

Guerilla Films
35 Thornbury Rd Isleworth Middx TW7
Tel: 0208 7581716 Fax: 0208 758 9364

Entertainment in Video
27 Soho Sq, W1V 6HU
Tel 0207 439 1979 Fax 0207 734 2483

Feature Film Company
4th Floor, 68-70 Wardour St, W1V 3 HP
Tel 0207 734 2266 Fax 0207 494 0309

Mayfair TV Entertainment Ltd
110 St Martins Lane, WC2N 4AD
Tel 0207 304 7911 Fax 0207 867 1184

**Medusa Communications &
Marketing Ltd**
Regal Chambers, 51 Bancroft, Hitchin,
Herts, SG5 1LL
Tel 01462 421818 Fax 01462 420393

Metro Tartan
79 Wardour St, W1V 3TH
Tel 0207 734 8508 Fax 0207 287 2112

Polygram Video Int
Oxford Hse, 76, Oxford St, W1N 0HQ
Tel 0207 307 1300 Fax 0207 307 1301

Twentieth Century Fox
31-32 Soho Sq, W1V 6AP
Tel 0207 437 7766 Fax 0207 434 2170

United International Pictures (UK)
Mortimer Hse, 37-41 Mortimer St,
W1A 2JL
Tel 0207 636 1655 Fax 0207 636 4118

film camera hire

Panavision
Metropolitan Centre, Bristol Rd,
Greenford, Middx UB6 8GD
Tel 0208 839 7333 Fax 0208 902 3273

GP Film Services
Unit 20, Wadsworth Business Centre,
21 Wadsworth Rd, Perivale, Greenford,
Middx, UB67LQ
Tel 0208 991 1026 Fax 0208 991 9845

Panavision Ireland
Ardmore Studios, Herbert Rd, Bray,
County Wicklow, Ireland,
Tel 010 3531 2 860811
Fax 010 3531 2 863425

Panavision Manchester
Manchester Rd, Kearsley, Bolton,
Lancs, BL4 8RL
Tel 01204 705794 Fax 01204 705780

Panavision Shepperton
Shepperton Studios, Studios Rd,
Shepperton, Middx, TW17 0QD
Tel 01932 572440 Fax 01932 572450

VFG (Michael Samuelson's Lighting, Camera Associates, Ronford Cameras)
8 Beresford Ave, Wembley HA0 1QN
Tel: 0208 9037933 Fax: 0208 9023273

Aim Image Camera Co Ltd
Unit 5 St Pancras Commercial Centre
63 Pratt St NW1 0BY
Tel: 0207 4824340 Fax: 0207 267 3972

Movietech Camera Rentals
7 Northfield Estate Beresford Ave
Wembley HA0 1NW
Tel: 0208 9037311 Fax: 0208 903 6713

AFL Television Facilities
Unit 5 181a Verulam Rd St Albans AL3
Tel: 01727 844117 Fax: 01727 847649

ARRI MEDIA
tel: 020 8573 2255
fax: 020 8756 0592
email:info@arrimedia.com

Awfully Nice Video Company
29 Kingsend Ruislip HA4 7DD
Tel: 07000 345678 Fax: 07000 45679

DPL Broadcast Hire Ltd
Unit 7 Wembley Pk Bus. Ctr North End
Rd Wembley HA9 0AG
Tel: 0208 7951866 Fax: 0208 7951868

Extreme Facilities Ltd
15-17 Este Rd SW11 2TL
Tel: 0207 801 9111 Fax: 0207 801 9222

Joe Dunton & Co
22c Abbey Works Mount Pleasant
Alperton Wembley HA0 1NR
Tel: 0208 324 2311 Fax: 0208 900 9840

Optex
20-26 Victoria Rd New Barnet Barnet
EN4 9PF
Tel: 0208 4412199 Fax: 0208 364 9235

Tattooist International
Westgate Hse Roman Way N7 8XH
Tel: 0207 7003555 Fax: 0207 700 4445

Hammerhead TV Facilities Ltd
42 Webbs Rd SW11 6SF
Tel: 0207 9243977 Fax: 0207 585 3463

KJP
93-103 Drummond St NW1 2HJ
Tel: 0207 380 1144 Fax: 0207 387 3354

MGB Facilities
Capital Hse Sheepscar Court
Meanwood Rd Leeds LS7 2BB
Tel: 0113 243 6868 Fax: 0113 243 8886

On-site Ltd
14/15 Berners St W1P 3DE
Tel 0207 637 0888 Fax: 0207 637 0444

Stowage Films
46 Gilbert Hse McMillan St Deptford
SE8 3DJ
Tel: 0208 4690512 Fax: 0208 806 6723

SVC
White City Motion Control 8 Silver Rd
W12 7SG
Tel: 0208 7491600 Fax: 0208 749 1700

The Picture Canning Company
3 Kimber Rd SW18 4NR
Tel: 0208 8749277 Fax: 0208 874 6623

The Video & Film Company Ltd
Unit 8 St Pancras Commercial Cent
Pratt St NW1 0BY
Tel: 0207 267 5111 Fax: 0207 485 3205

Transmission (TX) Ltd
Unit 2a Shepperton Studios Shepperton
TW17 0QD
Tel: 0208 7831972 Fax: 01932 572 571

WLC Broadcast
102 Dean St W1V 5RA
Tel: 0207 4372004 Fax: 0207 437 2021

Wood Visula Communications
Wood Hse Leeds Rd Bradford BD3 9RU
Tel: 01274 732362 Fax: 01274736 164

film editing

Anvil Post Production
Denham Studios, North Orbital Rd,
Denham, Uxbridge, Middx, UB9 5HL
Tel 01895 833522 Fax 01895 835006

Avid Technology
Charlotte Hse, 6-14 Windmill St,
W1P 1HF
Tel 0207 307 8000 Fax 0207 307 8001

De Lane Lea Ltd
75 Dean St, W1V 5HA
Tel 0207 432 3800 Fax 0207 437 0913

Edit Hire
Unit 1B, Shepperton Studios, Studios
Rd, Shepperton, Middx, TW17 0QD
Tel 01932 572253 Fax 01932 569899

Goldcrest Post Production Facilities Ltd
36-44 Brewer St, W1R 3HP
(Entrance in 1 Lexington St)
Tel 0207 437 7972 Fax 0207 437 6411

London Editing Machines
Twickenham Film Studios, St
Margaret's, Twickenham, Middx,
TW1 2AW
Tel 0208 744 9020 Fax 0208 744 0357

Lightworks Editing Systems Limited
38 Soho Sq, W1V 6LE
Tel 0207 494 3084 Fax 0207 437 3570

NATS Post Production
10 Soho Sq, W1V 6NT
Tel 0207 287 9900 Fax 0207 287 8636

Pinewood Studios
Pinewood Rd, Pinewood Rd, Iver,
Bucks
Tel 01753 651700 Fax 01753 656844

Rushes
66 Old Compton St, W1V 5PA
Tel 0207 437 8676 Fax 0207 734 3002

Salon Productions Ltd
10 Livonia St, W1V 3PH
Tel 0207 437 0516 Fax 0207 437 6197

Sam Sneade Editing Ltd
34-35 Dean St, W1V 5AP
Tel 0207 734 6901 Fax 0207 734 6765

Shears Post Production Services
Warwick Hse, Chapone Pl, Dean St,
W1V 5AJ
Tel 0207 437 8182 Fax 0207 437 8183

Solus Enterprises
35 Marshall St, W1V 1LL
Tel 0207 734 0645 Fax 0207 287 2197

The Film Editors
6-10 Lexington St, W1R 3HS
Tel 0207 439 8655 Fax 0207 437 0409

The Mill
40-41 Great Marlborough St, W1V 1DA
Tel 0207 287 4041 Fax 0207 287 8393

Soho Images
8-14 Meard St W1V 3HR
Tel 0207 437 0831 Fax 0207 734 9471

TSI Video Ltd
10 Grape St, WC2H 8DY
Tel 0207 379 3435 Fax 0207 379 4589

funding & development

The Film Council
Lottery Film Department 10 Little
Portland St, W1N 5DF
Tel 0207 973 5184 Fax 0207 973 5190

British Film Institute Productions
21 Stephen St W1P 2LM
Tel 0207 957 8984 Fax 0207 580 9456

British Screen Finance
14-17 Wells Mews, W1P 3FL
Tel 0207 323 9080 Fax 0207 323 0092

European Co-Production Fund
14-17 Wells Mews, W1P 3FL
Tel 0207 323 9080 Fax 0207 323 0092

Film Four International
124 Horseferry Rd, SW1P 2TX
Tel 0207 396 4444 Fax 0207 306 8361

First Film Foundation
9 Bourlet Close, W1P 7PJ
Tel 0207 580 2111 Fax 0207 580 2116

Glasgow Film Fund
249 West George St G2 4RB
Tel 0141 302 1752 Fax 0141 302 1714

**Northern Ireland Development
Fund & Film Commission**
21 Ormeau Ave, Belfast, Co Antrim,
BT2 8HD
Tel 01232 232444 Fax 01232 239918

**Scottish Screen Development &
Production Fund**
249 West George St G2 4RB
Tel 0141 302 1700 Fax 0141 302 1714

The Scottish Screen
74 Victoria Crescent Rd, Glasgow,
G12 9JN
Tel 0141 337 2526 Fax 0141 337 2562

Wales Sgrin The Bank
10 Mount Stuart Sq Cardiff Bay
CF10 5EE
Tel 01222 333300 Fax 01222 333320

film schools

**Bournemouth and Poole College
of Art and Design**
School of Film, TV and AV Production,
Wallisdown, Poole, BH12 5HH
Tel 01202 538204 Fax 01202 537729

Bristol University
Dept of Drama: Theatre, Film &
Television, Cantocks Close, Woodland
Rd, Bristol, BS8 1UP
Tel 0117 928 7838 Fax 0117 928 8251

Edinburgh College of Art
Lauriston Pl, Edinburgh, Midlothian,
EH3 9DF
Tel 0131 221 6000 Fax 0131 221 6001

**London College of Printing &
Distributive Trades**
Media Department, 10 Backhill,
Clerkenwell, EC1R 5EN
Tel 0207 514 6500 Fax 0207 514 6848

National Film & Television School
Beaconsfield Studios, Station Rd,
Beaconsfield, Bucks, HP9 1LG
Tel 01494 671234 Fax 01494 674042

**National Short Course Training
Programme**
National Film & Television School,
Beaconsfield Studios, Station Rd,
Beaconsfield, Bucks, HP9 1LG
Tel 01494 677903 Fax 01494 678708

Northern School of Film & TV
Leeds Metropolitan University, 2 Queen
Sq, Leeds LS2 8AF
Tel 0113 263 1900 Fax 0113 263 1901

**Ravensbourne College of Design
& Communication**
Walden Rd, Chislehurst, Kent,
BR7 5SN
Tel 0208 289 4900 Fax 0208 325 8320

Royal College of Art
School of Communications,
Kensington Gore, SW7 2EU
Tel 0207 590 4444 Fax 0207 590 4500

**The London International Film
School**
24 Shelton St, WC2H 9HP
Tel 0207 836 9642 Fax 0207 497 3718

**The Surrey Institute of Art &
Design**
Farnham Campus, Falkner Rd, The
Hart, Farnham, Surrey, GU9 7DS
Tel 01252 722441 Fax 01252 733869

University of Westminster
Harrow Campus, Studio M, Northwich
Park, Harrow, Middx, HA1 3TP
Tel 0207 911 5000 Fax 0207 911 5939

financial

**AON Entertainment Risk Services
Ltd**
Pinewood Studios Pinewood Rd Iver
SL0 0NH
Tel: 01753 658200 Fax: 01753 653 152

**Barclays Bank Media Business
Centre**
27 Soho Sq, W1A 4WA
Tel 0207 445 5700 Fax 0207 445 5784

Film Finances Services
1-11 Hay Hill, W1X 7LF
Tel 0207 629 6557 Fax 0207 491 530

Guinness Mahon & Co Ltd
32 St Mary at Hill, EC3P 3AJ
Tel 0207 623 9333 Fax 0207 528 0895

IFG International Film Guarantors
9 Hanover St
Tel: 0207 493 4719

The Bank Of Boston
39 Victoria St, Westminster, SW1 0ED
Tel 0207 799 3333 Fax 0207 222 5649

freight services

Aerly Bird Int courier & express service
Room 98G, Southampton Hse, Cargo Terminal, Heathrow Airport, Middx, TW6 9EN
Tel 0208 897 9291   Fax 0208 564 7553

DHL International
Hillbloom Hse, 1 Dukes Green Avenue, Faggs Rd, Feltham, Middx, TW14 OLR
Tel 0345 100 300   Fax 0208 818 8141

Jigsaw Freight
Unit B27, Calder Way, Poyle, Slough SL3 0BQ
Tel 01753 680616   Fax 01753 683016

Marken Worldwide Express
Unit 2, Metrol Centre, St Johns Rd, Isleworth, Middx, TW7 6NJ
Tel 0208 388 8500 Fax 0208 388 8500

Media Freight Services Ltd
Media Hse, Springfield Rd, Hayes UB4 0DD
Tel 0208 573 9999 Fax 0208 573 9592

Midnite Express
Unit 3, The Metro Centre, St Johns Rd, Isleworth, Middx, TW7 6NJ
Tel 0208 568 1568 Fax 0208 847 4418

The Pegasus Couriers
86-92 Stewarts Rd, SW8 4UG
Tel 0207 622 1111   Fax 0207 622 1616

Renown Freight
Unit 4, Central Park Estate, Staines Rd, Hounslow, Middx, TW4 5DJ
Tel 0208 570 5151 Fax 0208 572 2102

SamFreight Ltd
Technicolor Estate, Bath Rd, Harmondsworth, West Drayton, UB7 ODB
Tel 0208 750 2300 Fax 0208 750 2301

Team Air Express UK
Unit 8, Crown Way, Horton Rd, West Drayton, Middx, UB7 8HZ
Tel 01895 448 855 Fax 01895 448 851

XP Express Parcel System
Unit 6, Spitfire Way, Spitfire Industrial Estate, Middx, TW5 9NW
Tel 0208 813 5000 Fax 0208 813 5232

grips hire

A1 Grip Services
1 Hurstlands Hurst Green Oxted RH8 0HF
Tel: 01883 712 4260 Fax: 01883 712426

GP Film Services
Unit 20, Wadsworth Business Centre, 21 Wadsworth Rd, Perivale, Greenford, Middx, UB6 7LQ
Tel 0208 991 1026 Fax 0208 991 9845

Gripak
106 Noak Hill Rd Billericay CM12 9UH
Tel: 01277 656 759 Fax: 01277 656759

Griplet
Ltd 24 Woodland Drive Thorpe End Norwich NR13 5BH
Tel: 01603 702 779 Fax: 01603 702 779

Gripping Stuff Ltd
Pen Hse Grendon Rd Edgcott Aylesbury HP18 0TW
Tel: 01296 770 818 Fax: 01296 770 818

Grip Unit
29 Beechcroft Avenue Croxley Green Rickmansworth WD3 3EG
Tel: 01923 212 380 Fax: 01923 441 452

Panavision Grips Ltd
5-11 Taunton Rd, The Metropolitan Centre, Greenford, Middx, UB6 8UQ
Tel 0208 578 2382 Fax 0208 839 1640

Panavision Grips - North
Unit 5, Orchard Park Trading Estate, Maryville, Giffnock, Glasgow, G46 9XX
Tel 0141 638 8786 Fax 0141 638 8786

Media Film Service Ltd
4 Airlinks, Spitfire Way, Heston, Hounslow, Middx, TW5 9NR
Tel 0208 573 2255 Fax 0208 756 0592

Panavision Grips
Shepperton Studios, Studios Rd, Shepperton, Middx, TW17 0QD
Tel 01932 572440 Fax 01932 572450

The Grip Firm
Unit 12A, Isleworth Business Complex, St Johns Rd, Isleworth, Middx, TW7 6NL
Tel 0208 847 1771 Fax 0208 847 1773

insurance

Aegis Insurance Brokers
Collegiate Hse, 9 St Thomas St, SE1 9RY
Tel 0207 403 7188 Fax 0207 407 1076

AON Entertainment Risk Services
Pinewood Studios Pinewood Rd Iver SL0 0NH
Tel: 01753 658200 Fax: 01753 653 152

Bain Hogg Ltd
Digby Hse, Causton Rd, Colchester, Essex, CO1 1YS
Tel 01206 577612   Fax 01206 761202

Entertainment Brokers Intl
Sampson & Allen, 1 Kingly St, W1R 6HU
Tel 0207 287 5054 Fax 0207 287 0679

First Act Insurance Insurance Hse
Brighton Rd South Croydon CR2 6EB
Tel: 0208 686 5050 Fax: 0208 686 1933

Hanover Park Group Plc
Greystoke Hse, 80-86 Weston St, SE19 3AQ
Tel 0208 771 8844 Fax 0208 771 1697

Media & Entertainment Insurance Services Ltd
49 Glanville Rd Bromley BR2 9LN
Tel: 0208 460 4498

Parmead Insurance Brokers
Lion Hse Borough High St SE1 1JR
Tel: 0208 467 8656 Fax: 0208 295 1659

Robertson Taylor Insurance Brokers Ltd
33 Harbour Exchange Sq, E14 9SG
Tel 0207 538 9840 Fax 0207 538 9919

Stonehouse Conseillers
79-80 Margaret St, W1N 7HB
Tel 0207 636 3788 Fax 0207 636 5980

White & Wilson Insurance Brokers Ltd
3rd Floor, 48 Carnaby St, W1V 1PF
Tel 0207 734 2858 Fax 0207 734 2860

laboratories

Bucks Laboratories Ltd
714 Banbury Ave Slough SL1 4LR
Tel: 01753 576 611 Fax: 01753 691 762

Colour Film Services
10 Wadsworth Rd, Perivale, Greenford,
Middx, UB6 7JX
Tel 0208 998 2731 Fax 0208 997 8738

Lightning Strikes
3 Star Works Salter St NW10 6UN Tel:
0208 964 1232   Fax: 0208 964 3134

Metrocolor London Ltd
91-95 Gillespie Rd, N5 1LS
Tel 0207 226 4422 Fax 0207 359 2353

Playlight Hire
Ltd 860 Coronation Rd Park Royal
NW10 7PS
Tel: 0208 965 8188 Fax: 0208 961 6348

Rank Film Laboratories Ltd
North Orbital Rd, Denham, Uxbridge,
Middx, UB9 5HQ
Tel 01895 832323   Fax 01895 832446

Soho Images
8-14 Meard St, W1V 3HR
Tel 0207 437 0831 Fax 0207 734 9471

Technicolor Film Services
Bath Rd, West Drayton, Middx,
UB7 0DB
Tel 0208 759 5432 Fax 0208 759 6270

Todd-Ao Filmatic
Horley Crescent NW1 8NT
Tel: 0207 284 7900 Fax: 0207 284 1018

Ultralight Unit
17 Kings Park Kings Langley WD4 8ST
Tel: 01923 270 380 Fax: 01923 270 386

White Light North
Corporation St Halifax Sowerby Bridge
HX6 2QQ
Tel: 01422 839 651 Fax: 01422 839 773

lighting hire

AFM Lighting
12 Alliance Rd, W3 0RA
Tel 0208 752 1888 Fax 0208 752 1432

AFL Television Facilities
Unit 5 181a Verulam Rd St Albans
AL3 4DR
Tel: 01727 844117 Fax: 01727 847649

Arri Lighting Rental - Birmingham
Unit 73, Standard Ways, Gravelly Ind
Park, Birmingham, B24 8TL
Tel 0121 326 8118   Fax 0121 327 0403

Arri Lighting Rental - Cardiff
Unit 4, Excelsior Trading Estate,
Western Avenue Gabalfa, Cardiff,
CF4 3AT
Tel 01222 616160   Fax 01222 692383

Arri Lighting Rental - London
20A Airlinks Industrial Estate, Spitfire
Way, Heston, Hounslow, Middx,
TW5 9NR
Tel 0208 561 6700 Fax 0208 569 2539

Arri Lighting Rental - Manchester
Unit 6-8 Orchard St, Industrial Estate,
Salford, Lancs, M6 6FL
Tel 0161 736 8034 Fax 0161 745 8023

Backlight
18 West Harbour Rd Granton Edinburgh
EH5 1PN
Tel: 0131 551 2337 Fax: 0131 5520370

Cinequip Lighting
Orchard St Industrial Estate Salford
Manchester M6 6FL
Tel: 0161 736 8034 Fax: 0161 7458023

Direct Lighting
Units 11 & 12 North Western
Commercial Centre Bradfield Ln
NW1 9YS
Tel: 0207 424 0338 Fax: 0207 4240337

Electric Sun Unit
14 Parsons Green Depot Parsons
Green Ln SW6 4HH
Tel: 0207 731 0937 Fax: 0207 7312605

James Electrical Lighting Hire
Castle Studios Olmar St SE1 5AY
Tel: 0207 237 5332 Fax: 0207 2315030

John Hanlon Ltd
Hanlon Studio Minerva Rd Park Royal
NW10 6HJ
Tel: 0208 965 3335 Fax: 0208 9631250

Lee Lighting - Manchester
Manchester Rd, Kearsley, Bolton,
Lancs, BL4 8RL
Tel 01204 794000 Fax 01204 571877

Lee Lighting - Glasgow
110 Lancefield St, Glasgow, G3 8JD
Tel 0141 221 5175 Fax 0141 248 2751

Lee Lighting - London
Wycombe Rd, Wembley, Middx,
HA0 1QD
Tel 0208 900 2900 Fax 0208 902 5500

Lee Lighting - Bristol
Unit 4, Avon Riverside Est, Victoria Rd,
Avonmouth, Bristol, BS11 9DB
Tel 0117 982 7364 Fax 0117 923 5745

MGC Lamps Ltd
No 1 The Sovereign Centre Farthing Rd
Ind. Estate Ipswich IP1 5AP
Tel: 01473 461 875 Fax: 01473 240 081

Strathmore Film Lighting
49 Earlston Rd Stow Galashiels
TD1 2RL
Tel: 01578 730 398 01784 472 876

SPS Lighting
Manormead Risborough Rd Terrick Near
Wendover Aylesbury HP17 0UB
Tel: 01296 614 799 Fax: 01296 614798

**VFG - Michael Samuelson
Goleuadau Cymru**
The Media Centre, Culver Hse Cross,
Cardiff CF5 6XS
Tel 01222 599225 Fax 01222 599688

**VFG - Michael Samuelson Lighting
Leeds**
Unit 9, Maybrook Industrial Park, Armley
Rd, Loods, LS12 2EL
Tel 0113 2428232 Fax 0113 2454149

**VFG - Michael Samuelson Lighting
Ltd**
Pinewood Studios, Pinewood Rd, Iver,
Bucks, SL0 0NH
Tel 01753 631133 Fax 01753 630485

**VFG - Michael Samuelson Lighting
Southampton**
Meridian TV Centre, Northam,
Southampton, Hamts, SO14 0YS
Tel 01703 712056 Fax 01703 335050

VFG - The Electric Light Company
4 Royal Victor Place Bow E3 5SS
Tel: 0208 983 1666 Fax: 0208 215 0000

Web Lighting Ltd
Ravenscraig Rd, Little Hulton,
Manchester, M38 9PU
Tel 01204 862966/ 0208 744 0554
Fax 01204 862977/0208 744 2885

music libraries

Atmosphere Music Ltd
65 Maltings Pl, Bagleys Lane, Fulham,
SW6 3AR
Tel 0207 371 5888 Fax 0207 384 2744

Boosey & Hawkes Music Library
295 Regents St, W1R 8JH
Tel 0207 580 2060 Fax 0207 580 5815

Carlin Production Music
Iron Bridge Hse, 2 Bridge Approach,
Chalk Farm, NW1 8BD
Tel 0207 734 3251 Fax 0207 439 2391

Cavendish Music
295 Regents St, W1R 8JH
Tel 0207 580 2060 Fax 0207 436 5675

De Wolfe Music
80-88 Wardour St, W1V 3DF
Tel 0207 439 8481 Fax 0207 437 2744

Digiffects Sound Effects Library
5 Newburgh St, W1V 1LH
Tel 0207 434 9678 Fax 0207 434 1470

File Effects & JW Media Music Ltd
4 Whitfield Street, W1P 5RD
Tel: 0207 681 8900 Fax: 0207 681 8911

Independent Music Supervision
62A Warwick Gdns Kensington
W14 8PP
Tel: 0207 565 2665 Fax: 0207 6038431

KPM Music Ltd
127 Charing Cross Rd, WC2H OEA
Tel 0207 412 9111 Fax 0207 413 0061

Magmasters
20 St Anne's Court, W1V 3AW
Tel 0207 437 8273 Fax 0207 494 1281

Music Factor Ltd
42 Lucerne Rd N5 1TZ
Tel: 0208 802 5984 Fax: 0208 8097436

Music Hse International
5 Newburgh St, W1V 1LH
Tel 0207 434 9678 Fax 0207 434 1470

Music Matters
Crest Hse Church Rd Teddington
TW11 8PY
Tel: 0208 977 8499 Fax: 0208 977 6386

Music Sales
8-9 Frith St W1V 5TZ
Tel: 0207 432 4204

The Extreme Music Library Plc
Greenland Place Bayham St NW1 0AG
Tel: 0207 485 0111 Fax: 0207 482 4871

negative cutting

Mike Fraser Ltd
6 Silver Rd, White City Industrial Park,
W12 7SG
Tel 0208 749 6911   Fax 0208 743 3144

**Negative Cutting -
Computamatch**
Hammer Hse, 117 Wardour St,
W1V 3TD
Tel 0207 287 1316   Fax 0207 287 0793

PNC - Pro Negative Cutting
3 Carlisle St, W1V 5RH
Tel 0207 437 2025 Fax 0207 437 7036

Sylvia Wheeler Film Services Ltd
1 Woodlands Rd, Camberley, Surrey,
G15 3LZ
Tel 01276 63166   Fax 01276 684169

Tru-cut
11 Poland St, W1V 3DE
Tel 0207 437 7257 Fax 0207 734 4772

preview theatres

Bloomsbury Theatre
15 Gordon St, WC1H 0AH
Tel 0207 383 5976 Fax 0207 383 4080

Century Theatre
31-32 Soho Sq, W1V 6AP
Tel 0207 437 7766 Fax 0207 434 2170

Columbia TriStar Films UK
Sony Pictures, Europe Hse, 25 Golden
Sq, W1R 6LU
Tel 0207 533 1095 Fax 0207 533 1105

De Lane Lea Ltd
75 Dean St, W1V 5HA
Tel 0207 432 3800 Fax 0207 437 0913

Edinburgh Film & TV Studios
Nine Mile Burn, Penicuik, Midlothian,
EH26 9LT
Tel 01968 672 131   Fax 01968 672 685

Institute of Contemporary Arts
Nash Hse, The Mall, SW1Y 5AH
Tel 0207 930 0493 Fax 0207 873 0051

Metro Cinema
11 Rupert St, W1V 7FS
Tel 0207 287 3515   Fax 0207 287 2112

Mr Young's Preview Theatre
14/15 D'Arblay St, W1V 3FP
Tel 0207 437 1771 Fax 0207 734 4520

Odeon Cinema
The Broadway, Wimbledon, SW19 1QG
Tel 0208 540 9978 Fax 0208 543 9125

Rank Preview
127 Wardour St, W1V 4AD
Tel 0207 224 3339 Fax 0207 434 3689

The Royal Society of Arts
The Durham St Auditorium, 8 John
Adams St. WC2N 6EZ
Tel 0207 930 5115   Fax 0207 839 5805

Warner Brothers Preview Theatre
135 Wardour St, W1V 4AP
Tel 0207 734 8400 Fax 0207 437 5521

Watermans Arts Centre
40 High St, Brentford, Middx, TW8 0DS
Tel 0208 847 5651 Fax 0208 569 8592

production consultants

The Creative Partnership
13 Bateman St, W1V 5TB
Tel 0207 439 7762 Fax 0207 437 1467

Ex Post Facto
11 St Catherines Rd Winchester
SO23 0PP
Tel: 01962 627547 Fax: 01962 627547

production & location services

1st Call Location Vehicles
Bridge Hse, Three Mills Island Studios
Three Mill Lane, E3 3DZ
Tel 0208 227 1112   Fax 0208 227 1114

A & D Wheal Location Service Ltd
Unit 5, 13-15 Sunbeam Rd, NW10 6JP
Tel 0207 727 3828 Fax 0208 965 0699

A & J Exhibition & Film Service
44 Carlton Rd, Gidea Park, Romford,
Essex, RM2 5AP
Tel 01708 740341 Fax 01708 740341

A1 Mobile
2 Back Lane Cottages, Back Lane,
Halam, Nr Newark, Notts, NG22 8AG
Tel 01636 814063 Fax 01636 815737

GP Film Services
Unit 20, Wadsworth Business Centre,
21 Wadsworth Rd, Perivale, UB6 7JD
Tel 0208 991 1026 Fax 0208 991 9845

Location Facilities Ltd
St Albans Farm, Staines Rd, Feltham,
Middx, TW14 0HH
Tel 0208 572 3535 Fax 0208 572 6344

Michael Webb
Grasemere, Rosemary Lane, Thorpe
Village, Egham, Surrey, TW20 8PT
Tel 01932 568082 Fax 01932 568082

Mobile Toilets
Culverden, Crimp Hill Rd, Old Windsor,
Windsor, Berks, SL4 2RA
Tel 01753 866267 Fax 01753 866267

On Set Location Services
Clear Farm, Bassingbourn, Royston,
Herts, SG8 5NL
Tel 0208 840 9723 Fax 01763 244663

Rd Runner Film Services
1 Bradford Rd, Acton, W3 7SP
Tel 0208 742 9292 Fax 0208 749 7347

S & S Facilities Transport
The Old Cottage, Thomson Walk,
Calcot, Reading, Berks, RG31 7DP
Tel 0118 941 5250/0208 568 2173 Fax
0118 941 5250

Traylen Location Services
104 Bedfont Lane, Feltham, Middx,
TW14
Tel 0208 890 5029 Fax 0208 751 3581

Willies Wheels
Henry's Yard, Challenge Rd, Ashford,
Middx TW15 1AX
Tel/Fax 01784 240477

props

A & M Furniture Hire Ltd
The Royals, Victoria Rd, NW10 6ND
Tel 0208 233 1500 Fax 0208 233 1550

Animal Ark
The Studio, 29 Somerset Rd, Brentford,
Middx, TW8 8BT
Tel 0208 560 3029 Fax 0208 560 5762

Any Amount of Books
62 Charing Cross Rd, WC2H 0BB
Tel 0207 240 8140 Fax 0207 240 1769

Avant Gardener Ltd
16 Winders Rd, SW11 3HE
Tel 0207 978 4253 Fax 0207 978 4253

Beat About the Bush
Unit 23, Enterprise Way, Triangle
Business Centre, Salter St (off Hythe
Rd), NW10 6UG
Tel 0208 960 2087 Fax 0208 969 2281

Film Furniture
c/o Tomlinson Ltd, Moorside, Tockwith,
York, YO5 8QG
Tel 01423 359052 Fax 01423 358188

Floreal
7 Anglers Lane, Kentish Town,
NW5 3DG
Tel 0207 482 4005 Fax 0207 482 4006

Gimberts (div of Phoenix Hire)
Phoenix Hse, Whitworth St, Openshaw,
Manchester, M11 2GR
Tel 0161 223 6660 Fax 0161 223
6630

Granada TV Props General
Quay St, Manchester, Lancashire,
M60 9EA
Tel 0161 827 2020 Fax 0161 832 8809

Greenery Ltd
Bridge Farm, Hospital Bridge Rd,
Whitton, Twickenham, Middx, TW2 6LN
Tel 0208 893 8992 Fax 0208 893 8995

Jaysigns
10-12 Gaskin St, N1 2RY
Tel 0207 359 947 Fax 0207 226 3820

**Larsen & Laurens (scientific &
medical)**
6 Chase Rd, Park Royal NW10 6HZ
Tel 0208 453 1222 Fax 0208 453 1777

Laurence Corner
62-64 Hampstead Rd NW1
Tel: 0207 813 1010 Fax: 0207 813 1413

Living Props Ltd
Sevenhills Rd, Iver Heath, Iver, Bucks,
SL0 0PA
Tel 01895 835100 Fax 01895 835757

Neon Effects
Unit 5, Havelock Terrace, Battersea,
SW8 4AS
Tel 0207 498 1998 Fax 0207 498 0871

Newman Hire Co Ltd
16 The Vale, Acton, W3 7SB
Tel 0208 743 0741/0208 749 1501
Fax 0208 749 3513

Palmbrokers
Cenacle Nursery, Taplow Common Rd,
Burnham, Bucks, SL1 8NW
Tel 01628 663734 Fax 01628 661047

Phoenix Hire Ltd
20 Bethune Rd, NW10 6NJ
Tel 0208 961 6161 Fax 0208 961 6162

Piano Workshop
30a Highgate Rd, NW5 1NS
Tel 0207 267 7671 Fax 0207 284 0083

Pictures Props Company
Brunel Hse, 12-16 Brunel Rd, W3 7XR
Tel 0208 749 2433 Fax 0208 740 5846

Prop it Up
Basement, Design Bldg, BBC TV
Centre, Wood Lane, W12 7RJ
Tel 0208 576 7295 Fax 0208 576 7295

Props Galore
15-17 Brunel Rd, W3 7XR
Tel 0208 746 1222 Fax 0208 749 8372

Relic Antiques & Designs
The Old Rectory, Wellow, Bath,
BA2 8QZ
Tel 01225 833049 Fax 01225 837980

Rogers & Cowan
43 King St, Covent Garden, WC2E 8RJ
Tel 0207 240 4022 Fax 0207 240 1497

Scottish Props Enterprise West
24 Craigmont St, Maryhill, Glasgow,
G20 9BT
Tel 0141 946 0925 Fax 0141 946 0832

Simon Beardmore
Belmont Hse, Belmont Rd,
Leatherhead, Surrey, KT22 7EN
Tel 01372 372701 Fax 01372 361267

Studio & TV Hire
3 Ariel Way, Wood Lane, White City,
W12 7SL
Tel 0208 749 3445 Fax 0208 740 9662

Superhire
1-4 Bethune Rd, NW10 6NJ
Tel 0208 965 9909 Fax 0208 965 8107

Swans Music Ltd
3 Plymouth Court, 166 Plymouth Grove,
Manchester, M13 0AF
Tel 0161 273 3232 Fax 0161 274 4111

The Neon Circus
25 Enterprise Way, Salter St,
NW10 6UN
Tel 0208 964 3381 Fax 0208 964 0084

The Palm Centre
Ham Central Nursery, Ham St, Ham
TW10 7HA
Tel 0208 255 6191 Fax 0208 255 6192

Weird & Wonderful Prop Hire
Elstree Film Studios, Shenley Rd,
Borehamwood, Herts, WD6 1JG
Tel 0208 953 2468 Fax 0208 207 6762

publicity

BMS Barrington Marketing
Suite 5, 20 Molyneux St, W1H 5HU
Tel 0207 262 1976 Fax 0207 262 7899

Burston Marsteller Ltd
24/28 Bloomsbury Way, WC1A 2P
Tel 0207 831 6262 Fax 0207 430 1033

CKPR
42-44 Great Tichfiled St W1P 7AE
Tel 0207 637 7222 Fax 0207 637 7220

Corbett & Keene
122 Wardour St, W1V 3TD
Tel 0207 494 3478 Fax 0207 734 2024

Creative Publicity
22 Gibsons Hill, SW16 3JP
Tel 0208 764 8000 Fax 0207 629 2202

Dennis Davidson Associates Ltd
Royalty Hse, 72/74 Dean St, W1V 3DF
Tel 0207 439 6391 Fax 0207 437 6358

Ex Post Facto
11 St Catherines Rd Winchester
SO23 0PP
Tel: 01962 627547 Fax: 01962 627547

**JAC Publicity & Marketing
Consultants Ltd**
36 Great Queen St, Covent Garden,
WC2B 5AA
Tel 0207 430 0211 Fax 0207 430 0222

Joy Sapieka Associates
Piccadilly Mansions Shaftesbury
Avenue W1V 7RL
Tel: 0207 287 6839 Fax: 0207 287 840

Lowe Bell Good Relations
59 Russell Sq. WC1B 4HJ
Tel: 0207 631 3434 Fax: 0207 6311399

Mathieu Thomas Ltd
8 Westminster Palace Gardens,
Artillery Row, SW1P 1RL
Tel 0207 222 0833 Fax 0207 222 5784

McDonald and Rutter
14-18 Ham Yard, Great Windmill St
W1V 7PD
Tel 0207 734 9009 Fax 0207 734 1151

Orlando Kimber Public Relations
PO Box 5600, Newbury Rd, Berks
RG20 8YU
Tel 01488 608888 Fax 01488 608811

**Scope Communications
Management**
Tower Hse, 8-14 Southampton St,
WC2E 7HA
Tel 0207 379 3234 Fax 0207 240 7729

Shaw Thing Media
The Cambridge, 13-15 Mare St,
E8 4RP
Tel 0208 983 8644 Fax 0208 533 9295

Spirit Publicity
Lower Ground Floor 36 Langham St
W1N 5RH
Tel 0207 580 0909 Fax 0207 637 4055

The Creative Partnership
13 Bateman St, W1V 5TB
Tel 0207 439 7762 Fax 0207 437 1467

sales agents

Alliance Atlantis
184-192 Drummond St NW1 3HP
Tel: 0207 3916935 Fax: 0207 383 404

Avalon Publicity
Queens Hse Leicester Place Leicester
Sq. WC2H 7BP
Tel: 0207 7346677 Fax: 0207 437 3366

Centrestage Public Relations
20 Bryanstone Ave Guildford GU2 6UN
Tel: 01483 567572 Fax: 01483 67572

Ciby Sales
10 Stephen Mews, W1P 1PP
Tel: 0207 333 8877 Fax 0207 333 8878

Film Four International
124 Horseferry Rd, SW1P 2TX
Tel 0207 396 4444 Fax 0207 306 8361

First Independent Films
69 New Oxford St, WC1A 1DG
Tel 0207 528 7767 Fax 0207 528 7770

Handmade Films
15 Golden Sq, W1R 3AG
Tel 0207 434 3132 Fax 0207 434 3143

Intermedia Vision Ltd
104 Great Russell St WC1B 3LA
Tel: 0207 323 3444

**JAC Publicity & Marketing
Consultants Ltd.**
36 Great Queen St WC2B 5AA
Tel: 0207 430 0211 Fax: 0207 430 0222

J & M Entertainment
2 Dorset Sq, NW1 6PU
Tel 0207 723 6544 Fax 0207 724 7541

Janie New Public Relations
1 Northolme Rd N5 2UZ
Tel: 0207 704 2925 Fax: 0207 3548126

Mayfair Entertainment Int Ltd
110 St Martin's Lane, WC2N 4AD
Tel 0207 304 7911 Fax 0207 867 1184

Polygram Film International
Oxford Hse, 76 Oxford St, W1N 0HQ
Tel 0207 307 1300 Fax 0207 307 1301

The Sales Company
62 Shaftesbury Ave, W1V 7DE
Tel 0207 434 9061 Fax 0207 494 3293

solicitors

Davenport Lyons
1 Old Burlington St, W1X 2NL
Tel 0207 287 5353 Fax 0207 437 0216

Denton Hall
5 Chancery Lane, Cliffords Inn,
EC4A 1BU
Tel 0207 242 1212 Fax 0207 404 0087

Hammond Suddards
7 Devonshire Sq. Cutlers Gdns
EC2M 4YH
Tel: 0207 655 1000 Fax: 0207 6551001

Harbottle & Lewis
Hanover Hse, 14 Hanover Sq,
W1R 0BE
Tel 0207 667 5000 Fax 0207 6675100

Marriot Harrison
12 Great James' St, WC1N 3DR
Tel 0207 209 2000 Fax 0207 209 2001

Olswang
90 Long Acre, WC2E 9TT
Tel 0207 208 8888 Fax 0207 208 8800

Richards Butler
Beaufort Hse, 15 St Botolph St,
EC3A 7EE
Tel 0207 247 6555 Fax 0207 247 5091

Schilling & Lom
Royalty Hse, 72-74 Dean St, W1V 6AE
Tel 0207 453 2500 Fax 0207 453 2600

The Simkins Partnership
45/51 Whitfield St, W1P 6AA
Tel 0207 631 1050 Fax 0207 436 2744

---

sound equipment hire

AFL Television Facilities
Unit 5 181a Verulam Rd St Albans
AL3 4DR
Tel: 01727 844117 Fax: 01727 847649

**Audio Visual Asset Management
Ltd (AVAM)**
Little Orchard Hse Bears Den
Kingswood Tadworth KT20 6PL
Tel: 01737 830084 Fax: 01737 830 063

Better Sound Ltd
33 Endell St WC2H 9BA
Tel: 0207 8360033 Fax: 0207 4979285

Broadcast Film & Video Ltd
33 West Park, Clifton, Bristol, BS8 2LX
Tel 0117 923 7087   Fax 0117 923 7090

Birmingham Sound Hire Ltd
86 Wrottesley Rd Tettenhall
Wolverhampton WV6 8SJ
Tel: 01902 751 184 Fax: 01902 743 718

Dreamhire
Unit 5, Chapman's Park Industrial
Estate, 378 388 High Rd, NW10
Tel 0208 451 5544 Fax 0208 451 6464

Essential Pictures Ltd
222 Kensal Rd W10 5BN
Tel: 0208 696 7017 Fax: 0208 9608201

Fab
Unit 8 Rufus Business Centre
Ravensbury Terrace SW18 4RL
Tel: 0208 947 7738 Fax: 0208 9476608

Gearbox (Sound & Vision) Ltd
PO Box 99 Barnet EN4 9NF
Tel: 0208 449 6555 Fax: 0208 4495252

Hilton Sound
Unit 5 Chapmans Park Industrial Estate
High Rd Willesden NW10 2DY
Tel: 0208 459 1001 Fax: 0208 830

Osbourne Sound Eqpt
9 Meard St, W1V 3HQ
Tel 0207 437 6170 Fax 0207 439 4807

Richmond Film Services
The Old School, Park Lane, Richmond,
Surrey, TW9 2RA
Tel 0208 940 6077 Fax 0208 948 8326

**Skarda International Communica-
tions Ltd**
7 Portland Mews D'Arblay St W1V 3FL
Tel: 0207 734 7776 Fax: 0207 7341360

The Sound Design Co
Shepperton Studios TW17 0QD
Tel: 01932 572362 Fax: 01932 572 659

The Ware House Sound Services
23 Water St Leith Edinburgh EH6 6SU
Tel: 0131 555 6900 Fax: 0131 5556901

---

special effects

Action Firearms
152 Monega Rd, Forest Gate,
Tel 0208 471 3407   Fax 0208 4713407

ALL F/X Ltd
Little Orchard, Framewood Rd, Stoke
Poges, Slough, Berks, SL3 6PG
Tel 01753 662227   Fax 01753 663269

Any Effects
64 Weir Rd, SW19 8UG
Tel 0208 944 0099 Fax 0208 944 6989

Artem Visual Effects
Perivale Ind Park, Horsenden Lane, Sth
Perivale, Greenford, Middx, UB6 7RH
Tel 0208 997 7771 Fax 0208 997 1503

BBC Special Effects room G14
Park Western, 41-44 Kendall Avenue,
Acton, W3 0RP
Tel 0208 993 9434 Fax 0208 993 8741

Bickers Action
School Lane, Coddenham, Ipswich,
Suffolk, IP6 9PT
Tel 01449 760201   Fax 01449 760614

Cinesite (Europe) Ltd
9 Carlisle St, W1V 5RG
Tel 0207 973 4000 Fax 0207 973 4040

David Jones Fragile Ice & Water
Area No1, Riverside Works, Railshead
Rd, Isleworth, Middx, TW7 7BY
Tel 0208 568 7787 Fax 0208 568 7787

Effects Associates Ltd
Pinewood Studios, Pinewood Rd, Iver,
Bucks, SL0 0NH
Tel 01753 652007   Fax 01753 630127

Emergency House
Manchester Rd, Marsden, Huddersfield,
HD7 6EY
Tel 01484 846999   Fax 01484 845061

Especial Effects
86 Woodhurst Avenue, Petts Wood,
Orpington, BR5 1AT
Tel 01689 837251   Fax 01689 837251

Fantastic Fireworks Ltd
Rocket Park, Pepperstock, Luton,
LU1 4LL
Tel 01582 485555   Fax 01582 485545

Foxtrot Productions Ltd
Canalot Productions Studios, 222
Kensal Rd, Kensington, W10 5BN
Tel 0208 964 3555   Fax 0208 960 3811

FX Projects
Studio Hse, Rita Rd, SW8 1JU
Tel 0207 582 8750 Fax 0207 793 0467

Lightspeed Visual Effects
Cloudbase Marlow Rd Bourne End
SL8 5SP
Tel: 01628 525147 Fax: 01628 529 385

FUJIFILM'S SHOOTING RANGE

Fujifilm New Super F-Series		35mm	16mm
F-64D	Daylight Balanced	Type 8522	Type 8622
F-125	Tungsten Balanced	Type 8532	Type 8632
F-250	Tungsten Balanced	Type 8552	Type 8652
F-250D	Daylight Balanced	Type 8562	Type 8662
F-400	Tungsten Balanced	Type 8582	Type 8682
F-500	Tungsten Balanced	Type 8572	Type 8672

Fuji Photo Film (UK) Limited
Fuji Film House • 125 Finchley Road • London NW3 6HY

FUJIFILM
I&I – Imaging & Information

Contact Roger Sapsford • www.fujifilm.co.uk
Telephone 020 7586 5900 • Fax 020 7483 1419

Peerless Camera Company
32 Bedfordbury, WC2N 4DU
Tel 0207 836 3367 Fax 0207 240 2143

Ray Marston Wig Studio
Unit 24, 44 Earlham St, WC2H 9LA
Tel 0207 379 7953 Fax 0207 379 7953

Snow Business
56 Northfield Rd, Tetbury, Glos,
GL8 8HQ
Tel 01666 502857 Fax 01666 502857

Special Effects UK
Nr Crooked Billet Roundabout Uxbridge
Rd Iver Heath SL0 0LR
Tel: 01753 650658 Fax: 01753 650659

Theatrical Pyrotechnics Ltd
The Loop, Manston Airport, Ramsgate,
Kent, CT12 5DE
Tel 01843 823545 Fax 01843 822655

The Intrepid Aviation Company Ltd
Hangar 4 North Weald Aerodrome
Epping CM16 6AA
Tel: 01992 524233 Fax: 01992 524225

---

stock

3M
3M Hse, Bracknell, Berks, RG12 1JU
Tel 01344 858 385   Fax 01344 858 082

AGFA-GEVAERT Ltd
Motion Picture Division, 27 Great West
Rd, Brentford, Middx, TW8 9AX
Tel 0208 231 4310 Fax 0208 231 4315

Film Stock Centre BLANX
70 Wardour St, W1V 3HP
Tel 0207 494 2244 Fax 0207 287 2040

Fuji Photo Film (UK) Ltd
Fuji Film Hse, 125 Finchley Rd,
NW3 6HY
Tel 0207 586 5900 Fax 0207 722 4259

Kodak Ltd
Professional Motion Imaging, Station
Rd, Hemel Hempstead, Herts, HP1 1JU
Tel 01442 61122   Fax 01442 844458

Orchard Video Ltd
The Old School Hse, Barton Manor,
Bristol, BS2 0RL
Tel 0117 941 3898   Fax 0117 941 3797

Stanley Productions
147 Wardour St, W1V 3TB
Tel 0207 437 5472 Fax 0207 437 2126

Zonal
Holmethorpe Ave, Redhill, Surrey,
RH1 2N
Tel 01737 767 171 Fax 01737 767 610

---

studios

Bray Studios
Down Pl, Water Oakley, Windsor Rd,
Windsor, Berks SL4 5UG
Tel 01628 622111 Fax 01628 770 381

Ealing Studios
Ealing Green, Ealing, W5 5EP
Tel 0208 567 6655 Fax 0208 758 8658

Granada Television
Quay St, Manchester, M60 9EA
Tel 0161 827 2020 Fax 0161 827 2374

Millennium Studios
Elstree Way, Borehamwood, Herts,
WD6 1SF
Tel 0208 236 1400 Fax 0208 236 1444

Park Royal Studios
1 Barretts Green Rd, NW10 7AP
Tel 0208 965 9778 Fax 0208 963 1056

Pinewood Studios Ltd
Pinewood Rd, Iver, Bucks SL0 0NH
Tel 01753 651700 Fax 01753 656844

Shepperton Film Studios
Studios Rd, Shepperton, Middx,
TW17 0QD
Tel 01932 562611 Fax 01932 568989

Teddington Studios Ltd
Teddington Lock, Middx, TW11 9NT
Tel 0208 977 3252 Fax 0208 943 4050

Three Mills Island Studios
Three Mill Lane, E3 3DU
Tel 0207 363 0033 Fax 0207 363 0034

Twickenham Film Studios
The Barons, St Margaret's,
Twickenham, Middx, TW1 2AW
Tel 0208 607 8888 Fax 0208 607 8889

Yorkshire Tyne Tees Television
The Television Centre, Kirkstall Rd,
Leeds, LS3 1JS
Tel 0113 2438283 Fax 0113 2341293

3rd Millennium Studio
Church Farm (Office Village) High St
Eaton Bray LU6 2DL
Tel: 01525 221296

Capel Mawr Studio
Llanrug Caernarfon Gwynedd L55 4AE
Tel: 01286 678102 Fax: 01286 677410

Cobra Studios Ltd
Midland St Ardwick Manchester
M12 6LB
Tel: 0161 273 3828 Fax: 0161 2744209

Eastside Studios
40A River Rd Barking IG11 0DW
Tel: 0208 507 7572 Fax: 0208 5078550

HDS Studios
2e Eagle Rd North Moons Moat
Industrial Estate Redditch Nr
Birmingham
Tel: 01527 62822 Fax: 01527 68436

Studio Drama
Gaidhlig 54A Seaforth Rd Stornoway
HS1 2SD
Tel: 01851 701 125 Fax: 01851 701200

Westward Studios
Wroughton Park Swindon SN1
Tel: 0207 7290919 Fax: 0207 613 4729

---

stunts & weapons

Action Firearms
152 Monega Rd, Forest Gate, E7 8ER
Tel 0208 471 3407 Fax 0208 471 3407

Foxtrot Productions Ltd
222 Kensal Rd, Kensington, W10
Tel 0208 964 3555 Fax 0208 960 3811

Perdix Firearms Ltd
P O Box 1670 Salisbury SP4 6QL
Tel 01722 782402 Fax 01722 782790

Prop Farm
Grange Farm, Elmton, Nr Creswell,
Worksop, Notts, S80 4LX
Tel 01909 723100 Fax 01909 721465

Bapty & Co.
703 Harrow Road, NW10 5NY
Tel: 0208 9696671 Fax: 0208 960 1106

---

telecine & conversion

**Goldcrest Post Production
Facilities**
36/44 Brewer St, W1R 3HP (Entrance
no 1 Lexington St)
Tel 0207 437 7972 Fax 0207 437 6411

Midnight Transfer
15 Kingly Court, W1R 5LE
Tel 0207 494 1719 Fax 0207 494 2021

Rushes Post Production
66 Old Compton St, W1V 5PA
Tel 0207 437 8676 Fax 0207 734 2519

Salon Productions Ltd
10 Livonia St, W1V 3PH
Tel 0207 437 0516 Fax 0207 437 6197

Soho Images
8-14 Meard St, W1V 3HR
Tel 0207 437 0831 Fax 0207 734 9471

SVC Television
142 Wardour St, W1V 3AV
Tel 0207 734 1600 Fax 0207 437 1854

Telecine Ltd
Video Hse, 48 Charlotte St, W1P 1LX
Tel 0207 208 2200 Fax 0207 208 2250

Telefilm Video Services
Twickenham Film Studios, St
Margaret's, Twickenham, Middx, TW1
2AW
Tel 0208 744 9828 Fax 0208 744 0357

The Machine Room
54-58 Wardour St, W1V 3HN
Tel 0207 734 3433 Fax 0207 287 3773

The Mill
40-41 Great Marlborough St, W1V 1DA
Tel 0207 287 4041 Fax 0207 287 8393

Twentieth Century Video Ltd
2nd Floor, (unit 2-5), Wembley
Commercial Centre, East Lane,
Wembley, Middx, HA9
Tel 0208 904 6271 Fax 0208 904 0172

Vidfilm Europe
North Orbital Rd, Denham, Uxbridge,
Middx, UB9 5HL
Tel 01895 5835555 Fax 01895 835 353

Yorkshire Tyne Tees Television
Television Centre, Leeds, LS3 1JS
Tel 0113 243 8283 Fax 0113 234 1293

---

titles & opticals

FrameStore
9 Noel St, W1V 4AL
Tel 0207 208 2600 Fax 0207 208 2626

Cine Image Film Opticals
7a Langley St, Covent Garden,
WC2H 9JA
Tel 0207 240 6222 Fax 0207 240 6242

Cinesite (Europe) Ltd
9 Carlisle St, W1V 5RG
Tel 0207 973 4000 Fax 0207 973 4040

Filmoptic
Unit 10, Thames Hse, Middle Green
Estate, Middle Green Rd, Langley,
Slough, Berks SL3 6DF
Tel 01753 554955 Fax 01753 554955

General Screen Enterprises
Highbridge Estate, Oxford Rd, Uxbridge,
Middx, UB8 1LX
Tel 01895 231 931 Fax 01895 235 335

Howell Optical Printers Ltd
I-Mex Hse Wadsworth Rd Perivale
Middlesex UB6 7JJ
Tel 0208 564 9329 Fax 0208 564 8705

The Mill
40-41 Great Marlborough St, W1V 1DA
Tel 0207 287 4041 Fax 0207 287 8303

trade publications

BFI Film & Television Handbook
British Film Institute, 21 Stephen St,
W1P 2LN
Tel 0207 957 8922 Fax 0207 436 7950

KAYS UK Production Manual
Pinewood Studios, Pinewood Rd, Iver,
Bucks, SL0 0NH
Tel 0208 749 1214 Fax 0208 964 4604

KEMPS Directory
Cahners Publishing Company, 34-35
Newman St, W1P 3PD
Tel 0207 637 3663 Fax 0207 580 5559

Moving Pictures
151-153 Wardour St, W1V 3TB
Tel 0207 287 0070 Fax 0207 734 6153

PCR (Production & Casting Report)
PO Box 11, N1 7JZ
Tel 0207 566 8282 Fax 0207 566 8284

Screen Finance
Newland Hse, 40 Berners St,
W1P 3AA
Tel 0171 453 2800 Fax 0171 453 2802

Screen International
33-39 Bowling Green Lane, EC1R 0DA
Tel 0207 505 8080 Fax 0207 505 8116

The Hollywood Reporter
23 Ridgmount St, WC1E 7AH
Tel 0207 323 6686 Fax 0207 631 0428

The Knowledge
Miller Freeman Information Services,
Riverbank Hse, Angel Lane, Tonbridge,
Kent, TN9 1BR
Tel 01732 362666 Fax 01732 367301

The Spotlight
7 Leicester Pl, WC2H 7BP
Tel 0207 437 7631 Fax 0207 437 5881

The Stage Newspaper
47 Bermondsey St, SE1 3XT
Tel 0207 403 1818 Fax 0207 403 1418

Variety
34-35 Newman St, W1P
Tel 0207 637 3663 Fax 0207 580 5559

video duplication

Dubbs
25-26 Poland St, W1V 3DB
Tel 0207 629 0055 Fax 0207 287 8796

Holloway Film & Television
68-70 Wardour St, W1V 3HP
Tel 0207 494 0777 Fax 0207 494 0309

London Post
34-35 Dean St, W1V 5AP
Tel 0207 439 9080 Fax 0207 434 0714

M2 TV Ltd
74-80 Camden St, The Forum,
NW1 0EH
Tel 0207 387 5001 Fax 0207 387 5025

MetroSoho
6/7 Great Chapel St, Soho, W1V 3AG
Tel 0207 439 3494 Fax 0207 437 3782

Metrovideo Ltd
The Old Bacon Factory, 57-59 Great
Suffolk St, SE1 2BP
Tel 0207 928 2088 Fax 0207 261 0685

Molinare
34 Fouberts Place W1V 2BH
Tel: 0207 4787230 Fax: 0207 4787199

Northern Video Facilities
4th Floor, Central Buildings, 11 Peter
St, Manchester, M2 5QR
Tel 0161 832 7643 Fax 0161 832 7643

Rushes
66 Old Compton St, W1V 5PA
Tel 0207 437 8676 Fax 0207 734 2519

Soho Images
8-14 Meard St, W1V 3HR
Tel 0207 437 0831 Fax 0207 734 9471

The Machine Room Ltd
54-58 Wardour St, W1V 3HN
Tel 0207 734 3433 Fax 0207 287 3773

TSI Video Ltd
10 Grape St, WC2H 8DY
Tel 0207 379 3435 Fax 0207 379 4589

TVI Ltd
142 Wardour St, W1V 3AU
Tel 0207 878 0000 Fax 0207 878 7800

Video Time
22-24 Greek St, W1V 5LG
Tel 0207 439 1211 Fax 0207 439 7336

VMI Ltd
Unit 1 Granville Industrial Estate
Granville Rd NW2 2LD
Tel: 0208 209 1313 Fax: 0208 458 5047

West 1 Television
10 Bateman St, W1V 5TT
Tel 0207 437 5533 Fax 0207 287 8621

world film markets

AFM (American Film Market)
10850 Wilshire Blvd, 9th Floor, Los
Angeles, CA 90024 USA
Tel (1) 310 446 1000
Fax (1) 310 446 1600
Contact: Jonathan Wolf
email: jwolf@afma.com

CANNES
00 Boulovard Malochorboc
75008 Paris, France
Tel 33 1 45 61 66 00
Fax 33 1 45 61 97 60
www.Cannesmarket.com
www.festival-cannes.fr
Accreditation@festival-cannes.fr

MIFED
E.A. Fiera Milano, 20145 Milano, Largo
Domodossola 1, C.P. 1270 - 20101
Milan, Italy
Tel 39 02 48 01 29 20
Fax 39 02 49 97 70 20
Contact: Elena Lloyd
www.fmd.it/mifed

NATIONAL FUNDING BODIES

From April 2000, the Arts Council of England's Lottery Film Department will be merged into the Film Council, which will become a Lottery distributor in its own right, responsible for about £30m of Lottery funds to film every year. The Film Council will take on the functions and responsibilities of the British Film Commission and the BFI's Production Department and will work with the British Screen group of companies. The British Film Institute will continue as a charitable body delivering the cultural and educational objectives for film, but funded through the Film Council and responsible to it.

Film Council
Lottery Film Department, 10 Little Portland St W1N 5DF
Tel: 0207 973 5184
Fax: 0207 973 5190

Lottery Franchisees:
1. Pathé
Kent House Market Place W1N 8AR
Tel: 0207 323 5151
Fax: 0207 631 3568

2. DNA
Oval Rd Camden Town NW1 7DE
Tel: 0207 485 441
Fax: 0207 485 4422

3. Film Consortium
Flitcroft St WC2H 8DJ
Tel: 0207 691 4440
Fax: 0207 691 4445

Arts Council of Northern Ireland Lottery Department
MacNeice House 77 Malone Road Belfast BT9 6AQ
Tel: 01232 667000
Fax: 01232 664766

Arts Council of Wales / Cyngor Celfyddou Cymru
9 Museum Pl. Cardiff CF1 3NX
Tel: 01222 394711
Fax: 01222 221447

British Film Institute
21 Stephen St W1P 2LM
Tel: 0207 957 8984
Fax: 0207 580 9456

British Screen Finance
14-17 Wells Mews W1P 3FL
Tel: 0207 323 9080
Fax: 0207 323 0092

Channel Four International
124 Horseferry Rd, SW1P 2TX
Tel: 0207 306 8602
Fax: 0207 306 8361

Eastern Arts Board
Cherry Hinton Hall Cherry Hinton Road Cambridge CB1 8DW
Tel: 01223 215355
Fax: 01223 248075

East Midlands Arts Board
Mountfields House Epinal Way, Loughborough LE11 0QE
Tel: 01509 218 292
Fax: 01509 262 214

European Co-Production Fund
c/o British Screen Finance
14-17 Wells Mews W1P 3FL
Tel: 0207 323 9080
Fax: 0207 323 0092

European Media Development Agency (EMDA)
39c Highbury Place N5 1QP
Tel: 0207 226 9903
Fax: 0207 354 2706

Film Council
Queen's Yard 179a Tottenham Court Rd W1P 0BE
Tel: 0207 436 1357
Fax: 0207 436 1397

First Film Foundation
9 Bourlet Close W1P 7PJ
Tel: 0207 580 2111
Fax: 0207 580 2116

Glasgow Film Fund
249 West George St G2 4RB
Tel: 0141 302 1757
Fax: 0141 302 1714

Irish Film Board
Rockfort House St Augustine St Galway
Tel: 353 91 561 398

Isle of Man Film Commission
Illiam Dhione House 2 Circular Road Douglas IM1 1PJ
Tel: 01624 685864
Fax: 01624 685454

LFVDA (London Film and Video Development Agency)
114 Whitfield St W1P 5RW
Tel: 0207 383 7755
Fax: 0207 383 7745

MIDA (Moving Image Development Agency)
109 Mount Pleasant L3 5TF
Tel: 0151 708 9858

Northern Arts Board
9-10 Osbourne Terrace Jesmond Newcastle Upon Tyne NE2 1NZ
Tel: 0191 281 6334
Fax: 0191 281 2866

Northern Ireland Development Fund & Northern Ireland Film Commission
21 Ormeau Avenue Belfast BT2 8HD
Tel: 01232 232444
Fax: 01232 239 918

Scottish Arts Council Lottery Department
12 Manor Place Edinburgh EH3 7DD
Tel: 0131 226 6051
Fax: 0131 477 7240

Scottish Screen Development & Production Fund
74 Victoria Cres. Glasgow G12 9JN /249 West George St G2 4RB
Tel: 0141 302 1700
Fax: 0141 302 1714

Southern Screen
Brighton Media Centre 9-12 Middle St BN1 1AL
Tel: 01273 384211

South West Media Development Agency
59 Prince St Bristol BS1 4HQ
Tel: 0117 927 3226
Fax: 0117 922 6216

Wales Sgrin The Bank
10 Mount Stuart Square Cardiff Bay CF10 5EE
Tel: 01222 333300
Fax: 01222 333320

Yorkshire Media Production Agency
Workstation Paternoster Row Sheffield S1 2BX
Tel: 0114 272 0304
Fax: 0114 249 2293

WORLD FILM FESTIVALS

JANUARY

Int. Film Fest of India (Market)
The Directorate of Film Festivals, Ministry of Information and Broadcasting, 4th Floor, Lok Nayak Bhavan, Khan Market, New Delhi 110 003, India
Tel: 91 11 461 7226
Fax: 91 11 462 3430
Contact: Malki Sahai
dffiffi@bol.net.in

Int. Film Fest. Rotterdam
PO Box 21696, 3001 AR Rotterdam, The Netherlands
Tel: 31 10 890 90 90
Fax: 31 10 890 90 91
Contact: Carlie Janszen
tiger@iffrotterdam.nl

Film Fest. Brussels European Competition
Chaussée de Louvain 30, 1210 Brussels, Belgium
Tel: 32 2 227 39 80
Fax: 32 2 218 18 60
Contact: Christian Thomas
infoffb@netcity.be

The New York Fests.
780 King Street, Chappaqua, NY 10514 USA
Tel: 1 914 238 4481
Fax: 1 914 238 5040
Contact: Bilha Goldberg
info@nyfests.com

The Nortel Palm Springs Int. Film Fest.
1700 East Tahquitz Way, Suite 3, Palm Springs, CA 92262 USA
Tel: 1 760 322 2930
Fax: 1 760 322 4087
Contact: Jim Shearer
info@psfilmfest.org

Slamdance Film Fest.
6381 Hollywood Blvd #520, Los Angeles, CA 90028 USA
Tel: 1 323 466 1786
Fax: 1 323 466 1784
Contact: Henry Turner
mail@slamdance.com

Sundance Film Fest. LA Office
Sundance Insitute, 225 Santa Monica Blvd, Eighth Floor, Santa Monica, CA 90401 USA
Tel: 1 310 394 4662
Fax: 1 310 394 8353
Contact: Geoff Gilmore
la@sundance.org

Sundance Film Fest. UTAH office
Sundance Institute, PO Box 16450, Salt Lake City, UT 8411 USA
Tel: 1 801 328 3456
Fax: 1 801 575 5175
Contact: Nicole Guillemet
institute@sundance.org

Göteborg Film Fest.
PO Box 7079, 402 32 Göteborg, Sweden
Tel: 46 31 41 05 46
Fax: 46 31 41 00 63
Contact: Gunnar Bergdahl
goteborg@filmfestval.org

Max Ophüls Preis FilmFest.
Mainzer Strasse 8, D-66111 Saarbrücken, Germany
Tel: 49 681 93 674 21
Fax: 49 681 93 674 29
Contact: Gabrielle Bandel
filmfestSB@aol.com

Shanghai Int. Film Festival
11/F, STV Mansions, 298 Weihai Road, Shanghai 200041, P.R. China
Tel: 86 (0)21 62537115
Fax: 86 (0)21 62552000
siff@public4.sta.net.cn
www.siff.com

FEBRUARY

Portland Int. Film Fest.
Northwest Film Center, 1219 SW Park Avenue, Portland, Oregon 97205 USA
Tel: 1 503 221 1156
Fax: 1 503 294 0874
Contact: Bill Foster
info@nwfilm.org

AFM - American Film Market
10850 Wilshire Blvd, 9th Floor, Los Angeles, CA 90024 USA
Tel: 1 310 446 1000
Fax: 1 310 446 1600
Contact: Jonathan Wolf
jwolf@afma.com

Miami Film Fest.
Film Society of Miami, 444 Brickell Avenue, Suite 229, Miami, Florida 33131 USA
Tel: 1 305 377 3456
Fax: 1 305 577 9768
Contact: Pablo Pagan

Mardi Gras Film Fest.
Queer Screen, 12A/94 Oxford Street, Darlinghurst, NSW 2010 Australia
Tel: 61 2 9332 4938
Fax: 61 2 9331 2988
Contact: Richard King
info@queerscreen.com.au

MARCH

Valenciennes Action & Adventure Film Fest.
3 rue de Mons, 59300 Valenciennes, France
Tel: 33 3 27 29 55 40
Fax: 33 3 27 41 67 49
Contact: Patricia Riquet
ffav@wanadoo.fr

Cartagena Film Festival
A.A. 1834, Cartagena, Colombia, S.A.
Tel: 575 600 0966
Fax: 575 660 0970/575 373 0250
http://escape.com/~spyder/CART.html

Bradford Film Fest.
National Museum of Photography, Film & TV, Pictureville, Bradford BD1 1NQ UK
Tel: 44 1274 773 399
Fax: 44 1274 770 217
Contact: Lisa Kavanagh
filmfest@nmsi.ac.uk

Int. Women's Directors' Film Fest
Maison des Arts, Place Salvador Allende, 94000 Créteil, France
Tel: 33 1 49 80 38 98
Fax: 33 1 493 99 04 10
Contact: Jackie Buet
filmsfemmes@wanadoo.fr

New York Under-Ground Fest.
453 W 16th Street, office six, NYC 10011 USA
Tel: 1 212 675 1137
Fax: 1 212 675 1152
Contact: Ed Halter
festival@nyuff.com
www.nyuff.com

Brussels Int. Fest. of Fantasy Films
144 Avenue de la Reine, B-1030
Brussels, Belgium
Tel: 32 22 01 1713
Fax: 32 22 01 1469
Contact: Freddy Bozzo
peymey@skypro.be

Cleveland Int. Film Fest.
Cleveland Film Society, 2510 Market
Avenue, Cleveland
Ohio 44113, USA
Tel: 1 216 623 3456
Fax: 1 216 623 0103
Contact: Marcie Goodman
cfs@clevelandfilm.org

APRIL

Hong Kong Int. Film Fest.
Film Programmes Office, Level 7
Administration Building, Hong Kong
Cultural Centre, 10 Salisbury Road,
Tsim Sha Tsui, Hong Kong
Tel: 852 2734 2903
Fax: 852 2366 5206
Contact: Richard Lam
hkiff@hkiff.com.hk

Miller Genuine Draft Dublin Film Fest.
1 Suffolk Street, Dublin 2 Ireland
Tel: 353 1 679 2937
Fax: 353 1 679 2939
Contact: Joy Giovannelli
dff@iol.ie

Jamaica Film Fest.
African-Caribbean Institute of
Jamaica, Roy West Building, 12
Ocean Boulevard, Kingston Mall,
Kingston, JW1 Jamaica
Tel: 1 876 922 7415/4793
Fax: 1 876 924 9361
Contact: Bernard Jankee

Int. Istanbul Film Fest.
Istanbul Foundation for Culture and
Arts, Istiklal Caddesi, No 146 Beyoglu,
80070 Istanbul, Turkey
Tel: 90 212 293 3133
Fax: 90 212 249 7771
Contact: Hulya Ucansu
filmfest@istfest-tr.org

Cape Town Int. Film Fest.
Film Education Unit University of
Capetown, Private Bag, Rondesbosch
8001, Cape Town, South Africa
Tel: 27 21 4238 257
Fax: 27 21 4242 355
filmfest@hiddingh.uct.ac.za

Brasilia Int. Film Fest.
Academia de Teñis Resort, SCES
Trecho 4 Conj. 5 Lote 1-B Asa Sul,
Brasilia - DF - Brasil Cep 70200 - 150
Tel: 55 61 342 1177
Fax: 55 61 342 1178
Contact: Gustavo Galväo
toniriocinefest@hotmail.com

Palm Beach Int. Film Fest.
1555 Palm Beach Lakes Boulevard,
Suite 403, West Palm Beach, FL
33401 USA
Tel: 1 561 233 1044
Fax: 1 561 683 6655
Pbfilmfest@aol.com

Ankara Int. Film Fest.
Farabi Sokak 29/1, 6690, Ankara,
Turkey
Tel: 90 312 468 7745
Fax: 90 312 467 7830
Contact: Gokhan Erkihc

Aspen Shortfest
110 E. Hallam, Suite 102, Aspen, CO
81611 USA
Tel: 1 970 925 6882
Fax: 1 970 925 1967
Contact: Brad White
www.aspenfilm.org

London Lesbian and Gay Fest.
National Film Theatre, South Bank,
London, SE1 8XT UK
Tel: 44 207 815 1323/2
Fax: 44 207 633 0786
Contact: Carol Coombes
carol.coombes@bfi.org.uk

Minneapolis/St. Paul Int. Film Fest.
2331 University Ave. SE, Suite 130b,
Minneapolis, MN 55414 USA
Tel: 1 612 627 4431
Fax: 1 612 627 4111
Contact: Al Milgrom
filmsoc@tc.umn.edu

Los Angeles Independent Film Fest.
5455 Wilshire Blvd #1500, Los
Angeles, CA 90036 USA
Tel: 1 323 937 9155
Fax: 1 323 937 7770
Contact: Robert Faust
www.laiff.com

Singapore Int. Film Fest.
45A Keong Saik Road, Singapore
089149
Tel: 65 738 7567
Fax: 65 738 7578
Contact: Philip Cheah
filmfest@pacific.net.sg

Filmfest DC
PO Box 21396, Washington DC
20009, USA
Tel: 1 202 724 5613
Fax: 1 202 724 6578
Contact: Shirin Ghareeb
filmfestdc@aol.com

USA Film Fest.
6116 N. Central Expwy, Suite 105,
Dallas TX 75206 USA
Tel: 1 214 821 6300
Fax: 1 214 821 6364
Contact: Alonso Duralde
www.usafilmfestival.com

San Francisco Int. Film Fest.
San Francisco Film Society, 39 Mesa
Street, Suite 110, The Presidio, San
Francisco, CA 94129 USA
Tel: 1 415 561 5000
Fax: 1 415 561 5099
Contact: Hilary Hart
ggawards@sfiff.org
www.sfiff.org

Philadelphia Fest. of World Cinema
3701 Chestnut Street, Philadelphia, PA
19104, USA
Tel: 1 215 895 6571/6593
Fax: 1 215 895 6562
Contact: Dave Kluft
pfwc@ihphilly.org

Worldfest-Houston Int. Film Fest.
PO Box 56566, Houston TX 77256
USA
Tel: 1 713 965 9955
Fax: 1 713 965 9960
Contact: Hunter Todd
worldfest@aol.com

Taos Talking Pictures
7217 NDCBU, 1337 Gusdorf Road,
Suite B, Taos, New Mexico 87529
Tel: 1 505 751 0637
Fax: 1 505 751 7385
Contact: Kelly Clement
ttpix@taosnet.com

Fest. du Film de Paris
7 rue Brunel, 75017 Paris, France
Tel: 33 1 45 72 96 40
Fax: 33 1 45 72 96 41
Contact: Oliver Pélisson
festival@festival-du-film-paris.com

MAY

CANNES
99 Boulevard Malesherbes, 75008
Paris France
Tel: 33 1 45 61 66 00
Fax: 33 1 45 61 97 60/ 33 1 45 61 66 17
Contact: Gilles Jacob
Accreditation@festival-cannes.fr
www.festival-cannes.fr

Unifrance Film International
4 villa Bosquet, 75007 Paris
Tel: 33 1 47 53 95 80
Fax: 33 1 47 05 96 55
www.Cannesmarket.com

Toronto Jewish Film Fest.
33 Prince Arthur Ave. 2nd Floor, Toronto
Ontario M5R 1B2
Tel: 1 416 324 8226
Fax: 1 416 324 8668
Contact: Shlomo Schwartzberg
tjiff@interlog.com

Golden Rose of Montreux
c/o Television Suisse Romande, 20
Quai-Ernest-Ansermet c.p. 234, 1211
Geneva 8, Switzerland
Tel: 41 22 708 8998
Fax: 41 22 781 5249
Contact: Sarah Fancini
Sarahfancini @tsr.ch

Oberhausen Int. Short Film Fest.
Grillostrasse 34 D-46045,
Oberhausen, Germany
Tel: 49 208 825 2652
Fax: 49 208 825 5413
Contact: Lars Henrik Crass
info@kurzfilmtage.de

Seattle Int. Film Fest.
911 Pine Street, Suite 607, Seattle, WA
98101 USA
Tel: 1 206 4645 830
Fax: 1 206 2647 919
Contact: Carl Spence
mail@seattlefilm.com
www.seattlefilm.com

Toronto World Short Film Fest.
60 Atlantic Ave. Suite 106, Toronto,
Ontario, M6K 1X9 Canada
Tel: 1 416 535 8506
Fax: 1 416 535 8342
Contact: Brenda Sherwood
twsff@idirect.com

JUNE

Filmfest Emden
Postfach 23 43, D-26703 Emden, An
Der Berufsschule 3, D-26721 Emden
Tel: 49 49 21 91 55 31
Fax: 49 49 21 91 55 99
Contact: Thorsten Hecht
filmfest@filmfest-emden.de

**FantaFest. (European Fantasy Film
Festivals Federation)**
Viale Gioachino Rossini 9, 00198
Roma, Italy
Tel: 39 06 807 6999
Fax: 39 06 807 7199
Contact: Loris Curci

Out of Sight
Broadway Media Centre, 14-18 Broad
Street, Nottingham, NG1 3AL UK
Tel: 44 115 952 6600
Fax: 44 115 952 6622
Contact: Sarah Tutt
enquiries@broadway.org.uk

Florida Film Fest.
1300 South Orlando Avenue, Maitland,
Florida 32751 USA
Tel: 1 407 629 1088
Fax: 1 407 629 6870
Contact: Matthew Curtis
filmfest@gate.net

Midnight Sun Film Fest.
Malminkatu 36, 00100 Helsinki,
Finland
Tel: 358 9 685 2242
Fax: 358 9 694 5560
Contact: Kristina Haataja
kristina.haataja@msfilmfestival.fi

Sydney Film Fest.
PO Box 950, Glebe NSW, 2037
Australia
Tel: 61 2 9660 3844
Fax: 61 2 9692 8793
Contact: Jenny Neighbour
info@sydfilm-fest.com.au

JULY

Karlovy Vary Int. Film Fest.
Panská 1, 110 00 Prague 1 Czech
Republic
Tel: 420 224 23 54 12
Fax: 420 224 23 34 08
Contact: Jiri Bartoska
secretariat@iffkv.cz

**New Zealand (Auckland &
Wellington) Int. Film Fest.**
PO Box 9544, Marion Square,
Wellington 6035, New Zealand
Tel: 64 4 385 0162
Fax: 64 4 801 7304
Contact: Bill Gosden
festival@enzedff.co.nz

Giffoni Children's Film Fest.
Piazza Umberto 1, 84095 Giffoni Valle
Piana, Italy
Tel: 39 089 86 85 44
Fax: 39 089 866 111
Contact: Claudio Gubitosi
giffonif@giffoniff.it

Melbourne Int. Film Fest.
1st Floor, 207 Johnston Street, Fitzroy,
PO Box 2206, Victoria, Melbourne,
Australia
Tel: 61 3 9417 2011
Fax: 61 3 9417 3804
Contact: Sandra Sdraulig
miff@vicnet.net.au

Brisbane Int. Film Fest.
Level 3, Hoyts Regent Building, 167
Queen Street Mall, Brisbane QLD
4000, Australia
Tel: 61 7 3220 0333
Fax: 61 7 3220 0400
Contact: Anne Démy
anne@biff.com.au

AUGUST

The Montreal World Film Fest.
1432 de Bleury Street, Montreal, H3A
2J1 Quebec, Canada
Tel: 1 514 848 3883
Fax: 1 514 848 38869
Contact: Lorraine Caron
ffm@interlink.net

The Norwegian Int. Film Fest.
PO Box 145, N-5501 Haugesund,
Norway
Tel: 47 52 73 44 30
Fax: 47 52 73 44 20
Contact: Gunnar Johan Lovvik
info@filmfestivalen.no

Odense Int. Film Festival
Vindegade 18, DK-5000, Odense C,
Denmark
Tel: 45 66 13 1372
Fax: 45 65 91 43 18
Contact: Helle Nielsen
Off.ksf@odense.dk

Edinburgh Int. Film Fest.
Filmhouse, 88 Lothian Road, EH3
9BZ, Scotland
Tel: 44 131 228 4051
Fax: 44 131 229 5501
Contact: Penny Mills
info@edfilmfest.org.uk

Locarno Int. Film Fest.
Via B. Luini, 3/A - CH 6601,
Locarno, Suisse
Tel: 41 91 756 21 21
Fax: 41 91 756 21 49
Contact: Marco Muller
locarno@pardo.ch
www.pardo.ch/

Espoo Ciné Int. Film Fest.
PO Box 95, 02101 Espoo, Finland
Tel: 358 9 466 599
Fax: 358 9 466 458
Contact: Satu Elo
espoocine@cultnet.fi

Sâo Paulo Int. Short Film Fest.
C/o Zita Carvalhosa, Rua Simâo
Alvares, 748/2, 05417-020 Sâo Paulo
SP, Brazil
Tel: 55 11 852 9601
Fax: 55 11 852 9601
Contact: Zita Carvalhosa
spshort@att.global.net

**Venice Film Fest./La Biennale di
Venezia**
Ca'Giustinian, San Marco, Venice
30124, Italy
Tel: 39 041 521 8711
Fax: 39 041 522 7539
Contact: Felice Laudadio
das@labiennale.com

Rosebud Fantasy Filmfest
Veranstaltungs + Median GmbH,
Fregestrasse 36, D-12161 Berlin,
Germany
Tel: 49 30 861 45 32
Fax: 49 30 861 45 39
Contact: Frederike Berndt
rosebud-entertainment@t-online.de

SEPTEMBER

Telluride
379 State St #3, Portsmouth, NH
03801 USA
Tel: 1 603 433 9202
Fax: 1 603 433 9206
Contact: Stella Pence
tellufilm@aol.com

Boston Film Festival
PO Box 516, Hull, MA 02045 USA
Tel: 1 781 925 1373
Fax: 1 781 925 3132
Contact: Mark Diamond
GEMSAD@aol.com

Cinefest: The Sudbury Film Fest.
90 Elm Street, Sudbury, Ontario, P3C
1T2 Canada
Tel: 1 705 688 1234
Fax: 1 705 688 1351
Contact: Tammy Frick
cinefest@vianet.on.ca
www.cinfest.com

Aspen FilmFest
110 E. Hallam, Suite 102, Aspen, CO
81611 USA
Tel: 1 970 925 6882
Fax: 1 970 925 1967
Contact: Brad White
www.aspenfilm.org

Atlantic Int. Film Fest.
PO Box 36139, Halifax, Nova Scotia,
Canada, B3J 3S9
Tel: 1 902 422 3456
Fax: 1 902 422 4006
Contact: Lia Rinaldo
festival@atlantic film.com

Athens Int. Film Fest.
5 Benaki St, 152 35
Metamorphosi, Chalandri
Athens, Greece
Tel: 30 1 606 1363
Fax: 30 1 601 4137
Contact: George Krassakopoulos
festival@pegasus.gr

**Mostra Rio - Rio de Janeiro
Film Fest.**
Rua Fernandez Guimarâes 39,
222290-000 Rio de Janeiro,
Brazil
Tel: 55 21 295 1060
Fax: 55 21 295 4599
Contact: Iafa Britz
total@visualnet.com.br

San Sebastian Int. Film fest.
Plaza de Oquendo s/n 20004
Donostia, San Sebastián, Spain
Tel: 34 943 48 1212
Fax: 34 943 48 1218
Contact: Diego Galan
siff@sansebastianfestival.com

**LUCAS Int. Children's and
Young Peoples Film Fest.
(Kinder-und JugendfilmFest.)**
Deutsches Filmmuseum,
Schaumankal 41, D-60596
Frankfurt am Main, Germany
Tel: 49 69 620167
Fax: 49 69 6032185
Contact: Petra Diebold

**Independent Feature Film
Market**
12th Floor, 104 West 29th Street,
New York, NY 10001 USA
Tel: 1 212 465 8200
Fax: 1 212 465 8525
Contact: Milton Tabbot
ifpny@ifp.org

Toronto Int. Film Fest.
2 Carlton Street, Suite 1600,
Toronto, Ontario, M5B 1J3
Tel: 1 416 967 7371
Fax: 1 416 967 9477
Contact: Nuria Bronfman
tiffg@torfilmfest.ca

Vancouver Int. Film Fest.
1008 Homer Street, Suite 410,
Vancouver V6B 2X1, British Columbia,
Canada
Tel: 1 604 685 0260
Fax: 1 604 688 8221
Contact: Alan Franey
viff@viff.org

Filmfest Hamburg
Friedensallee 44 22765, Hamburg,
Germany
Tel: 49 40 399 19000
Fax: 49 40 399 190010
Contact: Kathrin kohlstedde
filmfest-hamburg@t-online.de

Temecula Valley Int. Film Fest.
27740 Jefferson Ave, suite 100,
Temecula, CA 92590, USA
Tel: 1 909 699 6267/ 1 323 462 5502
Fax: 1 909 699 8681
Contact: Jo Moulton
jmmoulton@earthlink.net
PJBFILM@aol.com
www.tviff.com

OCTOBER

Chicago Int. Film Festival
32 W. Randolph St. Suite 600,
Chicago, IL 60601, USA
Tel: 1 312 425 9400
Fax: 1 312 425 0944
Contact: Michael J Kutza
filmfest@wwa.com

The Hamptons Int. Film Fest.
609 Greenwich Street, Suite A-416,
NY 10014 USA
Tel: 1 212 905 1649
Fax: 1 212 905 1769
Contact: Corinne Militello
hiff@hamptonsfest.org

Sâo Paulo Int. Film Fest.
Mostra Internacional de Cinema - Sâo
Paulo, Alameda Lorena, 937 Apt 303,
01424-001 Sâo Paulo SP, Brazil
Tel: 55 11 308 351 37
Fax: 55 11 308 579 36
Contact: Leon Cakoff
info@mostra.org

British Film Festival of Dinard
2 Boulevard Feart, 35800 Dinard,
France
Tel: 33 2 99 88 19 04
Fax: 33 2 99 46 67 15
Contact: Sylvie Pauterel
fest.film.britan.dinard@wanadoo.fr

Kiev Int. Film Fest. "Molodist"
6 Saksagansky St. Kyiv, 252033,
Ukraine
Tel: 380 44 247 6798
Fax: 380 44 227 4557
Contact: Lyudmila Novikova
molodist@@oldbank.com

Pusan Int. Film Festival;
Pusan Yachting Center, #1393, Woo
1-dong, Haeundae - gu, Pusan 612-
021, South Korea
Tel: 82 51 747 3010
Fax: 82 51 747 3012
Contact: Kim Dong Ho
piffoo@chollian.net

Raindance Independent Film Fest.
Raindance Film Showcase, 81
Berwick Street, London W1V 3PF
Tel: 44 207 437 3991
Fax: 44 207 439 2243
Contact: Elliot Grove
info@raindance.co.uk

Flanders Int. Film Fest.
1104 Kortrijksesteenweg, B-9051
Ghent, Bolgium
Tel: 32 9 242 8060
Fax: 32 9 221 9074
Contact: Jaques Dubrulle
info@filmfestival.be

Denver Int. Film Fest.
1430 Larimer Square, Suite 201,
Denver, Colorado 80202, USA
Tel: 1 303 595 3456
Fax: 1 303 595 0956
Contact: Ron Henderson
dfs@denverfilm.org

Mill Valley Film Fest.
38 Miller Avenue, Suite 6, Mill Valley,
CA 94941, USA
Tel: 1 415 383 5256
Fax: 1 415 383 8606
Contact: Zoe Elton
Finc@well.com

British Independent Film Awards
81 Berwick Street, London W1V 3PF
Tel: 44 207 287 3833
Fax: 44 207 439 2243
Contact: Elliot Grove
info@raindance.co.uk

London Premiere Screenings
Single Market Events, 23-24 George
Street, Richmond, Surrey, TW9 1HY
Tel: 44 208 948 5522
Fax: 44 208 332 0495
Contact: Emma Lochery
lps@single-market.co.uk

Murphy's Cork Int. Film Fest.
10 Washington Street, Cork City, Rep.
of Ireland
Tel: 353 21 427 1711
Fax: 353 21 427 5945
Contact: Michael Hannigan
ciff@indigo.ie

Warsaw Film Fest.
WWF PO Box 816, 00-950 Warsaw 1,
Poland
Tel. 48 22 853 3636
Fax: 48 22 644 1184
Contact: Stefan Laudyn
festiv@wff.org.pl

Fort Lauderdale Int. Film Fest.
1314 East Las Olas Boulevard, Fort
Lauderdale, FL 33301 USA
Tel: 1 305 954 760 9898
Fax: 1 305 954 760 9099
Contact: Bonnie Adams
brofilm@aol.com

**MIFED - Milan (Cinema and
television Int. multimedia market)**
E.A. Fiera Milano, 20145 Milano,
Largo Domodossola 1, C.P. 1270 -
20101, Milan, Italy
Tel: 39 02 4801 2920
Fax: 39 02 4997 7020
Contact: Elena Lloyd
www.fmd.it/mifed

Tokyo Int. Film Fest.
3F, Landic Ginza Building II, 1-6-5
Ginza, Chuo-ku, Tokyo 104-0061,
Japan
Tel: 81 3 3563 6305
Fax: 81 3 3563 6310
Contact: Toshiyuki Horie
www.tokyo-film-fest.or.jp

Sitges Int. Film Festival of Catalonia
Avenida Josep Tarradellas 135, esc A
3r. 2a. 08029 Barcelona, Spain
Tel: 34 93 419 36 35
Fax: 34 93 439 73 80
Contact: Roc Villas
cinsit@sitgestur.com

Leeds Int. Film Fest.
The Town Hall, the Headrow, Leeds,
LS1 3AD, UK
Tel: 44 113 247 8398
Fax: 44 113 247 8397
Contact: Charlotte Fergusson
filmfestival@leeds.gov.uk

AFI Los Angeles Int. Film Fest.
2021 N. Western Avenue, Manor
House, Los Angeles, CA 90027, USA
Tel: 1 323 856 7707/ 323 856 7600
Fax: 1 323 462 4049
AFIfest@AFIonline.org

Vienna Film Fest. (Viennale)
Stiftgasse 6, A-1070 Vienna, Austria
Tel: 43 1 526 5947
Fax: 43 1 523 4172
Contact: Hans Hurch
office@viennale.or.at

NOVEMBER

Mannheim-Heidelberg Int. Film Fest.
Collini-Center, Galerie, D-68161
Mannheim, Germany
Tel: 49 621 10 29 43
Fax: 49 621 29 15 64
Contact: Michael Koetz
ifhm@mannheim-filmfestival.com

London Int. Film Fest.
National Film Theatre, South Bank,
London, SE1 8XT UK
Tel: 44 207 815 1323/2
Fax: 44 207 663 0786
Contact: Sarah Lutton
sarah.lutton@bfi.org.uk

Thessaloniki Film Fest.
40 K Paparigopoulou St, Athens 114
73, Greece
Tel: 301 645 3669
Fax: 301 644 8143
Contact: Michel Demopoulos
info@filmfestival.gr
www.filmfestival.gr

Int. Film Fest. de Amiens
MCA Place Léon Gontier F80000,
Amiens, France
Tel: 33 3 22 71 35 70
Fax: 33 3 22 92 53 04
Contact: Jean-Pierre Garcia
amiensfilmfestival@burotec.fr

Stockholm Int. Film Fest.
P. O. Box 3136 SE11 37, Stockholm,
Sweden
Tel: 46 8 677 5011/12
Fax: 46 8 200 590
Contact: Patrick Anderson
filmfestivalen.se

Int. Mountain & Adventure Film Fest.
Schonaugasse 3, A-8010 Graz,
Austria
Tel: 43 316 814 223-0
Fax: 43 316 814 223-4
Contact: Robert Schauer
mountainfilm@mountainfilm.com

Fest. of Jewish Cinema
27 Mary Street, Carlton North 3054,
Victoria, Australia
Tel: 61 3 9387 4707
Fax: 61 3 9387 4707
Contact: Les Rabinowicz

Independent Film Festival of Barcelona
C\ Montalegre 5 - 08001 Barcelona,
Spain
Tel: 34 93 306 41 00
Fax: 34 93 306 41 04
Contact: Tessa Renaudo/Marc Vaíllo
alternativa@cccb.org

Hawaii Int. Film Fest.
1001 Bishop Street, Pacific Tower
Suite 745, Honolulu, Oahu HI 96813
USA
Tel: 1 808 528 3456
Fax: 1 808 528 1410
Contact: Bruce Fletcher
bruce@hiff.org

Welsh Int. Film Fest.
Market House, Market Road, Cardiff,
CF5 1QE
Tel: 44 1222 406220
Fax: 44 1222 233751
Contact: Michelle Williams
enq@iffw.co.uk
www.iffw.co.uk

Cairo Int. Film Fest.
17 Kasr El Nil Street, Cairo, Egypt
Tel: 202 392 3962/3562
Fax: 202 393 8979
Contact: Hussein Fahmy
info@cairofilmfestival.com

Oslo Int. Film Fest.
Ebbellsgate 1 N- 0183, Oslo, Norway
Tel: 47 22 20 0766
Fax: 47 22 20 1803
Contact: Tommy Lordahl
filmfestival@eunet.no

The Southern African Film and TV Market
(Sithengi) PO Box 52120, Waterfront,
Cape Town 8002, South Africa
Tel: 27 21 430 8171
Fax: 27 21 430 8122
Contact: Meryl Ramsay
saftvm@hot.co.za

DECEMBER

Cinemagic - The Northern Ireland Int. Film Fest. for Young People
3rd Floor, Fountain House, 17-21
Donegall Place, Belfast, BT1 5AB
Tel: 44 28 903 11900
Fax: 44 28 903 19709
Contact: Frances Cassidy
info@cinemagic.org.uk

Index

The Film Producers Toolkit

The Producers Toolkit is a set of cost effective, yet extremely powerful software tools for film and TV. Designed especially for lower budget productions *The Producers Toolkit* empowers you to create and realise your dreams. Each module is self contained, but integrates with other modules. Developed by feature film makers who were frustrated by inflated price tags, un-intuitive interfaces and downright over complicated software, *The Producers Toolkit* is your solution to all your film making problems, from conception to completion.

Screenplay v2

A powerful screenplay formatter that takes the headache out of writing.

Features include... Automatic formatting in several industry standard layouts. Layout in any way you like, it's 100% customisable. Scene breakdown integration with the Schedule module*. Automatic scene numbering, page breaking, Cont' and More text addition etc. Hidden writers notes and a myriad of other features making Screenplay in incredibly powerful tool for creative writers. Requires MSWord v6, 95, 97 or 2000 for PC and MSWord v6 and 98 for Mac.

Budget v2

A powerful budget program that helps you formulate detailed budgets for your movie.

Features include... A powerful yet simple budgeting engine already customised for film and TV but suitable for any project. Extremely simple to use. Print your budget out in a professional way impressing investors and backers. Quick and clean to use, automatically calculating and totalling your budget with percentages. Requires MSExcel.

Schedule v1

A powerful scheduling suite designed to help you plan the way you shoot your movie. Automatically interfacing with the *Screenplay* module, *Schedule* will help you make the most out of the resources at hand and keep you organised. Under development and scheduled for delivery in the final quarter 2000.

Other modules are currently under development, check out our web site for more information at www.livingspirit.com

---